The Anglophone Question and Postcolonial Hegemony in Cameroon

The Anglophone Question and Postcolonial Hegemony in Cameroon

The Past that Did Not Pass

Volume One

Edited by

Lyombe Eko

SPEARS BOOKS

Denver, Colorado

Spears Books
An Imprint of Spears Media Press LLC
7830 W. Alameda Ave, Suite 103-247
Denver, CO 80226
United States of America

First Published in the United States of America in 2024 by Spears Books
www.spearsbooks.org
info@spearsmedia.com
Information on this title: www.spearsbooks.org/the-anglophone-question-vol1
© 2024 Lyombe Eko
All rights reserved.

ISBN: 9781957296418 (Paperback)
ISBN: 9781957296425 (eBook)

Designed and typeset by Spears Media Press LLC
Cover designed by Doh Kambem

Distributed globally by African Books Collective (ABC)
www.africanbookscollective.com

Dedicated to the following persons who fought for freedom of speech and expression in Cameroon and paid the penalty for it:

Mola Njoh Litumbe
Tataw Obenson (Ako Aya), pioneer West Cameroon journalist
Barrister Felix Agbor Nkongho (Balla), human rights lawyer
Nyo' Wakai, judge and author
Pius Njawé, Founder of Le Messager
Nyemb Ntoogue Paul (Nyemb Popoli), Cartoonist
Mancho Bibixy Tse, radio announcer and activist
Christian Penda Ekoka, Humanist
Cardinal Christian Wiyghan Tumi, Catholic Cardinal
Samuel Ajiekah Abuwe (Wazizi), journalist
Martinez Zogo, Journalist
All journalists detained or imprisoned in Cameroon.

Contents

Preface

LYOMBE EKO

> *O'oka teh oh rzuta eh wana*
> If you are sick, don't hide your mouth.
> Mokpe/Bakweri proverb, Cameroon

One of the fundamental pre-conditions of medical sciences, politics and practically all other domains of human endeavor is communication. Communication is perhaps the most effective problem-solving device human beings are endowed with. Since vocalization is part of the healing process, good-faith human dialogue is superior to, and often prevents the deadly, chaotic cacophony of firearms, bullets, and missiles. Bombast is preferable to bombs. The Anglophone Question, also known as the Anglophone problem in Cameroon, is a problem of communication, or lack thereof. Nay, it is a problem of the country's small-minded kleptocratic republican chief of state's refusal to communicate his willingness to engage in dialogue and counter-communication.

In effect, the Cameroon of the autocratic Ahidjo-Biya regime, which is best described by the neologism, *la chefferie républicaine* (republican chiefery), is the picture-perfect exemplar of a society where the body-politic is sick, and yet the patient refuses to communicate, to vocalize, to discuss, to dialogue, to facilitate diagnosis and treatment of the political disease. In his 50-plus years as Prime Minister and President, Biya became the Grand Chieftain of the *Chefferie Républicaine* du Cameroun (Republican Chiefery of Cameroon). President Biya is the: *Chef de l'État* (Literally, Chief of State) who was also crowned: "Fon of Fons" (Chief of the tribal chiefs of the Northwest region of Cameroon), Chief of the Bamileke Chiefs of the Western region, Chief of the chiefs of the Coastal Douala (Sawa), and *Nyamoto Kpwatolo*, chieftain of the tribal chiefs of his Central South region. Biya was also the chief of denial. Instead of communicating with its disgruntled citizens–and the Anglophones were not the only disgruntled citizens–the Biya regime chose the most potent form of counter-communication and counter-dialogue—denial. That was the official government policy. *La verité vient d'en* haut (truth comes from the top), President Biya once proclaimed. With the certainty of people who have a monopoly on power and on the truth, President Biya and his hand-picked sycophants have steadfastly and consistently repeated the chorus: "There is no Anglophone problem. Full Stop!" To them, the profound discontent and angst of the English and Pidgin-speaking minority of the former State of Southern Cameroons was a non-issue. In his dealings with the Anglophone minority, President Paul Biya, an ardent Francophile who never made a single speech in the English language to the Cameroonian nation on a national holiday, had two rules: "Rule 1: There is no Anglophone Problem, Rule 2: When in doubt, see Rule 1." All Cameroon government policies and actions centered around that mantra for decades. Case in point: the moribund, rubber-stamp Cameroon National Assembly. At the very onset of the Anglophone Revolt, on December 13, 2016, Honorable Joseph Wirba, Member of Parliament for Bui Division (county), in the English-speaking Northwest region, "subverted" a plenary session of the Cameroon National Assembly in Yaoundé by bringing up the massive government repression of demonstrating lawyers, teachers, students and members of the civil society in Buea, Bamenda and other towns in the English and Pidgin-speaking Southern Cameroons, that Biya had arbitrarily partitioned and renamed Northwest and Southwest provinces. The unrest in English-speaking Southern Cameroons and the massive repression was not on the agenda of the National Assembly. It had never been on parliament's agenda. It was as if it was not happening. Indeed, the president (Speaker) of the National Assembly, Hon. Cavaye Yeguié Djibril, strenuously resisted any attempts by English-speaking parliamentarians from the opposition Social Democratic Front (SDF) party to put the revolt on the agenda or even attempt to discuss it. Hon. Wirba had taken the floor to speak on a completely different topic when he suddenly delved into the Anglophone crisis that was shaking the country. Despite calls for him to yield the podium, Hon. Wirba stubbornly refused to stand down. He instead gave a fiery speech in which he decried the heavy-handed authoritarian repression that was going on in English-speaking Southern Cameroons and issued a clarion call for Anglophones to resist the attempted Francophone subjugation. Wirba told the National Assembly: "*When the people will rise, even if you take the whole French army* [the "*partenaire privilégié*" of the brutal and repressive Cameroon military] *and add it to yours, you will never bring them down.*" He quoted former American president, Thomas Jefferson, who had written that 'when injustice becomes law, resistance becomes duty.' The people of West Cameroon have a duty to resist," he thundered.

As the Anglophone Revolt widened, and the Cameroonian army and security forces led by the Israeli-trained and equipped *Bataillon d'Intervention Rapide* (BIR) unleashed a scorched-earth policy and wave after wave of terror in English and Pidgin-speaking Southern Cameroons, the SDF pleaded with the Speaker, Hon. Cavaye Yeguié Djibril to put the crisis on the agenda of the Assembly. They were met with a stony, contemptuous silence. On November 14, 2017, Honorable Banadzem Joseph and Senator Jean Tsomelou, heads of the SDF Parliamentary groups in the National Assembly and Senate, respectively, announced that the party was going to boycott the opening ceremony of the National Assembly on November 14, 2017. Their complaint was that National Assembly Speaker, Hon. Cavayé Yeguié Djibril, had brazenly ignored their appeals to include the Anglophone problem on the agenda, despite multiple entreaties by the SDF, and the reality of the rapidly deteriorating situation on the ground in Southern Cameroons, where the majority of their constituents lived.

The country was still discussing Cavayé Yeguié Djibril's determined efforts to play ostrich when, two days later, the top five floors of the National Assembly were destroyed by a fire. The offices of the SDF were among those completely destroyed by the blaze. The plenary hall of the National Assembly itself and the Speaker's offices were not destroyed. Though the cause of the fire was never determined, the situation looked like a Cameroonian version of the 1933 Reichstag fire, an arson attack on the German parliament planned and executed by the Nazis as a false flag operation designed to trigger the arrest of their opponents and consolidate Hitler's power.

On November 23rd, 2017, the world watched in wonderment as members of the opposition Social Democratic Front party brazenly disrupted proceedings in the National Assembly. It was an unusual sight to behold in the hallowed legislative precincts of the Cameroon Republic. Members of the SDF disrupted a session of parliament by standing up and occupying the front dais of the chamber. They burst out singing and dancing the Anglophone Pidgin English call and response protest song: "How many Pipo (people) Paul Biya go Kill?

Call: How many Pipo (people) Paul Biya go Kill?
Response: How many Pipo (people) Paul Biya go Kill?
Chorus:
Hoo, You go kill we tire
Hoo you go kill we tire
Hoo, you go kill we tire,
How many people Paul Biya go kill?

The mostly Anglophone MPs danced and waved peace plants and other symbols and brought parliamentary business to a standstill to protest Speaker Cavayé Djibril's categorical refusal to schedule a debate on the Anglophone crisis that had gripped the Northwest and Southwest regions. Members of the ruling Cameroon People's Democratic Movement (CPDM) party scampered out of the hall like frightened rabbits, afraid of being seen listening to the "subversive" anti-Biya chants of the SDF MPs. The SDF parliamentary revolt was tantamount to an attempt to beard the lion-man, Biya, in his den. Francophone Cameroonians, who are not used to the niceties of parliamentary democracy, were shocked that the protesting SDF members of parliament were not arrested and locked up on the spot. They would quickly learn that despite Biya's republican monarchy in which a climate of fear reigned, the SDF MPs knew that parliamentarians and senators in democracies have parliamentary immunity that protects them from arrest for things they say in parliament, including "speech acts" and expressive conduct like singing, blowing whistles, and drowning out the Speaker or other members of parliament (Cameroon: MPs stop parliament session over Anglophone crisis, 2017; SDF MPs Slam Parliament for Continuously rejecting Debate on the Anglophone Crisis, 2017).

On Wednesday, November 29, the SDF struck again! This time the opposition MPs disrupted the policy speech of Prime Minister, Philemon Yang (who happened to be Anglophone himself) when they rose up, took to the dais, blew whistles, clapped, and sang the Anglophone song of resistance, accusing Biya of being a killer: "Hoo, you go kill we tire, hoo, you go kill we tire, hoo, you go kill we tire, how many people Paul Biya go kill." Yang went through the motions of reading his speech, but the hapless Prime Minister was drowned out by the din and cacophony of the SDF members of parliament, his fellow Anglophones. In order to prevent the world from seeing this unprecedented display of defiance, impotence, powerlessness, and lack of vision, the security forces in the national assembly attempted to empty the chamber of journalists. The irony of the extreme tone-deafness of the Biya regime and its denialism was that the Anglophone Question in Cameroon had been discussed/debated in the Nigerian Senate, the House of Commons of the United Kingdom, the Canadian House of Commons Committee on Human Rights, the U.S. House of Representatives and the U.S. Senate, the German Bundestag, and the European Parliament. The Swiss Federal Parliament had issued a report on it, and the French Foreign Minister, Yves Le Drian, had responded to a question on the issue in the French National Assembly. If the inaction of the denialist Cameroon National Assembly is anything to go by, all these legislative bodies were debating a non-issue and interfering in the internal affairs of Cameroon.

This volume presents essays on the Anglophone problem that are written by different scholars from different disciplines and perspectives. The denial and willful amnesia of the Biya regime and the ruling elite, who saw the Anglophone Revolt as a challenge to their power, as well as the repressive excesses of the Cameroon security, led to one of the worst African human rights crisis of the first quarter of the 21st century. This volume demonstrates that the Biya regime had skillfully used the oil, natural gas, and other natural resources of Cameroon–and they are mostly from the Anglophone regions—to close the eyes, ears and mouths of four of the five members of the United Nations Security Council: France, the United Kingdom, China and Russia. The most the Americans, the fifth member of the Security Council, were able to do was organize an informal Arria-formula meeting on the humanitarian situation in Cameroon at the U.N. Security Council in 2019. The self-interest of the four members of the UN Security Council clearly trumped the lofty human rights principles of the Universal Declaration of Human Rights.

The Anglophone Question in Cameroon: A Definitional Note

A number of entries in this volume use the term "Anglo-Saxon" as an adjective that refers to the political, governance, legal, religious, and educational cultures inherited by the English and Pidgin-speaking peoples of the former British Southern Cameroons, now divided into the Northwest and Southwest regions of Cameroon. This usage raises eyebrows in multiple quarters. As a result, it is necessary to define the term as it is used in Cameroon. For starters, the term Anglo-Saxon or Anglo-Saxon is fraught with controversy. According to the *Encyclopaedia Britannica* (2024):

Anglo-Saxon is a "term used historically to describe any member of the

Germanic peoples who, from the 5th century CE to the time of the Norman Conquest (1066), inhabited and ruled territories that are today part of England and Wales... Their distinct dialects evolved into Old English... the term Anglo-Saxon seems to have been first used by Continental [Latin] writers in the late 8th century to distinguish the Saxons of Britain from those of the European continent...an informal synonym for English...

The term also has historical, ethno-linguistic, and classificatory meanings. In the United States, the term is an "ethno-racial" expression that is instrumentalized to denote white supremacy. The term White Anglo-Saxon Protestant (WASP) was an epithet used to describe "whiteness" in America (Rambaran-Olm & Wade, 2021). The term "Anglo" is now used in certain quarters to distinguish white Americans from Hispanics or Latinos.

In comparative law studies, the term Anglo-Saxon is used to distinguish the Common Law tradition of the UK and its former colonies from other legal families. Comparative Law scholars classify the French legal system as being in the Civil law "family," while the legal systems of the Anglosphere are classified as being in the Anglo-Saxon "family" of law (Zweigert & Kötz, 1998; van Hoecke, 2014). The English-speaking Cameroon Anglophone lawyers trained in the British common law tradition of the United Kingdom, whose diverse vestiges and iterations are the norm in the Anglosphere–Nigeria, Ghana, East Africa, the United States, Canada, India, Australia, New Zealand, the West Indies, Southern Cameroons, and so on–use the term *Anglo-Saxon* to distinguish themselves from their Francophone civil law counterparts. Both the French and English-language press in Cameroon use the term *Anglo-Saxon* in the French, geo-cultural sense. When Anglophone lawyers and teachers spearheaded demonstrations and strikes calling for respect for "Anglo-Saxon" cultural and identitarian specificity, they were using that term as it is used in comparative legal studies, as well as in the sense of the perpetual rivalries between French culture and English cultures in local and global arenas.

In France and Francophone Africa, the term *les Anglo-Saxons* is an identitarian epithet used to define the totality of the English-speaking *Other* from the French-speaking Self. It describes everything connected or related to the English language and culture anywhere in the world in the context of a perceived linguistic and cultural rivalry between *les Anglais* (the English) and *les Français* (the French). They speak of *le monde anglo-saxon* (the English-speaking or Anglophone world), and *le modèle anglo-saxon* (Chabal, 2017). At the global level, this distinction is embodied in the post-colonial linguistic and cultural groupings, the British Commonwealth of Nations and *l'Organisation de la Francophonie*, the competing, hegemonic groupings of British and French postcolonies respectively.

In Cameroon, parts of which were colonized by France and the UK for about 40 years, this linguistic and cultural rivalry is part of the Anglophone Question. The English-speaking Northwest and Southwest regions have been part of the global Anglosphere for centuries. The port of Bimbia was part of the West African slave trade network, from which Pidgin English emerged. It was the location where British-Jamaican missionary abolitionist, Rev. Joseph Merrick and his wife set up a mission in 1833, started an English school, and set up a printing press to publish religious literature for the mission. In 1858, British Baptist missionary, Rev. Alfred Saker founded Victoria, a missionary enclave named after Queen Victoria (1819-1901). When the Cameroons became German Kamerun under provisions of the Berlin Africa Conference of 1884-1885, the Germans did not tolerate missionaries of the English Baptist Missionary Society in their newly acquired territories. In 1885, the English Baptist missionaries were forced to abandon their work and mission stations and leave the entire Victoria Settlement to the Swiss-German, Basel Evangelical Missionary Society (the Basel Mission). The Basel mission was a missionary society of German-speaking Swiss Calvinists and German Lutherans based in Basel, Switzerland. The Basel Evangelical Missionary Society began work in German Kamerun in 1886. The Basel Mission was the founding mission of the current Presbyterian Church in Cameroon (PCC) (Wright, 1958, p. 31). Nevertheless, Southern Cameroons' anchorage in the Anglosphere survived German colonialism (1884-1919) and was revived under British Southern Cameroons (1919-1961). After the British and French defeat of Germany in Kamerun in World War I, the British colonial administration allowed German American Baptist missionaries into Southern Cameroons as early as 1935. American missionaries from the North American Baptist Conference, Karl Jacob Bender, Paul Gebauer, George Dunger, Ernest Zimbelman, their spouses and others, established missions, hospitals, schools, and colleges like Saker Baptist College, Victoria, and Joseph Merrick Baptist College, Ndu. The Roman Catholic Church was also prominent in the British Southern Cameroons. Saint Joseph's Missionary Society of Mill Hill (the Mill Hill Missionaries) started St. Joseph's College, Sasse, Buea, in 1939 as a replica of Saint Joseph's College, a seminary in Mill Hill, London. Catholic and Swiss (Basel) missionary societies also started hospitals and clinics, given that the British colonial administration did not consider these a priority. The churches were, therefore, the midwives of the State of Southern Cameroons, hence their role in the Anglophone Revolt.

After the reunification of French Cameroun and Southern Cameroons in 1961, the first tension was a religious one. French Cameroon had inherited the French secular republican, anti-religious, anti-clerical ideology spawned by the French Revolution of 1789. The ensuing Federal Republic of Cameroon, which had a strong, centralized, post-colonial Napoleonic administrative structure and culture, recognized all subjects in the General Certificate of Education examination, the high school diploma of the territory–except religion. This clashed with the religious grounding of Southern Cameroonian education and healthcare. But the Southern Cameroonian leaders–Foncha, Muna, Nfon Mukete, and others–did not raise any objections to this assertion of French post-colonial secular republican hegemony. Additionally, France saw the reunification as an opportunity to change le modèle anglo-saxon of Southern Cameroons, isolate the territory from the "Anglo-Saxon" cultural and industrial juggernaut, the United States, and assimilate it into la Francophonie. This policy failed because of the presence of American, British and Irish missionaries and the American Peace Corps in West Cameroon. The proximity of Nigeria and the ever-present American pop music that came with the emergence and globalization of pop music ensured that West Cameroon remained culturally anchored to the Anglosphere. Ultimately, attempts by the neo-Napoleonic regime of Yaoundé to erase the identitarian and cultural specificity of Anglophone Cameroon and assimilate the territory and its people into la Francophonie through the deceptively-sounding policy of harmonization triggered the Anglophone Revolt.

References

Rambaran-Olm, M. & Wade, E. (2021). The Many Myths of the Term 'Anglo-Saxon' Smithsonian Magazine, July 14th (Retrieved from: https://www.smithsonianmag.com/history/many-myths-term-anglo-saxon-180978169/).

The Editors of Encyclopaedia Britannica (2024). Anglo-Saxon (January 23). Retrieved from: https://www.britannica.com/topic/Anglo-Saxon

Van Hoecke, M. (2014). Do "legal systems" exist? The concept of law and comparative law. In *Concepts of Law*, Seán Patrick Donlan & Lukas Heckendorn Urscheler (eds.). London: Routledge.

Zweigert, K. & Kötz, H. (1998). *An Introduction to Comparative Law*, (T.Weir, transl.; 3rd ed.). Oxford University Press

ONE

Introduction

The Anglophone Question in Cameroon

LYOMBE EKO

"War made the state and the state made war."
Charles Tilly (1990)

"L'abus du pouvoir use le pouvoir, l'abus de la force use la force."
Abuse of power wears out power, abuse of force, spends and wears out force.
West African Proverb

Aeschylus, the ancient Greek master of dramatic tragedy, is believed to have said: "In war, truth is the first casualty." That was then. Today, in war, human rights, nay, human beings, constitute the first concrete casualties. Thereafter, historians, political scientists, and moral philosophers debate the truthfulness or falsity of information, misinformation, counter-information, and disinformation disseminated about the true causes of specific wars and their atrocities. With respect to the Anglophone crisis in Cameroon, information scientists, political scientists, military scientists, and ethicists have a lot of kernels to chew on. Here are some historical facts:

On October 1, 2017, at 4:33 pm, President Paul Barthélemy bi Mvondo, Head of State of the Republic of Cameroon since 1982 and Commander-in-chief of the Armed Forces, received reports of the first outcome of his decision to use military force to crush unarmed civilian political demonstrations demanding greater autonomy for the English and Pidgin-speaking (Anglophone) Northwest and Southwest regions of Cameroon. This was the result of years of tensions between the Anglophone minority, which felt marginalized, discriminated against, and oppressed by appointed prefects from the French-speaking majority in Cameroon, a country where millions of people live with perpetual food insecurity, have no clean drinking water, no access to healthcare, no decent schools, and no decent road infrastructure. The lot of Cameroonians in both parts of the country contrasted sharply with the reality of President Biya's *chefferie républicaine* (republican chiefery), the forty-two-year-long autocratic, kleptocratic, neo-patrimonial tribal cocoon which insulated the president from the day-to-day realities of the people. The military dispatch from Yaoundé arrived when the president was taking one of his usual lengthy vacations in the Swiss Alps, specifically, at the luxurious presidential suite of the Intercontinental Hotel, Chemin du Petit-Saconnex 7-9, 1209 Genève, Switzerland. Paul Barthélemy Biya bi Mvondo, then 84, and his wife, Chantal Pulchérie Vigouroux, then 48, were vacationing in the lap of luxury, accompanied by a large retinue of courtesans, security guards, aides, attendants, and hangers-on, who occupied a whole floor of the expensive, luxury hotel, at the expense of Cameroonian taxpayers… or Swiss and other companies doing business in Cameroon. Biya and his wife, Chantal, were regular private visitors at that well-appointed watering hole for presidents and high-flying diplomats, to the point where they were ridiculed by the international media (Hinshaw & Parkinson, 2018). Characteristically, the absentee, do-nothing president was on yet another vacation in Switzerland while his country was facing an existential crisis. The dispatch was from military headquarters at the *Ministre délégué à la Présidence, chargé de la défense* (The Minister Delegate at the Presidency of the Republic in Charge of Defense) in Yaoundé. Under the Biya regime, the president, Biya himself, was the Minister of Defense. He just delegated that portfolio to a minister delegate at the president's office, a person who was invariably from his tribe. The 1st October 2017 military dispatch from Yaoundé was crisp, clinical, and almost perfunctory. This is how it appeared verbatim on Facebook pages:

[01/10 à 16:33] +237 99104845: *Altercation armée au pont Satom à Mamfe contre une 50aine activistes brandissant leur gris-gris et tirant sur nous avec armes de chasse. bilan côté ennemi: 2 morts 5 arrêtés. Côté ami: RAS.*

[01/10 à 16:33] +237 99104845: Armed clash on the Satom bridge in Mamfe against about 50 activists brandishing traditional medicinal charms and shooting at us with hunting weapons. Casualty figures: On the side of the enemy: 2 dead, 5 arrested. On the friendly (Cameroon army side): Nothing to report.

[01/10 à 16:33] +237 99104845: *À Buea, les insurgés veulent prendre le palais du Gouverneur construit par les Allemands aujourd'hui avant 18h, car disent-ils, c'est leur capitale. Mais les FMO tiennent jusqu'à présent.*

[01/10 à 16:33] +237 99104845: At Buea, the insurgents want to take over the Governor's Palace built by the Germans today before 6 pm, because they say it is their capital but the military forces are holding firm up to the present moment.

[01/10 à 16:33] +237 99104845: *Survol à basse altitude et largage des grenades F4 à partir des hélicos*

[01/10 à 16:33] +237 99104845: Low altitude flight by helicopter gunships and dropping of F4 grenades [on the unarmed civilians] from helicopters.

[01/10 à 16:33] +237 99104845: *Dans le Nord-Ouest actuellement, la situation tourne au vinaigre. Le véhicule du préfet de Fundong vient d'être incendié. Plusieurs manifestants à Bamenda ont des grenades et des armes à feu.*

[01/10 à 16:33] +237 99104845: In the Northwest the situation is turning sour. The vehicle of the prefect of Fundong has been burnt. Many demonstrations in Bamenda have grenades and firearms.

[01/10 à 16:33] +237 99104845: *Matériel récupéré: 02 pistolets artisanaux et 35 cartouches*

01/10 à 16:33] +237 99104845: Equipment seized: 02 locally made pistols and 35 cartridges.

[01/10 à 16:33] +237 99104845: *Un Véhicule d'Intervention et de Dispersion (VID: Abraham) de la Gendarmerie mis hors d'état de fonctionner à Buea par les manifestants.*

01/10 à 16:33] +237 99104845: An Abraham Intervention and Dispersion Vehicle of the Gendarmerie [made by Soframe, Alsace, France] damaged in Buea by the demonstrators.

[01/10 à 16:35] +237 99104845: *Point fait par un ami de la Semil*

[01/10 à 16:35] +237 99104845: Clarification from a military colleague in SEMIL (Cameroun Military Security)

[01/10 à 16:35] +237 99104845: *Vives altercations à Mutengene entre manifestants et FMO. Au moins 3 morts déjà enregistrés côté adverse. Déploiement des renforts gendarmerie par le COLEGION.*

[01/10 à 16:35] +237 99104845: Serious altercations in Mutengene between demonstrations and Law Enforcement Officers. At least 3 dead recorded on the side of the adversary. Deployment of reinforcement by the commander of the gendarmerie legion.

[01/10 à 18:17] +237 99104845: *On tend vers 20 morts depuis le matin quand même hein. Ils ne rigolent pas en face*

[01/10 à 18:17] +237 99104845: We have about 20 dead since morning. The enemy is not laughing in our face

[01/10 à 18:17] +237 99104845: *Voilà le bilan actuel des morts par localité*

[01/10 à 18:17] +237 99104845: These are the deaths by locality

[01/10 à 18:17] +237 99104845: *Buea 2... Akwaya 1...Kumba 3...Kumbo 4 prison-niers...Mamfe 2....Muyuka 2....Mutenguene*

[01/10 à 18:17] +237 99104845: Buea 2…Akwaya 1…Kumba 3…Kumbo 4. Prison-ers…Mamfe 2…Muyuka 2…. Mutengene (English translation by author).

The telephone number: +237 99104845 is the official number of the Minister Delegate at the Presidency of the Republic in Charge of Defense.

This clinical, soldiery communication was confirmation that President Paul Biya had decided to employ deadly military force to solve a festering political problem, the so-called Anglophone Question in the two English and pidgin-speaking regions of Cameroon. In effect, as commander-in-chief of the Cameroon armed forces, Mr. Biya had ordered his troops to open fire on unarmed English and Pidgin-speaking civilians, who were demonstrating against what they perceived as their second-class citizenship in the French-dominated *la République du Cameroun*. The Cameroon army reported that on October 1, twenty persons were shot dead, and more than 500 were arrested (Amnesty International, 2018). That number rose exponentially as more bodies of the helicopter attack were found in the subsequent days. President Biya stayed at the Intercontinental Hotel in Geneva, unmoved by the crisis.

Figure 1.1. Israeli-trained *Bataillon d'Intervention Rapide* on May 20, 2018. Credit: Agence France Presse

The Anglophone Question has multiple international connections. The crackdown by security forces—the army, the gendarmerie, and the police, was led by the infamous, brutal, Israeli-trained, and armed *Batallion d'Intervention Rapide* (Rapid Intervention Brigade) that was popularly known by its French acronym (BIR) (Daoud, 2018). Cameroun and its security forces also have formal and informal military cooperation agreements with France, China, the UK, the United States, Russia, and other powers. The October 1, 2017 attacks constituted Biya's affirmative decision to violently suppress non-violent common law lawyers, teachers, and students demonstrating for democracy, equality, regional autonomy, and federalism in Bamenda, Buea, Kumba, Mamfe, and tens of other towns in the English and Pidgin-speaking regions of Cameroon. Their political demands were met with brutal repression, targeted killings, arrests, imprisonment, beatings, and torture by the Cameroon security forces. October 1 was a symbolic day for the English-speaking regions because it was the day the United Nations symbolically granted independence to Southern Cameroons in 1961 and gave the people of the territory the controversial choice of exercising their independence by joining *la République du Cameroun* or Nigeria.

Masterminding Human Rights Violations From the "Land of Human Rights"

The Cameroon military dispatch of its killings of unarmed civilian demonstrators in the English and Pidgin-speaking regions of Cameroon was intercepted by Western intelligence agencies and leaked to members of the press, who posted it on social media platforms. It was clear evidence that from his luxurious Swiss Alpine hide-away, President Paul Biya, Commander-in-chief of the Cameroon Armed Forces, had opted to use brute military force rather than reason and concertation to solve a political problem in faraway Africa. He had decided to crush the Anglophone Revolt, a peaceful uprising of the discontented English and Pidgin-speaking minority in the nominally "bilingual" country of Cameroon. The situation was pregnant with irony. Biya was masterminding the repression, subjugation, and human rights violations of the Anglophone minority in Cameroon from Swiss territory. Furthermore, his luxurious presidential suite at the Intercontinental Hotel was just a stone's throw from the *Palais des Nations*, the United Nations Office in Geneva (UNOG). Geneva is also the headquarters of the United Nations High Commissioner for Refugees (UNHCR), the agency that would later be called upon to address the refugee problem spawned by Biya's authoritarianism and human rights violations in Anglophone Cameroon. Geneva is also the headquarters of the United Nations Human Rights Council, an intergovernmental body within the United Nations system, whose mandate is to protect human rights around the globe. The subsequent membership of Cameroon in the United Nations Human Rights Council, despite the atrocities of the Cameroon military, made a mockery of the UN and the concept of human rights. As this book demonstrates, Biya, an absolute autocrat, had no patience with the niceties of human rights and humanitarian law. Indeed, one of the characteristics of the attempted subjugation of the English and Pidgin-speaking Cameroonians is that on multiple occasions, members of the notorious Israeli-trained and equipped *Bataillon d'Intervention Rapide* (BIR) and other units of the Cameroon security forces recorded their brutal torture, arson, and summary execution sessions on video and posted these damning images on Facebook and other social media. Some of these videos were featured on international broadcasting channels like the British Broadcasting Corporation (BBC) and Al-Jazeera, Qatar. As the bloodshed continued in Cameroon, Biya stayed unmoved in megalomaniacal self-absorption at the Intercontinental Hotel in Geneva. The Anglophone Question in Cameroon was also a Swiss problem inasmuch as the Swiss-German Basel Mission had historic colonial-era ties with Anglophone Cameroon since the European Partition of Africa at the Berlin Africa Conference of 1884-85. Furthermore, Swiss companies ranging from chocolate manufacturers to commodities traders (read oil, natural gas and other raw materials) maintain very lucrative, mutually beneficial personal ties with President Biya. As a result, Switzerland has, over the years, coddled the autocratic, kleptocratic, neo-patrimonial president to protect its economic interests in Cameroon.

Figure 1.2. Cameroonians demonstrating at the Intercontinental Hotel Geneva. Credit: *Agence France Presse*

Aim of the Volume

As the world marked the 100th anniversary of the Treaty of Versailles in 2019, the Southern Cameroons, a former British-administered United Nations Trust Territory that reunified with the former French administered *République du Cameroun,* was caught in a spiraling armed conflict fueled in part by struggles between and among, French, British, Israeli, Swiss, Russian, and Chinese governmental and corporate interests for control of the natural resources of the territory of Southern Cameroons, with the connivance of the autocratic regime of octogenarian President Paul Biya, who celebrated his 42nd year in power in 2024. This volume aims to explore, chronicle, analyze, describe, and explain the Anglophone Question–the problematic, subaltern status of the English and Pidgin-speaking minority of the formerly autonomous state of Southern Cameroons in the French-speaking *la République du Cameroun* from historical, political, cultural, economic, social and international perspectives. This book brings together diverse intellectuals who act as literal and figurative interpreters of the Anglophone Question and its multi-faceted "problematic situations" to borrow the expression of Atwood and Major (1993). The Anglophone Question is first and foremost a result of acute political tensions resulting from the unification of the contrasting governmentalities–conceptualizations, psychological variables, institutional logics, procedures, strategies of control, rationalizations and practices of "rulership" or the exercise of power (Foucault, 1994) – of the two postcolonial political components of what remained of the German colonial territory of Kamerun. The two postcolonial entities are the French-speaking *La République du Cameroun*, a former French United Nations-mandated territory, and the English and Pidgin-speaking British Southern Cameroons. The Anglophone Question is the political, cultural, and philosophical frictions that have arisen out of the clash between the centripetal (centralizing) authoritarian, governmentality of the French "postcolony" of *la République du Cameroun*, as Mbembe (2001) put it, on the one hand, and the centrifugal (decentralizing) governmentality of the politically fractious British Southern Cameroons, a once autonomous territory with a post-imperial, Anglo-African linguistic heritage. At its core, the Anglophone Question is thus an identitarian, politico-cultural conflict that emerged from a colonial past that has refused to pass. It was triggered by the postcolonial, authoritarian, neo-patrimonial Republic of Cameroon that has committed incredible human rights violations and crimes against humanity. The so-called "Anglophone crisis" in Cameroon has festered since 1961 due to the self-interested economic and strategic complicity of several countries–France, Israel, Switzerland, the United Kingdom, Russia, China, and Nigeria–under the impotent gaze of the African Union, the United Nations and the international community.

Definition of Terms

All discussions of the communitarian and identitarian conflict in Cameroon must begin with a definition of terms. What do we mean when we speak of "Anglophone" and "Francophone" in the multi-ethnic, multi-religious, multi-lingual, and multicultural context of Cameroon, a country of 25 million and more than 300 languages? The term "Anglophone" originates from "Anglo," the word-forming element of Latin origin, which means "pertaining to England or the English." It was part of the nomenclature of the Anglo-Saxon peoples. Etymologically, the word "Anglo" is a chameleonic adjective that takes on different linguistic, ethnic, and racial colorations to suit specific political, cultural, and ethnic environments. Indeed, the word "Anglo-Saxon" is an elastic term originating from the Latin *Anglo-Saxones,* which literally meant *"English Saxons"* or the Saxons of England as opposed to Continental European Saxons like those in Saxony, Germany. France has a different linguistic and cultural history and experience with the term "Anglo-Saxon." In French, the term Anglo-Saxon refers, first and foremost, to Germanic invaders (Angles, Saxons, Jutes, and their successors) of Great Britain and their language, Anglo-Saxon or Old English. When *Guillaume Le Conquérant* (William the Conqueror), Duke of Normandy conquered England in 1066, introduced Parisian French, and created the Common Law, French became part of the cultural landscape of England. The Latin and French-speaking scribes of that era used the term *Anglo-Saxones* to refer to the inhabitants who lived in the

British Isles before the Norman conquest. The term ultimately came to refer to British civilization and governance. Despite the Norman-French conquest of 1066 and its subsequent influence on the culture of England, France and England have historically had divergent governmentalities or mentalities of political governance. The French have always spoken of "*La notion anglo-saxonne de l'État*" (the Anglo-Saxon notion of the state) (Robert, 1992, p. 69). That term encompasses native English speakers in former British colonies–the United States, Canada, Australia, New Zealand, and South Africa. The Greek suffix "phone" or "phônos" means voice or sound. These suffixes are used to describe specific languages or linguistic groups based on their linguistic "articulations" (Petit Robert, 1992). Originally, the term Anglophone meant those who articulate or express themselves in some variant or iteration of English as their native language. The term has become elastic over time. It now includes speakers of any of the multiple forms of English or "Englishes" in the Anglosphere, the realm of English speakers. According to the *Cambridge Advanced Learner's Dictionary and Thesaurus*, the term Anglophone is often used in multicultural contexts. It refers to "a person who speaks English, especially in countries where other languages are also spoken." Former British colonies like India, Kenya, Zimbabwe, South Africa, Nigeria, Uganda, Namibia, Botswana, and so on, where English is the official language, alongside other languages, are considered Anglophone countries. The *Merriam-Webster English Dictionary* also highlights the multicultural context in which the term Anglophone is often used. It describes the term as an adjective that means, "consisting of or belonging to an English-speaking population especially in a country where two or more languages are spoken." It highlights the case of Canada, where a French-speaking or Francophone minority exists in an overwhelmingly Anglophone North America. Generally speaking, the term "Anglophone," which entered the French language in 1915, is more commonly used in French comparative cultural and linguistic contexts than in English scholarly milieux.

The term Anglophone is best understood by examining it with the word "Francophone," after which it was patterned. In the late 19th century, the expression "Francophone" entered the French language. It referred to people who spoke French as their mother tongue or as a second language. Due to colonial rivalries, Anglophone Africa is often defined in opposition to Francophone Africa. Indeed, the word "Anglophone" is the foil–with the adversarial connotations of the metaphor–of "Francophone" in the African colonial and postcolonial context. Both terms are used more often in French literature and usage than in English parlance. In the French African colonial and postcolonial context, the French refer to Africans who speak French as their mother tongue and use it as an official language, a lingua franca, or medium of communication as *les Africains francophones (Francophone Africans)*.

The handful of countries that have the difficult Anglophone/Francophone divide manage it in multiple ways. In Canada, the majority French-speaking or Francophone province of Quebec has a special, autonomous, politico-cultural self-governance that respects its cultural specificity. In Quebec, the term "Anglophone" is the nomenclature for the linguistic and cultural "Other." It refers to the minority English-speaking population of the province, as well as the majority English-speaking Canada as a whole. For their part, English-speaking Canadians generally refer to French-speaking Canadians from Quebec as French Canadians or *Francophones*. Mauritius, a multicultural former British colony, is an Anglophone country whose official language, English, is used alongside other languages, including French, Mauritian Creole, and multiple Asian languages. In the New England States and Upstate New York, which border the French-speaking province of Quebec, Americans of French or Quebecois descent prefer the nomenclature, "Franco-American," because they do not consider themselves "Anglos," in the ethnic sense in which the term is used in parts of the United States. In the Western and Southwestern states, the term "Anglo" is a subtly satirical descriptor used to distinguish white Americans in general, from Hispanics, Mexicans, or native Spanish speakers in general, irrespective of their race or ethnicity.

In the African colonial and postcolonial context, the French term *Africains Anglophones* refers to Africans who speak English as their mother tongue, and use it as an official lingua franca, a "vehicular language" or medium of communication and education (Petit Robert, 1992). French nomenclature for English speakers (Anglophones) and French speakers (Francophones) is the popular usage. Thus, to define one's self as Francophone is to define one's self in opposition to Anglophones. In Cameroon, the term "Anglophone" has a context-specific meaning. It is an unofficial, disparaging, epithet, a cultural adjective–often deliberately deformed into the insult, "Anglofous" (Anglofools), to describe Cameroonians who originate from the former British Southern Cameroons. The epithet is designed to relegate minority English and Pidgin-speakers, who do not master Parisian French, into the status of subalterns or second-class citizens (Gramsci, 1988). The most intriguing fact about the Anglophone/Francophone divide in Cameroon is that English is not the native language of most Anglophones–West African Pidgin is the lingua franca of the Northwest and Southwest regions– and French is not the native language of most Francophones. In the bi-lingual (French and English are the official languages) and multi-cultural situation of Cameroon (there are more than 300 different distinct languages and ethnic groups in Cameroon plus Pidgin English), the term refers to people whose ethnic origins are traceable to the former British Southern Cameroons, now divided and renamed the Northwest and Southwest regions. While the territory of the former British Southern Cameroons is inhabited by about 5 million people from a slew of African ethnolinguistic groupings, what unites them is a common lingua franca, a peculiar brand of pidgin English or creole. They are called English-speaking or Anglophones because they inherited English during their 40-year existence as a League of Nations Mandated Territory and a United Nations Trust Territory administered by the United Kingdom through Nigeria. In addition, there is a group of hyphenated Anglophones with ancestry in tribal or ethnic groups whose origin is outside the former British Southern Cameroons. These groups migrated from French Cameroon to British Southern Cameroons in the late 1950s and 1960s as refugees from the anti-French insurgency and fight for independence led by the outlawed *Union des Populations du Cameroun*. The children of these refugees attended English-medium schools and became part of the Anglophone mosaic. They include Bamileke-Anglophones (the so-called Anglo-Bami) whose ancestry is in the "Bamileke" area of the Western region, Bamun-Anglophones from the Bamun area of the Western region, the Douala, Bassa and Bakoko-Anglophones from the Littoral region. The term "Anglophone" therefore also includes persons from the Northwest and Southwest regions who migrated to French-speaking Cameroon cities like Bafoussam, Douala, and Yaoundé for political,

9

economic or security reasons. These people are always considered "Anglophones" despite the level of their mastery of the French language. The same is true of Francophones who originate from the territory of the former *Cameroun français* to the Northwest or Southwest region for whatever reason. They are always considered "Francophones" no matter their level of mastery of the English language.

From the Federal Republic to the *Chefferie républicaine* (Republican Chiefery)

The so-called "Anglophone crisis" in Cameroon results from a clash of governmentalities. Michel Foucault (2005) advanced the idea of *gouvernmentalité* (governmentality), a neologism formed from the words "government and mentality," which he defined as "a strategic field of power relations in their mobility, transformability, and reversability" (p. 252). Governmentality is the strategic conceptualization and deployment of governmental power within specific political and cultural contexts. It gives rise to different political regimes or diverse "arts of governance" (Foucault, 1994). The British Southern Cameroons and *la République du Cameroun* reunited in 1961 to form the bilingual *République Fédérale du Cameroun* (Federal Republic of Cameroon), without thinking through and conceptualizing the co-existence of a bi-cultural governmentality. The union turned out to be an unequal one due to a lack of conceptualization of the structure of the state, the geo-strategic ambitions of France, the Machiavellian disinterest of the United Kingdom, the naivety and fractiousness of Southern Cameroons politicians, and especially the unequal power dynamics between the majority French speakers and the minority English and Pidgin speakers. Before it attained independence from France on January 1, 1960, the fledgling *République du Cameroun* signed a series of *accords de coopération* (cooperation agreements) with the colonial Trusteeship power that created a postcolonial Francophone Cameroun republic whose national institutions, administration, monetary policy, armed forces, media and culture, secondary and higher education, as well as social policy, were put in place and managed by France. It is unclear whether John Ngu Foncha and his KNDP, Nfon Mukete, S.T. Muna, Ndeh Ntumazah of the One Kamerun Party, and other proponents of the One Kamerun idea were even aware of the existence of the *accords de coopération* between *la République du Cameroun* and France. One of the main dimensions of the Anglophone Problem is thus the structural and political imbalances between the two reunifying entities. In the run up to the re-unification, Foncha and the KNDP are famously said to have been indifferent at worst or had a certain "insouciance" and lack of concern at best, "concerning the actual form or content of the unification" they were championing and entering into (Ardener, 1962, p. 346). Through their political naivety, lack of sophistication and indifference towards the nature of the federation they were joining, Foncha, and his KNDP allies, as well as Ndeh Ntumazah's One Kamerun (OK) Party, implicitly endorsed extension of the *accords de coopération* between *la République du Cameroun* and France to Southern Cameroons, and participated with President Ahmadou Ahidjo, in creating a highly centralized, authoritarian, neo-patrimonial, single-party, *chefferie républicaine* (republican chiefery) in which Foncha and Muna served for a time as figure-head Vice Presidents. Thus, while French Cameroun inherited the centralizing French policy of secular republicanism, Southern Cameroons inherited a decentralized, federalist, faith-based localism and secularism from the British. In short, after reunification, each of the two Cameroon States brought to the table, "different interpretive schema," to borrow the expression of Campanini (2009, p. 6), with regard to the structure of the state, matters of religion and political governance. The expressions, "republican chiefery, chieftaincy, and chiefdom" are used interchangeably in this book (Willis, 2013).

Figure 1.3. Flag of the Federal Republic of Cameroon (1961-1972)

The Anglophone Question

The Anglophone Question, which French-speaking Cameroonians call it "*le problème anglophone*"- can be defined simply as the problematic role and place of the English and Pidgin-speaking minority in the hyper-centralized, authoritarian, neo-patrimonial, kleptocratic, majority French-speaking *chefferie republicaine* of Cameroon. As the newly independent *République du Cameroun* maneuvered to integrate the former United Nations Trust Territory of British Southern Cameroons, which was a functioning state with its own premiers, ministers, parliament, and independent judiciary, into its national territory after the UN-supervised Plebiscite of 1961, it partnered with its former colonial power, France, to assimilate the English and Pidgin-speaking territory into *la Francophonie*, the community of French-speaking countries. Since the reunification presented France an opportunity to extend its sphere of influence in Africa, the government of President Charles de Gaulle provided President Ahmadou Ahidjo of Cameroon, a man with no more than a three-year high school education, French legal advisers who drafted a rather centralized, "French-accented" federal constitution that was presented to Hon. John Ngu Foncha, Premier of Southern Cameroons, on the eve of reunification talks in Foumban in 1961. Despite the fact that this was a federal constitution designed for an emerging multicultural country with two distinct states that had both French and British colonial traditions, it had a very strong centralist, Napoleonic imprint. Indeed, the French Constitution of 1958 with its highly centralized system and its vague separation of powers, served as the rough template for the Cameroon federal constitution of 1961. The French-inspired, centralist, constitution of the Federal Republic of Cameroon was essentially an assimilationist death warrant for the state of Southern Cameroons.

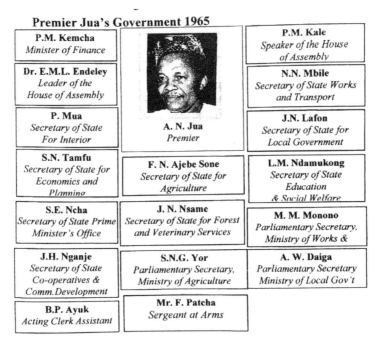

Premier Jua's Government 1965

P.M. Kemcha *Minister of Finance*		**P.M. Kale** *Speaker of the House* *of Assembly*
Dr. E.M.L. Endeley *Leader of the* *House of Assembly*		**N.N. Mbile** *Secretary of State Works* *and Transport*
P. Mua *Secretary of State* *For Interior*	**A. N. Jua** *Premier*	**J.N. Lafon** *Secretary of State for* *Local Government*
S.N. Tamfu *Secretary of State for* *Economics and* *Planning*	**F. N. Ajebe Sone** *Secretary of State for* *Agriculture*	**L.M. Ndamukong** *Secretary of State* *Education* *& Social Welfare*
S.E. Ncha *Secretary of State Prime* *Minister's Office*	**J. N. Nsame** *Secretary of State for Forest* *and Veterinary Services*	**M. M. Monono** *Parliamentary Secretary,* *Ministry of Works &*
J.H. Nganje *Secretary of State* *Co-operatives &* *Comm.Development*	**S.N.G. Yor** *Parliamentary Secretary,* *Ministry of Agriculture*	**A. W. Daiga** *Parliamentary Secretary* *Ministry of Local Gov't*
B.P. Ayuk *Acting Clerk Assistant*	**Mr. F. Patcha** *Sergeant at Arms*	

Figure 1.4. West Cameroon Government of Prime Minister Augustine Ngom Jua (1965)

Article I of the French Constitution of 1958 provides that: "*La France est une République indivisible, laïque, démocratique et sociale* (France is an indivisible, secular, democratic and social Republic). For its part, Article I of the 1961 Constitution of the Federal Republic of Cameroon provided that: "*La République Fédérale du Cameroun est démocratique, laïque et sociale*" (The Federal Republic of Cameroon is democratic, secular and social). As Paul Biya, Ahidjo's speech writer, Prime Minister, and President from 1982 admitted in 2019, the aim was to assimilate Southern Cameroons into French Cameroon. The Ahidjo-Biya regime quickly took the form of an authoritarian, hyper-centralized, neo-patrimonial, post-colonial, Napoleonic, Francophone regime. Cameroon evolved into a *chefferie républicaine* (a republican chiefery) in which the chief of state had absolute power, ruled by decree, controlled a subservient, rubber-stamp legislature, and an obsequious judiciary over which he presided (see preface). This was different from "*La notion anglo-saxonne de l'État*" (the Anglo-Saxon notion of the state) (Robert, 1992, p. 69), that the former British Southern Cameroons brought to the federation–a highly decentralized, federalist, governance that emphasized self-governance and localism. The nature of the Ahidjo/Biya regime can be determined by the status of its streets. The city of Buea, the former capital of Southern Cameroons has no formal street names. The streets belong to the central government in Yaoundé, which must approve all street names. No street names have been approved since 1961! Allowing Anglophone towns and cities to name their own streets was apparently viewed as a dangerous autonomist action.

The Anglophone Question arose because the Ahidjo/Biya regime imposed its authoritarian, neo-patrimonial, kleptocratic postcolonial Francophone *chefferie républic-aine* on the newly reunified Federal Republic of Cameroon. Presidents Ahidjo and Biya progressively eliminated the post-reunification Federal Republic of Cameroon, under which the once autonomous British Southern Cameroons maintained a certain level of autonomy, and imposed their hyper-centralized governance of *la République du Cameroun* on the whole territory. At the end of the chieftaincy of President Ahmadou Ahidjo, the new republican chieftain, President Paul Biya, signed a unilateral decree changing the name of the country to *La République du Cameroun,* the original name of French East Cameroon, thereby muting the politico-cultural identity and the very existence of the English and Pidgin-speaking Southern Cameroons. By a stroke of the pen, Paul Biya ensured that there was no past, there is no present, and there will be no future for the English-speaking Northwest and Southwest regions of Cameroon as distinct politico-cultural entities in Cameroon, which was renamed the United Republic of Cameroon and then *la République du Cameroun.* The Anglophone Question has been greatly complicated by the hardline autocracy of the Biya regime. Attempts by aggrieved English-speaking Cameroonians to resolve political problems through dialogue have, over the years been met with condescension, haughty dismissive-ness, and a refusal to engage in political dialogue. The All Anglophone Conferences of 1993 (AAC I), and 1994 (AAC II) that were held in Buea and Bamenda respectively, marked the beginning of the mass awakening of Southern Cameroonians to the intolerable injustices they suffered as citizens of a reunified Cameroon and laid the foundation for organized mass resistance to their domination, marginalization and assimilation into *la Francophonie.* Through the Buea Declaration (AAC I) and the Bamenda Proclamation (AAC II), Anglo-phones sounded the alarm that all was not well in the over-centralized, neo-patrimonial, autocratic, Napoleonic *chefferie republicaine* of Cameroon, called for a return to federalism and respect for the linguistic and cultural specificity of the former Southern Cameroons. These appeals were met with repression by the Biya regime. Instead of engaging in a frank and honest dialogue, the regime engaged in a series of bad-faith, authoritarian political maneuvers and pseudo-solutions that made the situation worse: militarization of the regions, political authoritarianism (the forced one-party state of Ahmadou Ahidjo), mar-ginalization, abolition of the state of West Cameroon and dividing it into Northwest and Southwest provinces, elimination of the United Republic of Cameroon with its two states, and replacing it with the highly centralized, tropical, Napoleonic, unitary, *la Republique du Cameroun,* the original name of the French Cameroun at independence, and instituting a flag with one star rather than the two stars of the federation. Harmonization of the Fran-cophone civil law and the Anglophone Common law (to the detriment of the Common law), led to the elimination of human rights protections like the presumption of innocence, habeas corpus, due process of law, and so on. Autocratic measures like nationalization of the natural resources and economic institutions of West Cameroon, harmonization of the sports and educational systems of British and French Cameroon to the detriment of British Southern Cameroons, elimination of freedom of speech and of the press, *la République du Cameroun's* membership in the British Commonwealth, the arrest, torture, imprisonment and murder of students, lawyers and teachers who demonstrated peacefully for change, and so on. This ultimately led to a clash of governmentalities, or conceptualizations of the very nature of the state, of governance, and of the rights of citizens (Foucault, 1994).

The authoritarian and neo-patrimonial actions of the Biya regime essentially sowed the seeds of the Anglophone Revolt, which ironically emerged in Foncha's home base of Bamenda in 2016 and transformed that city and most of the Northwest region into the bastion of Anglophone resistance. The Anglophone Question is thus a political, economic, cultural, identitarian, and geo-strategic problem that has been compounded by foreign interests. Besides France, which has had a long-term political and strategic goal of assimilating Anglophones into *la Francophonie*, a number of countries–Israel, the United Kingdom, Switzerland, China, Russia–to name just those–have propped up the Biya regime due to security, economic, political and other interests in Cameroon. The Anglophone Question is thus a crystallization of autocratic responses to the discontent of the English and Pidgin-speaking minority over the nature and structure of the state, and over its autocratic, non-inclusive governance, and blatant violations of human rights. Above all, it was compounded by the refusal of the authoritarian Ahidjo/Biya regime to listen to the political, economic, and human rights grievances of the English-speaking Southern Cameroons, whose territory had been divided into the Northwest and Southwest provinces, the better to dominate them and control their natural resources.

Not surprisingly, the Biya regime was blind to the fact that the Anglophone Question was a question of lack of democracy, that it was a problem of authoritarian governance and that the Anglophone Revolt was triggered by resistance to its divide and conquer policies towards the English and Pidgin-speaking Southern Cameroons, its assimilation and marginalization and especially by the hyper-centralized, autocratic, neo-patrimonial governance, the *chefferie républicaine*. When the Anglophone Revolt began in 2016, President Biya insisted on multiple occasions that under no circumstances, would the *forme de l'État* (the form of the state) be open to discussion. Instead, he opted for top-down bad-faith, *tromp l'oeil* solutions like "decentralization" and conferral of a dubious, French-style, "special status" on the restive Northwest and Southwest regions.

This clash of political worldviews soon became a bone of contention that was ignored in the flush of the totalitarian successes of the Ahidjo/Biya regime. It would ultimately degenerate into one of the triggers of Anglophone identitarian resistance. The Ahidjo/Biya neopatrimonialist system (Gabriel, 1999) facilitated French access to the natural resources of Southern Cameroons. Destruction of the Federal Republic of Cameroon, submergence, muting and dispersal of the English-and Pidgin-speaking Southern Cameroons into the Ahidjo/Biya *chefferie républicaine* (Republican chiefery), ultimately became the drivers of Anglophone discontent. Southern Cameroons had been transformed in half a century from a UN Trust Territory ripe for either independence or autonomy to a French postcolonial province. The authoritarian Biya regime's refusal to listen to Anglophone grievances–including pleas from Southern Cameroons reunificationist Vice Presidents, John Ngu Foncha and Solomon Tandeng Muna–and the cavalier insouciance with which he decided to use military means to solve the purely political Anglophone Question, led to the Anglophone Revolt in 2016. The regime's attempt to subjugate Anglophones with the military and financial assistance of France, the Israelis, China, the United Kingdom, Nigeria, and other countries, exacerbated the problem.

Additionally, as soon as the Federal Republic of Cameroon, made up of French East Cameroon and English-speaking West Cameroon came into existence in October 1961, France deployed a number of political, linguistic, and cultural tools aimed at politically and culturally assimilating the Anglophones of Southern Cameroons into *la Francophonie*. It accordingly implemented, with the collaboration of the East Cameroun regime of Ahmadou Ahidjo and Paul Biya–and with the cavalier imprimatur of West Cameroon Prime Ministers, John Ngu Foncha and Solomon Tandeng Muna–a number of measures that muted the identitarian specificity of English and Pidgin-speaking Cameroon, facilitated the destruction of the Federal Republic of Cameroon, eviscerated the autonomy of West Cameroon, and resulted in the highly centralized, authoritarian, neo-patrimonial (Gabriel, 1999), *chefferie républicaine* (Republican chiefery). This republican chiefery vested virtually all powers in the president, Ahmadou Ahidjo, who created a one-party state led by his party, the Cameroon National Union (CNU). He drafted a made-to-measure constitution loosely based on the French Constitution of 1958 and ruled by decree.

Figure 1.5. Left, Biya as Republican Chieftain - enthronement as chief of the SAWA (Douala)
Figure 1.6. Right, Biya as Republican Chieftain (enthronement in the Southern region).

French Assimilationist Policies and the Clash of Religious Establishmentalities

While the Ahidjo/Biya *chefferie républicaine* (republican chiefery) was putting together the building blocks of its neo-patrimonial autocracy, the French government took the opportunity to implement a policy of assimilation of the Southern Cameroons into *la Francophonie*, the community of French-speaking nations. As soon as the reunification of Cameroon was recognized by the United Nations, and British Trusteeship over Southern Cameroons was terminated, France set out to extend its *mission civilisatrice*, the Frenchman's civilizing burden to English-speaking Southern Cameroons by assimilating the territory into its Francophone African sphere of influence. In his confidential memorandum, French Ambassador to Cameroon, Monsieur Benard (1962) instructed the French Consul in Buea, Monsieur Yves Robin, that his task was to aid the French-style "unitary federalist" government of the Federal Republic of Cameroon (Anyangwe, 2008) in assimilating English and Pidgin-speaking West Cameroon into *La Francophonie*. This task involved: 1) "muting" the cultural and identitarian specificity of Anglophone Southern Cameroons, to use the expression of Ardener (1962, 2), isolating the territory from the

Anglosphere (the English-speaking world) by being wary of American initiatives that could be grounded in the linguistic commonality and cultural proximity between the United States and English-speaking Southern Cameroons, and 3) undertaking a crash political, cultural, economic, and pedagogical program that would modify the mentalities of Southern Cameroonians to accept the hegemonic imposition of the French language and culture, acquiesce to their assimilation into French Cameroon, and their cultural dispersal into the French-speaking world, *La Francophonie*. The expectation was that the English and Pidgin-speaking Southern Cameroons (renamed West Cameroon), which had a nearly 200-year-old, faith-based, Protestant secularism that pervaded its political, educational, medical, and social institutions, would vanish overnight and take on a French anti-clerical and anti-religious, secular republican coloration, which Morin (1991) called "Catho-secularism" after the reunification. The clash of mentalities over religion would become one of the points of friction between French and English-speaking Cameroon.

This French assimilationist strategy was a direct result of the transposition of the monocultural French Jacobine Revolutionary dogma of secular republicanism–and its anti-religious ethos– to the multicultural context of the reunifying Cameroon. The French-style secular republican provision of the 1961 Federal Constitution of Cameroon essentially sowed the seeds of the Anglophone Revolt because it represented an imposition, on the fledgling Federal Republic of Cameroon, of a legacy of the French Revolution of 1789 –French secular republican governmentality (logic of governance) (Foucault, 1991), and French counter-establishmentality–an anti-religious, anti-clerical worldview, mindset, and intellectual orientation. This counter-establishmentality is highly hostile towards the normative, spiritual, and public aspects of religion, especially its role and place in the life of the state and in the public sphere (Eko, 2012). Africanized French secular republicanism was manifested by hostility towards the study of religion in high schools and universities. Religion was systematically excluded as a subject that could be counted among the required number of subjects students had to pass to be considered successful in the single-subject examinations system of the General Certificate of Education. Religion was also excluded from the number of subjects that could be included among the number of subjects that applicants could include in the number of subjects that qualified them for participation in competitive examinations for civil service employment or higher education.

Anglophones as Subaltern Second-class Citizens

At the dawn of reunification, the French Cameroun perceived English-speaking Southern Cameroons as conquered territory and, with the assistance of France, set out to assimilate it into the French sphere of influence. The Anglophone Question is, therefore, a question of alterity or otherness, expressed in the governmentality of the inhabitants of that part of German Kamerun that was once a British League of Nations Mandate and a UN Trust Territory after World War I and became part of the British Empire for 40 years. After the reunification, the subalternity and alterity of English and Pidgin-speaking West Cameroonians stood in contradistinction to French Cameroun identitarian, political, socio-cultural, and economic hegemony. Over time, tensions between the two degenerated into a conflict of the "US," the hegemonic republican chiefery of French Cameroun, and the "Other than US"—the subaltern, minority, Northwest and Southwest regions, which were once the British Southern Cameroons. The tensions between the two Cameroons were exacerbated by authoritarian denialism, a strategic refusal to recognize and respect the cultural specificity of Anglophone Cameroon, and a long-term political and strategic goal of assimilating and dispersing the Anglophones into *la Francophonie*.

The Anglophone Question and the Anglophone Revolt

Southern Cameroons has been grafted into *la Francophonie* for a longer period than it existed under British benevolent but neglectful absentee colonialism. Nevertheless, those English-speaking "zones" have maintained an identitarian specificity that fueled the Anglophone Revolt that began in 2016 and evolved into an armed conflict in 2017, due to the tyrannous disregard for Anglophone pleas for democratic and equitable reforms to the over-centralized, authoritarian, neo-patrimonial, tribal, republican chiefdom that obtains in Cameroon. The identitarian specificity of the so-called Anglophone "zone" has been sustained by the following factors: 1) its religio-cultural and identitarian specificity, 2) its English-medium educational system, 3) its Anglo-American common law legal tradition, 4) its historic anchorage in the global Anglosphere, the English-speaking world, through popular culture and information and communication technologies. The Anglophone Revolt was spear-headed by two of the bulwarks of the culture and identity of the English-speaking regions of Cameroon–the legal profession and the educational sector. The English-speaking Common Law lawyers, and the English-speaking teachers' unions–and students– kicked off the Anglophone Revolt, with the blessing of their cultural, identitarian and spiritual partners, the Roman Catholic Church, the Presbyterian Church in Cameroon and the Cameroon Baptist Convention, whose work in the religious, educational, healthcare and other sectors, had molded a distinct English-language and Pidgin English culture grounded on African traditions in the two regions that had made up the former Southern Cameroons.

In its headlong rush to assimilate Southern Cameroons, the successive iterations of the Ahidjo/Biya regime–the Federal Republic of Cameroon, the United Republic of Cameroon and ultimately, the Republic of Cameroon–rejected the idea that English and Pidgin-speaking Cameroonians could be multiple subjects, simultaneously: Africans, Cameroonians and Anglophones. The government of Cameroon refused to recognize English-speaking Cameroonians as a distinct minority community, ignoring the fact that the State of Southern/West Cameroon was a self-governing entity that voluntarily joined the Republic of Cameroon in 1961. The main goal of *la République du Cameroun* was to assimilate and phagocyte the territory and resources of Southern Cameroons for the benefit of the elite of the kleptocratic, Napoleonic regime of Yaoundé. The Anglophone Question thus reflects political, philosophical, and social differences between *la République du Cameroun* and Southern Cameroons on the *scope* of the "reunification" of 1961. The Anglophone Question is now essentially the stubborn insistence of the English-speaking or Anglophone minority of Cameroon, citizens of the former state of Southern Cameroons in asserting their identitarian apartness, their peoplehood from the French-speaking or Francophone majority. The Anglophone Question is also the non-assimilability of the Anglophones of the former Southern Cameroons into the hyper-centralized, authoritarian, postcolonial, *chefferie républicaine* of *La Republique du Cameroun* despite more than half a century of French and Cameroon assimilationist policies, initiatives, and programs.

Structure and Content of the Volume

The Anglophone Question in Cameroon – French-speaking Cameroonians speak of *le problème anglophone* – is grounded in the history of European colonialism and imperialism in Africa. It is one of the few items of unfinished business of the First World War and the Treaty of Versailles of 1919. The Anglophone Question is more than a question of Africans fighting and killing each other over European colonial languages and cultures. It is an artifact of postcolonial hegemony and exploitation that has historical, cultural, identitarian, and collective memory dimensions. It is above all, a question of authoritarian denial. The Biya regime has never accepted that there is such a thing as an Anglophone Question or an Anglophone Problem. If there is no problem, there is no problem to solve, nothing to dialogue about. As such, the Anglophone Question in Cameroon is fundamentally a political question, a question of lack of democracy, of authoritarian governance. The Anglophone Question is essentially the stubborn persistence of the English and Pidgin-speaking minority of Cameroon, citizens of the former state of Southern Cameroons, in asserting their identitarian apartness, their peoplehood from the French-speaking or Francophone majority in the face of denial of same. It is the non-assimilability of the Anglophones of the former Southern Cameroons into the hyper-centralized, authoritarian, postcolonial, *chefferie républicaine* of *la République du Cameroun* despite more than half a century of French and Cameroon assimilationist policies, initiatives, and programs. This volume is concerned with the conceptual, historical, political, educational, legal, cultural, social, and national dimensions of the Anglophone Question, as well as its international, geo-strategic aspects, namely, the French, British, Israeli, Swiss, and Nigerian connections to the problem.

The volume is structured in three parts. The first part focuses on the conceptual, historical, and political aspects of the Anglophone Question. The second chapter defines the Anglophone Question and presents its historical and geo-strategic dimensions. It presents the two main theoretical perspectives that undergird, describe, and explain the Anglophone and Cameroonian governmental perspectives and postures on the Anglophone Question. The premise is that the constitutionally questionable assimilationist maneuvers used by President Ahidjo to transform the country from a two-state bilingual federal republic to a highly-centralized, autocratic, neo-patrimonial, Napoleonic chiefdom, the United Republic of Cameroon in 1972, and Chief of State, President Paul Biya's arbitrary erasure of the statal identity of the former British Southern Cameroons by partitioning it into two provinces, the Northwest and Southwest, and renaming the whole country, *la Republique du Camer-oun* (the Republic of Cameroon), the name of pre-unification French Cameroun in 1984, triggered the Anglophone Revolt in 2016. Furthermore, the tone-deafness and intolerance of the Biya regime, and its criminalization of the political philosophy of federalism, the political and systemic preference of most Anglophones, reinforced the perceptions of English and Pidgin-speaking people of Southern Cameroons that they were a subaltern, "muted group," mere "parenthetical citizens" who had no say in matters concerning their own governance (Ardener & Ardener, 2005, p. 53). They came to believe that they were the objects of a vast assimilationist conspiracy aimed at suppressing their identity as a people. The second theoretical perspective explored in chapter two is *le vivre ensemble* (living together), a theoretical framework advanced by the 19th century, French political thinker, Renan (1882). *Le vivre ensemble* has become the talismanic, political mantra of the Biya republican chieftaincy. At face value, this innocent-sounding phrase seems to denote tolerance, peaceful co-existence, and multi-culturalism; exactly what Cameroon needs to address the Anglophone Question. The reality on the ground is at variance with the sanctimonious and platitudinous pronouncements of the political elite of Cameroon. This chapter explores Renan's *vivre ensemble,* whose meaning has evolved over time, and shows that the phrase, which has become a buzzword in contemporary French sociology and politics, is actually an exhortation to immigrants–of which Muslims are the majority– to jettison their native cultures at the border and embrace the monocultural national ideology of French secular republicanism. This ideology, which is rooted in the French Revolution, is the actual antithesis of multiculturalism and cultural diversity. This political ideology is clearly misplaced and misapplied in Cameroon. It is the monocultural, assimilationist understanding of *le vivre ensemble* that deterritorialized to Cameroon and was on display at the Grand National Dialogue of September 30th to October 4th, 2019. This pseudo event ignored the crux of the Anglophone Question, namely, recognition of the cultural and identitarian specificity of the English and Pidgin-speaking former British Southern Cameroons (partitioned into the Northwest and Southwest regions), and their equal, bilingual, bicultural co-existence in a democratic, responsive federal state alongside the French-speaking peoples of *la République du Cameroon.* The Grand National Dialogue was an abject failure because it ignored the fact that Renan's concept of living together is grounded on the principle that the governed give the government their consent to be governed, not to be brutally subjugated. The "decentralization" that was "decreed" at this Grand National Dialogue, was actually a decentralization of the centralization of the administration of Chief of State-for-life, His Excellency, President Paul Biya who did not even bother to attend a single session of the "dialogue."

The third chapter focuses on the historical British connections and disconnections in the Anglophone Question. The main premise is that the Anglophone Question is unfinished business from World War I. Since the United Kingdom was the victorious "allied" power entrusted with managing the Southern Cameroons, and preparing it for self-determination under League of Nations mandates and United Nations trusteeships, the UK is directly responsible for the Anglophone problem. This chapter presents the chronology of the Anglophone Revolt, the mass uprising of lawyers, teachers, students, churches, and members of the Anglophone civil society, in response to the authoritarianism and repression of the Biya regime. The fourth chapter focuses on the historical and cultural aspect of the French connection to the Anglophone Question. Since the reunification of British Southern Cameroons and *la République du Cameroun* in 1961, France sought to extend the "Frenchman's burden," its colonial *mission civilisatrice* (civilizing mission) and postcolonial *exception culturelle* (cultural exception) (Betts, 1961; Eko, 2013) to the English and Pidgin-speaking population of Southern Cameroons by assimilating it into the French African community, *la Francophonie.* This aggravated the Anglophone Question.

Chapter 5 presents the genesis and evolution of one of the first bones of contention of the Anglophone Question, namely, the clash of legal cultures. This is the attempted co-existence of the French, Napoleonic, civil law system, which was deterritorialized into French Cameroun by France after it was mandated by the United Nations to take over most of former German Kamerun East of the Mungo River, and the British common law system that had been transferred into British Cameroons, slivers of former German Kamerun territories West of the Mungo, that had been handed over to the United Kingdom, under an identical League of Nations mandate and United Nations trusteeship. It was the judicial assimilationist maneuvers and systemic impositions of the Ahidjo/Biya regimes that transformed the once staid and placid Anglophone common law lawyers into activists that spear-headed the All Anglophone Conferences of 1993/1994 and the Anglophone revolt of 2016.

In Chapter 6, Barrister Tanjong Ashuntantang, a practicing Anglophone lawyer, presents the politico-legal dimension of the Anglophone Question. In his chapter, "Crossing the Red Line of Harmonization: How the Common Law went to War in Cameroon," Ashuntantang argues that one of the main causes of the Anglophone crisis and revolt was subtle Francophone legal assimilation through the vague, overbroad, and elastic policy of "harmonization." At face value, this musical metaphor suggests an aesthetically pleasing blend of multiple instruments. In the case of Cameroon, rather than blend the French civil law tradition that obtained in *La République du Cameroun*, with the Anglo-American common law system that existed in Southern Cameroons, for purposes of standardizing the law, harmonization became a Francophone tool for phagocytizing and erasing the common law system of Southern Cameroons. He argues that the outcome has been a paradigm shift in the legal culture of Anglophone Cameroon. This one-sided harmonization ignited a common law crisis and triggered an Anglophone Revolt in October 2016, when common lawyers launched a campaign of nonviolent action marked by a court boycott. The Cameroon government opted to crush and subjugate the Anglophone lawyers and teachers rather than hold talks with them. Violent repression of demonstrating Anglophone lawyers, teachers, students, and other members of the civil society by government forces led to a spiral of violence and bloodshed that subsequently triggered an armed conflict.

The second part of this volume consists of contributions by a diverse group of Southern Cameroonian scholars whose research and teaching focus on different aspects of the historical and politico-cultural aspects of the Anglophone Question and the Anglophone Revolt of 2016. In Chapter 7, Womai Song focuses on an aspect of the Anglophone Question that has not received much scholarly attention: the clash between Premiers Augustine Ngom Jua and Solomon Tandeng Muna that was one of the earliest symptoms of Anglophone disaffection in a reunified Cameroon and demonstrated that there was an influential minority in the Anglophone community that differed with the rush to disperse Anglophone specificity in the Francophone-dominated authoritarian federation. Chapter eight explores one of the main components of what has come to be known as the Anglophone Question – the very existence of the English-medium educational system that the state of Southern Cameroons had brought into the reunification with *La République du Cameroun*. This historical, political, cultural, and social survey uses case studies that describe and explain Anglophone struggles against attempts by the majority of French speakers to mute and erase the English-language educational sub-system through assimilation, harmonization, and authoritarian fiat. One of the main bones of contention was the attempted transformation and evisceration of the Anglophone General Certificate of Education (GCE), the main secondary and post-secondary school leaving examinations of Southern Cameroon. This chapter portrays the Anglophone educational system as one of the twin crucibles of Anglophone resistance–the other being the legal system–against assimilation and dispersal of Anglophone cultural and identitarian specificities into *la Francophonie*, the global French language community. The emergence and diffusion of the Internet and information and communication technologies (ICTs) from the United States, and the transformation of English into the global lingua franca demonstrated the importance of English to Francophones and probably saved the English language educational subsystem from total assimilation. In Chapter 9, Innocent Afuh Awasom presents a case study of the federal bilingual grammar school system. His essay is entitled, "Assimilationist Bilingual Education in Cameroon: The Case of the Federal Bilingual Grammar School, Molyko, Buea." Written from an insider's perspective, Awasom submits that the federal bilingual grammar schools in question were two highly selective secondary and post-secondary institutions located in Yaoundé and Man O' War Bay, near Victoria (the latter was soon transferred to Molyko, Buea). These institutions were built by a French construction company, Razel, with funding from the federal government of Cameroon and France. France also supplied a good number of French citizens to teach French to both Anglophone and Francophone students. The bilingual grammar schools had a dual system that combined the French Cameroon and Southern Cameroons secondary school models. The Federal Bilingual Grammar School in Buea enrolled mostly the children of the Southern Cameroons reunification elite, as well as the children of Francophone civil servants and military officials posted to Buea after the reunification. Awasom, a product of the bilingual grammar school system, suggests that the creation of the bilingual schools should be seen through the lens of the policy of assimilation. The best and the brightest children who had the necessary political or tribal connections were selected and put through rigorous bilingual training intended to transform them into an elite bilingual class fluent in both languages. This class would supply the lawyers, doctors, teachers, translators, administrators, and other professionals who would advance the assimilationist goals and aspirations of France and the Francophone-dominated Federal Republic of Cameroon.

In Chapter 10, which is entitled, "*#BringBackOurInternet: Cameroon Government Internet Shutdown and Digital Activist Resistance during the Anglophone Revolt*," Dibussi Tande, an author and international Information and Communication Technology consultant, describes and explains politically motivated Internet shutdowns in Africa as the backdrop for Internet and mobile telephone shutdowns in the context of the Anglophone Revolt in Cameroon. The Internet blackout was a wholesale transfer of the Cameroon government's notorious authoritarian repression and prior restraint (media censorship) from physical space to the dematerialized realms of cyberspace– the Internet and its networked social media platforms. In effect, the Anglophone uprising quickly became a social media-driven revolt that the government could not suppress. Anglophone activists used the Internet and social media applications on their mobile phones, to organize demonstrations in all parts of the English and Pidgin-speaking former Southern Cameroons (renamed the Northwest and Southwest regions). Anglophones in the diaspora–particularly the United States, the United Kingdom, Canada, South Africa, Nigeria, Belgium, Germany, and the Scandinavian countries joined the fray. This created an unprecedented global Anglo-Cameroon virtual community that could be called upon to hold demonstrations in Cameroon and Western countries. In response, Honourable Minette Libom Li Likeng, the Cameroon Minister of Posts and Telecommunications, ordered Camtel, the government-owned telecommunications operator and Internet service provider to carry out "suspension of Internet Services to certain sensitive regions [read the English-speaking region]" of Cameroon. This ministerial order essentially imposed a total mobile telephone and Internet blackout on the 5 million people of the English-speaking region of Cameroon. This 95-day blackout turned out to be Africa's longest Internet and mobile telephone blackout. In this chapter, Dibussi Tande surveys and analyzes the 2017 Internet shutdown in the English-speaking regions of Cameroon, he examines events leading up to the shutdown, shows how digital activists built a transnational multi-stakeholder coalition to pressure the Cameroon government to end the shutdown through the #BringBackOurInternet campaign, which placed the international spotlight on the Anglophone problem in Cameroon, as well as on the atrocities and human rights violations of Cameroon's Israeli-trained and equipped, army-within-the-army, the *Bataillon d'Intervention Rapide* (BIR).

One of the characteristics of the Federal Republic of Cameroon that emerged after the reunification of French Cameroon and Southern Cameroons in 1961 was a neo-patrimonial, national security state where there was the complete absence of freedom of speech and expression. Pre-registration of newspapers, prepublication censorship and post-publication punishment were the order of the day. Loss of freedom of expression was perhaps the steepest price Southern Cameroons paid for the ill-considered reunification. The Anglophone Revolt, spearheaded by lawyers and teachers, was an attempt to reclaim the lost right of freedom of expression. Chapter 11 is aptly entitled, "Killing the Messenger: The English-language Press and the Anglophone Crisis in Cameroon. In this chapter, Hansel Ngala, a budding scholar of communication studies, narrates and analyzes the repressive measures the Biya regime took to suppress freedom of expression, including the arrest, torture, imprisonment and murder of Anglophone journalists who reported on the crisis. Ngala carries out a case study on the arrest, torture and murder–with impunity–of Anglophone journalist, Samuel Ajiekah Abuwe, also known as Samuel Wazizi, 36, a presenter for Chillen Muzik and Television (CMTV). He was tortured to death while being held incommunicado in military detention. The reasons for the arrest, torture, and murder of Samuel Ajiekah Abuwe, 36, also known as Samuel Wazizi are unclear. Reliable sources within the Israeli-controlled military and security communications infrastructure of Cameroon suggest that the Cameroonian authorities were probably using Pegasus, spyware developed by an Israeli cyberwar company and stealthily deployed by authoritarian governments to monitor the communications of journalists, human rights activists, and dissidents, to surveil Wazizi's cellphone communications. It is believed he was arrested for allegedly setting up an interview with an alleged Ambazonian separatist supporter or sympathizer, but the truth will probably never be known given the mysterious circumstances of his arrest and murder in Cameroon military security custody.

In Chapter 12, Jude Fokwang, a professor of anthropology and sociology, analyzes the role and place of one of the distinctive institutions of Southern Cameroons, traditional rulers, in the Anglophone Question and the subsequent Anglophone Revolt of 2016. In effect, traditional rulers had been instrumental in the British system of indirect colonial rule in Southern Cameroons. Their transformation into "auxiliaries" of the administration under the Ahidjo/Biya federal and unitary regime, changed the dynamics of their relationships with their communities. Fokwang's chapter explores the thorny relationship between the Francophone-dominated regime of President Paul Biya and traditional leaders in the Anglophone regions. In the wake of the separatist conflict raging in the Anglophone territories, he interrogates the positions chiefs took at the onset and during the explosion of the Anglophone conflict, a political crisis that he argues is the outcome of the failure of the postcolonial state of Cameroon to manage the relationship between its constituent parts – *la République du Cameroun* (French Cameroun) and the former British Southern Cameroons.

The third part of this volume explores human rights aspects of the Anglophone crisis. Using as a springboard the famous aphorism attributed to ancient Greek master of tragedy, Aeschylus, "In war, truth is the first casualty" (Aeschylus, 550BC), Lyombe Eko suggests that the metaphor is applicable to the Anglophone crisis in Cameroon. In Chapter 13, Eko extends the metaphor and demonstrates that the second casualty of war is innocent men, women and children, and the third casualty is healthcare givers, and healthcare institutions. Lyombe Eko describes, explains and analyzes the travails of the healthcare workers and healthcare institutions that are caught between the Cameroon military, which does not care for the niceties of human rights, the Geneva Convention and the international laws of war, and Anglophone non-state armed groups who are ignorant of these principles and take out their frustrations on innocent citizens, healthcare workers and healthcare institutions. In the resulting anarchy, the innocent are caught in the crossfire, while military commanders and separatist warlords are having a field day.

Chapter 14 is written in dramatic, literary non-fiction style to convey the horrors of torture carried out by the Cameroon military on civilian women, men, and girls in the Northwest and Southwest regions of Cameroon, the former Southern Cameroons. It is informed by Nobel Prize winner, Wole Soyinka's conceptualization of "Climates of Fear," engendered by the authoritarian deployment of absolute power. The drama opens with the resistance of the women of Aghem, Wum, against the oppression they face at the hands of the Cameroon military. The damning accusation against women that amounted to an extrajudicial criminal indictment, conviction and sentence, is "Mama Amba!" (the mother of an Ambazonian separatist). The chapter then presents the mud torture of an accused Ambazonian separatist in Molyko, near Buea, and an identical mud bath torture of two young Anglophone girls near Cameroon Protestant College, Bali. The chapter is divided into four acts: Mama Amba, son of Mama Amba, daughter of Mama Amba, and President Macron and the Amba dilemma, the Anglophone Problem.

Conclusion

The idea that runs through this volume is that the Anglophone Question is a question of authoritarian governance and lack of democracy on the part of the Biya regime. It is the denial and diminishment of the cultural and political specificity and autonomy of the English-speaking State of West Cameroon, deceptively and forcefully declaring it part of a French-style, "one and indivisible" secular republican Cameroon– and that expression is lifted verbatim from Article I of the French Constitution. Dividing West Cameroon into two provinces/regions ruled by Francophone governors (pro-consuls), Napoleonic *préfets*, and sous-préfets appointed by President Biya without the consent of the people of Southern Cameroons all contributed to the problem. The dubious and deceptive strategy of assimilation of the State of West Cameroon and its English and Pidgin-speaking peoples and dispersing them into la Francophonie and the Biya regime's denial that there is an Anglophone problem in Cameroon, did more to aggravate the situation than the actions of Anglophone armed non-state groups, who call themselves "restoration forces." These ragtag groups claim to be fighting to restore the state of Southern Cameroons that was annexed by *La République du Cameroun* in 1961.

The Anglophone Revolt against the republican chiefdom, which Chiefs of State, Presidents Ahmadou Ahidjo and Paul Biya imposed on the multi-cultural nation of Cameroon, to the detriment of the politico-cultural identity, specificity, and economic well-being of the English and Pidgin-speaking minority territory of Southern Cameroons, officially began with the Buea Declaration issued by the All Anglophone Conference (AACI), held in Buea, on April 2-3, 1993. This was followed by the Bamenda Proclamation, issued by the All Anglophone Conference (AACII) held in Bamenda from 29th April to 1st May 1994. The Chief of State, President Paul Biya, turned a dictatorial glare and a deaf ear to the Anglophone calls for change and resorted to authoritarian police and military means to subjugate the Anglophone cause once and for all. Charles Tilly's clever dictum, *"War made the state, and the state made war" (1990),* is applicable to the Anglophone Problem. World War I led to the partition of German Kamerun into French Cameroun and British Southern Cameroons, and the injection of French and British colonial cultures on the former German territory. These forces led to the creation of the Cameroonian state, and that state made war on Anglophone identitarian and cultural specificity. In this book, we have argued that the Anglophone problem is the result of the failure of the authoritarian, neo-Napoleonic, republican chiefdom of Ahmadou Ahidjo and Paul Biya to manage the complications of the colonial and postcolonial biculturalism of Cameroon. The autocratic and bellicist posture of 92-year-old Chief of State, Paul Biya towards the Anglophones has weakened the State of Cameroon. The Anglophone crisis has consumed national resources that would have gone towards economic development and poverty alleviation. It has resulted in wanton destruction of public infrastructures and private property. It has decimated hospitals, schools and roads in the Anglophone regions and affected development in the rest of the country. The Anglophone crisis weakened the fabric of the nation, exposed the impotence of the rubber-stamp National Assembly, the utter lack of independence of the judiciary, the militarization of the system of justice, the entrenchment of the national security state, and the genesis of an oxymoronic, *tromp l'oeil* system of centralized decentralization.

The Anglophone crisis and its aftermath raise questions and uncertainties about post-Biya Cameroon. In his 2023 End of Year and 2024 New Year message to the Nation (2024), the Chief of State blamed economic difficulties and the lack of resources on the Ukrainian and Israel-Gaza wars rather than his own war against the Anglophones:

> As in the past, the said international context weighed heavily on our internal situation.
>
> The lingering war in Eastern Europe continued to disrupt the supply channels of the global consumer products market.
>
> Foodstuff and energy resource prices thus continued to rise as the conditions for accessing external financing tightened.
>
> The resurgence, last October, of the Israeli-Palestinian conflict worsened the rifts within the international community and is now monopolizing its attention.
>
> As expected, such a situation adversely impacted our country. It led to a general price hike in consumer products and, consequently, the cost of living. It also resulted in various types of shortages, including a shortage of petroleum products.

In Cameroon, the lessons of the past have not been learnt; have never been learnt. Since wars make nations as much as nations make wars, due to Paul Biya's failure to manage the Anglophone problem in a visionary democratic manner, he has merely postponed the problem to the next generation. As long as Pidgin English continue to be spoken in Cameroon, and English continues to be an "official" language, there will always be an Anglophone problem. One thing is sure, the Anglophone revolt has ensured that Cameroon will never be the same again, no matter who succeeds Paul Biya as president and Chief of State.

References

Aeschylus (550 BC). *The Oresteia*. E.D.A Morshead (trans.). Project Gutenberg. Retrieved from: http://gutenberg.net.au/ebooks07/0700021h.html

Anyangwe, C. (ed. 2010). *The Declassified British Secret Files on the Southern Cameroons*. Bamenda: Langaa

Albert, M. (1991). *Capitalisme contre capitalisme, (*Capitalism against capitalism*)*. Paris: Seuil.

Ardener, E. (1962). The Political History of Cameroon. *The World Today*, Vol. 18, No. 8. (pp. 341-350)

Ardener, S. (2005). Ardener's "Muted Groups": The genesis of an idea and its praxis. Women and Language, Vol. 28, (2), Pp. 50-54,72.

Ardener, E. (1970). Witchcraft, Economics, and the Continuity of Belief', in Mary Douglas (ed.), Witchcraft Confessions and Accusations (ASA Monographs No. 9), London: Tavistock, pp. 141-60.

Ardener, E. (1956). *Coastal Bantu of the Cameroons*. London: International African Institute.

Ardener, S. (1996). *Kingdom on Mount Cameroon: Studies in the History of the Cameroon Coast, 1500-1970*. Providence, R.I: Berghan Books.

Azuelos, M. (1996). *Le Modèle économique anglo-saxon à l'epreuve de la globalisation* (The Anglo-saxon economic model and the test of globalization). Paris: Nouvelle Sorbonne.

Baudrillard, J. & Guillaume, M.. (2008). *Radical Alterity* (Ames Hodges, Trans). Cambridge, MA: MIT Press.

Betts, R. (1961). *Assimilation and Association in French Colonial Theory, 1890-1914.* New York: Columbia University Press.

Clarke, S. (2010). *1000 Years of Annoying the French.* London: Transworld Publishers.

Crawford, J & Spoerndli, M. (2019). Cameroon's Biya: Why the Swiss Won't Stop His Geneva Stays. Swissinfo.ch. January 4. Retrieved from: https://www.swissinfo.ch/eng/who-foots-the-bill- cameroon-s-biya--why-the-swiss-won-t-stop-his-geneva-stays/44644510

Eko, L. (2010). "New Technologies, Ancient Archetypes: The *Boston Globe's* Discursive Construction of Internet Connectivity in Africa." *Howard Journal of Communications 21(2),* 182-198.

Eko, L. (2007). It's a Political Jungle Out There: How Four African Newspaper Cartoons Dehumanized and 'Deterritorialized' African Political Leaders in the Post-Cold War Era, *International Communication Gazette,* 69 (3), 219-238.

Eko, L. (2013). *American Exceptionalism, the French Exception and Digital Media Law.* Lanham, MD. Lexington Books.

Eko, L. (2012). *New Media, Old Regimes. Case Studies in Comparative Communication Law and Policy.* Lanham, MD: Lexington Books.

Eko, L. (2003). The English-Language Press and the 'Anglophone Problem' In Cameroon: Group Identity, Culture, and the Politics of Nostalgia. *Journal of Third World Studies*

Foucault, M. (1994), *Dits et Ecrits (Tome III), Sayings and Writings (Vol. III).* Paris: Editions Gallimard

Foucault, M. (1994a). *Dits et Ecrits (Tome II).(Sayings and Writings,* Vol. II*).* Paris: Gallimard.

Foucault, M. (2005). *The Hermeneutics of the Subject, Lectures at ehe Collége De France, 1981-1982* 252 (2005). (Arnold Davidson, ed., Graham Burchell, trans. Palgrave).

Foute, F. (2021). "The two Cameroons have still not been reunited." *The Africa Report.* March 4. Retrieved from: https://www.theafricareport.com/88389/the-two-cameroons-have-still-not-been-reunited-says-paul-ayah-abine/

Gaulle, Charles de. (1954). *Mémoires de guerre, l'appel, 1940-1942 (Memoirs of War, the Call, 1940-1942).* Paris: Plon.

Gramsci, A. (1988). *An Antonio Gramsci Reader,* D. Forgacs (ed.). London: Lawrence and Wishart.

Gründer, H. (1988). Christian Missionary Activities in Africa in the Age of Imperialism and the Berlin Conference of 1884-1885. In S. Förster, W. Mommsen & R. Robinson (eds.). *Bismarck, Europe and Africa: The Berlin Africa Conference 1884-1885 and the Onset of Partition (pp. 85-103).* Oxford: Oxford University Press.

Head of State's End-of-Year 2023, and New Year 2024 Message to the Nation (2024). Presidency of the Republic of Cameroon. Retrieved from: https://www.prc.cm/en/news/speeches-of-the-president/6958-head-of-state-s-end-of-year-2023-and-new-year-2024-message-to-the-nation

Herodotus (1925). *Book IV* (A.D. Godley, Trans.). Cambridge, MA: Harvard University Press.

Hochschild, A. (1999). *King Leopold's Ghost.* N.Y. Mariner Books.

Major, A. (1992) "Problematic" situations in press coverage of the 1988 US and French Elections. *Journalism Quarterly,* 69, 600-611

Mbembe, A. (2001). *On the Postcolony.* Berkley: UCLA Press.

Miers S (1988). "Humanitarianism at Berlin: Myth or Reality?" in *Bismarck, Europe and Africa:*

The Berlin Africa Conference 1884-1885 and the Onset of Partition, Stig Förster, Wolfgang Mommsen & Ronald Robinson, eds. Oxford: Oxford University Press, 333-345.

Morin, E. (1990). *Le trou noir de la laïcité* (The black hole of secularism). *Le Débat* No. 58, p. 38.

Mudimbe, V.Y. (1994). *The idea of Africa.* Bloomington, Indiana: Indiana University Press.

Nkafu Policy Institute (2019). Rt. Hon. Justice Ayah Paul Abine. Retrieved from: https://nkafu.org/experts/rt-hon-justice-ayah-paul-abine/

Purpose and Priorities (2024). The North American Baptist Conference. Retrieved from: https://nabconference.org/us/

Renan, E. (1882). *Qu'est-Ce Qu'une Nation?* (What is a Nation and Other Political Writings. Paris: Calman Levy.

Saker, E. (1908). *Alfred Saker, Pioneer of the Cameroons: By His Daughter.* London: The Religious Tract Society.

Ross, M. (2012). *The Oil Curse: How Petroleum Wealth Shapes the Development of Nations,* Princeton University Press, Oxford.

Tobin, S. (2002). Glencore UK subsidiary ordered to pay $310 mln over bribery, Reuters, (November 3). Retrieved from: https://www.reuters.com/world/uk/uk-court-approves-935-mln-pounds-confiscation-order-against-glencores-unit-2022-11-03/

Thomas, H. (1997). *The slave trade.* New York: Touchstone Books.

Tilly, C. (1990). *Coercion, Capital, and European States, AD 990-1990.* New York: Basil Blackwell.

Tocqueville, A. (1862). *De la démocracie en Amérique* (tome II) [Democracy in America. (Vol. II)]. (H. Reeve, Trans.). New York: J.H.G. Langley. (Original work published 1835).

Willis, J. (2013). 'Chieftaincy', in John Parker, and Richard Reid (eds), *The Oxford Handbook of Modern African History* (2013; online edn, Oxford Academic, 16 Dec. 2013), https://doi.org/10.1093/oxfordhb/9780199572472.013.0011, accessed 3 Nov. 2024.

Wright, J. Frantz, E. & Geddes, B. (2015). "Oil and Autocratic Regime Survival". *British Journal of Political Science.* 45 (2): 287–306. doi:10.1017/S0007123413000252.

Wright, J. & Frantz, E. (2017). How oil income and missing hydrocarbon rents data influence autocratic survival: A response to Lucas and Richter (2016). *Research & Politics.* 4 (3): 2053168017719794. doi:10.1177/2053168017719794

PART ONE

Conceptual and Historical Approaches

TWO

The Anglophone Question

History and Conceptual Approaches

LYOMBE EKO

> Men at some time are masters of their fates:
> The fault, dear Brutus, is not in our stars,
> But in ourselves, that we are underlings.
> *Julius Caesar*, Shakespeare

In Cameroon, the expressions "Anglophone" and "Francophone" are politico-cultural "lenses of perception" to use the expression of Marman (2016). These are existential worldviews, "in-the head" ways of seeing, being, and existing, that are grounded in language. They are inextricably linked with culture, and became part of the reality of Africans in the colonial and postcolonial periods. Trabant (2017) suggests that: "different languages yield different modes of thinking, or… different worldviews" (p. 4). Therefore, language is an element of the personality of nations and cultures…. Different languages yield different modes of thinking, different conceptualizations of political reality, different worldviews" (p. 5). The ideas that language is an intellectual product, an existential phenomenon that is a reflection of specific mentalities and worldviews, has far-reaching consequences. Trabant (2017) suggests that: "political consequences of the conception of language as 'work of the spirit' and of languages as 'worldviews' are obvious." Furthermore, it means resisting the idea that language is simply a tool of information transfer or of vocal signs (p. 5). Language is culture. In the postcolonial context, postcolonial subjects and actors for whom European languages were acquired as part of the colonial acculturation and educational process, are generally children of multiple linguistic and cultural worlds, which Trabant (2017) describes as a dual world of plurilingualism: "plurilingualism in its double sense… societal plurilingualism (the maintenance of the many languages) on the one hand, as well as individual plurilingualism (the knowledge of more than one language) on the other" (p. 5). The result is that the postcolonial subject is the subject of compartmentalization and hybridization. By his or her very multi-lingual and multicultural milieu, postcolonial subjects compartmentalize their existence into silos. They separate the following phenomena, pouring to ancestors in the village, during cultural festivals, and raising toasts in cocktail parties and galas in the city, seeing the diviner or herbalist in the countryside and seeing a medical doctor in a clinic or hospital in the city. In the realm of language, the multiple cultural milieux of the postcolonial subject means that he or she engages in constant linguistic code-switching and the production of multiple compartmentalized or hybrid works of the spirit, of mentalities and worldviews. This discussion is relevant to the "frozen" Anglophone crisis in Cameroon, which is at once a political, geographical, identitarian, social, and cultural question–in the philosophical sense of the term–that has international, geostrategic connections and dimensions.

One of the most deceptively cogent presentations of the Anglophone Question in Cameroon was provided by Cameroon's long-serving authoritarian ruler, President Paul Biya himself. The occasion was the Second Mo Ibrahim Foundation Peace Forum, organized from November 11 to 13th, 2019, under the auspices of French President, Emmanuel Macron. The location was La Grande Halle de La Villette in Paris. On the stage was President Paul Biya, Mr. Mo Ibrahim of the Mo Ibrahim Foundation, and Madame Louise Mushikiwabo, Secretary-General of the *Organisation Internationale de la Francophonie* (OIF), who was acting as facilitator and interpreter. The event turned out to be a public relations disaster. On Tuesday, 12 November 2019, President Paul Biya attended the opening ceremony of the Paris Peace Forum organized by the Mo Ibrahim Foundation and later participated in a panel discussion on the theme: "Recognizing the South for a more equitable global governance". The panel discussions were moderated by the Sudanese billionaire Mohamed "Mo" Ibrahim, President of the Mo Ibrahim Foundation. Louise Mushikiwabo, Secretary General of the International Organization of *la Francophonie*, translated certain questions into French for President Biya. The aging Mr. Biya, who had gone to Paris at the personal invitation of President Emmanuel Macron, brought a prepared speech to what was organized as a panel discussion. After a brief discussion between President Biya and Mr. Mo Ibrahim (interpreted by Madame Louise Mushikiwabo). President Paul Biya, who was prepared to read a speech on geopolitical issues, was confronted with questions about the crisis in the Anglophone Northwest and Southwest regions of Cameroon, a conflict that the Cameroon government pretended did not exist. It was in that semi-formal unguarded, off-script moment that President Biya made his most truthful statement on the Anglophone crisis. He declared in unexpected candor that German, French and British colonialism had bequeathed Cameroon a complicated postcolonial heritage:

> *...une juxtaposition de cultures et de civilisations qui rendent les choses assez délicates. Bon, on a tout fait pour mettre à égalité les deux langues, les langues anglaise et française. Mais, les mentalités, les systèmes scolaires, le système de la magistrature sont différents. Nous avons donc eu des conflits qu'on est en train de résoudre en ce moment, pour conserver à la partie de mon pays qui était sous colonisation britannique, un statut spécifique. On avait la possibilité de les [anglophones] intégrer directement dans le système francophone qui était celui de la majorité du peuple : 80%. Mais, je crois que*

les pays sont soucieux aujourd'hui d'affirmer leur identité et c'est pour ça que nous mettons sur pied un statut spécial qui reconnaît la spécificité de la zone anglophone, mais, elle reste dans l'intégrité territoriale du Cameroun.

The history of my country is a bit complicated…British and French colonialism resulted in a juxtaposition of cultures and civilizations, which makes things rather delicate. We have done everything to create equality between the two languages, but the mentalities, the educational systems, the judicial systems (the magistrature) are different. We have thus had conflicts that we are trying to resolve at the moment to give the part of my country which was under British colonialism a specific status. We had the possibility of directly integrating them [Anglophones] into Francophone system, which was that of the majority of the people (80%), but I think that countries are today conscious of affirming their identities. That is why we are setting up a special status which recognizes the specificity of the Anglophone zone, which remains an integral part of Cameroon. (President Paul Biya calls for Collective action to surmount the numerous challenges and uncertainties, 2019)

President Biya's statement was deceptively cogent because he gave the international community the impression that he understood the Anglophone problem and that his government was doing something about it. His assertion that the French Cameroun government had had the possibility of assimilating the English-speaking or Anglophone minority into *la République du Cameroun* but had apparently not done so because of awareness of the specificity of the Anglophone "zone" is a disingenuous misrepresentation. It expresses and yet dissimulates the Francophone "assimilative impulse," to borrow the expression of Betts (1961, p. 10), which had been the hallmark of the Ahidjo-Biya regime. The reality was, in fact, different from Biya's assertion. The facts show that from the beginning of the reunification of *La République du Cameroun* and British Southern Cameroons in 1961, the highly centralized, neo-patrimonial, Neo-Napoleonic regime of Yaoundé has done all in its power, in collaboration with France, to assimilate Southern Cameroons and disperse it into *la Francophonie*. It is the identitarian assertions and resistance of the Anglophone minority that have prevented a complete take-over and elimination of the specificity of the Anglophone minority in Cameroon. Indeed, granting the Anglophones zones a "special status," albeit a chimerical one, is recognition of the assimilationist project of *la République du Cameroun*. The so-called special status that Paul Biya was announcing to the international community was yet another act of political bad faith intended to maintain the authoritarian status quo. Though the Cameroon National Assembly passed a law conferring the special status on the English and Pidgin-speaking Northwest and Southwest regions, it has in reality been a top-down, chimerical special status. It was yet another demonstration of bad faith which proves that under the Ahidjo/Biya republican chiefery, the more things change, the more they become worse than they were.

Figure 2.1. Popaul (Poor Paul Biya) at the 2019 Paris Peace Forum. Paul Biya: "The Trip where everything failed." Biya speaking to Louise Mushikiwabo, Secretary General of the *Organisation Internationale de la Francophonie*, "Could you please translate? His Sudanese English slips through my ears." *Popoli* (Douala) November 13, 2019.

The "assimilative impulse" of *La République du Cameroun* vis-à-vis the State of Southern Cameroons is a postcolonial civilizational and cultural trait inherited from French colonialism. Indeed, the civilizational posture, the *raison d'être,* and master narrative of French colonialism and postcolonialism have always been the so-called *mission civilisatrice* (Betts, 1961). This is the enlightened politico-cultural civilizing mission that the French consider their destiny, the task they and they alone were assigned by fate to accomplish for humanity due to their exceptionalism, their civilizational and cultural superiority. Former French President Charles de Gaulle defined the French civilizational superiority as, *"une certaine idée de la France ou elle n'est réellement elle-même que quand elle est au premier rang"* (a certain idea of France where she is her real self only when she is at the forefront) (De

Gaulle, 1954). According to Betts (1961), French colonial theory was essentially a doctrine of assimilation. The policy of assimilation was a colonial "governing principle," (p. 10), a fundamental conquering and absorption doctrine that predated the French Revolution of 1789. Louis IV, and Cardinal Richelieu issued edicts in 1635 and 1642 that declared natives of French colonies who converted to Catholicism, "citizens and natural Frenchmen" (p. 12). Assimilation was thus a vague and abstract philosophic ideal of human legal and religious equality under God. It was the French Revolution that transformed assimilation into an indivisible French republic from a philosophical abstraction, and a religious principle, to a political one that embodied France's *mission civilisatrice* (civilizing mission) to humanity, and especially the less developed countries. Betts (1961) suggests that assimilation and the civilizing mission were based on the moralistic secular dogma of "the right of a 'superior' society to dominate and instruct a 'lesser' [barbaric] one…it was the 'white man's burden' translated into French by the word assimilation" (p. 30).

Figure 2.2. Paris Peace Forum: Biya's Anglophones "Assimilation Confession" Shocks Cameroonians, *The Post*, November 15, 2019

The former British Trust Territory of Southern Cameroons, whose official language was English, has been part of the predominantly French-speaking *La République du Cameroun* (Republic of Cameroon) since the reunification of the two United Nations Trust territories in 1961. In Cameroon, at the communitarian level, Anglophones and Francophones define themselves in opposition to each other. The Anglophone is the linguistic and cultural "Other," with a capital O, of the Francophone and vice versa. As the minority, the Anglophone community has existential fears of cultural submergence, assimilation and dispersal in the centralized, authoritarian nation. The authoritarian instincts and repressive reactions of the majority Francophone government, which has no patience with the niceties of democratic dialogue and respect for the minority, heightened the existential angst of the Anglophones and reinforced their need to highlight and attempt to protect their linguistic and cultural specificity.

Roots of the Anglophone Question: Slavery, Colonialism and Anglo-French Rivalries in Africa

The primeval European archetype of Africa has, from antiquity, been "The Dark Continent" (Herodotus, 1925). This archetype has been the prism through which Western politicians, missionaries, writers, and journalists have perceived Africa (Gründer,1988; Eko, 2010, Mudimbe, 1994). The perception that Africa represented the "geography of monstrosity," to borrow the expression of Mudimbe (1994), meant that Africa was the archetypal, exotic, uncivilized, unpredictable, marginal "Other Place." Western differential thinking about Africa, and classification of Africa as the "Other of humanity" was the justification for slavery and European colonialism (Tocqueville, 1862; Thomas, 1997). Portuguese, English, French, German, Spanish, and Arabic were introduced to Africa through European exploration, colonialism, Arabo-Islamic jihads, slavery, and Western missionary evangelization. These forces and movements triggered imperial rivalries. The most notable and most sustained European rivalry for control of territories, resources and peoples in Africa has been the Anglo-French rivalry that resulted in the United Kingdom and France colonizing vast swathes of territory on the African continent. The Anglophone Question in Cameroon is a colonial and postcolonial microcosm of the centuries-long Anglo-French colonial rivalry in Africa.

The genesis of the Anglophone Question in Cameroon can be traced to two historical phenomena: 1) abolition of slavery in the British colonies under the Slavery Abolition Act 1833, which provided for the immediate abolition of slavery in most parts of the British Empire, "promoting the industry of the manumitted Slaves, and for compensating the Persons hitherto entitled to the Services of Slaves" (Slavery Abolition Act 1833), and 2) the European scramble for, and ultimate partition of Africa in the last half of the 19th Century. Throughout that century, European powers sought, mostly under the pretext of humanitarian concerns (Miers, 1988), to use African territories as springboards for their imperial and great power ambitions. Controlling vast swathes of territories–and the natural resources and peoples in these territories ensured wealth and power on the world stage. This scramble for Africa followed the Age of Exploration when European powers explored the world in search of natural resources, trade routes, and territories that would expand their domains, enrich their countries, and give them dominance in the concert of Europe, the perpetual game of balance of power. The competition for African territories and their resources included the slave trade, which lasted from 1560 to 1850 (Farwell, 1986). The territory of *Rio dos Cameroes* (River of Prawns) that had been explored by the Portuguese in the 15th Century, was part of the so-called slave coast of West Africa. In the

19th century, it became one of the focal points of European interest in West Africa. The first political exchange between British Government representatives, and a native ruler in the coast of the Cameroons began in 1826 when King Bille (Williams) of Bimbia, surrendered the sovereignty of his chiefdom to England. For some reason, the British Government did not officially ratify this surrender of sovereignty (Wright, 1958). The Anglophone Question began when, in the 19th century, missionaries formally introduced the English language in the coast of what was to become German Kamerun, British Southern Cameroons, West Cameroon, and now the South West region.

Arrival of Anglo-Jamaican Missionaries

The first missionaries to settle in the territory were black missionaries of Jamaican extraction, who came to Africa under the auspices of the English Baptist Missionary Society, in furtherance of religious and humanitarian objectives in the wake of the Slave Abolition Act, 1833. The group was led by the Reverend and Mrs. Joseph Merrick. The Merricks and their missionary party settled in Bimbia, not far from a slave exporting port, in 1844. One of their aims was to stop the Portuguese slave trade from that coastal location. They established a Baptist mission and introduced the English language to the people. They translated parts of the King James Version of the Bible into the local Isubu language (Ardener, 1956; Wright, 1958). Rev. Merrick also started a printing press to spread literacy and the Gospel. That was the foundation of missionary work in the Cameroons slave coast.

Figure 2.3. Rev. Joseph Merrick Jamaican-English Missionary

Another missionary couple would follow in the footsteps of Rev. & Mrs. Joseph Merrick. Rev. Alfred Saker, a missionary of the English Baptist Missionary Society, who had started a mission in the Spanish island of Santa Isabel or Fernando Po, which is now known as Bioko, the capital of the Republic of Equatorial Guinea. Saker visited the Merricks in Bimbia and they worked together for a while before Saker returned to Fernando Po due to illness (Saker, 1909). In 1845, Rev. Alfred and Mrs. Helen Saker had started a Baptist mission in Akwa, Douala. They called it Bethel. They built a church, started an English school, learned the Duala language and proceeded to translate the King James Bible and English Hymnbooks into Duala (Saker, 1908). This was the second English settlement in the Cameroons. The British had signed trade agreements with two Douala chiefs in 1842. The aim was to substitute the slave trade, which the Cameroons coast was famous for, with trade in ivory, precious wood, and other tropical products. The very hot and extremely humid weather of the Cameroons coast made the location one of the most inhospitable locations on the continent. Indeed, many Europeans considered it "the white man's grave" (Farwell, 1986, p. 29). The natives of Douala were not highly regarded either. They were described with characteristic archetypal, missionary/explorer "Dark Continent" terminology: "… wild, turbulent cannibals. Their occupation for many years had been that of middlemen between the slave-hunters of the interior and the slave-ships on the coast" (Saker, 1908).

The Founding of Victoria

On May 24, 1858, Don Carlos Chacon, Governor-General of all Spanish Islands in West Africa, accompanied by six Jesuit priests, informed Rev. & Mrs. Saker, and the rest of the British and Jamaican missionaries in Fernando Po that their Protestant form of missionary work was not acceptable in the Spanish Catholic territory. The Spaniards were surprised that "heretic" English missionaries had settled on the Spanish colony and set up a mission, built a church, a school, and were using the island as their base to evangelize the Cameroons mainland. Governor-General Chacon solemnly proclaimed that Her Royal Catholic Majesty, Queen Isabella II of Spain recognized the Catholic faith as the only legal religious expression in Spain and its overseas territories. Governor-General Chacon proclaimed that the Spanish Crown had decreed that: "the religion of the Roman Catholic Church be the sole religion of Fernando Po as it was that of the Kingdom of Spain, to the exclusion of every other" (Saker, 1908, p. 143). As a result of this imperial order from Madrid, Don Carlos Chacon ordered Rev. & Mrs. Alfred Saker and all the Baptist mission personnel to leave the island of Fernando Po with immediate effect. The Baptist missionaries had ended up on a Spanish Catholic island off the coast of the Cameroons almost by accident. In her 1908 book, "Alfred Saker, the Pioneer of the Cameroons," the missionary's daughter, E.M. Saker, wrote that in 1843, Jamaican and British missionaries from the English Missionary Society had set up a mission in Clarence, a settlement of freed slaves and natives in Fernando Po (Equatorial Guinea) and used it as a base for religious and humanitarian activities in the Cameroons mainland, which was not a British colony or a colony of any European power for that matter, in the wake of the Slavery Abolition Act 1833.

After their expulsion from the Spanish island of Fernando Po, Rev. & Mrs. Saker and their English and Anglo-Jamaican missionary colleagues, moved their mission to Douala. However, the coast of Ambas Bay, with the majestic and picturesque Mount Fako (Cameroons peak), which was clearly visible from Fernando Po on clear days, offered Rev. Saker an alternative location for his missionary activities. It was just 20 miles across the bay on the mainland. The missionaries first went to Douala where Saker already had a mission and had started translating the Bible and Baptist hymns into the Duala language. Then they moved to Bimbia, where their colleagues from the Baptist Missionary Society, the Rev. and Mrs. Joseph Merrick and others, had started a mission. Rev Saker ultimately crossed Man

O' War Bay and headed west to Ambas Bay, the sheltered bay between present-day Down Beach Limbe, and Bota. After obtaining land from King Bille (Manga Williams), Rev. & Mrs. Alfred Saker and the Baptists who had been expelled from Fernando Po, founded the missionary settlement and colony of Victoria in honor of the British Empress, Queen Victoria, on August 9, 1858 (Wright, 1958; Ardener, 1956; Saker, 1908). Rev. Alfred Saker and his fellow missionaries, whose mainland headquarters were in the rather insalubrious settlement of Douala, decided to resettle "in a land where freedom of conscience and civil liberty could be enjoyed… [under] British protection, British capital and laws…a free port for the commerce of these rivers, and a refuge for the oppressed and the slave" (Saker, 1908, p. 147-148). They decided that their new settlement would be at the sheltered harbor at the foothills of the Cameroons or Fako Mountain, the Bay of the Amboises (Ambas Bay). The location was ideal because of the proximity of the Limbe River, whose clear, swift, pristine waters flowed from the Etinde Mountains to the north (Ardener, 1956; Victoria Centenary Committee, 1958; Thomson, 1871).

The Portuguese, who had explored the coast between Fernando Po and the mainland in the 15th century, had given the Mount Fako region and its people the name Amboizes, from which the name Ambas Bay was derived (Wright, 1958, p. 16). British social anthropologist and historian, Edwin Ardener (1956) wrote that: "From the beginning of the 16th century the inhabitants of the mountain area were known by variants of the name Ambozi, Ambos, Amboizes, after whom is named the present Ambas Bay, on which stand Victoria and Bota." The Cameroons Mountain itself was known for the next two centuries as *Alta Terra de Ambozi* (Highland of the Ambozi), and the region was known as the "province of Amboise" (p. 17). In the Kpe-Mboko language of the coast, that means Mountain of the Witchdoctors. In effect, the name Ambozi comes from the language of the Bantu-speaking Kpe-Mboko (Mokpe/Bakweri) people who inhabited the Eastern and Western slopes of the Cameroons (Fako) Mountain from Idenau to Ambas Bay (Bota and Victoria/Limbe coast), Tika'Molyko (Tiko and Mongo) up to the Ekona and Gbea (Buea) areas (Ardener, 1956).

The word Ambozi is a derivative of the Mokpe/Bakweri word, *Mborzi*, which means "traditional healer."[1] Before the arrival of the Europeans, the Kpe-Mboko venerated their ancestors by pouring libations and offering sacrifices to them, to ward off witchcraft, *liemba* or *nyongo* which was believed to be rampant (Ardener, 1996). They also venerated *Epharza Motɛ*, (literally, "Half Person") the god of the Cameroons Mountain, which the Kpe-Mboko people call "Fako [Hvako]." *Epharza Motɛ* was believed to be half-human and half-stone. Traditionally, when the Mborzi poured libations, and made incantations calling on the ancestors and *Epharza Motɛ* to protect the people from their enemies and from witchcraft, they ended with the word, "A'ambeh." This was a wish for good health

---

1 The word, Mborzi literally means "eye mucus" in the Mokpe or Bakweri language. In Kpe/Mboko tradition and culture, when a sick person goes to the Mborzi, a spiritual and physical healer whose totem is the spider, to beseech the healer to heal him or her by casting out demons or healing a specific disease, the patient is requiried to chant the following supplication: "Mborz'ono titowe, Mbo, Mbo-rzi Mbo, Ekuku luhwa, Mbo, Mbo-rzi Mbo," (Mborzi, the Spider who makes things out of nothing, cleanse me. I make this plea nine times (the magic number). The idea is that Mborzi the healer is the disease that contains the ingredients for its own eradication, like a modern-day vaccine which uses attenuated versions of an infection to prevent that infection.

and protection. That word comes from the Kpe-Mboko (Bakweri) verb, "l'aembeh," to be hale, hearty and protected from sickness and witchcraft. "A'ambeh" was thus an African equivalent of the Hebrew expression, "Amen." When Portuguese explorers saw the Mborzi (traditional healers) of the Kpe-Mboko people pouring libations to their ancestors and seeking protection from witchcraft by saying "A'ambeh!" they named the people the Ambozi (people ruled by the Mborzi or traditional healers), and the Fako Mountain *Alta Terra de Ambozi* (Highland of the Ambozi or traditional healers). They named the coast, Amboizes Bay (Bay of the Mborzi or traditional healers). In her 1908 book, "*Alfred Saker, the Pioneer of the Cameroons*," the missionary's daughter, E.M. Saker, wrote that the Kpe-Mboko people of the Cameroons coast "were superstitious, and dominated by their witch doctors [the Mborzi]. Everyman went in terror of his life from secret poison, sorcery, or open denunciation from these cruel men" (p. 42). British explorers, missionaries and cartographers Anglicized that geographic name Mborzi, to Ambozi, then to Amboises Bay and ultimately, Ambas Bay.

Figure 2.4. Left, Rev. Alfred Saker, English Baptist Missionary. Figure 2.5. Right, Mrs. Helen Saker

Victoria, the new settlement that Rev. Saker and other British missionaries had started on August 9th and 10th, 1858 in the land of the Kpe-Mboko (Ambozi) was a British missionary "republic" over which the British government never exerted full control. Somehow, despite the political exchange between British Government representatives, and King Bille (Williams) of Bimbia in 1826, during which Bille supposedly surrendered the sovereignty of his chiefdom to England, the British never officially ratified that surrender of sovereignty. The British Consuls in Clarence, Fernando Po, and Calabar (in modern-day Nigeria) never ensured that the Cameroons coast from Bimbia to Rio Del Rey were part of the British Empire because it was considered one of the most inhospitable stretches of the West African coast. They only got interested when the French Empire acquired vast territories in West Africa (Farwell, 1986). That disinterest would cost the British Empire the Cameroons territory–the Germans signed treaties with the Douala and Bimbia chiefs before the British Consul in Calabar could get to the Cameroons– and have a disastrous effect on British missionaries in Douala, Bimbia, and Victoria, when the major European powers partitioned Africa later in the 19th century. Nevertheless, the "little republic" of Victoria that Rev. Saker and other British missionaries had started on August 9th and 10th, 1858, had a system of administration of justice based on the British common law. It had its own Constitution, Supreme Court and Chief Magistrate who was also known as President of the Supreme Court of Victoria (Thomson 1881, p. 158). The system of justice of Victoria was based on the Victorian English interpretations of British common law and the 10 Commandments from the King James Bible, adapted to suit the local pioneering African context. Victoria was also essentially a Bible-style "city of refuge" to which people escaping slavery and persons the Mborzi or spiritual healers accused of witchcraft in the neighboring Kpe-Mboko villages escaped (Thomson, 1881, Saker, 1908). A.K. Wright notes that: "Although the settlement was not officially recognized as a British Possession, nevertheless, the Government was responsible for the welfare of the British nationals living there." A black man of Jamaican descent, Horton Johnson was appointed President of Victoria, and Acting Vice Consul in 1866 (Wright, p.20).

Figure 2.6. The Saker Centennial Memorial Monument erected in Victoria in 1958 (1858-1958)
Credit: author

The First Anglophone Problem (Kamerun, 1884-1885)

Just 25 years after Rev. & Mrs. Alfred Saker and their English and Jamaican colleagues had founded the English settlement of Victoria, on Ambas Bay, on 9th August 1858 in honor of Queen Victoria, the very status of the settlement as a British protectorate came into question. The English missionaries operated under the mistaken belief that Victoria was a free port, "a centre of civilization, freedom, and light" recognized and protected by the British government (Saker, 1908, p. 152-153; Wright, 1958, p.19). The fate of the settlement, Rev. & Mrs. Alfred Saker, the entire Anglo-Jamaican community, and the native Kpe-Mboko inhabitants of the settlement was changed forever by events in Europe. In effect, during the last quarter of the 19th century, European strategic territorial competition and balance of power realities resulted in the scramble and partition of Africa. As European countries rushed to acquire colonies in Africa for reasons of imperial expansion, balance of power equations, trade, natural resources, and diverse national interests in the wake of the abolition of slavery and the European slave trade, it became necessary to hold an international conference of the major Western powers to settle the myriads of territorial claims of these powers on the African continent. German Chancellor, Otto von Bismarck, leader of a unified, resurgent Germany, organized the Berlin Africa Conference from 1884-1885. The emerging United States was invited as an observer. At the Berlin Conference, the major European powers partitioned Africa into a patchwork of colonial territories often with scant knowledge of the physical realities on the ground in the vast continent.

Figure 2.7. European partition of Africa at the Berlin Africa Conference (1884-1885).

The Berlin Conference ratified German sovereignty and control of the whole of the Cameroons, on the basis of treaties signed between the German Commissioner for West Africa, Dr. Gustav Nachtigal, King Akwa of Douala and the King of Bimbia, territories where Rev. Joseph Merrick and Rev. Alfred Saker had established English Baptist missions but the British had not considered these territories strategic enough to formally transform into colonies or protectorates. The Portuguese had named the territory *Rio dos Cameroes* (River of Prawns), the English Anglicized it to the Cameroons, and the Germans "Germanized" the appellation of the territory to Kamerun. The German territory of "Kamerun" was a vast chunk of territory bigger than France and Germany combined. It stretched from the borders of modern-day Gabon, Congo Brazzaville, Central African Republic and Chad, to parts of

Nigeria (Farwell, 1986). Germany also obtained Togoland, Rwanda-Urundi, German East Africa (modern-day Tanzania) and German Southwest Africa (modern-day Namibia).

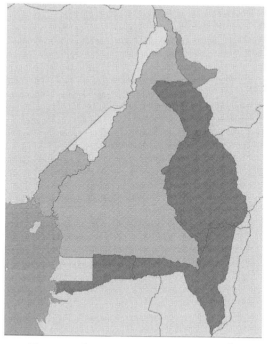

Figure 2.8. Map of German Kamerun (1884-1919). The territory stretched from parts of present day Nigeria to the Central African Republic and Congo (Brazzaville).

The British withdrew their claims in parts of the Cameroons West of the Mungo for strategic, balance of power reasons. They gave up seemingly inhospitable parts of the West African coast in order to consolidate other territories in West, Eastern, and Southern Africa. Since the Germans did not tolerate missionaries of the English Baptist Missionary Society in their newly acquired Kamerun territories, in 1885, the English Baptist missionaries were forced to abandon their work and mission stations and leave the entire Victoria Settlement to the Swiss-German Basel Evangelical Missionary Society (the Basel Mission), just as they had been forced to leave Clarence, Fernando Po by the Spaniards in 1858. The English Baptist Missionary Society would ultimately receive minimal compensation agreed to by the British and German governments. The Basel mission was a missionary society of German-speaking Swiss Calvinists and German Lutherans based in Basel, Switzerland. Interestingly, the Basel Evangelical Missionary Society had built a school to train Dutch and British missionaries in 1816, before the slave trade was abolished in the UK under the Slavery Abolition Act 1833. The Basel Evangelical Missionary Society began work in German Kamerun in 1886. The arrival of the Basel missionaries was the beginning of the Swiss connection in the Anglophone Question (see volume II). The Basel Mission was the founding mission of the current Presbyterian Church in Cameroon (PCC) (Wright, 1958, p. 31).

Figure 2.9. German advertisement for five-week journey from Hamburg to exotic German Kamerun by sea.

The transfer of the Cameroons from British to German sovereignty under international law led to the first "Anglophone" problem, the abolition of English as the official language of the Cameroons and its replacement with German. However, the arrival of the German Empire, and with it Swiss and German missionaries did not mean the end of the English language. It led to a period of flux that saw English and Duala survive in "native" or indigenous Baptist churches, alongside the lingua franca, Pidgin and Creole, as the Swiss and Germans started German-medium schools. Many of the "native" Baptist churches were led by converts who maintained the English language, the King James version of the Bible, the Baptist Hymnal, the famous *Sacred Songs and Solos,* popularly known as "Sankey & Moody" after its authors, the Book of Common Prayer of the Anglican Church, tracts and religious literature printed by the Religious Tract Society of London, as well as publishers in the United States. Some of the English/Jamaican Baptist churches in Victoria and the hinterland tenaciously maintained some English in their worship services through reading the King James Bible. They also used Duala language translations of the Bible that Rev. Saker and the English Baptist missionaries had published. Above all, many native Baptist Christians memorized the scriptures in English through the Baptist practice of "memory verses," whereby Christian converts are required to memorize key passages of the Bible that underpin the main dogmas and teachings of the Christian faith. In effect, the ministry of the English missionaries had included: "printing, translating, language study, brick-making, carpentry, agriculture, secular instruction and administration" (Wright, 1958, p. 31). Creole or Pidgin English, the lingua franca of Victoria that had emerged with the cultural mixtures brought about by slavery, the slave trade, and commerce between Europeans and Africans, became the language of many churches.

Das Wohnhaus des Gouverneurs von Kamerun in Buea. v.l.n.r. Gouverneur Dr. Seitz, Frau Seitz, Frl. von Cleve, Gesellschaftsdame, Adjudant Oberleutnannt von Puttkamer

Figure 2.10. The German Governor's Castle in Buea. Picture features Gov. Dr. Seitz & Mrs. Seitz, along with First Lieutenant von Puttkamer.

World War I, the Treaty of Versailles and the Partition of German Kamerun

The vast German colony of Kamerun lasted less than 30 years. In effect, the First World War (1914-1918) tolled the knell of the German Empire. When Great Britain declared war on Germany on August 5, 1914, that declaration resonated throughout the British Empire. The First World War was fought in West Africa (German Togoland), German Kamerun, German East Africa (modern-day Tanzania), and German Southwest Africa (Namibia). Since German Kamerun was sandwiched between British and French colonial territories, the British and the French set aside their political, cultural and territorial rivalries and became allies. Each country raised a colonial army led by British and French officers, to fight German colonial African armies that were also recruited, trained, and commanded by German officers (Farwell, 1986). A combined Anglo-French force led by a British commander captured Douala, landed in Victoria, marched up to Buea, the former German capital, captured Governor von Puttkamer's residence and looted its contents on November 16, 1914 (Farwell, 1986). By 1916, two years before World War I ended in Europe, Germany had been defeated and lost its colonies throughout Africa.

Since Germany was defeated in Europe and in multiple African battlefields, she was officially stripped of its African colonies. On March 4, 1916, the British and French proceeded to partition German Kamerun in accordance with their respective strategic interests in Africa. Two Franco-British agreements to partition German Kamerun were signed in 1916 and 1919. These were the Picot Line of 1916 and the Milner-Simon Declaration of 1919.

This partition took place under the zeitgeist and context of the 19th and early 20th century "Great power" imperial rivalries and compensatory diplomacy. This lopsided partition was intended to mollify the French, who had not been invited to share the battle and the spoils in German East Africa (modern-day Tanzania and Ruanda-Urundi). The British, who were the first Allied power to enter the German Kamerun cities of Douala and Yaoundé, during World War I, conceded these and other territories to France in exchange for most of German East Africa (except Ruanda-Urundi), and Southwest Africa (Namibia), which they considered more valuable and more vital to their interests. Under British compensatory diplomacy, the part of German Kamerun "enemy lands" they received close to the Nigerian border was nothing but a territorial bargaining chip in the Anglo-French geo-strategic chessboard (Elango, 2015). East Africa was considered the British sphere of influence, while French hegemony was recognized in Central Africa and large parts of West Africa.

Figure 2.11. Signing the Treaty of Versailles, Hall of Mirrors, Palace of Versailles, France (June 28, 1919).

The Treaty of Versailles of 1919, which regulated the global, post-World War I dispensation, put its stamp of approval on the partition of German Kamerun. Under provisions of the Treaty, France took four-fifths of German Kamerun and returned parts of the territory to Gabon, Congo, Central African Republic, and Chad. It renamed the core territory, *le Cameroun*, and governed it as a French League of Nations Mandates and later a UN Trust Territory as part of French Equatorial Africa. For its part, the British took the remaining fifth of German Kamerun and further partitioned it into Southern and Northern Cameroons, which they administered indirectly through Nigeria as League of Nations Mandate and UN Trust Territories for 40 years. *Deutsch-Ostafrika*, German East Africa (GEA), which included the mainland territory of present-day Tanzania went to the United Kingdom, while Ruanda-Urundi, out of which emerged the modern-day independent states of Rwanda and Burundi, became a Belgian territory in 1916. Furthermore, *Deutsch-Südwestafrika* (German Southwest Africa, modern-day Namibia) was placed under British-ruled South Africa as a League of Nations Mandate. Interestingly, under the influence of the emerging world Superpower, the United States, whose president, Woodrow Wilson was a proponent of the idea of self-determination for "non-self-governing territories," the former German territories were not immediately transformed into traditional British, French or Belgian colonies. Nevertheless, from 1916, the French introduced Napoleonic civil law in their portion of Cameroun, while the British reintroduced the common law in Southern and Northern Cameroons, by way of Nigeria. Naturally, the British and the French exported their linguistic and cultural rivalries to their new African colonial acquisitions.

The Anglo-French partition of German Kamerun turned out to be a messy exercise that led to an even messier politico-cultural geography for all Africans concerned, and sowed the seeds of the Boko Haram Islamist terrorist insurgency in British Northern Cameroons (now Northwest Nigeria) and the Anglophone Problem in British Southern Cameroons (now the Northwest and Southwest regions of Cameroon). The colonial territorial borders drawn on maps in European diplomatic conferences made no sense on the ground in Africa. The territories that emerged from the Anglo-French colonial boundary-making looked like the work of inebriated cartographers who could not understand each other. Edwin Ardener (1962), a British social anthropologist and expert on Southern Cameroons, described the outcome of the partition and especially the parts of German Kamerun that became British League of Nations Mandates in 1919, and United Nations Trust Territories in 1946, when the League of Nations ceased to exist, as follows:

> The British Mandate consisted of mere strips of territory on the Nigerian border, shaped like two penknife blades pointing at each other, the smaller down from the north, the longer up from the south. They did not touch however, the space between being occupied by the northern Nigerian town of Yola....

In a space of 30 years Southern and Northern Cameroons were transferred from German to British indirect colonial rule. The neglected, economically backward territory of Northern Cameroon was ultimately split into several Nigerian states and became the hotbed of the Islamist Boko Haram insurgency in 2009, while the neglected Southern Cameroons, which was annexed by French Cameroun in 1961 via a questionable UN plebiscite, erupted into the Anglophone Revolt of 2016. The Boko Haram insurgency in the former Northern Cameroons (today's northeast Nigeria), and the unrelated Anglophone Revolt in Southern Cameroons, are unfinished political businesses from World War I and the Treaty of Versailles. They amount to history's revenge against the Anglo-French Milner/Simon Declaration of 10 July 1919, British Machiavellian colonial policy in Nigeria and the Cameroons territories.

French Cameroun and British Cameroons: From League of Nations Mandates to UN Trusteeships

Following the Second World War, the fledgling United Nations set up a Trusteeship system whose main objective was "to promote the advancement of the inhabitants of Trust Territories and their progressive development towards self-government or independence." The Anglophone Problem in Cameroon represents the unfinished business of

World War I, the Treaty of Versailles and the UN Trusteeship system. In effect, the British and French mandates over the Cameroons were replaced by United Nations Trusteeship Agreements. That means both powers were to act as trustees of the territories on behalf of the peoples until such a time that these people would be ready to exercise the right of self-determination. These agreements referred to the line laid down by the Milner-Simon Declaration of 1919 to demarcate the respective territories placed under the trusteeship of the two European Powers. The trusteeship agreements for the British Cameroons and for Cameroun under French administration were both approved by the General Assembly on 13 December 1946. Pursuant to the Order in Council of 2 August 1946 providing for the Administration of the Nigeria Protectorate and Cameroons territories under British League of Nations Mandate, the regions placed under British trusteeship were divided into two for administrative purposes, thus giving birth to the Northern Cameroons and the Southern Cameroons. The 1946 Order in Council contained a series of provisions describing the line separating these two regions and provided that they would be administered from Nigeria. Nevertheless, French Cameroun was treated just like all other French colonies while the British treated Northern and Southern Cameroons as administrative appendages to their Northern and Southern Nigerian territories.

Southern Cameroons: From Pseudo–Independence to Subaltern of a French Postcolony

As the "wind of change" swept across Africa in the 1950s and 1960s, ushering in independence from the war-weary colonial powers, the United Nations began to prod the United Kingdom, France, and Belgium to grant independence to their non-self-governing Trust Territories. The idea of League of Nations mandates and UN Trust Territories was that the British, French, and Belgian Trusteeship powers were required to act as disinterested trustees of the territories, "the enemy lands" they had conquered from Germany. Because Britain ended up with two "strips of territory" from German Kamerun (Ardener, 1962) which did not even touch each other, it had further partitioned the territory into Northern and Southern Cameroons for purposes of indirect administration, and to strengthen the border in its Nigerian colony. It also wanted to use Northern Cameroons to shore up traditional feudal kingdoms in Northern Nigeria. As the UN Trusteeship approached its end in 1961, the British succeeded, through flawed UN plebiscites, to transfer Northern Cameroons to Nigeria and Southern Cameroons to *la République du Cameroun*, essentially denying the people of the Cameroons territories under its administration, the right of self-determination. The transfer of the Northern Cameroons territory from German colonial rule to British colonial rule and ultimately to Nigerian annexation, and Southern Cameroons from German colonial rule to indirect British colonial rule through Nigeria, and ultimately to direct annexation by an assimilationist *la République du Cameroun*, is the indirect cause of the Anglophone crisis in the Northwest and Southwest regions of Cameroon (the former British Southern Cameroons).

In effect, the Anglophone Question in Cameroon is, in part, a result of the short-sightedness of the United Nations and its Trusteeship Council, which gave short-shrift to the notion of self-determination and offered the people of Southern Cameroons and Northern

Cameroons a poisoned gift, independence by proxy rather than self-determination. When the United Nations Trusteeships of the United Kingdom and France drew to a close, the UN hastily organized plebiscites that gave the people of the territories of Southern Cameroons and Northern Cameroons, which in 40 years had been moved from German colonial administration to British colonial administration, a fatal choice between a rock and a hard place, a choice that would move them either to a third colonial experience, proxy French postcolonialism under *la République du Cameroun* or dispersal in the Nigerian politico-cultural and religious crucible. In effect, the people of Southern and Northern Cameroons were given a choice between two forms of African domination: Nigerian or French Cameroonian. The United Nations Trusteeship Council (1961) posed plebiscite questions that imposed outcomes which were deceptive pseudo exits from European colonial domination to independence. In reality, these questions were moving Northern and Southern Cameroonians from European colonialism to African domination:

(A) Do you wish to achieve independence by joining the independent Federation of Nigeria?

(B) Do you wish to achieve independence by joining the independent Republic of Cameroon?

It was clear that this was a no-win situation. There was no option of self-determination or independence for these former German colonial territories that were being moved once again from a colonial domination to a postcolonial one.

Genesis of the Anglophone Crisis: Reunification of British Southern Cameroons and *La République du Cameroun*

After 40 years of benevolent neglect through indirect colonial rule, the British decided that the means of granting self-rule to the territories that it had sub-partitioned into Northern and Southern Cameroons was to have them permanently incorporated and dispersed into Nigeria by all means possible (Anyangwe, 2010). Attaching the British Trust Territory of Cameroons to the British Nigerian Protectorate and Colony, sub-dividing it and administering it indirectly–without the consent of the people–made sense to the British who had obtained this territory as a spoil of war and wanted to use it to bolster the Northern region of Nigeria, while spending as little on it as possible. However, transferring the Cameroons territory to Nigeria was problematic for the peoples of the Southern Cameroons territory, who found themselves in a new country, among new peoples, the Igbos, who treated them with haughty condescension. It was also problematic for the British. The negative experiences of Southern Cameroonians who were treated as foreigners that the British had brought to Nigeria and incorporated into the Igbo-dominated Eastern region of Nigeria for reasons of balance of power in the colony resulted in the emergence of an identitarian and cultural consciousness that took the form of a so-called, "one Kamerun idea" (Johnson, 1965). In effect, Southern Cameroonian displeasure with their willy-nilly amalgamation into Nigeria and their second-class status there came to the fore in May 1953 when the 13 Southern Cameroons MPs in the Eastern Nigerian House of Assembly in Enugu, where the Cameroon territory was represented, asserted a right of cultural and political specificity, and proceeded to declare 'benevolent neutrality.' They henceforth refused to take part in

Nigerian partisan politics because they did not consider themselves Nigerians (Anyangwe, 2010). In July that year, at the London Constitutional Conference, Dr. EML Endeley, the leader of the Kamerun National Congress (KNC), and leader of British Southern Cameroons, citing fear of Nigerian domination–in Nigeria and Southern Cameroons– demanded a separate region for the Southern Cameroons in line with its trusteeship status, a demand that Britain acceded to. The territory thus gained a modicum of autonomy only after its leaders symbolically "seceded" from the Nigerian Federation to which the British had consigned them. The UN plebiscite was asking them to choose between Nigeria and *la République du Cameroun*. The Nigerians, and particularly the Igbo, drove the Southern Cameroonians, as it were, into the arms of French Cameroon

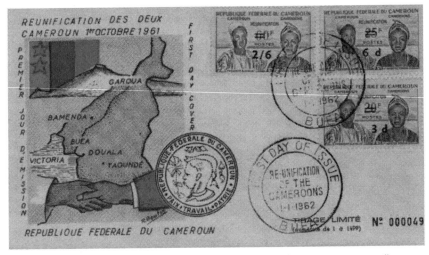

Figure 2.12. Federal Republic of Cameroon "reunification of the two Cameroons" postcard with Ahidjo and Foncha postage stamps, 1962.

The outcome of the United Nations Cameroons plebiscite of 1961 was mixed. The people of Northern Cameroons voted–twice– in a controversial plebiscite to attain independence by joining the fractious Federation of Nigeria, while the people of Southern Cameroons voted to obtain independence by joining the newly independent *la République du Cameroun*. French and French Cameroun surreptitious support for John Ngu Foncha and his reunificationist Kamerun National Democratic Party (KNDP) had tilted the scales in favor of Southern Cameroons' reunification with *la République du Cameroun* during the plebiscite. France essentially saw the reunification of *La République du Cameroun* and Southern Cameroons as an opportunity to enlarge the physical and cultural geography of *la Francophonie*, the French sphere of influence in Africa. The reunification essentially brought English and Pidgin-speaking Southern Cameroons (renamed West Cameroon) within the ambit of the pre-independence *accords de coopération* (cooperation agreements) signed between France and *la République du Cameroun* on the eve of the latter's independence on January 1, 1960. These agreements had essentially transformed *La République du Cameroun*, like other former French colonies, into dependent French postcolonies. By reunifying with *la République du Cameroun*, Southern Cameroons came under the ambit of these Franco-Cameroun agreements. The "reunification" of Southern Cameroons and *la République du Cameroun* did not turn out to be what its most fervent advocates had expected. Southern Cameroonians, who had revolted against Nigerian domination, were now forced to co-exist with their French Cameroun brothers and sisters, and become second-class or sub-altern citizens.

The *Chefferie Républicaine* (Republican chiefery) of Cameroon

The dream of the One Kamerun romantics—equality of citizenship—faded as the Ahidjo-Biya regime became a highly authoritarian, absolutist, neo-patrimonial, Napoleonic, republican chiefery where all institutions of the state, including the judiciary and the legislative were under the absolute sway of President Paul Biya and a handful of his Beti-Bulu tribal cronies. This totalitarian edifice has been held in place by a postcolonial straight-jacket stitched together by secret military defense and cooperation agreements, and especially the postcolonial currency, the CFA franc. This was part of the so-called "FranceAfrique," the postcolonial French domain of 14 former French colonies assembled under the UMOA, *l'Union Monétaire Ouest Africaine* (West African Monetary Union), created and managed by France, and for whom France printed the CFA, guaranteed its convertibility. France also managed the foreign exchange accounts of the 14 countries in the *Banque de France*. These postcolonial arrangements gave rise to a highly centralized, totalitarian, Napoleonic, republican chieftaincy whose politico-cultural matrix had no place for the niceties of the separation of powers between the executive, the legislative and the judiciary, and where the governmentality is one of rule by decree. When the French government and its postcolony (to use the expression of Mbembe, 2001), *la République du Cameroun* began their cultural assimilationist program in Southern Cameroons they were clearly oblivious to the fact that English and Pidgin-speaking West Cameroonians had certain "unmutable" global Anglophone cultural inter-connections. When Francophone intellectuals speak of *les institutions républicaines*, or *l'armée républicaine*, the republican ideology they have in mind is the French Jacobine republican ideology of popular sovereignty and the indivisibility of the French Republic that emerged during the Revolution of 1789 (Furet, 1978), and is set forth in Article I of the French Constitution: "*La France est une République indivisible, laïque, démocratique et sociale.*" (France is an indivisible republic, secular democratic and social). The Cameroon Constitution of 1996 copies this Jacobine creed almost verbatim: Article II: (2) *La République du Cameroun est un État unitaire décentralisé. Elle est une et indivisible, laïque, démocratique et sociale.*" (The Republic of Cameroon is a unitary, decentralized state. It is one and indivisible, secular, democratic and social). This was clearly a postcolonial parody of the French state. The governmentality of Jacobinism, as applied in Cameroon has resulted in an autocratic, Almighty State with an All-powerful *Chef de l'État* (Chief of State), and a made-to-measure Constitution. The Chief of State is above the law, rules by decree, and can rule indefinitely–President Biya ruled Cameroon for more than 40 years. The Chief of state was the Chief of all traditional chiefs, "the Fon of fons", as he was crowned in the Northwest region, and the chief of the Sawa, as he was crowned in the littoral region. The *chefferie républicaine* is the epitome of the rule of man rather than the rule of law. In the Cameroonian republican chiefery, there is no separation of powers. The Chief of State is also the Chief Magistrate–His Office is *La Magistrature Suprême* (the Supreme Magistrature)–and he presides over the *Conseil Superièure de la Magistrature* (Superior Council of the Magistrature), which controls the judiciary. The legislative–the National Assembly and Senate–are rubber-stamp bodies that put their imprimatur on the Republican Chieftain's *fénéantisme* (government by indolence). The Francophone Cameroon parody of Jacobinism is characterized by administrative and bureaucratic centralism, tribal elitism, glacial technocratic decision-making, and opaque management of the natural resources of the country. This is the tropical variant of French over-centralization–and all governance decisions–from street names in towns and cities to the selection of tribal chiefs–are taken in Yaoundé. In the republican chiefery of the Federal Republic of Cameroon, and especially, the unitary Republic of Cameroon, French became, for many English-speaking Cameroonians, a politico-cultural hurdle they had to scale in order to survive as a minority, nay, subalterns in the treacherous, opaque, and discriminatory, linguistic reality of the republican chiefery.

The totalitarian edifice of the republican chiefery was shored up by the military might of France (which benefits economically and politically from the neo-colonial arrangement), and the Israelis who created and trained a praetorian guard, (a presidential guard and an Israeli-style elite military corps), the *Batallion d'Intervention Rapide* or Rapid Intervention Battalion (BIR) commanded behind the scenes by former Israeli generals, whose official titles were "technical advisers" at the presidency of the republic, and provided a ready market for Israeli military weaponry. Investigative journalist, Emmanuel Freudenthal (2020) reported that Israeli mercenaries in Cameroon were "making a killing"–literally and figuratively–as the trainers of Cameroon's notoriously brutal military unit, the *Batallion d'Intervention Rapide* (BIR). The BIR is notorious for its crimes against humanity in Northern Cameroon and especially in the English-speaking Southern Cameroons ((Turse & Speri, 2022; O'Grady, 2019). Under this regime, not even the slightest dissent, whether from politicians, civil society, or the media is tolerated. The modus operandi of the government is to ignore dissident or even divergent political opinions, and brutally use the BIR, the military and the police to suppress and silence opponents. The France-Afrique regime of Ahidjo-Biya rules with an iron fist. There is no room for political deliberation, sincere dialogue, learning, compromise, or coming to a measure of understanding. The Ahidjo-Biya Napoleonic, republican chieftaincy regime of Cameroon, with its rule-by-decree methodology has no patience with dissent.

In the domain of Communication, the state-owned and controlled, taxpayer-funded Cameroon Radio and Television (CRTV) is the electronic media mouthpiece of the regime. Its print press counterpart, *Cameroon Tribune*, was the first mouthpiece of the government before the arrival of Television in 1985. *Cameroon Tribune* publishes verbatim official government decrees and bureaucratic communication. It mouths the official line and nothing but the official line on all issues. The only criticism that appears on its pages are critiques of the political opposition and dissidents. Critical voices from the fledgling independent media are routinely silenced by the *Conseil National de Communication* (CNC), a quasi-judiciary media regulatory body which routinely fines, suspends, and bans journalists who do not toe the government line. Those are the lucky ones. Those who are not so lucky are arrested, tortured, jailed without trial, or simply eliminated by the military, the Gendarmerie, the police or other security forces. As we see in chapter 11, TV journalist, Samuel Wazizi, was arrested by Cameroon military intelligence for allegedly associating with Anglophone separatists. He was tortured to death in military custody (Cameroon Journalist Samuel Wazizi died in Detention, 2020).

The English-speaking Community of Cameroon and the Global Anglosphere

Interestingly, in their rush to exercise their "assimilative impulse" (Betts, 1961) the French and their French Cameroon partners, were completely oblivious to the linguistic and multicultural legacy of Southern Cameroons. As a result of slavery and the slave trade on the West African "slave coast" from the 16th to the 19th Century, places like Bimbia became slave ports where contact between Portuguese, Spanish, English, French, Dutch, and other European slave traders and their Arabic and African suppliers led to the emergence of a West African lingua franca, English-based Pidgin or Creole (Krio), a trade language that is a mixture of African and European languages grounded in variations of English (standard and non-standard). Southern Cameroons was the Eastern-most linguistic frontier of Pidgin English or Krio. As early as 1792, Freetown, Sierra Leone was founded by abolitionists to settle poor blacks from London, England, freed slaves from North America (US and Canada) and the Caribbean. After the abolition of slavery, the British Royal Navy's West Africa Squadron, which was charged with enforcing the ban on the slave trade, intercepted slave trading ships and brought most of the slaves to Freetown, Sierra Leone, where they were freed. The population thus included descendants of many different peoples from all over the west coast of Africa. It was the perfect setting for the emergence of creole or Pidgin English. Further west in Liberia, American President, James Monroe's decision to send freed slaves back to Africa led to the founding of Monrovia in 1822 as a settlement for freed American slaves, most of whom arrived between 1830 and 1871. They spoke African American vernaculars, and intermingled with Africans from the interior. Pidgin or Creole thus became either the native language or the lingua franca of West Africa. With the movement of people, soldiers and workers under the British Empire, Pidgin English became the most widely-spoken lingua franca in the British colonial territories of West Africa—more so than proper English—though it had no official status in any of the British territories, including Southern Cameroons, which had officially become a British League of Nations Mandate under the Treaty of Versailles of 1919.

Furthermore, in their monomaniacal focus on secularism, and their rush to assimilate Southern Cameroons, the French, and their French Cameroon partners ignored or were completely oblivious to a third, and perhaps the most important cultural bulwark of English-speaking Cameroon, the Protestant Christian religion. With their Shakespearean era King James Version of the Bible, together with Roman Catholic doctrinal, catechistic and prayer books, Bible study and Sunday School manuals, and above all, a rich heritage of English and American hymnals and song books like the famous *Sacred Songs and Solos*, the *Baptist Hymn Book*, and others. Churches thus became the heir and custodian of the English-language culture of Southern Cameroons. Furthermore, in order to effectively reach the people with the Gospel, the early missionaries used a combination of languages.

English Baptist missionary, Rev. Alfred Saker, and other missionaries transformed Duala, their first language of contact in the Cameroon coast, into the lingua franca. They translated the Bible, English hymns and prayer books into Duala. They also started an English language school in Douala. The linguistic and cultural situation of the territory would later change with the arrival of Roman Catholic missionaries from the United Kingdom after World War I (Ndi, 2005). The Roman Catholics decided to use Pidgin or Creole, a mixture of English and various African dialects that had emerged from the slave trade and evolved into the lingua franca or "trade language" of the British colonies in West Africa, to evangelize the territory. In Buea, Victoria, Kumba, Bamenda, and other places, the Roman Catholic Church dispensed its catechism in the lingua franca, Pidgin English. The Basel Mission (Presbyterian Church) used Pidgin, and the Duala language in the coastal region. They used Pidgin and Bali (Mungaka) languages in the main churches in the Grasslands region. The Cameroon Baptist Mission, later renamed the Cameroon Baptist Convention (CBC), used a combination of languages: Duala, English and Pidgin in its coastal churches, Pidgin English and Lamnso' in Bui, Pidgin and Bikom in Menchum, Pidgin and Limbum in Donga Mantung, and so on. The Roman Catholic Church soon established educational and medical institutions, with, notably, the founding in 1939 of St Joseph's College, Sasse, the first secondary school in Southern Cameroons. The Catholic Bishops and leaders of the Presbyterian and Baptist Churches, which had dominated the educational and health-care sectors in Southern Cameroons, would later provide the moral and spiritual support for the Anglophone political, cultural, and identitarian resistance. It was therefore naïve and presumptuous of the French government and Francophone Cameroon to ignore the 175-year-old, largely faith-based Anglophone educational, and medical cultures, and expect them to vanish overnight and take on a French secular republican coloration that is hostile to the outward manifestations of religion, after the reunification in 1961. The problem is that French perceptions of their cultural superiority blinded them to the religious history of Southern Cameroons. The governments of General Charles de Gaulle and Georges Pompidou forgot a lesson that the French minority in Quebec, Canada, taught the world. The Roman Catholic Church became the heir and custodian of the French language and culture in Quebec after the British army defeated the French army at the Battle of the Plains of Abraham (*Bataille des Plaines d'Abraham*) in 1759, and France ceded most of its North American territories to Britain, under the terms of the Treaty of Paris of 1763. There are parallels between the Quebec experience and the culture of English-speaking Southern Cameroons. In the latter, the culture has four major bulwarks: the churches, the English-medium educational system, the Pidgin-English lingua franca, and the Common law system.

When they became part of the British Empire in 1916, Southern Cameroons and its citizens officially became part of the 20th Century Anglosphere. They became exposed to the various varieties of "Englishes" spoken in different parts of the Empire through educational and cultural exchanges. Southern Cameroons students studied in exotic places like Nsukka, Nigeria, Accra, Ghana, Freetown, Sierra Leone, Kampala, Uganda, Calcutta, India, and the UK, the West Indies, Canada, and the United States. Sometimes, the British posted administrators, teachers, doctors, and jurists from these places to Southern

Cameroons. Unbeknownst to France and French-Cameroun, Southern Cameroons' centuries' long linguistic and cultural history that had brought it in contact with multiple forms of "Englishes" and pidgins or creoles, had made the territory part of the Anglosphere. This is a global imagined community of official and unofficial speakers of multiple variations of English and Pidgins around the world. Indeed, Southern Cameroonians listened to Radio Nigeria, the British Broadcasting Corporation (BBC), the Voice of America (VOA), Radio Vatican, Radio Moscow, and others, in English, on a regular basis. Southern Cameroonians followed the American Civil Rights movement, and were inspired by the fiery speeches of Dr. Martin Luther King and other American Civil Rights leaders. They sang American "Negro Spirituals" that American missionaries had taught in their schools and churches, listened to news reports of Dr. King receiving the Nobel Prize, and joined the world in mourning his assassination in Memphis, Tennessee, in 1968. Additionally, the people of Southern Cameroons were culturally connected to the Anglosphere in multiple ways. They were exposed to the wave of American jazz, rock-and roll, rhythm and blues that was emerging from Motown, and sweeping across the world. They mouthed the words of James Brown, "Say it Loud, I'm Black and Proud", moved to the visceral, pounding rhythms, and inspiring lyrics of Jamaican reggae– Bob Marley and the Wailers' "Get up stand up, Stand Up for Your Rights," Jimmy Cliff's anti-war tune, "Vietnam", Peter Tosh's "Mama Africa" and others. They listened to Elvis Presley and The Beatles. They also listened to the exciting, exotic, and moving Xhosa and Zulu music of Miriam Makeba of South Africa, and swayed to the Afrobeats music of Fela Anikulapo Kuti of Nigeria, and repeated his defiant, anti-military, anti-authoritarian, pan-Africanist Pidgin English lyrics. They also sang and danced to the irresistible, anti-Apartheid tunes of Sonny Okosun, also from neighboring Nigeria. They also danced to Ghanaian Highlife music.

The centuries of existence of Cameroon Anglophones in the global Anglosphere, and exchanges with parts of it in the fields of religion, education, the law, and popular culture led to the emergence of a distinct cultural identity, a cultural geography where the English language-and it was a mixture of British, Southern Cameroonian, Nigerian, and American English– co-existed with Pidgin or Creole, the lingua franca of British West Africa, and multiple Bantu, Niger-Congo and Nilotic languages. The multi-cultural, Anglophone Cameroon culture was often defined in opposition to the Francophone culture, which had a different mentality of governance, the rule of law, human rights, and religion. Paul Verdzekov (2008), Roman Catholic Archbishop Emeritus of Bamenda wrote one of the most perceptive identitarian descriptions of the Anglophone community in Cameroon. Verdzekov noted that:

> In practical terms, the so-called Anglo-Saxon culture, actually a 'Southern Cameroonian Anglophone culture', was apparent in the offices, schools, hospitals, plantations, churches, on the highways, at formal and informal social occasions practiced by individuals in the discharge of their services both in private and public affairs. Initially, it was mistaken for naivety, especially by 'Francophone Cameroonians', but in reality it was a 'culture' identified with civility, broad-mindedness and moral probity,

forthrightness, duty consciousness, and above all, the assertive, fearless ability to stand up for one's rights and convictions in the face of all adversity (p. 347).

The African Natural Resource Curse and the Annexation of Southern Cameroons

One of the major paradoxes of African politics and economics is what has come to be known as the economic "resource curse." The fundamental premise is that in specific politico-cultural contexts, countries endowed with an abundance of natural resources, particularly oil, natural gas and minerals, tend to be neo-patrimonial, corrupt, have less economic growth, more conflicts, and poor economic outcomes than countries that are less endowed with natural resources (Smith & Waldner, 2021; Wright and Frantz, 2017, Wright et al. 2015; Ross, 2012). A number of African countries are classified as having a resource curse. They include the Congo, Congo Brazzaville, Gabon, Equatorial Guinea, the Central African Republic, Nigeria, and Cameroon (Berman et al, 2017; Kim & Woods, 2016). The centralized, republican chiefery of Cameroon has a unique case of the resource curse. Natural resources– oil, natural gas, minerals, and forestry resources–are exploited, controlled and spent by the republican chieftain (first Ahmadou Ahidjo, and after 1982 by his successor, Paul Biya and the ruling tribal elite), with utmost opacity and corruption, in true neo-patrimonial fashion, while much of the country lacks clean drinking water, and the public healthcare system is not worth the name (see Chapter 13). Many schools do not have classrooms and desks (see Chapter 7), the roads are deplorable death traps, and so on.

Research and experience have shown that the French "assimilative impulse" or its postcolonial variant in Cameroon, to use the expression of Betts (1961), was quickly put in place in the new Federal Republic of Cameroon. The new federation of East (Francophone) and West (Anglophone) Cameroon started off with a "one-country, two systems" ideology. The national flag was green, red, yellow, the flag of *la République du Cameroun*, to which two stars were added, symbolizing the two federated states. Both states maintained their respective systems of government, their executives (prime ministers), legislatures, and judiciaries. The easy decisions came first: the Federal Republic of Cameroon decided that all cars would drive on the right side of the road, rather than the left side as was the case in Nigeria and other former British colonies. The federation also adopted the postcolonial CFA franc like the rest of the Francophone countries of Africa. However, both states maintained their respective educational systems, though bilingual secondary schools were created in Yaoundé, the capital of East Cameroon, and Buea, the capital of West Cameroon, and other towns in West Cameroon, to enable students from both sides of the language divide to study together and become bilingual. Furthermore, the French government started the very first interactive French language distance education program in Africa, a radio program called *Français par la Radio* (French by Radio). This program was prerecorded. French teachers from France used the Radio Buea, the only radio station in West Cameroon, to teach French grammar (mostly conjugation) and conversational French.

Politicians, policymakers and educators on both sides of the language divide made moves to "harmonize" the laws of both states, and especially the penal code. This turned out to be tougher than anticipated because the legal philosophies of France and the United Kingdom, that had been introduced in both territories during colonization were incompatible, even contradictory. Under the Napoleonic civil law system that obtained in East Cameroon, there was no judicial independence, and no presumption of innocence. Accused persons were presumed guilty until proved innocent and the burden of proof of innocence was on them. By way of contrast, the Anglophone West Cameroon had the British common law system, an independent judiciary, and a high presumption of innocence. Persons accused of a crime were presumed innocent, and the burden of proof of guilt was on the government.

The Federal Republic of Cameroon was ultimately doomed by the natural resource curse. In 1971 French companies discovered huge oil and natural gas reserves in the Rio del Rey basin, in the territory of the State of West Cameroon. That information was kept secret from the leaders and people of West Cameroon. In a political sleight of hand designed to bring the oil and natural gas resources under the direct control of President Ahidjo and his cronies in Yaoundé, President Ahmadou Ahidjo violated the federal constitution and abolished the federation in 1972, through a referendum of dubious legality, creating a United Republic of Cameroon and splitting the state of West Cameroon into two provinces, the Southwest and Northwest provinces by decree. The authoritarian French Cameroon leader, Ahmadou Ahidjo soon imposed a highly centralized, autocratic Jacobin-style republic with a Napoleonic administration complete with appointed governors, prefects, and sub-prefects. That essentially ended the local government system of West Cameroon. These Machiavellian political moves also effectively transferred the oil, natural gas, and agricultural resources of West Cameroon to the control of Ahmadou Ahidjo, and ultimately, his successor, Paul Biya, his tribal and political cronies in Yaoundé. Reunification of Southern Cameroons and *la République du Cameroun* quickly turned out to be "lawful plunder" to borrow the expression of Bastiat (1998), who pointed out that "plunder is organized by law for the profit of those who make the law" (p.7). In the post-reunification Cameroon, Southern Cameroons became the object of lawful plunder. Ahidjo-Biya, and their French overseers used legal plunder to take the wealth of Southern Cameroons– its natural resources– oil, natural gas, timber, state-owned agricultural estates, agricultural cooperatives, educational institutions, and so on, and gave them to a few, while throwing a few crumbs to a handful of Anglophone leaders now and then.

In effect, Southern Cameroons became unequally yoked, and became the subject of the assimilationist mission of a *la République du Cameroun*, a highly centralized, republican chiefdom whose institutions, and governmentality mimicked Napoleonic authoritarianism, and employed a "republican" rhetoric that echoed the niceties of French secular republicanism but were in effect, a system of tribal patronage and rent-seeking writ large. In effect, the dispersal of Southern Cameroons into the *Francophonie camerounaise*, meant being grafted into a rent-seeking system which gradually transferred state power into an instrument for allocating public resources into private coffers, conferring economic and monetary advantages and benefits to the president, his ethnic group, and a handpicked, subservient elite, from other parts of the country, while imposing disadvantages on others. In time, the vague and overbroad vaporous metric– harmonization of the two legal systems, laws and legal procedures, educational and economic systems, and the like–became the thin edge of the wedge of assimilation.

The Anglophone Question is directly linked to the natural resource curse in Cameroon. In effect, the United Nations Trust Territory of Southern Cameroons, which became the state of West Cameroon in the Federal Republic of Cameroon had a variant of the natural resource curse. Southern Cameroons was doomed because of the vast natural resources (primarily oil and natural gas) within its territory, and the political naivety of its leaders, particularly the unsophisticated John Ngu Foncha, and the ambitious but equally unsophisticated Solomon Tandeng Muna. With the discovery of reserves of oil and natural gas reserves off the coast of what used to be British Southern Cameroons, the governments of *La République du Cameroun* and France embarked on a policy of assimilating the English-and Pidgin-speaking Southern Cameroons into *la Francophonie*. The reunification of Southern Cameroons and *La République du Cameroun* quickly turned out to be "lawful plunder", to borrow the expression of Bastiat (1998), who pointed out that in politics, especially in situations of unequal power dynamics, "plunder is organized by law for the profit of those who make the law" (p. 7). In the post-reunification Cameroon, Southern Cameroons became the object of lawful plunder. Ahidjo-Biya, and their French overseers used legal plunder to confiscate the natural resources of Southern Cameroons–oil, natural gas, timber, the Cameroons Development Corporation (CDC) and other state-owned agricultural estates, agricultural cooperatives, educational institutions, and so on, and gave them to their political cronies, while throwing a few Anglophone leaders here and there a bone to gnaw on. In effect, the attempted dispersal of English-speaking Southern Cameroons into the *Francophonie camerounaise*, meant grafting the territory into a neo-patrimonial, rent-seeking system which gradually transformed state power into an instrument for allocating public resources into private coffers, conferring economic and monetary advantages and benefits on the president, his Beti-Bulu tribe, and a handpicked, subservient elite from other parts of the country. These moves relegated the English-speaking minority for whom natural resources had become a curse, to second-class status, and triggered the identitarian and cultural resistance that became the Anglophone revolt of 2016.

The Anglophone Question in general and the Anglophone revolt of 2016 is the response of the plundered to the legal and illegal Francophone state and individual economic, social, and cultural plunder of Southern Cameroons and marginalization of its people. The fundamental problem of Cameroon is that the Ahidjo-Biya rule-by-decree regime converted postcolonial plunder into a system of governance, a governmentality. Thus, "in order to protect plunder, it converts lawful defense into a crime, in order to punish lawful defense," as Bastiat (1998, p. 5) put it. In this system of law and oppression, law and disorder, the law takes precedence over rights, and becomes an instrument of injustice (Bastiat, 1998, p. 15). The crisis is a reflection of the acute tensions between these Francophone and Anglophone governmentalities and their contrasting logics of the state, religion, culture, and the human person, the citizen.

Oil and natural gas thus became the grease that lubricated the wheels of the Ahidjo/Biya authoritarian, kleptocratic "neo-patrimonial" state, to adopt the usage of Fukuyama (2014), who describes such regimes as "governments staffed by the family and friends of the ruler, and run for their benefit…A neopatrimonial government has the outward form of a modern state, with a constitution, presidents and prime ministers, a legal system, and pretensions of impersonality, but the actual operation of the government remains a matter of sharing state resources with friends and family" (p. 287). The Ahidjo/Biya Napoleonic, *chefferie républicaine* with its ethos of rule-by-decree was perfect for the opaque control and mismanagement of the oil resources of the country. In effect, the oil and natural gas sector– and the funds accruing from it was a closely guarded state secret under the Ahidjo-Biya regime. The national oil refinery, SONARA started oil production in 1973 but it was kept secret until 1980, when President Ahidjo signed presidential decree no.80/86 of 12 March 1980, creating a state-owned oil company, the *Société Nationale des Hydrocarbures* (National Hydrocarbons Corporation), known by its French acronym SNH, a holding company based in Yaoundé. SNH controlled the only oil refinery in the country, *la Societe Nationale de Raffinage* (National Refinery Corporation), popularly known by its acronym, SONARA, that was inaugurated in 1981. SNH has subsidiaries, affiliations, opaque and dubious partnerships with a host of other companies in the oil and gas sector. What is interesting about the SNH is that the presidential decree of 1980, which created it stipulated that it would be legally a commercial and industrial enterprise that enjoyed "financial" autonomy and operated under the tutelage of the Secretary General of the Presidency of the Republic. This essentially meant that revenues from the oil sector would not be considered part of public revenues and would not go directly into the public treasury. In other words, the monies would be a slush fund controlled directly by the president and a few cronies like Adolphe Moudiki, whom he appointed Director General of the SNH in 1993 and has kept in that position as at the time of this writing in 2024. As we see elsewhere in this book, President Biya used these oil revenues as his personal slush fund to fund the Israeli-controlled national security system, as well as the system of neo-patrimonial patronage.

Managerial Opacity, International Corruption, and the Resource Curse in the Cameroon Hydrocarbons Sector

The oil and natural gas resources of Cameroon come mostly from the territory of the former Southern Cameroons. However, after the reunification, Anglophones were mere spectators who watched President Ahidjo treat the hydrocarbons from Southern Cameroons with extreme secrecy. President Biya essentially treated these natural resources as the instrument for the maintenance of his kleptocratic, neo-patrimonial regime. We have seen that the *Société Nationale des Hydrocarbures* (National Hydrocarbons Corporation) funds the Israeli-trained and equipped presidential guard and the notorious "army within the army," the *Bataillon d'Intervention Rapide* (BIR). The issue of oil revenues came up after the oil crash of the 1990s, when the Biya regime went before the IMF and the World Bank to negotiate loans and institute a structural adjustment program. The Bretton Woods institutions went through the motions of asking for transparency in the management of the oil revenues of Cameroon. Nevertheless, despite the lack of transparency and accountability in the management of the oil resources of the country, the Biya regime always got the money it needed to support its neopatrimonial budgets from the IMF and the World Bank. This is no surprise given that the managing directors of the IMF that the Ahidjo/Biya regime has had to deal with, have been mostly French citizens: Jacques de Larosière, Michel Camdessus, Dominique Strauss-Khan, and Christine Lagarde. In an extraordinary and unprecedented act of openness, a business law firm, Chazai and Partners, that is accredited at the bar of Paris and Cameroon, issued a press release on July 12, 2019 announcing that President Paul Biya had signed two decrees, No. 2019/342 changing the form of the SNH into a *"société à capital public"* a publicly traded company, and decree No. 2019/343, approving the statutes of the SNH. The Chazai and Partners statement stated that SNH had been transformed into *"société à capital public ayant l'État comme seul actionnaire,"* a publicly traded company solely owned by the state (emphasis in the original). The statement stated that SNH would continue having "financial autonomy" under the technical and financial tutelage of the Secretariat General of the Presidency, who will file an annual report to the President on the situation of the SNH. The management of the company would be carried out by a General Assembly, an Administrative Council, and a Directorate General. The decrees essentially transformed SNH into a state-owned publicly traded commercial and industrial corporation managed by the president, and his civil servant appointees. As we see in Volume II, "great power alliances," and postcolonial hegemonic national and corporate relationships made SNH and SONARA the center of what economists call the "natural resource curse" in Cameroon. The fundamental premise of the resource curse is that in specific politico-cultural contexts, countries endowed with an abundance of natural resources, particularly oil, natural gas, and minerals, tend to be neo-patrimonial, kleptocratic, have less economic growth, more conflicts, and poor economic outcomes than countries that are less endowed with natural resources (Smith & Waldner, 2021; Wright and Frantz, 2017; Wright et al., 2015; Ross, 2012). Where the resource curse is entrenched, the rent-seeking ruling elite of autocratic kleptocracies often colludes with international commodities (oil, natural gas, forest, agriculture, and mineral extraction) companies to further the interests of these companies. The ruling elite and controllers line their own pockets through bribery and corruption from Big Oil and Big Commodity trading companies, while their people are mired in poverty and misery (United States Foreign Relations Committee, 2008). Some of those persons responsible for the management of both the SNH and SONARA have been involved in high-level "bribery scheme" involving Swiss international commodities conglomerates, Glencore International A.G., and Glencore Ltd. That information was made public by the United States government. On May 24th, the United States Department of Justice announced that Glencore International A.G. had pled guilty in the Southern District of New York to violations under the Foreign Corrupt Practices Act (FCPA), while Glencore Ltd., pled guilty in the District of Connecticut to a commodity price manipulation conspiracy. The Department of Justice announced that the United States Attorney for the Southern District of New York, had entered into a plea agreement with Glencore International, A.G. and Glencore Ltd. The United States government had charged Glencore with bribing government and national oil company officials in multiple African countries including, the *Société Nationale des Hydrocarbures* (National Hydrocarbons Corporation) and the *Société Nationale de Raffinage,* National Refining Corporation (SONARA) in Cameroon, in furtherance of the interests of Glencore, a major commodities player in Cameroon and other African countries (*United States v. Glencore*

International AG, 2022).

The SONARA Fire of 2019 and its Aftermath

The reasons for the transformation of SNH, and its affiliate, SONARA into a state-owned "publicly-traded" company on July 9, 2019, are not unrelated to attempts to make management of these entities and their finances even more opaque than they had been for decades. This was probably due to a fire that crippled SONARA in 2019. In effect, on May 31, 2019, SONARA, the sole oil refinery of Cameroon, the main source of funding of the neo-patrimonial Ahidjo/Biya system, exploded into a catastrophic fireball that completely or partially destroyed seven out of the thirteen production units of the refinery, and knocked the facility offline. On June 1, 2019, the Director General of SONARA, Jean-Paul Simo Njonou issued a "*déclaration de FORCE MAJEURE*" (Njonou, 2019). Under business and contract law, a "*cas de force majeure*" or "unexpected, extraordinary or overwhelming circumstance" is a legal provision that relieves the declarants from fulfilling their contractual obligations to their clients, customers or patrons when specific, enumerated, unexpected circumstances beyond their control–such as war, terrorism or natural disasters– make fulfillment of their contractual obligations impracticable, or impossible. The common law equivalent of *cas de force majeure* is the less stringent doctrine of contractual "impracticability" (Ryan, 2011). To complicate matters further for SONARA, Anglophone non-state armed groups, who are fighting a war of insurgency for restoration of the statehood of Southern Cameroons, claimed responsibility for the explosion and fire at SONARA (Bole, 2019). The Cameroon government quickly denied the claim.

When it became clear that repair and rehabilitation of the refinery was expected to cost hundreds of millions of dollars, rumors swelled on social media to the effect that the managers of the refinery had failed to pay its insurance premiums to its insurer, Activa Insurance at the time of the explosion and fire. Five senior managers, including the chief finance officer, were arrested and held in detention at the Limbe police station. The narrative became further complicated when SONARA hastily published a call for tenders for insuring the refinery, its workers and automobile fleet, on its website after the catastrophic explosion and fire. The call for tenders was supposedly signed by the Director General of SONARA, Jean-Paul Simo Njonou on April 1, 2019–four months into the year–and just two months before the catastrophic incident. The call for tenders was for insuring the refinery for the three-year period 2019, 2020, and 2021. The call for tenders was, as usual, written only in French, the official language of SONARA (*Avis d'Appel d'Offres National*, 2019). There is no evidence that the refinery was insured before the catastrophic fire. The arrest of the five senior managers of SONARA was apparently not enough. On the 15th of July 2019, the Gendarmerie authorities summoned the Director General and managers of Activa Insurance, the insurer of SONARA, to report for questioning at the Judicial Police office in Limbe, Southwest region, in connection with the fire that ravaged the refinery. The assumption was that the SONARA officials and Activa had allegedly engaged in insurance fraud.

The reality was that without insurance coverage, the State of Cameroon, the sole owner of SONARA, had to bear the cost of repairing and rehabilitating the refinery. This was an uphill task given that the national treasury was virtually empty. In fact, in June 2017, 10 months after the start of the Anglophone crisis, the International Monetary Fund (IMF) had agreed to immediately disburse $171.3 million under its Extended Credit Facility (ECF) in order "to restore the country's fiscal and external sustainability and unlock job-rich, private sector-driven growth." A further aim of the loan was to ensure that the government initiate, "Reforms to maintain financial stability and boost financial inclusion, and address structural obstacles to competitiveness and economic diversification…" (IMF Executive Board Approves US$666.2 Million Arrangement, 2017). The IMF Executive Board further explained that the rationale for extending this loan to Cameroon for the three-year period–2017, 2018, and 2019– was that: "Cameroon, the largest economy in the Central African Economic and Monetary Union (CEMAC), has been hit hard since 2014 by shocks caused by a slump in oil prices and increased security threats. Oil revenue declined and security and humanitarian spending increased, while needed infrastructure programs continued, leading to widening fiscal and current account deficits as well as a rapid accumulation of external debt" (IMF Executive Board Approves US$666.2 Million Arrangement, 2017). The key phrase in the IMF agreement was "security and humanitarian spending," the euphemism for the wars against Boko Haram in north Cameroon, the security concerns along the border with the Central African Republic, and the Anglophone crisis, which had degenerated into a full-scale war.

Post-Cold War Liberalization and the All Anglophone Conferences of 1993 & 1994

This is how it all began. The fall of the Berlin Wall in 1989, and the collapse of the Soviet Union in 1991 brought an end to the East-West Cold War and changed the geo-strategic landscape not only in Europe but also in Africa. In effect, the end of the Cold War and its geo-strategic strictures on African nations triggered a fierce hurricane of instability over the African continent. Popular uprisings, strikes, sit-ins, demands for political freedom, and better standards of living broke out all over the African continent. This unprecedented phenomenon was a demonstration of what Monga (1996) called, "the anthropology of anger." In response to these massive uprisings, president after authoritarian president, seeing that France and other Western benefactors were no longer willing or able to provide unconditional support, legalized opposition parties, and allowed the press a modicum of freedom. Divergent voices began to be heard and many more people gained access to the mass media. This, in turn, led to demands for democratization, transparency, and accountability, which forced African regimes to grant more political freedoms to their people. The English-speaking minority in Cameroon took advantage of this "hurricane of change" that was sweeping across Africa. They demanded an end to the autocratic one-party, republican chiefery, and recognition of the cultural, identitarian and autonomist aspirations of English-speaking Cameroonians who lived primarily in the former Southern Cameroons, which was now divided into two provinces, the Northwest and Southwest regions. One of the results of the post-Cold War agitations and subsequent liberalization was that the independent press in Cameroon, which had been subject to draconian registration requirements and pre-publication censorship under the Ahidjo/Biya regime, was suddenly free to publish without governmental permission (Eko, 2003). One of the hottest topics in the liberalized, French-language, independent media space of Cameroon was the controversial pre-independence cooperation agreements signed with France in 1959. For the first time since independence, the independent media shone a spotlight on the financial provisions of these agreements, and especially the French African currency, the CFA (Franc of the French Colonies of Africa), which France had created in 1945, and bequeathed it to its postcolonies after independence (Mbembe, 2001). The independent press also commented on the military provisions of the pre-independence cooperation agreements that allowed France to intervene in African countries if pro-French regimes in power faced internal or external threats (Servenay, 2007).

The post-Cold War social activism of the 1990s saw the emergence of demands by English and Pidgin-speaking Cameroonians for national recognition of their identitarian and cultural specificity, that had been muted in the over-centralized, Napoleonic, neo-patrimonial republican chiefery of Cameroon. In effect, soon after the reunification of British Southern Cameroons and *la République du Cameroun* in 1961, France and the Ahidjo/Biya regime set out to assimilate the autonomous state of Southern Cameroons and disperse it into the French postcolonial, politico-cultural sphere of influence, *la Francophonie*. This created tensions and clashes between English and French-speaking Cameroonians in the domains of governmentality (the nature of the state, Southern Cameroons localism versus French Cameroon centralism, as well as the role of religion in the life of the state). There was also a clash of the educational and legal systems (the rule of law versus the rule of man); Anglophone adversarial legalism with a presumption of innocence versus Francophone inquisitorial justice without a presumption of innocence), civil rights (human rights over State's rights and rites, etc.,). The Anglophone Question, the role and place of minority English-speaking Cameroonians in the country, was thus present at the birth of the short-lived federal experiment in Cameroon.

With the realization that Francophone Cameroun and France were deliberately suffocating Anglophone identity and culture, and transforming English-language speakers from the former British Southern Cameroons into subalterns, second-class citizens, the Anglophone community, led by common law lawyers, engaged in collective political action aimed at securing reforms from the Biya regime. Collective Anglophone political demands were channeled through an umbrella organization, the All-Anglophone Conference (AAC) which met in Buea in 1993, and Bamenda in 1994. The first AAC issued the Buea Declaration and the second, the Bamenda Proclamation. Taken together, the two documents amounted to a ledger of grievances. It was a Declaration of Anglophone politico-cultural and identitarian specificity, and a Proclamation that described in great detail, the sub-altern status to which the Ahidjo-Biya regime had relegated the English and Pidgin-speaking minority. The AAC called for a return to the federal system of government and respect for the identitarian specificity and autonomy of the English-speaking former West Cameroon.

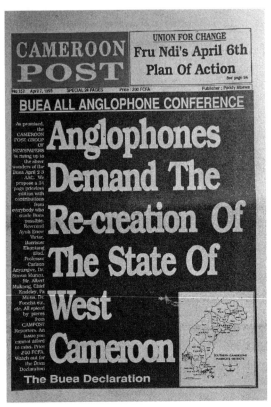

Figure 2.13. The All Anglophone Conference: Anglophones Demand the Recreation of the State of West Cameroon, *Cameroon Post*, April 7, 1993

The AAC conferences, the Buea Declaration and Bamenda Proclamation went to the heart of the Anglophone Question in Cameroon. The Buea Declaration was a ledger of grievances that stated in part:

> TODAY, NO GROUP OF PEOPLE who freely chose to join a political Union would want to be treated as a captive people. In 1961 the people of Southern Cameroons through a United Nations-supervised plebiscite decided to enter into a political Union with the people of La République du Cameroun whom they considered as their brothers and fellow countrymen. They did so, by the grace of God, FREELY and without the involvement or participation of the people of *La Republique du Cameroun*. Their aspiration was to establish a unique Federation on the continent of Africa, and to evolve a bicultural society in which the distinct heritage of each of the partners to the union would flourish. We believed that such a lofty goal could be achieved. During these past thirty-two years, however, our common experience in the Union leaves us in no doubt that far from attaining theses ends; we have become a people with a problem.
>
> Our problem, which the intolerant and hypocritical attitude of our Francophone brothers would rather suppress, springs from a breach of

trust on the part of Francophone leadership and from a lack of openness in matters of public interest. Within these thirty-two years, our Union accord has been violated. We have been disenfranchised, marginalized, and treated with suspicion. Our interests have been disregarded.

Our participation in national life has been limited to non-essential functions. Our natural resources have been ruthlessly exploited without any benefit accruing to our territory or to its people. The development of our territory has been negligible and confined to areas that directly or indirectly benefit Francophones. Through manoeuvres and manipulations, we have been reduced from partners of equal status in the Union to the status of a subjugated people.

The AAC delegates also wrote that they: DECLARE the preparedness of Anglophones to participate in the forthcoming Constitutional Talks with their Francophone brothers....

The AAC Buea Declaration concluded with the key grievance and demands of the Anglophone community (capital letters in the original):

1. THAT THE IMPOSITION OF THE UNITARY STATE ON ANGLOPHONE CAMEROON IN 1972 WAS UNCONSTITUTIONAL, ILLEGAL AND A BREACH OF FAITH.
2. THAT THE ONLY REDRESS ADEQUATE TO RIGHT THE WRONGS DONE TO ANGLOPHONE CAMEROON AND ITS PEOPLE SINCE THE IMPOSITION OF THE UNITARY STATE IS A RETURN TO THE ORIGINAL FORM OF GOVERNMENT OF THE REUNIFIED CAMEROON.

The All-Anglophone conferences of Buea and Bamenda were an unprecedented mass movement of English-speaking or Anglophone Cameroonians who assembled for purposes of expressing their collective rejection of the failed Southern Cameroons, French Cameroun reunification project championed by the United Kingdom, France, and the United Nations. It was the cry of anguish of a free people who had been forced into a union with the autocratic, republican chiefery, that was held together not by the consent of the people but by sheer force of arms. The constitutional conference that the Biya regime had floated turned out to be just a game of smoke and mirrors, an act of bad faith designed to maintain the over-centralized, kleptocratic status quo.

The Symbolic March at the Mungo Bridge

To underline their rejection of their subaltern and subservient status in *la République du Cameroun*, the Anglophone elite from both the Northwest and the Southwest regions, led by former Southern Cameroons Premiers and Federal Republic of Cameroon Vice Presidents, John Ngu Foncha and Solomon Tandeng Muna, assembled at the Mungo bridge, which marked the pre-independence border between Southern Cameroons and French Cameroun, brandished the flag of the United Nations and demanded restoration of the State of Southern Cameroons. In keeping with its autocratic nature, the Biya regime ignored the political demands of the Anglophone elite. This was one more step toward the

Anglophone Revolt, which ultimately occurred in 2016.

Figure 2.14. Anglophone leaders Muna, Foncha, Ekontang Elad, Munzu, Njoh Litumbe and others lead a symbolic march on the Mungo Bridge with the UN flag to symbolize failure of the Reunification between Southern Cameroons and *La République du Cameroun*, and a desire for the UN to intervene and solve the Anglophone Question.

This was not the first time Anglophones had campaigned for change in Cameroon.

The Ahidjo-Biya one-party system effectively ended when Mr. John Fru Ndi launched the Social Democratic Front (SDF) in Bamenda on the 26th of May 1990. Thereafter, Cameroon security forces opened fire on unarmed peaceful party members marching in Bamenda, killing six persons. Anglophone activism ultimately led to the end of the Ahidjo/Biya *Union Nationale Camerounaise* (UNC/CNU) one-party state.

Theoretical Approaches: The Muted Groups Theory and Living Together

The Anglophone Question in Cameroon was analyzed within the framework of Ardener's "muted groups" theory, which holds that in the African tribal societies and cultures they studied in Southern Cameroons, women and minorities were essentially "parenthetical citizens" (p. 53) who did not have a voice in the day-to-day management of society. They found that patriarchal and paternalistic social structures imposed heavy burdens on the expressive freedoms of women and minorities. The muted groups theory explains the unequal power dynamics at play in given authoritarian societies. The very nature of these oppressive societies silences the voices of women and minorities and reduces them to "relatively inarticulate groups." These "subdominant" groups are essentially "muted groups" because they are muted in relation to the dominant structures (Ardener, 2005, Ardener & Ardener, 1972). The premise is that in Cameroon, the Francophone majority has hegemonic constitutional, political, administrative, and economic control over the country and its natural resources, thereby relegating the English and Pidgin-speaking peoples, who live in the geographic area of the former state of Southern/West Cameroon, to the status of subalterns, second-class citizens who have no voice in the governance of the Napoleonic republican chiefdom of Cameroon. The second theoretical framework which sheds light on, and explains the unequal power dynamics between the Francophones and Anglophones is Renan's *le vivre ensemble* or living together idea. At face value, this looks like a call for peaceful co-existence, getting along, and cultural diversity in a multicultural society like Cameroon, but on closer examination, *le vivre ensemble* is actually part of the oppressive, assimilationist architecture that led to the Anglophone Question, and triggered the Anglophone Revolt. As such, the much talked about *le vivre ensemble* is ironically problematic in the Cameroonian politico-cultural context. Indeed, unreflecting deterritorialization and application of the French policy of *le vivre ensemble* as used in contemporary French politics is political and linguistic "apemanship," or "mental slavery" as Bob Marley put it.

The English and Pidgin-speaking Southern Cameroonians as a Muted Group in Cameroon

The Anglophone Question is a multi-dimensional, politico-cultural, identitarian, and linguistic problem. To get another perspective on it, we turn to social anthropology, which provides a useful tool, a theoretical approach to explaining it. This is the "muted groups" theory advanced by British social anthropologists, Edwin and Shirley Ardener (1972). In many societies around the world, there are sub-altern segments of society that exist as non-entities. In certain societies, they are there to be seen, not to be heard. In others, they exist neither to be seen nor heard. This is the case with the Islamo-patriarchal cultures of Afghanistan, Iran and other Muslim countries where women belong to an underclass, sub-citizens who must be covered and kept out of sight at all times. Most African societies have patriarchal or patrilineal cultures. These are male-dominated societies in which inheritance and leadership are based on male family lineages. There are a few matriarchal or matrilineal cultures where lineage and inheritance are traced through the mother's side, to be sure. However, even these cultures are male-dominated. In East Africa, the Swahili expression, "Wazee hukumbuka" (The old men who remember) and "Wazee wa kazi" (master craftsmen) emphasize the fact that male elders are the repositories of the collective memory, arts and crafts of the tribe, even though women live longer than men and do most of the passing of the traditions and cultures of society to their children. The cultural subordination of women in West African societies was the inspiration for a very influential social anthropological theory, the "muted groups" theory advanced by Ardener and Ardener (1975; 2005). It was one of the most influential theoretical perspectives to come out of British social anthropology in the 1960s and 1970s. This identitarian perspective emerged from the ethnographic fieldwork of British social anthropologists, Edwin and Shirley Ardener in what was then British Southern Cameroons (Ardner, 2005). They studied the role and place of women in a number of ethnic groups, and advanced certain theoretical speculations and interpretations that crystallized into the analytical framework that came to be known as the muted groups theory. The premise of this theory is that in the African tribal societies and cultures they studied, oppressive societies silenced the voices of women and reduced them to "relatively inarticulate groups," or "muted groups." These "subdominant" groups were essentially muted in relation to the dominant structures, which sometimes expected the muted subdominant groups to engage in "retraining" and "resocialization" to conform with the dominant groups. However, despite their different status in society, dominant groups and muted groups are not independent realities, they are often mutually reinforcing... 'simultaneities" (Ardener, 2005, p. 52) that cannot exist without each other. Muted groups had to find alternative outlets of symbolic individual or group self-expression. They found that muted women in Africa sometimes used body symbolism as symbolic speech or expressive conduct to make their case (Ardener, 1971).

Muted groups theory raises awareness of minority voices. Ardener (2005) suggests that there are multiple ways in which identitarian groups are muted: "Groups can be muted by the way society encodes its data, by the nature of its discourse, by the medium-not necessarily by the message-which may even contradict the medium," (p. 54). The theory also has a linguistic component. According to Ardener (2005), the basic linguistic argument of muted groups theory is that it:

> includes the question whether everyone in society has participated equally in the generation of ideas and their encoding into discourse. Have groups developed separate realities, or systems of values that do not get adequate recognition in the dominant representations of society? Are there mechanisms for devaluing their contributions, or squeezing them out from the arenas in which rewards are distributed?...While 'muting' may entail the suppression, or repression of speech, the theory, in its linguistic aspect, is concerned at least as much with *what* people say, and when they speak, and in what *mode,* as with *how much*...muting by dominant groups through control of dominant discourse is refracted through and embedded in many different spaces..." [and discourses]...the debate focuses on the fundamental question of the generation of categories of thought, of conceptualizations, and ideas concerning social structures (p. 5151).

Interestingly, Professor Edwin Ardener began his theory-building with a critique of social anthropology, a discipline which he believed viewed women through "dominant male systems of perceptions" (Ardener, 1975, p. xi). From there he wrote of societies "dominated or overdetermined by the model (or models) generated by one dominant group within the system. This dominant model may impede the free expression of alternative models of their world...and perhaps may even inhibit the very generation of such models...the latter might be relatively 'inarticulate' when expressing themselves through the idioms of the dominant group...." (Ardener, 1975, p. xi). This theory is prominent in women's and gender studies. It ultimately diffused to other disciplines, including political science, sociology, and media studies. It is very relevant in Southern Cameroons, which inspired it.

The Reality of *Le Vivre Ensemble* (Living Together) in Republican France

Multi-cultural, multi-ethnic, and multi-lingual states like Cameroon have to continually examine and reexamine themselves and renegotiate the terms of their, existence, which is nothing but political management of the co-existence of its various cultural and linguistic components. Multi-cultural nations that do not examine themselves in the light of internal political, economic, cultural, and demographic developments often degenerate into national security or police states. Cameroon is an instructive exemplar. When President Biya convened a Grand National Dialogue to tackle the intractable Anglophone Question, the motto of the conference was ironically, "Living together in PEACE." While the Biya regime turned a deaf ear and a blind eye to the identitarian demands of the Anglophone minority, its party and administrative cadres adapted the idea of *le vivre ensemble* (living together) from 19th century French political thinker, Ernest Renan. In his essay entitled, "What is a Nation?" Renan (1882) wrote that:

> A nation is a soul, a spiritual principle. Two things that, in truth are but one, constitute this spiritual principle. One is the past, the other in the present. One is the possession in common of a rich legacy of memories; the other is present consent, the desire to live together, the will to perpetuate the value of the heritage that one has received in an undivided form...the nation, like the individual, is the culmination of a long past of efforts, sacrifices, and devotion. The cult of ancestors is the most legitimate of all, our ancestors have made us who we are...A nation is therefore a vast solidarity, constituted by the sentiment of the sacrifices one has made and of those one is yet prepared to make. It presupposes a past; it is however summarized in the present by a tangible fact: consent, the clearly expressed desire to continue a common life. A nation's existence is...an everyday plebiscite... (p. 186).

Renan (1882) emphasized the old principle of democratic governance according to which governments govern by the consent of the governed. He added that since people can only be governed to the extent they consent to be governed, "forgetting, or ignoring foundational understandings undermines the possibility of a common history by excluding an entire class of memories...Forgetting destroys the historic inheritance and current consent to be governed." (p. 186). In contemporary France, Renan's idea of *le vivre ensemble* has been actualized and re-presented to suit the political needs of the moment, to the point where it has become a political buzzword. It is used to present anew the French ideology of secular republicanism and monoculturalism as an assimilationist ideology directed at new waves of mostly Muslim immigrants in France. *Le vivre ensemble* in the contemporary French secular republican context is not a pluricultural or multicultural concept. It is premised on the utopian ideal of a single French national, Gallic culture that is believed to be universal and open to all who come to France, jettison their native cultures, and embrace French secular republican along with its enlightenment ideals. *Le vivre ensemble* is thus, by nature, hostile to British or American-style multiculturalism. Federalism, as it functions in Switzerland, the United States, Germany or even Mexico, presupposes the co-existence of multiple cultures, and is thus the anti-thesis of French secular republican *vivre ensemble,* which is French emphasis on national unity over cultural and religious pluralism (Bernand, 2006, Lawrence & Viasse, 2006). This emphasis on secularism and individualism over religious and cultural pluralism has led to a unique system of cultural integration and assimilation in France: citizens are *French* first, and members of cultural and religious groups second. French secular republicanism has no place for the multiple subject, persons with multiple cultural allegiances, or for cultural diversity. Immigrants are supposed to abandon their cultural identity at the border when they become French citizens, and adhere to the French secular republican creed of *liberté, égalité, fraternité (laïcité)* (Laurence and Viasse, 2006). French rejection of the Islamic veil is based on the idea, nay the legal justification that ostentatious and public displays of symbols of religious membership were tantamount to a rejection of French secular republicanism and its ideology of *le vivre ensemble,* the politico-cultural and social tie that binds French secular republican society. *Le vivre ensemble* essentially means living together in this French mono-cultural model, while adhering to the national ideology of secular republicanism.

Le Vivre Ensemble (Living Together) In the Republican Chiefdom of Cameroon

Renan's 19th-century expression, *le vivre ensemble,* or living together, has become a political, social, cultural, and sociological ideology and creed that the contemporary French political class bandies about to justify assimilationist immigration and social integration policies. It has evolved from traditional democratic concepts like the idea that people should not be governed without their consent, to a buzzword for monocultural secular republicanism. In France, it is therefore not synonymous with the peaceful co-existence of cultures, multiculturalism, tolerance of, and respect for linguistic and cultural diversity. It does not stand for respect for how different cultures organize themselves, how they exercise their establishmentalities (postures towards religion and its place in the life of the State and in the public sphere). It does not stand for respect for systemic diversity in educational and legal systems, which are the main bones of contention of the Anglophone Revolt.

While chanting the mantra of *vivre ensemble,* the Ahidjo/Biya regime ignored the federalist foundations of the Cameroon nation in order to control the natural resources of the Anglophone region and use them corruptly to maintain a lavish lifestyle in an authoritarian neo-patrimonial regime. Government ministers, hand-picked administrative apparatchiks, ruling party cadres, and agents of the Biya republican chiefdom took Renan's phrase "*vivre ensemble*" (living together) out of its original context, deliberately ignoring the fact that the concept of living together is grounded in the principle of the governed giving the government consent to be governed rather than to be brutally subjugated:

> a nation has no more right than a king does to say to a province: You belong to me, I am seizing you... A province, for us, is its inhabitants, if anyone has the right to be consulted in such an affair, it is the inhabitant. A nation never has any real interest in annexing or holding on to a country against its will...Nations are not something eternal. They had their beginnings, they will end (Renan, 1882, p. 187).

When President Paul Biya convened the so-called Grand National Dialogue to look for solutions to the Anglophone Question in 2019, he gave the meeting the motto: of *le vivre ensemble* en *PAIX* (Living Together in PEACE). The Grand National Dialogue clearly used the contemporary French assimilationist sense of the expression. The agenda had no items on the peaceful co-existence of Anglophone and Francophone cultures, respect for Anglophone identitarian specificity, tolerance of, and respect for linguistic and cultural diversity as well as respect for systemic diversity in the Francophone and Anglophone educational and legal systems of Cameroon. *Le vivre ensemble* of the Grand National Dialogue of 2019 turned out to be empty sloganeering. It was clearly a facile and farcical misapplication of a French assimilationist political slogan for purposes of maintaining the status quo–President Biya's autocratic, neo-patrimonial republican chiefdom– without making any concessions to Anglophone federalists and independentists and non-state armed groups. The Grand National Dialogue of 2019, which President Biya did not even bother to attend, will go down in history as a colossal failure, sheer waste of time and resources.

Conclusion

Cameroon is a member of both *la Francophonie*, and the British Commonwealth of Nations. English and Pidgin-speaking Southern Cameroons, which has since been split into the Northwest and Southwest regions for purposes of assimilation into la Francophonie, is still solidly Anglophone. It has an Anglophone sub-system of education, and a legal and civil rights culture that is different from the Francophone system. English is the medium of instruction in the Anglophone sub-system of education, from kindergarten to university, and a specific variant of the Anglo-American common law is still generally applicable despite attempts to assimilate into *la Francophonie* through a process of transposition through eclectic harmonization. This is a process of selective adaptation, centralization, bureaucratization, and homogenizing of educational and legal systems that have different, even contradictory worldviews. For example, in the postcolonial Francophone legal system of Cameroon, there is no separation of powers, and no checks and balances between the Executive, the judiciary and the legislative. The president of Cameroon is the Supreme Magistrate who presides over *Le Conseil Superieure de la Magistrature* (the Supreme Council of the Magistrature). He appoints and dismisses judges at will in a system where there is no judicial independence, no security of tenure and no presumption of innocence. Accused persons are presumed guilty until proven innocent, and the burden of proof is on them. The Anglophone sub-system in the Northwest and Southwest regions still has a semblance of presumption of innocence. The 2016 strikes by Anglophone lawyers and teachers that sparked the Anglophone Revolt were triggered by attempts by the Francophone central government in Yaoundé to assimilate the educational and legal systems of the Anglophone regions into the Francophone secular republican educational system, and Napoleonic civil law systems, respectively, through a process of over-centralization, bureaucratization, and harmonization.

The Anglophone Question is the diminishment of the cultural and identitarian specificity and autonomy of the English-speaking State of West Cameroon, declaring it part of a French-style, "one and indivisible" ethno-republican chiefery–that expression is lifted verbatim from Article I of the French Constitution– annexing and dividing it into two provinces/regions called (Northwest and Southwest) ruled by Francophone governors (pro-Consuls), and French-style Napoleonic era *préfets* and *sous-préfets* (*chef de terres*) appointed by President Biya without the consent of the people of Southern Cameroons. The Anglophone Question was brought to the fore by a dubious and deceptive strategy of assimilation of the State of West Cameroon and its people, and their dispersal in the over-centralized authoritarian, institutions of *La République du Cameroun*, as well as the plunder of the resources of West Cameroon. The Anglophone Question is thus the uneasy, subaltern status of the English-speaking minority in the majority French-speaking nation of Cameroon. It is also the history of attempts by lawyers and other members of the legal profession in the English-speaking regions to maintain what Nforbin (2019) calls, "the oneness of the English as a judicial language in the Southern Cameroons jurisdiction of Cameroon." (p. 504). The desire by teachers and student to maintain the integrity and standard of the English language in the Anglophone educational sub-system in the face of assimilationist moves by the majority Francophone government of Cameroon, converged with the aspirations of the lawyers. This led to the creation of the Cameroon Anglophone Civil Society Consortium (CACSC), and the beginning of the so-called Anglophone crisis in 2016. The Anglophone Question in Cameroon is grounded in the history of European colonialism and imperialism in Africa. The Anglophone Question has been accentuated by the progressive diminishment, over time, of the cultural and political specificity and autonomy of the two English-speaking regions of the country, as postcolonial *la République du Cameroun* has morphed into a highly centralized, Jacobin/Napoleonic system of government, and drawn closer to France and *la Francophonie*, the organization of French-speaking countries.

In effect, the Reunification of Southern Cameroons and *la République du Cameroun* quickly turned out to be "lawful plunder" to borrow the expression of Bastiat (1998), who pointed out that "plunder is organized by law for the profit of those who make the law" (p.7). In the post-reunification Cameroon, Southern Cameroons became the object of lawful plunder. Ahidjo-Biya, and their French overseers used legal plunder to take the wealth of Southern Cameroon—its natural resources—oil, natural gas, timber, state-owned agricultural estates, agricultural cooperatives, educational institutions, and so on, and gave them to a few, while throwing a few Anglophone leaders here and there a bone to gnaw! In effect, Southern Cameroons had become unequally yoked, the subject of the assimilationist mission of *la République du Cameroun*, whose institutions and governmentality mimic Napoleonic authoritarianism, and employs a "republican" rhetoric that echoes the niceties of French secular republicanism but is in effect, a system of tribal patronage and rent-seeking writ large. The dispersal of Southern Cameroons into the *Francophonie camerounaise*, meant being grafted into a rent-seeking system which gradually transferred state power into an instrument for allocating public resources into private coffers, conferring economic and monetary advantages and benefits to the president, his tribe, and a hand-picked, subservient elite from other parts of the country, while imposing disadvantages on others. In time, the vague and overbroad vaporous metric– harmonization of the two legal systems, laws and legal procedure, educational and economic systems, became the thin edge of the wedge of assimilation.

The Anglophone Question in general and the Anglophone Revolt of 2016 are the responses of the plundered people to the legal and illegal Francophone state and individual economic, social, and cultural plunder of Southern Cameroons and marginalization of its people. The fundamental problem of Cameroon is that the Ahidjo-Biya rule-by decree regime converted neocolonial plunder into a system of governance, a governmentality, "in order to protect plunder. And it has converted lawful defense into a crime, in order to punish lawful defense," as Bastiat (1998, p. 5) put it. In this system of law and injustice, the law takes precedence over rights, and becomes an instrument of injustice (Bastiat, 1998, p. 15). The crisis is a reflection of the acute tensions between these Francophone and Anglophone governmentalities and their contrasting identitarian logics. The Anglophone Question, which has been triggered by postcolonial Francophone hegemony and autocracy, is all about the distant colonial past, and the past of the reunification that has not passed. The traumas of the past have become the glue that holds together the different strata of Anglophone identitarian history and contemporary lived experience as subaltern citizens under Francophone hegemony (Gramsci, 1988) in the French "postcolony" of *La République du Cameroun* (Mbembe, 2001), which has been progressively transformed into a *chefferie républicaine*, a republican chiefery.

References

Albert, M. (1991). *Capitalisme contre capitalisme,* (Capitalism against capitalism*).* Paris : Seuil.

Anyangwe, C. (ed. 2010). *The Declassified British Secret Files on the Southern Cameroons*. Bamenda: Langaa

Appiah, A. (1994). Appiah A. (1994). Identity against culture: Understandings of multiculturalism. UC Berkeley, Townsend Center for Humanities. Retrieved from: https://escholarship.org/uc/item/20x1c7s2

Ardener, E. (1962). The political History of Cameroon. *The World Today*, Vol. 18, No. 8. (pp. 341-350)

Ardener, S. (2005). Ardener's "Muted Groups": The genesis of an idea and its praxis. Women and Language, Vol. 28, (2), Pp. 50-54,72.

Ardener, E. (1970). Witchcraft, Economics, and the Continuity of Belief', in Mary Douglas (ed.), *Witchcraft Confessions and Accusations* (ASA Monographs No. 9), London: Tavistock, pp. 141-60.

Ardener, E. (1956). *Coastal Bantu of the Cameroons*. London: International African Institute.

Ardener, S. (1996). *Kingdom on Mount Cameroon: Studies in the History of the Cameroon Coast, 1500-1970*. Providence, R.I: Berghan Books.

Azuelos, M. (1996). *Le Modèle économique anglo-saxon à l'épreuve de la globalisation (The Anglo-saxon economic model and the test of globalization)*. Paris: Nouvelle Sorbonne.

Bastiat, F. (1998). *The Law* (2nd edition). Foundation for Economic Education.

Berman, N., Couttenier, M., Rohner, D. & Thoenig, M. (2017). "This Mine Is Mine! How Minerals Fuel Conflicts in Africa." *American Economic Review*, 107 (6): 1564-1610.DOI: 10.1257/aer.20150774

Bernand, C. (2006). The Right to be Different: Some Questions about the "French Exception." In Kathleen Perry Long (Ed). *Religious Differences in France*. (p. 201-219). Kirksville, Mo.: Truman State University.

Betts, Raymond (1961). *Assimilation and Association in French Colonial Theory, 1890-1914*. New

York: Columbia University Press.

Cameroon Journalist Samuel Wazizi died in Detention (2020) Reporters Without Borders, June. Retrieved from: Retrieved from: https://rsf.org/en/news/cameroonian-journalist-samuel-wazizi-died-detention

Clarke, S. (2010). *1000 Years of Annoying the French.* London: Transworld Publishers.

Eko, L. (2010). "New Technologies, Ancient Archetypes: The *Boston Globe's* Discursive Construction of Internet Connectivity in Africa." *Howard Journal of Communications 21(2),* 182-198.

Eko, L. (2007). It's a Political Jungle Out There: How Four African Newspaper Cartoons Dehumanized and `Deterritorialized' African Political Leaders in the Post-Cold War Era, *International Communication Gazette,* 69 (3), 219-238.

Eko, L. (2003). The English-Language Press and the 'Anglophone Problem' In Cameroon: Group identity, Culture, and the Politics of Nostalgia. *Journal of Third World Studies*

Foucault, M. (1994), Dits et Ecrits (Tome III), Sayings and Writings (Vol. III). Paris: Editions Gallimard

Foucault, M. (1994a). *Dits et Ecrits (*Tome II*).(Sayings and Writings,* Vol. II*).* Paris: Gallimard.

Foucault, M. (2005). *The Hermeneutics of the Subject, Lectures at the Collége De France, 1981-1982,* 252 (2005). (Arnold Davidson, ed., Graham Burchell, trans. Palgrave).

Freudenthal, E. (2002). Making a killing" Israeli mercenaries in Cameroon. *African Arguments,* June 23. Retrieved from: https://africanarguments.org/2020/06/making-a-killing-israeli-mercenaries-in-cameroon/

Fukuyama, F. (2014). *Political Order and Political Decay: From the Industrial Revolution to the Globalization of Democracy.* New York: Farrar Strauss and Giroux.

Furet, F. (1978). *Penser la Révolution française (Conceptualizing the French Revolution).* Paris: Gallimard.

Gaulle, Charles de. (1954). *Mémoires de guerre, l'appel, 1940-1942 (Memoirs of War, the Call, 1940-1942).* Paris: Plon.

Gramsci, A. (1988). *An Antonio Gramsci Reader,* D. Forgacs (ed.). London: Lawrence and Wishart.

Gründer, H. (1988). Christian Missionary Activities in Africa in the Age of Imperialism and the Berlin Conference of 1884-1885. In S. Förster, W. Mommsen & R. Robinson (eds.). *Bismarck, Europe and Africa: The Berlin Africa Conference 1884-1885 and the Onset of Partition (pp.* 85-103). Oxford: Oxford University Press.

Herodotus (1925). *Book IV* (A.D. Godley, Trans.). Cambridge, MA: Harvard University Press.

Hochschild, A. (1999). *King Leopold's Ghost.* N.Y. Mariner Books.

Kim, I. & Woods, J. (2016). Gas on the Fire: Great Power Alliances and Petrostate Aggression" *International Studies Perspectives,* Volume 17, Issue 3 (August), Pages 231–249, https://doi.org/10.1093/isp/ekv004

Laurence, J. & Vaisse J. (2006). *Integrating Islam: Political and Religious challenges in Contemporary France.* Washington D.C., Brookings Institution.

Major, A. (1992) "Problematic" situations in press coverage of the 1988 US and French Elections. *Journalism Quarterly,* 69, 600-611

Mbembe, A. (2001). *On the Postcolony.* Berkley: UCLA Press.

Miers S (1988). "Humanitarianism at Berlin: Myth or Reality?" in *Bismarck, Europe and Africa: The Berlin Africa Conference 1884-1885 and the Onset of Partition,* Stig Förster, Wolfgang

Mommsen & Ronald Robinson, eds. Oxford: Oxford University Press, 333-345.

Mudimbe, V.Y. (1994). *The idea of Africa.* Bloomington, Indiana: Indiana

Monga, C. (1996). *The Anthropology of Anger: Civil Society and Democracy in Africa.* Boulder: Lynne Rienner Publishers.

Ndi, A., (2005). *Mill Hill Missionaries in Southern West Cameroon (1922-1972): Prime Partners in Nation Building,* Paulines Publications Africa, Nairobi

Renan, Ernest (1882). *Qu'est-Ce Qu'une Nation?* (What is a Nation and Other Political Writings. Paris: Calman Levy.

Ross, M. (2012) *The Oil Curse: How Petroleum Wealth Shapes the Development of Nations,* Princeton University Press, Oxford

Saker, E. (1908). *Alfred Saker, Pioneer of the Cameroons: By His Daughter.* London: The Religious Tract Society.

Smith, B. & Waldner, D. (2021). *Rethinking the Resource Curse. Cambridge University Press*

Thomas, H. (1997). *The slave trade.* New York: Touchstone Books.

Tocqueville, Alexis (1862). *De la démocracie en Amérique* (tome II) [Democracy in America. (Vol. II)]. (H. Reeve, Trans.). New York: J.H.G. Langley. (Original work published 1835).

United States Foreign Relations Committee (2008). Petroleum and Poverty Paradox: Assessing U.S. and International Community Efforts to Fight the Resource Curse". Washington DC, U.S Printing Office. Retrieved from: https://www.govinfo.gov/content/pkg/CPRT-110SPRT44727/pdf/CPRT-110SPRT44727.pdf

United States v. Glencore International AG, Docket No. 22-CR-297 (May 24, 2022). United States Department of Justice, United States Attorney for the Southern District of New York. Retrieved from: https://www.justice.gov/criminal-fraud/united-states-v-glencore-international-ag

Wright, J., Frantz, E. & Geddes, B. (2015). "Oil and Autocratic Regime Survival". *British Journal of Political Science.* 45 (2): 287–306. doi:10.1017/S0007123413000252.

Wright, J. & Frantz, E. (2017). How oil income and missing hydrocarbon rents data influence autocratic survival: A response to Lucas and Richter (2016). *Research & Politics.* 4 (3): 2053168 017719794. doi:10.1177/2053168017719794

THREE

The British Connection and (Dis)connection in the Anglophone Question in Cameroon

LYOMBE EKO

Monday, March 12, 2018, was celebrated as Commonwealth Day in all former British colonies (with the notable exception of the United States). On that day, the United Kingdom and its postcolonies celebrated the links between the UK and the countries where the British monarch is still the titular "Head of State," as well as former British colonies and territories. The day was marked with a solemn religious service at Westminster Abbey, the site of memory par excellence, of the British Empire, and a reception at Marlborough House, where the headquarters of the Commonwealth of Nations and the seat of the Commonwealth Secretariat is located. These celebrations were led by Queen Elizabeth II, Head of the British Commonwealth. The solemn, majestic, colorful, politico-multicultural event was celebrated with the pomp, pageantry, and circumstance that the British are known for. As the Commonwealth flagbearers marched out of Westminster Abbey at the end of the political high mass, attention turned to four clusters of Cameroon Anglophone political "pallbearers," each carrying a rough-hewn, home-made "coffin," the type of cheap funerary contraptions in which paupers are buried, on their shoulders. The men carrying the coffins were Anglophone Cameroon "political pallbearers." They walked slowly, to the surprise of curious onlookers, from Westminster Abbey to Marlborough House, their faces as solemn as the coffins on their shoulders. They were heading to a demonstration at the official Commonwealth Day reception and cocktail party at Marlborough House. A group of police officers moved cautiously towards the approaching "pallbearers" and stopped them from advancing and blocking the entrance of Marlborough House with their coffins. The pallbearers slowly and reverently lowered their burdens on the sidewalk beside the entrance of the Commonwealth Secretariat and draped them with the blue and white Ambazonian flag. English and Pidgin-speaking Cameroonian activists, teachers, lawyers, students, and some church leaders whose calls for a return to their illegally squashed federalism and regional autonomy had been ignored for decades, had adopted the name Ambazonia, as the nomenclature for a separate Anglophone state in Cameroon.

The name was derived from Ambas Bay, the piece of coastal territory from Down Beach, Limbe to Bota in Southern Cameroons, where Rev Alfred Saker had founded the English settlement of Victoria in 1858.

At the Commonwealth Day demonstration in London, a police officer could be heard telling the "pallbearers":

> "We are glad you are here, but we are a bit concerned…can we see what's inside the coffins?"

Whereupon the pallbearers opened the makeshift coffins. They were empty. One demonstrator explained that the coffins were carried to Marlborough House as a symbolic representation of the death and destruction visited on the English and Pidgin-speaking community of Southern Cameroons by the authoritarian Biya regime, a member in good standing of the British Commonwealth. He displayed a picture of Sam Soya, a disabled Anglophone Rastafarian musician who was arrested in Menchum county by Cameroon security forces and decapitated for supporting Anglophone self-determination.

Figure 3.1. Screenshot of members of the Southern Cameroons Community of the UK (SCCUK) demonstrating in front of the Commonwealth headquarters with their makeshift coffins on Commonwealth Day, March 12, 2018.

As the distinguished heads of government and diplomats from British Commonwealth countries like India, Sri Lanka and Nigeria were dropped from their luxurious cars at the entrance of Marlborough House, they were met at the gated entrance by Anglophone Southern Cameroons demonstrations. In effect, the pallbearers were part of an anti-Commonwealth demonstration staged by the largest Southern Cameroons Diaspora community, the Southern Cameroons Community in the UK (SCCUK). Members of SCCUK assembled in noisy but dignified defiance on the street in front of Marlborough House. The noisy, chanting, singing demonstrators, who showed remarkably restrained anger, held protest signs that denounced the political and human rights hypocrisy of the British Commonwealth. Clearly, the Southern Cameroonians were not at Marlborough House to commemorate Commonwealth Day 2018, but to protest against what they called the "Commonwealth of Hypocrisy," an organization which wined and dined with the Biya regime whose human rights violations flew in the face of every tenet of the charter of the Commonwealth. The demonstrators vehemently denounced the double standards of the British Commonwealth, which cuddled the autocratic regime of Yaoundé despite its atrocities and crimes against humanity, which directly affected members of the SCCUK and their families in their home country, *la République du Cameroun*. The Anglophone Cameroon demonstrators carried signs that read "Commonwealth of Hypocrisy: We Demand Justice for the Over 350 Villages Burnt by the Cameroon Army," "Stop the Torture, Stop the Rape, Stop the Killings, Cameroon Must Stop Executing Women and Children," and "Stop the Colonization of Former British Southern Cameroons," "Dismiss Cameroon from the Commonwealth."

The demonstrators soon burst into an Anglophone song of protest and nostalgia that British naturalist, Gerard Durrell (1954) had memorialized in his Southern Cameroons travelogue, *The Bafut Beagles*:

> Home, my home, my home
> Home, my home, my home
> When shall I see my home?
> When shall I see my native land?
> I will never forget my home!
>
> Ambazonia, Home, my home, my home
> Home, my home, my home
> When shall I see my home?
> When shall I see my Mammy?
> I will never forget my home!

That migrant workers' song, which emerged from the camps of Southern Cameroons agricultural workers who had left their villages in the Grasslands of Cameroon and moved to the coast to work in the German plantations, became a musical "site of memory" to use the expression of Nora (1995), for Southern Cameroonian immigrants scattered in the Anglosphere from the United Kingdom and the United States, to Canada, South Africa, Australia and New Zealand. It was quite stunning to hear African immigrants and refugees in Europe singing about, and yearning to return home to Africa.

The Cameroon Anglophone immigrants presented the main obstacle to a return to their cherished homeland in a Pidgin call and response lament against the murderous Biya regime:

Call: How many (pipo) people Paul Biya go kill?
Reply: How many pipo Paul Biya go kill?

Chorus: Hey, you go kill we tire,
Hey you go kill we tire
Hey' eh you go kill we tire
How many pipo Paul Biya go kill.

This catchy song underlined the danger members of the Southern Cameroons English-speaking diaspora faced if they dared to return to the home they yearned for with such earnestness.

As if to provide additional information to the police and the British onlookers who had stopped to watch the curious coffin protest, the Southern Cameroons demonstrators continued with an Africanized call-and-response version of the famous African American song of resistance against slavery, the "Negro Spiritual," *Go Down Moses*:

These are the words of the Mighty Lord
Let my people go!
These are the words of the Mighty Lord
Let my people go!
Go down Moses, go down to Yaoundé
Go tell Biya, Biya let my people go

Biya with his Mighty Head
Let my people go
Biya Mr. chop broke pot
Let my people go
Go down Moses, go down to Yaoundé
Go tell Biya, Biya let my people go

Figure 3.2. British police woman talking to Southern Cameroons Community of the UK (SCCUK) Demonstrators on 2018 Commonwealth Day (London).

In this rendition of the famous African American song of resistance, the protesters likened President Paul Biya, the nonagenarian, autocratic ruler of Cameroon's republican chieftaincy, to the hard-hearted, egomaniacal Egyptian Pharaoh of the Old Testament who enslaved the Israelites and stubbornly refused to let them go despite the plagues and catastrophes that God visited on Egypt. Biya, who is described as having a "Mighty Head," was Cameroon's metaphorical Pharaoh. Ironically, the autocratic Pharaoh of Cameroon was being propped up by the State of Israel through lucrative contracts with former Israeli military intelligence officials, with the imprimatur of the Israeli Ministry of Defense and Israeli defense and security industries (see Volume II, Chapter 17). The demonstrators also described Biya's complete lack of vision with the Pidgin English epithet, "chop broke pot" (the one who eats to his fill and breaks the pot in which the food was cooked, forgetting that he will be hungry the next day). The emphasis is on Biya's lack of vision, his tendency to "eat, drink and make merry today, tomorrow be damned!"

Figure 3.3. Mancho Bibixy (in yellow shirt), founder of the Anglophone "Coffin Revolution" addressing a crowd in Bamenda, while standing in a real white coffin (2016).

The empty coffins that the demonstrators were carrying in front of the Commonwealth headquarters were an extension of the so-called "coffin revolution" that had been launched in Bamenda by radio personality and Anglophone federalist-turned separatist activist, Mancho Bibixy, aka Mancho BBC. After Cameroon security forces killed tens of unarmed civilian demonstrators in Bamenda in 2017, Mancho Bibixy told French international television broadcaster, France24 that the Biya regime had turned a deaf ear to the pleas of the English-speaking community, which had tried to use the political and trade union process to request a return to the federal system of government that had been illegally squashed in 1972 under president Ahidjo. Mancho told the French broadcaster that the government of Cameroon had two choices: 1) either reform the constitution to return to a federal system or 2) face the consequences of a separate Anglophone state. From then on, Mancho held rallies in which he stood inside an open, white coffin and spoke to thousands of angry, disaffected, and disgruntled young people. Mancho and his followers called the Anglophone Revolt, "the Coffin Revolution, meaning that they were ready to die for it" (France24, 2017). After the France24 interview, Mancho Bibixy was arrested in Bamenda, deported to the dungeons of the *Secretariat d'état de la Défense (SED)* in Yaoundé, and locked up in the Kondengui Maximum Security Prison. He was ultimately tried before the French language-only *Tribunal militaire* (Military Tribunal) in Yaoundé and sentenced to 15 years in prison. The coffin the Anglophone demonstrators carried in front of Marlborough House in London also symbolized the thousands of unarmed, peaceful demonstrators, civilians, and villagers that the Cameroon security forces had killed in cold blood in Southern Cameroons since 2016.

Aim of the Chapter

This chapter aims to describe and explain the role of the United Kingdom in the Anglophone Question in Cameroon in general, and specifically in the Anglophone crisis that began in 2016. The premise is that the United Kingdom is, historically, the most deeply connected Western country in the Anglophone Question in Cameroon. Its indirect governance of the territory, its refusal to extend the Wilsonian principle of self-determination to Southern Cameroons, and especially its tepid reaction to the atrocities and crimes against humanity visited on the English-speaking minority that was once British Southern Cameroons, reflects a post-Brexit Machiavellian posture that emphasizes British economic interests at the expense of the historic human rights values and posture of the United Kingdom and the British Commonwealth of Nations. The premise is that the United Kingdom historically saw the former German colonies in Africa, and specifically the United Nations Trust Territory of Cameroon, as a pawn in the Concert of Europe, the Great Powers' rivalries, and the perpetual search for a balance of power between Germany, France, the United Kingdom, Spain, and Portugal. As a result of this imperialist mindset, Southern Cameroons was viewed as an expendable and valueless bargaining chip that was bargained away to France to balance gains in what the UK considered more valuable parts to Africa, namely East and South Africa. Ironically, the United Nations Trust Territory of British Southern Cameroons, which the British had concluded was nothing more than a territorial bargaining chip in the post-World War I, and post-World War II Anglo-French geo-strategic chessboard, and was given to President Charles de Gaulle of France, who considered it *"un petit cadeau de la reine d'Angleterre"* (A little gift from the Queen of England) (Anyangwe, 2010. p. 742) turned out to be rich in natural resources, namely oil and natural gas. The British subsequently made lucrative economic deals with the post-independence, neo-patrimonial, authoritarian, kleptocratic, Francophone-dominated government of the Republic of Cameroon, to exploit the natural resources in its former Trust Territory, that was now owned by French Cameroon.

There are thus historical continuities between contemporary British policy -luke-warmness towards the identitarian, cultural, and linguistic claims of former English and

Pidgin-speaking British Southern Cameroons (now partitioned by the Ahidjo/Biya regime into the Northwest and Southwest regions) and historical British disinterest in the territories and peoples of those territories. In effect, after World War I, Britain had ended up with–it is probably more accurate to say it was saddled with– two disjointed "strips" of German Kamerun territory. These territories, which stretched from Lake Chad to the Atlantic Ocean, resulted from post-war territorial settlements between France and Britain. This was compensatory diplomacy that involved the United Kingdom ceding captured former German territories in Central and West Africa to France in exchange for French quiescence over British control of former German territories in East Africa (Tanganyika) and Southwest Africa (modern-day Namibia) (Elango, 2015). However, the war had changed the global geo-strategic calculus. The UK and France could not annex these territories outright as colonial "possessions." The rising global power, the United States, which had an anti-colonial mindset, ensured that these German African territories would be administered as League of Nations Mandates under provisions of the Treaty of Versailles of 1919 (Ardener, 1963). The ultimate aim of these mandates was to prepare the peoples of these territories for eventual self-determination (independence). The United Kingdom proceeded to partition and rename these spoils of war "Southern Cameroons and Northern Cameroons" and administered them indirectly through its Nigerian colony.

Figure 3.4. The United Kingdom partitioned its share of German Kamerun into Southern Cameroons and Northern Cameroons, and administered them indirectly through its Nigerian colony. Queen Elizabeth II with Southern Cameroons Grassfields Chiefs during visit to Nigeria (1956).

As we see later, the British considered Southern Cameroons an economically nonviable, expendable territory that they wanted to get off their hands as expeditiously as possible (Phillipson, 1959). It turned out that Southern Cameroons, which was now unhappily yoked with the repressive, assimilationist republican chieftaincy of French Cameroun, was rich in natural resources, namely oil, natural gas, rare earth, agricultural and forestry products. At the turn of the 21st century, the British government and British companies made deals with the corrupt and neo-patrimonial Biya regime to exploit these resources and turned a blind eye and a deaf ear to the atrocities perpetrated against the people of the former British Southern Cameroons.

Figure 3.5. Queen Elizabeth II with British Cameroons Leaders at Government House, Lagos, February 1956.

The Anglophone Revolt

The Anglophone Revolt of 2016 that was triggered by the common law lawyers, teachers, university lecturers, students, and members of the civil society from the minority English-speaking former Southern Cameroons was a response to decades of majority Francophone political repression, linguistic and cultural assimilation, and marginalization. The revolt was kicked off when lawyers and teachers in the English and Pidgin-speaking Northwest and Southwest regions, formerly British Southern Cameroons, revolted against decades of dictatorial administration of justice, and muting of their cultural and identitarian specificity in the law by the Ministry of Justice. The system included military tribunals, which were part of the Ministry of Defense and had jurisdiction over civilians in cases involving the vague notion of "national security.. The sparks that set off the revolutionary crisis were dictatorial, top-down rule by decree measures that threatened the very existence of the English-medium legal and educational systems of Southern Cameroons that, together with the English and Pidgin medium churches, form the backbone of the identitarian and cultural specificity of Southern Cameroons. The heavy-handed repression of Anglophone civilian demonstrations by the Biya regime –security forces killed tens of unarmed, peaceful demonstrators on September 22 and October 1, 2017 in multiple locations in the former Southern Cameroons–shocked the English and Pidgin-speaking minority, whose diaspora around the world quickly internationalized the conflict through the Internet and social media.

When the English and Pidgin-speaking minority of Southern Cameroons revolted against the authoritarian French Cameroon government, demanding recognition of their identitarian and cultural specificity, their political demands were met with harsh repressive measures, atrocities, and violations of their basic human rights. Due to its economic interests and ties to the authoritarian Biya regime, the United Kingdom did not flinch. It continued to be a partner in crimes against humanity with the brutal Biya regime that had been in power for close to 40 years at the time of the Anglophone revolt. Cameroon was a member of the British Commonwealth, the postcolonial assembly of the United Kingdom, and her former colonies. Though the Commonwealth had expelled Nigeria, Zimbabwe, Fiji, and Pakistan for less weighty human rights violations, it made no move to invoke its charter and numerous declarations against the murderous regime of President Paul Biya. British economic interests in the post-Brexit era outweighed the niceties of the Universal Declaration of Human Rights. This chapter explores the origins of the Anglophone problem in British colonialism and its continuation in the 21st century as a result of the marriage of economic convenience between the British government, which had been strategically "bribed" with oil and natural gas, electricity, military and other contracts by the authoritarian Biya regime to turn a blind eye and a deaf ear to its former Trust Territory that was being subjugated.

The 2018 Commonwealth Day demonstration in London was the latest demonstration of the failed political marriage between the British Southern Cameroons and French-speaking *la République du Cameroun* that had taken place in 1961. Both parties had come to this political marriage with different governmentalities (philosophies of government). Southern Cameroons had a decentralized, federal, common law experience, while French-speaking *la République du Cameroun* came to the marriage with a highly centralized, authoritarian Napoleonic civil law system. Due to political bad faith on the part of *la République du Cameroun*, and the naivety of Anglophone leaders, the Anglophones were "swallowed" into *la Francophonie* and became marginalized, subaltern citizens of *La République du Cameroon*. In the meantime, Cameroon became a member of the Commonwealth in 1995 due to pressure from Anglophones who complained that Cameroon was a member of *la Francophonie* but not the Commonwealth. To the disappointment of English-speaking Cameroonians, Cameroon never subscribed to, adopted, or applied Commonwealth norms and values of human rights, democracy, and good governance. That had been just fine with the British Commonwealth. By 2015, all hopes that Cameroon would adopt the values of the Commonwealth: democracy, the rule of law, respect for human rights, separation of powers, and so on, had evaporated.

To the Southern Cameroonian demonstrators on Commonwealth Day, 2018, it was incomprehensible that the Biya regime could commit such atrocities against unarmed civilian demonstrators and still remain a member in good standing of the Commonwealth. The reasons for this state of affairs can be found in the strategic economic relations between the two strange bedfellows, the kleptocratic, authoritarian, republican chiefdom of President Paul Biya and the government of the United Kingdom.

March 12, 2018 was Commonwealth Day, the successor holiday to British Empire Day, which the government of the former British Trust Territory of Southern Cameroons, part of the British Empire, celebrated with pomp and pageantry. In the early 1960s and 1970s, citizens participated in parades that included ex-servicemen, veterans who had fought for the British Empire in World War II. In the afternoon, memorial services were held at the Commonwealth Graveyard in the Botanic Gardens in Victoria (now Limbe), where government officials and veterans solemnly placed flowers on the Commonwealth graves. Southern Cameroonians expressed pride in being part of the British Commonwealth.

Figure 3.6. 1958 British colonial stamp issued through Nigeria, commemorating the Centenary of the founding of Victoria by British Missionary, Rev Alfred Saker.

Fast forward to 2016. English-speaking Southern Cameroonian lawyers, teachers, and students, who had essentially been relegated to the status of second-class citizens in *la République du Cameroun*, took to the streets and demonstrated peacefully, calling on the Napoleonic regime of Cameroon, which had illegally dissolved the Federal Republic of Cameroon, to recognize their political and cultural identity and specificity. They were met with extreme violence, imprisonment, and trial at the Yaoundé French-language-only Military Tribunal. Anyone suspected of having federalist or separatist tendencies or ideologies that were at variance with the over-centralized one-man rule of Biya was thrown in jail. Hundreds were still in prison at the time of publication of this book in December 2024. The Internet was cut off in the English-speaking parts of Cameroon in order to hide the atrocities of the Cameroon army. The marginalization of English-and Pidgin Southern Cameroonians, and lack of opportunities in the French Cameroon government meant the emigration of hundreds of thousands of Anglophones to the Anglosphere: the UK, Ireland, the United States, Canada, South Africa, Australia, and New Zealand. One of the largest Southern Cameroon Diaspora communities is the Southern Cameroon Community in the UK (SCCUK).

The Ironies of the United Kingdom and its Cameroons Territorial "Bargaining Chip"

Historically, British policy towards the English and Pidgin-speaking Northwest and Southwest regions of Cameroon, its former United Nations Trust Territory of Southern Cameroons, can be defined as a policy of benign neglect of the territory and its people it was mandated to prepare for self-determination. The British Trust Territory of Southern Cameroons was part of the spoils of World War I. It was carved out of the German colonial territories that were ruled under the name Kamerun, the Germanized form of the Portuguese name *Rio dos Cameroes* (River of prawns). We have seen elsewhere that the European powers partitioned Africa at the Berlin Africa Conference presided over by Germany's "Iron Chancellor," Otto von Bismarck, from 1884-1885. One of the pretexts for the partition of Africa was humanitarian, namely, ending the vestiges of the slave trade and undertaking a Western 'civilizing mission" that would lead to the development and betterment of African natives (Förster et al., 1988). Under the terms of this partition, Germany's African colonial Empire included Kamerun, a vast territory that included parts of present-day Cameroon, as well as territories that are now part of Nigeria, Chad, the Central African Republic, and Congo. Germany also took control of Togoland, German East Africa (most of modern-day Tanzania), Rwanda-Urundi, and Southwest Africa (modern-day Republic of Namibia) (Förster et al., 1988). The partition of Africa took place within the framework of the so-called "concert of Europe," the balance of power between the major powers, global imperial rivalries, and compensatory diplomacy (granting territorial concessions in one geographic region in order to gain territories in another). It was the apogee of Western colonialism, the era when "Britannia ruled the waves."

When World War I broke out in Europe, it quickly spread to the European colonial territories in Africa. Germany, Britain, France, and Belgium raised colonial African military divisions and corps that were trained and commanded by European officers. The African armies of Britain, France, and Belgium invaded German Kamerun in 1914 and effectively defeated the German army and its native African troops in 1916, two years before the end of the war in Europe. Even before the defeat of Germany, the French and British agreed to divide German Kamerun along a so-called "Picot Provisional Partition Line" that gave Britain one-fifth of the German colony situated along the Nigerian border, while France gained the majority of the former German territory of Kamerun (Alvarez-Juimenez, 2012). This was the result of territorial horse-trading that followed purely balance of power logics and did not at all take the interests of African natives into consideration (Elango, 2014). The overall principle that guided British post-World War I negotiations with France over these captured German "enemy lands" in Africa was a long-standing "globalist" imperial policy of conceding West African territories to France in order to secure East and Southwest African territory, which was considered more vital to British interests (Robinson et al., 1961). The British, the first Allied power to enter the German Kamerun cities of Douala and Yaoundé during World War I, conceded these and other territories to France (Elango, 2014). The French, who controlled Madagascar, the Comoros, and the Reunion Islands off the coast of East Africa, had desired a share of German East Africa on the African mainland but were content to settle for a greater share of German Kamerun and Togoland. East Africa was considered the British sphere of influence, while French hegemony was recognized in Central Africa and large parts of West Africa. Thus, under British compensatory diplomacy, Southern Cameroons was nothing but a territorial bargaining chip, a pawn in this Anglo-French geo-strategic chessboard (Elango, 2015). The Treaty of Versailles of June 28, 1919, put its imprimatur on this provisional Anglo-French partition of Kamerun. The partition, therefore, followed the Zeitgeist and ethos of 19th Century Western imperialism and compensatory diplomacy, where territories changed hands in accordance with the strategic interests of the imperial powers and never in the interests of the peoples in those territories. This was contrary to the guiding ethos of the Treaty of Versailles of 1919. In his famous Fourteen Points, the statement of principles upon which post-World War I peace negotiations were based, President Wilson of the United States had stated that European colonial powers had to take the interest of the native African populations into consideration when they settled colonial claims and transferred territories from one colonial power to the other (Point V). Wilson preferred a system that would give African natives the right of self-determination through the creation of League of Nations mandates (Wilson, 1919). Thus, German Kamerun did not become colonial annexations as the British and French had wanted. The territory was split and apportioned into French and British League of Nations Mandates. The idea was that the British and the French were required to act as disinterested trustees over the territories they seized from Germany. Their task was to aid the native populations until they were in a position to govern themselves.

Dividing and Demarcating the West African Spoils of World War I

The British Trust Territory of Southern Cameroons that the United Kingdom had acquired as part of the spoils of World War I and the subsequent territorial horse-trading with France, was a bit of a geographic anomaly. The first issue was that the United Kingdom was not allowed to annex the territory outright and make it part of the British colonial empire. Thus, the United Kingdom was essentially an international colonial trustee that administered the territory under the auspices of the League of Nations. Geographically, the territory of Southern Cameroons was roughly based on border demarcations that had been the subject of Agreements between Great Britain and Germany in 1913. The first of these agreements was the "Anglo-German Agreement of 11 March 1913," which settled the frontier between Nigeria and the Cameroons from Yola to the Sea, and the second was the "Anglo-German Agreement of 12 April 1913" that demarcated the border between Nigeria and the Cameroons from Yola to the Cross River (Cameroon v. Nigeria, 2002). The town of Yola was thus the demarcation point, the colonial boundary line that separated the British Nigerian Protectorate and Colony, and the western border of the German Kamerun colony. We have seen that after World War I, the UK and France apportioned to themselves the German colonial territory of Kamerun. This amounted to colonial sub-partition, a territorial modification of the partition of Africa at the Berlin Conference of 1884-1885. The partition of German Kamerun was enshrined in international law by a Franco-British Declaration signed on 10 July 1919 by Viscount Milner, the British Secretary of State for the Colonies, and Henri Simon, the French Minister for the Colonies. The Declaration is commonly known as the "Milner-Simon Declaration." It that enlarged the scope of French Equatorial

Africa, buttressed, and ultimately enlarged the British colony of Nigeria. The independent States of Cameroon and Nigeria that subsequently emerged from the post-World War I European colonial territorial line-drawing ultimately solicited the legal remedies of the International Court of Justice to resolve long-running border disputes that originated from Anglo-German colonial border agreements and declarations (Cameroon v. Nigeria, 2002).

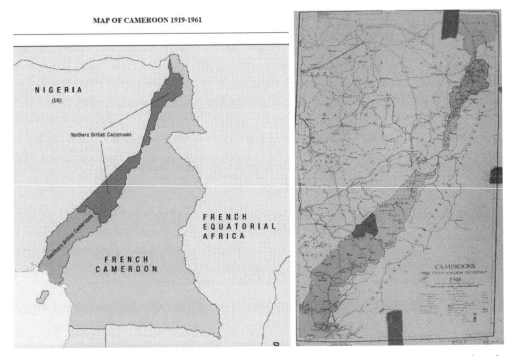

Figure 3.7. Left, Cameroons under United Kingdom Trusteeship, 1948 / drawn & reproduced by Survey Department. Scale 1:2,000,000. Lagos, Nigeria: Survey Department, 1949. Figure 3.8. British Northern and Southern Cameroons (1948).

British Indirect Governance of the Southern Cameroons Territorial "Spoils of War"

One of the realities of 19th and early 20th century European colonial territorial acquisitions, apportionments, and demarcations in Africa is that the territorial maps drawn in European colonial conferences did not always coincide with realities on the ground in Africa. This was particularly true of maps of the border between German Kamerun and British Nigeria, now the republics of Cameroon and Nigeria. Additional Anglo-French Declarations, such as the Thomson-Marchand Declaration, as incorporated in the Henderson-Fleuriau Exchange of Notes (1929-1931), attempted to but did not completely clarify, the uncertainties and ambiguities in the Anglo-French demarcation of the Cameroon/Nigerian border. Indeed, the International Court of Justice would later recognize that some of the maps on which the Milner-Simon Declaration of 1919 was based were problematic because they contained inaccuracies and ambiguities. These Anglo-French agreements essentially dismembered that part of the territory of German Kamerun closest to the Nigerian border into strips of often discontiguous territories that touched Lake Chad in the North and the Atlantic Ocean in the South but were discontinuous in the middle. They were drawn without the slightest regard to the wishes or welfare of the Africans who inhabited those territories. The Northern Cameroonian territories were used chiefly to bolster the Nigerian border and the political strength of the Northern rulers of British Nigeria to counterbalance the South. Edwin Ardener (1962), a British social anthropologist and expert on Southern Cameroons, described the territories that became British League of Nations Mandates in 1919 and United Nations Trust Territories in 1946 as follows:

> The British Mandate consisted of mere strips of territory on the Nigerian border, shaped like two penknife blades pointing at each other, the smaller down from the north, the longer up from the south. They did not touch however, the space between being occupied by the northern Nigerian town of Yola....

As we saw above, the Nigerian town of Yola was the central point of Anglo-German territorial demarcations in 1913. The Anglo-French partition of German Kamerun of 1916 was ratified by a Royal Commission and the British Governor General of Nigeria was appointed the Chief Administrator of the part of the German Kamerun territory closest to the Nigerian border (Elango, 2014).

In this territory, which was renamed British Cameroons, the German language was abolished, and English became the official language of the colonial administration, the courts, and the educational system. British administrators and education officials from Nigeria seized all German books from the handful of schools that existed in the former German territory and destroyed them. The French did the same in French Cameroun. When the British and French completed their partition of German Kamerun, Britain did not change its position with respect to indirectly administering Southern Cameroons, which it had obtained through its policy of substitutionary diplomacy. It did not wish to administer these "two strips" of former German territory as a stand-alone colony, they were treated as mere appendages designed to strengthen the border of Britain's Nigerian Protectorate and Colony (Ardener, 1962). Nevertheless, British colonial administrators kept separate administrative, financial, and legislative records for Cameroons territories for purposes of making periodic reports to the League of Nations and the United Nations (Callahan, 2004). On 2nd August 1946, the realities of that part of the German Kamerun territory placed under British trusteeship were further complicated by the British government. Under the 1946 Order in Council Providing for the Administration of the Nigeria Protectorate and Cameroons, the part of German Kamerun placed under British trusteeship was further sub-partitioned into Northern and Southern Cameroons for administrative purposes. Even though the League of Nations Mandates were underpinned by the ideals of President Woodrow Wilson, whose Fourteen Points for regulation of the post-World War I dispensation included a rejection of colonial territorial annexation of captured territories, extension of colonial sovereignties, as well as a greater regard for the rights and welfare of Africans who lived in the territories that were changing hands (Callahan, 2004), the reality on the ground was different. The British saw these former German territories as "Nomanslands" (Callahan, 2004. P. 24), disposable burdens that could be easily absorbed into its Nigerian Protectorate. The wishes of the peoples of both territories were never sought. These two "strips" of indirectly administered territory essentially became neglected, insignificant extensions of the British Nigerian Protectorate from 1919 to 1961 (Budi, 2019). Indeed, Southern and Northern Cameroons ultimately became two of the most backward and underdeveloped parts of the British Protectorate and Colony of Nigeria (Phillipson, 1959). Ironically, the transfer of the Western parts of German Kamerun to indirect British colonial administrative control amounted to returning the territory to the Anglosphere (the English-speaking world) where it had belonged in the 18th and 19th Century through 1) British and Continental European (French, Portuguese, Spanish, Dutch) and Arab slavery and the slave trade which facilitated the emergence of Creole (Krio) or Pidgin English as the lingua Franca of West Africa.Proper English came with 19th century British Christian missionary evangelistic activity in what is today the coast of Cameroon. Indeed, the natives of Southern Cameroons, what is today the Northwest and Southwest regions of Cameroon, were Anglicized and became "Anglophones" as a result of these two historical phenomena.

The Abortive British Trusteeship and Decolonization of Northern and Southern Cameroons

One of the realities of British Cameroons, the territory that the United Kingdom obtained as spoils of World War I from Germany, it never became an independent nation because the line of demarcation drawn by the British and French in 1919, the Milner-Simon Declaration, created a territory, or rather two-non-contiguous territories that were suitable for incorporation into the British Colony of Nigeria, but not considered viable for independence. The UK subsequently amalgamated and dispersed these Cameroons territories into its Nigerian protectorate and colony after obtaining the imprimatur of the Treaty of Versailles of 1919, and of the United Nations in 1946. As a result, these two "strips" of territories, which were bigger than Gabon, Gambia, the State of Israel, Togo, Benin, Swaziland, Lesotho, and others, were consigned to the periphery of the Nigerian colony. The Anglophone crisis is a direct result of this European colonial willy-nilly transfer of territory from one colonial jurisdiction to another. Indeed, some scholars claim that the Anglophone crisis of 2016 was due to the fact that the UK failed to meet its international obligations under the Trusteeship Agreement of 1919, and the UN Mandate it assumed in 1946 (Anyangwe, 2010). In 1959, Sir Phillipson, the colonial official whom the British government had assigned to study the economic and political viability of the Southern Cameroons, noted that: "Southern Cameroons has been, and still to some extent is, one of the less developed, more backward areas embraced within the Federation" (Cited in Anyangwe, 2010, p. 555). Certainly, this was not what the League of Nations and the United Nations had intended when they endorsed the British Trusteeship and Mandate in 1919 and 1946, respectively.

Article 22 (1) of the Covenant of the League of Nations, which endorsed the Anglo-French partition of German Kamerun, provided that:

To those colonies and territories which as a consequence of the last war have ceased to be under the sovereignty of the States which formerly governed them and which are inhabited by peoples not yet able to stand by themselves under the strenuous conditions of the modern world, there should be applied the principle that the well-being and development of such peoples form a sacred trust of civilization and that securities for the performance of this trust should be embodied in this Covenant.

Clearly, the British did not seek "the well-being" and development of the peoples of the former German Kamerun territories it had seized as spoils of war. It sub-partitioned the territory and actively sought to incorporate both of these "strips" into its Nigerian colony for political reasons rather than for reasons of self-determination. Phillipson, who wrote a report on the viability of Southern Cameroons as an independent territory, concluded that the trusteeship and mandate system were partly responsible for British neglect of Southern Cameroons:

The special status of the Southern Cameroons as a Trust Territory is not without some bearing on the foregoing arguments. Trust Territories do not form part of the territory of the states entrusted with their administration. The Southern Cameroons is not, and has never been, a part of Nigeria; it has only been administered as part of Nigeria. This arrangement was made not by the will of either Nigeria or the Southern Cameroons, but as a result of decisions made, after the First World War, by the League of Nations and the Mandatory Power and, after the Second World War, by the United Nations and the [British] Administering Authority (Cited in Anyangwe, 2010, p. 556).

Figure 3.9. Flag of British Southern Cameroons (1916-1961).

Controversial British Decolonization of Southern Cameroons

After 40 years of benevolent neglect through indirect rule, the British decided that the means of granting self-rule to the territory that it had sub-partitioned into Northern and Southern Cameroons territories was to have them permanently incorporated into Nigeria by all means possible (Anyangwe, 2010). Attaching the British Trust Territory of Cameroons to the British Nigerian protectorate and colony, sub-dividing it and administering it indirectly—without the consent of the people—made sense to the British who had obtained this territory as a spoil of war and wanted to use it to bolster the northern region of Nigeria, while spending as little on it as possible. However, transferring the Cameroon territory to Nigeria was problematic for the peoples of the Southern Cameroons territory, who found themselves in a new country and among new, negative, politico-cultural realities. It was also problematic for the British. The negative experiences of Southern Cameroonians, who the Nigerians treated as foreigners—they had been brought to Nigeria by the British, incorporated into the Igbo-dominated Eastern region, and promptly neglected—resulted in the emergence of an identitarian and cultural consciousness that took the form of a so-called, "one Kamerun idea" (Johnson, 1965). The cornerstone of this idea was reunification with the Trust Territory of French Cameroon, which the French had acquired as spoils of war from Germany under the auspices of the Treaty of Versailles of 1919, the League of Nations, and the United Nations in 1946. The "Kamerun idea" was prevalent in Southern Cameroons politics. All the political parties were Kamerun parties. They used the German appellation, Kamerun, in their names: The Kamerun National Democratic Party (KNDP), Kamerun National Congress (KNC), Kamerun People's Party (KPP), and One Kamerun Party (OK). This emphasis on Kamerun was to highlight their identity and cultural specificity with regards to Nigeria. However, the Kamerun idea went beyond mere identitarian considerations for two political parties. It became the political ideology of the Kamerun National Democratic Party (KNDP) that was led by John Ngu Foncha. It was also shared by Solomon Tandeng Muna, Nfon Mukete, E.T. Egbe, Ndeh Ntumazah, founder of the One Kamerun (OK) Movement, and other proponents of reunification with *La Republique du Cameroun*. Even Dr. EML Endeley, who was very skeptical of reunification with French Cameroun, was the leader of the Kamerun National Congress, which later merged with other parties to form the Cameroon Peoples' National Congress (CPNC). Incorporating Southern Cameroons in the British protectorate and colony of Nigeria had not muted the politico-cultural specificity of the former German territory, whose inhabitants now spoke English and Pidgin. The first formal indication of Southern Cameroonian displeasure with their willy-nilly incorporation into Nigeria came in May 1953 when the 13 Southern Cameroons MPs in the Eastern Nigerian House of Assembly based in Enugu asserted a right of cultural and political specificity and proceeded to declare 'benevolent neutrality.' They henceforth refused to take part in Nigerian partisan politics, claiming that they did not consider themselves Nigerians (Anyangwe, 2010). In July of that year, at the London Constitutional Conference, Dr. EML Endeley, the leader of the Cameroon Peoples' National Congress (CPNC) and leader of British Southern Cameroons, citing fear of Nigerian domination, demanded a separate region for the Southern Cameroons in line with its trusteeship status, a demand Britain acceded to. The territory thus gained a modicum of autonomy only after its leaders symbolically "seceded" from the Nigerian Federation. In January 1954, the Nigerian Constitutional Conference agreed that Southern Cameroons Trust Territory should become a separate autonomous unit within a proposed federation of Nigeria. The Southern Cameroons soon had its own House of Assembly, like the rest of the regions in Nigeria. It was also allowed to have an Executive Council and a High Court of Justice located at Buea. The Southern Cameroons Executive Council met in Buea for the first time in 1954. In 1958, Southern Cameroons became an autonomous region with a premier, Dr. EML Endeley, leader of the Kamerun National Congress, the CPNC (Anyangwe, 2010). However, British Colonial Secretary, Oliver Lyttleton, decreed that Northern Cameroons, whose leaders had not expressed a wish to leave Northern Nigeria, as Southern Cameroons had done, would remain part of the Northern region of Nigeria, and that the British Governor General of Nigeria in Lagos, would have to assent to all Southern Cameroons legislation (Nigeria talks set role of Cameroon, 1954). The quasi-statehood of Southern Cameroons was a hard-won status that had been secured from the British through resistance against relegation to the status of an appendage to the British protectorate and colony of Nigeria. Having essentially settled the issue of Northern Cameroons arbitrarily, the British now had to deal with the more complicated case of Southern Cameroons, whose leaders had expressed a decidedly "Kamerun" nationalistic bent and led a symbolic secession from Nigeria, where the British had dumped them since 1919.

Figure 3.10. The Southern Cameroons Executive Council with Samson Adeoye (Mamfe), Solomon Tandeng Muna (Bamenda Division), Rev. Jeremiah Chi Kangsen, Wum Division, and Dr. Endeley, Victoria Division, Leader of Government Business) (1954).

The British had thus swallowed Northern Cameroons, one of the two "strips" of non-contiguous territories, the spoils of World War I that had been carved out of German

Kamerun by early 20th century British and French surveyors who either did know what they were doing or deliberately created two territories to facilitate British incorporation of Northern Cameroons into its Nigerian colony, and French incorporation of Southern Cameroons into its French Cameroun Mandate, and ultimately into French Equatorial Africa. The British now turned to Southern Cameroons, the more complicated of the two Cameroons territories. This territory had a "Kamerun," nationalist orientation, unlike Northern Cameroons. Southern Cameroons political leaders—and both major opposition parties had the identitarian nomenclature, "Kamerun" in their names—had symbolically "seceded" from Nigeria in 1953. The "sacred trust" Britain had assumed under the League of Nations included the obligation to lead these two territories to independence. Under provisions of article 76 (b) of the Charter of the United Nations, colonial Trusteeships like the former German Kamerun territories granted the United Kingdom and France under the Treaty of Versailles were supposed to be led to autonomy (self-rule or independence).

Since the United Kingdom had relegated those parts of the German Kamerun territories that it had obtained in 1919 to the status of insignificant appendages to its Nigerian colony, no significant development had taken place in Southern Cameroons. In the 40 years of British colonial rule, the Southern Cameroons Trust Territory relied on Nigeria for everything–education, transport and communication, broadcasting, defense, international relations, and so on. The territory and its capital, Buea, had no roads, no named streets, no sewers, no electricity, no hospital or clinics worth the name, and no water system. Baptist, Catholic, and Presbyterian missionary organizations created and controlled most primary schools. Under international law, Britain was obligated to permit missionaries from all member countries of the League of Nations into its mandated territories (Callahan, 2004). Native Authorities set up a few other schools, which British colonial educational officers in Nigeria inspected from time to time. There was only one secondary school in the whole of the territory, St. Joseph's College, Sasse, which was started in 1939. After British amalgamation of Northern Cameroon with Nigeria, the very strident "One Kamerun" ideology of the majority of Southern Cameroons political leaders, and their dramatic "secession" from the Eastern Nigerian regional assembly in Enugu, the British became convinced that Southern Cameroons' destiny lay with either Nigeria or French Cameroon, not as an independent country. The main reason why the UK did not even consider granting Southern Cameroons the option of independence was the fiction that the territory was an underdeveloped basketcase that would not be economically viable as an independent country. From the British perspective, the Anglo-French partition of Cameroon of 1916 had not created two "viable" territories. Britain had merely acquired the two "strips" of Cameroon territory to strengthen its Nigerian protectorate and colony and to mollify the French, who had designs on territories in British East Africa.

The Wind of Change and the "End" of European Colonialism in Africa

In the late 1950s and early 1960s, a so-called "wind of change" swept across Africa. African liberation movements and international, anti-colonial ideals sounded the death knell of European colonialism in Africa. The major European colonial powers, exhausted by the ravages of World War II and pressured by global anti-colonial and human rights sentiments, began a process of decolonization. As Britain prepared to grant independence to Nigeria, it kept its eyes on the ultimate goal of the "Sacred Trust," the League of Nations Mandate for its Cameroons territories, independence, or self-determination for the territories. Britain decided that neither of its Cameroons territories, Northern and Southern Cameroons, would be viable entities as independent countries, never mind that Britain had smaller territories like Gambia, Swaziland, Lesotho, etc. The ultimate goal was for both territories to become part of an independent Nigeria, since both territories were already being indirectly administered as part of Nigeria. To achieve this outcome, Northern Cameroons remained part of Northern Nigeria. To quash independence sentiments in Southern Cameroons, which had obtained a modicum of autonomy within Nigeria in 1954, the British Government invented a myth that an independent Southern Cameroons would not be an economically viable country (Anyangwe, 2010, p. 591). Declassified confidential correspondence between the British Ambassador in Yaoundé, *La Republique du Cameroun*, His Excellency, Mr. Johnston, and Mr. C.B. Boothby, Head of the African Department in the Foreign Office reveals the thinking of the British diplomats with respect to the future fate of Southern Cameroons:

> …we are not attracted by the idea of an independent Southern Cameroons because it would certainly not be able to pay its way and, as you suggest, we are not at all anxious to have to do so on its behalf. We cannot expect to get any advantage from being foster—mother to an independent Southern Cameroons and it is clear that it would have to be fostered by somebody. The responsibility would only be likely to embarrass us with the Nigerian and Cameroun Governments in turn. In fact, the sooner we can provide decently for the future of the Southern Cameroons and wash our hands of it, the more pleased we shall be (cited in Anyangwe, 2010, p. 590).

Having come to the conclusion, albeit erroneous, that Southern Cameroons had the geo-political and geo-strategic disease of "economic non-viability," the British made that argument forcefully and persistently at the United Nations. Southern Cameroonians hold one British colonial administrator and diplomat, Sir Andrew Benjamin Cohen, responsible for thwarting their desire for independence and consigning them to the authoritarian, Napoleonic, *chefferie républicaine* (republican chieftaincy) of French Cameroun under President Ahmadou Ahidjo. Sir Andrew Cohen is held responsible for the Anglophone crisis in Cameroon because the Anglophone Revolt is an attempt to undo the annexation of Southern Cameroons that he masterminded and facilitated. Sir Andrew Cohen is an unlikely candidate to play the role of villain of the Anglophone oppression in Cameroon. Cohen was an Anglo-Jewish colonial administrator and diplomat who served as Assistant Undersecretary for African Affairs in the Colonial Office. Having been traumatized by the Holocaust, he was an anti-racialist who supported African rights in the British Southern African colonies. He was against the rising menace of racism in South Africa, preferring British settler paternalism to radical Afrikaner white supremacy. In 1952, he was appointed Governor of Uganda, and tasked with the responsibility of preparing that country for independence. He made the mistake of deposing the Kabaka of Buganda, thereby triggering anti-colonial sentiments. The Kabaka was ultimately restored and became president of Uganda in 1962.

The Myth of the Economic "Nonviability" of Southern Cameroons

The UK soon turned to its "sacred trust" of preparing the Cameroons for self-determination and independence. The nature of the independence that was to be granted to these neglected territories was decided first and foremost by the Colonial Administrative authority, the United Kingdom, with the approval of the United Nations Trusteeship Council. From 1957, Sir Andrew Cohen was appointed the UK representative to the United Nations Trusteeship Council. In that capacity, he opposed independence for Southern Cameroons, claiming the territory would not be an economically viable country. He spearheaded the sustained British campaign against independence for the Southern Cameroons, a campaign in which British diplomats did not hesitate to resort to duplicity and arm-twisting to achieve their goal (Anyangwe, 2010, p. 592). In declassified internal diplomatic correspondence, Ambassador Cohen wrote:

> I think it may be necessary to tell Field firmly that the policy of H.M.G. is to discourage any tendency towards a "third question' very strongly because this could not lead to any reasonable solution of the territory's problems and could only involve the United Kingdom and I think the Southern Cameroons as well as Nigeria and the Cameroun Republic in embarrassment (Sir Andrew B. Cohen, cited in Anyangwe, 2010, p. 592).

The UK then used its immense influence to persuade the United Nations to adopt the argument that Southern Cameroons was a non-viable entity. Even recently independent former colonies like India were swayed by the British position on the incurable political disease of "economic non-viability." In October 1959, the Fourth Committee of the General Assembly of the United Nations ruled out the possibility of 'separate' independence for the Southern Cameroons based on the alleged economic non-viability of the territory. Anyangwe (2010) concluded that the UN Committee was, in effect, "ordaining that the Southern Cameroons would continue to be a colonial territory so long as it remained what it called 'economically non-viable' (p. 507). Interestingly, the UN would later repudiate economic viability as a criterion or excuse for according or denying territories and peoples' self-determination and independence (Anyangwe, 2010).

Economic Non-Viability of the Southern Cameroons: Sir Phillipson's Report (1959)

It is interesting how Ambassador Cohen obtained evidence of the economic non-viability of Southern Cameroons. In order to find evidence to support this conclusion, the British government commissioned Sir Sydney Phillipson, a veteran British colonial official to assess the economic viability of Southern Cameroons but not Northern Cameroons since it was a foregone conclusion that the strip of territory that made up Northern Cameroons was going to be incorporated into the independent federation of Nigeria. In his report, Sir Phillipson noted that: "Southern Cameroons has been, and still to some extent is, one of the less developed, more backward areas embraced within the Federation" (cited in Anyangwe 2010, p. 555). Nevertheless, the report proceeded to paint a realistic picture of the state of the Southern Cameroons economy, which was based on a sound and rapidly expanding mixed agricultural regime made up of plantation agriculture, cooperatives and peasant farmer production of cash crops. The plantain agricultural base included the vast plantations of the Cameroon Development Corporation (CDC), which an International Bank Mission Report on the Economic Development of Nigeria (and Southern Cameroons) had described in glowing terms:

> The Mission wishes to record the opinion that the establishment and operations of the Corporation have been of great benefit. It has made available the economic and technical advantages of plantation production, has provided for the social and educational welfare of its workers and the earnings of the enterprise it has built up will continue to contribute to the development of the Southern Cameroons (Cited in Phillipson, 1959; Anyangwe, 2010, p. 544).

The CDC had plowed its profits back into the territory by building the Tiko and Bota wharves.

Phillipson also noted that the following agricultural concerns that contributed to the economy of Southern Cameroons: Elders and Fyffes, Ndongo (engaged in banana plantation agriculture), Cadbury and Fry Limited, (engaged in Cocoa plantation agriculture, in Ikiliwindi, Meme), Estates and Agencies Limited (engaged in tea plantation agriculture in Ndu, Donga Mantung), the Southern Cameroons Development Agency (engaged in the Santa Coffee Estate, Mezam), the Cameroon Development Corporation (CDC) Tea Estate in Tole, which began growing, processing and packaging tea in April 1958, while the Bakweri Co-operative Union of Farmers was a cooperative whose members grew and marketed bananas. For its part, the Southern Cameroons Marketing Board marketed agricultural products. Additionally, the following agricultural products were produced and sold by peasant farmers: palm kernel in the Mamfe Division, coffee (both Arabica and Robusta), that had been introduced and was spreading rapidly in the Grasslands region. Rubber, tea, and palm oil were also estate-produced (Phillipson, 1959). The Phillipson report was cursory at best. It did not pay much attention to industries like fisheries, cattle-rearing, and forestry.

The Report (1959) contained this ominous conclusion:

> As a completely independent state the Southern Cameroons, at its present stage of development, would not be viable. A further period of Trusteeship, if adequate, might afford the Southern Cameroons the time it needs to develop and test its financial strength (Cited in Anyangwe, p. 575).

The Phillipson report demonstrated the scope of British neglect of the Cameroons territories it had obtained from Germany after World War I. Northern Cameroons was economically even less developed than Southern Cameroons. Nevertheless, the conclusion of the Phillipson report became the basis for the official British policy of opposing the independence of Southern Cameroons. As we see later, the Phillipson Report's conclusions were wide off the mark. Besides its rich, emerging agricultural and forestry economy, the teritory has vast offshore oil and natural gas reserves. These natural resources would later attract British, French, Swiss, Chinese, and Russian companies. Ironically, the economic stone that the British Colonial Office cast away in Southern Cameroons, turned out to be one of the cornerstones of their post-Brexit global economic engagement under *la République du Cameroun*.

The UN and the Myth of Southern Cameroons Economic Non-viability

Having decided that the economic non-viability of Southern Cameroons made it unsuitable or unprepared for independence, the British decided to stick with their original policy of considering both Northern and Southern Cameroons as "mere strips" of territory that had to be annexed by Nigeria or *la Republique du Cameroun*, both of which were scheduled to obtain their independence from the UK and France respectively in 1960. No consideration whatsoever was paid to the identitarian and cultural specificity of both territories. The fact is that the crumbling British Empire was eager to liquidate its West African territories, including Nigeria no later than 1st October 1960. Colonialism was very expensive for the weakened post-World War II Empire. Therefore, the expedient thing to do was to dispense with the Trust Territory as soon as possible. According to Anyangwe (2010), the British, in furtherance of the aim of dispensing with the burden of this Trust Territory which they had essentially neglected for forty years, set the agenda for dispensing with Southern Cameroons in accordance with the conclusion it had arrived at and used its influence as a permanent member of the UN Security Council and a colonial power, albeit a waning one, to take advantage of the unequal power dynamics of the moment. Neither Southern Cameroons nor the United Nations were in a position to challenge or question British decolonization policy. This campaign against Southern Cameroons independence, which consisted of decolonizing the territory on British terms was spearheaded by Sir Andrew B. Cohen, the UK representative to the United Nations Trusteeship Council. Cohen and other British diplomats used their influence in the United Nations to persuade other members of the United Nations to adopt their conclusion that Southern Cameroons would not be an economically viable independent nation. At all the Committees of the UN General Assembly held in 1958 and 1959, Mr. Cohen emphasized the British mantra of the non-viability of Southern Cameroons as an independent country. In the face of this unequal power dynamics, some of the Southern Cameroonian politicians like Ndeh Ntumazah, leader of the One Kamerun Party, and N.N. Mbile, leader of the Kamerun People's Party, naively agreed with Cohen's assessment. From that point, the stage was set for decolonization on British terms.

The UN Cameroon Plebiscites: Between the French Postcolony of *La République du Cameroun* or the Cacophonous Federal Republic of Nigeria

United Nations General Assembly Resolution 1350 (XIII, 794th Plenary Session) of 13th March 1959 concerning the future of the Trust Territory of the Cameroons under United Kingdom Administration essentially put its imprimatur on British sub-partition of its spoils of war, the former German territories closest to the Nigerian border into Northern Cameroons and Southern Cameroons. The resolution also ignored the principle of self-determination when it endorsed a plebiscite as the means of ascertaining the wishes of the people of both territories. However, the plebiscite questions did not include an option of independence. They essentially gave the people two options: 1) decide whether they wished to join the Federation of Nigeria (to which the UK had consigned them as marginal backwaters for 40 years) when Nigeria became independent in 1960 or 2) decide whether they wanted to decide the fate of Northern Cameroons at a later date. The wording of the plebiscite was confusing and subject to multiple interpretations. This attempt to put a veneer of democracy on British colonial territorial annexation did not go as expected. Despite the fact that the people of Northern Cameroons voted in 1959 by a substantial majority to decide their future at a later date, the UN and the UK, in their haste to end the Trusteeship of Northern Cameroons, held another plebiscite in which the two alternatives presented to the people were:

> "(a) Do you wish to achieve independence by joining the independent Federation of Nigeria?"
> "(b) Do you wish to achieve independence by joining the independent Republic of the Cameroons?"

The people of Northern Cameroons were being asked to pick their poison–decide between colonization by Nigeria or colonization by France via French Cameroun. Both countries turned out to be autocratic kleptocracies. Britain used all means at its disposal to ensure that it obtained the results it desired. The people of Northern Cameroons ultimately voted as the British desired to join the independent Federation of Nigeria, the lesser of two evils, in the 1961 plebiscite.

The case of Southern Cameroons was a bit more complex. United Nations General Assembly Resolution, 1350 (XIII, 794th Plenary Session) of 13th March 1959 called on all parties concerned in the Southern Cameroons Trust Territory, the British Colonial Administration, the Premier of quasi-autonomous Southern Cameroons, John Ngu Foncha, the leader of the opposition, Dr. E.M.L Endeley, and the leaders of other parties, to reach an agreement on the alternatives to be put in the plebiscite in Southern Cameroons and qualifications for voting in it. They were given six months to make this decision and report to the UN before the opening of the fourteenth session of the General Assembly in October 1959. This resolution essentially gave the British Colonial Office a freehand to pressure the Southern Cameroonian leaders to ratify its conclusion that Southern Cameroons would not be economically viable as an independent country and that they should work within the parameters of the British decolonization plan, which was to: 1) join the Federation of

Nigeria when it became independent in 1960, or 2) join *la République du Cameroun* when it became independent in 1960. The Nigerian option was the most problematic, given the second-class status to which the people of Northern and Southern Cameroons had earlier been relegated in the British Nigerian colony. This had led to the "secession" of Southern Cameroonian politicians from the Eastern House of Assembly in Enugu in 1953 and led to rumblings of discontent among the politicians of Northern Cameroons. The second option, joining French Cameroun, was not without its foreseen and unforeseen problems. It actually meant consigning the people of Southern Cameroons to the status of a minority in the French African sphere of influence. The Kamerunist identitarian nomenclature of the Southern Cameroons political parties was essentially a way of defining themselves in opposition to the alien and subaltern Nigerian reality to which Britain had consigned them in 1916. It did not necessarily mean they were all clamoring to join *la République du Cameroun*. Indeed, except for Ndeh Ntumazah's One Kamerun party, which was affiliated with the *Union des Populations du Cameroun* party in French Cameroun, the Southern Cameroons leaders wanted to leave Nigeria but desired more time to contemplate whether to join la *République du Cameroun* or become independent. They were never given that option since it had backfired on the British in the first plebiscite in Northern Cameroons.

By giving the United Kingdom and Southern Cameroonian leaders the task of coming up with only two alternatives to be put to the people in the plebiscite–and this was taking place in the context of unequal power dynamics between the colonizer and the colonized–the UN abandoned all pretext of following the Wilsonian ideal of self-determination, and essentially put its imprimatur on the "Southern Cameroons economic non-viability" mantra that the British were preaching at the UN. The UN thus gave the British the green light to take advantage of the unequal power dynamics between itself and its underdeveloped Southern Cameroons Trust Territory to advance its Southern Cameroons decolonization without a self-determination policy. Indeed, the British government had already rejected any idea of prolonging the Trusteeship over Southern Cameroons. They also rejected outright, the third option, "secession from Nigeria without reunification" with *la République du Cameroun*. This was the independence option. As we saw above, Sir Andrew Cohen, the British Colonial Administrator who represented the UK at the Trusteeship Council, categorically rejected that third option, and argued strenuously against it. Being in a position of weakness vis-à-vis the British colonial behemoth, the Southern Cameroonian leadership was too divided and too unsophisticated to realize the gravity of the situation or to challenge the "decolonization" roadmap the British had set out for them. Given their antipathy towards Nigeria and their uncertainties regarding joining French Cameroun without a well-defined internationally guaranteed legal framework, it is no surprise that the Southern Cameroons parties could not see eye-to-eye on what the two alternative questions that could be put on the plebiscite would be. The result was a fatal deadlock that played into the hands of the British. Interestingly, this appears to have been the only instance where the UN used the "economic non-viability" criteria to deny self-determination to a colonized territory created by European imperialism. Anyangwe (2010) suggests that "the so-called economic non-viability of the Southern Cameroons was a bogey created by the British Government in 1959 for the purpose of influencing the plebiscite vote so that the people of the Southern

Cameroons return to the political and economic backwater of Nigeria where the British had caged them for almost half a century" (p. 609).

The Southern Cameroons Plebiscite of February 11, 1961

After the failure of the UK and its Southern Cameroons colonial subjects to come up with two questions that would present the two alternatives that would be put to the people in the proposed plebiscite, the United Nations proceeded to present the British decolonization plan to all concerned. The UN General Assembly ruled out 'separate' independence for the Southern Cameroons because of the supposed limited economic potential of the territory. UN General Assembly Resolution 1352 (XIV): "The Future of the Trust Territory of the Cameroons under United Kingdom Administration – Organization of the Plebiscite in the Southern Part of the Territory" of October 1959 stated that:

> 1. ... Noting the statement made by the representative of the Administering Authority, by the Premier of the Southern Cameroons and by the Leader of the Opposition in the Southern Cameroons House of Assembly to the effect that no agreement was reached before the fourteenth session of the General Assembly as to the alternatives to be put in the plebiscite and the qualifications for voting in it,

> 2. Recommends that the two questions to be put at the plebiscite should be:
> "(a) Do you wish to achieve independence by joining the independent Federation of Nigeria?"
> "(b) Do you wish to achieve independence by joining the independent Republic of the Cameroons?"

The wording of the Southern Cameroons plebiscite was identical to that of the second Northern Cameroons plebiscite. It was confusing and subject to multiple interpretations. For example, the second option called *la République du Cameroun*, "the independent Republic of the Cameroons." Due to the insistence of the British, the plebiscite omitted the third option, "secession from Nigeria without reunification with *la Republique du Cameroun*." Having decided that an independent Southern Cameroons would not be economically viable and being unwilling to extend the duration of its Trusteeship, the UN and the British government gave the Southern Cameroonians two choices–become subalterns in Nigeria, a status they had rejected in 1953, or join French Cameroun and become a linguistic and cultural minority subject to assimilation into "FranceAfrique," the Franco-African sphere of influence. It was tantamount to asking the Southern Cameroonians and the Northern Camerooonians to choose between being engulfed by a python or being swallowed by a crocodile. According to Anyangwe (2010), the UN was stating that the "Southern Cameroons would continue to be a colonial territory as long as it remained 'economically non-viable.'" However, "the UN did not extend the British Trusteeship in Southern Cameroons until such a time as the territory became 'economically viable.' It instead decided to make Northern and Southern Cameroons the colony of either Nigeria or French Cameroun, which were both scheduled to become independent in 1960" (p. 507). The plebiscites contradicted the letter and spirit of the Treaty of Versailles of 1919. They were clearly contrary to the spirit of the Wilsonian post-World War I principles that emphasized self-determination and rejection of colonial annexations and extensions of national sovereignty (Callahan, 2004).

Nevertheless, the Southern Cameroons politicians returned home and picked their respective poison. The "One Kamerun" politicians, led by John Ngu Foncha and the KNDP, Ndeh Ntumazah, Nfon Victor Mukete, E.T. Egbe and others, campaigned for reunification with *la République du Cameroun*, albeit with a reckless disregard for the kind of reunification they were championing. Some "one Kamerunists" like Nfon Mukete even harbored the naïve notion that they could wean French Cameroun from undue French influence. Dr. EML Endeley, leader of the opposition CPNC, campaigned to join Nigeria, arguing that Southern Cameroons was culturally and linguistically proximate to Nigeria rather than to French Cameroon. Their idea was to become an autonomous region of the federation of Nigeria. People who had seceded from Nigeria in 1953 and gained autonomy in 1954, were now placed in the untenable situation of campaigning for a return to Nigeria as the British wished. The campaign styles and slogans of both sides of the plebiscite were different. The rallying cry of Foncha's emotionally charged populist KNDP was a simple Pidgin English slogan that became popular:

> Small nobi sick, Cameroon na we Country
> Small nobi sick, Cameroon na we own oh.

For his part, Dr. EML Endeley of the CPNC published a rather visceral–and prescient– manifesto that highlighted the linguistic and systemic proximities between Southern Cameroons and Nigeria, as well as the lack of respect for human rights in French Cameroun. It stated inter alia:

> ... if you vote for Cameroon Republic, you will invite a new system under which everyone lived under fear of the Police and the Army. You will not be free to move about, you cannot lecture freely or discuss your political views in public, you must carry your tax receipt round your neck like a dog, and you can be arrested and flogged by the Police and even imprisoned without a fair trial.
>
> ...
>
> But under the French system, you cannot have a fair trial. Anyone accused of an offense in the Cameroon Republic is manhandled and flogged and is generally treated as a guilty criminal. Even the most junior policeman there seems to have the power of "life and death" over the common people. This is a bad system and must be rejected by the voters.

Historical events, especially the Anglophone Revolt of 2016 and subsequent events, proved that Endeley's characterization of *la République du Cameroun* was right on target (see volume II).

While it opposed independence for Southern Cameroons, the UK set out to work with France to ensure the amalgamation of Southern Cameroons into French Cameroun and, by extension, *la Francophonie*, the Franco-African sphere of influence. This was tantamount to a modification of the Milner/Simon agreement of 1919 that had partitioned German Kamerun into French and French territories in 1919. Southern Cameroons would ultimately become a British gift to the French. It was what President de Gaulle of France would call, "*un petit cadeau de la Reine d'Angleterre*" (a little gift from the Queen of England) (Anyangwe, 2010, p. 735). Northern Cameroons ultimately voted to achieve independence by joining the independent federation of Nigeria, while Southern Cameroons voted to gain independence by joining the French postcolony, *la République du Cameroun* in 1961. When the United Nations gave Southern and Northern Cameroonians the possibility of gaining independence through unification with either the independent *la Republique du Cameroun* or Nigeria, it did not do due diligence to determine the nature of "independence" the people stood to gain by joining either of the two countries.

As a result, when the people of Southern Cameroons voted to join their "brothers and sisters" in the former French Trusteeship territory of Cameroon, that became independent in 1960 as *la République du Cameroun*, they had no idea that they were joining a territory whose pre-independence *Accords de Cooperation* with France, made the country a virtual postcolony of France (Mbembe, 2001). As we saw in earlier chapters, Southern Cameroonians soon became a marginalized minority in French Cameroon and the subject of intense pressure to assimilate into *la Francophonie*. History and subsequent events show that the UN and the UK actually impeded the self-determination of the people of both Northern and Southern Cameroons.

The plebiscites essentially transferred half of the British Cameroons territory to Nigeria and the other half to *La République du Cameroun*. The results has been disastrous. Northern Cameroons had been administered indirectly (essentially neglected) by the British until 1961, when it was subsequently incorporated into the independent Nigerian federation via the questionable plebiscite. From 1961, Northern Cameroons became a neglected part of the Nigerian federation and has since been sliced and diced into a number of states. The territory of the former Northern Cameroons is the stronghold of Boko Haram. Some analysts argue that the Boko Haram terrorist organization took on an anti-Western, Islamist coloration that obscures multiple economic and political grievances, namely, the Northeast (former Northern Cameroons) has the poorest population in the country. The region is marked by low education rates, high unemployment, high underemployment, and people who lack basic infrastructures like clean drinking water, basic health services, schools, electricity, and so on. Boko Haram emerged out of these circumstances as well as what Adibe (2014) has termed "a sense of alienation" and a "retreat from the "Nigeria project"—the idea of fashioning a nation out of the disparate nationalities that make up the country—and instead construct meanings in primordial identities, often with the Nigerian state as the enemy." With respect to Southern Cameroons, history would ultimately prove Sir. Cohen and the British government wrong. Their claim of Southern Cameroons being economically non-viable was false, inaccurate and misleading. The state of affairs was due in part to their failure to fulfill the 'Sacred trust' they had obtained from the League of Nations in 1919.

Fast forward to the twenty-first century. As we see later, since the 1970s, it has been a known fact that Southern Cameroons is endowed with vast reserves of natural resources, including oil and natural gas that British, French, Swiss, Chinese, Russian, and other companies are exploiting under license from the secretive neo-patrimonialist autocratic and kleptocratic Biya regime considers these natural resources as the personal property of President Biya and his tribal cronies and controls them accordingly. West Cameroon, with its parliamentary system of government, was quickly swallowed by the bigger, highly centralized, authoritarian, kleptocratic Napoleonic regime of *La Republique du Cameroun*, which has zero respect for human rights. President Ahidjo transformed Cameroon into a highly centralized, autocratic, neopatrimonial, kleptocratic, clientelist state, a republican monarchy of sorts. Ahidjo became the authoritarian dictator of the Federal and United Republic of Cameroon. President Paul Biya, who had a monarchical or chieftaincy bent, took things one step further (Du Pont, 2019). As soon as he became president, his hand-picked tribal elite ensured that he was crowned traditional ruler of traditional rulers, the chief of all traditional chiefs in Cameroon, in keeping with his official title of *"Chef de l'État"* (Literally Chief of State). Biya essentially became the Grand Chieftain of the autocratic *Chefferie Républicaine* du Cameroun (Republican Chiefery of Cameroon).

The 2016 Anglophone Revolt in the former Southern Cameroons is a direct result and evidence of the failure of the United Nations and British decolonization of the territories that were carved out of German Kamerun during World War I. As such, the Anglophone Revolt in Cameroon is unfinished business of World War I and the Treaty of Versailles of 1919. The Anglophone crisis in Cameroon is the result of the failure to heed the Wilsonian caution against moving territories from jurisdiction to jurisdiction and from sovereignty to sovereignty without reference to the interests of the peoples of those territories. That is part of the genesis of the Anglophone problem in Cameroon.

Conclusion

Though variants of the lingua franca of West Africa, Pidgin English or Creole, had emerged with the West African slave trade in the 18th and 19th centuries, the seeds of the Anglophone Question in Cameroon were planted in Bimbia, near modern-day Limbe in 1844 when English Baptist missionary, Rev. Joseph Merrick began missionary work in the area. The spread of the English language was accelerated when Rev. Alfred Saker founded the colony of Victoria (named after Queen Victoria) in 1858. The European partition of Africa at the Berlin Africa Conference (1884-1885) resulted in the emergence of German Kamerun, a vast territory that included parts of the present-day Central African Republic, Congo, Cameroon, and Nigeria. As the German colonial administration of Kamerun moved to replace English with German, that transition led to the first Anglophone crisis. That first Anglophone "problem" arose when Germany annexed the English settlement of Victoria as part of its colony of Kamerun. Alfred Saker and his colleagues were forced to turn over the Victoria settlement to Germany and the Swiss-German Basel Mission (with minimal compensation). When the British missionaries left Victoria, they left the English language, the King James version of the Bible, and English Baptist hymn books with their Christian converts, who included persons of Jamaican and West African Creole origin (Sierra Leone, Ghana, Togo, Dahomey, and Nigeria). These "native" Baptist churches maintained their Anglo Pidgin/Creole culture and identity despite the imposition of German as the official colonial language in Kamerun.

Fast forward to World War I (1914-1918). The defeat of Germany by British and French forces in Kamerun in 1916 and the partition of German Kamerun into French and British League of Nations mandates under provisions of the Treaty of Versailles of 1919 meant the official return of the English language to what was to become British Cameroons. The British further partitioned the territory into British Northern and Southern Cameroons in 1946 to facilitate their colonial administration through Nigeria. The controversial, UN-supervised Southern Cameroons plebiscite of 1961 and reunification of English and Pidgin-speaking Southern Cameroons with French-speaking *La République du Cameroun* revived the Anglophone Question, which ultimately morphed into an identitarian and cultural question of the place of the English and Pidgin-speaking minority in the authoritarian, over-centralized, Napoleonic republican chiefdom of Cameroon. The Anglophone Question was compounded by the fact that France and French Cameroon perceived the reunification of British and French Cameroun as an opportunity to mute and erase the Anglophone culture of Southern Cameroons and assimilate the territory and its people into la *Francophonie*, the French politico-cultural sphere of influence in Africa. Since 1961, France has attempted in vain to mute the linguistic and cultural specificity of Southern Cameroons, stifle its cultural identity, and assimilate it into la *Francophonie*.

The Anglophone Question in Cameroon has thus persisted due to five historical phenomena: 1) 19th century European colonialism and post-World War I British and French strategic imperial rivalry and compensatory diplomacy in Africa, 2) French and British post-World War II and pre-independence entente over the United Nations Trust Territories of French Cameroon and British Cameroons that they had created out of German Kamerun, 3) the cultural assimilationist measures undertaken by France and its authoritarian French Cameroun postcolony, la *République du Cameroun* to mute the identitarian and cultural specificity of Southern Cameroons and disperse it into the French African sphere of influence, la *Francophonie*, 4) the discovery of large reserves of oil and natural gas in Southern Cameroons that led President Ahmadou Ahidjo to deceptively and illegally abrogate the post-reunification two-state federal republican system in favor of a centralized, autocratic system, in order to control these natural resources, and 5) French, Israeli, British, Chinese, Russian, Swiss, World Bank and International Monetary Fund support for the authoritarian Biya regime despite its horrendous repression and crimes against humanity in Anglophone Southern Cameroons. The British have been the most Machiavellian of the lot. The post-Brexit UK is clear-eyed about its interests but clearly lacking in moral clarity about international human rights and humanitarian norms. History shows that the British have abandoned Southern Cameroons at every turn.

By an ironic twist of history, the German Kamerun territories acquired by the UK under the Treaty of Versailles and partitioned into British Northern and Southern Cameroons have become centers of armed conflict. The poverty and economic deprivation of the British Northern Cameroons territories that were attached to the postcolonial Federal Republic of Nigeria, led to the emergence of the Boko Haram Islamist insurgency in these former German "enemy" territories. The Anglophone Revolt of 2016 represented a failure of British and United Nations decolonization policies in Southern Cameroons. The name "Cameroon" now stands for the colossal failure of an international experiment to unite the former French and British-administered UN Trust territories of Southern Cameroons and East Cameroon into a bilingual union of two equal states and equal citizenship. The failure of British and French post World War I balance of power politics and the failure of United Nations decolonization policies led to a virtual black-on-black annexation and colonization of Southern Cameroons by the autocratic, kleptocratic, republican chiefery, that can best be described as *la chefferie républicaine du Cameroun*.

References

Adibe, J. (2014). Explaining the Emergence of Boko Haram, The Brookings Institution (May 6). Retrieved from: https://www.brookings.edu/blog/africa-in-focus/2014/05/06/explaining-the-emergence-of-boko-haram/" https://www.brookings.edu/blog/africa-in-focus/2014/05/06/explaining-the-emergence-of-boko-haram/

Alberto Alvarez-Jimenez (2012). Boundary Agreements in the International Court of Justice's Case Law, 2000–2010, *European Journal of International Law*, (23), 1, Pp. 495-515 Retrieved from: https://doi.org/10.1093/ejil/chs015" https://doi.org/10.1093/ejil/chs015

Anyangwe, C. (ed. 2010). *The Declassified British Secret Files on the Southern Cameroons*. Bamenda: Langaa

Anyangwe, C. (2008). *Imperialist politics in Cameroon: Resistance and the Inception of the Restoration of the Statehood of Southern Cameroons*. Bamenda: Langaa.

Ardener, E. (1962). The Political History of Cameroon. *The World Today, Vol. 18, No. 8. (pp. 341-350)*

Ardener, S. (2005). Ardener's "Muted Groups": The genesis of an idea and its praxis. *Women and Language*, Vol. 28, (2), Pp. 50-54,72.

Ballard, W. (2020). The Irony of Southern Cameroons' "Poverty" Medium, April 11. Retrieved from: https://medium.com/@wbam/the-irony-of-southern-cameroons-adfc67eb940d

Callahan, M. (2004). *A Sacred Trust: The League of Nations and Africa, 1929-1946*. Brighton: Sussex Academic Press.

Centre for Human Rights and Democracy in Africa (CHRDA) and Raoul Wallenberg Centre for Human Rights, "Cameroon's Unfolding Catastrophe: Evidence of Human Rights Violations and Crimes against Humanity in the Anglophone Regions of Cameroon" (2019). Retrieved from: Online and www.rwhrc.org

Durrell, G. (1954). *The Bafut Beagles*. New York: The Viking Press.

Eko, L. (2003). The English-Language Press and the 'Anglophone Problem' In Cameroon: Group Identity, Culture, and the Politics of Nostalgia. *Journal of Third World Studies*. Vol. XX (1), 79-102.

Elango, L. (2015). "Anglo-French Negotiations Concerning Cameroon during World War I, 1914-1916: Occupation, "Condominium", and Partition," *Journal of Global Initiatives: Policy, Pedagogy, Perspective*: Vol. 9: No. 2, Article 10. Available at: https://digitalcommons.kennesaw.edu/jgi/vol9/iss2/10

France24 (2017). *La Colère des Anglophone de Bamenda*. January 2. Retrieved from: https://www.youtube.com/watch?v=0zfvcnbapSU» https://www.youtube.com/watch?v=0zfvcnbapSU

Johnson, W. (1965). The Cameroon Federation: Political Union Between English and French-Speaking Africa. In William Lewis (ed). *French-Speaking Africa*. New York: Walker and Co.

Monga, C. (1996). *The Anthropology of Anger: Civil Society and Democracy in Africa*. Boulder: Lynne Rienner Publishers.

Nforbin, E. (2019). The Push to Protect the Oneness of English as a Judicial Language in the Southern Cameroons Jurisdiction of Cameroon, *International Journal on Minority and Group Rights*, 20, 503-574.

Nigeria Talks Set Role of Cameroon (1954). The New York Times, January 22.

Norwegian Refugee Council (2020). Africa is home to nine of ten of the world's most neglected crises. Retrieved from: https://www.nrc.no/news/2020/june/africa-is-home-to-nine-of-ten-of-the-most-neglected-crises/

Nyo'Wakai, (2009). *The Law and My Times: Under the Broken Scale of Justice* (pp. xiii-xx). Bamenda: Langaa Research and Publishing

Osuntokun. J. (1978). Anglo-French Administration of the Mandated Territory of the Cameroons 1923-1939: A Case Study in Comparative Administration. *Quarterly Journal of Administration*, 12(3) pp. 257-270.

Phillipson, S. (1959). Report of the Financial, economic and administrative consequences to the Southern Cameroons of separation from the Federation of Nigeria. Lagos: British Protectorate and Colony of Nigeria. OCoLC)654552976. Retrieved from: https://www.worldcat.org/title/financial-economic-and-administrative-consequences-to-the-southern-cameroons-of-separation-from-the-federation-of-nigeria-report/oclc/34571687

Roberts, C. & Burton, B. (2020). Cameroon's Government is Deceiving the West While Diverting Foreign Aid. *Foreign Policy*, November 22. Retrieved from: https://foreignpolicy.com/2020/11/22/cameroons-government-is-deceiving-the-west-while-diverting-foreign-aid/#

Robinson, R., John Gallagher, and Alice Denny. *Africa and the Victorians: The Climax of Imperialism* (1961). Garden City, N.Y.: Anchor Books, 1968.

Stinson, N. (2019). UK signs £1.5 Billion trade deal as Brexit Britain expands on world stage. *Express News.* June 9.

The Future of the Trust Territory of the Cameroons Under French Administration [1959] UNGA 1; A/RES/1349 (XIII) (13 March 1959)

The Future of the Trust Territory of the Cameroons Under United Kingdom Administration [1959] UNGA 2; A/RES/1350 (XIII) (13 March 1959)

UN Economic and Social Council (2019), Committee on Economic, Social and Cultural Rights Concluding observations on the fourth periodic report of Cameroon. Retrieved from: http://docstore.ohchr.org/SelfServices/FilesHandler.ashx?enc=4slQ6QSmlBEDzFEovLCuW6UZeww1QFihQBrUmR7Q0x%2b7sQ3AZSm%2bA7QNvS6tVnTh9k59MkRMQNGRUXQ4pLgokni08NG2SuYYEhZyG%2bBU%2foxSIz6SX6TVFRb4CoPNYWEU"http://docstore.ohchr.org/SelfServices/FilesHandler.ashx?enc=4slQ6QSmlBEDzFEovLCuW6UZeww1QFihQBrUmR7Q0x%2b7sQ3AZSm%2bA7QNvS6tVnTh9k59MkRMQNGRUXQ4pLgokni08NG2SuYYEhZyG%2bBU%2foxSIz6SX6TVFRb4CoPNYWEU

Wilson, W. (1919). The Fourteen Points. The National World War I Museum. Retrieved from: https://www.theworldwar.org/learn/peace/fourteen-points

FOUR

The French Connection in the Anglophone Question

Extending the Frenchman's Civilizational Burden to Southern Cameroons

LYOMBE EKO

It was one of the most surreal and most dramatic public moments of the presidency of French President, Emmanuel Macron. It was the kind of unscripted, uncontrollable occurrence that political handlers, image managers, public relations officers, and spinmeisters dread. It happened on February 22, 2020, at the *Salon de l'Agriculture de Paris*. As reported by the French government's international broadcaster, *Radio France Internationale* (2020), when President Emmanuel Macron was touring exhibitions at the agricultural fair, the national and international press in tow, a loud male voice from the crowd that had been cordoned off by metal security barriers loudly interpellated him with an air of fierce and desperate urgency:

> *"Monsieur Macron…Monsieur Macron," the voice shouted in desperation.*

President Macron paused and instinctively looked in the direction from which his name was being shouted. He hesitated a moment, his eyes scanning the crowd to find out who was shouting his name. The President's aides and the media followed the president's cue and paused. That brief pause gave the desperate male voice in the crowd a little opening, which the shouter deftly exploited:

> *Il y a Paul Biya qui tue les Camerounais Monsieur Macron…. Il y a un génocide au Cameroun Monsieur Macron…Paul Biya tue les Camerounais M. Macron…*
> *Nous sommes des Camerounais et nous sommes des morts Monsieur Macron…*
> *Monsieur Macron, Monsieur Macron s'il vous plait!*
> *S'il vous plait, Monsieur Macron!*

Mr. Macron, Mr. Macron. Paul Biya is killing Cameroonians, Mr. Macron. There is a genocide in Cameroon, Mr. Macron. Biya is killing Cameroonians, Mr. Macron. We are Cameroonians and we are the dead, Mr. Macron, Mr. Macron, Mr. Macron. Please, please, Mr. Macron.

The Anglophone Question in Cameroon had gate-crashed a political exercise that President Emmanuel Macron was going through in the heart of Paris. The voice was that of Abdoulaye Thiam a.k.a. 'Calibri Calibro,' a Cameroonian immigrant who was one of the leaders of a Europe-based group known as *le Brigade Anti-Sardinard* (BAS). The group consisted of Cameroonians whose residency status in Europe ranged from dissidents, political asylum seekers and exiles, to immigrants of all states of legality or lack thereof. Calibri Calibro was referring to the horrendous crimes against humanity visited on innocent people and villages in the Anglophone regions of Cameroon. Specifically, he was referring to the gruesome massacre of 38 innocent women and children at Ngarbuh in the Donga Mantung Division of the Northwest region on February 14, 2020. The atrocities were carried out by members of the Cameroon army and their Fulani herdsmen militias and partners. France's direct and indirect role in the human rights violations of Anglophone citizens was thus the cause of the dramatic interpellation of President Macron in Paris on February 20, 2020. To everyone's surprise, President Macron turned and walked towards the voice, his eyes scanning the crowd. As Macron approached, Abdoulaye Thiam a.k.a. 'Calibri Calibro" waved his hands excitedly and continued his denunciation of the Biya regime:

Monsieur Macron, il y a un génocide au Cameroun M. Macron...

(Mr. Macron, there is a genocide in Cameroon, Mr. Macron).

"*Oui*," (yes), answered President Macron, standing near the security perimeter surrounded by a phalanx of reporters and cameras, audio and video recording devices of all kinds. Calibri Calibro was speaking, a voice from the crowd on the other side of the security barrier.

"*Il y a un génocide au Cameroun M. Macron...C'est un enorme plaisir de vous voir Monsieur Macron...*"

(There is a genocide in Cameroon, Mr. Macron...It is a pleasure to see you, Mr. Macron).

"*Moi aussi*" (Me too), responded President Macron.

The activist lowered his voice and stopped his frantic waving once he was certain he had attracted President Macron's attention. The man struggled to cram as much information as possible into the fleeting moment he was granted.

"Il y a plus de 22 morts... qui sont morts calcines, Monsieur Macron"

(There are more than 22 dead... who were burned to death, Mr. Macron").

"Je sais...Je sais ça..."

(I know... I know that), responded President Macron

"Nous sommes des Camerounais et nous souffrons...J'ai pris la Méditerrané et je vous ai écrit et vous avez répondu..."

(We are Cameroonians and we are suffering...I came through the Mediterranean [as an illegal immigrant]. I wrote you and you responded).

President Macron then expressed his position on the politico-cultural situation in Cameroon:

Vous savez mon engagement sur ce sujet...J'ai mis la pression sur Paul Biya pour que d'abord, il traite le sujet de la zone Anglophone et ses opposants. J'avais dis que je ne vais pas le recevoir à Lyon, tant que Kamto n'a pas été libéré. Il a été libéré parce qu'on a mis la pression. La, la situation est en train de se redégrader...Je vais appeler la semaine prochaine Monsieur Biya et on mettra le maximum de pression pour que cette situation cesse. Je suis totalement au courant et totalement impliqué sur les violences qui se passent au Cameroun et qui sont intolérable donc je voudrais, je fais le maximum... (Radio France Internationale, 2020).

You know my commitment on this issue. I have put pressure on Paul Biya to first of all deal with the matter of the Anglophone zone and his [Francophone political] opponents. I said that I did not want to see him at Lyon [at the international conference for Refinancing of the Global Fund to Fight AIDS, Tuberculosis and Malaria], as long as [jailed opposition leader] Kamto had not been freed. He was freed because we put pressure. The situation [in the Anglophone region] is deteriorating again. I am going to call Mr. Biya next week and we will put maximum pressure in order for this situation to stop. I am totally aware and totally concerned about the violence that is taking place in Cameroun and which is intolerable. So, I would like...I do the maximum...

Calibri Calibro took advantage of this unprecedented moment granted to him by fate to squeeze in as many questions as possible, questions that expressed the anguish of the helpless immigrant in the face of human rights abuses in Cameroon, the home he had fled, and atrocities about which he could do nothing. Skillfully, and subtly, Calibri Calibro transformed this opportunity into a critique, nay, a subtle denunciation of French postcolonial policy in Africa in general, and English-speaking Southern Cameroons in particular:

"Je vous remercie Monsieur Macron…mais il y a plus de douze mille morts aujourd'hui,"

(Thank you, Mr. Macron…but there are more than twelve thousand dead today).

"Je sais"

(I know), responded Macron.

"Nous, les jeunes Camerounais nous prenons la Méditerranée par ce que nous avons a la tête de nos états des dictateurs…Monsieur Macron, la France est un état de droit, la France est un pays de droits de l'homme. Elle ne peut pas soutenir les dictateurs" (Radio France Internationale, 2020).

We, young Cameroonians, take to the Mediterranean [to immigrate to Europe] because our countries are ruled by dictators…Mr. Macron, France has the rule of law, France is a country of human rights. It must not support dictators [in Africa].
"Non!" (No!) President Macron responded firmly.

"L'Afrique a besoin du soutien de la France, Monsieur Macron," Calibri Calibro said.

Africa needs the support of France, Mr. Macron.

The French President took the opportunity to explain the Africa policy of France.

"Là-dessus, …Nous sommes très clair…simplement, la France est, si je peux dire, pris dans un rôle compliqué en Afrique…Nous sommes un état de droit, nous défendons un état de droit partout, mais quand en Afrique un président Français dit tel dirigeant n'est pas démocratiquement élu, les Africains dissent de quoi venez-vous vous mélez? Vous n'avez pas a nous donner des leçons. Donc mois je dis partout je veux des dirigeant démocratiquement élu et là ou ils ne sont pas démocratiquement élu, je travaillerai avec la société civile. Je mets la pression sur chacun, je travaille avec l'Union Africaine et les organisations régionale pour mettre la pression… Sur le président Biya, je lui ai dit, il doit ouvrir le jeu, il doit décentraliser, il doit libérer les opposant politiques… il doit fait respecter les droits. Je mettrai tous qui est en mon pouvoir…il faut que vous le sachiez."

On that…We are very clear. Simply stated, France is, if I may say so, caught in a complicated role in Africa. We are a country of the rule of law. We defend the rule of law everywhere, but when in Africa, a French president states that such and such a leader is not democratically elected, the Africans ask us, why are you interfering? It is not your place to lecture us? Thus, I say everywhere I want democratically elected leaders and where they are not democratically elected, I will work with civil society. I put pressure on everyone, I work with the African Union and regional organizations to put pressure…. As concerns President Biya, I told him that he had to open up the political space, that he has to decentralize, that he has to free political opponents, that he must ensure that rights are respected. I will do all in my power. You must know that.
"*Merci, Monsieur Macron.*"

(Thank you, Mr. Macron).

"*Ce n'est pas la France qui va faire la démocratie au Cameroun à la place des Camerounaises et des Camerounais, voilà.*"

It is not the place of France to create democracy in Cameroon for Cameroonians, that's it!

Calibri Calibro continued the dialogue by countering President Macron's point of French non-interference in the affairs of Africa nations by obliquely referring to French support for African dictators:

"*Je le comprends, Monsieur le Président, sauf que quand ils viennent prendre de l'argent en Afrique, quand ils viennent vous prendre de l'argent, c'est ne pas une ingérence…La France donne de l'argent aux présidents africaines…*"

I understand, Mr. President, except that when they come and take money in Africa, when they come and take money from you, it is not interference. France gives money to African presidents.

"*Non, non…l'action est très vigilant…Nous finançons des projets, on ne donne pas de l'argent à un président ou à un gouvernant.*"

No, no, our actions are very vigilant. We finance projects, we don't give money to a president of a government.

Calibri Calibro continued by complaining that funds sent to Cameroun by the French for development projects were misappropriated. President Macron asked the activist to let him know cases of embezzlement, instances where funds destined to finance non-governmental organizations that aid the people are embezzled. The BAS activist made a last request. He asked the French president to intervene with President Biya to secure the release of political prisoners, including Mamadou Mota, Vice President of the MRC political party. President Macron asked his aides to take the names of political Cameroonian prisoners and detainees mentioned by the activist. An aide stepped forward and gave Calibri his card, with a number he could call at the president's office at the Champs Elysée. President Macron then reached out and shook hands with Calibri Calibro and other African activists in the crowd, and the encounter was over.

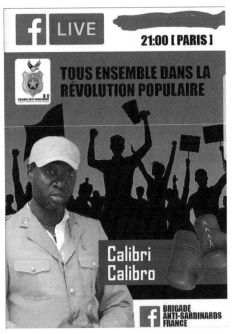

Figure 4.1. Calibri Calibro (aka Abdoulaye Thiam) featured in an online poster of the *Brigade Anti-Sardinard* France (The Anti Sardine Corruption Brigade). This was a reference to Cameroon RDPC/CPDM politicians who distribute loaves of bread and tins of sardines during campaigns to buy the votes of hungry citizens. The ruling elite are known as "Sardinards", those who buy the votes of the hungry with bread and sardines.

The French and international media reported this surreal exchange between a French president, Emmanuel Macron, and an obscure, insignificant immigrant and political refugee from Cameroon at the *Salon de l'agriculture* (Agricultural Fair) in Paris. The Anglophone Question in Cameroon, the resultant Anglophone Revolt, the heavy-handed repression, and the crimes against humanity committed by the Biya regime in his attempt to subjugate Anglophone Cameroon, had intruded on the public political agenda of the French president. The significance of the improbable Macron/Calibri Calibro dialogue on the fringes of the *Salon de l'agriculture de Paris* was that it brought to the fore of international public opinion, the role of France, which enjoys a "special partnership" with Cameroon and its notorious military establishment under bilateral defense agreements, in the Anglophone problem in Cameroon. Indeed, the French government states that "*la France bénéficie d'un rang de partenaire privilégié*" (France occupies the position of a privileged partner) in its relations with Cameroon. Thus, the atrocities and human rights violations of the Cameroon military and security forces, which are mostly trained, armed and equipped by France, in the English-speaking regions of Cameroon reflected negatively on France. Since independence in 1960, France has been a "strategic partner" of Cameroon under bilateral (*accords de coopération*). Calibri Calibro's complaints therefore raised the matter of the direct and indirect involvement of the Macron government in the human rights violations that were being perpetrated by the Biya regime on the English-speaking regions, as well as on his political opponents in the French postcolony of Cameroon, to use Mbembe's (2001) expression.

The fierce urgency of the pleas of Calibri Calibro seemed to prick the conscience of President Macron, whose references to the crisis in the "zones anglophone," had a tone of humanistic candor that belied the historic, Machiavellian machinations of France that had made the English-speaking Northwest and Southwest regions a laboratory of French linguistic and cultural assimilation. The reasons for Macron's uncharacteristic display of humanism in the face of the Biya regime's gross violations of human rights in the English-speaking regions of Cameroon are not hard to discern. English-speaking Southern Cameroonians and a segment of the French-speaking public opinion viewed France as a partner in crimes against humanity in Southern Cameroons. President Macron, President of France, the self-styled country of human rights, freedoms, and civil liberties, was being asked in public by an immigrant whose status was unknown, to strike a balance between the pull of his country's historic, moral philosophical and humanistic rhetoric, and the push of its national, economic, and cultural self-interest in Africa. As we see below, when Calibri Calibro accosted President Macron on the Anglophone crisis, the scales were tipped in favor of French national politico-cultural economic self-interest. That is to say, France supported the Biya regime, despite its horrendous human rights violations, to protect its economic and cultural interests in Cameroon.

The Official French Posture Towards the Anglophone Crisis in Cameroon

It is not as if President Macron had not spoken to President Paul Biya about the Anglophone Revolt. President Macron's off-the-cuff remarks on the *crise anglophone* (Anglophone crisis) at the *Salon de l'agriculture de Paris* was the first time he publicly spoke of the crisis. In fact, Macron seemed to be talking about the Anglophone crisis in public because formal, diplomatic overtures to President Paul Biya to resolve the crisis had fallen on deaf ears. One such occasion came in the aftermath of the stage-managed, hotly contested, and controversial October 2018 presidential elections. The main opposition candidate, Maurice Kamto, and his MRC party claimed that the elections were rigged, but Biya's hand-picked Constitutional Council ruled in favor of Biya, who had been in power for 37 years at that time, granting him another 7-year term. In a congratulatory letter dated 25 October 2018, President Emmanuel Macron had urged Biya to resolve the Anglophone crisis expeditiously:

> *S'agissant des régions anglophones du Cameroun, la France est prête à apporter son appui aux initiatives que vous pourriez prendre pour progresser*

vers un règlement politique et pérenne de la crise qui y sévit. Je forme le vœu que de telles initiatives prennent corps au plus vite car l'aggravation continue de la situation dans ces régions est une préoccupation profonde pour la France et l'ensemble des partenaires extérieurs de Cameroun.

With respect to the Anglophone regions of Cameroon, France is ready to assist with initiatives that you could undertake to progress towards a lasting political solution of the crisis which is raging there. I hope that these initiatives are undertaken as soon as possible because the continued degradation of the situation in these regions is a matter of deep concern for France and the rest of the external partners of Cameroon.

The Anglophone problem was internationalized because it had essentially reached an impasse in Cameroon due to the extreme lack of leadership shown by President Biya, the reclusive, absentee president who had ruled the country for over 40 years. Rather than address the root causes of the Anglophone Revolt—Anglophone demands for restoration of the political autonomy of their regions as well as calls for respect for their linguistic and cultural specificity—President Paul Biya had opted for a two-pronged authoritarian strategy—military subjugation and manifestly deceptive, bad-faith, cosmetic measures aimed at showing the world that he was doing something to stop the tit-for-tat war of insurgency.

President Macron's Letter of 2019

As the situation in the English-speaking regions degenerated into a cauldron of massive human rights violations, complete with massive extrajudicial killings, the burning down of whole villages and the displacement of thousands of people (Agbor Balla, Raoul Wallenberg Center, 2019), in 2019, President Macron again wrote to President Biya and urged him to make urgent efforts to resolve the Anglophone crisis. This time, his solicitude and concerns about the deteriorating crisis in the English-speaking regions of Cameroon were conveyed in the traditional diplomatic letter that countries send each other to congratulate them on their national holidays. Macron wrote on Cameroon's national day, 20th May, 2019, which ironically commemorates, not the anniversary of the independence of *la République du Cameroun* (January 1st, 1960) nor the reunification of the two States of East and West Cameroon (October 1st, 1961) but the anniversary of President Ahmadou Ahidjo's controversial and unconstitutional referendum that eliminated the Federal Republic of Cameroon in 1972, ushered in the highly centralized United Republic of Cameroon, and sowed the seeds of the Anglophone Revolt. In his May 20, 2019 letter, President Macron turned a blind eye and a deaf ear to the blatant human rights violations of the French, Israeli, and American-trained and funded Cameroon army—and specifically the BIR—in the English-speaking Northwest and Southwest regions of Cameroon:

Je souhaite également vous dire la solidarité de la France face aux crimes commis contre, notamment, des représentants de l'État, dans le contexte de tensions que connaissent les régions anglophones du Cameroun. Je forme le vœu que ces tensions puissantes être résorbées de manière pacifique et concertée, dans le strict respect de l'unité et l'intégrité de votre pays.

I would also like to express the solidarity of France in the face of crimes committed against, notably, representatives of the State, in the context of the tensions in the English-speaking regions of Cameroon. I wish that these tensions can be reduced peacefully and in a concerted manner, while strictly respecting the unity and integrity of your country.

This statement of resounding support by Macron, the young, newly elected president of France, exemplified the old saying, "the more things change the more they stay the same." Macron hued to the old French statist, neo-colonial line and made no bones about French support for the Biya regime despite the horrendous human rights violations that the Cameroon military was committing in Anglophone Cameroon. To Macron, the Anglophone Revolt amounted only to "tensions," despite the fact that international human rights groups had found that thousands of civilians and armed, non-state actors had been killed, that at least sixty thousand Anglophones had become refugees in Nigeria, Ghana and other places, that hundreds of thousands of people had been displaced internally due to the conflict, and despite the fact that more than one thousand Cameroonian soldiers, paramilitary gendarmerie, government officials, and police had been killed in the civil war. Macron's predecessors in the Champs-Élysées were a little less explicit in their support for their authoritarian postcolonies and their wanton disregard for human rights in Africa. Calibri Calibro's interpellation of President Macron and his claim that there was a genocide going on in Anglophone Cameroon contrasted sharply with Macron's official communication to President Paul Biya that the Anglophone conflict in Cameroon amounted only to "tensions." President Macron waded into the Anglophone question in Cameroon because France had been one of the key international entities involved in the Anglophone Question since the reunification of Cameroon in 1961. Before we discuss the direct French connection to the Anglophone Problem, we need to explore French colonial and postcolonial ideology and policy.

Historical Background: French Postcolonial Cultural Assimilationist Policies in Africa

French colonial and postcolonial policies in Africa were grounded in a Gallic version of what Kipling (1940, p. 321) called "The Whiteman's Burden." This was a French "*mission civilisatrice* (civilizing colonial mission) (Gavin and Bentley, 1973, p. 169), whose fundamental principle was the assimilation of African peoples into the French linguistic and cultural sphere, *la Francophonie*, the French language being the passport and entry visa into that imagined superior civilizational community (Betts, 1961). France essentially assigned unto itself, a self-interested "linguistic and civilizational burden" in Africa. This burden was described and explained by a French colonial military officer, Lieutenant Paulhiac in 1905. In his book, *Promenades Lointaines: Sahara, Niger, Tombouctou, Touareg (Distant Promenades: Sahara, Niger, Timbuktu, Touareg)* Paulhiac wrote:

Notre langue s'implantera par la force des choses et ne l'oublions pas, c'est un des moyens les plus sûrs qui fera pénétrer le progrès dans nos colonies, comme ce sera le seul qui saura nous conserver à jamais les colonies mêmes... C'est dans notre langue que résidera notre force, comme elle sera, plus tard, la base de notre indestructible influence dans les pays que nous aurons façonnés à notre image ... (Paulhiac, 1905, pp. 406-407).

Our language will implant itself by force of circumstances and let us not forget that it is one of the surest means of making progress penetrate our colonies, just as it will be the only means of ensuring that we maintain the colonies themselves for ever...It is in our language that our power resides, as it will be, later, the basis of our indestructible influence in the countries that we will have shaped in our image.

Paulhiac's idea was that French colonization had a quasi-religious, secular mission—propagation and vulgarization (imposition of widespread and popular use) of the French language, and through it, French culture, mentality, and way of life in the colonized territories of Africa. French colonial and postcolonial policy in Africa was grounded in the idea of the French language as the gateway to civilization, culture, and development in Africa. It was a matter of conversion and transformation, with secular missionary zeal, of African mentalities such that they accept the exceptionalist superiority of the French language and culture. The peoples in French territories were taught to see France as their home, *les Gaulois* (the Gauls) as their ancestors, French culture as their culture, French history as their history, to claim ownership of the French language as *"notre langue"* (our language) and make it the medium of expression of their mentalities, their thought lives, their angst and aspirations. It never occurred to the French colonialists that Africans were embodiments of multiculturalism, that each African is, anthropologically, linguistically, and socially, a composite of multiple cultures and multiple cultural belongings.

The most enlightened pre-independence expression of French cultural assimilation of Africans was penned by celebrated French existentialist philosopher, Jean-Paul Sartre (1947). In an article entitled *Présence Noire* (Black Presence), Sartre advanced an interesting, though Franco-centric perspective on Francophone African intellectuals in France and how they negotiated their encounter with the French language and culture that had been imposed on them by colonialism. On the occasion of the launching of the intellectual journal, *Présence Africaine* by French-speaking African intellectuals in France on the eve of independence, Sartre (1947) wrote:

Gardons-nous de voir dans ces productions de l'esprit un hommage rendu à la culture française. Il s'agit de tout autre chose. La culture est un instrument; ne pensons pas qu'ils ont élu la nôtre... La vérité, c'est que les noirs tentent de se rejoindre eux-mêmes à travers un monde culturel qu'on leur impose et qui leur est étranger ; il faut qu'ils retaillent ce vêtement tout fait... et pourtant ils ont appris à utiliser jusqu'aux insuffisances de cet outil. Une langue étrangère les habite et l'eur vole leur pensée ; mais ils se retournent, en eux-mêmes, contre ce vol, ils maîtrisent en eux ce bavardage européen et, finalement, en acceptant d'être trahis par le langage, ils le marquent de leur empreinte. Pour ma part, je considère avec admiration l'effort qu'ont fourni ces auteurs…, pour se conquérir dans et par le langage hostile des colonisateurs. Je souhaite que nous apprenions à lire ces œuvres et que nous sachions gré aux noirs d'enrichir notre vieille culture cérémonieuse… chaque noir qui cherche à se peindre au moyen de nos mots et de nos mythes, c'est un peu de sang frais qui circule en ce vieux corps (Sartre, 1947).

Let us be careful to not to see, in these productions of the mind [published in *Présence Africaine*] a homage rendered to French culture. It is something completely different. Culture is an instrument; let us not think that they have selected ours…The truth is that black people try to reach themselves through a cultural world that is imposed on them, that is strange to them. It is necessary for them to refashion this ready-made attire…and yet they have learned to use even the insufficiencies of this tool. A foreign language inhabits them and robs them of thought. But they turn inwards against this theft. They master this European chatter, and, finally, by accepting to be betrayed by the language, they put their imprint on it. As for me, I consider, with admiration, the efforts made by these authors… to conquer themselves in, and through the hostile language of the colonizers. I wish that we would learn to read these works and that we would be grateful to the blacks for enriching our old ceremonious culture… each black person who seeks to paint himself through our words and through our myths, is a bit of fresh blood circulating in this old body.

The focus of French foreign policy in the post-independence era (after 1960) was the maintenance of French linguistic and cultural hegemony in its African postcolonies. This was crucial, given the geo-strategic, Cold War rivalries with the United States, the linguistic behemoth that was transforming English into the global lingua Franca, and to a lesser extent with Russia. Progressive and humanistic French intellectuals like Sartre welcomed the "new blood" that African intellectuals like Leopold Sédar Senghor and others, who were educated in France, were bringing to the French language and increasing its global reach.

The Pre-Independence Bilateral Cooperation Agreements Between France and its African Colonies

On the eve of independence in the 1960s, France signed the famous *Accords de coopération* (bilateral cooperation agreements) with all its former colonies. These pre-independence agreements—and some of them had secret provisions—set forth the relationships between France and its former colonies in situations of unequal, one-sided power dynamics. These bilateral agreements were part of what Kodjo-Grandvaux (2016) calls *"l'indépendance négociée,"* (negotiated independence). This system of dependence led to what French and

Francophone scholars call *la Françafrique*, the neo-colonial system of unequal power-re-
lations and dependence that transformed French-speaking colonies into independent
"postcolonies" (Mbembe, 2001). These agreements had a striking Gallic cultural touch.
They embodied the mentality of French President, General Charles de Gaulle, champion
of French greatness, who proclaimed a Gallic politico-cultural exceptionalism: *"une certaine idée de la France ou elle n'est réellement elle-même que quand elle est au premier rang"*
(a certain idea of France where she is her real self only when she is at the forefront) (De
Gaulle, 1954, p. 1).

The French National Assembly and Senate debated and ratified these Franco-African
cooperation agreements, which had a very pronounced imprint. French government ministers who presented these agreements to the National Assembly and Senate explained that
all the agreements were based on a common Gallic template, which was adopted to suit the
national context of each country to which France was granting independence. During the
parliamentary debates, the French government unsurprisingly framed these agreements as
vehicles for promoting *la grandeur de la France* (French greatness), the French language,
French culture, and French economic interests.

> *Tous les États d'Afrique et de Madagascar demeurent ainsi liés à la Répub-
> lique Française par des accords de coopération. La langue française demeure
> obligatoire en matière d'enseignement*

> *La grandeur de la France, c'est bien plus la présence intellectuelle française à
> l'étranger, et notamment dans tous ces territoires avides de nos ingénieurs,
> de nos experts, de nos professeurs. Songez que nous avons encore à l'heure
> présente, dans les républiques africaines, 4.500 enseignants. N'est-ce pas un
> actif considérable ? N'est-ce pas le moyen d'apprendre aux jeunes africains
> la philosophie et les techniques de la France ? En formant ces jeunes gens à
> notre langue, en les amenant à faire ici leurs études supérieures, leurs études
> du troisième cycle, ils seront nos messagers quand ils retourneront dans leur
> pays, car connaissant mieux nos techniques c'est à nous qu'ils s'adresseront*
> (Débats Parlementaires, 1960).

All the [French-speaking] States of Africa and Madagascar will thus remain
tied to the French Republic by cooperation agreements. The French language will remain obligatory in education.

The greatness of France, it's the intellectual presence of France abroad,
and notably in all these territories that are hungry for our experts, our
professors. Imagine that we still have, at the present moment, in the African
republics, 4500 teachers. Isn't that a considerable asset? Isn't it the means
of teaching young Africans the philosophy and techniques of France?
By training these young people in our language, by bringing them here
to pursue higher education, to do their university studies here, they will

become our messengers when they return to their countries, because knowing our techniques better, they will refer to us.

The United Nations Trust Territory of French Cameroun was required to sign a cooperation agreement with France before the government of President Charles de Gaulle granted the territory independence as *La République du Cameroun*. The Franco-Cameroun pre-independence cooperation agreement was based on the template that France provided to the other French-speaking African countries. In its debate of the agreement, the French Senate stated that:

> ...*il consacre la permanence des méthodes administratives et des techniques françaises au Cameroun. En étroit parallèle avec cet accord, la convention culturelle prend acte de l'usage, du français comme langue officielle du nouvel État...Par un enseignement dont le caractère français est garanti... Puisque, dans les considérants, figure aussi l'affirmation que l'enseignement de caractère français est devenu pour le peuple camerounais, dans la fidélité à ses traditions nationales, l'instrument de son développement culturel, politique, économique et social. Voilà une affirmation qui a pour nous une valeur singulière et particulièrement importante. Ainsi la langue française est une langue véhiculaire qui peut permettre à un État, grâce à cette langue même, d'assurer son propre développement suivant son propre souhait* (Débats Parlementaires, 1960).

> ...it [the accord] establishes the permanence of French administrative and technical methods in Cameroon. In close parallel with this agreement, a cultural convention notes usage of French as the official language of the new State...through an educational system whose French character is guaranteed...Since in the recitals (preamble) there is also the affirmation that French-style education has become for the people of Cameroon, within their national traditions, the instrument of cultural, political, economic, and social development. This is an affirmation that has for us, a singular and particularly important value. Thus, the French language is a vehicular language that can enable a State, through this very language, to ensure its development as it sees fit.

These Gaullist, jingoistic sentiments expressed during the French National Assembly and Senate debates on the *accords de coopérations*, as well as the legislative intent of the lawmakers in assenting to these bilateral agreements, demonstrate a clear desire for France to create a *chasse gardée* (closed hunting preserve) in Francophone Africa. This was a postcolonial French African sphere of influence, *La Francophonie*, that critics call "FranceAfrique" (France and its African postcolonial territories). The assimilationist French language sphere of influence created by France in conditions of unequal power dynamics is political, cultural, economic, and military.

Figure 4.2. Ahmadou Ahidjo and French President, Charles de Gaulle

French Cameroun: From French Colony to Francophone Postcolony

Cameroonian intellectual, Achille Mbembe has described Francophone African countries as *postcolonies* (2001) because virtually all of them acceded to what can be called illusory independence. The most concrete and visible demonstration of French postcolonial hegemony in its Africa postcolonies is the financial and economic provisions of the *accords de coopération*. The economies of the 12 French African postcolonies (and eventually one former Portuguese territory, Guinea-Bissau, and one former Spanish territory, Equatorial Guinea), were tethered and assimilated into the French monetary orbit through the colonial currency, the franc CFA. This acronym originally stood for *Colonies Françaises de l'Afrique* (the Franc of the French Colonies of Africa). In effect, the CFA franc was created in December 1945 by the French government to serve as the economic and financial umbilical cord of "FranceAfrique," (Signé, 2019). After independence, the meaning of the CFA acronym was changed to *Communauté Financière Africaine* (African Financial Community). The Franc CFA has become a controversial bone of contention in Africa and Europe where it is seen in some quarters as an albatross around the necks of French-speaking African countries. In 2019, Luigi Di Maio, Italy's former deputy prime minister and minister of foreign affairs accused France of using the colonial franc CFA to exploit and impoverish its former colonies, thereby retarding the economic development of these 14 African states. Di Maio claimed that this neo-colonial arrangement contributes to the flood of illegal immigrants and refugees into Europe (Specia, 2019; Signé, 2019). Di Maio added that, "The EU should sanction France and all countries like France that impoverish Africa and make these people leave, because Africans should be in Africa, not at the bottom of the Mediterranean Sea" (Cited in Giles & Goodman, 2019). This heated rhetoric resulted from the fact that the franc CFA is printed in France under the auspices of the *Banque de France*. In return for guaranteeing the currency, the Banque de France holds 50 percent of all the foreign exchange reserves of the 14 CFA franc countries. In January 1994, the CFA was devalued from 50 CFA francs to 1 French Franc to 100 CFA francs to 1 French franc. Interestingly, the CFA franc survived the French franc, which was replaced by the single European currency, the euro in 1999. The CFA is now pegged to the euro. While some

African politicians and elite who benefit from the financial status quo consider the CFA franc as a stabilizing force, others see it as a colonial relic, a tool of neocolonialism that has left countries without control of their own currencies and economies, a currency that allows France to continue its monetary imperialism in Africa (Specia, 2019; Signé, 2019).

The "Dependent" Independence of *La République du Cameroun*

When French Cameroun nationalists started agitating for independence in the 1950s, France launched a psychological and bloody anti-insurgency campaign against anti-colonial groups and their leaders. It also decided to reluctantly grant French Cameroun, a territory that was not a traditional French colony, "negotiated" independence in 1960. On December 26, 1959, France's hand-picked leader of French Cameroun, President Ahmadou Ahidjo, and a representative of General Charles de Gaulle of France, signed decolonization agreements, which included secret economic and military clauses that put the politics, education, army, and economy of the country under French tutelage. On January 1, 1960, France granted *la République du Cameroun* independence in the presence of United Nations Secretary General, Dag Hammarskjöld, to signify the end of the United Nations Trusteeship over French Cameroun.

Figure 4.3. Stamp commemorating the Independence of *la Republique du Cameroun*, January 1, 1960. Cameron does not celebrate this independence day.

This "independence" was "illusory" (Kodjo-Grandvaux, 2016; Deltombe, Domergue, & Tatsitsa, 2016; Deltombe, Domergue, & Tatsitsa, 2011). This was because the lopsided agreements that France imposed on the new republic made it nothing more than a French "postcolony" (Mbembe, 2001). The *accords de coopérations* were designed to ensure perpetual French political, economic, linguistic, and cultural influence in Cameroon. They included military provisions that guaranteed postcolonial Cameroon French military assistance in case of external aggression or internal rebellion. This explains the military assistance that France continued to provide the Biya regime despite the horrendous crimes against humanity committed by the Israeli-trained and equipped *Bataillon d'Intervention Rapide* (BIR), the Cameroon army, gendarmerie and police in the English-speaking Northwest and Southwest of Cameroon. Furthermore, the French ambassador was guaranteed to be the dean of the diplomatic corps in Yaoundé. Indeed, a former French ambassador, Yvon Omnes became a special adviser to President Biya at the end of his diplomatic career (with the approval of the French government of course).

French Postcolonial Cultural Policy: Extending the French Exception to Francophone Africa

The pre-independence, bilateral agreements that the government of President Charles de Gaulle signed with the emerging, French-speaking African countries was a new development in relations between the colonial power and its soon-to-be independent postcolonies. These agreements, which were presented to the emerging French-speaking African countries, were clearly "negotiated" and signed in situations of unequal power dynamics between the colonizer and the colonized. The pre-independence agreements between Cameroon and France were patterned after exclusive colonial protectorate agreements that the European colonial powers signed with African chiefs and chieftains in the 19th Century. These colonial agreements generally specified that the colonial power offering the agreement: Great Britain, France, Germany, Portugal, and Spain, undertook to extend its protection to specific, mostly coastal tribal chiefs, who in turn agreed and promised, inter alia, to refrain from entering into any agreements or treaties with any other foreign nations or Powers without the prior approval of the protecting colonial government (ICJ, 2002). The end result was, as Jean-Paul Sartre put it, "the new State, in spite of its formal sovereignty, remains in the hands of the imperialists" (p. 10). However, the Cold War context made these agreements different from the pre-colonial agreements signed during the 19th-century European partition of Africa. The postcolonial agreements were designed to keep French-speaking African countries within the ambit of the French geo-strategic, politico-cultural sphere of influence during the East-West Cold War.

These agreements were not so much a change from the assimilationist, colonial-era *mission civilisatrice* of France (Betts, 1961), as a transition to a new dispensation, a French postcolonial *mission de stabulation culturelle permanente* (mission of cultural zero-grazing). This was a postcolonial *mission rassemblementatrice*, the corralling of French-speaking (Francophone) African "postcolonies" (Mbembe, 2001) into a French political, economic and cultural *chasse gardée* (exclusive hunting preserve). The fundamental ideological premise of this postcolonial ideology was furtherance of the Gaullist *rayonnement culturelle* (French cultural radiance and influence). This was the deterritorialization of the French exception, the declaration of French politico-cultural difference, which President Charles de Gaulle (1954: 1) defined as: "*une certaine idée de la France ou elle n'est réellement elle-même que quand elle est au premier rang*" (a certain idea of France whereby she is her real self only when she is at the forefront). The French cultural exception was thus an ideological declaration of Gallic linguistic and cultural specificity and difference in response to perceptions of rising global "Anglo-Saxon" (read Anglo-American) cultural globalization and homogenization. The French exception is the ancient worldview under which France emphasizes the uniqueness and specificity of its language, culture, and civilization, in opposition to other languages and cultures (Godin and Chafer 2005; Rosanvallon 2004).

In the eighteenth century, Alexis de Tocqueville (1843) situated the French exception, the '*specificité française*' (French specificity), in a historical continuum traceable to the *ancien régime* that was overthrown by the Revolution of 1789 (Rosanvallon 2004: p. 109). The French exception and its corollary, *l'exception culturelle francaise* (the French cultural exception) are synonymous defensive mechanisms erected against perceived cultural threats from globalized American "fast culture," (identical to unhealthy fast food) disseminated by the mass media, cinematic entertainment, global information and communication technology corporations, their digital and linguistic capitalism, free enterprise religion, and excessive electronic commerce (Kuisel 1993). The French exception is thus an official, nationalistic ideology that promotes the *rayonance* (the spreading abroad) of French culture, while protecting it at home from perceived threats posed by the "Anglo-Saxon" (Anglo-American) media and popular culture.

The Cultural Provisions of the Franco-African Cooperation Agreements: *La Francophonie*

The most prominent provision of the postcolonial bilateral agreements signed between France and the newly independent French-speaking countries of Africa was the cultural provision that the government of President Charles de Gaulle required each country to agree to in a context of flux and unequal power dynamics. On March 20, 1970, the French government, led by President Georges Pompidou created a French-led organization of French-speaking African Countries, *l'Agence Culturelle et Technique* (the Cultural and Technical Agency, popularly known by the French acronym, ACCT), at Niamey, in Niger. The aim of ACCT was to promote French language and culture in Africa. That French agency was renamed *l'Organisation Internationale de la Francophonie* (The International Organization of French-speaking Countries, with the French acronym, OIF) or *la Francophonie*, for short. The French-speaking countries that are members of *la Francophonie* launched a *Journée internationale de la Francophonie* (an international French cultural day) celebrated in March each year.

In 1974, Marie-Elisabeth Cousin carried out a textual, thematic, and grammatical analysis of these pre-independence *accords de coopération* that France signed with the colonial territories to which it was granting independence. The main template of the agreements was identical for all countries. However, it was slightly modified to suit the political and cultural specificities of each country (*Débats Parlementaires*, 1960). Cousin (1974) found that the vocabulary and grammatical constructions of the agreements generally framed postcolonial Franco-African relationships in Gallic, identitarian, moral-philosophical, and metaphysical terms. In these agreements, the French language and culture were framed in religious, evangelical terms. Indeed, the French language was framed as a "sacred," consecrated vessel through which the sacred culture of France had been revealed to Africans. Now that French-speaking Africans had been assimilated into the sacred *fraternité* (brotherhood and fellowship) of *la Francophonie*, the gospel of the French language and culture had to be preached to the succeeding generations of Africans in the French post-colonies. Education was the designated quasi-religious field in which the diffusion of the gospel of French culture was to take place. By signing these agreements, French-speaking

African countries agreed that when they attained independence, France would guide and shape their educational systems to ensure that they would have "*l'enseignement de caractère français ou d'inspiration française*" (French-style or French-inspired educational systems) (Débats Parlementaires, 1960; Cousin, 1974). The French language was also presented as the historic instruments of economic, cultural, social, and human development that needed to be localized and made the medium of instruction of specific national educational and cultural systems. This intellectual and cultural zero-grazing (*l'elevage culturelle à l'enclos*), which was adapted to suit diverse African realities, became the French and Francophone idea of cultural diversity vis-à-vis the so-called Anglo-Saxon countries. The former French African countries agreed to make the French language tower above their multicultural specificities:

> La langue française, moyen d'étude et d'expression, ne peut servir au développement africain que si elle s'apprend et se parle en dehors de toute référence à la civilisation de l'ancienne métropole (Cousin, 1974, p. 328).

> The French language, the medium of education and expression, can only serve African development if it is studied and spoken outside all references to the civilization of the former colonial power [France].

The idea was that postcolonial French-speaking African countries would use the French language as their instrument of political, administrative and cultural expression, as well as the medium of education in their postcolonial regimes. *La Francophonie*, an imagined, international, community of French-speaking peoples grounded in colonial linguistic and cultural continuities, became the visible and audible embodiment of this new type of post-colonial identitarian reality. The agreements essentially meant that each French-speaking African country was linked to France by special cultural and civilizational bonds, "*des liens particuliers qui unissent librement leurs deux nations*" (special links that freely united their two nations) (Cousin, 1974, p. 328). The pre-independence agreements thus framed *la Francophonie* as an interlinked metaphysical, identitarian, "imagined community," to borrow the expression of Benedict Anderson (1983), whose main contextual parameter was the specificity of the exceptional French language and culture, which African countries had been bequeathed by French colonialism and had in common. The texts of the pre-independence *accords de coopération* framed *la Francophonie* as an exceptional, trans-national, quasi-religious, moral, spiritual "space," a cultural imaginary—albeit one grounded in unequal power dynamics—whose "contextual matrixes," to borrow the expression of Pierre Legrand (2003) is the French language and culture. These agreements essentially transformed the idea of *la Francophonie*, which had been advanced in the 19th century by French intellectuals, into international cultural law. Indeed, former Senegalese president, Leopold Sédar Senghor, an eminent Francophone and "Negro-African" poet and cultural theorist, who also happened to be the first person of African descent to be admitted into the hallowed assembly of the sainted "immortals" of the venerable *Académie Française*, defined *la Francophonie* in religious and identitarian terms:

"La Francophonie se présente comme la communauté spirituelle des nations qui emploient le français, soit comme langue nationale, soit comme langue officielle, soit comme langue d'usage" (cited in Cousin,1974, p. 327).

La Francophonie presents itself as the spiritual community of nations which use the French language, either as the national language, the official language or the common language.

The French language and culture were thus deployed as the instruments, par excellence, for projecting and propagating French geo-strategic, economic, and political interests and objectives in Africa (Mpegna, 2016). The *Organisation Internationale de la Francophonie* (OIF) is thus a postcolonial, hegemonic, linguistic and cultural organization that is grounded on the supremacy and preeminence of the French language and culture in particular, and Western civilization in general, of which France is an exemplary palimpsest. However, the OIF sees itself differently. It states that its major role is:

…d'accompagner ses États membres face aux défis multiformes auxquels ils sont confrontés. Aujourd'hui, c'est une Organisation en pleine capacité, qui entend apporter sa contribution au développement et à l'épanouissement des peuples dans l'espace francophone en particulier et dans le monde en général. Dans sa volonté d'accompagner les États, elle les assiste dans le renforcement de la démocratie et la consolidation de l'État de droit, la lutte contre le terrorisme et l'extrémisme violent… (Francis, 2021).

to assist member states confront the multiple challenges they face. Today it is a full capacity organization, which hopes to contribute to the development and growth of peoples in the Francophone space in particular and in the world in general. In its wish to assist states, it assists them in the reinforcement of democracy and consolidation of the rule of law, the struggle against terrorism and violent extremism…

France is a composite, nay, a palimpsest of Gallo-Roman, Frankish (German), Celtic, Norman, and other European cultures and influences. Interestingly, *La Francophonie* has no formal cultural institutions dedicated to the study of African languages and cultures.

Muting the Federal Republic of Cameroon and Transforming Anglophone Cameroon into a Theatre of French Cultural Assimilation

As the newly independent *République du Cameroun* maneuvered, with Machiavellian dexterity, to integrate the United Nations Trust Territory of British Southern Cameroons into its national territory after the UN-supervised Plebiscite of 1961, it partnered with its former colonial power, France, in the process. For France, this was a geo-strategic opportunity to extend the geographic and economic frontiers of its sphere of influence in Francophone Africa because its postcolony, *La Republique du Cameroun*, would be bringing a former British territory into *la Francophonie*. The governments of President Charles de Gaulle and George Pompidou therefore provided President Ahmadou Ahidjo legal advisers who assisted with drafting a rather centralized, "French accented" federal constitution for Cameroon that was presented to Hon. John Ngu Foncha, Prime Minister of Southern Cameroons, on the eve of reunification talks in Foumban in 1961. Even though this proposed federal constitution was designed for an emerging multicultural country that had both French and British colonial traditions—in addition to its African cultures and traditional systems of governance, the document had a very strong centralist, Gallic/Napoleonic imprint. Indeed, the French Constitution of 1958, with its highly centralized system of government and its vague separation of powers, served as the rough template for the Cameroon federal constitution of 1961. Article I of the French Constitution of 1958 provides that: "*La France est une République indivisible, laïque, démocratique et sociale* (France is an indivisible, secular, democratic and social Republic). For its part, Article I of the 1961 Constitution of the Federal Republic of Cameroon provided that: "*La République Fédérale du Cameroun est démocratique, laïque et sociale*" (The Federal Republic of Cameroon is democratic, secular and social).

This article was a verbatim transposition of the monocultural French Revolutionary dogma of unitary secular republicanism to the multicultural context of the emerging Cameroon, which had African, German, French, and British political and cultural legacies. The French-style, secular republican provisions of the Federal Constitution of Cameroon made Cameroon a centralist, pseudo-federation. This constitution essentially sowed the seeds of the Anglophone Revolt because it represented an imposition on the fledgling Federal Republic of Cameroon, of the legacy of the French Revolution of 1789—a highly centralized French secular republican governmentality (Foucault, 1991), and French counter-establishmentality—a militant, anti-religious, anti-clerical worldview, mindset, and intellectual orientation. This counter-establishmentality is highly hostile towards the normative, spiritual, and public aspects of religion, and especially its role and place in the life of the state, and in the public sphere (Eko, 2012). It is the opposite of the faith-based secular parliamentarian system that existed in Southern Cameroons.

The Constitution of the Federal Republic of Cameroon, drafted by French constitutional lawyers, created what Anyangwe (2008) calls a system of "unitary federalism." This template and roadmap guided President Ahmadou Ahidjo as he progressively moved towards asphyxiating Southern Cameroons and assimilating its English and Pidgin-speaking population into *la Francophonie*. That federal constitution made a couple of concessions to the minority English speakers. It recognized both English and French as official languages of the federal republic and allowed Southern Cameroons to have its own government and prime minister. Nevertheless, the Ahidjo regime removed a Prime Minister, Augustine Ngom Jua, whom the president could not manipulate, and replaced him with Solomon Tandeng Muna, a highly maleable politician he could control. Nevertheless, the working language of the Cameroon government and East Cameroon was French. The rest of the provisions of the constitution indirectly put its imprimatur on the *accords de coopération* between *la République du Cameroun* and France in terms of national institutions, and in the domains of administration, monetary policy, the armed forces, culture and the media, secondary and higher education, as well as social policy. Though President Ahmadou Ahidjo often presented Canada as a successful model of English/French bilingualism, and biculturalism, Southern Cameroons (renamed West Cameroon in the Constitution), did not have anything near the political, economic, and linguistic autonomy of the province of Quebec with its minority French-speaking population. Ultimately, through political subterfuge, in 1972, President Ahmadou Ahidjo orchestrated a referendum in the country. This resulted in the abolition of the Federal Republic of Cameroon, along with the autonomous federal state and government of West Cameroon. The country became the United Republic of Cameroon.

The French Posture Towards the State of Southern Cameroons After Reunification

At the end of World War II, France was one of the victorious allies that formed the North Atlantic Treaty Organization (NATO). For France, the Allied defeat of Nazi Germany was a pyrrhic victory at best. French-speaking Africa provided it the best avenue to reassert its status as a global power. This was the geo-strategic context of the bilateral pre-independence cooperation agreements that France entered into with its former colonial territories. These agreements cemented French hegemony in French-speaking Africa, and gave France political, economic, cultural and diplomatic gravitas—a reliable voting block—on the world stage, and especially in the United Nations and its specialized agencies. As the Western powers—Britain, France, Portugal, and Spain—were obliged to decolonize their African territories, it was in the best interest of France to transition its colonial African empire to a postcolonial sphere of influence, *la Francophonie*.

The reunification of United Nations Trust Territories of French East Cameroon (*La République du Cameroun*) and the smaller British Southern Cameroons provided France an opportunity to extend *la Francophonie*, French hegemony into a former British colonial territory in Africa. French diplomats in Cameroon thus closely watched and actively participated in the reunification of Cameroon and the evolution of the newly independent *La République du Cameroun* to the Federal Republic of Cameroon (1961-1972). Under their watchful eye, and with their active participation, President Ahmadou Ahidjo embarked on the constitutionally questionable abrogation of the Federal Republic of Cameroon, and its transformation into a centralized, authoritarian, one-party *chefferie republicaine* (republican chiefery), the United Republic of Cameroon (1972-1983). This change took place after Total, a French multinational oil company that had been operating in French Cameroon since 1947, discovered oil and natural gas reserves in the waters off the territory of Southern Cameroons—and kept it a secret from the Prime Ministers of West Cameroon, Augustine Ngom Jua, John Ngu Foncha and Solomon Tandeng Muna. The French government was also a party to President Paul Biya's highly controversial transformation of the United Republic of Cameroon back to the original name of the French Cameroon, *la République du Cameroun*, further entrenched a highly centralized, authoritarian, one-party, kleptocratic, tribalistic, Napoleonic, *chefferie républicaine*. The renaming of the country as *la République du Cameroun*, signified the total assimilation of English-speaking Southern Cameroons into French postcolonial hegemony, *la Francophonie*, and symbolically erasing its political and cultural identity. The constitutions of the United Republic of Cameroon and the Republic of Cameroon all bear the hallmarks of French secular republicanism. They all repeat in slightly modified form, Article I of the French constitution: *La France est une République indivisible, laïque, démocratique et sociale* (France is an indivisible, secular, democratic and social Republic). For their part, Article I of the 1961, 1972, and 1996 Constitutions of Cameroon provide that: "*La République Fédérale du Cameroun, la République Unie du Cameroun, La République du Cameroun est démocratique, laïque et sociale*." This Machiavellian political "apemanship" peaked when the Anglophone Revolt began in 2016. Instead of engaging in a frank and sincere dialogue to resolve the root causes of the Anglophone problem, the Biya regime opted to use military means to solve the political problem. When he decided to subjugate the rebellious English speakers, he added the indivisibility provision of the French Constitution to governmental declarations: *Le Cameroun est un et indivisible* (Cameroon is one and indivisible).

French Ambassadors and the Cultural Assimilation of Anglophones (1962-2017)

French Ambassadors in Yaoundé, and the former French Consulate in Buea, the capital of West Cameroon observed these developments keenly, with a view to expanding the frontiers of French "civilization" in Africa—spreading the French language and culture among the English-speaking minority of Southern Cameroons, and safeguarding French economic interests in the oil, natural gas, timber and other natural resources in Southern Cameroons. Immediately after reunification of *la République du Cameroun* and English-speaking West Cameroon, France opened the first diplomatic mission, the French Consulate in Buea, capital of West Cameroon. Barely three months after the reunification, the French Ambassador in Yaoundé, Jean-Pierre Benard, who was considered the "real president" of Cameroon because of his pervasive influence over President Ahidjo and all aspects of the government of the newly independent and reunified Federal Republic of Cameroon (Deltombe et al., 2019), wrote a confidential letter to Yves Robin, the French Consul in Buea, giving him instructions and the terms of reference of his assignment.

In his Confidential letter No. 27 of 8 January 1962, copies of which were sent to the French Secretary of State for African Affairs, the Directorate of African and Malagasy Affairs, in the French Ministry of External Affairs, the Ministry of Cooperation, the French Embassy in London, the Trade Representative, and the Liaison on Foreign aid and Cooperation, Ambassador Jean-Pierre Benard (1962) wrote the following instructions to French Consul, Yves Robin in Buea:

> The mission to which you have been assigned in West Cameroon is essentially political in nature. You are called upon to carry out your functions in a territory that was for 40 years under British administration before rejoining in the framework of a federation, *la République du Cameroun* which during the same period was under French tutelage.

The Ambassador attributed the success of the reunification vote to nationalistic sentiments on the part of Southern Cameroonians. He noted that the decision of the inhabitants of Southern Cameroons to vote for reunification with *la République du Cameroun* on 11 February 1961 represented a true desire of Southern Cameroonians to destroy the artificial borders erected by European colonial powers, France and Britain after World War I, and to restore true political unity based on ethnic, geographic and economic realities and similarities between the peoples of both States. Nevertheless, the ambassador warned his consul in Buea that for half a century, the two states had evolved under profoundly different colonial administrative systems, economic approaches, and human resource training. He noted that these administrative differences posed a serious challenge to the desire for unity between both States of Cameroon. Benard (1962) proceeded to caution the consul what to expect in Buea:

> You will quickly have the occasion to discover that after crossing the Mungo [the border between English and French-speaking Cameroon] that for the moment the dissimilarities between the two parts of the Federal Republic of Cameroon are more numerous than the similarities. Such a situation is likely to create serious difficulties for the [federal] Cameroonian government, either it threatens national unity in case of a crisis, or it hampers the daily work of administration.

The general tone of Ambassador Benard's confidential instructions to his consul in Buea was one of strategic recapture. It gave the impression that *la République du Cameroun* had recaptured West Cameroon, a part of its territory that had been sliced off by unnamed European colonialists and evolved under the British colonial administration for close to half a century. The French government, therefore, had the task of aiding the French-style unitary federalist government of Cameroon in reabsorbing and assimilating West Cameroon into the fold of *La Francophonie*, where it rightfully belonged. After these preliminary words of caution about the enormity of the task ahead of the consul, France and the fledgling Francophone-dominated Federal Republic of Cameroon, the ambassador assured his consul that the government had resolved, while "respecting the personality of the State of West Cameroon," to undertake major initiatives to unify the two parts of the country in a number of crucial areas. The Ambassador then proceeded to spell out the policy, a virtual road map of French policy and actions in the Federated State of West Cameroon. It was essentially an assimilationist mission, an extension of the French colonial *mission civilisatrice* to the West Cameroon. The goal of France was to assimilate the English-speaking State of West Cameroon into the French sphere of influence, *la Francophonie*, and ultimately transform English-speaking West Cameroonians into speakers of the French language. Ambassador Benard (1962) favorably compared French-speaking East Cameroun and English-speaking West Cameroon. He believed that since West Cameroon was the less developed of the two states in the federation, the bigger, richer, French Cameroon would ultimately assimilate the smaller, less developed "former British zone":

> ...*Étant donné l'importance relative du Cameroun Oriental par rapport au Cameroun Occidental, la différence du chiffre de population, de richesses, de*

degré d'évolution des habitants, il est évident que cette politique d'unification aboutira en définitive et dans la plupart des cas à implanter au Cameroun occidental la langue, les méthodes administratives, les structures économiques de l'ancienne République du Cameroun.

Given the relative size of East Cameroon compared to West Cameroon, differences in the size of their populations, of wealth, the degree of cultivation (civilization) of its inhabitants, it is evident that this policy of unification will eventually lead in most cases, to the implantation in West Cameroon, of the language, the administrative methods, and the economic structures of the former [French] *République du Cameroun.*

Ambassador Benard stated that the French government would be willing to assist the assimilationist goals, objectives and policies of the French Cameroon government as it set out to diffuse French culture and civilization to the territory of West Cameroon. "We cannot ignore the will of the Cameroon government to enable the former British zone to benefit from the achievements of 40 years of French administration. We must on the contrary, help it and give it our entire support. It is in this perspective that your actions must be oriented" (Benard, 1962). The irony is that in less than ten years, the French oil company, Total, would discover large deposits of oil and natural gas in the territory of West Cameroon. This and other considerations accelerated the evisceration of the autonomy and the cultural specificity of Southern Cameroons.

The French Ambassador's Confidential Letter No. 27 of January 1962 was a clear roadmap for the extension of the French colonial *mission civilisatrice* to English-speaking West Cameroon, which the French considered rather backward and uncivilized. It was, above all, a roadmap for Ahidjo's nullification of the political autonomy of West Cameroon. Interestingly, the various permutations and nomenclature of the nation of Cameroon were arrived at without the consent of the people of Southern Cameroons. Presidents Ahmadou Ahidjo and his selected Prime Minister and successor, Paul Biya, changed the independent French *La République du Cameroun* to the bilingual Federal Republic of Cameroon (where Southern Cameroons was renamed West Cameroon), to the centralized United Republic of Cameroon that merged the governments and civil services of Southern Cameroons with the Napoleonic administration of *la République du Cameroun.* They also masterminded the divide and conquer strategic move of splitting West Cameroon into two separate Northwest and Southwest regions via presidential decree, and the ultimate renaming of Cameroon, *la République du Cameroon* (the Republic of Cameroon), via another presidential decree. The French Ambassador's 1962 confidential letter suggests that all these nomenclatural gymnastics and gyrations were grounded in an existential, fear of disunity, and emergence of crises between the two States that could lead to a dissolution of the union. The French and French Cameroon solution to this fear was the dissolution of the political autonomy, erasure and muting of the cultural identity, and specificity of Southern Cameroons in the Francophone Cameroon nation and ultimately *la Francophonie.* This was the political and cultural equivalent of a suffocating python's hug. In hindsight, the Ahidjo/Biya regime followed this French roadmap to the letter!

Figure 4.4. French Ambassador to Cameroon, Bruno Gain with Fon of Bafut before the Anglophone Crisis (2015).

French and French Cameroon "Muting" of the Federal State of West Cameroon

The French Ambassador also instructed the Consul in Buea that he had the delicate task of informing, educating and "sensitizing" the government of West Cameroon about the marvels, and positive advantages of the civilizational activities of France in Africa in order to "soften" it and prepare it for assimilation into the *Francophonie*. The assumption was that West Cameroon was a cultural *tabula rasa*, a blank slate to be assimilated and filled with French culture. Ambassador Benard instructed Consul Yves Robin that his relations with the West Cameroon had to be inspired by the following considerations:

> The government of West Cameroon has up till today, known little in fact, of the policies followed by France in its former Overseas territories, and the achievements that have taken place in these territories. It would thus be necessary that in your contacts with it (the government) you inform it exactly how the African territories that were under French sovereignty were led to independence, the considerable efforts that have been made to endow them with economic and social infrastructures, as well as to promote their development. You are to indicate to them the sizeable amount and the modalities of the aid France continues to provide them. You will not fail to correct prejudices that your interlocutors could have in this regard.

The ambassador stated that even though the government in Buea did not have competence in international affairs, the Prime Minister, John Ngu Foncha, as Vice President of the Federal Republic of Cameroun could be called upon to influence the foreign policy of Cameroon. It was, therefore, necessary for the consul to keep him informed of the position of France on the different world problems that particularly concerned it. Ambassador Benard (1962) then turned to France's greatest fear, difficulties and tensions between Southern Cameroons and the "Central Government" in Yaoundé over the interpretation of the Constitution and understandings over the nature of the federation:

> *Des difficultés ne manqueront sans doute pas de surgir entre le Gouvernement Central et celui de BUEA sur l'interprétation de la Constitution et l'étendue des pouvoirs laissés aux autorités locales.* **La réunification s'est faite sur une** équivoque. **Yaoundé considérant que la Fédération ne constituait qu'une phase transitoire, alors qu'Outre-Mungo, l'on voyait dans la réunification la consolidation d'une très large autonomie à** l'égard **de toute métropole européenne ou africaine** (Benard, 1962, emphasis added).

> Difficulties will without doubt not fail to arise between the Central Government and that of BUEA on the interpretation of the Constitution and the extent of power left to local authorities. **The reunification took place under an equivocation[1] Yaoundé considering that the Federation was only a transitory phase, while across the Mungo, the reunification was seen as the consolidation of a very broad autonomy from all European** [read French] **and African metropolises.**

This paragraph is very revelatory because it describes the state of mind of President Ahidjo, President Paul Biya, and their French overseers with respect to the deliberate ambiguity of the unitary federalism that France designed for Cameroon, as well as the hidden assimilationist agenda behind the ambiguous federal experiment—it was programmed to fail. The French government saw the federation as nothing more than a transitory phase in the evolution of Cameroon towards a centralized Napoleonic, French-speaking country within *la Francophonie*. Federalism is an alien concept in France. There are no federal French-speaking countries in Africa. The federal experiment in Cameroon was not designed to be sustainable in the long term, like the union between Tanganyika and Zanzibar that made up Tanzania. The policies and actions that Presidents Ahmadou Ahidjo and Paul Biya took to eviscerate the autonomy of Southern Cameroons and destroy the federation demonstrated that they, along with their French postcolonial partners, considered the federation transitory at best. This was a deceptive gambit. Ahidjo and Foncha never discussed or agreed on the nature of the federation, and there was no formal union treaty between *la République du Cameroun* and Southern Cameroons. It was "understood" by the "parties" (Ahidjo and Foncha), but never put down in writing, that the Federal Republic of Cameroon would steer clear of both *la Francophonie* and the British Commonwealth, the

---

1 The use of ambiguous language to conceal the truth or to avoid committing one's self; prevarication. Oxford Living Dictionaries, https://en.oxforddictionaries.com/definition/equivocation

Franco-Cameroun *accords de coopération* notwithstanding. It is unclear whether Foncha was even aware of those agreements between France and *la République du Cameroun*.

The dictatorial actions of Ahidjo and Biya that led to muting of English-speaking Cameroon include elimination of the federation—and Anglophone autonomy—and the division of Southern Cameroons into two provinces, the Northwest and Southwest. This political and cultural muting conformed to the French perspective on the reunification, as expressed by Ambassador Benard in his Confidential letter No. 27 of 8 January 1962. There were four milestones in the muting and assimilation of English-speaking Southern Cameroons into French Cameroon and *la Francophonie*. These were characterized by nomenclatural permutations of the nation of Cameroon that were decreed and imposed by Yaoundé without the consent of the people of Southern Cameroons: 1) President Ahmadou Ahidjo and his French overseers changed the independent French *la République du Cameroun* to the ambiguous, bilingual, centralist Federal Republic of Cameroon to accommodate English-speaking Southern Cameroonians—Southern Cameroons was renamed West Cameroon in the process, 2), Ahidjo imposed an unconstitutional referendum on May 20, 1972 that changed the form of the country from a federal republic to a centralized, authoritarian Napoleonic state, the United Republic of Cameroon, that engulfed the government and civil service of Southern Cameroons, 3) application of a divide and conquer strategy by splitting West Cameroon into two separate provinces, the Northwest and Southwest, via a presidential decree, and 4) Ahmadou Ahidjo's successor, President Paul Biya's renaming of the whole country, *la République du Cameroun* (the Republic of Cameroon), the original name of French Cameroun via a presidential decree. The French ambassador's 1962 confidential letter suggests that all these nomenclatural gymnastics and gyrations were grounded in an existential fear of a dissolution of the union. The French and French Cameroon solution to this fear was erasure of the political autonomy, cultural identity and specificity of Southern Cameroons.

However, Ambassador Benard foresaw some transitional problems regarding British expatriates who worked in Southern Cameroons under the British colonial administration. The impression was that these British citizens would be phased out and French expatriates faced in.

> *Bien que des nombreux agents britanniques soient encore restés en fonction au titre de l'assistance technique, il n'apparait pas que le Gouvernement de Londres envisage de faire un effort important pour maintenir dans l'État du Cameroun Occidental son influence. Les fonctionnaires qui y servent actuellement le font à titre individuel. Il est explicable que certains d'entre eux éprouvent de l'amertume à se voir éliminer progressivement par des Camerounais de formation française. Dans vos rapports avec les éléments britanniques vous voudrez bien éviter tout propos ou toute position qui pourrait laisser croire que nous considérons que le referendum du 11 Février a constitué une victoire de la France sur la Grande Bretagne, ni que nous poussons le Gouvernement de Yaoundé à effacer toutes les marques de*

l'influence britannique...

Though numerous British civil servants are still working [in West Cameroon] in the context of British technical assistance, it does not seem that the Government of London plans to make an important effort to maintain its influence in the state of West Cameroon. The functionaries that serve there do so on an individual basis. It is understandable that some of them feel bitter that they are being progressively eliminated by French-trained Cameroonians. In your relations with British citizens, do well to avoid all expressions and all views that could leave the impression that we consider the referendum of 11 February a victory of France over Great Britain, or that we are pushing the Government of Yaoundé to erase all traces of British influence.

The impression was that the civilized, French and French-trained, French-speaking Cameroonians from East Cameroon would progressively replace British expatriates in West Cameroon in place of the unsophisticated Anglophones. There was no place for muted English-speaking Cameroonians in West Cameroon, except of course those who assimilated into *la Francophonie* and were trained in France. The post-independence transition also involved the private sector. British businessmen and trading companies like John Holt, and especially shipping company Elders and Fyffes (E&F) Ndongo, near Tiko, were essentially put out of business. E & F, which was famous for its banana boats which maintained regular services that ferried bananas, mail, and first-class passengers between Southern Cameroons and the United Kingdom, were caught in the crossfire of the reunification, and the transition from the British pound as the legal tender in Southern Cameroons to the franc CFA. Many of these companies abandoned or sold their properties at fire sale rates and left the territory, spelling the doom of the banana trade on which native farmers on the coast relied for income.

Finally, since West Cameroon had political autonomy, the ambassador was concerned with keeping other countries, particularly the United States and Nigeria out of Southern Cameroons as the territory was progressively assimilated into *la Francophonie*. The fear was that the United States would control the educational system of West Cameroon, and use it to perpetuate the English language, to the detriment of the French Cameroun assimilationist project. Ambassador Benard wrote:

Other countries can also have a special interest in the State of West Cameroon. The United States, which up to the present has not had much success in its efforts to ensure a certain "credit" with the Government of Yaoundé, could be tempted to interest itself particularly in West Cameroon, where use of the English language could facilitate the implantation of their influence. The US could supply them technical assistance personnel, finance economic infrastructure projects and take charge of certain sectors of education there.

136

The French had concluded that the British had no interest in maintaining the cultural specificity of Southern Cameroons. The territory thus became the subject of French political and cultural assimilation. As a result, the French ambassador told the French Consul in Buea, Monsieur Robin, that France was emphatically opposed to all attempts by English-speaking countries, particularly Nigeria and the United States, to maintain the identitarian and cultural particularity of the former British Southern Cameroons. He therefore instructed the Consul as follows:

> *Il conviendrait que vous suiviez attentivement toutes les tentatives faites en ce sens, qui tendraient ainsi à perpétrer le particularisme de l'ancienne zone britannique, et que vous m'en teniez régulièrement informé (Benard, 1962).*

> It is necessary that you attentively follow all attempts made [by the United States and Nigeria] in this sense, which would tend to perpetuate the particularity of the former British zone, and that you keep me regularly informed about it (emphasis added).

This French policy perspective explains the concerted efforts made by the Francophone-led government of Cameroon to isolate English-speaking Southern Cameroons internationally and diplomatically and mute it culturally in order to facilitate its assimilation into the French sphere of influence. The British, American, German, Swiss, and other Consular representations were withdrawn from Buea, the capital of Southern Cameroons and moved to either Yaoundé or Douala. At the diplomatic level, an English-speaking Cameroonian has never been a Cameroon Ambassador to the United Nations, the United States or France. It also explains, as we see in Chapter 8, the concerted efforts of France in multiple domains to spread its culture to the English-speaking Southern Cameroons through the educational system and the cultural activities of French cultural centers in Buea, Limbe, Bamenda, and other parts of Southern Cameroons. It also explains the concerted efforts of the French-dominated government of Cameroon to "harmonize" (read disperse) the cultural bulwarks of English-speaking Southern Cameroons—the English-medium educational system, and the common law legal system—into the Napoleonic Francophone "national" reality. As we see in Chapter 8, a concerted attempt was made to eliminate the specificity of the General Certificate of Education, the principal exam taken by high school and post-secondary students in the English-speaking Southern Cameroons. The Ministry of Education led a concerted effort to transform that examination into a French-style baccalauréat. This became a bone of contention that was only resolved with the creation of an independent GCE Board in Buea. Indeed, attempts to water down and dissolve these two cultural bulwarks ultimately led to the Anglophone Revolt of 2016. The third Anglophone identitarian bulwark, the informal Pidgin English lingua franca, sustained the Anglophone Revolt.

Interestingly, the French and their French Cameroon partners completely ignored the linguistic and cultural legacy of Southern Cameroons in their heady rush to assimilate the territory. As a result of slavery and the slave trade on the West African coast from the

16th to the 19th Century, places like Bimbia became slave ports where contact between Portuguese, Spanish, English, French, Dutch, and other European slave traders and their Arabic and African suppliers led to the emergence of a West African lingua franca, English-based Pidgin or Creole (Krio). This is a trade language that is a mixture of African and European languages. Southern Cameroons was the Easternmost linguistic frontier of Pidgin English or Krio.

As early as 1792, Freetown, Sierra Leona was founded by abolitionists to settle poor blacks from London, England, freed slaves from North America (US & Canada) and the Caribbean. After the abolition of slavery, the British Royal Navy's West Africa Squadron, which was charged with enforcing the ban on the slave trade, intercepted slave trading ships and brought most of the slaves to Freetown, Sierra Leone, where they were freed. The population thus included descendants of many different peoples from all over the West coast of Africa. It was the perfect setting for the emergence of Creole or Pidgin English. With the movement of people, soldiers and workers under the British Empire, Pidgin English became the most widely-spoken lingua franca in the British colonial territories of West Africa—though it has no official status in any of the British territories, including Southern Cameroons, which had become a British League of Nations Mandate under the Treaty of Versailles of 1919.

Progress Report from Buea: The French Consul's Assimilationist Initiatives

Five years after the reunification of East and West Cameroon, the French Consul in Buea, Monsieur Michel Moreux, did a stock-taking of French initiatives in pursuance of the political and cultural objectives assigned him by the French diplomatic mission in the Federal Republic of Cameroon, to mute and assimilate the English-speaking former British Southern Cameroons into French Cameroun and *la Francophonie*. In his Confidential Report of 22 August 1967, Mr. Moreux wrote to the *Chargé d'Affaires* at the French Embassy in Yaoundé that five years after the reunification of Cameroon, the assimilation of Southern Cameroons into *la Francophonie* was not going as quickly or as easily as the French government had hoped in 1962. Moreux (1967) reported that:

> *Le Cameroun Occidental est encore un État Anglophone et la francophonie,*
> *emploi général et usuel de la langue française n'est pas à la veille de s'imposer.*
> *Il faudra une génération pour parvenir au bilinguisme et plusieurs décades*
> *seront probablement nécessaires pour généraliser l'usage de notre langue, la*
> *rendre "usuelle" dans la masse occidentale.*

> West Cameroon is still an English-speaking State and *Francophonie*, the generalized and common use of French is not on the verge of imposing itself. It will take a generation to arrive at bilingualism and several decades shall probably be necessary to generalize the use of our language [French], render it common usage among the West Cameroon masses.

The Consul then presented what he considered to be the obstacles to *"l'installation du*

138

français dans cet Etat." (Installation of French as the primary language in this state). By that, he meant the general adaptation of the French language and culture in English-speaking West Cameroon. In other words, the installation of the French language meant the muting of English and transformation of French into the *lingua franca* of English-speaking Cameroon. He stated that at the time of the reunification of the two federated States of Cameroon, the presence of many Englishmen in West Cameroon, and the "habits" adopted by English-speaking Cameroonians during their 40 years of British colonial tutelage gave France little chance of penetrating "this British fief" as quickly as the French had hoped (Moreux, 1967). Monsieur Moreux ignored the fact that West Cameroon was the successor state of Southern Cameroons, a territory that included Bimbia and Ambas Bay regions (from present-day Limbe to Bota). This region had, at the time of reunification, a centuries-old history of English and Pidgin English (Creole) language contact and culture. It was the height of political and cultural hubris for the French government to expect to mute these centuries-long Anglophone histories and cultural vestiges and replace them overnight with the supposedly superior French language and culture.

These realities did not prevent the French government and its diplomats in Yaoundé and Buea from redoubling their assimilationist efforts in Southern Cameroons. To move the assimilationist agenda forward, Mr. Moreux gave his nod to a Cameroon Federal Government policy of *"intrusions du français"* (intrusion of French) into English-speaking West Cameroon through posting of high-level French-speaking federal officials to Buea. The aim of these postings was to assert control over the territory, and make the Federal offices circles of French language, cultural expression and promotion. More than that, from 1962, France sent a good number of French teachers to West Cameroon under provisions of the pre-independence bilateral *accords de cooperation* signed between *la République du Cameroun* and France in 1959. The French Consul stated that the cultural assimilationist activities of Francophone government officials posted to Southern Cameroons included: *"les efforts des professeurs enseignant au Centre Linguistique et sur les ondes de Radio Buea promet d'être efficace"* (Moreux, 1967).

This was a reference to the French government's creation of a "Linguistic Center" in Buea to teach West Cameroon civil servants French, as well as a radio program called *Français par la Radio* (French by Radio). This was an interactive French language distance education program for the major primary schools in the English-speaking State of West Cameroon. The consul reported that France had three primary methods of teaching French: "the classical method, the audio-visual method [French films and television programs shown to the public at the Centre Culturel Français, the French Cultural Center in Buea and Limbe], and teaching through radio" (discussed in detail in Chapter 8. The French Cultural Center were centers of French culture whose libraries carried only books in the French language. In Buea, where there was no public library, the library of the French Cultural Center was open to the public and served as a reading and study location for English-speaking students as well as French-speaking students from the Lycée Bilingue de Buea (Bilingual Grammar School) and the *Ecole Francophone de Buea*, the French-language primary school for Francophone civil servants, members of the military and other Francophones who had moved to Southern Cameroons. The French Cultural Centers also had a program of literature distribution to Francophone and Anglophone children who visited the center to participate in cultural activities.

After the first five years of cultural programming in West Cameroon, the French Consul in Buea concluded that of the two federated states, West Cameroon will probably be the first to reach bilingualism:

> *Mais son intégration totale dans la Francophonie sera longue. Il faudra pour y accède un complet remaniement des méthodes d'enseignement à partir du cycle premier et une évolution psychologique qui changeât les inclinaisons même de sa population (Moreux, 1967).*

> But its total integration in the *Francophonie* will take a long time. It will require, to reach this goal, a complete overhaul of the methods of teaching from the first cycle (high school) and a psychological evolution which will change the very inclinations of the population" [to turn towards London rather than Paris].

He concluded that, "Forty years of British tutelage has left an elite whose habits and traditions are closer to those of London than those of Paris." He added that West Cameroonian civil servants in Buea were not interested in studying French because they were: "*imprégné de l'héritage, bien modeste cependant, légué par l'administration britannique, pour se lancer dans l'étude du Français*" (Permeated by the heritage, albeit modest, bequeathed by the British administration, to begin studying French).

Figure 4.5. *Kouakou* magazine. French comic book of African cultural stories produced by the French Foreign Ministry for free distribution to African youth. The French Cultural Center in

Buea distributed *Kouakou* free to Anglophone and Francophone youth.

Monsieur Moreux suggested the Linguistic Center had not been a resounding success. He therefore proposed that the French assimilationist project target the younger generation of English-speaking Cameroonians who would be more amenable to French culture and come under the sway of the French language: *"En revanche, la génération montante sera soumise rapidement à l'influence de la langue française si nous poursuivons, si nous amplifions notre activité culturelle..."* (In contrast, the upcoming generation will be rapidly subject to the influence of the French language if we continue, if we increase our cultural activities) (Moreux, 1967). He said French cultural assimilation efforts should be directed at the younger generation, those who were 18-30 years old, because they were a generation that is ready to dialogue, is malleable, has a curious spirit, has no prejudices, and is ready to assimilate what will be taught to them.

The Confidential Report of French Consul, Monsieur Moreux, demonstrated the misguided evangelistic zeal with which France set out to "convert" Southern Cameroonians who were ensconced in an unofficial global Anglosphere into true believers in French secular religion—the French language and culture.

French Ambassador's Perspective on Ahidjo's Abolition of the Federal Republic of Cameroon

On May 6th, 1972, President Ahmadou Ahidjo of the Federal Republic of Cameroon carried out a political sleight of hand. He announced in the National Assembly that he was submitting a new Constitution that would eliminate the Federal Republic of Cameroon, and replace it with a highly centralized, Napoleonic regime to be called the United Republic of Cameroon, to a popular referendum of the people of Cameroon. The referendum was scheduled to take place in two weeks. There was no discussion of Ahidjo's proposed Constitution. With this announcement, President Ahidjo launched what he called a *"revolution pacifique"* (peaceful revolution) that changed the nature of the Federal Republic of Cameroon. The problem is that Ahidjo carried out this Machiavellian maneuver without consulting the "junior partner" in the federation, the English-speaking State of West Cameroon, and its political leaders, John Ngu Foncha and Solomon Tandeng Muna, with whom he had "negotiated" the reunification of Cameroon, and promised not to annex the English-speaking State. The result of the referendum was known in advance. The question in the referendum was: "Do you approve, with the intent of consolidating national unity and to accelerate economic, social, and cultural development of the nation, the draft constitution submitted to the people of Cameroon by the President of the Federal Republic of Cameroon, creating a one and indivisible republic [copied from article I of the French Constitution] to be named the United Republic of Cameroon?" There were, in effect, just two options on the ballot: *Oui* and Yes. The ballot was not secret, and individuals could vote for their whole families. Military commanders could vote for their men (Dupuy, 1972). The results were a foregone conclusion. In one fell, dictatorial swoop, Ahidjo had eliminated the autonomy of English-speaking Cameroon. His new Constitution created a hyper-centralized, highly authoritarian, neo-patrimonial, one-party, Napoleonic, *Chefferie républicaine* (Republican Chiefdom). *La République du Cameroun* had essentially annexed the State of Southern Cameroons, and its newly discovered oil and natural gas resources. Ironically, the statehood of Southern Cameroons, which Ahidjo had just eliminated, was a hard-won status that had been secured from the British colonial administration. In effect, when Britain took possession of Southern Cameroons under the terms of the Treaty of Versailles of 1919, it lumped the territory with its Nigerian colony, where it became a neglected, insignificant part of Nigeria under indirect British administration (Budi, 2019). Southern Cameroonian politicians in Nigeria resisted the marginalization, and domination of their territory and succeeded in obtaining significant autonomy to have their own Premier, Dr. EML Endeley, in 1958. Ahidjo's excuses for the annexation of Southern Cameroons included the cost of operating three governments (East Cameroon, West Cameroon, and the Federal government). Interestingly, Ahidjo's *revolution pacifique had* occurred despite Federal Constitutional provisions to the contrary. In effect, Article 47 of the Federal Constitution of 1961 stated that: *"Toute proposition de révision de la présente Constitution portant atteinte à l'unité et à l'intégrité de la Fédération est irrecevable"* (All proposals for revision of this Constitution that are detrimental to the unity and integrity of the Federation are inadmissible).

This controversial change in the form and structure of the State of Cameroon was of great interest to the French. They recognized it as a major milestone in the history of Cameroon, a milestone they had orchestrated with the Ahidjo regime and anticipated. Nevertheless, though the change served French interests and assimilationist objectives set forth as early as 1962, there were concerns about how the English-speaking Cameroonians would perceive the loss of their autonomy. As we saw earlier, the French Ambassador to Cameroon in 1962, Monsieur Jean-Pierre Benard, had observed that the federal Republic of Cameroon was grounded on a deliberately and legally ambiguous foundation. At the time of the reunification in 1961, France and *la République du Cameroun* viewed the Federal Republic of Cameroon as a transitory phase in the march towards a centralized, unitary, French-style, Napoleonic, secular republican state within *la Francophonie*. For its part, English-speaking Southern Cameroons viewed the referendum as a consolidation of a broad autonomy from all European powers—including France (Benard, 1962).

The outcome of the 1972 referendum, which asked the people of Cameroon to vote on whether to change the nature of the state from a federal republic to a centralized, united republic, without public discussion, was considered a very bitter pill by English-speaking Cameroonians. To them, the referendum was essentially a deceptive, authoritarian, political maneuver that was intended to nullify their hard-won autonomy—and natural resources. Former West Cameroon Prime Minister and Federal Vice President, John Ngu Foncha would later write that the referendum was imposed on Southern Cameroonians without consultation or discussion, in an authoritarian political atmosphere that was characterized by an absolute lack of freedom of speech and expression (Foncha, 1993).

On 25 May 1972, five days after the constitutional referendum that abolished the Federal Republic of Cameroon, the French Ambassador to Cameroon, His excellency Jacques Dupuy wrote to the Directorate of African and Malagasy Affairs of the French Ministry of Foreign Affairs, analyzing the political implications of the referendum of May 20, 1972, and the creation of the United Republic of Cameroon:

> *Ainsi que j'ai eu l'occasion de le signaler au Département, il y a avait un point sur lequel ce referendum ne pouvait manquer de susciter certaines inquiétudes ; on pouvait en effet interpréter la réforme constitutionnelle propose aux Camerounais comme une atteinte au particularisme du Camer- oun Occidental. Les Anglophones ont bien senti que la nouvelle constitution consacre, quoiqu'elle en dise, la prééminence du français. Si la République Unie de Cameroun doit être un État "unitaire" et "pluriculturel", certains appréhendent qu'avec le temps celui-ci soit de moins en moins "bilingue."*

As I have had the occasion to inform the Department [of African and Malagasy Affairs]. There is a certain point where this constitutional reform could not fail to raise certain concerns: one could in effect interpret the constitutional reform submitted to Cameroonians as an attack on the specificity of West Cameroon. The Anglophones felt that the new consti- tution establishes, no matter what it says, the preeminence of French. If the United Republic of Cameroon has to be a "unitary" and "pluricultural" state, some are apprehensive that with time, it [the country] will be less and less "bilingual."

The French ambassador read the Cameroonian political "tea leaves" very well. He saw clearly that the English-speakers saw the change of form of the Cameroonian state as an attack on their political autonomy and cultural specificity. Despite the fact that France and the French cultural assimilationist policy were well-served by this constitutional sleight of hand, Ambassador Dupuy (1972) was cautious. He rightly predicted that the new consti- tution would make Cameroon less bilingual and more monolingual, that is to say, more French-speaking. He was right on target because a few years later, John Ngu Foncha, former Prime Minister of West Cameroon, and former Vice President of the Federal Republic of Cameroon, the self-styled "architect of the reunification," wrote a lengthy open letter in the form of a printed booklet. Foncha was very critical of the political evolution of Cam- eroon from a federal republic to an overcentralized, one-party autocratic state that did not respect the human and civil rights of its citizens. In the booklet entitled, "An Open Letter Addressed to the Government of the Republic of Cameroon on the Operation of Unification 1961-1971" Foncha (1993) expressed disappointment and regret that the reunification he had ardently championed had not gone as planned because the Federal Republic of Cameroon, and its successors, the United Republic of Cameroon as well as the Republic of Cameroon, had shown a total disregard for the human and civil rights of citizens. He accused the government of turning a blind eye and a deaf ear to the pleas of the marginalized English-speaking people of West Cameroon, who had been reduced to the status of second-class citizens.

Ambassador Dupuy (1972) put Ahidjo's transformation of the State from a two-state federation to a one-party unitary state within the framework of a grand design to gradually transform the country into a centralized, unitary state and assimilate the English-speaking West Cameroon into the French system, *la Francophonie*.

> *Le referendum du 20 Mai 1972, semble bien être le terme du grand dessein que s'était fixé M. AHIDJO lors de l'accession de son pays à l'indépendance. Après l'avoir réunifié en 1961, il vient de la faire passer du stade fédéral au stade unitaire…Il avait su préalablement au 6 Mai obtenir ou conserver le secret, notamment des juristes français auxquels il avait demandé de lui préparer le projet de constitution qu'il a ensuite étudié lors de retraites fréquentes qu'il effectue chez lui à Garoua dans le Nord.*

> The referendum of 20 May 1972 seems to be the termination of the grand design that Mr. Ahidjo set out to accomplish upon accession of his country to independence. After having unified it in 1961, he has moved to the unitary stage…he had made sure to obtain from French jurists, before 6th May, and kept in secret, a draft constitution that he had asked them to prepare, and which he studied during his frequent retreats at his home in Garoua in the North.

The Constitution of the United Republic of Cameroon made Ahidjo a dictator. It eliminated the Federal Assembly, the West Cameroon House of Assembly, the West Cameroon House of Chiefs, and the East Cameroon parliament, and replaced them with one Cameroon National Assembly. The Constitution also eliminated the principle of "separation of powers," and replaced it with a vague and ambiguous "collaboration of powers."

Ambassador Dupuy (1972) revealed that France had participated in the Constitutional sleight of hand, and that the Constitution of the new United Republic of Cameroon had been drafted by French jurists and submitted in secret to President Ahmadou Ahidjo just two weeks before the referendum to abolish the Federal Republic of Cameroon and adopt that French-drafted Constitution. President Ahidjo did not see it fit to present the proposed Constitution of the United Republic of Cameroon to the Federal Assembly, the main legislative body of the land or to the West Cameroon House of Assembly, the West Cameroon House of Chiefs, or the East Cameroon parliament before the referendum. In hindsight, the Ambassador's tone of caution was not misplaced. The elimination of the Federal Republic of Cameroon, and with it the autonomy of West Cameroon, can be considered one of the major root causes of the Anglophone Revolt of 2016. Ahmadou Ahidjo's coerced transformation of the country into a one-party state under the umbrella of his political party, the Cameroon National Union (CNU) was one more step towards the Anglophone crisis.

The Anglophone Question and the French Ambassador Turned Technical Adviser at the Presidency of Cameroon

Fast forward to November 4, 1982. At the apogee of his rule, President El Hajj Ahmadou Babatoura Ahidjo, who had reigned single-handedly, and in an authoritarian fashion for

22 years as the uncontested, *Chef de l'État* (Chief of State), the *président à vie* (the president-for-life) of the Napoleonic *Chefferie républicaine* (Republican Chiefdom) of Cameroon, went on Radio Cameroon, the national broadcast network and abruptly, unexpectedly announced that he had decided to resign as president of Cameroon. He had governed the country with an iron, dictatorial fist, together with a small Foulbé/Peuhl elite from his North Cameroonian bastion, the so-called "*Grand Nord*." The Chief of State and leader of the one-party, Union Nationale Camerounaise (Cameroon National Union), announced to the shocked nation that he was handing over power to his "Constitutional successor," Prime Minister Paul Biya. He left in place his personal praetorian guard, the French-trained, *guarde républicaine* (republican guard), composed almost entirely of officers who were Toupouri or Tupuri, a fiercely loyal ethnic group from the Far North. To many Africans, Ahidjo had become an exemplar of the West African proverb: *L'abus du pouvoir use le pouvoir, l'abus de la force, use la force* (Abuse of power wears down power, abuse of force wears down force). Ahidjo had been worn out by his over-centralized, absolutist, one-man rule. Officially, he was resigning for unspecified health reasons.

The Biya Regime Aggravates the Anglophone Problem

French Ambassador, Yvon Omnes, coined the term "Anglophone Problem" to refer to the identitarian and cultural specificity of the English-speaking minority in the State of West Cameroon and the challenges of assimilating that minority into French Cameroon, and by extension *la Francophonie*. President Paul Biya aggravated the problem. As soon as he came to power, it became clear that he would be reading from the French assimilationist playbook. It did not take long for him to continue implementing the Franco-Ahidjo post-reunification, assimilationist agenda in Southern Cameroons. Biya actually took some fateful steps that hastened the dispersal of Southern Cameroon into *la Francophonie*, and watered the seeds of the Anglophone Revolt that had been sown by Ahidjo's abolition of the federation and nullification of the identitarian and cultural specificity of English and Pidgin-speaking Southern Cameroons. In August 1983, in a bid to submerge the identitarian rumblings of the English-speaking minority into the Francophone national, he set in motion a divide-and-rule strategy. This took the form of a partition of the former federated English and Pidgin-speaking State of West Cameroon into two provinces, the Northwest and Southwest provinces. He appointed, by presidential decree, French-speaking governors, who played the role of imperial proconsuls in these new provinces. He also abandoned the name United Republic of Cameroon in favor of the original name of French Cameroun, *la République du Cameroun* (Republic of Cameroon) at independence in 1960, President Ahidjo had already removed the second star that represented the State of West Cameroon from the national flag of Cameroon in 1972. President Biya reinforced the centralist, neo-patrimonial regime put in place by President Ahidjo, replacing the ruling Northern elite with elite from his Beti/Bulu ethnic group. This essentially transformed Cameroon into a kleptocratic, *clientéliste chefferie républicaine* (republican chiefdom) "entombed in egomania", to borrow the expression of (Douthat, 2024). In his more than 40 years in power, Biya neither spoke English in public nor read any of his official National Day speeches in English. He ignored the political and identitarian pleas of the English-speaking minority, which called for constitutional reforms that would lead to a restoration of its autonomy as a territory. These appeals were formulated by the All Anglophone Conferences in 1993 and 1994 (See Chapter 1). The dispersal of English and Pidgin-speaking Southern Cameroons into *la Francophonie* was complete, or so it seemed.

The Aftermath of the Attempted Coup d'État of April 1984 and the Anglophone Question

On April 6, 1984, Ahidjo's praetorian guard, *la guarde républicaine* (republican guard), and a number of Northern Foulbé/Peuhl elite, backed by the former President, who was now residing in France, attempted a *coup d'état* against President Paul Biya. The coup attempt failed, Biya survived because he was hidden in a secret toilet in the basement of the Presidential palace in Yaoundé by Ivo Desancio Yenwo, an officer from Bui division in the English-speaking Northwest region. When the Anglophone Revolt began in 2016, Yenwo would ultimately be promoted to the rank of General in the Cameroon army. Ironically, his home county, Bui, would become one of the theatres of the Anglophone revolt and the ensuing military conflict. The Cameroon army razed tens of Bui villages to ashes, killed hundreds of civilians, thousands more became refugees in Nigeria, the French-speaking Noun division and other parts of Cameroon.

Meanwhile, after the 1984 coup, Biya disbanded Ahidjo's mutinous republican guard. A bloodbath ensued. Members of the now-defunct republican guard, the military, gendarmerie, and government officials from Ahidjo's Northern bastion who were accused of supporting or sympathizing with the coup attempt were massacred and buried in mass graves on the road to Mbalmayo. Former President Ahidjo was quickly tried in a military tribunal and sentenced to death in absentia. President Biya quickly filled the government, parastatal corporations and diplomatic missions with loyalists from his Bulu/Beti ethnic group. The Northern, Muslim elite who survived the post-coup purges were reduced to secondary roles in the Biya government (Dougueil, 2013). The failed coup d'état led to tensions in the relations between Cameroon and France. Ahidjo had lived in France and announced support for the coup plotters on the French-government international broadcaster, *Radio France Internationale*. The French government of President François Mitterrand was caught between loyalty to French friend and partner, Ahmadou Ahidjo, and long-term French interests in Cameroon. The French chose their interests and persuaded Senegalese President, Abdou Diouf to take in Ahidjo, whose residence in France had become politically problematic. The former president moved to Dakar, Senegal, where he lived with his wife, Germaine, until his death in 1989. Former Senegalese President, Abdou Diouf is reported to have said that President Biya refused to take his call to discuss the burial place of Ahidjo. The former president is buried in Dakar.

The failed *coup d'état* severed the cozy military and security relationship between Cameroon and France that had been set in place by the bilateral *accords de coopération* of 1959. Distrust of France caused President Biya to turn to the Israeli government for military, logistical and tactical assistance in rebuilding the presidential guard and an elite army-within-the Cameroon army, the *Bataillon d'Intervention Rapide* (BIR). The BIR was to become infamous for its horrendous human rights violations and crimes against humanity in the

146

fight against Boko Haram in North Cameroon, and during the Anglophone Revolt in the English-speaking regions of Cameroon (See Vol. II, Chapter 17, The Israeli Connection). Due to this failed attempt to unseat Biya, the regime took a sharp authoritarian, tribalistic turn that ultimately resulted in the Anglophone crisis.

A French Ambassador's View of the Anglophone Problem in the Biya Era

As President Biya's authoritarian regime consolidated power and redoubled measures to assimilate English-speaking Southern Cameroons into French Cameroon and la Francophonie, rumblings of discontent began to be felt over the progressive loss of Anglophone identity and culture. On October 13, 1985, the French Ambassador to Cameroon, Yvon Omnes, wrote Report No. 332/DAM, entitled "Le Problème Anglophone" (The Anglophone Problem) to the Minister of External Relations in Paris with a copy to the attention of the Directorate of African and Madagascan Affairs. The main thrust of Ambassador Omnes' report was that more than 20 years after reunification, the English-speaking Southern Cameroons, now divided into the Northwest and Southwest provinces, had not been entirely assimilated into French Cameroon and la Francophonie. His report contained an undertone of French discomfort with cultural diversity, the multiple subject who could be bilingual and multicultural—Anglophone and Francophone, an African with multiple ethnic and linguistic identities, affiliations, and capabilities. The ambassador reported that there was political agitation among Anglophones for a change of the form of the government, for a return to federalism and restoration of the autonomy they had lost in 1972, when the Federal Republic of Cameroon had been abolished and replaced with a hyper-centralized Republic of Cameroon. He stated that the bones of contention were the exploitation of the natural resources in Anglophone Cameroon (oil and natural gas, water, forestry and other resources for "enrichment of other part of the country" (Omnes, 1985). In his 1985 report, Ambassador Omnes raised one of the key components of the Anglophone problem, the gradual dismantling and assimilation of the Anglo-American Common Law system that was one of the cultural and identitarian bulwarks of the English and Pidgin-speaking population of Southern Cameroons:

> L'administration est d'autre part en grande partie aux mains des francophones qui s'efforcent de remettre en cause le système juridique locale, dernier bastion du particularisme Anglophone (Omnes, 1985).

> The [government] administration is, mostly controlled by French-speakers who make efforts to question and change the local [Common law] judicial system, the last bastion of Anglophone specificity.

Ambassador Omnes stated that Anglophones had successfully resisted attempts by the Francophone Minister of Justice and Keeper of the Seals, Ngongang Ouandji to tamper with the "common law" in the English-speaking regions under the policy of harmonization.

He reported that an English-speaking Cameroonian jurist, Benjamin Itoe, had been appointed Minister of Justice to calm things down. Unfortunately, that was all Mr. Benjamin

Itoe could do. The French-speaking Justice ministers who came after Itoe, particularly the long-serving Laurent Esso, redoubled efforts to harmonize (read assimilate) and dilute the common law legal system in the English-speaking regions into the Francophone civil law. This consisted of posting French-speaking magistrates and judges to preside (using French civil law and the French language) over criminal and civil trials in the English-speaking regions (See Chapter 9). Since Cameroon does not have a jury system, where one is theoretically tried by a jury of one's peers, most often than not, criminal and civil defendants could not understand the proceedings because the judge spoke only French. Criminal defendants often had no clue what they were charged with and did not know whether they had been convicted or acquitted and for which crimes. Those convicted did not even know the length of their prison sentences. These concerted political and administrative efforts to dilute and assimilate the common law system, which Ambassador Omnes reported on so accurately in 1985, flared up during the All Anglophone Conference of 1993, and turned out to be one of the triggers of the Anglophone Revolt in 2016. In effect, Anglophone lawyers' strikes in 2016 turned out to be the spark that set off the Anglophone Revolt.

Ambassador Omnes' 1985 report touched on the other major component of what he called the Anglophone Problem in Cameroon, the educational system. It had begun to dawn on the French and Francophone Cameroon political leadership that assimilation of English-speaking regions into *la Francophonie* could not be successful if the educational system in English-speaking Cameroon continued to be primarily an English-medium enterprise. The Constitution of the Federal Republic of Cameroon had specified that primary education would be the province of the two state governments. This guaranteed that basic education would be in English. However, abolition of the federation essentially nationalized and centralized education at the primary, secondary and university levels in Cameroon. Ambassador Omnes reported that harmonization of the two educational systems of Cameroon through the creation of a single system of education by governmental decree "raised Anglophone suspicions" because they saw it as assimilation (Omnes, 1985). In reality, despite centralization and harmonization, the English-medium, "mission-school" dominated Anglophone educational system did not disappear. It just continued as a beleaguered sub-system that ultimately became the theatre of Anglophone identitarian resistance. As we see in Chapters 8 & 9, nationalizing and centralizing education in Cameroon led to political and cultural tensions and conflicts in which Anglophones used injustices of the past to score points in the present. This resistance ultimately resulted in the attainment of a certain level of hard-won autonomy for the Anglophone educational sub-system at the primary and secondary levels.

In his 1985 report, Ambassador Omnes concluded that there was a certain political disquiet in Cameroon. He said Anglophones felt like marginalized, second-class citizens. He suggested that: "Erosion of the political weight of Anglophones" could be the main reason for their disquiet. The decision of Paul Biya in January 1984 to transform the United Republic of Cameroon to *la Republique du Cameroun* was the last step in the grand design of Ahidjo and Biya to assimilate English-speakers into the French-speaking sphere. Ambassador Omnes stated that the language of instruction in the French-style *grandes écoles* was French and that bilingualism, which he seemed to frown upon, was, in reality, only "for

Anglophones" because they had to learn French to cope with the French-medium higher education system, *grandes écoles,* government bureaucracy, administration, and courts in most of Cameroon.

> *"L'incompréhension est en train de faire place à l'agacement. Le risque existe d'un durcissement des autorités de Yaounde, certains pensant déjà que l'agitation pourrait être entretenue de l'extérieur (Omnes, 1985).*

> Misunderstanding is giving way to annoyance. There is the possibility that the authorities in Yaoundé would take a tough stance, some of them think the agitation could be instigated from abroad.

The ambassador's remarks demonstrated the French and French-Cameroonian mentality with regard to English-speaking Cameroonians. The perception is that they lacked political agency; they did not know what was good for them; they could not speak for themselves. As such, they had to be pawns in some regional, geo-strategic game, and their very existence as a distinct linguistic community threatened French cultural interests. Nevertheless, Ambassador Omnes' observations were surprisingly prescient. He concluded with an ominous, cautionary statement that is as true in 2024 as it was in 1985: "It is up to the authorities in Yaoundé to know the aspirations of, and to dialogue with the Anglophones." Ambassador Omnes' letter explains the hardline, intransigent posture of the Biya regime towards the political demands of the Anglophone lawyers and teachers. Of the two options outlined by the French diplomat, the Biya regime took the authoritarian route—with the full support of the French, Israelis, Russians, and Chinese. In practical terms, this was a tough, uncompromising stance against Anglophones. Biya ignored their identitarian aspirations and demands for greater autonomy. He turned a deaf ear to the international community, and especially to Pope Francis, who called for dialogue and respect for the identitarian specificity of the Anglophone minority. The result was the prolonged Anglophone Revolt. Ambassador Yvon Omnes retired as French Ambassador to Cameroon and in an ironic, unprecedented move that raised eyebrows among English-speaking Cameroonians, President Biya appointed the retired French diplomat as his special adviser—with the imprimatur of the French government.

Conclusion

The French connection is one of the causes of the Anglophone Revolt in Cameroon. The reunification of the two Cameroon States: French East Cameroon and British West Cameroon was grounded on a deliberately vague and ambiguous constitutional foundation through the Machiavellian machinations of Cameroon's authoritarian, postcolonial president Ahmadou Babatoura Ahidjo, and his French postcolonial advisers on the one hand, and on the political naivety, insouciance and reckless disregard of constitutional and governance structures by John Ngu Foncha, Emmanuel Tabi Egbe, Nfon Mukete, Ndeh Ntumazah, and other unsophisticated "Kamerunists," on the other hand. For the authoritarian, neopatrimonial, republican chiefdom of Francophone Cameroon and France—whose governmentality has no room for minorities and multiculturalism—Southern Cameroons was a territory that had to be emptied of its identitarian and cultural specificities and assimilated into *la Francophonie*. Foncha, Muna, and the English-speaking Kamerunists were so blinded by nationalist and pan-Africanist rhetoric, big egos, and selfish interests that they were oblivious to the cultural, identitarian and geo-strategic dimensions of the reunification they were championing. For their part, Presidents Ahidjo, Biya, and the French, overestimated the strength and superiority of their culture and the weakness and inferiority of the English and West African Pidgin multi-culture of Southern Cameroons. The French connection in the Anglophone Question was thus facilitated by Francophone and Anglophone political disconnection. These connections, disconnections, and miscalculations were the direct causes of the Anglophone problem, and the Anglophone Revolt of 2016.

References

Ambassade de France (2017). *Discours prononcé par l'Ambassadeur de France, Gilles Thibault, lors de la réception de la fête nationale du 14 juillet 2017 à la Résidence de France á Yaoundé* (Speech presented by the Ambassador of France, Gilles Thibault, during the reception on the occasion of the national holiday of 14 July 2017 at the Residence of the Ambassador of France, Yaoundé). Retrieved from: https://cm.ambafrance.org/L-Ambassadeur-de-France-dans-le-Nord- Ouest

Anyangwe, C. (2008). *Imperialist politics in Cameroon: Resistance & the Inception of the Restoration of the Statehood of Southern Cameroons.* Bamenda: Langaa.

Assemblée Nationale (2011). Avis: La commission de la Défense Nationale et des Forces Armées Sur le projet de loi (N° 3194), adopté par le Sénat, *autorisant l'approbation de l'accord entre le Gouvernement de la République française et le Gouvernement de la République du Cameroun instituant un partenariat de défense.* (Opinion of the Commission on National Defense and Armed Forces on Draft Law No. 3194 adopted by the Senate, Authorizing Ratification of the Agreement Between the French Government and the Republic of Cameroon, Instituting a Defense Partnership). Retrieved from: https://www.assemblee-nationale.fr/13/rapports/r3289.asp#P166_22005

Ardener, E. (1962). The political History of Cameroon. *The World Today,* Vol. 18, No. 8. (pp. 341-350)

Ardener, S. (2005). Ardener's "Muted Groups": The genesis of an idea and its praxis. Women and Language, Vol. 28, (2), Pp. 50-54,72.

Bayart, J. (1989). *L'Etat en Afrique* (The State in Africa). Paris: Fayard.

Benard, J-P. (1962). Confidential letter No. 27 of 8 January 1962. French Embassy Yaoundé, Cameroon.

Betts, R. (1961). *Assimilation and Association in French Colonial Theory, 1890-1914.* New York: Columbia University Press.

Budi, R. (2019). Colonial Administrative Integration of African Territories: Identity and Resistance in Nigeria's Southern Cameroons, 1922-1961. *IAFOR Journal of Arts & Humanities* 691): 109-122. DOI: 10.22492/ijah.6.1.09

Débats Parlementaires (Parliamentary Debates) 1960-1961, Sénat (French Senate), Journal Officiel No. 73 S du 15 December 1960. Retrieved from: http://www.senat.fr/comptes-rendus-seances/5eme/pdf/1960/11/s19601126_1_1997_2004.pdf

De Gaulle, C. (1954) *Mémoires de guerre, l'appel, 1940-1942* [War Memoirs, the Call, 1940-1942]. Paris: Plon.

Deltombe, T., Domergue, M., Tatsitsa, J (2019). *Kamerun! Guerre cachée aux origins de la Franca-frique, 1948-1971 (Kamerun! Hidden war that at the origins of France-Afrique, 1948-1971).* Paris: Editions la Decouverte.

Dougueil, G. (2013). *Cameroun: Les Foulbés, condamnés aux seconds rôles?* (The Foulbes, doomed to play secondary roles?). *Jeune Afrique*, 18 March. Retrieved from: https://www.jeuneafrique.com/138137/politique/cameroun-les-foulb-s-condamn-s-aux-seconds-r-les/

Douthat, R. (2024). The Question is Not if Biden Should Step Aside. It's How. *The New York Times* (February 10). Retrieved from: https://www.nytimes.com/2024/02/10/opinion/joe-biden-convention-2024.html

Dupuy, J. (1972). *Referendum Constitutionnel du 20 Mai 1972* (Constitutional Referendum of 20th May, 1972). Diplomatic Correspondence between French Ambassador in Yaoundé, Cameroun and French Ministry of Foreign Affairs, Paris.

Eko, L. (2001) Many Spiders, One World Wide Web: Towards a Typology of Internet Regulation. *Communication Law and Policy*, 6, 448-460.

Eko, L. (2012) *New Media, Old Regimes: Case Studies in Comparative. Communication Law and Policy*. Lanham, MD: Lexington Books.

Eko, L. E. (2019). Couching Political Criticism in Humor: The Case of Musical Parodies of the Military in Cameroon and Congo Brazzaville, in Uche Onyebadi (ed). *Music and Messaging in the African Political Arena* pp 87-107. Hershey, PA.: IGI Global Group identity, Culture, and the Politics of Nostalgia. *Journal of Third World Studies*. Vol. XX(1), 79-102.

Eko, L. (2004). Internet Connectivity and Development in Africa: Look before you "leapfrog!" In J. M. Mbaku and S.C. Saxena (Eds.). *Africa at the Crossroads*. Westport, CT.: Greenwood Press (pp. 211–231).

Eko, L. (2013). *American Exceptionalism, the French Exception and Digital Media Law*. Lanham, MD. Lexington Books.

Eko, L. (2003) Freedom of the Press in Africa, *Encyclopedia of International Media and Communications*: Donald Johnston, (ed.).

Foncha, J.N. (1993). *An Open Letter Addressed to the Government of the Republic of Cameroon on the Operation of Unification, 1961-1971*. Bamenda: Cam Press.

Gavin R.J. and Bentley J.A. (1973). *The Scramble for Africa: Documents on the Berlin West Africa Conference and Related Subjects 1884/1885*. Ibadan, Nigeria: Ibadan University Press.

Fandio, P., Amoko, M., Tchaya, Z., Tamo, C., & Batoum, S. (2017). Au Cameroun, carnet de guerre en «Ambazonie» TV5 Monde. December 27. Retrieved from: https://information.tv5monde.com/afrique/au-cameroun-carnet-de-guerre-en-ambazonie-211446

Foucault, M. (1994). *Dits et Ecrits* (Tome III), Sayings and Writings (Vol. III). Paris: Editions Gallimard

Foucault, M. (1994a). Dits et Ecrits (Tome II). (Sayings and Writings, Vol. II). Paris: Gallimard.

Francis, J. (2021). *Cameroun-La Francophonie: Cinquante Années Ensemble* (Cameroon-La Francophonie: Fifty Years Together). Cameroon Tribune, 22 March. Retrieved from: https://www.cameroon-tribune.cm/article.html/39001/en.html/cameroun-la-francophonie-cinquante-annees-ensemble

Gabriel, J. (1999). Cameroon's Neopatrimonial dilemma. Beiträge, 20 (2).

Gaulle, Charles de. (1954). *Mémoires de guerre, l'appel, 1940-1942 (Memoirs of War, the Call, 1940-1942)*. Paris: Plon.

Hammer, J. (2016). Hunting Boko Haram: The U.S. Extends its Drone War Deeper into Africa with Secretive Base. The Intercept, February 25. Retrieved from: https://theintercept. com/2016/02/25/us-extends-drone-war-deeper-into-afric

Kipling, R. (1940 "The White Man's Burden," in Rudyard Kipling's Verse (New York, Double Day,)

Kodjo-Grandvaux, S. (2016). *Le Cameroun a été le laboratoire de la Françafrique*, Le Monde, November 18. Retrieved from: https://www.lemonde.fr/afrique/article/2016/11/18/le-cameroun-a-ete-le-laboratoire-de-la-francafrique_5033354_3212.html

Kuisel, R. (1993) *Seducing the French: The dilemma of Americanization.* Berkley, CA: University of California press.

Legrand, P. (2003). The Same and the Different. In Pierre Legrand and Roderick Munday (eds.). *Comparative Legal Studies: Traditions and Transitions* pp. 240-311. Cambridge, UK: Cambridge University Press,

Loi no. 2011-423 du 20 avril 2011 autorisant l'approbation de l'accord entre le Gouvernement de la République française et le Gouvernement de la République du Cameroun instituant un partenariat de défense et textes afferents (Law No. 2011-423 of 20 April 2011, authorizing the agreement between the Government of the French Republic and the Government of the Republic of Cameroon instituting a partnership of Defense and related texts) JORF no.0094 du 21 avril 2011.

Mbembe, A. (2001). *On the Postcolony.* Berkley: UCLA Press.

Moreux, M. (1967). Confidential Consular Report, French Consul Buea, 22nd August (French Diplomatic Correspondence).

Morin, E. (1990) *Le trou noir de la laïcité* [The black hole of secularism]. *Le Débat* No. 58, 38.

McLuhan, M. (1964). *Understanding Media.* New York: McGraw-Hill.

Monga, C. (1996). *The Anthropology of Anger: Civil Society and Democracy in Africa.* Boulder, CO.: Lynne Rienner Publishers.

Paulhiac H. (1905). *Promenades Lointaines: Sahara, Niger, Tombouctou, Touareg.* Paris: Libraire Plon.

Radio France Internationale (2020). Massacre au Cameroun: Le Président Macron dit qu'il appelera Paul Biya. (Massacre in Cameroon, President Macron Says he will Call President Paul Biya). February 22. Retrieved from: http://www.rfi.fr/fr/afrique/20200222-france-cameroun-massacre-zone-anglophone-emmanuel-macron-paul-biya

Richard, F. (2017). Cameroun anglophone: aux origines de la crise. France 24, October 4th. Retrieved from: https://www.france24.com/fr/20170518-cameroun-region-anglophoanglophone-paul-biya-manifestations-origine-crise

Rosanvallon, P. (2004). *Le Modéle Politique Français: La société civil contre le jacobinisme de 1789 à nos jours [The French Political Model: Civil society against Jacobinism from 1789 to the present].* Paris: Éditions du Seuil.

Sartre, J-P. (1963). Preface. In Frantz Fanon, *The Wretched of the Earth.* Pp. 7-26. Constance Farrington (trans). Middlesex, UK: Penguin Books.

Sartre, J-P. (1947). *Présence noire* (Black presence), in *Presence Africaine*, vol. 1 (pp. 28-29).

Servenay, D. (2007). Les accords secrets avec l'Afrique: encore d'époque ? (The Secret Agreements with Africa: Still Relevant?). L'Observateur, 26 July. Retrieved from: https://www.nouvelobs. com/rue89/rue89-politique/20070726.RUE1127/les-accords-secrets-avec-l-afrique-encore-d-epoque.html

Signé, L. (2019). How the France-backed African CFA franc works as an enabler and barrier to development. *Quartz Africa*, December 7

Specia, M. (2019). The African Currency at the Center of a European Dispute. *The New York Times.* January 22. Retrieved from: https://www.nytimes.com/2019/01/22/world/africa/africa-cfa-franc-currency.html

Tocqueville, A. (1843). *De la démocracie en Amérique (tome II) [Democracy in America. (Vol. II)]*. Translated by H. Reeve. New York: J.H.G. Langley.

FIVE

Resisting the Frenchman's Burden

The Clash of Legal Cultures and the Anglophone Question

LYOMBE EKO

We have seen that the "Frenchman's burden" was the French government's concerted efforts to extend its traditional, colonial, *mission civilisatrice* (civilizing mission), to the English and Pidgin-speaking State of West Cameroon after reunification in 1961. The purpose of the French civilizing mission was to transform Africans into Francophones for whom the French language would become the gateway to French culture and, by extension, to *la Francophonie*, the global French-language sphere. We have seen that President Charles de Gaulle of France considered Southern Cameroons as, "*un petit cadeau de la reine d'Angleterre*" (A little gift from the Queen of England) (Anyangwe, 2010. p. 742). De Gaulle and his successors essentially had a *mission assimilatrice*, an assimilationist mission, that consisted of muting the English and Pidgin-speaking territory's cultural and identitarian specificity, assimilating and dispersing into *la Francophonie*. However, the assimilationist task was a bit complicated because France and their French Cameroon postcolony did not, unfortunately, appreciate the magnitude of the task. They were unaware of or completely ignored the fact that the people of Southern Cameroons were informally anchored to the global Anglosphere due to reasons of historical, linguistic, cultural, and religious proximities with the Anglo-Saxon world—tenuous as some of these may have seemed in 1961. Furthermore, post-World War II emerging and globalizing Anglo-American popular, and Nigerian, African American, and Jamaican culture (literature, recorded music, cinema, international broadcasting, and globalized popular religion), complicated the muting and erasure of English in the former Southern Cameroons. Above all, American information and communicational technologies (ITCs), the Internet, its associated social media platforms, as well as global mobile telephony, made English and Pidgin-speaking Southern Cameroons assimilation proof. The Anglophone Revolt in Cameroon was triggered by the failure of the Ahidjo/Biya regime and France to come to terms with the reality of globalization, the identitarian turn in societies around the world, and the rise of English as the global lingua franca in the post-Cold War era.

The Clash of Legal Philosophies and Cultures in Cameroon

At first blush, the Anglophone/Francophone divide in Cameroon appears to be a matter of Africans fighting over two colonial languages (English and French). Indeed, researchers have concluded that language, language policy, and language protection were the bones of contention in the Anglophone Revolt (Nforbin, 2019). While there is an obvious divide between English and Pidgin-speaking Southern Cameroons and French-speaking *la République du Cameroun*, the conflict goes beyond language. It is a clash of worldviews, political postures, religious orientations, and cultures that pits the numerical and cultural minority, the English and Pidgin-speakers in Southern Cameroons (divided and renamed "Northwest and Southwest regions") and the majority French-speakers in the Republic of Cameroon. Globalization of the English language made recognition of Anglophone cultural and identitarian specificity on the one hand, and postcolonial Franco-African authoritarian cultural assimilation on the other hand, inevitable. This resulted in a clash of cultures. This clash involved the centripetal political acceleration, the centralizing governmentality of the French-dominated *République du Cameroun*, and centrifugal political deceleration, the decentering pressures of demands for recognition of the identitarian and cultural specificity of the English and Pidgin-speaking (Anglophone) minority. This clash of worldviews and cultures manifested itself primarily in political and trade union disputes over the English-medium educational system and especially in the English-medium, common law legal system of Southern Cameroons. This clash of cultures, which had been simmering beneath the seemingly placid surface of Cameroon politics, burst into the surface like molten magma from Mount Fako in 2016.

Aim of this chapter

Attempts by the Francophone-dominated government of *la République du Cameroun* to harmonize away and disperse the common law legal system of the English-speaking Southern Cameroons into the Napoleonic, civil law national system was one of the major triggers of the Anglophone Revolt of 2016. At the beginning of the Revolt, the perception of Anglophone common law lawyers was that the common law–and common law lawyers—had been relegated to a position of "sub-alternity or marginality," to borrow the expression of Legrand (2003, p.244), from where they were being gradually squeezed out of existence in the overwhelmingly French civil law system of Cameroon. That perception of hegemonic marginalization had been growing steadily since the 1980s when the Francophone-dominated government of President Paul Biya took a crucial centralizing turn, a deliberate policy to eradicate the identitarian and cultural specificity of the English and Pidgin-speaking minority West Cameroonians and dissolve it in the imagined "Kamerun" nation. This chapter compares and contrasts the philosophical and systemic differences between the British common law systems of Anglophone West Cameroon and the Napoleonic civil law system of French Cameroun. It describes and explains how the law in the books and the law in action in both parts of the country differentially approach issues of human rights, the rule of law and the administration of justice, leading to conflicts of law.

The chapter analyzes how the Cameroon government's refusal to resolve these political and philosophical conflicts contributed to the Anglophone Revolt of 2016. The premise of this chapter is that the Anglophone Revolt emerged from a clash between the common law legal system of West Cameroon, and the civil law legal regime of French Cameroon over fundamental philosophical and legal issues like the separation of powers, the rule of law versus the rule of man, human rights, the applicability of military law and civilian law in non-military situations, the tension between law and rights, and issues of human dignity, sanctity, and freedom of expression. The identarian, systemic, institutional, and professional grievances of the Anglophone common law lawyers were part of the ferment in English and Pidgin-speaking West Cameroon that, taken together, brought about generalized dissatisfaction with the authoritarian, assimilationist turn of events and a feeling of marginalization on the part of Anglophones.

Ladies and Gentlemen of the Common Law Versus the Forces of Law and Disorder

One of the unprecedented and incongruous sights of the Anglophone Revolt that began in Cameroon in 2016 was the image of striking, English-speaking learned men and women, common law lawyers parading the streets of Bamenda, Kumba or Buea, in full court dress – black advocates' ceremonial robes and white court wigs on their heads – marching silently in the hot tropical sun. The learned men and women of the law marched silently and solemnly, carrying banners and signs that proclaimed their grievances: "Anglophones Should Stand Up to Save the Anglo-Saxon English System of Education from Complete Eradication. Only a Two-state Federation or Outright Independence Can Save the Common Law and Anglophones." Other signs read: "Stop the Injustice Against Anglophone Cameroonians. Don't Destroy the Anglo-Saxon Universities of Buea and Bamenda. They are the Nurseries of Common Law Lawyers" and "We reject the abuse of human rights in Cameroon." The English-speaking common law lawyers who had formed a Common Law Bar Association, which defined itself in opposition to the Napoleonic Civil law system in force in French Cameroon, also held signs that read: "Our New Common Law Bar Association Will Ensure the Protection of Common Law, Respect for Rule of Law and Stand Against all Forms of Injustice." These unprecedented demonstrative processions on the street represented active resistance against the introduction of the French language, French-speaking judges and magistrates–and by extension, the Napoleonic civil law system–in court proceedings in English-and Pidgin-speaking West Cameroon, which had, due to indirect British colonialism, become part of the imagined global Anglosphere where the common law legal system was the norm. Crowds of onlookers stared silently at the learned men and women of the law, who had decided to boycott the courts in order to publicly protest the intolerable wrongs that the highly centralized, Napoleonic civil law legal regime of the kleptocratic, authoritarian, *cheffferie républicaine* had inflicted upon them..

Since Cameroon is a national security state in which law and order trump rights, specifically the rights of freedom of assembly, freedom of expression, and freedom to air grievances, the forces of law and order were not amused by these solemn demonstrations of common law lawyers. The omnibus paramilitary gendarmerie, who are essentially forces of law, violent enforcement, and disorder, confronted the protesters, riot shields, helmets, tear gas, guns, and truncheons at the ready. The lawyers and gendarmes stood face-to-face for a short period of time. Without warning, the gendarmes charged the unarmed, peaceful, protesting men and women of the law. They proceeded to brutalize the lawyers who had naively entertained the illusion that they were acting under the color of law and that their peaceful demonstration was within the ambit of the right of freedom of expression set forth in the Constitution of Cameroon, the African Charter on Human and Peoples' Rights and the UN Universal Declaration of Human Rights. The gendarmes beat up the men and women of the law, tore off the wigs and gowns of those they could reach, seized their cellphones, and proceeded to search the law firms of those lawyers whom they considered the ring leaders of the demonstration. In some cases, they seized properties and documents without valid search warrants. Attempts by the lawyers to hold press conferences were banned by the unelected administrators appointed by the president. The bans were enforced by gendarmes and police officers. This strike was the culmination of a series of actions undertaken by the government, and counteractions undertaken by the common law lawyers of the English-speaking Northwest and Southwest regions, who viewed these governmental actions and decrees as attempts to undermine and eradicate the common law regime and disperse common law lawyers into the Jacobine/Napoleonic civil law system that obtained in the rest of the country. This discontent had been simmering in the English and Pidgin-speaking Southern Cameroons, at least since the All Anglophone Conference of 1993. However, the immediate cause of the revolt of the common law lawyers was a proposed transformation of the administration of justice in the English-speaking regions into a Napoleonic, civil-law-style regime. When news got out that the system was about to be "civilized" (Francophonized), the common law lawyers, advocates and notaries public strenuously resisted it. On 16 April 2014, they wrote a protest statement to the government entitled: "Petition against the imminent appointment of notaries-public and the extension of the French Civil Code to the Anglophone regions of our country." In this petition, the advocates/notaries of the North West and South West Regions complained that "unfortunately, the past forty-two (42) years have witnessed a systematic and unmitigated dismantling of the Southern Cameroons heritage. This could be seen in all spheres of our national life whereby the identity of the Cameroonian Anglophone is systematically being annihilated." (cited in Nforbin, 2019). The men and women of the law received no formal response from the Ministry of Justice and Keeper of the Seals or any other government official.

The Clash of Cultures of Due Process and Human Rights: The British Common Law of Southern Cameroons Versus the Napoleonic Civil Law of French Cameroun

The fundamental issue of the Anglophone Question in Cameroon is the diverse, even contrasting conceptualizations of the rule of law, due process of law, and the rights of the citizen between the common law system of Southern Cameroons (the Northwest and Southwest regions) and French Cameroun. As we saw above, the United Kingdom administered the UN Trust Territory of British Southern Cameroons from its Nigerian colony and protectorate. The territory thus inherited principles of the rule of law that are traceable to the Magna Carta: habeas corpus, a presumption of innocence, adversarial legalism, due process of law, and independence of the judiciary. For its part, French Cameroun inherited the highly centralized, inquisitorial, Napoleonic civil law system where law is more important than rights. In this system, there is no presumption of innocence, no due process of law, and no independence of the judiciary. Attempts to "harmonize" both systems into a system suitable for a bilingual, multicultural Federal Republic of Cameroon were stymied by the assimilationist mentality of France and French Cameroon, which attempted to diminish English and Pidgin-speaking Southern Cameroons' cultural and identitarian connection with the Anglosphere, in order to assimilate it into the French sphere of influence, la Francophonie. President Ahidjo instituted an authoritarian, neo-patrimonial, kleptocratic, one-party, *chefferie républicaine* (Republican chiefdom) where there was no separation of powers, and the authoritarian president ruled by decree. Administratively, the Federal Republic of Cameroon adopted the French system of unelected Napoleonic *préfets* and *sous-préfets*, who are appointed by presidential decree and reported to no one but the President of the Republic. They have the power to authorize or ban political and social gatherings and evict whole villages, as we see in the chapter on the Nigerian connection. Orders of the préfet are law in all jurisdictions.

Figure 5.1. President Ahmadou Ahidjo and Prime Minister Paul Biya, creators of the "republican chiefery" of Cameroon.

The authoritarian turn of Cameroon ultimately led to a clash of its two legal systems. In October 1992, Cameroon held its first multi-party presidential elections. This was a major development after thirty years of the Ahidjo/Biya dictatorial, one-party *chefferie républicaine* (republican chieftaincy). In effect, the fall of the Berlin Wall, the dissolution of the Warsaw Pact and the collapse of the Soviet Union between 1989 and 1991 had unleashed a fierce whirlwind of of instability over the African continent. One of the consequences was relative political liberalization and an exponential growth of independent newspapers, tabloids, and magazines (Eko, 2007). However, the "democratization and liberalization" of the post-Cold War period did not transform all African countries into liberal democracies. The relative freedom of the media was enough to cause discomfort to the ruling elite, but in time, these old dictatorships were able to regroup and continue their authoritarian, neo-patrimonial ways. The Biya regime in Cameroon is one of those regimes that paid lip service to democracy, but the more things changed, the more they stayed the same.

Figure 5.2. Left, Vice President John Ngu Foncha and Prime Minister Paul Biya. Figure 5.3. Right, Prime Minister Paul Biya and Vice President Solomon Tandeng Muna.

The 1992 presidential election was a case in point. At the end of the hotly contested, chaotic, and opaque affair, the chief justice of the Supreme Court acknowledged serious irregularities in the election process but stated that there were no formal complaints over which it could assert jurisdiction at that time. He, therefore, proceeded to announce that President Biya had won the elections with 39.9% of the vote, that the candidate for the opposition Social Democratic Front (SDF) had obtained 35.9%, and that the UNDP candidate, Bello Bouba Maigari, had obtained 19.2% of the vote. The SDF refused to accept the results, claiming that they were fraudulent. National and international observers like the National Democratic Institute for International Affairs (NDI) concluded that the Cameroon government had manipulated the electoral process, that the elections were far from free and fair, and that they were tainted by many irregularities to the point that they could not be viewed as reflecting the will of the Cameroonian people. As such, the results announced by the partisan Ministry of Territorial Administration, giving President Biya the victory, were highly questionable and non-verifiable (NDI, 1992). In short, the conclusion of the opposition and many observers was that the elections had been rigged by the hardline Biya regime.

The announcement of the disputed results triggered a rash of violence, looting, arson, and killings in Bamenda, as well as other parts of the Northwest, the home region of John Fru Ndi, the losing presidential candidate of the opposition Social Democratic Front. In response, the president-elect, Paul Biya, declared a state of emergency. As a result, a leading SDF member and former judge, Nyo'Wakai and 172 other political activists were arrested and detained in what has been described as highly insalubrious and "absolutely dehumanizing conditions" at the *Brigade Mixte Mobile* (BMM), a notorious military, paramilitary gendarmerie, and police detention center in Bamenda, for committing unspecified "common law offenses." In response, twenty-two English-speaking common law lawyers filed a motion at the High Court of Mezam, Bamenda, on behalf of the political detainees. The lawyers requested the court to grant the detainees bail, pending charges that may be filed against them. Their rationale was that the detentions were arbitrary and flagrantly irregular. The issue before the court was whether the detention of Justice Nyo'Wakai and the 172 SDF political activists was irregular. The court answered in the affirmative, stating that none of the detainees were implicated in the events that followed the proclamation of the 1992 election results, and ordered that all the detained persons be either released forthwith or released on bail pending charges that may be brought against them (Nyo' Wakai and 172 Others v. State of Cameroon, 1992). The Minister of Justice in Yaoundé was furious. He claimed the Bamenda High Court ruling was illegal because the Court did not have jurisdiction over "administrative acts" (detentions ordered by the unelected *sous-préfets*, *préfets*, governors or the Minister of Justice himself). He, therefore, ordered the Minister of Territorial Administration not to release the detainees as ordered by the Mezam High Court. This was an authoritarian Francophone civil law action in which "administrative law" trumped the common law right of presumption of innocence, freedom from arbitrary arrest, and wrongful detention. The action also made a mockery of a common law court in English-speaking Cameroon. This was a major clash between the common law system, with its heightened ethos of protection of individual rights, and the Francophone civil law system, which had no presumption of innocence and gave unelected administrative officers absolute power over citizens (Tande, 2017).

Figure 5.4. "War Continues in Bamenda," *Cameroon Post*, December 29, 1992 (reporting the conflict of laws between the Anglophone common law and the Francophone Civil/Administrative law).

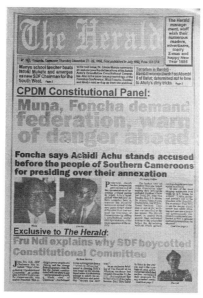

Figure 5.5. Muna, Foncha demand federation, warn of danger ahead, *The Herald*, December 1994.

In an act of absolute contempt of the Anglophone common law system in force in Southern Cameroons, as well as the Mezam High Court that was applying it, on the night of December 27, 1992, the 173 detainees that the Mezam High Court had ordered released were bundled into Cameroon government public transport buses and deported to Yaoundé, essentially removing them from the jurisdiction of the Anglophone common law system and its protection of individual rights (War Comes to Bamenda, 1992; Tande, 2017). That was the beginning of the French Cameroon government's practice of arresting political activists, demonstrators, members of civil society, students and so on, in the English and Pidgin-speaking Southern Cameroons, and deporting them to detention centers, military tribunals, and prisons in French-speaking Cameroun. This practice, which essentially eviscerated the courts in Anglophone Southern Cameroons, was one of the reasons why common law lawyers were at the forefront of the Anglophone Revolt in 2016.

The Spark that Set off the Anglophone Revolt: Assimilationist Presidential Decree of December 18, 2014

The Anglophone crisis was triggered by a number of actions that common law lawyers viewed as affronts to the English-medium common law system in Southern Cameroons. On 17 November 2014, a Francophone judge of the administrative court of the English-speaking South West Region delivered a judgment in French, l'affaire Theodore Leke c. Etat du Cameroun (*Theodore Leke v. the State of Cameroun*). This systemic line-crossing scandalized the common law legal community, which protested strenuously against it because two of the three judges were English-speaking, and the defendant was an English-speaking person who did not speak or understand French. However, this case was a sore reminder to the common law lawyers that Cameroon's administrative law is mostly of French inspiration (Nforbin, 2019). However, the most radical act of legal assimilation and dispersal in the legal history of post reunification Cameroon, the occurrence that was the figurative equivalent of throwing a lit matchstick into the long, smoldering powder-keg of Anglophone common law lawyers' discontent took place on December 18, 2014. On that fateful day, the Biya regime demonstrated utter contempt for the common law lawyers and their spirited submissions, petitions and protests by turning a deaf ear to their insistent pleas. More than that, it took an affirmative step that escalated the cultural tensions between Anglophone and Francophone Cameroon. After a meeting of the *Conseil Supérieure de la Magistrature* (Supreme Judicial Council, a body that we discuss below) presided over by President Paul Biya entirely in French, the president issued a presidential decree posting magistrates and judges who had recently graduated from the French-style *grande école, l'École Supérieure de l'Administration et de la Magistrature* (Higher Institute of Administration and Magistracy, that is popularly known by its acronym, ENAM). This decree, which was read on national radio and TV like all other decrees, posted new magistrates to different court jurisdictions around the country. The decree also reshuffled the judiciary by transferring magistrates and judges already in service to various jurisdictions. The decree was controversial because it did something unprecedented. It did not consider the bi-jural nature of the country. French-speaking judges and magistrates who were trained in, and practiced in the Jacobine/Napoleonic civil law system, and knew little or no English, were posted to preside over court jurisdictions in the English and Pidgin-speaking former Southern Cameroons, divided and renamed the Northwest and Southwest regions. Some English-speaking magistrates were also posted to French-speaking jurisdictions. This was the ultimate act of muting, assimilation, and dispersal of the common law system into la Francophonie. The dilemma posed by this decree was how French-speaking magistrates and judges could fairly and impartially administer justice to English and Pidgin-speaking litigants and advocates. Though this practice of posting French-speaking judges to preside over cases in the English-speaking regions was common in the Military Tribunal system–resulting in monumental miscarriages of justice–this was the first time this assimilationist practice was being extended to civilian courts. One of the most incomprehensible results of this deliberate act of administrative authoritarianism was that all the judges in the North West Court of Appeal (an English-speaking, common law jurisdiction) turned out to be Francophone judges trained in the French civil law tradition.

The Anglophone common law lawyers were taken aback. They saw in this decree, an arbitrary, top-down imposition designed to "civilize" (read assimilate and Francophonize) the administration of law in the English and Pidgin-speaking former Southern Cameroons. They saw this as an attack on the identitarian and cultural specificity of the English and Pidgin-language common law system, a move to undermine the very foundation of Cameroon as a bilingual, bi-jural country. They wasted no time making known their dissatisfaction to the government of Cameroon. In a memorandum dated 13th March 2015, and addressed to: "appropriate government and judicial officers" the common law lawyers of the South West region, represented by the Fako Lawyers' Association (FAKLA) and the Meme Lawyers' Association (MELA), denounced the government's ham-handed way of dealing with "issues which adversely impinge on our common law practices and usages and call to question the bi-jural foundations of our judicial system." The men and women of the law gave the authorities in Yaoundé 30 days to redress these grievances, "failing which we shall consider further appropriate action." (Nforbin, 2019).

According to human rights lawyer, Nkongho Felix Agbor Balla, President of the Fako Lawyers' Association, a collective of self-described common law lawyers in the Southwest region of Cameroon, the Ministry of Justice in Yaoundé, exhibited a haughty indifference and reckless disregard towards the concerns and submissions of the Anglophone lawyers. The Francophone government essentially turned a blind eye and deaf ear to the identitarian and human rights pleas of the Anglophone men and women of the law. In a 2017 interview on the independent television station, Equinoxe of Douala, Barrister Nkongho Felix Agbor Balla, Anglophone lawyer, human rights activist, and federalist told his audience that for the English and Pidgin-speaking minority linguistic community of Cameroon: "French is the language of oppression." He then proceeded to present a chronology of events and counter-events, occurrences and counter-occurrences that ultimately led to a breakdown in communication between Anglophone teachers, lawyers and the government. The resulting stalemate led to the Anglophone Revolt.

The Common Law Lawyers' Bamenda Memorandum of May 2015

The common law lawyers of the Southwest and Northwest soon responded formally to the presidential decree of December 18, 2014 that had symbolically erased the linguistic, philosophical and cultural differences between the bi-jural common law and civil law judicial regimes in Cameroon. The willy-nilly transfer of magistrates and judges across the two systems without references to appropriate training and linguistic competence essentially negated the cultural and identitarian specificity of the common law and the common law lawyers. On 9th May 2015, 700 English-language common law Lawyers met in Bamenda to, "address a wide range of issues affecting the nature and quality of the administration of justice and the rule of law in Cameroon, especially as they negatively impact the minority English-speaking members of this Bi-Cultural, Bi-Jural, reality in Cameroon." At the end of the heated deliberations, the men and women of the common law wrote a "Bamenda Memorandum" to the President, the Prime Minister, the National Assembly, the Senate, the National Bar Council, the Nigerian High Commission, and others. The Bamenda Memorandum reiterated the philosophical, systemic, linguistic, institutional, and practical issues that the lawyers believed needed to be addressed by the Cameroon government to avoid work stoppage and mass civil disobedience in the English and Pidgin-speaking Northwest and Southwest regions. The strongly worded memorandum was accusatory in tone. It addressed not just purely legal matters. It ventured into broader Anglophone identitarian matters and issues of the cultural specificity of the community in Cameroon. The Memorandum, which sounded like a pre-revolutionary *cahier de doléances* (litany of grievances) proclaimed in part:

> We note the deliberate and well-planned program of whittling away and replacement of the Common Law-inspired rules of Criminal Procedure, Civil Procedure, and of Evidence, with a system and culture of French-inspired or copied Civil Law and strongly and unequivocally reject this process and practice and demand the restoration of the referred Common

Law-inspired Rules of practice and Procedure...

We oppose and reject the progressive replacement of Common law inspired rules and principles of substantive law in such areas as contract, tort, land law, family law, etc. and call for their restoration within the Common Law jurisdiction in strict respect of the bi-jural nature of our country and in keeping with the Country's Constitution...

We strongly condemn the absence of independence of the Country's Judiciary and the domination and control of the judiciary by the executive with the resulting loss of a truly transparent, credible and independent system of administration of justice and its attendant unpredictability and call for an immediate review of the justice sector of the country with a view to rendering it more Just, Functional, more credible, less corrupt, independent, dependable and reliable in the service of justice and a truly democratic society...

The two Divisions of Common Law and Civil Law be clearly defined and operated side by side in ENAM and the quota of intake in both divisions known in advance. Only common law trained Magistrates to be posted in the South West and North West Regions and Civil Law Trained Magistrates to the Civil Law Jurisdictions.

The men and women of the English-language common law then ventured outside the domain of strictly legal issue to address wider Anglophone identitarian, cultural and communitarian issues and grievances that they felt were pertinent to the administration of justice and their role as legal practitioners. They talked about the other major bulwark of Anglophone cultural and identitarian specificity in Cameroon. They appealed to the government to ensure the linguistic autonomy of the Anglophone regions and insisted:

That the Educational System in the South West and North West Regions should not be adulterated, English-speaking citizens should have their studies in the English language from cradle to professional life. That all Public Examinations be organized in two Poles; English and French, with none being translated from the other, and the quota in both poles known in advance.

We have observed with utter dismay that there has been and continues to be a lack of protection with regard to the rights of the minority (Anglophone Cameroonians) as provided for in the constitution of this bi-jural, bilingual and bi-cultural nation. It is obvious that the rights of the Anglophones in Cameroon in the spheres of education, socio-cultural values, administrative setups etc., are continuously and systematically being eroded with a view of imposing the socio-cultural and administrative views of the French and or Civil law heritage of the majority Francophone Cameroon.

The lawyers ended their memorandum with a sensitive political demand that raised the hackles of the Francophone majority–a reexamination of the form of the dysfunctional, over-centralized, authoritarian, neo-patrimonial State of Cameroon, and restoration of a decentralized federation.

> We demand that the State should exercise its Constitutional duty to protect the Anglophone minority and, by so doing, protect our history, heritage, education and cultural values. Consequently, for the better protection of the minority Anglophone Cameroonians and the Common Law heritage, we strongly demand a Federation.

The government of Cameroon did not respond to the Bamenda Memorandum. On 13 February 2016, Common Law Lawyers met in Buea and issued the Buea Declaration that decried the continued erosion of the common law in Anglophone Cameroon and asked for linguistic autonomy in the courts and educational system. The government did not see it fit to respond to this new plea.

In the face of governmental indifference towards their pleas and demands, the Anglophone common law lawyers wrote another petition on 6th October 2016. This open letter was entitled a "Joint Communiqué of the Leadership of the Constituent Associations of the Cameroon Common Law Lawyers" to President Paul Biya. It decried the fact that the lawyers' previous correspondences had not elicited any responses whatsoever from the government. They then proceeded to restate their request to President Biya "in his capacity as Head of the Judiciary, the Head of the Executive and principal initiator of legislation in both legislative houses." That thinly veiled sarcastic formulation suggested that there was no separation of powers in Cameroon, that Biya was the "be all and end all," the republican chieftain who had absolute power and control over the executive, legislative and judicial branches of government. The insinuation was that Cameroon was a state of law and disorder in which the rule of man trumped the rule of law, and the law took precedence over rights. The common law lawyers demanded that:

> That Your Excellency should hold an emergency session of the Higher Judicial Council and redeploy All Civil Law Magistrates from the two Common Law jurisdictions of the Northwest and Southwest Regions and, in the same vein, redeploy All Common Law Magistrates from the Civil Law jurisdictions to the Common Law jurisdictions of the Northwest and Southwest Regions.

The lawyers then proceeded to give the president notice that if their requests were not accommodated, all common law lawyers would hold a "sit-down strike from all court actions" from Tuesday, 11th of October 2016, to the 14th of October 2016.

The Biya government once more ignored the open letter from the common law lawyers, who began their sit-down strike from all court activities on Tuesday, the 11th of October 2016. This action of the men and women of the common law essentially marked the beginning of the Anglophone Revolt. The government created an Inter-ministerial

Ad-hoc Committee to dialogue with the common law lawyers regarding their strike. The committee quickly deadlocked, and no solution was found to end the lawyers' strike.

Barrister Felix Nkongho (Agbor Balla) told Equinoxe TV, Douala, that the Anglophone common law lawyers met Justice Minister Laurent Esso to discuss their grievances, but all they got from him was disrespect. The minister did not hide the fact that he thought the common law lawyers were being insubordinate, a threat to national unity and coercion. The Biya-appointed Senior Divisional Officer for Fako, Mr. Zang III, then issued an order banning the Fako Lawyers' Association. The lawyers next met with Prime Minister Philemon Yang and requested him to open a commission of inquiry to investigate atrocities security forces had visited on lawyers in Bamenda, Buea, Limbe and Muyuka. Nothing came of the meetings.

Enter the Cameroon Anglophone Civil Society Consortium

One of the major developments of the Anglophone Revolt was the emergence of the Cameroon Anglophone Civil Society Consortium, an organization made up of the leaders of the common law lawyers, Anglophone teachers' trade unions, university students, churches, and activists opposed to the assimilation and marginalization of the English and Pidgin-speaking minority in Cameroon. While lawyers protested the imposition of Napoleonic French civil law and criminal procedure on English-medium courts, teachers and students went on strike to protest the assimilation and "Francophonization" of the English-medium educational system of the Northwest and Southwest regions. The consortium spearheaded resistance against the Cameroon government's arrest, torture, deportation, persecution, and prosecution of Anglophone dissidents and activists. On January 17, 2017, Minister of Territorial Administration (Interior), Réné Sadi issued a decree declaring the Anglophone Civil Society Consortium a threat to national unity and banned it. All its activities were declared illegal. The Cameroonian authorities were also not amused by the activism of Barrister Felix Nkongho Agbor Balla, a federalist, human rights, and common law activist who was president of the banned Fako Lawyer's Association, as well as president of the banned Cameroon Anglophone Civil Society Consortium (CACSC). On January 17th, the same day the Consortium was banned, Barrister Felix Agbor Balla Nkongho, and Dr. Fontem Neba, Secretary General of the Consortium, were arrested in Buea, blindfolded and driven to the dungeons at the Gendarmerie Headquarters, the *Secretariat d'État à la Defense* (Secretariat of State for Defense) in Yaoundé and detained incommunicado. On 20 January 2017, they were charged with "terrorism, hostility against the motherland, secession, insurrection, contempt of public authorities, and collective rebellion"; "incitement to civil war by bringing the inhabitants of the South- and Northwest regions to arm themselves against other citizens"; and "attempt[ing] to modify the constitutional laws, notably the federalist system, through violence." Though Agbor Balla and his English-speaking co-accused are civilians, they were charged in the French-language-only Yaoundé Military Tribunal because their alleged offenses fell under Law No. 2014/028 of 23 December 2014 on the Suppression of Acts of Terrorism. They faced the death penalty if found guilty. Though Agbor Balla and his co-accused are part of the Anglophone linguistic and numerical minority, the Military Tribunal's proceedings were carried out entirely in French, and they did not have the benefit of English interpreters (See Volume II Chapter 27 for trial observation report written by the Law Society of England and Wales). This essentially meant that they and hundreds of other Anglophone political prisoners were transferred from the adversarial common law jurisdiction of Southern Cameroons, where there was still a modicum of a presumption that accused persons were innocent until proven guilty—and the burden of proof is on the prosecution— to the inquisitorial civil law jurisdiction of Francophone Cameroun where there is no presumption of innocence and the burden of proof was on the accused. This is exactly the type of cross-system, boundary-crossing that the English-speaking common law lawyers had been denouncing. For these Anglophones, oppression came in French. Political activists are arrested in French, they are tortured in French, tried in French-language courts, and imprisoned in French language prisons.

Multiple governments, international human rights organizations, law societies, and other non-governmental societies around the world criticized the arrest and prosecution of Agbor Balla, Dr Fontem Aforteka'a Neba and others. The French-language Yaoundé Military Tribunal denied defense pleas to release the accused on bail and remanded them for detention at the Kondengui Prison in Yaoundé. After multiple appearances before the Military Tribunal, and multiple adjournments, international pressure on the Cameroon government became so intense that President Biya issued a decree in French – ordering the release of Felix Nkongho Agbor Balla, Dr. Fontem Aforteka'a Neba, Justice Paul Ayah Abine and 53 other Anglophone detainees who had been arrested between October 2016 and January 2017 (Amnesty International, 2019). Agbor Balla and his colleagues had spent eight months in prison. Though more than 1000 other Anglophones remained in detention or had been sentenced to long prison terms over the crisis, Cameroonian cartoonist, Nyemb Popoli published a cartoon presenting the Anglophone crisis as a David versus Goliath conflict. Biya was depicted as the fallen Goliath.

Figure 5.6. David vs. Goliath as depicted by cartoonist, Nyemb Popoli

Agbor Balla Nkongho's Dismissal from the University of Buea and International Recognition

When Agbor Balla was released from prison, he resumed his position as an adjunct professor at the University of Buea. He was assigned to teach a course entitled "Political and Constitutional History of Cameroon (Law 243)." He would soon learn that academic freedom was one of the casualties of the Anglophone crisis due to the prominent role he and other lawyers and teachers had played in it. An examination he set for this class got him into trouble with the Cameroon government. In effect, he gave his students the following highly "sensitive" examination questions that focused on the Anglophone Question:

1. The Anglophone Crisis since 2016 was caused by the lawyers' and teachers' strike. Assess the validity of this statement
2. Discuss the Special Status within the framework of the Special Status in Cameroon.
3. Between 1961 and 1972, Cameroon had Federation. Discuss (Bisong, 2020).

In a breathtaking act of violation of academic freedom, the Minister of State for Higher Education in Yaoundé, Jacques Famé Ndongo, who is the boss of all universities in Cameroon, ordered the Vice Chancellor of the University of Buea to punish Agbor Balla for transforming the classroom into a platform for political advocacy in breach of the ethical and deontological code of the university which demands that all courses, including political science and law courses be "apolitical." The international human rights lawyer said he believed his examination questions fell "within the confines of the course." The Cameroon government did not think so. Since arresting Agbor Balla and sending him back to prison would have been condemned by human rights activists around the world, the government chose the less painful option. Agbor Balla was promptly dismissed, and all his courses and students withdrawn with immediate effect (Bisong, 2020). This exam controversy was a case study in Francophone violation of academic freedom in the English-speaking regions of Cameroon. The authoritarian republican chiefery has no room for freedom of thought or expression.

Fast forward to 2022. The Anglophone crisis ground on, taking more and more lives as the Biya regime took shelter in denial, trying one bath faith, half-baked idea after another rather than attack the root of the crisis, extinguishment of the autonomy of the English and Pidgin-speaking minority of the former British Southern Cameroons. He adamantly refused to recognize their identitarian and cultural specificity, and their claim to a share of the natural resources in their territory. After his release from prison, Barrister Felix Nkongho Agbor Balla formed the Center for Human Rights and Development in Africa (CHRDA), which is dedicated to the promotion of human rights, the rule of law, and democracy in Africa. CHRDA has partnered with international human rights organizations in monitoring, documenting, and reporting human rights violations perpetrated by the Cameroon security forces as well as the non-state armed groups, in the context of the Southern Cameroons crisis. CHRDA has trained civil society actors to protect the human rights of women and children, as well as prisoners in the volatile region. The international community has recognized Barrister Felix Nkongho Agbor Balla's human rights work. He has been given multiple awards including the Robert F. Kennedy Human Rights Award by the RFK Center in Washington DC.

Figure 5.7. Barrister Felix Agbor Nkongho (Balla) Gets RFK Human Rights Award, *The Advocate*, June 2022.

The Clash of Legal Cultures and Mentalities in Cameroon: Historical and Colonial Origins

We have seen that the Anglophone Revolt was caused for the most part by a clash of legal cultures and mentalities– the French Jacobin/Napoleonic civil law system, iterations of which obtain in the French-speaking world (*la Francophonie*) and in the French regions of Cameroon on the one hand, and the Anglo-Saxon common law legal system that obtains in the Anglosphere, and in the Northwest and Southwest region of Cameroon, on the other hand. Both systems were introduced to Cameroon after the German territory of Kamerun had been partitioned between the British and the French following their joint victory over the German colonial army during World War I. Four-fifths of the territory became the French Mandated Territory of Cameroun, while one fifth became the British Mandated Territory of Southern Cameroons. Both territories were thus colonized by France and Britain for 40 years. This section compares and contrasts the two legal systems – civil law and common law mentalities, cultures, and procedures that were introduced into French and British Cameroons respectively, by these colonial powers. Assimilation and harmonization of the two systems would become one of the major bones of contention between the two territories after they reunited in 1961. As we saw in earlier chapters, attempts by France and French Cameroon to mute the English-medium common law system of Anglophone Cameroon would ultimately lead to the Anglophone Revolt, the so-called Anglophone crisis in Cameroon. The immediate spark that set off the powder keg of the English-speaking common law lawyers' discontent, resentment, and resistance was what they perceived as Francophone attempts to mute, marginalize and assimilate the minority common law regime into the majority civil law regime. To understand this bone of contention, we will now carry out a comparative analysis of the French, Napoleonic civil law system of which an iteration is practiced in the English-speaking former Southern Cameroons (the North-west and Southwest regions). The two legal systems–the Napoleonic Civil law system and the British Common law system–were inherited by the States of East and West Cameroon from France and the United Kingdom, respectively, after a relatively short, 40 years of colonial Trusteeship under the United Nations. That was long enough for iterations of the two legal systems to be imprinted and emerge in the two territories. Legrand suggests that "law is culture" (1999) because the law reflects the ideologies, religious and moral values, cultural norms, mentalities, and community standards of specific countries and jurisdictions. As such, the law is a highly "structured and structuring system," to use the expression of Bourdieu (1994).

Comparative law scholars traditionally classify British common law–and its iterations in the Anglosphere (the United States and the British Commonwealth countries), and French law–and its iterations in (French former colonies and post-colonies regrouped under the *Organisation Internationale de la Francophonie*) as belonging to two different "Western" legal traditions, viz, the Anglo-American Common Law (French scholars generally refer to the common law system of the Anglosphere, as Anglo-Saxon) and the Continental European Civil or Romanistic Law tradition respectively (Stark et al., 2000; Zweigert & Kötz, 1998). However, Legrand (2003) cautions that: "'Civil law' and 'Common Law' do not exist *a priori* as kinds of essences, but only *a posteriori* in multiple incarnations–none of which is pure" (p. 244). The common law, as practiced in Commonwealth countries, is judge-made law based on the rule of stare decisis (Latin for "let the past decision stand"), a form of legal precedent that originated in the British common law. Under this system, jurisprudence is based on general principles found in judicial decisions (Holmes, 1881). It is therefore, judge-made law for the most part.

France is part of the Continental European civil law system, which stands in contra-distinction to the Anglo-American common law system. Historically, civil law is grounded in legal codes, which originated with the Romans (Zweigert & Kötz, 1998). Contemporary civil law is generally based on the codification and interpretation of general legal rules and principles of law constructed by legislators. In civil law countries, judges interpret articles of the code in order to arrive at legal decisions in specific cases. Such interpretations do not however, become authoritative legal precedent for subsequent cases. All future cases are based on fresh interpretations of the code without reference to prior judicial interpretations.[1] This statute-law system is different from the case-law system that obtains in the common law countries (Zweigert & Kötz, 1998).

Zweigert and Kötz (1998) suggest that *Le Code des Français*, Napoleon's *Code civil* of 1804, is the model of the branch of continental European civil law that they call the

---

1 John Crabb, The French Civil Code (1977) At 9. (Not sure what at 9 stands for)

"Romanistic legal family" (p. 174). In France, and Francophone countries, the *Code civil* and other legislative enactments in areas as diverse as freedom of expression, individual privacy and hate speech are not known for the exactitude, completeness or clarity of their language. Courts therefore have some leeway in interpreting their provisions in the light of changing society and new technologies (Zweigert and Kötz, 1998). David and Brierley suggest that French legal rule (doctrine) is related to moral philosophy and is much wider in scope than its Anglo-American equivalent. Some scholars note that the seeming rigidity of precedent and *stare decisis* (in comparison with the more flexible, interpretative French system) is attenuated by the technique of distinguishing cases (Stark et al., 2000). The Cameroonian iteration of the civil law is grounded on presidential rule-by-decree. Presidential decrees or executive actions that regulate all domains of national life are the primary form of law-making in Cameroon.

In criminal law, the common law is adversarial and accusatorial while the civil law system is inquisitorial. A very important difference between the two legal systems, as it is practiced in Cameroon, is their different postures on the presumption of innocence of accused persons. In the common law, adversarial system, an accused person is, in theory, presumed innocent until proven guilty, and the burden of proof is on the prosecution. Presumption of innocence is not very pronounced in the inquisitorial system of the civil law as transplanted in Francophone African countries (Nyo'Wakai, 2010). Judges are not impartial arbiters of legal disputes. The presumption is that anyone who is arrested or brought before a court is considered culpable.

The Frenchman's Burden: Diffusion of the Napoleonic Civil Law in the British Common Law Jurisdiction of West Cameroon

Law is an expression of politico-cultural mentalities and ideologies. This is what Legrand (2001) calls "law as culture." We have noted that the Napoleonic civil law and the British common law systems are different in terms of legal philosophy and their respective approaches to jurisprudence and the administration of justice. Legrand (2003) argues that: "law is a performance (whether voluntary or involuntary)–not a 'being' but a 'doing'–such that what makes civil law 'civil law' and what makes 'common law 'common law' takes place in a constituting process in which civil law and common law call upon each other as other in order to be able to fashion themselves and be what they are in difference from one another" (p. 244). The fundamental problem raised by the Anglophone Common Law Lawyers' Association was the clash between the iteration of the common law that obtained in English-speaking Cameroon and the iteration of the Napoleonic civil law that is practiced in the French-speaking part of Cameroon. These tensions were exacerbated by the fact that the civil law was introduced to the English and Pidgin-speaking State of West Cameroon in the context of the unequal power dynamics. After the reunification of the two States of Cameroon in 1961, France began a post reunification *mission assimilisatrice*. This was a mission to assimilate West Cameroon into *la Francophonie* and extend the French colonial "civilizing mission" across the Mungo River. This policy, that was operated from the French Consul in Buea, consigned the English and Pidgin-speaking West Cameroon and its common law tradition to a position of "sub-alternity and marginality" to borrow the expression of Legrand (2003), vis-à-vis French-speaking East Cameroon and its Napoleonic civil law system. In the 60 years after reunification, the official policy of harmonization of the two legal systems never produced the hybrid, mixed legal system that the Anglophone proponents of reunification and harmonization–Foncha, Muna, Nfon Victor Mukete, Emmanuel T. Egbe, Ndeh Ntumazah, and others–had hoped for (Nyo'Wakai, 2008). As it turned out, the ultimate goal of harmonization was not the creation of a hybrid, bilingual, multicultural legal system that respects the multiple subject and its multiple belongings. It was to assimilate English-speaking Cameroonians into the monoculturalism of *la Francophonie*. This was because the terms of the reunification between the two States were left deliberately vague to ensure assimilation of the common law system into the civil law system (Benard, 1961). The French/Francophone Cameroon assimilationist posture was based on the technique of "hierarchization of governmentalities" (Legrand, 2003, p.260, 261). To the French and their French Cameroun partners, the English and Pidgin-speaking Southern Cameroons and its common law tradition were, to borrow the expression of Legrand (2003, p. 260), "an imperfect approximation" of French civilization, culture and civil law. The crux of the Frenchman's jurisdictional burden in West Cameroon was thus cultural assimilation as the method of "civilizing" the less developed Anglophone State and its less refined iteration of the British common law. The Anglophone Revolt was thus the culmination of a clash of politico-cultural and legal cultures that not only affects the rule of law and the administration of justice, it affects the core of the identities and cultural specificity of the Anglophone and "Piginophones" minority of Cameroon. The Revolt represented a failure of the Biya regime to manage cultural difference. Biya opted to use the argument of deadly military force rather than the niceties of the force of political argument to address the Anglophone Question, which is essentially discontent discontent over the subaltern status of the minority Anglophone Community in Cameroon.

How it all Began: The Civil Law and Common Law systems in the Emerging Federal Republic of Cameroon

The genesis of the Anglophone crisis, which is actually the Cameroon crisis because it is a crisis of the form and governmentality (mentality of governance) of the nation of Cameroon, can be traced to the following factors: 1) the deliberately ambiguous constitutional and institutional pillars on which President Ahidjo and his French partners grounded the reunified nation, 2) the assimilationist linguistic and cultural mission of France in West Cameroon, 3) the reckless political nonchalance of John Ngu Foncha and the "One Kamerun" Anglophone leadership with regard to the nature and structure of the federation they were partnering with Ahidjo in creating, 4) the Machiavellian indifference of the exhausted and waning British empire, which considered Southern Cameroons an expendable burden, and 5) the ethno-authoritarian turn of the country under President Ahmadou Ahidjo and especially under President Paul Biya. The February 11, 1961 UN-supervised plebiscite where the people of Southern Cameroons were given the choice to decide whether to become independent through amalgamation with Nigeria or with French Cameroun (*la République du Cameroun*) did not decide the constitutional structure of the emergent nation. The political leaders of French East Cameroon and English and

Pidgin-speaking West Cameroon merely decided that a new nation, a constitutionally ambiguous country to be styled the Federal Republic of Cameroon would come into existence. The discussions that later ensued were about the detailed constitutional arrangements that arose after the vote. No union treaty was ever signed between the two States. It was a question of adapting the Constitution of the *République du Cameroun*–whose template was the French Constitution of 1958– to suit the circumstance of the emerging centralist Federal Republic of Cameroon. *La République du Cameroun* had become independent from France just one year earlier. This vagueness and uncertainty made it possible for President Ahmadou Ahidjo to assume an authoritarian, hegemonic, posture, and with the help of France and French lawyers, abolish the Federal Republic through a constitutional sleight of hand in 1972 (Benard, 1962; Dupuy, 1972). Justice Nyo'Wakai (2010, p. 111) suggests that the constitutionally ambiguous and vague nature of the reunification sowed the seeds of the Anglophone crisis because the so-called basic law [the Federal Constitution of 1961] essentially laid the foundation for the emergence of a dictatorship rather than a democracy. Indeed, the strong presidential regime ultimately evolved into a Francophone *chefferie républicaine* (republican chieftaincy).

The mindset of the midwives and powers-that-be of this new federalist experiment–President Ahmadou Ahidjo, Prime Minister, Paul Biya (and their behind-the-scenes partner, France), Hon. John Ngu Foncha, Prime Minister of Southern Cameroons and subsequent Vice President of the Federal Republic, Hon. Solomon Tandeng Muna, Prime Minister of West Cameroon, and subsequently Speaker of the National Assembly, and others—seems to have been, from the outset, that the survival of the emerging Federal Republic of Cameroon hinged on muting the identitarian and cultural specificity of English-speaking Southern Cameroons. This mindset was evident in the subsequent actions that Presidents Ahmadou Ahidjo and Paul Biya took to mute and assimilate Southern Cameroons and disperse it in the Francophone Cameroon national. That was the genesis of the Anglophone problem. Justice Nyo'Wakai (2008) suggested that the Anglophone problem arose because of the deliberate muting of the identitarian and cultural specificity of the numerical and linguistic minority, the people of the English and Pidgin-speaking Southern Cameroons (renamed West Cameroon, and later the Northwest and Southwest regions). In Justice Nyo'Wakai's view, the Anglophone problem was the fusion of a people with a distinct common culture and heritage into a national union where they are barred from asserting their identitarian and cultural distinctiveness. The problem also included "the refusal of their rightful due in the natural resources of the patrimony" (p. 111), by Presidents Ahidjo and Biya. The Anglophone Problem therefore manifested itself from the very beginning of the new Federal Republic of Cameroon. The role and place of the legal systems that the two States brought into the Federal Republic ultimately became a bone of contention that triggered the Anglophone Revolt. We now turn to that dimension of the legal history of Cameroon.

The Federal and State Legal Systems in West Cameroon after the Reunification

Since the history, political, cultural, identitarian, and legal specificity of the State of West Cameroon has been muted as part of the assimilationist program of the Ahidjo and Biya governments, not much is known of it outside the small circle of aging legal scholars.

This section is informed by the excellent book, *The Broken Scales of Justice: The Law and My Times* published by late Justice Nyo'Wakai who served in the office of the Federal *Procureur Général* of West Cameroon and under the Ministry of Justice in the centralized United Republic of Cameroon, and the Republic of Cameroon. This book fills a huge gap in the constitutional and judicial history of West Cameroon. In 1961, during the Foumban talks over provisions of the constitution of the emerging Federal Republic of Cameroon, the States of East and West Cameroon were represented by Ahmadou Ahidjo and John Ngu Foncha respectively. It soon became clear that there was a need to ensure that the reunification of East and West Cameroon would not amount to mere submergence of the identity and cultural specificity of the numerical and linguistic minority, West Cameroonians, in the majority Francophone sea. In order to assuage the fears of Anglophones who feared that reunification would also mean a loss of autonomy, thereby serve as a political guise for the annexation of Southern Cameroons by *la République du Cameroon*, it was agreed that the Constitution of the Federal Republic of Cameroon would contain a provision that would guarantee the long-term existence of the federation and the autonomy of West Cameroon. The vaguely-worded Part X of the Constitution of the Federal Republic of Cameroon (1961) provided:

> 47 (1) No bill to amend the Constitution may be introduced if it tends to impair the unity and integrity of the Federation.

Nevertheless, president Ahidjo would, in an act of extreme bad faith, ultimately go round this Constitutional provision by hurriedly proposing a national referendum in 1972 that essentially submerged the voice of the Anglophone minority, and eliminated the Federal Republic of Cameroon. This political sleight of hand accelerated the process of muting of the identitarian and cultural specificities of West Cameroon, and assimilating it into *la République du Cameroun*. This change of the form of the state is one of the bones of contention in the Anglophone crisis.

Balancing the Federal and the State Legal Systems

On October 1, 1961, when the Southern Cameroons united with the Republic of Cameroon to form the Federal Republic of Cameroon, West Cameroon had a Supreme Court, but due to a lack of trained lawyers and jurists, virtually all the judges and magistrates were from the United Kingdom or other countries of the Commonwealth. The situation was identical in East Cameroon, where virtually all the legal experts were French expatriates. Postcolonial Cameroon therefore had to import legal talent–from both the civil law and common law traditions–to meet the immediate personnel needs of the transplanted legal systems since there were very few trained legal experts, magistrates and judges in either French East or British West Cameroon. The persons charged with laying the foundation of the legal system of the Federal Republic of Cameroon were Hon. Sanda Oumarou, a Francophone, who was a French-style Minister of Justice and Keeper of the Seals, and the honorable Emmanuel Tabi Egbe, an Anglophone, English trained lawyer, who was Vice Minister of Justice. They kept the two transplanted legal traditions separate and developed them separately. While Hon. Oumarou recruited French jurists to serve as legal advisers and trainers for the Federal and East Cameroon civil law systems, Hon. E.T. Egbe recruited West Indian (Caribbean) common law lawyers of mostly African descent. Apparently, Mr. Egbe had met many Caribbean barristers in London during his legal studies there (Nyo'Wakai, 2008).

Since West Cameroon was a State, it had its own constitution, the West Cameroon Constitution. Though under the federal constitution, justice was a federal matter, there actually existed a parallel system of federal and State law in West Cameroon. The government of West Cameroon set up its own Legal Division, and had its own Attorney General, who participated in cabinet meetings. The Supreme Court of West Cameroon was also established to determine matters at first instance (High Court) and on appeal. The Honorable Justice S. M. L Endeley was the first Cameroonian to be appointed to the Supreme Court of West Cameroon. He ultimately became the Chief Justice of West Cameroon. Thus, in West Cameroon, both the Federal and West Cameroon State law officers came out of the common law tradition and worked hand-in-hand in that tradition. Indeed, prior to 1966, the Attorney General's Chambers in Buea carried out legal functions for the government of the Federated State of West Cameroon and that of the Federal State (Nyo'Wakai, 2008). In 1968, the Federal government appointed Frederick Ngomba Eko, a common law lawyer, *Procureur Général* for West Cameroon. Nyo'Wakai (2008) suggests that the federal law officer of the State of West Cameroon was known as the *Procureur Général* because "common lawyers in West Cameroon did not find, from his functions, an adequate appellation." Additionally, the law officers in the Procureur Général's Chambers were called Federal Counsel (F.C.). The arrival of a federal legal official from the French civil law tradition did not cause a stir because that official was a civil law lawyer who practiced civil law. This demonstrates that in West Cameroon, the emerging federal law took on a common law coloration, while in East Cameroon, federal law took on a civil law complexion. The bi-jural system in action.

Harmonization of the Civil Law and Common Law Systems

Under the Constitution of the Federal Republic of Cameroon, the administration of justice was a federal matter, a federal responsibility. However, in order to assure Anglophones and Francophones that they were not entering into the Federal Republic as legal and legislative tabula rasa on which an "alien" legal tradition could be imposed, Article 46 of the Constitution of the Federal Republic of Cameroon (1961) recognized the legislation, legislative history, and law reports of both Southern Cameroons and East Cameroon:

> Previous legislation of the Federated States shall remain in force in so far as it does not conflict with the provisions of this Constitution.

This constitutional provision essentially recognized the bi-jural nature of the Federal Republic of Cameroon. Despite the fact that the Federal Republic was a centralist French-style republic (Anyangwe, 2008), those who were responsible for developing a federal system of justice in Cameroon set out to build it on a nearly non-existent foundation. The civil law and common law systems that had been transplanted from France and the UK to French Cameroon and Southern Cameroons respectively, during their colonial Trusteeships, were still in their infancy. The leaders first had to develop and strengthen both systems side-by-side from the ground up. They did not have the time, the expertise or the political will to engage in the niceties of developing a brand-new, single, legal regime for the multi-cultural, bi-jural Federal Republic of Cameroon. Since the French and British United Nations Trusteeships over parts of Cameroon lasted only for a relatively short 40-year period, compared to the average 80 or more years of colonial administration in Nigeria, Ghana, Ivory Coast or Congo, the legal profession was under-developed in both parts of Cameroon (Nyo'Wakai, 2008).

Indeed, French East Cameroun had relied heavily on French lawyers, provided by France, to help it navigate and negotiate pre-independence *accords de coopération* (bilateral agreements) … with France on the eve of independence. French lawyers had also helped President Ahmadou Ahidjo draft the federal constitution that was the subject of negotiations with John Ngu Foncha and his team of "One Kamerun" Anglophone politicians. In contrast, Southern Cameroonians clearly lacked sound legal advice from constitutional law experts. Foncha and his team paid lip service to that reunificationist ideology, but exhibited a surprisingly reckless nonchalance with regard to the nature of the federation to which they were bringing West Cameroon (Johnson, 1965). Foncha's lack of transparency with his Anglophone colleagues with respect to Ahidjo's constitution only compounded the problem. The result is that the whole vague, federal constitutional edifice was built on a structure of unequal legal power dynamics. As such, the Federal Republic of Cameroon that emerged from talks between Ahidjo and Foncha was a French-style "unitary federalist" government that drew heavily on the Gaullist French Constitution of 1958 (Anyangwe, 2008).

After the plebiscite of 1961, efforts were to be made to create a nationally and culturally relevant hybrid system that reflected the multi-cultural and bi-jural nature of the Federal Republic of Cameroon. There was thus a need at the federal level, to fuse or harmonize both systems and begin the task of creating a Cameroon federal law regime that that would meet universal ideals of human rights and freedom of expression enshrined in the Universal Declaration of Human Rights, and also reflect the specificity of the multicultural, bilingual, and bi-jural nature of the country. The official policy of legal fusion was called "harmonization." Harmonization was intended to bring about legal approximation, certainty and predictability rather than uniformity (Andenas & Anderson, 2012). In Cameroon, harmonization can be conceptualized as legal and regulatory unity in diversity in the bi-jural legal and legislative context. This harmonized federal law would be a national system of converged laws that would transcend the traditional civil law and common law distinction, and include Cameroon customary law. The government adopted a program of harmonization of the legal and educational systems of both of the Federated States of Cameroon. The intent was to blend elements of the Napoleonic civil law and the British common law to create a new, hybrid system of law and legal procedure that would be relevant to the new postcolonial realities of Cameroon (Nyo'Wakai, 2008). However, the term harmonization meant different things to lawyers on both sides of the linguistic and legal divide. For Francophones trained in the civil law tradition, it meant legal assimilation, unification of laws, sameness, and uniformity of the entire law–in the image of Napoleonic civil law– while for Anglophone lawyers, it meant limited legal hybridity that would go no further than necessary to create consistency of laws, legal principles, regulations, standards and practices in specific domains and circumstances, while respecting the specificity of the common law tradition of the Anglophone West Cameroon.

The Anglophone common law lawyers' strike and the Anglophone Revolt are indications that the policy of harmonization was a dismal failure. The failure of harmonization–the emergence of a hybrid legal system that incorporates French civil law, British common law, and African customary law–is attributable to a number of factors: 1) the not-so-subtle assimilationist agenda of France and French Cameroon, 2) a clash of transplanted legal cultures between the two systems, and 3) the sharp authoritarian turn of the Ahidjo/Biya regime, which became anti-federalist, vitiated the independence of the judiciary, and quashed freedom of expression.

Franco-Cameroon Assimilationist Governmentality and the Legal System

During the Second Mo Ibrahim Foundation Peace Forum that took place in Paris, France, from November 11 to 13th, 2019, President Paul Biya made an unexpected off-script comment on the Anglophone crisis in response to a question from Mr. Ibrahim. The president suggested that French and British colonialism had bequeathed the country a poisoned gift of sorts: "A juxtaposition of cultures and civilizations that make things rather delicate. Well, we first tried to put the two languages on an equal footing, the English and French languages. But the mentalities, educational systems, and judicial systems are different. We then had conflicts that we are trying to resolve at the moment, to grant the part of my country that was under British colonialism [Southern Cameroons] a special status. We had the possibility of integrating them directly into the Francophone system, which is the system of the majority of the people; 80% of the population, but I think that countries are today conscious about affirming their identity" (Mo Ibrahim Foundation, 2019). This unusually candid statement from President Biya supports the fact that one of the long-term goals of France and the Francophone-controlled government of Cameroon was to assimilate the English and Pidgin-speaking minority into the French-speaking majority, and by extension into the French-speaking world, la Francophonie. However, Anglophone assertions of identitarian and cultural specificity, as well as differences in governmental-ities (mentalities of governance), educational, and judicial systems in the two States had resulted in the Anglophone crisis. President Biya's analysis was right on target. As we see elsewhere in this volume (Chapter 4), from the beginning of the Federal Republic of Cameroon in 1961, France and French Cameroon made a concerted and sustained effort to assimilate English and Pidgin-speaking West Cameroon into the Franco-African sphere of influence. As a result, there was no political will to seriously engage in the creation of a novel, hybrid, indigenous legal system that would include elements of the civil law, the common law and African customary law. The same can be said of the educational sector. Since law is geo-cultural, and law is language, the tradition-bound common law system that obtained in Anglophone West Cameroon, turned out to be one of the bulwarks–along with the English-medium educational system and English & Pidgin-medium Christianity– of Anglophone Cameroon cultural and identitarian specificity. If the harmonization of the two legal systems and cultures was supposed to involve the fusion of the best elements of the French civil law tradition and the British common law tradition, and adapting them to the realities of the Federal Republic of Cameroon, it failed. Indeed, the major Anglophone movements that sought to preserve Anglophone specificity and the bi-jural system, the All Anglophone Conference of Buea (1993), the Second All Anglophone Conference (AAC II 1994) of Bamenda, the Cameroon Anglophone Civil Society Consortium, and the Common Law Lawyers' Association, were all spearheaded by men and women of the common law tradition in West Cameroon. They were joined in 2016 by the Anglophone Cameroon Teachers' Trade Union, CATTU, and the Teachers' Association of Cameroon (TAC) and together their actions resulted in the Anglophone Revolt.

The Clash of Legal Cultures

The existence of mixed, civil and common law jurisdictions, which operated autonomously side-by-side in East and West Cameroon, led to a clash of cultures and even conflicts of law (Tumnde, 2010). Before too long, tensions began to emerge between these two antipodal legal systems and cultural paradigms. There were conflicts over judicial concepts, procedures and usages, conflicts of mentalities over the presumption of innocence and over judicial independence. As a result, the powers that be decided to subtly assimilate the common law system. Nyo'Wakai (2008) states that this amounted to the Francophone judicial system imposing itself on the common law system. France and the Ahidjo/Biya government had engaged in a centripetal acceleration, as part of the march towards assimilation of the common law system into *la Francophonie*. The Cameroun common law lawyers essentially became a metaphorical decelerating force that resisted the assimilating and centralizing actions of the Cameroon government.

The Anglophone Revolt that was spearheaded by common law lawyers was the tragic outcome of a failed process of post-reunification harmonization of the two legal systems inherited from the French and the British colonial regimes (Nyo'Wakai, 2008). The irony is that the legal regime that began to emerge in the Federal Republic of Cameroon, reflected the dual-statehood and bi-jural nature of the reunified Cameroon. However, the good intentions expressed by the lawyers of both States failed under the concerted and sustained assimilationist political pressures of France and the Cameroon government, under Presidents Ahmadou Ahidjo and Paul Biya over time. Assimilationist impulses tended to highlight differences and divergences between the two systems rather than their convergences. Harmonization was an opportunity to creatively pay respect to alterity. Unfortunately, for the majority Francophones, harmonization was an opportunity to assimilate and eliminate the Anglophone common law "Other", with a capital O. Nyo'Wakai laments that as a result of assimilationist pressures, harmonization was never achieved: "We failed the test of enacting laws that reflected our newly achieved sovereignty. Where we dared venture, we merely adopted our peculiar heritage…. We spent the time adapting the laws received from our colonial master. This I believe, made our administration look so different in each component of the union…" (p. 91). Unfortunately, rather than harmonize both sub-systems

178

they essentially copied the legal systems of France and the UK, did not do much to harmonize and create a new system suitable for the new Federal Republic (Nyo'Wakai, 2010). This essentially left the bi-jural regime intact. This situation lasted until the early 2000s, when in an assimilationist urge, President Biya decided to cross legal and systemic lines and treat both systems as one bureaucratic unit.

The Authoritarian Turn and Diminishment of Judicial Independence

So far, we have seen that the Anglophone Revolt was triggered by a number of factors. Perhaps the most important of these was the democracy deficit, the transformation of the Federal Republic of Cameroon into an authoritarian, neo-patrimonial, tribalistic, kleptocracy, first under President Ahmadou Ahidjo and subsequently under his successor, President Paul Biya. The abolition of the Federal Republic of Cameroon and its transformation into an over-centralized, bureaucratic "republican" (in the French Revolutionary sense of the term) chieftaincy meant not only the loss of the statehood of West Cameroon. but also, the loss of a robust of multi-party parliamentary democracy, separation of powers, independence of the judiciary, freedom of speech and of the press, and individual liberties. The problem is that both Presidents Ahmadou Ahidjo and Paul Biya were oxymoronic, authoritarian, republican (again in the French *anti-ancien regime* sense of the term) chieftains who had no patience with the niceties of political dialogue, dissent, and concertation.

Issues of Separation of Powers and Independence of the Judiciary

One of the major grievances of the Anglophone common law lawyers was the lack of separation of powers and the resultant lack of judicial independence in the country. They clearly stated that the system they had inherited from British colonialism, the common law system, could not function in an environment where there was no judicial independence. Indeed, in their memorandum of 6th October 2016, addressed to President Paul Biya, the Anglophone Common Law Lawyers' Association stated that the men and women of the law were addressing their grievances to President Paul Biya in his capacity as: "Head of the Judiciary, the Head of the Executive and principal initiator of legislation in both legislative houses." It was a thinly veiled sarcastic reminder of the lack of separation of powers and judicial independence in Cameroon. Institutionally, the French civil law system—and its multiple iterations in the Francophone postcolonies of Africa—is different from the Anglo-American common law system. The role of the president in the United States or Prime Ministers in other countries is an expression of the governmentality of each country. In the United States and other Anglophone countries, there are multiple iterations of the concept of checks and balances between the Executive, the Legislative and the Judiciary. Interestingly though this concept originated from French philosopher Baron de Montesquieu, throughout its history, France has struggled with the problem of separation of powers and independence of the judiciary. Under the French Constitution of 1958, the President of the Republic is the guarantor of the independence and authority of the judiciary. Furthermore, in France, the presidency is *la Magistrature Suprême* (the Supreme Magistrature), and the president is the Chief Magistrate. He was assisted in this task by the *Conseil supérieur de la magistrature* (Higher Council of the Magistrature, popularly known by its French acronym CSM). The president appointed the members of the CSM and presided over their meetings. The CSM provided advisory opinions as requested by the President of the Republic, appointed and disciplined judges, made decisions on matters of judicial ethics, and ensured the smooth functioning of the system of administration of justice. The problem of separation of powers was especially compounded by the fact that the President of the Republic chaired the Higher Council of the Magistrature. At independence, this system was exported wholesale to all French-speaking African countries.

However, France made strides to reform the system in the 1990s. As a result of the constitutional reforms advanced by President Nicolas Sarkozy in July 2008, the President of the Republic ceased to be the chairman of the CSM. This gave the French courts greater independence and autonomy. However, these reforms did not diffuse to the former French colonies in Africa. In virtually every Francophone country, the President of the Republic continues to play a preponderant role in the judiciary, and in matters of administration of justice. In Cameroon for example, Article 37 (3) of the Constitution of 1996 was copied and pasted from the French Constitution of 1958. It provides as follows:

> The President of the Republic shall guarantee the independence of judicial power. He shall appoint members of the bench and legal department.
> He shall be assisted in this task by the Higher Judicial Council [CSM] which shall give him its opinion on all nominations…

The President of the Republic presides over the CSM, assisted by the Minister of Justice. He presided over the CSM for 39 of the 40 years he has been in power. He missed the 2020 meeting due perhaps to the COVID-19 pandemic. In practice, President Paul Biya appoints all magistrates and judges, including judges of military tribunals that handle cases connected to terrorism, by decree. Judges and magistrates have no security of tenure and can be removed from office for any reason, including political ones. This has greatly compromised the independence of the judiciary. As Nyo'Wakai (2008) noted, the President of Cameroon, head of the Executive branch of government crafted a made-to-measure constitution which made the President the Chief Magistrate. In that capacity he presided over the Higher Judicial Council whose members were appointed by himself. This Council had the responsibility of appointing, promoting, disciplining, transferring and dismissing Magistrates and judges, who are career civil servants. This situation seriously undermined the independence of the judiciary. That is the status quo in the republican chieftaincy of Cameroon.

The case in point is the Ayah affair. Justice Paul Ayah Abine a former member of the National Assembly of Cameroon, a former vice president of the Court of Appeal in Buea in the Southwest region, and a sitting justice of the Supreme Court of Cameroon. He was arrested on 21 January 2017 on suspicion of advocating that Cameroon return to the federal system of government that it had from 1961-1972. He was never brought before the Yaoundé Military Tribunal like Felix Nkongho Agbor Balla, president of the banned Fako Lawyers' Association, and President of the banned Cameroon Anglophone Civil Society Consortium (CACSC) who was charged with terrorism for advocating federalism.

All attempts by lawyers to have the justice produced in court or freed, were unsuccessful. Justice Paul Ayah Abine was sent on forced retirement from the Supreme Court via a presidential decree issued while he was in detention. After a lot of international pressure, he was released from prison by another presidential decree on the 30th of August 2017, along with 51 other Anglophone detainees, after spending more than eight months behind bars in Yaoundé. The government of Cameroon never stated why the justice was arrested nor why he was never brought before a court of law during the eight months in which he was detained. The arrest and detention without trial of Justice Paul Ayah Abine sent a clear message to the judiciary.

Ahidjo's imposition of one-party rule on 1st September 1966, made Cameroon a *parti-État* (one-party State) in which the government and the sole political party, *L'Union Nationale du Cameroun*, (the Cameroon Nation Union, CNU) constrained the political environment, increased the scope of the powers of the President of the Republic, the Chief of State, who also happened to be the president of the CNU. This development further reduced the independence of the judiciary. This one-party dictatorship ultimately led to a clash of cultures between Anglophone common law practitioners, who believe that judges and magistrates are a professional corps that should be completely independent of any control by the political class or the public administration, and the civil law magistrates who, as career civil servants trained in a *grande école* (ENAM), were used to having the president of the republic as the Chief Magistrate (Nyo'Wakai, 2008). Despite post-Cold War liberalization that led to multiparty elections (all won by President Biya), and relative freedom of the press, the Cameroon judiciary remained shackled in the "hermetic grip of absolutism", to borrow the expression of Soyinka (2004). Retired Justice Nyo'Wakai (2008) concluded that Cameroon was an unfortunate combination of bad laws and an authoritarian political context that essentially transforms judges into automatons, cogs in the machinery of the autocracy, agents of neo-patrimonialism who do not have judicial independence.

Fast forward to 2003. The Anglophone Question in Cameroon became the subject of international law when 14 English and Pidgin-speaking Southern Cameroonians lodged a complaint with the African Commission on Human and People's Rights on their behalf and on behalf of the people of the former British Trust Territory of Southern Cameroons against *la République du Cameroun*, a State Party to the African Charter on Human and Peoples' Rights. They alleged that they were relegated to the status of second-class citizenship, and many of their fundamental rights were violated by the government of Cameroon. Their enumerated complaints included, inter alia, that:

1. The UN Cameroon plebiscite of 1961 which gave them a choice to attain independence by joining *la République du Cameroun* or Nigeria ignored a third alternative, namely the right to independence and statehood for Southern Cameroons.
2. The September 1961 federal constitution of Cameroon did not receive the endorsement of the Southern Cameroons House of Assembly.
3. The people of Southern Cameroons remained a separate and distinct people. Their official working language is English, whereas the people in *La République du Cameroun* are Francophones. The legal, educational, and cultural traditions of

the Southern Cameroons and *La République du Cameroun* remained different, as did the character of local administration.

4. That the political unification and the application of the Napoleonic civil law system in Cameroon resulted in the discrimination against Anglophones in the legal and judicial system. Southern Cameroonian companies and businesses were forced to operate under the civil law system…that many Southern Cameroonian businesses went bankrupt, following the refusal by Francophone banks to lend them finances, in some cases, unless their articles of association were drafted in French.

5. Anglophones facing criminal charges for speaking out against Francophone domination were transferred to the Francophone zone for trial, under the Napoleonic Code, thereby adversely affecting their civil rights. The Complainants stated that the common law presumption of innocence upon arrest was not recognized under the civil law tradition, since guilt is presumed upon arrest and detention. Furthermore, the courts in French Cameroon conduct trials of English and Pidgin-speaking Southern Cameroonians in the French language without the aid of interpreters. They also alleged that Southern Cameroons court decisions were ignored by the Cameroon government.

The plaintiffs claimed that these and other acts of the Cameroon government violated multiple provisions of the African Charter of Human and Peoples' Rights. The African Commission of Human and Peoples' Rights declared that it had jurisdiction in the matter and decided that the complaints of the Southern Cameroonians were admissible. After receiving the submissions of the parties and hearing oral arguments, the Commission ruled in 2009 that:

1. Refusal by regional, transnational multilateral organizations to register companies established by Southern Cameroonians on account of language, amounted to a violation of Article 2 of the African Charter.2

2. Cameroon's ratification of the multilateral Francophone treaty known as *Organisation pour l'Hamonisation des Droits d'Affaires en Afrique* "(the Organization for the Harmonization of Business Law in Africa), otherwise known as (OHADA)" had led to discrimination against the people of Southern Cameroons on the basis of language in as much as the sole working language of OHADA was French. The Commission ruled that ratification of OHADA resulted in discrimination

---

2 The latest manifestation of discrimination against the English language and its speakers in the business arena occurred in April 2020. The so-called *Banque des Etats de l'Afrique Centrale* (BEAC) affair was a controversy where a financial services company, Cameroon Postal Services (CAMPOST) applied to BEAC, the central bank of the Francophone Central African region, for authorization to launch financial services in the region. The governor of BEAC, Abbas Mahamat Tolli, wrote to CAMPOST stating that its application could not be processed because it was "irregular." The bank explained what it meant by irregular: "*En effet, intégralité du dossier de votre demande est redigée en langue anglaise, et non pas en langue française qui est la langue de travail de la BEAC et de la COBAC.*" (In effect, the entire packet of your application is drafted in the English language, and not in the French language, which is the working language of the BEAC and COBAC.). The bank stated that it would process the application once it is resubmitted in the correct language, French.

against Anglophone owned companies and businesses, which could not open bank accounts unless they registered in French under OHADA: "the Respondent State [Cameroon] failed to address the concerns of Southern Cameroonian businesses, which were forced to re-register under OHADA, and as such violated Article 2 of the African Charter. Notwithstanding the translation of OHADA into English, it was wrong for institutions, such as banks to force Southern Cameroons based companies to change their basic documents into French.

3. Cameroon violated Article 4 of the African Charter which protects the right to life, inviolability of the human being, and the integrity of the person through security force killing of unarmed participants in a Social Democratic Front (SDF) political rally in Bamenda.

4. Cameroon violated Article 5 of the African Charter by subjecting Anglophone suspects to torture, cruel, inhuman and degrading punishment and treatment.

5. Cameroon violated Article 6 of the Charter by arresting and detaining persons for long periods of time without trial before releasing them.

6. Cameroon violated Article 7(1) (b) of the African Charter of Human and Peoples' Rights, which is concerned with the right to fair trial. The Cameroon government systematically transferred Anglophone civilians from Southern Cameroons to French Cameroon for trial by the Yaoundé and the Bafoussam Military Tribunals, which are extensions of the executive, rather than the judiciary. The Commission noted that military tribunals are not intended to try civilians.

7. Cameroon violated Article 7(1)(b) (c) and (d) of the Charter, which is concerned with a fair trial, specifically the responsibility of African states to ensure that accused persons are tried in a language they understand, or with the assistance of interpreters, if they do not understand the language in which they are being tried.

8. Cameroon violated Article 11 of the African Charter which provides for freedom of assembly when it detained demonstrators, applied excessive force to enforce law and order, and in some cases killed demonstrators.

Figure 5.8. Barrister Nkongho Felix (Agbor Balla) and civil law lawyers demonstrating in Bamenda (2016).

Interestingly, events show that when the Anglophone Revolt began in 2016, seven years after the ruling of the African Commission on Human and Peoples' Rights, the Cameroon government had not remedied the situation. All the human rights violations that the Commission had determined were committed by the Cameroon government in 2009, were repeated without qualms by the government from 2017 to 2021. It used the heaviest of heavy-handed repression measures in its attempt to subjugate English-speaking Southern Cameroons demonstrators. The right to peaceful assembly was openly violated. Lawyers who were demonstrating for change were beaten, and their wigs and phones seized by the authorities. Many Anglophone leaders were arrested, and transferred to French-speaking jurisdictions despite the existence of Anglophone common law courts of competent jurisdiction in the English-speaking Northwest and Southwest regions. Those detained included Barrister Nkongho Felix Agbor Balla, President of the Cameroon Anglophone Civil Society Consortium (the Consortium), who was also President of the Fako Lawyers' Association, and vice president of the African Bar Association, as well as Professor Fontem Aforteka'a Neba, Secretary General of the Cameroon Anglophone Civil Society Consortium.

The Consortium was banned by the government of Cameroon on January 17, 2017 and its leaders detained at the infamous dungeons of the *Secretariat d'états à la Defense* (Secretariat of State for Defense SED). These civilian leaders, teachers, students, and journalists were later moved to the Kondengui Maximum Security Prison in Yaoundé. They were subsequently court-marshaled at the Yaoundé Military Tribunal, where they faced the death penalty. Though Nkongho Felix Agbor Balla, and Fontem Aforteka'a Neba were released after international pressure on the Cameroon government, their cases were not dismissed. Other Anglophone leaders including Sisiku Ayuk Tabe, Elias Ayamba, and Nfor Ngala Nfor, as well as journalists Mancho Bibixy and Penn Terence were convicted by the Yaoundé Military Tribunal and sentenced to life imprisonment. Striking teachers and lawyers were beaten, arrested, detained, tortured, and tried at the French language-only military tribunals in Yaoundé, Douala, Bafoussam, and Buea. Most were given long prison sentences. Others fled the country and became refugees in Nigeria, Ghana, and other countries. On October 1, 2017, helicopter gunships opened fire on unarmed civilian demonstrators in Buea killing 21 people. Journalists who reported on these events were arrested, detained and tortured. One of them, Samuel Wazizi died in military custody, but his corpse was never released to his family for burial. In effect, the human rights situation had not changed since the African Commission's 2009 ruling against the litany of human rights violations perpetrated against Anglophones in Cameroon (See Law Society of England and Wales, 2018).

Militarization of the Legal System

At the onset of the Anglophone Revolt, President Paul Biya signed a decree creating a Code of Military Justice. This decree created a military tribunal in each of the 10 regions of Cameroon. The decree granted the president the power to create more than one military tribunal in certain regions. Article 4 of the decree stipulates that "In exceptional circumstances set forth in article 9 of the Constitution, serious threat to public order, to the security of the State, or of terrorism, the Yaoundé Military Tribunal may exercise jurisdiction on the entire national territory." Additionally, the judges and investigating magistrates (prosecutors) of the Military Tribunal may be "either Military Magistrates or Civilian Magistrates." They are appointed by a decree of the President of the Republic" (Presidency of the Republic, 2017). Additionally, the Minister in charge of military justice, has the power to transfer military judges–and civilian judges drafted to serve in military tribunals–to other jurisdictions for a maximum of six months. In situations where a civilian magistrate presides over a case, the decree stipulates that he must be assisted by two military judges/assessors. Military Tribunals have competence to judge all cases of terrorism, state security, cases involving firearms or armed robbery, and importation of military attire and equipment. The Yaoundé Military is a jurisdiction of first and last instance. Its decisions cannot be appealed to the civilian Supreme Court. The President of the Republic and the Minister in charge of Military Justice (the Minister of Defence) can, at any moment, order the termination of cases before military tribunals at any stage of the proceedings (Law No. 2017/012, 2917). This decree essentially militarized justice in Cameroon, blurred the lines between military and civilian justice, brought the judiciary further under the ambit and control of the executive (the Republican Chieftain), and eliminated the presumption of innocence. It essentially removed the biggest legal and constitutional issue in the history of Cameroon, the Anglophone Revolt, from the jurisdiction of the civilian courts. It was yet another nail in the coffin of the comatose common law system in the former Southern Cameroons (Northwest and Southwest regions). The procedures and modus operandi of the Yaoundé Military Tribunal are described in the Trial Observation Report of Dr. Brilman of the Law Society of England and Wales (Chapter 26).

As if to underline the fact that five years into the Anglophone Revolt, the Napoleonic instructional structures and their functions had not changed, French-language military tribunals were still actively dispensing military justice to civilians. On September 7, 2021, the Military Tribunal in Buea, in the English and Pidgin-speaking Southwest region, sentenced four accused persons, all civilians, to death by firing squad after convicting them of "acts of terrorism, hostility against the fatherland, secession, insurrection, murder and illegal possession of firearms and ammunition" under provisions of the Law on the Suppression of Acts of Terrorism adopted on December 19, 2014. According to the Buea-based Center for Human Rights and Democracy in Africa (CHRDA, 2021), the trial, which was presided over by Lieutenant Colonel Tchinda Jackson, was conducted entirely in French, the official language of the military and military tribunals in Cameroon. This was the harshest sentence imposed on any accused person in connection with the Anglophone crisis. The four were part of a group of 12 persons who had been arrested and charged with the alleged murder of seven students and causing injury to 13 others during a shooting at the Mother Francisca International Bilingual Academy in Kumba, on 24 October 2020. The accused included the proprietor of the high school, the principal, the vice principal, the discipline master, and the security guard. These persons were all detained for long periods of time before the trial. Four of the accused were sentence to five months imprisonment and ordered to pay a fine of about $100, and four others were discharged and acquitted (2021). The trial in the military tribunal brought to the fore the human rights violations highlighted by the African Commission on Human and Peoples' Rights. The accused were tried and convicted by a Francophone, Napoleonic, military tribunal in the Southwest region, bypassing

Anglophone common law courts of competent jurisdiction. The fact that the accused, who were all English-speaking civilians, were tried by Francophone military officers in a military tribunal, which is part of the executive (the Ministry of Defense) and whose official language is French, raised serious concerns about the independence of the Buea Military Tribunal, and the fairness of the trial and conviction of the accused. This verdict marked a grim milestone in the miscarriage of justice in the Anglophone Revolt. The steamroller of military injustice continued its inexorable journey of human rights violations in the Anglophone Northwest and Southwest regions. By September 2021, Cameroon military tribunals had accumulated an unenviable record of travesties of justice in the Anglophone Revolt, which they have prosecuted since 2016 under provisions of the infamous Law of Suppression of Acts of Terrorism of 2014: They sentenced four Southern Cameroonians to death by firing squad, 30 to life imprisonment in French Cameroon prisons, sentenced 25 suspects to 30 years imprisonment, sentenced 6 to 20 years imprisonment, and sentenced dozens of others to terms ranging from 10 to 15 years. Hundreds of other Anglophones continue to be detained without trial.

Conclusion

The Anglophone Revolt began because common law lawyers complained that the administration of justice was being impaired by a lack of judicial independence and forced assimilation of the common law system of the English-speaking former British Southern Cameroons into the Napoleonic civil law system of French Cameroon that is notable for its sheer careerism, corruption, and emphasis of law over rights. This was in total disregard of the lessons of history, the identitarian and cultural specificity of Anglophone Southern Cameroons. President Biya and the Minister of Territorial Administration, Paul Atanga Nji, dismissed the cultural, identitarian, and autonomist aspirations of the English-speaking common law lawyers out of hand by simply ignoring them. The tragedy is that President Biya opted to use military means–subjugation of the English-speaking regions– to solve a political problem.

Epilogue

On March 30, 2017, nearly two years after the Cameroon Common Law Lawyers Association made its identitarian and cultural demands, the Minister of Justice, Laurent Esso, held a press conference in which he outlined some cosmetic administrative "measures" that would be taken to address the grievances and demands of the Anglophone lawyers. The structural, identitarian and regional autonomy demands of the lawyers were not addressed.

At the end of 2024, the announced administrative measures had not been implemented.

References

Amnesty International (2019). *Cameroon: 2017/2018 Report*. Retrieved from: https://www.amnesty.org/en/countries/africa/cameroon/report-cameroon/

Andenas, M., & Anderson, C. (2012). *Theory and Practice of Harmonisation*. Cheltenham, UK: Edward Elgar Publishing.

Anyangwe, C. (2008). *Imperialistic Politics in Cameroun: Resistance and the Inception of the Restoration of the Statehood of Southern Cameroons*. Bamenda: Langaa Research and Publishing.

Ardener, S. (2005). Ardener's "Muted Groups": The genesis of an idea and its praxis. Women and Language, Vol. 28, (2), Pp. 50-54,72.

Asonganyi, T. (2009*)*. Preface II in Nyo'Wakai: *The Law and My Times: Under the Broken Scale of Justice* (pp. xiii-xx). Bamenda: Langaa Research and Publishing

Benard, J.-P. (1962). Confidential letter No. 27 of 8 January 1962. French Embassy Yaoundé, Cameroon.

Bisong, N. (2020). Agbor Balla Suspension Saga: "I am only being celebrated," Balla tells *The Sun. The Sun* (May 7th), Retrieved from: https://thesunnewspaper.cm/agbor-balla-suspension-saga-celebrated-balla-tells-sun-2/

Betts, R. (1961). *Assimilation and Association in French Colonial Theory, 1890-1914*. New York: Columbia University Press.

Bouddih, A. & Mbunwe, C. (2016). After Gov't Snubs Ultimatum, Anglophone Lawyers Begin Strike October 11. *Cameroon Post*. October 11. Retrieved from: https://cameroonpostline.com/after-govt-snubs-ultimatum-anglophone-lawyers-begin-strike-oct-11/%E2%80%8B

Bourdieu, P. (1994). *L'emprise du journalisme*, (Pressures on Journalism) *Actes de la Recherches en Sciences Sociales*, 101 (1), 3-9.

Crabb, J. (1995). *The French Civil Code*. Dordrecht, Netherlands, Wolters Kluwer Academic Publishers

David, R., & Brierley J. E. (1985). *Major Legal Systems in the World Today*, (3rd ed.). London: Stevens & Sons.

Dupuy, J. (1972). Referendum Constitutionnel du 20 Mai 1972 (Constitutional Referendum of 20th May 1972). Diplomatic Correspondence between French Ambassador in Yaoundé, Cameroun and French Ministry of Foreign Affairs, Paris.

Eko, L. (2012). *New Media, Old Regimes. Case Studies in Comparative Communication Law and Policy*. Lanham, MD: Lexington Books.

Holmes, O. (1881). *The Common Law*. Cambridge, MA: Harvard University Press.

Johnson, W. (1965). The Cameroon Federation: Political Union Between English and French-Speaking Africa. In William Lewis (ed). *French-Speaking Africa*. New York: Walker and Co.

Kipling, R. (1940) "The White Man's Burden," in *Rudyard Kipling's Verse* (New York, Double Day).

Legrand, P. (1999). *Fragments on Law-as-Culture*. Deventer: W.E.J. Tjeenk Willink.

Legrand, Pierre (2003). The Same and the Different, in Pierre Legrand and Roderick Munday (eds.). *Comparative Legal Studies: Traditions and Transitions* pp. 240-311. Cambridge, UK: Cambridge University Press

Mbembe, A. (2001). *On the Postcolony*. Berkley: UCLA Press.

Ngwang Gumne v. Cameroon, Comm. 266/2003, 26th ACHPR AAR Annex (Dec 2008 – May 2009).

Mo Ibrahim Foundation (2019). Paris Peace Forum 2019: Four takeaways. Retrieved from: https://mo.ibrahim.foundation/news/2019/paris-peace-forum-2019-four-takeaways

National Democratic Institute for International Affairs (NDI, 1993). An Assessment of the October 11, 1992 Election in Cameroon. Retrieved from: https://www.ndi.org/node/23441

Nforbin E. (2019). The Push to Protect the Oneness of English as a Judicial Language in the Southern Cameroons Jurisdiction of Cameroon. *International Journal of Minority and Group Rights*, 26, 503-574.

Nyo'Wakai, (2009). *The Law and My Times: Under the Broken Scale of Justice* (pp. xiii-xx). Bamenda:

Langaa Research and Publishing

Nyo'Wakai and 72 Others v. State of Cameroon, *Juris Periodique*, No. HCB/19, CRM/92 (1992).

Presidency of the Republic (2017). Loi No. 2107/012 of 12 July 2017. Creating a Code of Military Justice. Retrieved from: https://www.prc.cm/fr/multimedia/documents/5695-code-justice-militaire

Soyinka, W. (2005). *Climate of Fear: The Quest for Dignity in a Dehumanized World*. New York: Random House.

Stark, B., Roland, H. & Boyer, L. (2000). *Introduction au Droit, 5ème edition (Introduction to Law, 5th edition)*. Paris: Litec.

Tande, D. (2017). Memory Lane (December 1992): Bamenda Erupts as 173 Detainees are "Kidnapped" to Yaoundé. Scribbles from the Den. Retrieved from: https://www.dibussi.com/2017/01/bamenda-detainees-to-yaounde.html

The Centre for Human Rights and Democracy in Africa (CHRDA) (2021). CHRDA Statement on the Death Sentence Handed to 04 accused by the Buea Military Tribunal. Retrieved form: https://www.facebook.com/chrda.org

Tumnde, M. (2010). Harmonization of Business Law in Cameroon: Issues, Challenges and Prospects. *Tulane European and Civil Law Forum* 25, pp. 119-137.

War Continues in Bamenda (1992). *Cameroon Post*. No. 141 December 29, p. 1.

Zweigert, K. & Kötz, H. (1998) *An Introduction to Comparative Law* (3rd. ed.). (Tony Weir trans.). Leicester, UK: Clarendon Paperbacks

SIX

Crossing the Red Line of Harmonization

How the Common Law Went to War in Cameroon

TANJONG ASHUNTANTANG

The territory of Kamerun (Cameroon) was born in the late 19th century out of the expansionist ventures of imperial Germany and other European powers. The clash of Western imperialist forces during the First World War and the defeat of Germany saw the territory partitioned between two contending European powers, Great Britain, and France. This was a sequel to mandate agreements signed between the League of Nations and His Majesty's government of Great Britain on the one hand and between the League of Nations and France on the other hand. Per those agreements, the British took possession of discontinuous strips of land on the territory's westerly border with Nigeria while the French occupied the remaining portion to the East. Per Article 2 common to the Mandate agreements, each of the two colonial powers was enjoined:

> To be at liberty to apply its laws to the territory under the mandate…and to constitute the territory into a custom, fiscal or administrative union or federation with adjacent territories under its sovereignty or control.

Pursuant to "Proclamation N° 41" issued by Sir Hugh Clifford, the British Governor-General of Nigeria on the 18th of January 1922, the British administered their acquisition as part of the neighboring British Colony and Protectorate of Nigeria. The appendage of the British part of divided German Kamerun to Nigeria subjugated the territory to British colonial governance in Nigeria until the demise of the League of Nations after the Second World War. With the coming of the United Nations Organization (UNO) in 1945, a trust agreement was executed between His Majesty's Government of Great Britain and Northern Ireland over British Cameroons. A similar agreement was executed with France over the neighboring territory of French Cameroun. Article 76(b) of both agreements urged the two colonial powers to:

Promote the political, economic, social and educational advancement of the inhabitants of the trust territories, and their progressive development towards self-government or independence as may be appropriate to the particular circumstances of each territory and its people.

Per Order 6 of Nigeria (Protectorate and Cameroon) Order in Council 1946, the British partitioned "British Cameroons" horizontally into "Northern Cameroons" and "Southern Cameroons." Northern Cameroons was administered as part of the British Protectorate of Northern Nigeria while Southern Cameroons was administered as one of the provinces of Southern Nigeria.

"Ethnic" Construction and the Anglophone Legal Identity

The operative clauses of the League of Nations Mandate and United Nations Trusteeship agreement over the erstwhile German Kamerun gave the British and French a socio-cultural leverage over their respective enclaves. This led to separate colonial state formations in either territory. The outcome was the development of territorial differences in language and culture between them. So, "as a result of their different colonial experiences with British and French rule, the two Cameroons developed two distinct, albeit opposing styles and attitudes in matters of language, governance and basic freedoms" (Nfi, 2014, p. 121). In Southern Cameroons, the imprints of British colonialism were evident in English customs, usages and practices that prevailed in the territory (Konings and Nyamnjoh, 2004). As a consequence, the administrative traditions, community management, education, legal tradition, and perception of government and governance in Southern Cameroons were inspired by "Anglo-Saxon traditions"[1] (Acha, 2016). The same was true in French Cameroun, which was inspired by French Revolutionary secular republicanism, centralism, and Napoleonic administration, and legal codification. To this end, the average Cameroonian on either side of the colonial divide differed mentally, intellectually, socially and psychologically (Nyansako Ni Nku, 1993). This would in due course lead to the emergence of the term Anglophone for someone having his or her ancestral roots in Southern Cameroons and Francophone for those from French Cameroun.

As a result of its colonial experiences and its place in the Anglo-Pidgin sphere, the Anglophone community in Cameroon came to be perceived and treated as an "ethnic" group, similar to the other major ethnic groups in Cameroon. Bobda (2001) put it succinctly when he wrote that:

The term Anglophone, as is understood in Cameroon, has mostly an ethnic

---

1 Editor's note: The term Anglo-Saxon is used to describe everything connected or related to the English language and culture, in the context of a perceived linguistic and cultural rivalry between the English (Anglophone) and French (Francophone) cultures. English-speaking Anglophone lawyers trained in the "Anglo-American" common law tradition, use the term Anglo-Saxon to distinguish themselves from their Francophone Civil Law counterparts. Both the French and English-language press in Cameroon use the term in the French, geo-cultural sense, and the comparative law tradition, given the lawyers spear-headed the Anglophone revolt (see preface)

connotation. It refers to a member of an ethnic group in North West and South West Provinces which were formally part of British Cameroons... the term Anglophone has very little to do with knowledge of the English Language; indeed, an Anglophone in the Cameroon sense does not need to know a word of English.

Therefore, even though there are ninety-five ethnic groups and a corresponding number of ethnic languages spoken in the Northwest and Southwest regions, Anglophones have a collective identity and memory that emerged from their historical and cultural heritage, which includes the English language and Pidgin, a "broken" variant of English. Anglophones have become an "ethnic group" (Ashuntantang, 2020).

Cameroon and Comparative "Legal Families"

One of the bones of contention in Cameroon is the co-existence of a French and a British postcolonial legal systems, in the former French Cameroun and the former British Southern Cameroons respectively. Comparative Law scholars classify the French legal system as being in the Civil Law "family" of law, while the legal systems of the Anglosphere are classified as being in the Anglo-Saxon "family" of law (Zweigert & Kötz, 1998; van Hoecke, 2014). This is one of the origins of the use of term "Anglo-Saxon" to describe the common law system that operated in the Northwest and Southwest regions. Perceived threats to, and erosion of that system led English-speaking lawyers to demonstrate in defense of the system. One of the realms in which Britain and France exercised their leverage over their mandated and later trust territories was law. The Civil Law and common law systems thus came to French Cameroun and Southern Cameroons respectively through post-World War I League of Nations Mandates. Article 9 of the Mandate Agreement actually gave Britain and France blank checks to export their laws to their respective mandates. It read:

> The mandatory shall have full powers of administration in the area subject of the mandate. This area shall be administered in accordance with the laws of the mandatory as an integral part of its territory.

Thanks to the above provision, the two imperial powers transposed their respective legal systems to their mandated territories. In this light, the British sowed the seeds of the English legal system based on the Common Law in Southern Cameroons while the French implanted French Civil Law based on the Napoleonic code in French Cameroon. The transposition of each of the two legal systems to either colonial enclave was predicated on an enabling Act legislated by each colonizing authority.

At the time British Cameroons was appended to Nigeria in 1922, the enabling act that allowed for the application of English law in British Overseas Territories was the Foreign Jurisdiction Act of 1897. It was under this Act that the Nigerian Supreme Court Ordinance of 1914 was passed. The Ordinance was meant to regulate legal issues in Nigeria. The laws administered under that ordinance included the Common Law of England, doctrines of equity and statutes of general application applicable in England on January 1, 1900. Per a

1924 Order in Council, the jurisdiction of the Nigerian Supreme Court ordinance of 1914 was extended to British Cameroons. From then on, Nigeria and Cameroon had the same legal system (Asuagbor, 2008). That was how the Common Law of England, doctrines of equity and statutes of general application in England on the 1st of January 1900 first became applicable in British Cameroons.

Pursuant to the Nigerian (Constitution) Order in Council of 1954, Nigeria became a federation of 3 regions - and a federal territory (Lagos). Per that Order in Council (otherwise known as the MacPherson Constitution), Southern Cameroons attained the status of a quasi-federal territory. This gave it some degree of autonomy. The MacPherson Constitution of 1954 established for the whole colony of Nigeria and its appendage, Southern Cameroons, a court known as the Federal Supreme Court. A High Court was also established in each of Nigeria's three regions, Lagos and the quasi-federal territory of Southern Cameroons. In addition, Magistrate Courts were set up in each of the four jurisdictions under their respective High Court and Magistrate Court Laws. For Southern Cameroons, it was the 1955 Southern Cameroons High Court Law and the 1955 Magistrate Court Law. These laws specifically sanctioned the application of the Common Law system in Southern Cameroons. Article 10, 11 and 15 of the Southern Cameroons High Court law are of particular importance here. Article 10 provides:

> The jurisdiction vested in the High Court shall, so far as practice and procedure are concerned be exercised in the manner provided by this law or any other written law, or by such rules and others in court as may be pursuant to this law or any other written law, and in the absence thereof, in substantial conformity with the practice and procedure for the time being of Her Majesty's High Court of Justice in England.

What this section implied was that recourse could be had to the current practice and procedure in England in situations where local laws and rules were silent. However, the Article of the 1955 law that imported English law into Southern Cameroons wholly is Article 11. It reads:

> Subject to the provisions of any written law and in particular of this section and sections 10, 15 and 22 of this law…
> a. The Common Law
> b. The doctrines of Equity, and
> c. The Statutes of General Application which were in force in England on the 1st day of January 1900, shall in so far as they relate to any matter with respect to which the legislator of Southern Cameroons for the time being is competent to make laws, be in force within the jurisdiction of this court.

The application of English law in Southern Cameroons was further legitimised by Article 15 of the 1955 law which was to the effect that:

The jurisdiction of the High court in Probate, Divorce and Matrimonial Causes and Proceedings, may subject to the provisions of this law, and section 27, and to Rules of Court, be exercised by the courts in conformity with the law and practice for the time being in England.

Going by sections 10, 11 and 15 of the Southern Cameroons High Court law 1955, English-type courts were set up in the territory of Southern Cameroons. This led to the gradual relegation of local laws and customs. It was the emergence of a new society consisting of indigenous people who had embraced the English culture including the English Common law.

Like the British, France also exhibited legal leverage over French Cameroun by imposing French Civil Law on that territory through French codes. In procedural matters, the basic texts were the Code of Civil and Commercial Procedures, promulgated by the Decree of 16th December 1954 and the Code of Criminal Instruction promulgated in 1938. While the latter governed Criminal Procedure, the former was concerned with Civil Procedure. In substantive law the applicable law in French Cameroun was the Code Civil otherwise known as Code Napoleon of 1804 and the Code of Commerce that came into force on the 7th of December 1850.

Distinguishing the Common Law and Civil Law legal systems, Fombad (2016) holds that both systems are "divergent and potentially antagonistic, each with a strong colonial cultural baggage, identification and loyalty." For Legrand (1997) the differences between Common Law and Civil Law "predominate over their similarities." Caslav Pejovic (2001), for his part, opines that "While there are many legal issues which are dealt with in the same way by the Common Law and Civil Law systems, there remain also significant differences between these two legal systems related to legal structure, classification, fundamental concepts and terminology." He goes further to draw a comparison between the two systems in these words:

> The Common Law and the Civil Law are the products of two fundamentally different approaches to the legal process. In Civil Law, the main principles and rules are contained in codes and statutes, which are applied by the courts. Hence, codes and statutes prevail, while case law constitutes only a secondary source of law. On the other hand, in the Common Law system, the law has been dominantly created by judicial decisions, while a conceptual structure is often lacking. The difference is the result of the different role of legislator in Civil Law and Common Law. The Civil Law is based on the theory of separation of powers, whereby the role of the legislator is to legislate, while the courts should apply the law. On the other hand, in Common Law, the courts are given the main task in creating the law (Caslav Pejovic, 2001 p. 820).

Reunification and Bijuralism in Cameroon

In conformity with the United Nations Trusteeship Agreement, France granted independence to French Cameroon on 1st January 1960 under the baptismal name *La République du Cameroun*. Nigeria for its part attained independence (without Southern Cameroons) on the 1st of October 1960. Per resolution 1352XIV of the 6th of October 1959 the people of Southern Cameroons voted in a plebiscite on the 11th of February 1961 to join independent *La République du Cameroun*. On Sunday the 1st of October 1961, Southern Cameroons merged with *La République du Cameroun* to form the Federal Republic of Cameroon, a federation of two states - West Cameroon and East Cameroon. West Cameroon comprised the erstwhile Southern Cameroons while East Cameroon constituted the territory of the moribund *La République du Cameroun*.

Because of their disparate socio-cultural baggage, the union between Southern Cameroons and *La République du Cameroun* on the 1st of October 1961 was a mélange of the Gallic, Civil Law traditions of East Cameroon and the Common Law of West Cameroon, which was part of the Anglo-Saxon legal family. So, aside their territorial delineations, West and East Cameroon could be distinguished by the components of their respective socio-cultural heritage. For either side, these components became their identity markers and included language, the legal system, the educational system, values, their postures towards religion, the system of governance, and social organization.

Owing to the disparity between Common Law and the Civil Law, the rule-based laws, legal system, and legal culture of West Cameroon were diametrically different from those of East Cameroon at the dawn of reunification in 1961. It was left to be seen which system of law would be applicable in the nascent postcolonial state. To put it differently, what would become of the received English common law of Southern Cameroons and the received Civil Law of French Cameroon? This question was aptly answered in two principal enactments, notably: the Cameroon Federal Constitution of 1st September 1961, and the West Cameroon Constitution of 26th October 1961. Section 53 (1) of the West Cameroon constitution stipulated as follows:

> Subject to the provisions of this section, the existing laws shall have effect after the commencement of this constitution as if they had been made in pursuance of this constitution and shall be read and construed with such modifications, adaptations, qualifications and exceptions as may be necessary to bring them into conformity with this constitution.

Subsection 4 went ahead to state that:

> For the purpose of this section, "the existing laws" means all ordinances, laws, proclamations, Rules, Regulations, orders and other instruments having effect as part of the law of the state immediately before the 1st day of October 1961.

The above provisions saved the received Common Law in West Cameroon, at least, for the time being. These saving pronouncements were also contained (albeit tersely) in section 46 of the federal constitution promulgated on the 1st of September 1961 in these words:

> In so far as they do not conflict with the provisions of this constitution, the existing laws of the federated states shall remain in force.

Based on the foregoing, West Cameroon continued with the Common Law after 1st October 1961; just as Civil Law was the applicable legal system in East Cameroon (Konings, 1999). Bijuralism being the co-existence of two legal systems in one country, the postcolonial state of Cameroon was born as a bijural country. Against this background, Federal Ordinance No. 61-of-9 of 16th October 1961 set up the Supreme Court of West Cameroon. The Supreme Court of West Cameroon consisted of the High Court and Court of Appeal of West Cameroon. The High Court derived its jurisdiction from the Southern Cameroons High Court Law, 1955, Federal Ordinance No 61-DF of 16th October 1961, the Southern Cameroons (Constitution) Order in Council of 1960 and the constitution of the Federal Republic of Cameroon. Based on the above constitutional provisions, the Common Law flourished in West Cameroon throughout the federal era as did French Civil Law in East Cameroon.

Figure 6.1. 1967 French language *République Federale du Cameroun* Stamp Commemorating the Solemn Proclamation of the Independence of *La République du Cameroun* on January 1, 1960. This was not problematic because West Cameroon was autonomous.

National Integration and Harmonization

Following the outcome of a referendum held in 1972, Cameroon moved from a federal to a unitary state. The country's official appellation changed from Federal Republic of Cameroon to the United Republic of Cameroon. The States of West and East Cameroon became moribund. Administratively, the country was split into seven provinces; two of which were carved out of the defunct West Cameroon and respectively named the Southwest province and the Northwest province. The coming of the unitary state in 1972 completely changed the Common Law narrative in West Cameroon. Following what Asuagbor (2008) tags "Cameroon's ambitions for national unification," Cameroon adopted a policy of national integration. In the legal realm this saw the promulgation of Ordinance N°72/4 of 26th August 1972 on Judicial Organization. Under this law, Anglophone Cameroon lost its judicial autonomy as the West Cameroon Supreme Court became moribund. Appeal Courts were set up in each of the seven provinces to entertain appeals from the lower courts of each province while appeals from the provincial courts of appeal went to the Yaoundé-based Supreme Court. Per Article 13 (2) of law N°75/16 of 8th December 1975 this was the national Supreme Court in Yaoundé. Unlike the West Cameroon Supreme Court that was a court of judicial review with powers to review the findings of fact and inferences in the court below, the Supreme Court in Yaoundé was a French-style, *Cour de Cassation* that examined only points of law and form. To make matters worse for Common Law practitioners, the Supreme Court in Yaoundé had no Common Law bench. This meant that appeals from the two Anglophone legal jurisdictions were at the mercy of non-English-speaking Francophone judges not trained in the Common Law. Under the same law the Magistrate Courts of West Cameroon became Courts of 1st Instance, an appellation unknown to Common Law.

Along the same line, the government began a process of replacing inherited laws hitherto applying in West Cameroon with standard laws applying to both the Anglophone and Francophone legal jurisdictions. In legal theory, this process is known as "harmonization." Harmonization arises exclusively in comparative law. Its purpose is law reform. Law reform means improving the laws by making changes or corrections so that the laws will be in harmony with constant demands by democratic norms (Mohammad, 2016). Conventionally, harmonization is limited to rule-based laws. Under the Civil Law system, rule-based laws are found in codes, decrees, and ordinances. In the case of the Common Law, they are found in statutes and decisions of superior courts. Harmonization entails the replacement of existing rule-based laws with common rules. Such laws that have since been put in place under the Cameroon harmonization scheme include:

1. Ordinance N°72/4 of 26th August 1972 on Judicial Organization
2. Ordinance N°74/1 of 6th July 1974 on Land Tenure.
3. Law N° 74/14 of 27th November 1974 on the Land Tenure
4. Ordinance N°81-2 of 29th June 1981 on Civil Status
5. Law N°89/019 of 29th December 1989 on Judicial Organization dropped Certiorari
6. Law N° 89/019 of 29th December 1989 introduced the *Partie Civile* Procedure
7. Law N°89/019 of 29th December 1989 on the Simplified Recovery

8. Ordinance Nº89-005 of 13th December 1989 on Insurance law
9. The CIMA Insurance Code of 1992
10. Law Nº 92-007 of 14th August 1992 on the Labor Code
11. 1998: The OHADA Uniform Acts ratified by Cameroon
12. The Criminal Procedure Code Law Nº 2005/007 of 27th July 2005

Flawed Harmonization

The Cameroon harmonization scheme has generally not found favor with Common Law lawyers. For Common Law lawyers, the scheme is flawed. This is not surprising. Going by the norms of harmonization per the literature, the Cameroon harmonization scheme is problematic; its methodology is defective, its application is prescriptive, and its outcome is assimilative. Here are some considerations why the Cameroon harmonization scheme is flawed.

Absence of diversity, harmony, and consonance in harmonized laws

Harmonization in the literature means standardization of rule-based norms. Such harmonized laws should have diversity, harmony, and consonance. For Common Law lawyers, harmonized laws in Cameroon lack diversity, harmony, and consonance. For them, harmonized laws are not a hybrid as they should be. Rather they are a transcription of the French Civil Law status quo in Francophone Cameroun before the 1972 transition. For this reason, harmonized laws are laden with Civil Law norms, concepts, and terminologies to the near exclusion of Common Law variants. The application of such norms, concepts, and terminologies in the Common Law jurisdictions of Cameroon has actually been problematic. This may not be surprising as culturally dependent norms are thought to be transferrable only between legal systems with similar legal cultures (Legrand, 2001). Being of Civil Law extraction, most of the norms and concepts in harmonized laws are culture-dependent. That is why applying them in Common Law Cameroon has been a problem.

Harmonization of Legal systems

Another problematic about harmonization in Cameroon is that it goes beyond rule-based laws to include harmonization of legal systems. Rather than limit harmonization to rule based laws, which is the norm, the government extended harmonization to the Common Law legal system. This is unconventional. A legal system is an operating set of legal institutions, procedures, and rules (Tetley, 2000). It refers to the nature and content of the law generally, and the structures and methods whereby, it is legislated upon, adjudicated upon, and administered within a given jurisdiction (Tetley, 2000). The distinguishing feature between the Common Law and Civil Law legal systems is their sources of law. While Civil Law is found in codes, Common Law is based on the doctrine of precedence or *stare decisis*. As a result, Civil Law is termed codified law while Common Law is tagged, judge-made law. The coming of the OHADA Uniform Acts led to the codification of the entire realm of mercantile law. Statistically, the putting in place of the codified Uniform Acts and the Criminal Procedure Code meant that the realms of law regulated by codes in Anglophone Cameroon outnumbered those based on the Common Law doctrine of precedence. Since

197

codification is a signpost of Civil Law, the packaging of harmonized laws in codes was seen by Common Law lawyers as a veiled attempt by government to replace the Common Law in Anglophone Cameroon with the Civil Law variant. In fact, the wanton codification of national laws tipped the balance of legal systems in Cameroon in favor of Civil Law.

Harmonization of Legal cultures

In each society, the legal system forms part of the culture, civilization, history, and life of its people (Boodman, 1998). For Van Hoecke (2014), legal systems are one aspect of the culture to which they belong. In this regard the Common Law as a legal system is an integral part of the culture of Anglophone Cameroon. Ipso facto, the Civil Law is entrenched in the culture of Francophone Cameroon. Accordingly, Dainow (1966) submits that a legal system is part of the life of the people for whom it functions. Panel-beating the legal system of a given community is therefore tempering with its legal culture. Legal culture here is defined as a specific way in which values, practices and concepts are integrated into the operation of legal institutions and the interpretation of legal texts (Bell, 1995). It entails everything that influences the making, interpretation and application of norms including those things not necessarily thought to be in the realm of law (Lundmark, 2012). Legal culture can be internal or external. Internal legal culture is perceived as:

> The process of law-making and law-finding, the method of legal reasoning of judges, the structure of the legal system and the administration of justice in a given society or jurisdiction and the training and organization of the legal profession (Banakas, 2002, p. 179).

External legal culture, for its part, implies "ideas, values, attitudes and opinions people in society hold with regard to law and the legal system" (Friedman, 1994). This will include the language of the court, the dressing of lawyers and judges, juristic styles, legal philosophies, and the system of legal education. Because of the disparity in their legal systems, language preferences and colonial grooming (Anglophone Common Law lawyers continue to wear wigs to court), the internal and external legal culture of Anglophone Cameroon is different from that of Francophone Cameroon. In the language realm, the language of the court in Anglophone Cameroon was always English while the legal education orientation of its judges and magistrates was always English Private law based on Common Law traditions. Conversely, the language of the court in Francophone Cameroon was French and the legal education and orientation of its judges and magistrates was always French Private Law based on Napoleonic Civil Law traditions. This was the state of affairs in Cameroon until the Cameroon government started a tradition of posting Francophone magistrates to Anglophone Cameroon under its harmonization scheme. The language preference of such judges is French while their legal education orientation is French Private Law based on Civil Law. As would be expected, the legal culture of these Francophone judges as espoused in their language preference and other cultural attributes is out of tune with the legal culture of Anglophone Cameroon. For this reason, Common Law lawyers opine that harmonization in Cameroon is a smokescreen for Anglophone assimilation, a mechanism to blur the Anglophone identity in Cameroon, suppress cultural plurality under the guise of fostering civic nationhood.

Legal culture is part of general culture and general culture is at the core of identity and identity is the character-making element of an identitarian group. In social anthropology, Anglophone Cameroon is an identitarian group. Like other cultural groups, Anglophones have cultural identity markers that distinguish them from Francophones. The legal culture of Anglophone Cameroon (based on Common Law) is one of such identity markers. Conceiving it as an assault on the Anglophone legal culture, Common Law lawyers perceived harmonization as an attempt to destroy one of their major cultural identity markers – the Common Law. For them, this was an affront to their Anglophone heritage. Harmonization had crossed the red line.

Structural Violence in the Cameroon Harmonization Scheme

Like many Anglophones, Common Law lawyers have the feeling their right to a local legal identity precedes the overriding claims of national integration. As a result, Common Law lawyers have for over four decades been decrying the systematic erosion of the Common Law in Cameroon through harmonized laws. Their lamentations hinge on the fact that harmonized laws are having a toll on their professional wellbeing. The systematic erosion of Common Law via harmonization has subjected them to certain deprivations and social injustices that have taken them out of their Common Law professional comfort zones. Such social injustices and deprivations are known in conflict studies as "structural violence." Structural violence is defined as "Avoidable impairment of fundamental human needs or to put it in more general terms, the impairment of human life which limits the actual degree to which someone is able to meet their needs below that which would otherwise be possible" (Galtung, 1969, p. 173). Elsewhere, Galtung describes social violence as injustices embedded in social and institutional structures within society that results in harm to individuals (Galtung, 1969). Since Galtung's 1969 conceptualization of structural violence, other peace scholars have also sought to give a definitional clarity to the term.

Farmer (2003) defines structural violence as any violence or suffering caused by the structures and institutions of society. For him structural violence is perpetuated by social arrangements that put individuals and populations in harm's way. It comes when societal resources are being distributed unfairly, leading to gross disparities in income, literacy, education and access to health services (Farmer, 2003). Howes (2016) opines that it can be difficult to see structural violence in everyday life because it is perpetuated by large structures that hide behind their massive size and careful wording. George Kent (2018) conceives of structural violence as harm imposed on others indirectly through the social system, as they pursue their own preferences (Kent, 2011). He posits that such harm is inflicted through a slow and steady process with no clearly identifiable perpetrators and that structural violence is not visible in specific events and cannot be photographed. He however notes that the effects of structural violence are observable at societal level in the form of shortfalls in the quality of life of certain groups of people (Kent 2011). Winter and Leighton (2001) have also enriched the discourse on structural violence. For them structural violence occurs whenever people are disadvantaged by political, economic, legal or cultural traditions.

From the above postulations, structural violence signifies injustice, inequality and discrimination built into the fabric of society. In other words, it is the harm done to people by injustice and discrimination in society, leading to denial of their basic rights. As Common Law lawyers blame the Anglophone Common Law crisis on a flawed harmonization scheme, structural violence in the context of the Anglophone Common Law crisis encapsulates the injustices entrenched in respective harmonized laws and allied initiatives. These injustices (structural violence) have resulted from what Common Law lawyers describe as:

> A prolonged arbitrary super-imposition of the Civil Law legal system as practiced in the former East Cameroon in all its manifestations over the Common Law legal system practiced in the former West Cameroon (Common Law Lawyers Memo, 1993).

The structural violence occasioned against Common Law lawyers by harmonization is multi-dimensional. What follows is a non-exhaustive exposition of harmonization – related structural violence perpetuated over the years against the Anglophone population at large, and Common Law lawyers in particular.

Obsolescence of accumulated Legal Knowledge

One of the greatest social injustices or structural violence resulting from Common Law erosion in Cameroon is the obsolescence of legal knowledge accumulated by Common Law lawyers in many years of legal advocacy under the Common Law system. This is explained by the fact that, with the coming of a new law, the old law is replaced. The implication is that all knowledge based on the old law becomes obsolete or redundant. This is worse when the new law is predicated on a different legal system. That is the case with harmonized laws in Cameroon from a Common lawyer's perspective. The frustrations of Common Law lawyers hinge on the fact that all the years of their university studies (where they studied English private law) and years (or even decades) of legal practice have now come to naught as most terms, norms, and concepts in harmonized laws are Civil Law inspired. Taking the case of the CPC that replaced the CPO, Common Law concepts like "No Case Submission," "Proof beyond a reasonable doubt," "Striking out a matter for want of diligent prosecution," "Notice and grounds of Appeal" and "Subpoena" have suddenly become obsolete.

Obsolescence of Secondary Sources of Law

Just as knowledge acquired by lawyers over the years becomes obsolete in the face of harmonized laws, so too are practice books and law reports. This is because whenever a law is repealed, secondary sources of that law become obsolete. The obsolescence of Common Law practice books, casebooks and law reports means that a sizeable number of books in Common Law lawyers' libraries become obsolete each time a new harmonized law comes into force. In fact, with the acceleration of harmonization within the past few years most books in common law lawyers' offices nowadays are just decorating the shelves.

Harmonization Costs

Akin to the obsolescence of knowledge accumulated by Common Law lawyers over the years is their lack of legal knowledge of the new Civil Law terms, norms and concepts contained in harmonized laws. For example, Civil Law concepts in the CPC like "Proof by any means," "Proof beyond doubts," "tendering of case files in the case of an absent accused person" are strange to Common Law lawyers. Under this state of affairs, seniority at the Bar and experience does not count. Senior lawyers become legal neophytes while younger lawyers with more receptive brains become masters. This is an aberration in Common Law where seniority is sacrosanct. This is one of the reasons why the senior Common Law lawyers abhor harmonization in the Cameroon context.

Another facet of structural violence imputed on Common Law lawyers by harmonization is the cost they have to bear in renewing their stock of secondary sources. Whenever new laws are put in place, secondary sources of the new law like books quickly emerge to facilitate understanding of concepts in the new laws. In the case of the repealed Common Law realms, Common Law lawyers had in their libraries, standard practice books, case books and law reports from various Common Law realms. This is not the case with harmonized laws, whose Civil Law content means that secondary sources in English are rare and hard to come by. New laws bring new information. So, to be abreast with the new (harmonized) laws, the Common Law lawyers also have to invest money in refresher courses, seminar and workshops. So, the transposition of Civil Law to the hitherto Common Law jurisdiction of Cameroon enjoins Common Law lawyers to replace their Common Law practice books with Civil Law ones now and then. This is where the real problems begin. Firstly, law books are very expensive. Renewing a law library entails high costs. Secondly, existing books and legal authorities on harmonized laws are mostly written in the French language. An example is the regulated updated annotated text on OHADA laws. The obsolescence of accumulated knowledge and practice books on Common Law realms and the dearth of practice books on harmonized laws in English means that no matter their experience and years of practice Common Law lawyer cease to be an expert in any realm of law once it is harmonized. This may lead to loss of earnings as a result of dwindling clientele.

Location of CEMAC and OHADA Courts in French-speaking countries

Furthermore, Superior courts of harmonized treaty laws like the CEMAC laws and OHADA Acts are in French-speaking African countries—Ivory Coast for OHADA and Ndjamena for CEMAC. The binding authorities emanating from the OHADA Supreme Court in Abidjan are in French. The full judgments are in the French language and cannot be found anywhere in English as law reporting is not known in Civil Law. Again, the Civil Law style of writing judgments is sketchy. It also goes without saying that Common Law practitioners in Cameroon who are English-speaking will have a natural handicap pleading in those countries. Aside from the language problem, the procedure in those courts is equally Civil Law oriented. The transport costs to the venue of those courts can also be prohibitive.

Figure 6.2. BEAC slaps Cameroon's bilingual status, *The Sun*, April 20, 2020 (reporting that the Bank of Central African States, whose French acronym is BEAC, rejected a request from Cam-Post, the government corporation responsible for postal services in Cameroon, because the request was in English).

Cultural Cost of Harmonization

Harmonization has also imputed cultural costs on Common Law lawyers and Anglophones at large. Common Law being an Anglophone identity marker in Cameroon, its systematic eradication through harmonization is an attack on the Anglophone cultural identity in Cameroon. That is to say, since Common Law practices are part of the Anglophone legal culture, the erosion of Common Law is a dent on the Anglophone legal culture and *ipso facto* a denigration of the Anglophone cultural identity in Cameroon. Harmonization is therefore a threat to the culture and history of Anglophone Cameroon since legal culture is a part of general culture. The next issue Common Law lawyers decry is the fact that a number of harmonized laws exist only in the French language. This is the case with some CEMAC and OHADA laws. With this state of affair, Common Law lawyers do not know where to turn to. Even harmonized texts that have been translated into English are not very reliable as the translation is problematic. In many cases there are no terminological equivalents in Common Law. There are also no interpretation acts. This has put Common Law lawyers at difficult crossroads.

Another vexing issue for Common Law lawyers is that the manner of citing cases in OHADA textbooks, court judgments and rulings is alien to Common Law. In fact, it is everything but Common Law. Rather than having the names of the adversaries, followed by a citation, it begins with a French word "Arret," followed by a number. It does not say where the case is reported or where it can be found. Also, there is no *ratio - decidendi*, there are no quotations from the judgment/ruling and the name of the presiding judge is never stated. This is psychologically very painful to Common Law lawyers who see their age-old case law culture disappearing. Again, interpretation of harmonized texts follows the Civil Law spirit. By this is meant that the interpretation is very narrow and strict. The rules of statutory interpretation known to Common Law do not have a place in Civil Law. And since harmonized laws are Civil Law oriented and with no case law to explain them, the strict interpretation of the Civil Law is the way out. Equally, with codified law, there is no equity. Equity being an integral part of the Common Law, discarding it is a big handicap to common law lawyers who were brought up to spice their arguments and submissions with equitable maxims where necessary. So, the non-regard of equity and rules of statutory interpretation in the construction of harmonized codes is a constraint to Common Law lawyers which fits into the bracket of structural violence.

Loss of Earnings

Harmonized laws have also had an effect on Common Law practice in pecuniary terms. This is because some harmonized laws have taken away "work" from Common Law lawyers. As one common lawyer puts it, "Harmonization has affected our bread and butter." In this regard, Common Law lawyers cite the various Land Ordinances, the Labor Code and the CIMA code. For land matters the lawyers hold that the harmonized land law has taken away matters of title to land from the law courts and handed to the administration with President Biya's appointed *Sous-prefets* (Divisional Officers or D.O.) and *Prefets* (Senior Divisional Officers, S.D.O.) at the head. In typical Common Law jurisdictions, a "declaration of title to land" is a claim entertained in law courts on a daily basis. Under harmonized Cameroonian land law, it is a preserve of the "Land Consultative Board" headed by a D.O. This has no doubt robbed Common Law lawyers who traditionally prosecute matters of title to land from earning money. The same thing goes for the harmonized labor code. Under the labor code, the labor inspectorate and the labor inspector are the first port of call for aggrieved workers. It is only when the labor inspector can't resolve the dispute that the matter goes to court. Even then, it is the "statement of non-conciliation" issued by the labor inspector that seizes the court and not a lawyer's writ.

The "sins" of the labor code against the Common Law extend to the sum of money that can be claimed as general damages in a labor claim. While under Common Law such general damages have no stated amount, the harmonized labor code limits it to what the aggrieved worker's monthly earnings are, multiplied by the 12 months of the year. This has caused labor suits to gradually reduce from case lists in Anglophone courts. The same goes for insurance claims. The compensation rates for accident victims under the CIMA code is drastically lower than what obtained under the repealed Fatal Accidents Act. The exportation of the 5% deposit for civil claims to Common Law Cameroon has also affected common law practice in the Anglophone regions of Cameroon. As a result, many intending plaintiffs have simply reneged when told of this deposit. The combined effect of all these professional constraints on Common Law lawyers is that it has reduced their workload and invariably their earnings.

Another aspect of structural violence which Common Law lawyers have been subjected to is the posting of French-speaking Civil Law trained "magistrates" to the Common Law jurisdiction of Cameroon. Not groomed in Common Law and lacking a mastery of the English language, their professional output can only be sloppy. In fact, most Common Law lawyers hold that the handicaps of the Civil Law trained magistrates are very glaring in the prosecution of criminal matters, especially when it comes to cross-examination. Language constrains and lack of mastery of the art of cross examination means that their professional output is poor. This has led to their inability to prove the ingredients of offence through cross examination on many occasions. The resultant effect is that Common Law lawyers with civil claims attached to the criminal protection are hard done. Common Law lawyers have also faced dwindling earnings as a result of limited realms of legal practice. Unlike their Civil Law colleagues, Common Law lawyers have constraints in practicing in certain realms of harmonized laws. This is the case with certain CEMAC laws and the OHADA Uniform Acts. The reason being that the codes of these realms of law were conceived with a Civil Law mindset, written in French and have never been translated. Matters are worse with the CEMAC Laws. The ultimate CEMAC court is in Ndjamena and the language of the court is French. This no doubt limits the practice scope of the common law lawyer materially and geographically. In the West Cameroon days when common law reigned supreme in Anglophone Cameroon, all laws relevant to legal practice were conceived in English, drafted in English, and applied in English. Common Law lawyers of that generation had no language constrains. Above all, the West Cameroon Supreme Court was in Buea in Anglophone territory.

Common Law Lawyers Resist Harmonization

Burdened by the multidimensional structural violence occasioned against them by harmonization, Common Law lawyers began raising their voices in the early 1990s. The government was however uncompromising. With harmonization reaching new depths in the first decade of the new millennium, Common Law lawyers gathered in Bamenda on the 15th of May 2015 for a crisis meeting. The outcome of the meeting was an SOS addressed to the government in a rigorous memorandum. Going by its content and wordings, *The Post*, a local English language newspaper tagged the memorandum "a Riot Act." The memo was a huge statement of intent by Common Law lawyers which the government once more ignored. Construing government silence as a resolve to continue with its obnoxious harmonization scheme, Common Law lawyers went on the offensive. On the 17th of October 2016, they commenced a campaign of nonviolent action marked by a court boycott. This was followed by a cultural mobilization demonstration in Bamenda. A similar demonstration in Buea was foiled by a brutal assault on Common Law lawyers by the police even before it started. The lawyers' identitarian mobilization campaign seemingly paid off as Anglophone teachers queued up with a school boycott. Sympathetic members of the Anglophone civil society equally joined in. For better coordination of the growing movement, the Anglophone Civil Society Consortium (CCSC) was born. Not long afterwards Anglophone Cameroon was engulfed in a civil disobedience campaign characterized by a court boycott by lawyers, school boycott, ghost towns and protest marches. Disproportionate use of force by the military on protesters provoked reprisals from Anglophone activists. The spiral of violence continued until it attained the threshold of an armed conflict per International Criminal Tribunal for the Former Yugoslavia (ICTY) jurisprudence. There is no end in sight to the Anglophone crisis.

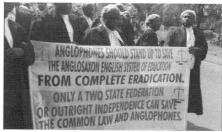

Figure 6.3. Left, "Common law lawyers begin week-long strike today." *The Guardian Post*, October 2016. Figure 6.4. Right, Anglophone lawyers on strike in October 2016. This was the beginning of the Anglophone Revolt.

Conclusion & Discussion

The official reason for harmonization is national integration. The purpose of national integration is usually to eliminate cultural differences. It is meant to forge a national identity by suppressing diversity. So, in theory the purpose of harmonization in Cameroon is to suppress diversity of laws and promote uniformity. In most countries where assimilation is practiced, the official excuse for it is the quest for "national unity" or "national integration." This is in line with Stavenhagen's assertion that:

> Assimilation occurs when there is a dominant model of what constitutes a nation, usually furthered by a strong nationalist ideology, and when specific measures are adopted with the purpose of incorporating members of distinct ethnic groups who do not originally conform to this model into the world of what is defined as a nation (Stavenhagen, 1996, p.3).

The key phrases in the above definition are dominant model, nationalist ideology, specific measures, and members of a distinct ethnic group. Taking the Common Law crisis as a case study the dominant model is Civil Law, the nationalist ideology is centralization, the specific measure is harmonization and the members of a distinct cultural group are Anglophone Common Law lawyers. It can thus be said that harmonization is aimed at eroding Common Law to the benefit of Civil Law. This is assimilation.

One of the outcomes of assimilation is cultural genocide. Novic (2006) perceives cultural genocide as the systematic destruction of traditions, values, language, and other elements that make one group of people distinct from another. Since what distinguishes one ethnic group from another are its ethnic identity markers, including cultural values and language. For Nersessian (2005),

> Cultural genocide extends beyond attacks upon the physical and/or bio-logical elements of a group and seeks to eliminate its wider institutions. This is done in a variety of ways, and often includes the abolition of a group's language, restrictions upon its traditional practices and ways... and attacks on academics and intellectuals (p. 7).

Cultural Genocide is therefore the destruction of a group's identity makers or the constitutive elements of its ethnicity. To put it differently, it is the intentional destruction of social, racial, religious, ethnic and linguistic groups through cultural assimilation and otherwise. This falls in line with the postulation of Sautman (2003: 177) that Cultural Genocide is the "extermination of a culture that does not involve physical extermination of its people." The term "Cultural Genocide" is sometimes used interchangeably with "Ethnocide," which is perceived as the intentional and systematic destruction of an ethnic culture. Planned compulsory assimilation of a minority ethnic group or an element of their culture will fall within this concept. There is no gainsaying that harmonization in Cameroon has eroded and destroyed the internal and external legal culture of Anglophone Cameroon. It is both "Ethnocide" and "Cultural Genocide." Since no group of people would like to lose their cultural identity, minority groups usually detest and resist assimilation, Ethnocide and Cultural Genocide. Thus, the grievances of Common Law lawyers who took to the streets in November 2016 resulted from, and was resistance to assimilation through harmonized laws. This was perceived by the government to be dissidence, hence its heavy-handedness.

References

Ashuntantang, J. (2020). Anglophone Cameroon Literature: Writing from the Margins of the Margin. In Tanure Ojaide and Joyce Ashuntantang (eds.). *Routledge Handbook of Minority Discourses in African Literature* (pp. 52-67). London: Routledge.

Banakas, S. (2009). The Contribution of Comparative Law to Harmonization of European Private Law. In Andrew Harding and Esin Örücü (eds). *Comparative Law in the 21st Century*. (pp. 179-192). London: Kluwer Academic.

Bell, J. (1995). English Law and French Law –Not so different? *Current Legal Problems*, 48 (2), 63-101.

Bobda, A. (2001). Varying Statuses and Perceptions of English in Cameroon: A diachronic and synchronic analysis. *Internet-Zeitschrift für Kulturwissenschaften.* Retrieved from: https://www.inst.at/trans/11Nr/bobda11.htm

Boodman, M. (1991). "The Myth of Harmonization of Laws," *American Journal of Comparative Law*, 39, pp. 699-724.

Dainow, J. (1966). The Civil Law and the Common Law: Some Points of Comparison. *American Journal of Comparative Law*, 15, pp. 419-435.

Farmer, P. (2004). An Anthropology of Structural violence. *Current Anthropology*, 45 (3), 305–317.

Fombad, C. (2016). Some Reflections on the prospects for the Harmonisation of international Business law in Africa: OHADA and Beyond. *Africa Today* 59(3) 51-80.

Fombad, C. (2016) *Separation of Powers in African Constitutionalism*, Oxford: Oxford University Press,

Galtung, J. (1969). Structural violence: Violent, Peace, and Peace Research, *Journal of Peace Research*, Peace Research Institute, Oslo, 6(3), 167-191.

Howes, D. (2016). *Bad Language: A study of structural Problems through language policies in Australia.* Capstone project and Master's Theses. California State University, Monterey. Retrieved from: https://digitalcommons.csumb.edu/caps_thes_all/2

Kent, G. (2011). Structural Violence. In *Experiments with Peace: Celebrating Peace on Johan Galtung's 80th Birthday*, Jorgen Johansen (ed., pp. 111-140). Oxon, UK: Pambazuka Press.

Konings, P. & Nyamnjoh, F. (2004). President Biya and the "Anglophone Problem" in Cameroon. In Mbaku J.M., Takougang, J. (Eds.) *The leadership challenge in Africa: Cameroon under Paul Biya* (pp. 191-234). Trenton, NJ: Africa World Press.

Konings P. (1999). The Anglophone Struggle for Federalism in Cameroon. *Federalism and decentralization in Africa: The multicultural challenge*, L.R. Bastia et J. Ibrahim (eds). Fribourg: Institut du Fédéralisme

Legrand, P. (1997). Against a European civil code. *The Modern Law Review.* Vol 60 (I) 44-63.

Lundmark, T. (2012). *Charting the Divide Between Common and Civil Law.* Oxford: Oxford University Press

Nfi, L. (2014). *The Reunification Debate in British Southern Cameroons: The Role of French Cameroon Immigrants*, Bamenda: Langaa Research and Publishing Common Initiative Group (Langaa, RPCIG).

Nersessian, D. (2005). Rethinking cultural genocide under international law, *Human Rights Dialogue*, 2 (12) 7-8

Novic, E. (2001) *The Concept of Cultural Genocide, An International Law Perspective.* Oxford: Oxford University Press.

Ni Nku, N. (1993). *Cry Justice: The Church in a Changing Cameroon.* Limbe: Pressbook.

Pejovic, C. (2001). Civil Law and Common Law: Two Different Paths Leading to the Same Goal. *Victoria University of Wellington Law Review*, 32(3) pp. 817-841

Sautman, B. (2003). "Cultural Genocide and Tibet." *Texas International Law Journal*, 38: 173- 248.

Shahabuddin, M. (2016). *Ethnicity and International Law: History/Politics and Practices.* Cambridge: Cambridge University Press.

Stavenhagen, R. (1996). The Ethnic Question in the World Crisis. In: *Ethnic Conflicts and the Nation-State.* Palgrave Macmillan, London. https://doi.org/10.1007/978-1-349-25014-1_1

Tetley, W. (2000). *Mixed Jurisdictions: Common Law v. Civil Law (Codified and Uncodified)*, Louisiana

Law Review, 60 (678-738). Available at: https://digitalcommons.law.lsu.edu/lalrev/vol60/iss3/2

Treaty of the Organisation for the Harmonisation of Business Law in Africa (OHADA) 17th of October 1993.

Van Hoecke, M. (2014). Do "legal systems" exist? The concept of law and comparative law. In *Concepts of Law*, Seán Patrick Donlan & Lukas Heckendorn Urscheler (eds., pp. 1-13). London: Routledge.

Wakai, N. (2008). *Under the Broken Scale of Justice: The Law and My Times*. Bamenda: Langaa Research and Publishing Common Initiative Group (Langaa, RPCIG).

Winter, D. & Leighton, D. (2001). Structural Violence. In D.J. Christie, R.V. Wagner and D.D. Winter (eds.). *Peace Conflict and Violence: Peace Psychology in 21st century* (99-101). New York, Prentice Hall.

Zweigert, K. & Kötz, H. (1998). *An Introduction to Comparative Law*, (T. Weir, transl.; 3rd ed.). Oxford: Oxford University Press

Laws

CIMA Insurance Code of 1992

Criminal Procedure Ordinance

Criminal Procedure Code

Federal Ordinance No. 61-of-9 of 16th October 1961

Federal Ordinance No 61-DF of 16th October 1961

Law N° 92-007 of 14th August 1992

Law N° 74/14 of 27th November 1974

Law N° 89/019 of 29th December 1989

Law N° 89/019 of 29th December 1989

Law N° 89/019 of 29th December 1989

Law N° 65-LF-24 of 12th November 1965

Law N° 2019/014 of 24th December 2019

Law N° 2005/007 of 27th July 2005

The League of Nations Mandate document

OHADA Uniform Acts

Ordinance N°72/4 of 26th August 1972

Ordinance N° 74/1 of 6th July 1974

Ordinance N° 81-2 of 29th June 1981

Ordinance N° 89-005 of 13th December 1989

Quebec Act of 1774

The Colony of Nigeria "Proclamation No 41 of 18th of January 1922,

The Nigeria (Protectorate) and Cameroon Order in Council of 1946

The British Foreign Jurisdiction Act of 1897

The Nigeria (1924) Order in Council,

The Nigeria Supreme Court Ordinance of 1914

The Nigerian (Constitution) Order in Council of 1954,

The Southern Cameroons High Court Law of 1955

The Southern Cameroons Magistrate Court Law of 1955

The French Cameroon Code of Civil and Commercial Procedures of 16th December 1954

The French Cameroon Code of Criminal Instruction of 1938

The Code (Civile) Napoleon of 1804

The French Cameroon Code of Commerce of 7th of December 1850.

The Cameroon Federal Constitution of 1st September 1961

The West Cameroon Constitution of 26th October 1961.

The 1706 Act of Union between Scotland and Great Britain

The Labour Code, 1968

Newspaper

The Post, 18th May 2015

PART TWO

Historical, Cultural and Political Dimensions of the Anglophone Problem

SEVEN

Early Symptoms of Anglophone Discontent in Post-Reunification Federal Cameroon

The Jua-Muna Power Tussle

WOMAI I. SONG

Colonized by the Germans in 1884, Kamerun was partitioned between Britain and France after the First World War with Britain taking one-fifth and France having four-fifth of the territory. Baptized by the League of Nations as Mandated Territories and later by the United Nations Organization as Trust Territories, Britain administered her share as part of her adjacent colony of Nigeria (with the southern section administered as part of the Eastern Region and the northern section as part of the Northern Region), while the French-administered her portion as an entity within the French Community. At the advent of decolonization in Africa, French Cameroun acquired independence on January 1, 1960 as the Republic of Cameroun with Ahmadou Ahidjo as its president. On the other side, British Southern Cameroons, which had acquired internal self-government from the Eastern Region of Nigeria in 1954 voted in a plebiscite on February 11, 1961 to reunify with her sister territory of the Republic of Cameroun. British Northern Cameroons voted in the same plebiscite to remain in the Nigerian federation (Elango, 1987; Levine, 1970, pp. 119-130; Delancey, 1989, pp. 7-45). Southern Cameroons and French Cameroun then engaged in negotiations led respectively by John Ngu Foncha and Ahmadou Ahidjo to seek a consensus on the nature of a reunified Cameroon.

A Federal Republic of Cameroon of two states was eventually proclaimed on October 1, 1961, following the June 1961 Bamenda All Parties Constitutional Talks, the July 1961 Foumban Constitutional Conference, and the August 1961 Yaoundé Tripartite Conference. By Article 1 of the Federal Constitution, the Republic of Cameroun became known as East Cameroun (further divided into four provinces), and Southern Cameroons was styled West Cameroon (further divided into two provinces – the Northwest and Southwest provinces) with its capital in Buea. Still in accordance with the federal constitution, there was to be a president and vice president, each from a different state. While the president and vice president headed the federal superstructure in the federal capital in Yaoundé (also doubling as the East Cameroun's state capital) with the assistance of a federal house of assembly comprised of elected members from both states, article 38 of the constitution ruled for each federated state to be led by a prime minister and a legislature elected by the people of the respective states (Mbile, 2011, pp. 133-144).

Figure 7.1. Foncha and Ahidjo

Figure 7.2. Stamp showing the Federal Republic of Cameroon

As one of the colonial legacies, the young Cameroon federation was in sync with the postcolonial African federal experiences of the 1950s and 1960s. It was an inter-state federation similar to the political arrangements between Ethiopia and Eritrea, Senegal and French Sudan, Tanganyika and Zanzibar, and the mooted proposals between Ghana, Mali, and Guinea. In this light, it was very different from the contemporary intra-state African federations of the likes of Nigeria, Kenya, Uganda, and Zaire (Burgess, 2012, p. 9). The type of federation notwithstanding, the young Cameroon federation constituted one of the most attractive experiments of nation-building in postcolonial Africa. As Walter Samah (2010) puts it, the "Cameroon [federation] provided a unique experience in Africa of the coming together of French and English-speaking territories. As it was a blend of two contrasting

214

traditions, the entire world looked up to the Cameroonian experience for lessons that could be emulated elsewhere. The union was of particular interest to Pan-Africanists, notably Kwame Nkrumah of Ghana, who saw the Cameroon example as the beginning of a new era in Africa – that which was to culminate in a United States of Africa" (p. 247).

Despite the hopes of Pan-Africanists and the outside world, as Cameroonians cele-brated the advent of a reunified nation, the country's political aristocracy felt burdened with the challenges that lay ahead. Prominent among such challenges were: inculcating a sense of a Cameroon identity, bridging the politico-socio-economic differences between West and East Cameroon, bringing along those who had staunchly believed in alternative options to reunification, reconciling those who saw the federation as the final solution to the reunified Cameroon and those who secretly viewed it as a temporary arrangement on the road to the unitary state; and dealing with French neo-colonial interests. Such challenges were common to many African states emerging from close to a century of colonial rule and often created the fear of potential disintegration in the process of nation-building. The independence debacle that culminated in the assassination of Patrice Lumumba and the subsequent Biafran War were stark reminders of the unpredictability and "painful" process of "growing" that is often associated with new nations and awaited newly independent African countries in the early 1960s (Lipset, 1967, p. 18).

Given the divergent opinions that had characterized Cameroon's journey to indepen-dence, the Federal Republic of Cameroon inevitably consisted of many individuals, groups, and institutions with conflicting loyalties and different levels of tension. Carrying over issues from one historical period to another created a political atmosphere characterized by bitterness and frustration rather than tolerance and compromise. Men and parties differed, not simply on ways of settling postcolonial cleavages, but on fundamental and opposed outlooks. Consequently, the whole Cameroon federal political system in 1961 lacked effective value integration. This was further complicated by the major features that subsequently animated the political transition from federalism in 1961 to unitarism in 1972. Some of these features included: constitutional amendments, changes to the electoral system, reallocation of political power, transition from multi-partism to monolithism, economic harmonization, experimentation, and authoritarianism.

In the Federated State of West Cameroon, the dynamics of the relations between the opposition and the government, the degree of conflict and/or cooperation between the political actors, and the extent of interaction with federal authorities, defined the tune and ramifications of transition on the state. As far as political actors were concerned, Augustine Ngom Jua and Solomon Tandeng Muna had emerged after Foncha as the two most influential political figures in West Cameroon after independence and reunification. Their political resources included: political apprenticeship in the British Trusteeship administration in Nigeria and/or Southern Cameroons; a rich resume of political positions; friendships; political efficacy; political consciousness; social status; political charisma; support bases; limited but very impactful formal education; healthy body systems; social/political con-nections; relatively rich economic backgrounds; knowledgeability on factual information about the state; and a strong belief of their relevance and indispensability in the building of the young federation in general and the Federated state of West Cameroon in particular

(Donovan et al., 1986, p. 13).

Further epitomized by their occupation of conspicuous political positions in the ruling party (KNDP) at the state and/or federal levels, Jua and Muna competed for the limited political influence in Anglophone Cameroon during the transition period. In this competition, they had conflicting perspectives on: the need for peace and political unity in West Cameroon, the place of the opposition in the West Cameroon parliamentary system of government, the role of the single party in the federation, the preservation of the state's autonomy and Anglophone personality; the direction of transport infrastructure; the place of the Federal Inspector of Administration in West Cameroon; the role of the federal government; bilingualism; the solution to the West Cameroon Bank crisis; and the future Cameroon federal polity. Rooted in the mutual mistrust that had characterized their relationship in the run-up to independence, this competition was further driven by vaulting personal ambitions, stubborn convictions, the pressure of respective supporters, and the interests of external actors.

As Ruth First (1970) put it, "politicians are men who compete with one another for power and seeking to exercise power in the pursuit of policy objectives constitute the cornerstone of the science of politics," Jua and Muna sought to subordinate the ends that each other favored to their own respective favored ends by maneuvering to successfully wield political authority or legitimate power in West Cameroon between 1961 and 1972 (p. 9). This political power rested in the West Cameroon's Prime Minister's office. Their tussle would see them in and out of this office in indelible dramatic episodes in early post-independence Cameroon's transition history.

This chapter puts the Jua-Muna clash into proper perspective in the genesis of the ongoing crisis in Cameroon. It focuses on the struggle between these two high-profile West Cameroon politicians to occupy the highest office in the state between 1961 and 1972 in the context of early symptoms of Anglophone Cameroon disenchantment in the country's federal experiment. It is divided into three major sections. The first concentrates on the first duel culminating in the rise of A.N. Jua as the Prime Minister of West Cameroon in 1965. The second part focuses on the conditions that precipitated the second duel and the rise of Muna as Premier of the state in 1968. These are followed by a third section that examines the role of the federal president in this mesmerizing political schism. The conclusion is an analysis of the ramifications of this political drama on the Anglophone Cameroonians and its meaning in the subsequent Anglophone Problem.

The First Duel and the Rise of Jua as Premier

The genesis of the political clash between A.N. Jua and S.T. Muna in postcolonial Cameroon was the federal constitutional requirement (Article 9) of the separation of the office of the Prime Minister of West Cameroon from that of the office of the Vice Presidency of the Federal Republic of Cameroon before the April 1965 presidential elections. As the end of the constitutionally allotted transition from colonial rule to independence drew nearer, it was clear that J.N. Foncha, who had held both positions according to the dictates of Article 52 of the Federal Constitution, would prefer the prestigious office of the Vice President. This was indicative following a meeting with his closest confidants and advisers at Isogo, during which he refused to make a declaration on the issue against their pressure for him to retain the position of Prime Minister as early as 1963. Because he was seemingly leaning toward the federal Vice Presidency, camps began to develop within the ranks of KNDP cadres in West Cameroon who had prospects of succession to the office of the West Cameroon Prime Minister (Johnson, 1970, p. 268). Ngunjoh Tafoh – the Organizing Secretary of the KNDP (as cited in *Day Down: Cameroon's Authoritative Newspaper*, August 1990, p. 9) confirmed this sense of euphoria.

Figure 7.3. Augustine Ngom Jua

The competition amongst West Cameroonians for the prospective vacancy in the office of West Cameroon's Prime Minister gathered momentum at the KNDP party convention in Bamenda in mid-August 1963. Since it was the unspoken assumption within the party that whoever occupied the post of the party's First Vice President would automatically be the party's nominee to replace Foncha as Prime Minister of West Cameroon, all aspirants had to first audition for that position within the party's administrative hierarchy (G. Atem, personal communication, March 7, 1999; J. Gwellem, personal communication, March 15, 1999). Against such unexpected developments, the Bamenda convention drew an unusual turnout of delegates as several party heavyweights declared their candidacies for that position. These included Peter Kemcha (incumbent), Secretary of State for labor from Mamfe; Johannes Bokwe, the Secretary of State for Transport and Public Works from Kumba; Joseph Noni Lafon, Secretary of State for Local Government from Nso; A.N. Jua, Secretary of State for Finance from Kom; and S.T. Muna, Federal Minister of Transport, Mines, and Power (J. Gwellem, personal communication, March 15, 1999; Johnson, 1970, pp. 270-271). But as the campaign machinery set in motion, the field quickly narrowed to Jua and Muna, both of whom had bases of strength in the important Grassfields constituencies. Emmanuel Tabi Egbe, who campaigned for the post of the Secretary General of the party, joined the Muna camp while his challenger Nzo Ekangaki allied with Jua.

Figure 7.4. Solomon Tandeng Muna

For purposes of analysis and substantiation of the thesis of this study, it is important to consider some of the motivations behind Jua and Muna's aspirations for the post of the First Vice President of the KNDP party and, ultimately, the premiership of West Cameroon at this moment in Cameroon's transition history. For Jua, besides the apparent personal ambition for higher office that has often driven a majority of politicians in any political system, it was a patriotic calling for him to continue to live the life of service that had inspired him throughout his political career (Vb/a1965/2, National Archives Buea). He considered his occupation of the office of the Prime Minister of West Cameroon as an opportunity to fulfill the best service for his people that he had committed to since the colonial days in British Southern Cameroons. Having been lukewarm to the idea of reunification with French Cameroun and subsequently highly disappointed by the second-class citizenry position of his people in the early days of reunification, Jua is said to have seen his occupation of the highest office in the federated states of West Cameroon as the most singular opportunity to make a difference for his people (Vb/a1965/2, NAB).

Jua's competition for the position was further instigated by his sense of justice and belief that he was the next most qualified party official after J.N. Foncha. This was particularly the case given that he was the co-founder of the KNDP and had been a dedicated, able, and most loyal lieutenant of the "Life President" since the party's formation on the floor of the British Southern Cameroons House of Assembly in 1955. In this regard, he believed that he had paid his dues and earned his place as the most senior West Cameroon ruling party member by 1963. To him, by virtue of the longevity of party affiliation and experience as a party official, he was the next in command. Furthermore, Jua's subtle claim for the premiership of West Cameroon in the early 1960s was propelled by the massive support base he enjoyed within the KNDP. His patriotism to the West Cameroon State, his no-nonsense attitude vis-à-vis the federal officials, his political charisma, his experience with party business and administration, and his party founding member status, had won him profound admiration, respect, and the confidence of a cross-section of his party comrades (Song, 1999, pp. 49-55).

On his part, Muna has not left any explicit record explaining why, despite the fact that he was a high-ranking federal minister, he decided to contest for the First Vice President of the KNDP and, ultimately, the premiership of the Federated State of West Cameroon in the early 1960s. But the allegation at the time that he was Ahidjo's man sent on a secret special mission to West Cameroon to secure the state, protect Ahidjo's most cherished project of transitioning to a unitary state, and protect French neo-colonial interest gained credence over the years per the assertions of J. N. Foncha, Atem George, V. T. Lainjo, Albert Mukong and A. N. Ngwa in 1999 (personal communications, cited in Song, 1999). Proponents of this school of thought argued that there was no other palpable reason for Muna's decision to contest that position. Mukong and Atem argued that Muna was fully aware that there was insufficient political power left in the Prime Minister's office in Buea. This, they insisted, was particularly the case given that the federal constitution had rendered the position not only very powerless but more ceremonial. This was rendered even so by the appointment of a federal inspector of administration whose office had arrogated most of the power-based services in West Cameroon under the federal jurisdiction. Foncha's seeming abandonment of the position in preference for the Yaoundé-based Vice Presidency was telling enough (personal communications, cited in Song, 1999).

Suffice it to state that this argument might be convincing to many. This may be particularly so in the context of the fact that Muna was relatively more powerful and influential than the Prime Minister of West Cameroon as per the federal arrangements. From his prominence in pre-unification and post-plebiscite talks, he had been appointed the only West Cameroon full federal minister. This was unlike Jua, who was just a deputy federal minister of health. As a federal minister based in Yaoundé, Muna was closer to the center of political power and intimately shared Ahidjo's vision of a reunified Cameroon. Even the inference of acquisitiveness as a motivation was remote, given that cupidity in conflict relations is intrinsically power-driven. Some may, therefore, see no tangible motivation or interest in Muna's position in West Cameroon's premiership except to serve Ahidjo's will. Besides, the French are alleged to have preferred Muna leading West Cameroon to ensure that the wells of the crude oil which had just been discovered in the West Cameroon southern shores did not fall into wrong hands (Vb/a1968/03, NAB). Although there is still not ample documented evidence to substantiate these assertions further, one is forced to stand by them by virtue of the French neo-colonial grandstanding and economic exploitative maneuvers and tendencies in postcolonial Africa in general and Cameroon in particular.

Notwithstanding Muna and Jua's motivations to fill the impending vacancy in the West Cameroon Prime Minister's office, the competition between them continued amidst tension and excitement. It became an open secret that the victor and vanquished could only be separated in the ballot box. In reference to the ramifications of this clash, an observer stated that:

> Unfortunately, the threat of their political struggle for power spread with real sinister effect within the rank and file of the party, and as a result, the party which was looked upon as the MOSES OF CAMEROON UNIFI-CATION (SIC), was adversely caught entangled in this fray of leadership

struggle, which developed into real political devastating hurricane which not only swept throughout the KNDP but also in all other political parties in the country.... Supporters and well-wishers of the party. . . helplessly bit their fingers with grinding teeth, with the only consolation of turning their eyes on the leader of the party. He in turn found his hands tied by the party constitution as such had no other alternative than to constitutionally ask the convention of the party to decide on this issue, in order also, to exonerate himself from the woes of the Angels of blessings and the calamities of the devil of favoritism (Vb/1968/3, NAB).

Foncha who could not decide or vote by virtue of his returning officer status recoiled to a neutral position. According to him:

Despite the fact the two candidates [Muna and Jua] vying for the post of the First Vice-President of the party [KNDP] were my supporters, they could only get to that position through elections by the [Bamenda] Convention delegates. As a matter of fact, elections was [sic] and remain the general rule by which people get into positions in political parties and political positions in a nation. Thus, I could not prefer one against another because this would have made my party to be no longer democratic and I would no longer have been a person who hated discrimination.... It was therefore left for the delegates to choose their vice-president which I think was supposed to be based on competence (personal communication cited in Song, 1999, p. 47).

Foncha's claim on the Jua-Muna tussle in 1999 was largely consistent with his statements in the *Cameroon Times* of April 1965. In a reply to a question on his preference, he had stated that his preference was irrelevant considering that the appointment of his successor was "solely within the ambit" of the president following the decision of his party's "convention and West Cameroon Legislature" (*Cameroon Times*, April 7, 1965, NAB).

Foncha's claim of fairmindedness in the Jua and Muna feud is, however, challenged by some scholars and politicians. Willard Johnson, Jacques Benjamin, Albert Mukong, Phillip Ewusi, and Nicolas Ade Ngwa firmly held that Foncha was never evenhanded in the succession debacle. They were all of the opinion that Foncha, at least initially, backed Muna and even subsidized his campaign against Jua with the sum of 40,000FCFA (*Cameroon Life*, October 1990; Johnson, 1970, p. 269; personal communication with A. Mukong and A. Ngwa cited in Song, 1999). Although this school of thought lacks palpable evidence, it cannot be discarded entirely especially when one takes a look at the camaraderie between Foncha and Muna between 1957 and 1963. Despite his neophyte status, the Foncha-Muna esprit de corps had given Muna undue influence in the KNDP Party. This was particularly so given that Foncha had led secret meetings with Muna and Ahidjo in Douala and Yaoundé shortly after the plebiscite, during which Ahidjo had promised Foncha the post of the vice president and Muna a federal ministerial position (*Cameroon Outlook*, April 24th – 30th,

1961, NAB). During most of Foncha's several trips abroad, Muna had also unexpectedly deputized as the Prime Minister of West Cameroon (Johnson, 1970, p. 268). More credence was given to the allegation of Foncha's support for Muna by A. T. Ngunjoh when he stated that "Foncha misled Muna by accepting to Muna that he was going to fight to make Muna the Prime Minister [of West Cameroon].... I told Foncha that this was wrong" (personal communication cited in *Day Down*, August 29th, 1990, p. 9). Muna himself admitted that he had initially enjoyed the support of Foncha, who later changed his mind for reasons he had never fully comprehended (personal communication, cited in Song, 1999, p. 74).

Foncha's position notwithstanding, the delegates overwhelmingly voted in favor of Jua with 175 votes against 73 for Muna. Ekhangaki defeated Egbe by 159 votes against 95 as the Secretary General of the KNDP. Jua's victory for the party's vice presidency was consolidated in the party's 1964 ninth convention in Kumba when the party's constitution was amended to ensure that the holder of that position in the absence of the "life president" of the KNDP party from the West Cameroon House of Assembly should automatically be the party's nominee as Prime Minister of the Federated State of West Cameroon. Although Foncha was not in favor of this amendment, he consulted with each of his fellow West Cameroon Assembly men to find out which of the two candidates commanded the support of the majority. In this consultation, Jua again triumphed over Muna. Jua's popularity by the end of 1964 in West Cameroon was no longer a secret as meeting after meeting in West Cameroon confirmed his victory and called on Muna to surrender (Johnson, 1970, pp. 272-273; Ngoh, 1987, p. 249).

Jua's Popularity over Muna: An Explanation

One of the fundamental explanations for Jua's popularity over Muna was his lifelong dedication to a position of dignity for the English-speaking state of Cameroon. Even before reunification, Jua's position was that Southern Cameroons first server its links with Nigeria and become an independent state in its own right before opening negotiations for reunification on a federal basis. Consequently, he stood to make integration and secession the only questions in the 1961 plebiscite. Thus, when Foncha was pressured at the United Nations (UN) in September 1959 to compromise his position in favor of reunification in the plebiscite, Jua wired him to indicate that the KNDP leadership considered such a compromise unacceptable. It is even alleged that Jua and close collaborators contemplated replacing Foncha as the leader of the KNDP and insisting on integration and secession as the only plebiscite options. But he was persuaded to abandon his plans after assurance by the territory's traditional rulers that Foncha would be able to secure reunification on the basis of a loose association or, at worst a confederacy (*Annals of the Faculty of Arts, Letters, and Human Sciences*, 1&2, January-July 1990, p. 3).

After reunification, Jua was very disappointed in the federal constitution which deprived West Cameroon of political and economic autonomy. His autonomist statements in the WCHA as Finance Minister earned him a lot of popularity amongst the majority of the KNDP militants. Popular traditional rulers of the likes of the Fon of Bali sympathized with Jua's autonomist vision for West Cameroon. Suffice it to submit that Jua's popularity over Muna was partly based on his unapologetic "states-rights" candidacy. Although Muna had earlier shared Jua's sentiments by stating that "Unification between the Southern Cameroons might take the form of a loose federation with the aim of preserving the individuality of the Southern Cameroons State," he had greatly diverged from this position after reunification (*West African Press Release*, No. 618, 1959, November 25th, NAB). Attempts at explaining Muna's change of heart ranged from greed and personal ambition to opportunism. Increasingly viewed as a "bellytician" in West Cameroon, Muna, unlike Jua was generally viewed as a "centralist" or a "federation man" with "an image of political adventurism" (Hazlewood, 1967, p. 333; Johnson, 1970, p. 269; personal communications with O. Inglis and P. Ewusi cited in Song, 1999, p. 74). Jua's edge over Muna based on their opposing perspectives on the status of West Cameroon in the Cameroon federation was expressed by Commissioner J.O. Field in a 1961 dispatch to the Colonial Office stating that:

> ... All is not well in the KNDP. Jua's influence in the party has been increasing ... at the expense of Muna. This is of course, a clash between those who are strong for re-unification (Muna) and those who are not (Jua). At a recent party congress, Jua was elected 1st Vice-President and Muna failed to secure any office at all. I understand matters came to a head when it came to light that during the Foncha and Muna's recent visit to Yaoundé, Okala had secret talks with Muna and persuaded him to agree that the police and the army should be federal subjects on the understanding that Muna would be Minister of Defense.... If Foncha had anything to do with it, he has now swung away from it and is firm with Jua in demanding that the police shall be federal, that no forces of the Republique [sic] shall be permitted to enter the Southern Cameroons without the Southern Cameroons Government's consent and that the new security force, if it materializes, shall be under Southern Cameroons' control to start with (Southern Cameroons Restoration Movement – SCARM, "Renotification of Decision", March 1999, p. 2).

Muna and Jua's contrasting positions on the future of Southern Cameroons were again demonstrated in the Bamenda "All Parties Constitutional Conference" later in June. Unlike Jua, Muna strongly disagreed with the Fon of Bali's caution that "we should be careful to build a house without windows and doors." Muna, in effect, meant that he saw no need for the inclusion of a clause in the Southern Cameroons' constitutional proposals, which called for secession of the territory in case the union proved unworkable. In this light, Muna, unlike Jua, was very contented with Article 47 of the Federal Constitution, which, amongst other things, stated that any proposal for the revision of the constitution that could impair the unity and integrity of the federation was inadmissible.

Another factor that edged Jua over Muna was the former's KNDP founding father status. It is even alleged that Jua was the main brain behind the formation of the party in 1955 and that he had ceded leadership to Foncha because he respected him as an elder (personal communications with P. Ewusi, N. Jua, and V. Lainjo cited in Song, 1999, p. 74). The KNDP militants believed that Jua was more abreast with the party's manifesto and founding principles/philosophy than his rival – Muna, who had just joined the party in September 1957. Within the circles of the party, Muna was looked upon as an opportunist. He was not in the good books of the party's cadre, especially as his close friendship with Foncha had given him considerable influence in the party. Up to the 1963 national convention, he deputized as premier of West Cameroon during Foncha's several trips abroad.

This offended the "elder" KNDP politicians who thought that Jua was the appropriate person to assume such duties in terms of seniority within the party. Thus, when Muna pleaded with Ngunjoh in June 1963 to support him against Jua to become the Vice President of the party and Prime Minister of West Cameroon, Ngunjoh bluntly retorted "sir, if you had crossed the carpet from the KNC to the KNDP or the opposition together with Foncha, I would have supported you. I think only Jua who joined him is qualified to take over from Foncha. That is the nature of politics.... I believe in first come first served" (*Day Down*, August 1990, pp. 7-10). Although this sounds conflicting with democratic principles, it reflected the general feeling, especially amongst the enlightened KNDP militants, and contributed enormously to Jua's victory over Muna in the first round of their political conflict in West Cameroon between 1961 and 1972.

Jua's popularity within the rank and file of the KNDP could equally be attributed to his firm character. He is believed to have been fearless, forceful, direct, shrewd, hot-headed, and impetuous. With these character threats, West Cameroonians saw in him the person more likely to push hard against any opponent to satisfy the needs of the state. This was particularly the case as there was growing disappointment with Foncha's defense of West Cameroon's interests at the federal level and an increasing malaise about changes occasioned by reunification. The West Cameroonians, therefore, saw much hope in Jua, who had demonstrated the extent to which he could confront the federal government in 1964 during Foncha's absence. Acting as Deputy Premier of West Cameroon, Jua is alleged to have stopped the Federal Inspector of Administration's car and instructed him to personally remove the Cameroon flag that his car was flying. This, the Federal Inspector shamefully did in public and to the satisfaction of elated West Cameroon onlookers (Henry Bain, Personal communication, cited in Song, 1999, p. 53). This abrasive personality seemed to have been in complete contrast to that of Muna whom many West Cameroonians considered to be unpredictable and very gullible. The rapidity with which he had changed his political affection in the 1950s did not make him a competent candidate for the Prime Minister of the State of West Cameroon at a very crucial moment in its history (A. Mukong, personal communication, cited in Song, 1990, p. 53).

Jua's progressive inclination was an added advantage over Muna. In the 1963 Bamenda Convention, it was evident that the party had fractured into two ideological factions: the progressives and the conservatives, supporting Jua and Muna respectively. The majority of progressives advocated for radical changes in the party so as to give it a machinery powerful enough to confront the federal government and check the growing ethnic and nepotistic sentiments within the party. The conservatives, on the other hand, stood for the status quo. Jua won the hearts of the civil servants and the Anglophones of the forest region when he allegedly led a crusade for the reinstatement of Eric D. Quan and Peter M. Efange into the civil service. These were Bakweri civil servants who had been summarily dismissed apparently because someone had accused them of having given aid and support to the CPNC in early 1961 (Johnson, 1970, p. 272). Although Jua never succeeded because of opposition from Foncha and Muna, he left an impression that if given the opportunity, appointments, and promotions of civil servants in the West Cameroon government would be based on merit and not on ethnic, regional, or former party affiliations. This certainly made him more popular than Muna whose close association with Foncha attracted the party's disdain towards his candidacy.

Lastly, Jua's popularity over Muna stemmed from his charismatic nature. He was a forceful speaker and a man of mesmeric personality with the knack of holding his audience spellbound (*Cameroon Times*, May 13, 1965; J. Gwellem, personal communication, cited in Song, 1990, p. 54). It was in this context that he had cultivated a number of important branch organizations at the level of the constituencies so that their delegations to the national conventions were often filled with his supporters. This was unlike Muna whose local base support was very thin. This contrast between these claimants was demonstrated at the local level elections in February 1965 during by-elections to fill the seats of those state assembly men who had been elected the previous April to seats in the Federal Assembly. The fact that Muna's handpicked candidates for his own former assembly seat were defeated, pointed to his detachment from and lack of touch with the KNDP grassroots politics at the time (Johnson, 1970, 271).

Despite the fact that all these factors had tilted the balance in favor of Jua at the party's ninth convention in Bamenda, tenth convention in Kumba, in the West Cameroon House of Assembly, and in the May 9, 1965 joint parliamentary meeting, Muna still refused to surrender. He instead stressed the constitutional prerogative of the president of the Federal Republic of Cameroon to nominate the State's Prime Minister. He strongly believed that the West Cameroon Parliamentary wing of the KNDP would back him if he was appointed by Ahidjo. Nicolas Ade Ngwa argued that by pressing his candidacy after the Bamenda and Kumba conventions, Muna ignored the "will of the people" and was at that point driven by self-centeredness – a view shared by many political analysts (personal communication, February 15, 2014). But enslaved by his belief that he could emerge victorious in the midst of all odds, Muna increased pressure on his former ally – Foncha. Foncha, who at that moment saw the need for party discipline, advised Muna to "step down". The hidden Foncha-Muna pact had collapsed at this juncture as the latter accused the former of being the party's "number one devil" insisting the president would nominate him if given the opportunity (Johnson, 1970, p. 273; *L'Effort Camerounaise*, 508, October 3, 1965, p. 3).

The competition between Jua and Muna had a chilling effect not only in the KNDP but in West Cameroon. As the constitutional deadline for Foncha's replacement drew near, Muna and his followers stepped up their subterranean campaign, spreading the propaganda of assurances from Ahidjo. This brought a cloud of anxiety and uncertainty throughout West Cameroon. Frustrated party members accused these "rebellious, scandalous bunch of party men," "confuscionists", and "traitors", of a calculated attempt to assassinate the party for the benefit of a third party. The political uncertainty and uneasiness over the Jua-Muna tussle was vividly captured by a publication in May 1965. It amongst other things stated that:

> This [tussle] caused sensation in the whole of West Cameroon and raised anxiety both in the Federal capital and in parts of East Cameroun.... It became the subject of silent conversations in every office, in every pub, in every home, in every street in West Cameroon. The people turned to pages of the Federal and Federated State Constitutions to find out whether it was possible for the president to arbitrarily appoint a person of his own choice as Prime Minister of West Cameroon.... When president Ahidjo arrived to consult popular opinion, ... people became more anxious than ever. Buea was crowded with people from other parts of the territory and interested persons from East Cameroun. The dark alleys of the town became popular rendezvous for strategic meetings. There were swift and secret movements.... The big question mark that overhung the whole Buea remained in its place – [who was going to be the next Prime Minister?].
> (Vb/a1965/3, NAB – Cameroon)

Against such a tense political backdrop, the Federal President's power to affect the course of politics was never real than at that moment of the Jua-Muna political tug-of-war. Interestingly enough, Ahidjo for once in his post-independence leadership of Cameroon acted democratically. On arrival in West Cameroon on Tuesday May 11, 1965, he immediately indulged into consultative meetings. For two days he consulted both individuals and groups of West Cameroon politicians (Johnson, 1970, p. 273; *L'Effort Camerounaise*, Oct 1965, p. 3). On the much-awaited day of the appointment of Foncha's successor in the West Cameroon's Prime Minister's office, "anxious and vexed people with throbbing hearts began to assemble within and outside the West Cameroon House of Assembly. They jostled for places and only murmured in low tones. Some sat around the only loudspeaker outside the house and supported their cheeks in their palms." (Vb/a1965/3, NAB – Cameroon). At 3:30 pm, Ahidjo by Decree No 65/DF/170 nominated A.N. Jua as the Prime Minister of West Cameroon in the following words:

> The President of the Federal Republic of Cameroon, mindful of the constitution of the Federal Republic of Cameroon of 1st September 1961 and in particular Article 39 thereof; considering the letter of the 12th May 1965 from the Speaker of the House of Assembly of West Cameroon giving notification of the investiture obtained by the Prime Minister Augustine Jua at its session of the same date; hereby decree as follows: that Mr. Augustine Ngom Jua shall be appointed Prime Minister, Head of Government of the Federated State of West Cameroon (Vb/a1965/2, NAB, Cameroon).

At 4:20 pm, the Speaker of the WCHA, P.M. Kale, officially communicated the nomination to the anxious assembly which quickly confirmed. After the oath of office and the investiture, the new Prime Minister pledged in an inaugural speech to serve the people of West Cameroon faithfully and to the best of his ability. He then drove off the assembly ground escorted through cheering crowds as his vanquished rival looked on with disappointment and in contemplation of his next option (Vb/a1965/3, NAB – Cameroon).

Jua's victory over Muna in his ascendancy to the post of the Prime Minister of West Cameroon received the widest acclamation throughout the length and breadth of the territory. The West Cameroon civil servants in a message signed by its Secretary General N.N. Nsiong Enang exhorted him to be the defender of the constitution and democracy and to transform the West Cameroon State into a socialist state, first by setting up farming schemes to check the influx of youth from rural areas into cities (*Cameroon Times*, May 18, 1965, p. 2).

Fully aware of the challenges before him as reflected in the succession crisis that had brought him to power, the new prime minister quickly recommended a cabinet to the president. In response to his recommendations, the president on May 13, 1965 approved a "short term" government which managed the affairs of the state until August 1965 when the Prime Minister re-organized the ministries following the KNDP–CPNC alliance and formed a much more permanent executive. The "short term" government was composed of the Prime Minister, seven secretaries of state, and four parliamentary secretaries. The Secretaries of State included: Peter Mboya Kemcha, John Henry Nganje, Joseph Noni Lafon, Lucas Mbo Ndamukong, Francis Myang Ajebe-Sone, Patrick Mua, and Simon Eno Cha; while the Parliamentary Secretaries were A.W. Daiga, S.N.G. Yor, M.M. Monono, and R.N. Namme (*House of Assembly Debates, Official Report Comprising 10th to 14th May 1965*, NAB -Cameroon, p. 5).

A more permanent West Cameroon executive bench was established after the August 1965 cabinet reshuffle. The KNDP-CPNC "unity cabinet" that resulted from this reshuffle was largely maintained until its demise in January 1968. It was made up of the Prime Minister, a Leader of Government Business, ten Secretaries of State, and three Parliamentary Secretaries. In the permanent cabinet P.M. Kemcha from Mamfe was appointed Secretary of State for Finance; L.M. Ndamukong from Ndop was entrusted with the Ministry of Primary Education and Social Welfare; N.N. Mbile from Kumba was in charge of the Ministry of Works and Transport; F.N. Ajebe-Sone from Kumba was appointed Secretary of State for Agriculture; J. Msame from Nkambe became Secretary of State for Forests and Veterinary Services, assisted by a Parliamentary Secretary – S.N.G. Yor from Nkambe; E.M.L. Endeley from Victoria became Leader of Government Business with a cabinet rank; S.N. Tamfu from Nkambe was assigned matters relating to economic affairs in the Prime Minister's office; and S.E. Ncha from Mamfe was appointed Secretary of State at the Prime Minister's office (Federal Ministry of Information and Tourism, West Cameroon Press Releases, no. 4244, Government Press, Buea, 1965, p. 5).

At the head of the government was, of course, A.N. Jua –the Prime Minister from Kom. Besides the functions of the Head of Government, he was to directly ensure the coordination and control of internal economic activities for which the authorities of the Federated State of West Cameroon were responsible in the federal constitution. For this purpose, he was where applicable, to undertake a re-organization of the services, participate in different capacities and in various secretaries of state in the administration of such matters. In this case, he was to oversee the functioning of existing industries, internal marketing, collection of statistical data, and participation in attaining the objectives of the National Economic and Social Development Plan. The Prime Minister was equally to coordinate and control the internal economic activities in close collaboration with the Ministry of Economic Affairs of the Federal Government whenever the economic activities in question were likely to affect the exercise of the jurisdiction of the federal authorities (Federal Ministry of Information and Tourism, West Cameroon Press Releases, no. 4244, Government Press, Buea, 1965, p. 6).

Jua's fifteen-strongman cabinet, while carrying out their ministerial responsibilities, was to be guided by the new government's policies. These policies aimed at salvaging the West Cameroon State from the dislocations occasioned by reunification were given passive attention by his predecessor. Amongst other objectives, Jua's government dedicated itself to encouraging responsible opposition in West Cameroon. Such opposition was going to be one "energetic in spotting, in an enlightened manner, the shortcomings of the government of the day, so that the electorate could be appraised of the manner in which government was failing or succeeding in carrying out its mandate." To stress the importance which his government was to attach to this co-operation, Jua made it clear that "unscrupulous elements were not going to be allowed to multiply West Cameroon's internal problems" (*Federated State of West Cameroon House of Assembly Debates*, Buea, Government Press, 1965, p. 13).

By "unscrupulous elements" in West Cameroon, Jua was referring more specifically to Muna and his supporters whose most recent and relentless succession competition with the new Premier had culminated in the political becoming intensely personal, creating powerful enemy camps and threatening to dismember the ruling party. The effect of the acrimonious Jua-Muna political battle on party and personal relations was an apt reflection of Bynander and Hart's (2006) view that "Leader succession involves considerably personal and political risks for the people and parties involved, and the processes by which leaders are chosen often disrupt the fragile social network that maintain party cohesion and organizational culture" (p. 708).

The Jua-Muna rift had reached a point of no return. This was particularly so given that shortly after Jua's victory, he recommended that Muna and his staunch supporters be suspended from the KNDP (cited in Kofele-Kale ed., 1980, p. 118). Notwithstanding the democratic soundness of such a suggestion, the party's national executive quickly embraced it. In announcing the suspension, Foncha stated thus:

> ... I regret to inform you that... certain parliamentarians of our party and Secretaries of State led by Hon. S.T. Muna showed an unusual bad and stubborn conduct and refused to yield to my nomination... I cannot therefore tolerate this new idea of a minority wishing to work their will on the majority. The fault of these gentlemen lies in that they wanted Hon. S.T. Muna and no other person to be the Prime Minister of West Cameroon. I have accordingly suspended all of them from the Parliamentary Wing meetings and the 3 Secretaries of State concerned in this misbehavior have lost their ministries. Those concerned...are: Hon. S.T. Muna, E.T. Egbe, W.N.O. Effiom, J.M. Bokwe, M.N. Ndoko, Sam Mofor, L.I. Umenjoh, J.K.N. Tataw, and B.T. Sakah. (Vb/a1965/2, NAB – Cameroon).

In response to the "scapegoating and flagrant injustice," Muna resigned from the KNDP on August 2nd, 1965, in solidarity with his other eight supporters whose suspension sentence had been converted to dismissal from the party shortly before his return from mission in Montreal. He later formed the Cameroon United Congress (CUC) with him as the president and E.T. Egbe as its Secretary General. As the only opposition party, the CUC turned out to be one of the major stumbling blocks to Jua government's scheme for a West Cameroon united front. This was particularly the case as he and his backers in an endeavor to canvas for support, embarked on a mass campaign to discredit Jua, his government, and the KNDP. Rather than projecting their party as a new movement expressing a new ideology, Muna's CUC, in its utterances and writings, complained mostly of injustice and lack of democracy in the KNDP (Johnson, 1970, p. 274). It also assailed the Jua government for corruption, favoritism, nepotism, and victimization. Such persistent and consistent onslaught against Premier Jua by Muna's camp with President Ahidjo's full but disguised support would be largely responsible for the fall of Jua as the Prime Minister of West Cameroon in 1968.

The Final Battle and the Rise of Muna as Premier

The appointment of Jua as Prime Minister of West Cameroon in 1965 only ended the first round in the struggle for power between him and Muna. Muna largely held Jua responsible for his ousting from the KNDP and was determined for a comeback soonest. As he blatantly stated,

> ... after reunification, I was obliged to remain at Yaoundé as Federal Minister. Knowing fully well that I was supported by Mr. Foncha, Mr. Jua began a dirty campaign against me in the party in order to be nominated Prime Minister.... It is people who do not have clear hands who opposed me becoming Prime Minister, because if I was nominated as Prime Minister, I would have unmasked certain things since they knew I was strict. But this will not last for long (*L'Effort Camerounaise*, October 3, 1965, p. 3).

In his quest for political revenge, Muna's most potent strategy was an unholy alliance with Ahidjo in fostering his travesty of a "centralized federation." To this effect, Muna, declared that "... their expulsion from the KNDP was not because they loved the party less but because they loved the federal constitution more (V/b/b1966/16, NAB, Cameroon). Muna's disposition of being very subservient and sympathetic to Ahidjo's course of centralization was very assuring to Ahidjo.

Besides reassuring Ahidjo of his loyalty, Muna, with the tacit blessings of the latter, is believed to have been at the forefront of orchestrating the formation of a single party in the federation as the surest route to prominence in the federation. Consequently, he led the bandwagon for creating the Cameroon National Union (CNU) in September 1966 (*Cameroon Times*, September 1, 1966). In his practical assistance to the single-party project, Muna took part in the first meeting in Yaoundé on June 11, 1966, where the decision to dissolve all political parties in favor of the CNU was made. After the meeting, he was the first to dissolve his party in Bamenda on August 5-6, 1966. On this occasion, Muna called on the people of West Cameroon to promote the CNU party because it guaranteed a better life for all. He declared, "We cannot say we love Cameroon and fail to give the CNU party our first support" (*Cameroon Times*, September 1966).The speed with which Muna and the CUC embraced the single party concept in the face of Jua's initial opposition was clear evidence of their lust for power and influence within the changing power constellation in the Federated state of West Cameroon in particular and the Cameroon federation in general.

Besides this political scheme of isolating Jua, it is believed that Muna was equally at the center of an elaborate but secret campaign that sought to smear his administration. Subsequent rumors, such as that of Jua's ambition to form a rival political party, were associated with Muna and his close collaborators. This rumor was quite intense in 1967 when it was circulated that Premier Jua and close collaborators were organizing a new political party to challenge the CNU (CF/1966/1, NAB, Cameroon; Aa/1966/79, NAB, Cameroon). Besides these, it was reportedly circulated by Muna that Jua and Victor Kamga were planning to assassinate President Ahidjo. Although this particular rumor was baseless, as asserted by Jua and many others, Ahidjo did not take it lightly as he considered it a possible pointer to a new dimension of what had become known as *Le Problème Bamiléké* in Cameroon. Most perturbing to Ahidjo was Jua's Catholic orientation. In this case, a Catholic conspiracy against him could not be completely ruled out, considering that a prominent Catholic faithful like Archbishop Jean Zoa, as well as the newspaper *L'Effort Camerounaise*, had remained very critical of Ahidjo's regime (Levine, 1971, pp. 129-130). Most distressing was the alleged connection of a prominent Bamileke prelate, Msgr. Albert Ndongmo with the UPC nationalists (Le Vine, 1971, pp. 131-132). To Ahidjo, replacing a Catholic Jua with a protestant Muna as Prime Minister of West Cameroon was undoubtedly the best means for his personal survival, the survival of his authority, and a peaceful transition to the unitary state. Fully aware of the dynamics and implications, Muna seemed ever willing to play the game of his protégé irrespective of its impact on what was clearly the early symptoms of Anglophone Cameroon discontent in post-reunified Cameroon.

Furthermore, the alleged secession designs of Premier Jua discredited his government to the federal authorities. When the Nigerian civil war broke out in 1967, it was rumored that Jua was planning to lead West Cameroon in imitating Biafra. The alleged Muna propagated rumor held that Jua was importing arms for this purpose through the Victoria seaport (Foncha, Ewusi, Lainjo, personal conversations cited in Song, 1999, p. 213). The situation was further complicated by the adjacent location of Biafra. More alarming to Ahidjo was that a majority of West Cameroonians made no secret of their sympathies for the Biafran course (Le Vine, 1971, p. 175). Ahidjo is said to have paid serious attention to this particular allegation, given that about 2,000 rounds of ammunition had been reported missing at the Muyuka police post earlier in 1965. In addition, it had earlier been reported that at its liquidation, *Elders & Fyffes* had put at the disposal of the West Cameroon government ammunition, which was later sold to West Cameroonians without the knowledge of the federal authorities (personal conversation with P. Ewusi, cited in Song, pp. 213-214 & 239-240). In the light of this secession rumor, Ahidjo, a die-heart exponent of African unity at the time, saw the removal of Jua as the sure means of preserving a united Cameroon. As he stated, "No head of state who is in his right frame of mind and who is worth his name would allow one part of his country to secede" (Jotanga, 1972, p. 63).

Against this background of constant rumors intended to blackmail Jua's person and his administration, the Prime Minister mounted an investigation that allegedly implicated Muna. In connection with this, Premier Jua, on October 1, 1967, rebuked Muna's attitude. He stated that:

> ...The CNU is a party that reacts fatally against blackmail and character assassination. In it, blackmail aimed at running others down in order to shine is as intolerable as it is suicidal and people who spurn this blackmail and hand it to their stewards to spread while they stealthily wait to see the results are certainly digging their graves. Those who think that they can act this way and yet go unnoticed are not only fooling themselves but are seeking a fall and when the fall will come, it will be colossal (Federal Ministry of Information and Tourism, West Cameroon Press Release, October 3, 1967, p. 4).

Even as Jua admonished Muna for scheming to undermine and oust him as Prime Minister of West Cameroon, he failed to appreciate the extent to which the political damage had already been done by Muna with the complicity of his political godfather. This was more so as Foncha this time had reversed his support in favor of Muna for the post of the Prime Minister of West Cameroon (G. Atem, personal conversation, cited in Song, 1999, p. 216). As if this was not enough, the alleged Muna designs, unfortunately, had the blessings of his own nominee as Speaker of the WCHA – W.N.O. Effiom. Hon. Effiom admitted to having schemed with Muna and Ahidjo to dethrone Jua because "Jua always left the impression that everything started with him and ended with him" (cited in Waindim, 1997, p. 23). Muna equally exploited to his political advantage some of the lapses of the Jua government.

One of such was the economic and social scandals that bedeviled his administration. Prominent amongst these was the near collapse of the West Cameroon Bank in February 1966. A.S. Ngwana's letter of January 19, 1966 accusing the Jua government of being largely responsible for the liquidity crisis in the Bank constituted a major gift to its Muna-led detractors (QB/D/1966/10, PMO 491, Vol. 2, NAB, Cameroon). In addition, the Jua government is reported to have pampered and encouraged corruption. It was common knowledge that leading government members were involved in corruption scandals. In reference to this, an editorial of *Cameroon Times* of February 18, 1966, stated without calling names that:

> we know there are some people in positions of trust whose stock in trade now is to use their good offices and political positions to grab wealth . . . and become businessmen in disguise. We know there are those of them who indirectly have interests in companies connected in one way or the other with their offices. To these men we...in keeping with the code of morals in western democracy [call on them] TO RESIGN THEIR OFFICES IMMID- IATELY AND VOLUNTARILLY. RESIGN THEY MUST [sic]. (p. 2)

Cases of corruption and embezzlement especially by government officials also undercut the credibility of Jua's administration and provided additional ammunition to Muna and its other critics. The Secretary of State for Finance, P.M. Kemcha, reportedly used his good office to cripple the Cameroon Commercial Cooperation (CCC). Through his influence, goods were given out by various stores of the CCC to his family, relatives, and friends on credit, debts which the company hardly recovered (*Cameroon Times*, March 1968, p. 3; *Cameroon Mirror*, November 11, 1969, p. 2). Similarly, Jua was accused in 1966 by a prominent West Cameroon lawyer, Gorji Dinka and Tataw Obenson for fraudulently exhausting West Cameroon funds in taking care of his wife in a London hospital. Although Jua sued Dinka and Obenson for defamation and later won the case, Muna and his enemies used it to discredit him to the federal authorities. Even more damaging was the rumor that Jua had fraudulently used state money to construct his personal property in Kom (*Cameroon Times*, November 5, 1966, pp. 1-3; *Cameroon Times*, November 10, 1966, pp. 1-2; *Cameroon Star*, July 15, 1966, p. 3).

Corruption equally characterized the ranks of West Cameroon parastatals during the premiership of A.N. Jua. It was common knowledge that prominent officials like M.O. Njanfa, manager of the Santa Coffee Estate; Mbiwan, the Managing Director of POWER-CAM; and Libanga, the Managing Director of the West Cameroon Development Authority (WCDA), diverted the labor, property, and funds of corporations for personal use. A peculiar case was that of Mbiwan, who corruptly used his corporation's labor, material, transport, and money in the construction and maintenance of his personal buildings known today as the Miramare and Park Hotels (*Report of the Commission of Inquiry on WCDA*, 1969, pp. 82-108; *Federated State of West Cameroon, House of Assembly Debates*, July 1965, pp. 12-22; *Federated State of West Cameroon, House of Assembly Debates*, July 1966, pp. 73-79). Similarly, Mr. D.W. Njikam was at the center of a corruption racket in the Department of Lands and Surveys. This was particularly the case as he leased government land for financial compensation. In 1967, for instance, Njikam was involved in a 15,000,000 CFA francs deal to sublease land in Bamenda to AGIP Petrol Company. So, too, did he lease a plot to Mobile Petrol Company at Mile 17, Buea, for a financial compensation of 120,000 CFA (*Cameroon Times*, April 1967, p. 2). Similarly, his colleague, Emmanuel Chimmy got 130,000 CFA francs and a bottle of whisky to give land to Peter Igani and Stephen Osheoture in the same year (*Cameroon Times*, November 5, 1966, p. 3).

These and other cases of corruption and government's inaction seriously reduced the prestige of the Jua government in the eyes of the federal authorities. By implicitly condoning corruption, the Jua government gave Muna and its other detractors another opening to discredit it further. There is no gainsaying that the August 1966 article by Dinka in *Cameroon Star* was very damaging to the Jua government. Captioned, "in an open letter Dinka tells Jua honor demands your resignation (yes)," the article left the impression that the Jua government was a corrupt one (*Cameroon Times*, November 5, 1966, p. 3). This constituted a big blow from the Muna camp. Even more damaging was the 1967 sex scandal. A prominent West Cameroon polygamist Secretary of State, John Henry Nganje had a sexual encounter with a nurse in the Buea General Hospital. He was subsequently forced to relinquish his position by Premier Jua (Personal conversations with Lafon, Lainjo, and

Mukong, cited in Song, 1999, p. 220). Though this may be considered a trivial incident, it was effectively used by the Muna camp to highlight the moral bankruptcy of the Jua administration.

It was against this background of the Muna-led ferocious attacks on the Jua government and a general cloud of political uncertainty in West Cameroon that elections into the state's House of Assembly were scheduled for December 31, 1967. With the political chessboard of West Cameroon firmly in his hands, with Muna having done the dirty job as instructed, and with a well-thought-out strategy to oust the Jua government from West Cameroon, President Ahidjo through the political bureau of the CNU nominated thirty-seven out of the 347 candidates who had applied to run for the 1967 parliamentary elections in West Cameroon (*Cameroon Times*, December 1967, p. 1). But before the nominations, Ahidjo notified candidates that "...it is necessary that candidates understand that they are not going to be elected because of their popularity, their competence in this or that domain or because of their level of education. They will be elected solely on the basis of their fidelity to the party, that is to say, to the regime – for their capacity to be efficient and loyal pawns in the chessboard of the party" (cited in Joseph ed., 1978, p. 106). By implication, Ahidjo clearly indicated that his political leverage over West Cameroon had increased with the advent of the single party and the list system. With this leverage, he could decree policies detrimental to the interests of West Cameroon without much effective formal opposition as in the days of multi-party competitive elections. This implied that the delicate balance of West Cameroon politics, which Jua had needed to ward off Muna and his pro-Ahidjo forces, had been swept aside.

Consequently, the list of the nominated thirty-seven candidates was largely in Muna's favor as it included every one of the expelled KNDP supporters in 1965 with the single exception of John Tataw, who had earlier rejoined the ranks of Jua's supporters (West Cameroon Press Release, N0. 1021, December 18, 1967). By returning to the WCHA, it was but certain that Muna's supporters would do everything in their power to avenge the defeat of 1965. However, by retaining twenty-four of West Cameroon House of Assembly incumbents, Ahidjo gave the false impression to the Jua government that everything was alright. Before the list was submitted as a single slate to the voters, Jua tried to explain and defend the concept of nomination by stating that

> ...It would... be unwise to believe that the nomination by the political bureau amounts to an election. The true position of this question is that nomination by the political bureau is rather a pre-election and the people are therefore called upon to signify their approval by voting. The power of nomination possessed by the political bureau to propose lists of party candidates to the electorate is of utmost significance. The basic aim of this power is to transform elections into a kind of public service and to avoid a struggle for power by people without a consciousness of the national interest. Once nominations have been made, the CNU militants must accept and sponsor the party's list and abide by it... ("Prime Minister's Address to the Prefects in Victoria", November 16, 1967, NAB, Cameroon).

Since West Cameroonians were obliged to 'accept,' 'sponsor,' and 'abide' by the party list, the voting on Sunday, December 31, 1967, was merely ceremonial. The elected members subsequently took their oath of office on January 8, 1968, during the maiden session of parliament. In this session, the incumbent speaker, W.N.O. Effiom, was re-elected. Remarking about the December 1967 elections at Bokwango on January 10, 1968, Ahidjo reiterated that:

> The results of the...elections into the WCHA constitute a success not only for the CNU, not only for the Federated State of West Cameroon, but for the entire Republic. Members of the newly elected assembly have therefore to justify the confidence placed in them by the people of West Cameroon by showing their own contribution towards the national reconstruction (*Cameroon Times*, 8/5, January 11, 1968).

The issue of a new prime minister and a new government had preoccupied most West Cameroonians since the December 31, 1967 elections. This was particularly so because the appointment of the prime minister and the new government was to be done within the context of the single party for the first time since reunification. Although the president still had the constitutional mandate to appoint a prime minister, there was still some fuzziness over whether the candidate was to be recommended by the WCHA or the political bureau of the CNU. This worry was expressed by *Cameroon Times* when it stated that:

> Following the recent political evolution in the country which brought about one party thus making it necessary for only one list of candidates in the election, the question of the leadership of government still remains obscure in the face of the sweeping changes.... It is however, understood from unofficial sources that the very steering committee which nominated the party's list of candidates may also name the prime minister and cabinet. Other sources believe that the prime minister will be allowed to be chosen by the thirty-seven members themselves (*Cameroon Times*, January 6, 1968, p. 1).

Within the context of the cloudy political atmosphere, the new political alignment in the WCHA, and the relentless political battery suffered by Jua's camp, Jua become nervous. This was demonstrated by his repeated consultations with President Ahidjo and Vice-President Foncha on the issue of the premiership of West Cameroon between January 1st and 11th, 1968. In all of such consultations, he was allegedly given double assurance by Ahidjo and Foncha of his reappointment as the Prime Minister (Nfor, 1998, p. 44). Based on these unmistaken assurances, Jua took pains to dismiss the rumors about his imminent replacement. It is even alleged that as late as 11 am on January 11, 1968, Hon. A.N. Jua, amidst growing rumor and increasingly cautious warnings from his intimate friends residing at Yaoundé, met the president again and secured his assurance (personal communications with N. Ngwa, J. Foncha, P. Ewusi, cited in Song, 1999, p. 226).

Despite the reassurances, the tense atmosphere around the Assembly grounds in the afternoon of Thursday, January 11, 1968, indicated the contrary. The WCHA premises were unusually littered with fierce-looking soldiers and gendarmes. Amidst an anxious-looking crowd, the new parliamentarians took their seats, awaiting the president's decision. At about 5:15 pm, the unexpected happened. Mr. Solomon Tandeng Muna was appointed the new prime minister of West Cameroon in a letter from President Ahidjo that read, "I have the honor to inform you that in conformity with terms of Article 39 of the constitution, I have appointed Mr. Muna, Prime Minister of West Cameroon (Ngwane, 1994, p. 11; *Cameroon Times*, January 9, 1968).

As the West Cameroon House of Assemblymen burst into thunderous applause, Mr. S.T. Muna, who had earlier arrived from Yaoundé and stayed unnoticed and out of the assembly premises, was ushered into the assembly by soldiers and gendarmes under the close supervision of J.C. Ngoh. Summing the unexpected and tense events, an editorial stated that:

> The day then dawned. At ten o'clock in the morning in the West House of Assembly at Buea, where Jua, the then Prime Minister looked so sure of himself of being reappointed Prime Minister of the State of West Cameroon. But little did he know that overnight his friends and backers had been snatched from his camp the previous night for Muna instead of him. And though he was greeted on his arrival to parliament by them, it was all hypocrisy of Judas to Christ. And little did he know that Mr. S.T. Muna who was believed to be in Yaoundé, was instead taking shelter in the Buea Ministerial Rest House, awaiting to have his pound of flesh from him. And little did he know that even his official car will be immediately taken from him (V/ba1968/3, NAB, Cameroon).

Muna's political revenge against Jua was concretized when his streamlined government comprised only two members of the latter's government. This new government included: A.N. Elangwe, Secretary of State for Finance; B.T. Sakah, Secretary of State for Interior; B.T.B. Foretia, Secretary of State for Public Services; and S.N. Tamfu, Secretary of State for Public Works. J.C. Wanzie, J.C. Kangkolo, N.N. Mbile, and M. Luma were also appointed Secretaries of State for Primary Education, Natural Resources, Land and Surveys, and the Prime Minister's Office respectively. In addition, a parliamentary bureau was set up, headed by W.N.O. Effiom as Speaker; Fon S.A.N. Angwafor II as First Deputy Speaker; Mr. Sam Mofor as Second Deputy Speaker; Mrs. G.E. Burnley as Secretary; and Hon. C.M. Njumbe as Treasurer (*Cameroon Times*, January 13, 1968, p.1).

The triumph of Muna and his camp over Jua in 1968 highlighted the victory of Muna's "Godfather" or "Big brother" politics over his rival's belief in "grassroots" and "popular" democracy in postcolonial Cameroon. It equally demonstrated Muna and Ahidjo's political treachery in the context of the single party federation. In Richard Joseph (1978), it is aptly emphasized that "unlike the procedures followed in 1965 at the time of the elevation of Jua, Muna was chosen by Ahidjo in 1968 with hardly any show of prior consultation with

West Cameroonian legislators and political figures" (p.88). Since political and constitutional powers were in Ahidjo's hands, thanks to Article 35 of the CNU constitution and Article 39 of the Federal Constitution, Ahidjo sought to reward his most West Cameroon loyal and political allies and, in so doing, quicken the move towards the establishment of a unitary state. Whether it was ideology, opportunism, or vindictiveness that drove the Muna-Ahidjo alliance in the politics of transition, there was little doubt that it paid off with his victory in 1968.

Just how acrimonious the Jua-Muna had become, they hardly communicated nor cared about its effects on each other. Just as Jua had maneuvered with Foncha to oust Muna from the KNDP in 1965, Muna machinated with Ahidjo for a return blow in one of the most godawful political coups in Africa of the 1960s. Jua's response was telling enough of a disgruntled loser. During the inauguration of the Muna government on Saturday, January 13, 1968, he said the handing-over ceremony was different as no handing-over notes had been prepared because of the nature of the change of government. He advised the new premier to pry the files for updates and left the same evening amidst mounting tension for his home village of Njinikom (*Cameroon Times*, January 16, 1968).

As expected, the reaction of West Cameroonians was mixed. A majority received the news with consternation, shock, and disgust. As aptly put by Anyangwe (2008), "The people of the state were devastated. For most of them, Muna's appointment was nothing short of a coup d'etat and an act of provocation" (p. 67-68). Although Jua's government had faltered in some avenues, Jua was still the favorite candidate of West Cameroonians. A majority of the populace in the state's nine divisions expressed disapproval and disappointment with the change of government. In some divisions, disappointment was expressed by the mass boycott of Youth Day celebrations. However, a minority received the news with excitement. This was particularly the case with Muna's supporters and those whom Jua's government had aggrieved. But many stakeholders, including Albert Mukong held that those who welcomed Jua's replacement were a minority, self-seeking, and power-mongering West Cameroonians who had put self and ethnic affinity above West Cameroon state interest (personal conversation, cited in Song, 1999, p. 229).

The nature of reactions notwithstanding, the basic fact was that the Muna-Ahidjo concept of federalism had triumphed to the indignation of the archenemies of the early symptoms of Anglophone assimilation. With the appointment of an exponent of centralist federalism as prime minister of West Cameroon, Juaism was temporarily eclipsed. With a single political movement effectively controlling men and events in both states, the assimilation of West Cameroonians entered a new phase characterized by little or no opposition in West Cameroon. Beholden and accountable to Ahidjo, Muna's premiership set out to achieve the mission for which it was created (Anyangwe, 2008, p. 68). With its total cooperation, between 1968 and 1970, the federal government took over almost all that had been temporarily reserved for the West Cameroon Government by *Article 6* of the Foumban Constitution which had not yet been federalized. Prominent amongst these were the status of civil servants, tax rates, police, land law, roads, and prisons (cited in Kofele-Kale, ed., 1980, pp. 120-121).

In 1970, the unity moves that Jua had fought against received an additional impetus when, in the presidential elections, Foncha was replaced with Muna as the running mate of Ahidjo for the post of Vice-President of the Federal Republic of Cameroon. This was in accordance with a 1969 federal law that had made it possible for one person to hold both that position and that of the West Cameroon Prime Minister (cited in Kofele-Kale, 1980, pp. 122-125; Chem-Langhee, 1990, pp. 22). With the impending dissolution of both states and federal parliaments in 1970, politicians in West Cameroon stepped up secret campaigns for the post of Premier in West Cameroon. Although Jua's name was again circulated as a viable candidate, despite the law's specifications, West Cameroonians did not believe that the two offices could be merged by virtue of their weighty responsibilities.

But in this third duel, Muna again emerged victorious, relegating Jua to the corridors of power in the federation until his passing in 1977 (Vb/a1970/1, NAB, Cameroon). With the replacement of the original proponent and symbolic exponent of the Cameroon federation, it was clear that the dismemberment of the West Cameroon State was just a matter of time. Consequently, on May 20, 1972 the federation which Jua and his government had spared no effort to protect in the interest of Anglophone Cameroonians came crashing with an Ahidjo-Muna organized referendum in which a majority of Cameroonians purportedly voted to replace the Federal Republic of Cameroon with the United Republic of Cameroon.

It is, however, important to note Jua's volte face in joining the political bandwagon in 1972 to campaign for the very unitary state that he had fought ferociously against. This turnabout has attracted conflicting interpretations. One school of thought holds that Jua was halfheartedly committed to his campaign (personal conversations with C. Munteh, J. Lafon, A. Mukong, cited in Song, 1999, p. 231). This view might seem tenable considering a confidential letter addressed to Jua by the Divisional Officer of Fundong Sub-division (copying the National Secretariat of the Political Bureau of the CNU and West Cameroon Regional Inspector of Administration). In the June 19, 1972 letter, J.A. Fominyen accused Jua of having disrupted the 20th May referendum campaign in Fundong Sub-division. Fominyen accused Jua of having told the people of Kom that he would have blocked the transition to the unitary state if he had still been prime minister of West Cameroon ("Bobe A.N. Jua: Petitions and correspondences concerning, 1972", pp. 9-11, NAB, Cameroon). In this regard, Mr. Fominyen stated:

> Would you deny the fact that you interfered in the May 20th referendum? The Northern team led by His Excellency the Vice President of the United Republic of Cameroon Mr. S.T. Muna in which you were a member was to visit Fundong but you interfered and the team could no longer visit this place.... On the 18th of May 1972, while the divisional team led by Hon. S. Nji – Menchum Section President and Hon. J.C. Kangkolo were at Fundong, and known to you, you cunningly rushed and dispersed the heavy crowds at Njinikom, Sho, and Belo telling them that there was no campaign team visiting the area on that day.... You told people that... if you were in authority, you would not have allowed the president to change the constitution ("Bobe A.N. Jua: Petitions and correspondences concerning, 1972", pp. 9-10, NAB, Cameroon).

The authenticity of this excerpt as a pointer to Jua's unenthusiastic commitment to the unitary state campaign becomes doubtful when put vis-à-vis Jua's often robust refutations of such accusations. In one of such surrebutters addressed to the Senior Divisional Officer of Njinikom in 1972, he denied these accusations by stating that:

> You will agree with me that hear-say is dangerous and that it is important for you to sift the truth from falsehood.... You heard false stories about me to the effect that I was turning people back from coming for lectures and you hastily reported me to Mr. Muna without hearing from me.... This is quite serious.... I hope you will change for the better for the new nation needs truth and service. ("Bobe A.N. Jua: Petitions and correspondences concerning, 1972", p. 8, NAB, Cameroon)

Jua's letter further stated that such notorious falsehood about him had no meaning but to discredit him and the people of Kom.

The excerpts from Jua's responses seem to support the competing flip-flop perspective, which holds that he was totally committed to campaigning for the unitary state in 1972. Proponents of this school explain that his turnaround was dictated by politico-economic frustration, especially in the context of being betrayed by some prominent Anglophone Cameroonians to Ahidjo. But judged against his forceful nature, adherents of the about-face perspective must consider that it was risky and sometimes suicidal to popularize dissent in the context of Ahidjo's authoritarian, monolithic, and coercive state of Cameroon. As stated by Doh (2008),

> Ahidjo... had in place a gestapo which was used as an intimidating force to coerce West Cameroonian rivals into submission. For fear of losing their lives in the hands of Ahidjo's bloodcurdling gestapo or rotting in jail, many Anglophone politicians stayed mute in the face of Ahidjo's atrocious coup against the state of West Cameroon.... The West Cameroonians [who] could stand their ground in the face of Ahidjo, and they were numerically not up to the number of fingers on one hand, went to an early grave (p. 23).

Irrespective of characterization, the fact remains that Jua campaigned in 1972 to dismantle the very federation he had fought to preserve. The dawn of a unitary state, it can be argued, constituted a major success for Ahidjo, who, with the tacit approval of France, had turned Jua and Muna into helpless figures in his political calculus regarding the marginalization of the minority English-speaking Cameroon during the first decade of Cameroon's independence.

The Ahidjo Factor in the Jua-Muna Tussle

The Jua-Muna political wrangling cannot be fully understood without thoroughly appreciating President Ahidjo's role. Contrary to the views of Konings & Nyamnjoh (1997), Rubin (1971), Ngoh, and Bayart, that Ahidjo only exploited a conflict of ambitious West

Cameroon politicians to his political advantage, the argument can be made that he was its instigator. A student of Machiavelli, Ahidjo orchestrated, perpetuated, pursued, and sustained the Jua–Muna tussle with tactfulness, shrewdness, patience, and vigor. Masterfully employing the colonizer's strategy of "divide and conquer," Ahidjo surreptitiously engrafted cynicism, discord, and pandemonium amongst Anglophone Cameroon's political heavyweights in the early years of the federation. This diabolic strategy was conceived in the context of his hidden unitary state agenda, which was similar to the French system, to further French neo-colonial interests, obliterate the virulent UPC threat, and guard his political authority. Having humbled the opposition in the Federated State of East Cameroon during the decolonization process, Ahidjo's major stumbling block in his grand design was West Cameroon, where there were sporadic but persistent articulations of its particularistic identity. Sensing Foncha's virtuous politics, Ahidjo then targeted the next most sophisticated and politically savvy leaders of Anglophone Cameroon – Muna and Jua. In their "do or die" struggle for the Premiership of West Cameroon, these political rivals found themselves at the mercy of Ahidjo, who constituted the bastion of political and constitutional power, especially after forming a single political party in 1966. By playing them against each other, he hoped to neutralize them as competing political challengers, project the incidence of disunity, conquer West Cameroon, and, most importantly, liquidate the Cameroon federation. Although in his political ploy, he struggled to avoid leaving any fingerprints, historical discernment is very implicating of him.

The first pointer of Ahidjo's centrality in the Jua-Muna struggle was his alleged sponsor of Muna in a "special mission" to contest for the position of the Vice President of the KNDP between 1964 and 1965. Although not supported by documented evidence, this premise is deductively convincing. This is particularly so given that Muna at the time was closest to the center of power in his relationship (as Ahidjo's trusted friend) and in his federal responsibility as the only fully-fledged Anglophone federal minister. Closely related to this was the fact that the post of the Prime Minister of West Cameroon had been largely rendered ceremonial by the very centralized Foumban Constitution. Foncha's surrender of this position in favor of the Vice Presidency further indicated the relative power impotence of the West Cameroon's Prime Minister's office. That Muna wanted that position even though he did not need it could not be explained in the context of the drive for political power as has been insinuated in the literature. This argument is bolstered by Atanga's (2011) view that "Muna... was far ahead of the others in understanding in whose hands political power was" in the Cameroon Federation (p.72). Ahidjo's role as Muna's sponsor to run for the Premiership of West Cameroon becomes very plausible in this light. Considering that he knew and trusted Muna, Ahidjo sent him to challenge Jua in the race for the premiership of West Cameroon, given that Muna would be more sympathetic to the neutralization of English-speaking Cameroon's influence in postcolonial Cameroon than Jua.

In addition, Ahidjo's role in appointing West Cameroon's Prime Minister in 1965 was further indicative of how ready he was to sustain the Jua-Muna struggle for his long-term subjugation plan. Although frustrated by the parliamentary system in West Cameroon, within which Jua's popularity vis-à-vis Muna's was evident, Ahidjo played for time by appointing Jua despite his preference for Muna. This is vividly expressed by Johnson (1970):

> Ahidjo could have nominated Muna despite the party's decision, and by challenging the dominant power in the state, incur its utter hostility. Perhaps such a move would have spurred some assemblymen to change their votes, but more likely it would have produced an impasse, with the president nominating and the assembly failing to elect the candidate. Under such circumstances, the president could then dissolve the assembly and call for new elections, which might or might not have been honest ones, or perhaps declare a state of special emergency and established a government under his own authority. In either case, Cameroon would have reproduced conditions similar to those that were leading to such a great tragedy in neighboring Nigeria (p. 273-274).

But rather than doing that, he smartly sustained the struggle by appointing Jua with respect to the wishes of the West Cameroon Assemblymen and the KNDP majority. Ahidjo knew that the four-year-old federation was still too fragile for such a move. This was particularly the case given the strong fervor of particularistic tendencies in the Federated State of West Cameroon. By appointing Jua, knowing fully well that Muna was the man for the "job," Ahidjo postponed the struggle when the conditions would be more propitious for the latter.

To ensure the coming of that time, Ahidjo tactfully retained Muna and his close supporters in their federal responsibilities against the advice of the KNDP leadership. He did not "demonstrate his independence from regional and personal pressures" in this action, as claimed by Johnson (1970, p. 274). One can argue that it was a well-calculated move and Ahidjo at his political best. Doing so provided Muna and Egbe, around whom the rest clustered, with the financial support and political platform that saved them from complete political liquidation in West Cameroon. By refusing to relinquish them of federal portfolios which they had acquired on the KNDP ticket, Ahidjo made clear that he valued his long-term unity project rather than party tranquility in West Cameroon. If the surest route to that project was political chaos in West Cameroon, he was determined to pursue it. Sure, he did at the most convenient time. In an apt description of Ahidjo's status as a political power-player in perpetuating and sustaining the Jua-Muna clash, Bayart writes:

> [Ahidjo] played skillfully...between Muna and Jua, letting the former know that he was the favored one, yet accepting the latter as Western Prime Minister, all the while permitting the temporarily eclipsed aspirant continued access to federal resources. Muna was therefore kept in reserve for the opportune moment when Ahidjo would pull the rug from under Jua. Ahidjo had therefore neutralized Jua in the same way he had mentalized many of his other opponents Assale, Mayi Matip, Kamdem-Ninyim, and Foncha, that is, by accepting them as temporary expedients until their power base had been eroded (cited in Joseph ed., p. 86).

Thirdly, Ahidjo's political gamesmanship during the Jua-Muna competition for the premiership again pointed to the fact that he was an intimate factor in the struggle between these West Cameroon politicians. He repeatedly assured the incumbent Prime Minister of his reappointment in 1967 and 1968 despite rumors to the contrary. That he did not only dishonor his promise but replaced him with his nemesis in the most notorious acts of political deceit and treachery in Cameroon history was indicative enough of his role in driving a wedge between Jua and Muna.

The last indicator of Ahidjo's integral role in the Jua-Muna clash between 1961 and 1972 was his perceived indifference to the complaints submitted by Jua about his victimization by Muna. After being ousted as Prime Minister of West Cameroon, Jua wrote directly to Ahidjo, complaining of persecution by his adversary. In some of the most somber words contained in one of such petitions, he wrote:

> His Excellency,....
>
> The story of my forming a new political party has been revived by the Prime Minister of West Cameroon, Mr. S.T. Muna and his gangsters. ...This again is not true.... These are vicious and diabolic lies against me for no reason whatsoever. It is to be recalled that just when the CNU was formed, Mr. Muna and Mr. Ngoh...in order to...create falsehood...said I had formed a new party in Mamfe. I mounted an investigation and, in the end, it was discovered to my dismay that it was nothing but the work of Mr. Muna and his gangsters. The discovery of this vicious falsehood made him to switch onto others such as: (1) That I was plotting to assassinate the Head of State. (2) That I had sent Nangah to West Germany to organize secret importation of arms into the country for an uprising. (3) That I had no respect for Federal Institutions and that I did not believe in the federation. (4) That I borrowed 4,000,000frs from the federal government for the service of West Cameroon Bank which was at the time in great financial difficulties, thereby lying and so dishonestly dubbing Your Excellency. (5) That I was pro-British and anti-French....
>
> Mr. Muna and his gangsters. . . have sworn to liquidate me politically and economically. I pray Your Excellency to examine my petition with patience...I am seeking protection from you my patron, for without you, I shall be liquidated willy-nilly ("Bobe A.N. Jua: Petitions and Correspondences concerning, 1972, NAB, Cameroon; Song, 2015, appendix B).

That Ahidjo failed to respond, let alone address complaints from a man of Jua's political status, further strengthens the argument that he was intimately involved in the Jua-Muna tussle in the Cameroon Federation in the period in question. The central role of Ahidjo notwithstanding, the Jua-Muna contest was metastasizing given its far-reaching repercussions on the Jua-Muna relationship and, most importantly, in Anglophone Cameroon.

Conclusion

The Jua-Muna political tussle remains one of the most contentious political disputes in Cameroon's postcolonial history. Although Jua emerged as the loser in this duel, his bold actions catapulted him not only to the position of the most popular political figure of his generation but also as the most deserving flagbearer of Anglophone separatist tendency and grandfather of modern Anglophone Cameroon nationalism. Reverberated by some of his most audacious Anglophone intellectuals and political contemporaries, such as Dr. Bernard N. Fonlon (*Cameroon Times*, 1964-1966; *The Task of Today*, 1966, p. 7), anti-assimilation restiveness in West Cameroon continued to gather momentum throughout the 1960s and early 1970s. As aptly captured by Anyangwe (2008), "the informed view was that the Southern Cameroons had become more or less an internal colony of Cameroun Republic and that the former's salvation and that of its people could only be found in withdrawing . . . and proclaiming separate independence" (p. 93). Although one may question the intended purpose of the 1971-1972 federal intelligence report stressing that secession sentiments in West Cameroon at this time were "expressed by those within high circles and even by the ordinary woman in the street" (cited in Anyangwe, 2008, p. 94) the veracity of that report could not be contested.

As Jua ebbed into the political wilderness and finally joined his Anglophone Cameroon ancestors in 1977, Anglophone Cameroon's sensitivity to marginalization continued to metamorphose. The political liberalization process in the early 1990s brought with it the strengthening of "Juaism" by a growing number of Anglophone Cameroonians. Under the canopies of various pressure groups, these Anglophones expressed views similar to those of the 1960s about the politico-socio-economic domination of English-speaking Cameroonians. In the context of the continuous denial of the problem by the Biya government and the lukewarm response by the international community, the SCNC declared the independence of Anglophone Cameroon in 2017 (Korieh and Mbanaso, 2010, pp. 16-17).

While the academic discourse, the armed struggle, and diplomatic efforts continue in search of a solution to the Anglophone Problem in Cameroon, what remains clear is that an Anglophone political minority has remained a problem to Anglophones in the Anglophone Problem (here I mean that there are a few English-speaking Cameroonians who have consistently thwarted the majority's search for freedom in post-colonial unified Cameroon). Inaugurated by the Jua-Muna political warfare in the 1960s, a minority of English-speaking politicians have always served as a force majeure in the subjugation of Anglophone Cameroon by Cameroon's postcolonial regimes. The alliance of Muna and the other seven minority Anglophone Cameroon politicians with Ahidjo constituted a heavy blow to the Jua-led Anglophone Cameroon budding autonomist culture. As rewarding as this might have been to this minority, the impact on the Anglophone community of Cameroon was very considerable. Muna, in particular, was seen as the West Cameroon Prime Minister who, in connivance with Ahidjo, masterminded the demise of the State of West Cameroon and facilitated the annexation of Anglophone Cameroon. To his detractors, he was a "traitor" or "Mr. in-between" who made the idea of a unitary form of government a reality in West Cameroon (*The Post*, January 25, 2002). Anthony Ngunjoh held that through greed for power, selfishness, and sabotage, Muna became the Prime Minister of West Cameroon and eventually abandoned the federal form of government, thereby opening the doors wide open for Ahidjo to carry on with his unitary ambition hitch-free (*The Herald*, January 13-20, 1993). To legendary UPC leader, Ndeh Ntumazah, Muna was a political mercenary. In his own words, "I have placed him better in his historical context where he belongs, in mercenaries' rule in Kamerun." He saw Muna as a survivalist who went into politics with no other purpose than to line his private pocket and educate his children (*The Post*, January 25, 2002).

Muna's actions after his retirement in 1988 seem to give some credence to the views of his Anglophone Cameroon detractors. In another interesting twist in this fascinating chapter of Anglophone Cameroon political history, Muna joined the bandwagon of the Anglophone problem in protest against the guileful subjugation of the Anglophone minority. The high point of his late activism was leading an SCNC delegation to New York in 1995 to petition the UN to intervene on behalf of the Anglophone minority. Konings and Nyamnjoh (1997) argue that these "missions to the United Nations may not have yielded any tangible results, but it [gave] wide publicity to the Anglophone course and helped to discredit Biya's regime" (p. 221). This action by the Anglophone architect of integration was, by implication, indicative of having sacrificed his Anglophone brethren in the course of serving Ahidjo. Whether his ultimate embrace of "Juaism" was conviction-driven or just another of his calculated ploys towards salvaging the image of a "sellout" and having a peaceful retirement, it was too little too late as the assimilation and marginalization of Anglophones in Cameroon was deeply institutionalized by his successive political protégés.

Besides pointing to the dictum that in politics, there are no friends but interests, Muna's self-realization after 1988 speaks to some fundamental issues in his political conflict with Jua. Beneath the surface of Ahidjo's threatening totalitarian role, France's overbearing neo-colonial design, and the struggle for political power was the question of political culture. Despite their impressive political resumes, what did they really know about democracy and the political craft/art? The background of headmasters in colonial denominational schools seemed to have crept into some of their actions. This was particularly so as they tended to be more authoritative in their temperament during their feud. The expulsion of Muna and his group from the KNDP in 1965 was an apt example. Though rooted in the KNDP party rules, it was not only misguided but also one of the most deleterious miscalculations of Prime Minister Jua, who was the de facto leader of his party at that time. He failed to learn from the circumstances that led to the Eastern Regional Crisis in 1953 and precipitated the British Southern Cameroons' search for independence. Even more problematic was the fact that their expulsion took place at a time when all hands were needed on deck to mitigate the dissipating linguistic and cultural identity of West Cameroon in the Cameroon federation.

The expulsion constituted a resounding political blow that Muna and his minority Anglophone co-conspirators subsequently found difficult to forgive, let alone forget. Most importantly, it worsened an already worse situation by driving Muna totally into Ahidjo's arms and militated against any chance of an Anglophone united front vis-à-vis France's driven Francophone stratagem of domination. Muna, on his part, failed to see beyond the horizon of personal interest and safeguarding of Ahidjo's patronage. In pursuing Ahidjo's centralization vision, he did so blindly, unable to appreciate his ulterior motive of lording over the Anglophones in a united Cameroon. But if Jua and Muna were inept because they lacked political sophistication, what accounted for Ahidjo's political savvy in successfully playing them against each other in this political conspiracy? Although a diligent disciple of Machiavelli, there is no doubt that the French, unlike the British, were intimately the driving force behind Ahidjo's political craftsmanship in this hell-bent struggle.

The most consequential significance of the Jua-Muna clash in Anglophone Cameroon was the formation of the single party in 1966. Jua's obsession with checking Muna's influence, on the one hand, and Muna's determination, on the other hand, to revenge his defeat led them to the bottomless pit of the single party in the Cameroon federation. The search for peace and political unity was in itself very welcome, but in stretching his hand too far in search for peace and unity, Jua, in particular, lost his dynamism and sense of mission and un-sagaciously further compromised the status of West Cameroon by embracing the CNU (Nfor, 1998, p. 43). As Ngwane (1994) felicitously put it, he failed to decipher beyond the bare facts to understand that in Ahidjo's mind, the one-party system meant one nation (united Cameroon), one flag (single star), one constitution (unitary), and one voice (Ahidjo) (p. 10). An important stage in maximizing Ahidjo's power, he could now intervene directly via the list system in West Cameroon more than ever before. In the legislative elections of December 1967, Ahidjo used the list system to reward Anglophone politicians like Muna, who were sympathetic to his cause of centralization, preparing the way for the ousting of Jua and his autonomist supporters.

Evidently, some West Cameroonians were far ahead of these political titans as they considered the idea of the single party very abhorrent. This was particularly the case with Fonlon, who, in early 1966, excoriated the idea of a single party. As he pointed out, "Everywhere in Africa, people are being told that in order to speed up the social and economic development of the continent, the one-party state has become a must. But almost everywhere this system is implemented, we witness the suppression of liberty, the elimination of debate, the imposition of silence, and the rise of despotism" (cited in Zartman & Schatzberg eds., 1986, p. 115). Echoing Fonlon's admonishment, Muyuka-based Moses E. Enoh addressed a thought-provoking letter to all West Cameroonians on November 17, 1967. In the letter, copies of which were published in *Cameroon Times*, *The Iroko*, and *Cameroon Star*, he articulated the implications of the single party more than those who were considered the political ideologues of West Cameroon. Enoh questioned the *raison d'*être of the single party in the following questions:

> Has the CNU come to strengthen our state federation or it has come to weaken our state federation? If to weaken our State federation, East and West Cameroon, which will become subordinate to the other? Is the formation of a national party in a federal country to strengthen the state federation? Is list system voting on the people's choice or voting on dictation [sic]? Should West Cameroon assume that minus one-party system in a state or in a federal state such as ours, there can be no peace and harmony for all? What has this Jua and Muna struggle done to our

state? ("Let West Cameroon Know", 1967, p. 2, NAB).

In the context of the general euphoria within the political class in West Cameroon for the CNU, Enoh's publication earned him an immediate arrest and eight days of detention "pending investigation" in accordance with Prefectorial Order No. 6/1967 of December 19, 1967. Mr. Nicholas Ade Ngwa, who had ordered the arrest in his capacity as the Divisional Officer of Victoria at the time, insisted that he was acting on the instructions of his political superiors (personal communication, 1999).

Given that most ordinary West Cameroonians were generally opposed to the single party and raised their voices in published letters and articles, its endorsement constituted the most far-reaching outcomes of the Jua-Muna rift in Anglophone Cameroon. It is incomprehensible how Jua, in particular, thought his government could effectively protect the autonomy of the West Cameroon State in the context of the single party. As he would subsequently watch in indignation, the CNU instead erased the last vestiges of West Cameroon autonomy in the Cameroon federation. Foremost in this regard was the eclipse of its British-bequeathed system of parliamentary democracy – a system in which political power was ultimately in the hands of an elected majority, not a minority. In the context of the single party, Ahidjo could disregard the Westminster political model by which all ministers first had to be elected members of parliament, with only the majority party called upon to form a government. In introducing the Presidential System by which ministers were appointed as a reward for loyalty, Ahidjo had a greater say in political developments in West Cameroon. As president of the federation, the chairman of the CNU, and the chairman of the main decision-making body of the CNU (the Political Bureau), Ahidjo was in complete possession of political and constitutional authority to shape the nation in the direction France wanted.

Between June 1966 and May 1972, Ahidjo, through the CNU, effectively executed his most cherished project of the liquidation of the Cameroon federation. The most unfortunate thing was that Ahidjo used the very CNU that Jua had assisted in its formation to unseat him, who represented the hopes and aspirations of a majority of West Cameroonians. With the end of the federation, West Cameroon ceased to exist as a state. It was divided into two provinces: North West and South West, with its provincial capitals in Bamenda and Buea, respectively. The divide-and-rule policy, effectively tested and consolidated in the Jua-Muna tussle, would be sustained by Ahidjo and his successor in the endless neutralizing political strategy of playing the Anglophone politicians against one another.

The minority Anglophones have since lived with a deep feeling of trepidation against the dominant Francophones, who have more or less treated them as second-class citizens in postcolonial Cameroon. Although Muna was embraced as Anglophone Cameroon's prodigal son after he resigned from government and activism in popularizing the Anglophone problem until he died in 2002, Jotanga's view that "with the exception of Augustine Jua, who…had argued for the continuation and strengthening of the federal system… most West Cameroonian elites found that it benefitted their public careers to become political clients of the president", is reflective of the feelings of a majority of Anglophone Cameroonians forty-three years since the climax of the Jua-Muna conflict.

Most concerning is that the new generation of obsequious Anglophone Cameroon politicians learned little from the costly misapprehensions of their predecessors. Prominent among these were Simon Achidi Achu, Peter Mafany Musonge, Ephraim Inoni, Philemon Yang, Nfon Victor Mukete, Fon Angwafor III, Fonka Shang Lawrence, John Ebong Ngolle, Peter Agbor Tabi, Francis Wainchom Nkwain, Dorothy Limunga Njeuma, Pauline Nalova Lyonga, Paul Atanga Nji, and Joseph Dion Ngute. They continued to sycophantly espouse integration at the expense of subordination and second-class citizenship for the minority Anglophones in modern Cameroon. As the battle for and the debate over the future of Anglophone Cameroon progresses, a united front amongst its stakeholders remains improbable as it has been since reunification.

References

Archival Material - National Archives Buea (NAB)

Bobe A.N. Jua – petitions and correspondences concerning 1972, Od(1972). File No: None.

Cameroon Bank, Qb/d /1966/10, File No. PMO 491 Vol. 2.

Cameroon United Congress activities and population reaction- security reports by the police staff, Vb/b/1966/16. File N0: None

Federal Ministry of Information and Tourism: West Cameroon Press Release No. 780, October 3rd, 1967. File No: None.

Federal Ministry of Information and Tourism: West Cameroon Press Release No. 1021, December 18th, 1967. File No: None.

House of Assembly Debates: Official Reports. Buea; Government Press, 1962 – 1972.

Prime Minister's Office Buea: Jua's personal papers, Oa/b(Jua)1. File No: 31/5/65

Prime Minister's Address to the Prefects in Victoria, November 16, 1967. File No: None.

Prime Minister's Speeches, Va/d /1965/ 5, File No.F.797/S.1

Security Reports: Politics of West Cameroon Government 1968, Vb/b/1968/3. File No: None.

Situation/Intelligence Reports, Aa(1966)79. File No: P22.

The Man in the Schloss: S.T. Muna – A.N. Jua Political Tussle for Power, Vb/a /1968/ 3. File No: None.

Why A.N. Jua is the people's choice instead of Hon. S.T. Muna, 1965, Vb/a(1965)2. File No: None.

II: Secondary Sources

Books

Anyangwe, C. (2008). *Imperialistic Politics in Cameroon: Resistance and the inception of the statehood of Southern Cameroons*. Bamenda: Langaa Publishers.

Atanga, M. (2011). *The Anglophone Cameroon Predicament*. Bamenda: Langaa Research & Publishing.

Benjamin, J. (1972) *West Cameroonians: The minority in a bi-cultural State*. Translated by Jotanga, J Montreal: Montreal University Press. Translated by Jotanga, J (1998).

Delancey, M. (1989). *Cameroon: Dependence and independence*. Boulder: West View Press.

Doh, F. E. (2008). *Africa's Political Wastelands: The bastardization of Cameroon*. Bamenda: Langaa Research & Publishing.

Donovan, C. J, Morgan E. R., Pothholm, C. P., Weigle, Marcia A. (1986). *People, Power, and Politics:*

An introduction to political science. 2nd ed. New York: Random House.

Elango, Z. L. (1987). *The Anglo-French Condominium in Cameroon, 1914-1916: History of a Misunderstanding.* Limbe: NAVI-Group Publications.

First, R. (1972). *The Barrel of the Gun: Political Power in Africa and the Coup d'état.* Harmondsworth: Penguin Books Ltd.

Hazlewood, A. (1967). *African integration and disintegration: case studies in economic and political Union.* London: Oxford University Press.

Kofele-Kale, N. ed. (1980). *An African experiment in nation building: The bilingual Cameroon since reunification.* Boulder: Westview Press.

Johnson, W. (1970). *The Cameroon Federation: Political Integration in a Fragmentary Society.* Princeton: Princeton University Press.

Joseph, R. ed. (1978). *Gaullist Africa: Cameroon Under Ahmadou Ahidjo.* Enugu: Fourth Dimension Publishers.

Le Vine, V. (1970). *The Cameroon Federal Republic.* Ithaca: Cornell University Press.

Lipset, S. M. (1967). *The First Nation: The United States in historical and comparative perspective.* New York: Anchor Books.

Mbanaso, U. M. & Korieh J. C. eds. (2010). *Minorities and the State in Africa.* New York: Cambria Press.

Mbile, N. N (2000). *Cameroon Political Story: Memories of an Authentic Eye witness.* Limbe: Press Print.

Nfor, N. (1998). *The Hidden Agenda.* NP.

Ngoh, V. J. (1988). *Cameroon 1884-1985: A Hundred Years of History.* Yaoundé: CEPER.

Ngwane, G. (1994). *The Anglophone File or the Study of the Gulf between the "coastal" and the "Graffi" in the Anglophone Cameroon.* Limbe: Press book.

Rubin, N. (1971). *Cameroon: An African Federation.* New York: Praeger Publishers.

Waindim J. (1997). *Bobe Jua: Spiritual Legacy of a Great Man.* Yaoundé: N.P.

Zartman W & Schatzberg M. eds. (1986). *The political economy of Cameroon.* New York: Praeger.

Articles

Bynander, F. & Hart, P. (2006) When Power Changes Hands: The Political Psychology of Leadership Succession in Democracies. *Political Psychology,* 27, no. 5, 707-730.

Burges, M. (2012). Federalism in Africa: An Essay on the Impacts of Cultural Diversity, Development, and Democracy. *The Federal Idea,* 1-20.

Chem-Langhee, B. (1990). The Road to the Unitary State of Cameroon, 1959-1972. *Annals of the Faculty of Arts, Letters, and Social Sciences,* VI, Nos. I and 2, 3-22.

Konings, P. and Nyamnjoh, F. (1997). The Anglophone Problem in Cameroon. *The Journal of Modern African Studies,* 35, No. 2, 207-229.

Newspapers

Cameroon Life, Vol. 1, No. 5, October, 1990.

Cameroon Outlook, Vol. 9, No. 4, April 24th – 30th, 1961.

Cameroon Times, Vol. 1 No. 52, April, 1965.

Cameroon Times, Vol. 5, No. 62, May 13, 1965.

Cameroon Times, Vol. 5, No. 63, May 18, 1965.

Cameroon Times, Vol. 6, No. 19, February 18, 1966

Cameroon Times, Vol. 6, No. 79, September 1, 1966.

Cameroon Times, Vol. 6, No. 8, November 5, 1966

Cameroon Times, Vol. 6, No. 9, November 10, 1966

Cameroon Times, Vol. 7, No. 41, April, 1967

Cameroon Times, Vol. 7, No. 59, December, 1967

Cameroon Times, Vol. 8, No. 51, January 11, 1968.

Cameroon Times, Vol. 8, No. 2, January 6, 1968.

Cameroon Times, Vol. 8, No. 13, January 9, 1968.

Cameroon Times, Vol. 8, No. 6, January 13, 1968

Cameroon Times Vol. 8, No. 7, January 16, 1968

Cameroon Times, Vol. 3, No. 21, March 1968.

Day Down: Cameroon's Authoritative Newspaper Vol. 10, No. 29, August 29th, 1990.

L'Effort Cameroonaise, Vol. 508, October 3rd, 1965.

The Herald, No. 022, January 13-20, 1993.

The Post, No. 0343, January 25, 2002.

Dissertations, Long Essays, and unpublished papers

Song, W. (1999). The Premiership of A.N. Jua in West Cameroon, 1965-1968: An Assessment. M.A. Thesis: University of Buea,

Song, W. (2015). The Clash of the Titans: Augustine Ngom Jua, Solomon Tandeng Muna, and the politics of transition in post-colonial Anglophone Cameroon, 1961-1972. PhD Dissertation, Howard University.

Reports

Federated State of West Cameroon: House of Assembly Debates, Official Report comprising 10th–14th May 1965. NAB.

Federated State of West Cameroon: House of Assembly Debates, July 1965. NAB

Federated State of West Cameroon: House of Assembly Debates, July 1966, NAB.

Report of the Commission of Inquiry on West Cameroon Development Authority, 1969.

EIGHT

Educational Aspects of the Anglophone Question in Cameroon

English-Medium Education as Bulwark Against the French Man's Burden

LYOMBE EKO

One of the most touching viral videos of the Anglophone crisis was a French-language video that was uploaded and distributed widely on French-language versions of social media platforms and discussion groups: Facebook, Twitter, and WhatsApp in 2017. It featured a French-speaking teacher who had been posted to teach at a government primary school in a small town outside Bamenda, in the English-speaking Northwest region of Cameroon. The video, directed at French-speaking Cameroonians, was the lament of a trained and qualified French-speaking teacher, a university graduate who felt out of place in the English-medium school where the Ministry of Primary Education had posted her. In effect, the anonymous young female teacher, who described herself as a "pure Francophone," said she had grown up in the French-speaking part of Cameroon, was educated entirely in French, spoke only French, had graduated from the mostly French University of Yaoundé, and the *Ecole Normale Superieure* (Advanced Teacher Training College), Bambili. Upon completion of her teacher-training course, the Ministry of Primary Education had posted her to teach third grade (class three) at a government primary School in the English region of Cameroon. The video was captivating. It showed long shots of unidentifiable school children dressed in the traditional sky-blue uniforms of children in English-speaking government primary schools. The young teacher told her audience she had felt like a fish out of water from the first day she reported for work in her new school. The problem was that she spoke only French and could only teach in French, but the students she was supposed to teach did not understand a word of French. They had just been introduced to the basics of the English language. The results of this linguistic and pedagogical mismatch were distressing for the teacher, the pupils, and their parents. The teacher taught nothing, and the children learned nothing. The disoriented teacher stated that she had pleaded in vain with the centralized bureaucracy at the Ministry of Primary Education to transfer her to a French-speaking school in Francophone Cameroon, where she was trained and qualified to teach. This Cameroonian parody of education could be repeated thousands of times throughout the English-speaking Northwest and Southwest regions of Cameroon, which used to be the state of Southern Cameroons in the federated state of West Cameroon before it was split. This parody of education and teacher-training was at best, an example of linguistic and cultural assimilation, and at worst, it was an object lesson, a demonstration of the failure of the idea of bilingualism and harmonization of the two postcolonial educational sub-systems. This cautionary tale of pedagogical and linguistic failure, lack of preparedness, incompetence, and bureaucratic failure is an example of what the Cameroon Teachers' Trade Union (CTTU), the organized interest group of the Anglophone educational sub-system called "marginalization." The CTTU and the Anglophone community in Cameroon saw marginalization as a deliberate attempt to eradicate English-medium education, assimilate the Anglophone sub-system of education, and disperse it into the postcolonial Francophone educational system of Cameroon. Anglophone teachers who do not master the French language are never sent to teach Francophone children.

The mass transfer of French-speaking teachers to the English-speaking Northwest and Southwest regions represented a failure of the policy of bilingualism and harmonization. According to the Anglophone Teachers' Association of Cameroon (TAC), this Francophone bureaucratic practice was viewed as an assimilationist ploy designed to mute and destroy the English-language educational system in the Northwest and Southwest regions and reinvent it in the image of the Francophone system. The high-handed actions of Francophone ministers and administrators reinforced the perception that the English-speaking population was being forced to adopt the French language and culture against its will. This was one of the sparks that lit the fire of Anglophone resentment against Francophone domination and perceived assimilation. This mass resentment morphed into the Anglophone Revolt of 2016.

Purpose of this Chapter

The purpose of this chapter is to explore one of the main components of what has come to be known as the Anglophone Question – the existential issues facing the English-medium educational system that the state of Southern Cameroons brought into the reunified Federal Republic of Cameroon. This historical, political, cultural, and social exploration uses case studies that describe and explain Anglophone struggles against muting of the English-language sub-system through assimilation, harmonization, authoritarian fiat, as well as attempted transformation and evisceration of the General Certificate of Education (GCE), the secondary and post-secondary school-leaving examinations. This chapter thus portrays the Anglophone educational system as one of the crucibles of Anglophone resistance against the assimilation/dispersal of its cultural and identitarian specificities into la Francophonie. Topics covered include French assimilationist cultural diplomacy in West Cameroon, French (East) Cameroun government attempts to assimilate the English and Pidgin or Creole-speaking population (which came to be known as Anglophones in contra-distinction to Francophones) into *la Francophone* (French culture), the philosophical differences of the two sub-systems with regard to the role and place of religion in the educational system, the problem of technical education and examinations, the Anglophone Revolt of 2016, school strikes, massacres and transformation of schools into zones of conflict.

Historical Background and Contemporary Realities

After World War I, the Treaty of Versailles of 1919 ratified the partition of German Kamerun into French Cameroun and British Southern Cameroons under the League of Nations Mandate system. After the League of Nations collapsed and the United Nations' was founded after World War II, both territories became UN Trust Territories under French and British colonial control, respectively. Both colonial powers extended their national establishmentalities to the two colonies. Since Great Britain has an established church, the Church of England, the British colonial posture towards religion was therefore different from the French secular republican posture. In British Southern Cameroons, the first secondary school, Saint Joseph's College Sasse, was started in 1939. The medium of instruction was English, but Duala, the lingua franca of the Cameroon coast, was also taught at Sasse College. Nevertheless, some Southern Cameroonians went to Nigeria to pursue secondary education and later university studies in English.

British, German, Swiss, and American missionaries opened schools in many locations and used their educational institutions as instruments of evangelism and conversion of as many children as possible. This differed from the goal of French colonial education, which was to train a small administrative elite. Competition between the Catholic, Basel (later Presbyterian), and Baptist missions in Southern Cameroons led to the opening of many primary and secondary schools. To this day, the most famous high schools in Southern Cameroons are so-called mission schools: Saint Joseph's College Sasse, Saker Baptist College, Victoria, Presbyterian Secondary School, Kumba, Queen of the Holy Rosary College, Okoyong, Mamfe, Cameroon Protestant College (CPC), Bali, Seat of Wisdom College (Fontem), Our Lady of Lourdes (Mankon), Sacred Heart College (Mankon), Joseph Merrick Baptist College (Ndu), to name just those early ones. It is clear from this partial list that the dominant educators in English-speaking Southern Cameroons were church and missionary primary and secondary schools. They were actively encouraged by the British colonial administration which did not want to take full responsibility for education in Southern Cameroons. This Christian missionary educational "competition" to build more and better schools led to better educational outcomes in British colonial Africa than in French colonies (Dupraz, 2015).

After the reunification of French-speaking East Cameroon and English-speaking West Cameroon to form the Federal Republic of Cameroon in 1961, the Federal Constitution of Cameroon stipulated that French and English would be the official languages of the Federal Republic. The postcolonial Federal Republic of Cameroon set out to "harmonize" the two educational systems inherited from British and French colonialism, respectively. The Federal Government stipulated that educational institutions would be the spaces where a bilingual Cameroon would be forged. In 1962, the policy of bilingualism was kicked off by Cameroon's first president, the authoritarian El Hajj Ahmadou Ahidjo, with inauguration of the French-funded *Lycée bilingue fédérale* (the Federal Bilingual Grammar School) at Man O' War Bay, Victoria (the school was later moved to Molyko, Buea). Ahidjo (cited in

Yaro, 2020) told his audience in French: "By bilingualism we mean the practical usage of our two official languages, English and French, throughout the national territory." Yaro (2020) suggests that in the Cameroonian context, bilingualism refers to the ability to communicate alternatively in French and English, "the acquisition of proficiency in English by francophones and of French by anglophones," while bilingual education refers to the use of English and French as the media of instruction for part of, or for the entire school curriculum. The Bilingual Grammar School, where students from the English-speaking and French-speaking states of Cameroon studied French and English together, was supposed to be the template for a bilingual, bicultural educational system for the Federal Republic of Cameroon.

Primary Education Policy in Cameroon

Under the Federal Republic of Cameroon, primary education was a matter for each federated state. In the old Southern Cameroons, state competence extended to secondary schools. Parent Teacher Associations (PTA) were powerful institutions that ensured quality education at the local level. However, primary and secondary school education soon became a matter for the national government. Native Authority (NA) and Council Schools were soon transferred to the centralized ambit of the Ministry of National Education in Yaoundé, especially after the abrogation of the federation in 1972. Anglophones have struggled to regain control of their educational system ever since, while the Francophone government has sought to assimilate the English-medium system into the majority French system. While the Bilingual Grammar School, Buea, and the Bilingual Grammar School Yaoundé, as well as other schools, produced a bilingual elite that served the language needs of the centralized bureaucracy in Yaoundé, bilingualism never really took hold in the centralized government bureaucracy, especially in the educational sector. Both systems co-existed as hermetically sealed co-systems despite the national lip service to bilingualism. The reality is that the English-language sub-system was relegated to the place of a subaltern system. Since reunification in 1961, the highly centralized Ministry of National Education has always had a French-speaking minister. Even when the ministry was split into three, the Minister of Higher Education, the Minister of Secondary Education, and the Minister of Primary Education were all French-speaking Cameroonians. This was an indicator of the marginality of English-speaking Cameroonians in policy-making positions in the educational section. This situation continued until 2018 when an Anglophone Minister of Secondary Education was appointed in a bid to end the Anglophone revolt. In this kind of top-heavy, French-style bureaucracy, bilingualism never really took hold in the government bureaucracy or the curriculums of the two educational sub-systems of Cameroon. Despite top-down orders and policies from the centralized bureaucracies of the three government ministries responsible for education, it appears that only teachers and students in the English-language sub-system were expected to be bilingual. Examples of top-down, unfunded, unimplemented bureaucratic fiats, decrees, and mandates from Yaoundé to the "provinces" include the following:

1. Ministerial Order N⁰ 21/E/59 of 15 May 1996 organizing the Grade I teacher certificate examination. This Order stipulated that 'every primary school teacher

would henceforth teach every subject on the school syllabus, including the second official language subjects."

2. Law N⁰. 98/004 of 14 April 1998, laying down guidelines for education in Cameroon, stated that "the State shall institute bilingualism at all levels of education as a factor of national unity and integration' (Part 1, section 3).

3. Ministerial Order N⁰.62/C/13 MINEDUC/CAB of 16th February 2002 introduced the teaching of English and French from classes 1 to 6 in all primary schools. These subjects were also made compulsory in both the written and oral parts of the First School Leaving Certificate examinations and the Francophone *Certificat d'Études Primaires*. It did not matter that the First School Leaving Certificate has no oral parts as opposed to French exams, which generally have both written and oral parts.

Despite these policy directives, French-only primary schools, known as "*écoles Francophones*," emerged in the English-speaking West Cameroon to serve the children of Francophone bureaucrats, military officers, and ordinary Francophones who were resident in the territory. Bilingualism was not for them. The most famous of these schools is *l'École francophone de Buea*. Likewise, English-only primary schools, which used the nomenclature "bilingual" to appease the authorities, emerged in French-speaking towns like Yaoundé, Douala, and Bafoussam to serve the children of Anglophone parents who had moved to those towns as civil servants, military officers or businessmen and women.

English-speaking Teachers' Resistance to French Assimilation

Anglophone teachers, teachers' unions, and students, who had been on the receiving end of the authoritarian presidential decrees and ministerial orders from Yaoundé in the last 60 years, attempted over the years to provide input into the educational and especially bilingual policies being enacted and imposed on Anglophones without their input (Eko, 2003). As such, Anglophone teachers became, over time, the heirs and custodians of the Anglophone educational sub-system in Cameroon (Nyamnjoh & Akum, 2008). As tensions rose and the Anglophone revolt began to be felt, in October 2016, the CTTU, led by its Secretary General, Wilfred Tassang, issued an 11-point memorandum of grievances that ultimately led to the Anglophone teachers' strike. This strike, along with the strike of Anglophone common law lawyers over the appointment of Francophone judges and court officials in English-speaking Southern Cameroons courts, were the kick-off events of the Anglophone crisis. The CTTU issued what amounted to a memorandum that enumerated the grievances of the Anglophone community in matters of Education (The 11 Reasons for the Anglophone Teachers' Strike, 2016). The list of grievances included systemic inequalities, identitarian, linguistic bias, and issues of fairness and lack of equity that were the lot of Anglophones and their educational sub-system in the Republic of Cameroon. The CTTU memorandum confirmed the viral video anecdote discussed above. It stated in part:

1. Government continues to send Francophones who do not master English to teach in Anglophone schools. The teachers teach in broken English, thereby confusing the students. As a result, many do not perform well in their final examinations.

2. The Universities of Buea and Bamenda have been Francophonized, and admissions

into key faculties have been taken to Yaoundé so that admission lists can be doctored.

3. Our children are compelled to write *Certificat d'Aptitude Professionnelle* (CAP), *Probatoire*, and *Baccalaureat* [French examinations] in technical schools, with a tradition of poorly translated questions and massive failures on their part. [These are the] qualifications into professional schools and the universities, what a mockery to our certificates! (The 11 Reasons for the Anglophone Teachers' Strike, 2016).

4. The 1998 Law on the Orientation of Education in Cameroon provides for the creation of an Education Board, but we are asking for separate boards which can address the needs of each subsystem....

The writers of the memorandum indicated that the problems were brought about by a dictatorial and repressive Napoleonic Francophone state and its nepotistic, inefficient, and suffocating educational bureaucracy that stifled Anglophone aspirations, creativity, and innovation at all levels of the educational system:

> Francophones outnumber Anglophones in the professional schools in Anglophone Universities of Buea and Bamenda by a ratio of up to 90:10% in HTTTC Kumba, 90:10% in Medical School in Buea, 80:20% in HTTTC Bamenda whereas there are no Anglophones in these schools in Francophone Universities.

This memorandum synthesized one of the twin areas of grievance of the Anglophones. The other set of grievances centered on the inequitable legal system, and its maladministration of justice in the Anglophone Southern Cameroons. When the government of Cameroon turned a blind eye and a deaf ear to the pleas of the Anglophone teachers and lawyers, the grievances percolated to the top. The Cameroon Anglophone Civil Society Consortium (CACSC), an umbrella organization of lawyer and teacher trade unions led by Felix Nkongho Agbor Balla, Professor Fontem Neba, and Wilfred Tassang of CTTU, initiated a sit-down strike on October 6, 2016. All Anglophone teachers joined the strike action in November 2016. The Anglophone Revolt had begun.

Anglophone Revolt Over Educational and Judicial Grievances Lead to Civil War

The Cameroon Anglophone Civil Society Consortium (CACSC) had been banned, and its members arrested, imprisoned, and tried at the Yaoundé Military Tribunal; President Paul Biya had opted for a military solution to the political problem by dispatching the Cameroon military, led by the notorious-Israel trained and equipped *Bataillon d'Intervention Rapide* (BIR), the paramilitary *Gendarmerie Nationale,* and the police to crush the Anglophone revolt, and subjugate English-speakers. Anglophone resistance/restoration forces emerged, using traditional hunting rifles and later sophisticated weapons captured from the military. Thousands of people were killed, including hundreds of resistance fighters and at least 1500 government soldiers. The civil war caused hundreds of thousands of civilians to become internally displaced persons or refugees in Nigeria.

Fast-forward to 2024. The Anglophone crisis continues unabated and is ignored by the international community because at least four members of the United Nations Security Council (France, the UK, China, and Russia) have economic and strategic interests in propping up the authoritarian, neo-patrimonial regime of 92-year-old President Paul Biya. Education in the Anglophone regions (Southern Cameroons) is still one of the twin bones of contention of the Anglophone crisis (Sheppard, 2018). Monday "ghost town" strikes continue throughout the territory. Though some schools in the urban areas have timidly resumed classes, the school boycott in the Anglophone regions has not been officially lifted by the teachers' trade union. A large proportion of schools were still closed. Armed, self-styled independentist "Ambazonia restoration forces" continued to use extreme, senseless violence to enforce the boycott of education in the Anglophone regions, trying to pressure the government to support their call for dialogue to address the root causes of the Anglophone discontent or pave the way for the independence of Anglophone regions, which they call Ambazonia. In November 2017, when attempts to crush the uprising led by civil society groups had failed and Ambazonian "restoration forces" had taken up village hunting rifles to resist the BIR, the Cameroon army, gendarmerie, and police, leading to casualties on both sides, President Paul Biya opted for a military "solution" to the Anglophone political problem. He announced that he had instructed the military to eradicate "terrorists" who failed to lay down their arms. In the face of Cameroon government intransigence, violent repression, and military destruction of Anglophone villages suspected of harboring independentists, Ambazonia non-state fighters attacked military and police installations, government buildings, and schools that refused to take part in the boycott. Schools quickly became the theater on which the Anglophone Civil War was fought. Non-state armed groups who had lost sight of the objectives of the Revolt, kidnapped innocent students and teachers who refused to respect the boycott. They also used abandoned schools as bases. Government forces attacked and burned down many of these schools and arrested, tortured, or killed anyone suspected of harboring or aiding separatist fighters. They also committed other serious human rights violations, including against children in multiple locations such as Kupe Muanengube, Muyuka, Kumba, Manyu, Bali, Bafut, Ndu, Ngarbuh, Babanki, Boyo, Wum, Buea, Limbe, Ekona, and other locations.

Schools as Military Targets and Temporary Barracks

To control as much territory as possible, the military occupied primary and secondary schools and health centers in remote areas of the Northwest and South regions and transformed them into temporary barracks. The United Nations Office for the Coordination of Humanitarian Affairs, the UN agency responsible for international responses to complex emergencies and natural disasters, reported that non-state armed groups attacked some of these non-operational primary school buildings being used by the military at Nchum (Mezam division) in Bafut (Mezam division) in the NW (UN OCHA Reports, 2020). On February 14, soldiers massacred 21 people, including 13 children, in Ngarbuh village, Donga Mantung county, in a reprisal attack aimed at punishing the population accused of harboring non-state fighters (UN OCHA Reports, 2020). After initially denying involvement in the Ngarbuh massacre, the government finally admitted that the Cameroon military had carried it out.

One of the most savage attacks on an educational institution in the bloody civil war over the educational and legal systems in Southern Cameroons (the Northwest and Southwest) took place on October 24, 2020, at the Mother Francisca Bilingual Academy, Bamileke Street, Kumba, Southwest region. Unidentified gunmen stormed this private high school, whose motto is ironically, "Knowledge for a Brighter Future," killing seven children and injuring at least 13 others. The Cameroon government and military blamed Ambazonian separatists for the attack, while the leaders of the non-state armed groups in the Diaspora blamed government forces for carrying out the attack. Interestingly, an alleged viral WhatsApp text exchange between a Cameroon government administrator and military officer left the impression that the military carried out the massacre in order to lay the blame on the non-state armed groups. It is unclear whether the text exchange was fake or real. Schools and school children continue to be caught in the crossfire of the atrocities of the Anglophone crisis. The school shootings in Kumba were clear manifestations of the educational aspects of the Anglophone revolt.

On September 7, 2021, the Military Tribunal in Buea, in the English and Pidgin-speaking Southwest region, sentenced four accused persons, all civilians, to death by firing squad after convicting them of "acts of terrorism, hostility against the fatherland, secession, insurrection, murder, and illegal possession of firearms and ammunition" under provisions of the Law on the Suppression of Acts of Terrorism adopted on December 19, 2004. The trial, which was presided over by Lieutenant Colonel Tchinda Jackson, was conducted entirely in French, the official language of the military and military tribunals in Cameroon. This was the harshest sentence imposed on any accused person in connection with the Anglophone crisis. The four were part of a group of 12 persons who had been arrested immediately after the massacre. They included the proprietor of the high school, the principal, the vice principal, the discipline master, and the security guard. These persons were all detained for long periods of time before the trial. Four accused were sentenced to five months' imprisonment and ordered to pay a fine of about $100, and four others were discharged and acquitted. The fact that the accused, who were all English-speaking civilians, were tried by Francophone military officers in a Military Tribunal, which is part of the executive (the Ministry of Defense) and whose official language is French, raised serious concerns about the fairness of the trial and conviction of the accused.

Origins of the Anglophone Revolt: The Problematic Situation of Religion in Postcolonial Cameroon

As we have seen above, it is generally believed that the Anglophone identitarian revolt of 2016 was triggered by teachers, lawyers, students, and members of civil society in response to Francophone assimilation, dilution, and dispersal of the two institutions that represent the bulwark of Anglophone culture and identity – the education system and the common law tradition. But there is a third pillar that often goes unmentioned. This third cultural bulwark is religion. In effect, the two Cameroonian States that were reunited in 1961, *la République du Cameroun* and British Southern Cameroons, inherited fundamentally different establishmentalities or national ideological postures towards the role and place of religion in the public sphere and the life of the state (Eko, 2012). That is to say, after reunification, each of the two states brought to the table, what Campagnini calls "different interpretive schema," with regard to matters of religion (Campanini, 2009, p. 6). Postcolonial *République du Cameroun* inherited the French revolutionary ideology of secular republicanism. Under this pseudo-religious ideology, the state is a counter-Church whose official dogma is secularism. The fundamental creed of secular republicanism is that there is a sacred right to blaspheme religion (Berkowitz & Eko, 2007). Nevertheless, since France is historically and culturally Catholic, Morin (1990) described France as *"Catho-laique"* (a Catho-secular state) where there is *de jure* separation of faith and politics. The government does not recognize the church's spiritual, normative, doctrinal, and institutional aspects in the political arena. However, there is also *de jure* inseparability between the state and the cultural aspects of Roman Catholicism because the state owns and operates tens of historic cathedrals and religious edifices dating back to the *ancien régime* and puts these cultural edifices at the disposal of the Roman Catholic Church (Eko, 2013).

The French state's indifference towards God and religion was exported to French colonies. In the colonial territories, the French language and culture were "the gospel," the religion that was the object of evangelism of the French government's *mission laïque* (secular mission). In this context, the Catholic religion and Catholic missionaries were recognized as instruments for the propagation of the "gospel" of *"notre langue et culture"* – French enculturation and cultural assimilation. This policy was implemented in colonial public education. According to (Dupraz, 2015), in Cameroon, the centralized French colonial government turned a blind eye to its numerous inherited mission schools that were mostly unsupervised and unsubsidized. The French colonial administration established a weak, centralized network of free, public, nonreligious schools where the only permitted medium of instruction was French. The first secondary school opened in 1945. The goal of French colonial education was to train a small administrative elite. Even after the first secondary school was created in French Cameroon, many children, mostly of the elite, went to France for secondary education (Dupraz, 2015).

The French disinterest in religion was illustrated in 2009 after the signature of a partnership agreement between France and Cameroon. In order to "moralize" and professionalize its armed forces, the Cameroon government decided to start a religious chaplaincy system. The Cameroon Ministry of Defense requested the French military to assist in establishing the chaplaincy and training of chaplains. Something that came naturally in the U.S. and other militaries was problematic for the Catho-secular French army. During parliamentary debates, the French lawmakers expressed regret at the missed opportunity to provide chaplains and chaplaincy training for the Cameroonian military. In effect, French secular republicanism did not work well with military chaplaincy. The French National Assembly (*Assemblée Nationale*, 2011) lamented that:

> *D'après les informations communiquées à la commission de la défense, nos forces armées n'ont par exemple pas été en mesure de répondre à une demande de soutien des forces armées camerounaises, qui souhaitaient que la France mette à disposition un aumônier du culte pour accompagner la construction*

de leurs aumôneries militaires. Le motif apparemment invoqué – le fait que cela corresponde pas à la politique de coopération habituelle – paraît regrettable : il s'agissait d'une occasion pour envoyer un signal fort à peu de frais, dans un domaine essentiel pour l'unité du Cameroun.

According to information communication to the commission on defense, our armed forces were not, for example, in a position to favorably respond to request for assistance from the Cameroon armed forces, who wished that France make available to them chaplains to accompany the creation of their military chaplaincies. The reason given – that it did not fit our traditional cooperation policy – seems regrettable; it was an opportunity to send a strong signal at little cost in an area essential to the unity of Cameroon.

The Cameroon GCE Board: Symbol of Linguistic and Cultural Resistance

After the formal termination of the London GCE in 1976 and the take-over of the system by the Ministry of National Education in Yaoundé, the Cameroon government began to impose its French-style secular republicanism on the Anglophone educational system. In competitive examinations for admission to the University of Yaoundé (known initially as "l'Université fédérale du Cameroun" (the Federal University of Cameroon), French-style *grandes écoles*, or recruitment into the civil service or government parastatal companies, announcements always specified that candidates had to pass a certain number of subjects at the GCE Ordinary or Advanced Levels – excluding religion. The Cameroon government mimicked the French government, which had set itself up as a counter-Church. They expected the 175 years of largely faith-based Anglophone educational culture to vanish overnight and take on a French secular republican coloration. Naturally, this flew in the face of the Anglophone educational culture, which has a strong tradition of missionary religious education in addition to regular academic subjects.

The Anglophone Question in Cameroon is a story of the attempts by Francophone and Anglophone politicians and policymakers to meld and harmonize the two philosophically different educational systems that both states brought to the reunified Cameroon from their different colonial legacies and experiences. The French Cameroun educational system was a highly structured, centralized system inherited from French colonialism. It was assimilationist in nature in that its goal was to "civilize" and assimilate Africans into *la Francophonie*, the French-speaking world (Betts, 1961). As such, it had a strong emphasis on teaching the French language and culture (French was the only language of instruction allowed), had elements of French secular republicanism, and was designed to train a cadre of elites to run the postcolonial administration within the framework of secret pre-independence cooperation agreements signed between France and the Ahidjo regime. For its part, the educational system of the State of West Cameroon was marked by two main features: decentralization and the dominance of religious/missionary institutions. The colonial and postcolonial educational system in the former Southern Cameroons was based on mission schools started by the Catholic, Baptist, and Basel (Presbyterian) missions. Since Christian missionary education had an underlying evangelical purpose, schools were open to all children. Later, Native Authority (NA) and Council Schools were added to the mix. These conflicting philosophical perspectives were soon brought together after reunification in 1961. One of the major bones of contention in the unequal, problematic power dynamic between the Francophone and Anglophone educational subsystems of Cameroon was the high school examination system and the certificates they awarded successful students – the BEPC, *Probatoire & Baccalauréat* in Francophone Cameroon and the General Certificate of Education (GCE Ordinary and Advanced Levels) in Anglophone West Cameroon. Both systems were inherited from France and the United Kingdom, respectively.

Conflict over Harmonization of the GCE and the French Baccalauréat

The crowning achievement of French and Francophone secondary school education (lycée) is the standardized Baccalauréat, which qualifies students to enter university or specialized *grandes écoles* (professional schools). The Baccalauréat or bac is a French educational milestone, a diploma created by Napoleon in 1801 and exported to all French colonies. In Francophone Cameroun, students who sat for the baccalauréat at the time of reunification chose different series (streams): bac A1, A2, A3, B, C or D (modified over the years). Each stream results in a specialization that prepares students to work in specific fields and carries different weights (coefficients) associated with each subject. The bac also has an oral final test. Each baccalauréat stream has its own set of subjects that carry a different weight (coefficient). That means some subjects are more important than others because they impact the mean grade more. Passing the bac is thus determined by *la moyenne* (aggregate score). The bac is a passport for entry into universities and professional education institutions.

The Postcolonial General Certificate of Education: Historical Origins

This postcolonial Francophone bac system differed greatly from the postcolonial General Certificate of Education (GCE) Ordinary Level and Advanced Level inherited from the British colonial examinations system. The first secondary school, St. Joseph's College Sasse, was opened in 1939. Since World War II, students in Southern Cameroons have taken a number of examinations in accordance with changing political realities. These have ranged from the University of Cambridge Local Examinations Syndicate, the West African School Certificate (WASC), and the University of London General Certificate of Education (GCE). The University of London administered the examinations in Cameroon from 1963 to 1977 (GCE Board Policy and Procedure Manual, 2017). The GCE was more flexible than the *baccalauréat*. It focused on qualifications in particular subjects (English, Mathematics, History, Geography, etc.), had no series (streams), no weights (coefficients), and no passing mean. It was roughly divided into two groups: the arts, sciences and mathematics. Students who qualified in any subject received a certificate attesting that they had passed in that subject. Students had to qualify in five subjects to pass the GCE at the Ordinary Level and two subjects to pass at the Advanced Level. Policymakers in Yaoundé decided to harmonize both systems for multiple reasons. The French-style professional schools or *grandes écoles* were based on the Francophone baccalauréat series that did not exist in the Anglophone system. The result is that very few Anglophones were admitted into these prestigious institutions, and the plum government jobs graduates of these schools automatically secured. Francophone politicians and policymakers decided that in order to ostensibly give Anglophones better chances of gaining admission to the French-style *grandes écoles*, whose primary language of instruction was French, the baccalauréat and the GCE had to be harmonized.

In 1983, just one year after President Paul Biya took office, the Minister of National Education, René Ze Nguele, issued an order restructuring the GCE. The so-called New GCE was nothing more than a transformation of the Anglophone GCE into an Anglicized form of the Napoleonic baccalauréat, complete with series (streams), weights (coefficients), and *moyens* (aggregate scores). All kinds of religious studies –philosophy of religion, history of religion, comparative religious studies, and the like, were eliminated from the New GCE. This was a reflection of the legacy of French secular republicanism, secularism and anti-clericalism. The New GCE contained three compulsory subjects at both the Ordinary and Advanced Levels: English, French, and Mathematics. The restructuring was to be implemented by the Director of Examinations of the Ministry of National Education, who also oversaw Francophone examinations throughout the country. This top-down, assimilationist governmental restructuring, drafted without input from the stakeholders and published in the government newspaper, *Cameroon Tribune*, without fanfare, stunned the Anglophone community. Anglophone students of the University of Yaoundé demonstrated against it on campus and at the Ministry of National Education in Yaoundé, where Anglophone intellectuals and workers in government ministries in the capital joined them. The demonstrators stated that the GCE restructuring was "a grotesque defiance of Anglophone public opinion…an absolutely vicious and calculating attempt at subordinating or effacing the Anglophone educational system to the advantage of the Francophone system of education." They saw the restructuring as an attempt to "radically assimilate acquiescent" Anglophones (Nyamnjoh, 2009, p. 3). The students took the opportunity to write a formal petition to the Ministry of National Education in which they complained that "the lecturers of the University of Yaoundé were too preponderantly Francophone to warrant the institution being termed bilingual" because by forcing Anglophone students to study in French and write examinations in French, a language over which most of them did not have mastery when they enrolled at the university, the situation systematically resulted in high rates of frustration, failure, and drop out (Nyamnjoh, 2009, p. 32). The students emphasized that they did not want to be second-class citizens. The demonstrating students were met by riot police, who beat them with clubs and truncheons and forced them from the Ministry of National Education. Nevertheless, the students were able to hand in a petition that listed their grievances to a senior government official. The petition was addressed to President Paul Biya, the Prime Minister, the Speaker of the National Assembly, the Minister of Education, and the Chancellor of the University of Yaoundé (Nyamnjoh, 2009, p. 3). In response to these demonstrations, the Minister of National Education went on Radio Yaoundé and confirmed the worst fears of the Anglophone community. He told the Francophone national audience that reforms of the GCE were just "retouches" (retouchings), minor alterations aimed at making the GCE Advanced Level look a little bit like the baccalauréat, in order to conform to the Nation's bilingual policy and to make it possible for Anglophones to gain admission to the French-style, French-language only professional schools (*grandes écoles*) that train civil servants. These institutions included the Polytechnic, the School of Agriculture in Ngaoundéré, the School of Administration and Magistracy (ENAM), the military academy (EMIA), *Ecole Normale Superieure,* the *Ecole Fédérale des Postes et Télécommunications,* which had been changed to *Ecole Nationale Supérieure des Postes et Telecommunications* (Higher School of Posts and Telecommunications) in 1982, the *Ecole de Police* (Police College), *le Centre Hospitalier et Univerisatire* (CHU) de Yaoundé (Yaoundé University Teaching Hospital), the *Institut des Relations Internationales du Cameroun* (International Relations Institute of Cameroon (IRIC), etc., where Anglophones had so far been conspicuously absent (Nyamnjoh, 2009, p. 17). After further intense pressure, the nomenklatura of Anglophones in the regime: former Prime Minster of West Cameroon, former Vice President of the Federal Republic of Cameroon, and Grand Chancellors of National Orders, Dr. John Ngu Foncha, former West Cameroon Prime Minister, and Speaker of the National Assembly, Solomon Tandeng Muna, Emmanuel Tabi Egbe, Minister of Posts and Telecommunications, Dr. Victor Anoma Ngu, Dr. Bernard Fonlon, mediated between the striking students and the government. Other Anglophone actors engaged in the fight to prevent harmonization, assimilation, and "Napoleonization" of the GCE included the Teachers' Association of Cameroon (TAC), the churches (primarily the Catholic, Baptist, and Presbyterian missions), which were the foremost educators in Southern Cameroons, and had worked with the colonial administration to build primary and secondary schools during the colonial and postcolonial period. The government of Cameroon ultimately withdrew the order to restructure the GCE, which was an attempt to mute the identitarian specificity of the English-language sub-system in Cameroon. Anglophones had won the first identitarian, communitarian battle against Francophone assimilation of their educational system and culture.

Creation of the Cameroon General Certificate of Education Examination Board

Other battles won by Anglophones under the leadership of the Teachers' Association of Cameroon (TAC) included the attempt to harmonize the number of years in high school by reducing the duration of Anglophone secondary school education from 8 years to 7 years, punctuated by promotion exams as was the case in the Francophone system. However, the most important and sustained act of resistance that Anglophone teachers engaged in was the fight to create an examination board for the English language sub-system of education in Cameroon. In 1975, the Cameroon government transferred the General Certificate of Education, which had been set and graded by the University of London as the "London GCE" to the Directorate of Examinations at the Ministry of National Education in Yaoundé. The result was widespread abuses and numerous irregularities in the conduct of the GCE exams. This forced the Anglophone community to demand a GCE board independent of the bureaucracy of the Ministry of National Education in Yaoundé. This demand came in the form of a resolution passed by the All Anglophone Conference (AAC), which was held on April 2–3, 1993, in Buea. The fight for the GCE Board was spearheaded by secondary and high school (post-secondary) teachers under the auspices of the Teachers Association of Cameroon (TAC). The teachers framed the GCE crisis as a "government-led Francophone crusade against Anglophone education in Cameroon." Other Anglophone organizations that joined the fight included the Confederation of Anglophone Parent-Teacher Associations of Cameroon (CAPTAC), the Confederation of Parents Teachers Association (COPTA) of the North West and South West, the Anglophone press, which was the repository of Anglophone collective memory in Cameroon (Eko, 2003), and the churches (Catholic, Baptist and Presbyterian), which operate the oldest and most prestigious educational institutions in Anglophone Cameroon (Nyamnjoh & Akum, 2008). TAC framed the confrontation in military and religious terms: "Anglophones will fight on land, in the air, in the oceans, in the rivers, at sea, up the hills and down the valleys to preserve their culture. We will fight the battles of Tiko and Santa to keep the heathen at bay" (p. 91). The much-censored, English-language press joined the fray. It published stories of the Anglophone community's drive to restore its autonomy through federalism as expressed in the All Anglophone Conference (AAC) of 1993. The English-language press played the role of the collective memory of the Anglophone community and used the injustices of the past to advocate for justice in the present (Eko, 2003). The English-language press framed France as the villain of the Anglophone Question in Cameroon. In August 1993, the venerable *Cameroon Post*, published by Paddy Mbawa, ran a rather prescient front-page story entitled, "Mitterrand Instructs Biya to Reject Two-State Federation: Suggests Army Intervene to Crush Anglophone Resistance" (Mbawa, 1993). The story was accompanied by a caricature of Mitterrand sitting on a chair that was too big for him.

After the government created the *Office du Baccalaureat du Cameroun* for Francophone examinations, Anglophone teachers, acting under the umbrella of TAC, demanded an independent examination board and went on strike, refusing to mark the GCE under what they considered intolerable conditions (Nyamnjoh & Akum, 2008, p. 51). For its part, as TAC intensified its demand that the government create a credible, independent Examination Board in Buea for the Anglophone Examination system. In 1993, TAC forced the hand of the government. It created the Cameroon Examination Board (CEB), which the Ministry of National Education promptly declared illegal. However, months later, President Biya signed a decree creating a GCE Board without specifying how it would actually function and how it would be financed (Nyamnjoh & Akum, 2008, p. 51). Mr. Azong Wara, chairman of the Teachers' Association of Cameroon (TAC) and first registrar of the Cameroon GCE Examinations Board, described the bureaucratic hurdle Anglophone teachers and parents had to scale to actually get the GCE Board instituted in the context of Cameroon's Francophone rule-by-decree bureaucracy:

> Presidential decrees in Cameroon tend to be very brief and ambivalent. Their real scope is usually defined in a document called the text of application. In general, this text emanates from the office of the Prime Minister and Head of Government and is based on the recommendations made by a study committee set up under the auspices of the titular Minister. The interpretation and implementation of the decree depends on both the Manager and Supervisory Minister of the Institution (in the case where the decree creates an institution as the GCE Board) (Wara, 2008, pp. 319-320).

In this case, the Minister of National Education, Robert Mbella Mbappe, was very reluctant to cede any independent authority to the Anglophone educationists and parents for fear that it would be the beginning of a slippery slope to much feared Anglophone iden-titarian autonomy. Ironically, the harder the Yaoundé regime fought to prevent any kind of devolution of power and authority, the more strident the identitarian and autonomist demands became. The fears of the authoritarian regime in Yaoundé were partially real because, in hindsight, it is evident that the identitarian and communitarian sentiments that triggered the Anglophone Revolt of 2016 were present at the launching of the Cameroon GCE Board in 1993 in Buea. However, the more the government insisted on maintaining the assimilationist status quo, the more strident opposition to it became. In his speech at the GCE Examinations Board launching in 1993, Mr. Azong Wara, president of the Anglo-phone Teachers' Association of Cameroon (TAC) and first registrar of the GCE Board, declared: "The occasion is the beginning of the process of the restoration of the identity of a people. Through the installation of the GCE board we are proud to be able to tell our children tomorrow that we were there" (Nyamnjoh & Akum, 2008). However, Wara (2008) saw the GCE Board affair as part of an ongoing "Anglophone struggle for freedom, social justice and equality in Cameroon" (Nyamnjoh & Akum, 2008, p. 312). For his part, Mr. Sylvester Dioh who was installed as Chairman of the GCE Board said obtaining of the GCE Board was a victory, "a clear signal that Anglophones are determined to assert their cultural identity as a people who, on attaining independence on 1st October 1961, volun-tarily opted to join *La République du Cameroun*... as a STATE in a two State Federation." For his part, Mola Njoh Litumbe, a chartered accountant, Anglophone nationalist, and founder of the Liberal Democratic Alliance (LDA), denounced the senseless repression and violence that the government had deployed in order to prevent the emergence of the GCE Board and called for: "the political Resurrection of a State [Southern Cameroons] which attained independence and voluntarily entered a Union [with *la République du Cameroun*], only to be annexed, marginalized and brutalized." Ultimately, the GCE Board retained the historic practice whereby the GCE Examination is a single-subject certificate examination. The Board issues certificates to every student who passes at least one subject (GCE Board Manual). However, for students to qualify for admission to universities, or other institutions of higher education in Cameroon and abroad, and to be considered for the American Diversity Lottery, they must pass at least five subjects. This differs from the Francophone system, where the baccalauréat and other examinations are group certificate examinations where a pass depends on obtaining a certain predetermined average score.

The GCE Board's Relations with the Universities of London and Cambridge University

Ironically, Cameroon was admitted into the British Commonwealth the same day the Cameroon General Certificate of Education Board was installed in Buea. This was probably calculated to show the British that Cameroon respected Anglophone minority rights. As the chapter on the British connection to the crisis recounts, when the Cameroon govern-ment started carrying out atrocities and crimes against humanity in Anglophone Southern Cameroons in the wake of the Anglophone Revolt in 2016, the British Commonwealth was heavily criticized for maintaining *La République du Cameroun* as a member in good standing of the Commonwealth, when Fiji, Zimbabwe, and Nigeria had been expelled from that postcolonial association of English-speaking countries for less substantial violations of human rights. Due to the territorial realignments of Cameroon after World Wars I and II, Southern Cameroons used the University of Cambridge Local Examination Syndicate (UCLES) and later the West African School Certificate Examination (WASC). After reunification, West Cameroon adopted the University of London GCE Examinations and used it as the main assessment tool for its secondary school education at the Ordinary and Advanced level until 1975, when the Francophone–dominated Cameroon Ministry of National Education took over the conduct of the examinations for political and nationalistic reasons. Presidential decree No. 76/555 created the Cameroon GCE. The British contributed in creating, organizing, and implementing the Cameroon GCE. The University of London was to ensure international recognition of the Cameroon GCE results and certificates in the Anglosphere. This was crucial since, from a geo-political and geo-strategic perspective, Anglophone Cameroonians had essentially become part of *la Francophonie*. International recognition of certificates from this entity was not guaranteed, making study abroad, international academic recognition and cooperation almost impossible. However, things did not work out as expected. From 1984, the GCE began to experience acute irregularities. In 1990, the University of London Examination and Assessment Council withdrew from participating in the GCE due to the Ministry of National Education's failure to meet the agreed terms of its participation in the Cameroon GCE and failure to pay for its services (Wara, 2008). Things quickly went downhill after that. The GCE experienced acute irregularities that ranged from poor printing, poor examination content, shortages of examination questions, to examination leakages, and postponements of some subjects (GCE Board Manual, 2017). As we saw above, the struggle by the Anglophone Teachers Association of Cameroon (TAC), parent-teacher associations, and religious denominations to pry these examinations out of the grip of the ineffectual Francophone Ministry of National Education's bureaucracy took close to 20 years. The coalition that led these fights and successfully resisted Francophone governmental attempts to vitiate the particularity of the Anglophone educational system, assimilate it, and disperse it into *la Francophonie*, laid the foundation for the Anglophone Revolt which exploded in 2016. Anglophone common law lawyers, teachers, university professors, students, and civil society actors rebelled against Francophone assimilation and dispersal under the umbrella of the Cameroon Anglophone Civil Society Consortium. The GCE Board maintains good relations with the University of London Examinations and Assessment Council (ULEAC). The Cameroon Ministry of National Education and the University of London Examinations and Assessment Council still have relations. The University of London Board still prints the certificates for the Cameroon GCE; it does the examination vetting (examines the GCE setting that Anglophones have done and checks the marking to ensure that it meets international standards). The GCE Board also collaborates with the Department of Foreign Examinations at Cambridge University, which vets the Technical GCE. These relations aim to maintain international standards and recognition of the Cameroon GCE Examinations

Technical Education in the Anglophone Sub-system

In the 1993 struggle to create the GCE Board, the Minister of National Education, Robert Mbella Mbappe, opposed including examination of technical education in the terms of reference of the GCE Examinations Board (Wara, 2008). Though the GCE Technical Ordinary and Advanced Level examinations were within the ambit of the GCE Examinations Board, in 1997, just four years after the creation of the board, the government of Cameroon had a change of heart. President Paul Biya signed two decrees that broadened the scope of the GCE Examination Board and changed its character as an Anglophone cultural institution. In effect, decree No. 97-45 of March 1997 gave the GCE Board the task of organizing English versions of a number of French technical high school examinations that were being organized by the French language examinations board, *l'Office du Baccalauréat du Cameroun*. These French examinations, which the GCE Board was mandated to organize were collectively known as Bacc et al.; they were English versions (often poorly translated) of examinations that led to the following French Cameroun certificates: The *Baccalauréat Technique*, the *Brevet de Technicien*, the *Brevet d'études Professionnelles*, and the *Brevet Professionnelle*. Interestingly, these examinations are very different from the GCE's traditional single-subject certificate examination system. They are structured into 14 *options* (series and specialties). A pass in each series or specialization is determined by an aggregate score of the candidate on the 14 subjects in the series or specialization, taken together. The passing aggregate score and pass/fail decisions are determined by a jury of lecturers and National Inspectors from the Ministry of National Education in Yaoundé. The Bacc et al. essentially tethers the GCE Examinations Board to the centralized bureaucracy of the Ministry of National Education in Yaoundé. The question development and validation are carried out by officials of the Ministry of National Education (GCE Board Policy and Procedure Manual, 2017). The Bacc et al. English versions of French technical examinations organized by the GCE Board make it a unique institution in Africa. In Cameroon, secondary and post-secondary school students in technical and other schools can choose to sit their final examinations in French or English.

This development is interesting because the *Office du Baccalauréat du Cameroun* (OBC) is the government department that manages all Francophone general and technical secondary school examinations. The OBC had been created two months after the creation of the GCE Board and has no mandate to offer French versions of English certificate examinations. This was probably intended to resolve the problematic status of secondary technical education and examinations in the Anglophone educational sub-system, where educators had complained for decades that Francophone technical high school standards were being imposed on Anglophones. They claimed examination questions were set in French and translated – often poorly – into English, thereby imposing the Francophone technical education system and syllabi on Anglophone technical education students.

The Presidential decree of 1997 that gave the GCE Board the task of organizing English language versions of French technical education examinations and issuing certificates for these French examinations, using their original French nomenclature, essentially transferred Francophone-style technical high school education and assessment to the Anglophone sub-system. This was in response to the proliferation of French-style technical high schools that were filling the vacuum in Anglophone secondary technical education. These French Cameroon examinations ostensibly give English-speaking students the opportunity to have identical secondary school technical certificates as those in Francophone Cameroon in order to facilitate their integration into the Francophone *grande écoles* system. Nevertheless, large numbers of Francophone students take the English versions of the original French examinations. It was, therefore, a bureaucratic expression of the national policy of harmonization and assimilation of sorts. Studying technical school subjects initially developed in French and translated into the English language, writing examinations for those subjects in the English language while maintaining the French names of those certificates might sound strange almost everywhere in the world. But in Cameroon, bureaucratic centralism, assimilation, and dispersal of Anglophone culture in *la Francophonie* results in unique problematic situations. Nevertheless, given that the lingua franca of global science, information, and communication technology, as well as business, is English, studying in English in order to earn a French certificate is not anathema to culture-conscious Francophone Cameroonians as it was in the past.

Conclusion

Education is one of the foremost seedbeds of culture identity formation and propagation. The bilingual and multicultural educational reality of postcolonial and post-reunification Cameroon was one of the bones of contention between the majority French-speaking *la République du Cameroun* and the English and Pidgin-speaking Southern Cameroons, which came together to form the Federal Republic of Cameroon in 1961. Tensions arose between the two educational systems due to international geo-strategic and national superiority perceptions on the part of French Cameroon towards English and Pidgin-speaking Southern Cameroons. In effect, France saw the reunion of the two parts of Cameroon as an opportunity to extend its African geo-cultural sphere of influence by assimilating English-speaking Cameroon into *la Francophonie* and transforming Southern Cameroonians who had centuries-long linguistic and cultural proximities and continuities with the English-speaking world, into Francophones. The Anglophone Revolt is the result of more than half a century of French and French Cameroon refusal to recognize the identitarian and cultural specificity of Southern Cameroons. Interestingly, through the Anglophone educational subsystem, the cultural identity of English-speaking Cameroon was inadvertently strengthened by the Biya regime. The public University of Buea (founded 1993) and its associated campus, the University of Bamenda (founded 2011)–which ironically saw the light of day as a result of the Biya regime's 1993 nationwide reform and expansion of the university system – soon became bastions of English-language educational culture. French-speaking Cameroonians used the derisive, geo-cultural epithet *"les Anglo-Saxons"* that the French historically use to describe their British rivals, to describe and differentiate the universities of Buea, and Bamenda from the French-style Francophone universities in Yaoundé, Douala, Dschang, Ngaoundéré and elsewhere. English-speaking Cameroonians embraced the epithet and celebrated it, thereby turning it on its head. The English-medium Catholic University Institute of Buea (CUIB), and other English-medium institutions in the English-speaking regions ultimately reinforced this English-medium educational and identitarian culture, essentially complicating the assimilationist goals of the Cameroon government.

Postscript

Three of the most jarring images to emerge from the Anglophone Revolt were taken by the Cameroon Army in Muyuka, Southwest region, on September 6, 2021. They showed a heavily armed Cameroonian soldier in combat gear, an AK 47 rifle slung over his bullet-proof vest, teaching a classroom full of children who have no books and no writing material "mathematics".

Figure 8.1. Cameroon soldier "teaches" a class in Muyuka. The children have no books, pens or pencils.

Though the Cameroon military meant these images to convey the message that the military was doing its part to ensure that school children who had been deprived of education for five years by a senseless boycott were being protected and schooled by the military, the pictures actually told a tale of failure and futility.

The 2024-2025 school year had come by, and the Anglophone crisis stalemate had continued. The pictures, which seemed staged, showed that the Cameroon government had failed to resolve the Anglophone Question, and was imposing its will by force of arms. According to the Cameroon government, the argument of force trumps the force of argument, and education can be dispensed by soldiers through the barrel of the gun. It is unclear whether the Cameroon army will take over all educational institutions in Southern Cameroons and assign professional soldiers to teach in all the schools.

References

Adebile, R. (2011). "Language Policy and Planning for Education in Cameroon and Nigeria," Academic Leadership: *The Online Journal*: Vol. 9: Iss. 2, Article 22. Available at: https://scholars.fhsu.edu/alj/vol9/iss2/22

Ardener, S. (2005). Ardener's "Muted Groups": The genesis of an idea and its praxis. *Women and Language*, Vol. 28, (2), PP. 50-54,72.

Ardener, E. (1962). The Political History of Cameroon. *The World Today*, Vol. 18, No. 8. (pp. 341-350)

Berkowitz, D. & Eko, L. (2007). Blasphemy as a Sacred Rite/Right: The Mohammed cartoons affair and maintenance of journalistic ideology, *Journalism Studies*, 8 (5), 779-797.

Betts, R. (1961). *Assimilation and Association in French Colonial Theory*, 1890-1914. New York: Columbia University Press.

Decree No. 76-555 of 24 November 1976 instituting the GCE Examinations in Cameroon.

Débats Parlementaires (Parliamentary Debates), 1960-1961, Sénat (French Senate), *Journal Officiel* No. 73 S du 15 December 1960

Decree No. 93/172 of 1 July 1993 to create the General Certificate of Education Board.

Dupraz, Yannick (2015). French and British Colonial Legacies in Education: A Natural Experiment in Cameroon most recent version: http://www.parisschoolofeconomics.eu/IMG/pdf/jobmarket-paper-dupraz-pse.pdf

Eko, L. (2003). The English-Language Press and the 'Anglophone Problem' In Cameroon: Group Identity, Culture, and the Politics of Nostalgia. *Journal of Third World Studies*

Fon, N. (2019). Official Bilingualism in Cameroon: An Endangered Policy? *African Studies Quarterly*, 18 (2). February.

Mbawa, P. (1993). "Mitterrand Instructs Biya to Reject Two-State Federation, Suggests Army Intervene to Crush Anglophone Resistance." *Cameroon Post*, No. 178, August 23-29.

Nyamnjoh, F. (2008). Anglophone Students of the University of Yaoundé Petition against Introduction of a New Cameroon GCE Scheme for Anglophone Schools. In Francis Nyamnjoh Richard Fonteh Akum (eds.). Pp. *The Cameroon GCE Crisis: A Test of Anglophone Solidarity,* pp. 1–48. Bamenda, Cameroon: Langaa Publishing.

Nyamnjoh, F. B. and Richard Fonteh Akum (eds., 2008). *The Cameroon GCE Crisis: A Test of Anglophone Solidarity*. Bamenda, Cameroon: Langaa Books and Publishing.

Wara, A. (2008). The Problem. In Francis Nyamnjoh & Richard Akum (eds., 2008). The Cameroon GCE Crisis: A Test of Anglophone Solidarity, pp. 313-341. Bamenda, Cameroon: Langaa Books and Publishing

Yaro, L. (2020). Optimising Post-Colonial Bilingual Education in Cameroon's Primary and Secondary Schools: A Critic on School Practice, *Asian Journal of Education and Social Studies*, 9(3): 39-53. DOI:10.9734/AJESS/2020/v9i330250

NINE

Assimilationist Bilingual Educational Experience in Cameroon

The Case of the Federal Bilingual Grammar School, Molyko, Buea

INNOCENT AWASOM

They Tried to bury us.
They did not know that
We are like seeds
Scattered through explosive mechanism
Some falling on rocks and dying
Others fell on fertile soil and blossomed
We will rise and come back to our motherland
And claim what is ours for our progenitors
Some may never see the promised motherland
But we all took the first step
Go home in our name. Go home sweet home"
(Adapted and Modified from an anonymous Mexican Proverb)

The French and the British colonial legacy are still entrenched in Africa and can be seen clearly in the socio-cultural, political and especially the educational systems of the former colonies. While the French policy according to Clignet and Forster (1964), can be characterized as "assimilationist and aimed at creating an elite group, cherishing metropolitan values" (p.191), the British system of indirect rule favored the cultural adaptation of programs to local political and socio-cultural contexts thereby creating an educated core group of Africans rooted in their culture. The colonial policies, therefore, had direct implications on the educational development of the colonies as the school systems, as well as the curricula, were reflective of those policies. The dawn of independence, therefore, saw the acceleration of the training of interpreters, copy clerks, teachers, and administrators to take over from the colonial administration as opposed to the pre-independence curriculum that was focused on agriculture for export and home consumption as well as practical schooling to keep the locals in check and under colonial rule. This reality is particularly true in the case of Cameroon.

The historiography of the evolution of the Cameroons as a nation-state navigating through the German, British and French colonial powers and leading up to independence has been well documented (Devenois, 1959, 1960; Amaazee,1994; Awasom, 2002, 2020; Terreta, 2012), yet it remains an intriguing subject of debate as the Anglophone minority wants out of this unholy union (Eko, 2003; Tiewa & Vibo, 2015; Awasom, 1998, 2000, 2003, 2020; Konings, 2006; Jua et al., 1997; Ngoh, 1999; Okereke, 2018). The educational system has been studied extensively, especially in grey literature from graduate students' theses and dissertations and scholars like Konings 2006; Mengot, 1967; Ndille, 2015 2020; Clignet & Forster, 1964; Gwanfogbe, 1996. However, both educational systems (Francophone and Anglophone) have been studied extensively on a standalone basis as well as the cohosting of separate Francophone and Anglophone educational institutions in the same premises. The promise of a bilingual country came at the dawn of independence and the country's first president, Ahmadou Ahidjo, on the instruction of the French. This led to the creation of a model bilingual grammar school (ironically for boys only) as exemplified by the Federal Bilingual Grammar School (BGS) Man O'War Bay/Molyko Buea. Official bilingualism was given its most unequivocal definition by Cameroon's first President, Ahmadou Ahidjo, who underscored: "By bilingualism, we mean the practical usage of our two official languages, English and French, throughout the national territory" (Gonondo & Djiraro, 2016). This bilingual educational experiment has not received as much attention as it deserves, for it represents the much-cherished ideals that, if followed to the letter, would have created a great country according to the dreams of the pioneer President of the Federal Republic of Cameroon.

Anchimbe (2015) posits that Cameroon's adoption of bilingualism at independence aimed to shape the country's unique identity. Cameroon's first President, Ahmadou Ahidjo echoed this:

> [W]e must in fact refrain from any blind, narrow nationalism, and avoid any complex when absorbing the learning of other countries. When we consider the English language and culture and the French language and culture, we must regard them not as the property of such and such a race, but as an acquirement of Bilingualism in Cameroon| the universal civili-zation to which we belong. This is in fact why we have followed the path of bilingualism since...it offers us the means to develop this new culture... and which could transform our country into the catalyst of African unity.

Despite Ahidjo's best efforts at bilingualism, regional balance in development and employment, as well as national integration, the socio-political evolution of the landscape in Cameroon under his successor, President Biya, who continued Ahidjo's pro-French foreign policy, degenerated. It is apparent that the total assimilation of the Anglophones of the former Southern Cameroons was the long-term goal of the bilingual educational system set in motion through the creation of bilingual grammar schools, linguistic centers, and other avenues of assimilating and transforming Anglophones into Francophones as admitted by President Paul Biya during an event in France in 2019 (Fofung, 2019). In hindsight, the creation of the bilingual grammar school can be seen through the lens of the assimilationist policy. The best and the brightest students were selected and put through a rigorous bilingual training program to transform them into an elite bilingual class that would be comfortable in advancing the goals and aspirations of the French. The teachers were, in most cases, French citizens. Britain was neither invested in nor interested in education in Cameroon.

The bilingual educational system, therefore, was hegemonic and assimilationist and can be explained by the theory of hegemony as well as Stephens Krascher's theory of second language acquisition. Gramsci (1996), an Italian Marxist philosopher, advanced the theory of hegemony. The main idea of Gramscian hegemony is that hegemony is a negotiated, consensual process whereby dominant political and cultural classes provide values, worldviews, political leadership, and cultural meanings to subordinate classes or subaltern groups in specific historical and political contexts (Gramsci & Buttigieg, 1996). In hegemonic situations, the dominant leadership class thrived through forming alliances with various factions within the socio-cultural and political groups to dismantle any political opposition. Pessoa (2003) concludes that the theory of hegemony helps explain socio-political and cultural order in societies. In Cameroon, the majority of Francophones are the dominant ruling cultural and political group, while Anglophones are the subalterns or dominated group. The idea of a bilingual country was to create a cadre of citizens who would be able to acquire the ability to learn, speak, and communicate fluently in a second language - French for Anglophones and English for Francophones. The bilingual class would have the role of defending and maintaining the system.

Stephens Krascher's theory of second language acquisition has greatly impacted all areas of second language research and teaching and is extremely critical for kids ages 11-16. This is the age of children in secondary schools in Cameroon. Krashen further posits that linguistic competence is enhanced when it is subconsciously acquired during spontaneous events like sports and other social settings. It heavily depends on the learner's mood, as learning is impaired when the subject is under duress or not interested in learning the language. Based on the above framework, this chapter looks at the evolution of the traditional Anglophone educational system and how the bilingual grammar school experience was different from it. It will also explore the educational infrastructure (libraries and information centers, sports and clubs) as well as the experience of Anglophone students from the English-speaking regions of Cameroon who move to Yaoundé, Douala, Dschang, or Ngaoundéré to attend Francophone universities.

The Traditional Anglophone Educational System

Konings and Nyamnjoh (2003) opined that in Cameroon, "separate colonial state formation and the development of territorial differences in languages and cultural legacies laid the spatial and historical foundation for the construction of Anglophone and Francophone identities" (p. 10). The traditional Anglophone educational system was modeled after the British colonial educational system that was implemented across the board in all the British colonies in Africa and consisted of:

- 2–3 years of Vernacular or Bush school,
- 2 years at the infant department,
- 4 years of elementary school,
- 2 years of senior primary school,
- 2 years of Middle school and
- 4 years of Secondary school

After completing secondary school, graduates were qualified to work for the Local Government or Native Authority. The top students in all the schools were shortlisted, and the best selected underwent a further 2–3 years of training to become highly respected teachers in the communities. Emphasis in the curriculum was on the philosophy of adaptation based on whether the schools were in rural or urban settings. Ndille (2015) states that the Colonial Office prescribed the three Rs – Reading, wRiting and aRithmetic, British and European History, Literature, and Geography. For schools in the rural areas–and they were in the majority– in addition to the three Rs, emphasis was put on the types of activity in which school leavers would be engaged. This centered around agriculture; hence, rural science and domestic science were emphasized. The results of this dual system subsequently led to curriculum adaptations that emphasized technical, vocational, and agricultural training at the expense of more traditional subjects. The new system ultimately led to the creation of government technical and trade schools like Government Technical College, Ombe, as well as other Christian mission and private-led initiatives across West Cameroon.

The traditional Francophone educational system was similar to the Anglophone system but shorter. It was 12 years as opposed to 17 years for the British system, which spent more time preparing the local government staff in secondary schools. In contrast, the French were closely involved as expatriates in running local affairs in French colonies. Major emphasis was placed on the study of the French language and culture, history, and philosophy, as well as mathematics. Upon reunification of British Southern Cameroons and *la République du Cameroun*, the federal government gradually shifted towards harmonizing the two separate systems, as seen in Table 8.1 below. The British colonial educational system followed the 2 – 8 – 5 – 2 - 3 system (2 years of nursery education, 8 years of primary education, 5 years of secondary education, 2 years of post-secondary, and 3 years of education at the tertiary level). The Francophone system was 2 – 6 – 4 - 3 - 4. It therefore took at least 20 years for an Anglophone to get a university degree, while it took the Francophones 19 years. The technical or vocational education systems were similar. However, they had the added advantage that successful Anglophone candidates were ready to enter the job market after the Ordinary Levels or City and Guilds professionals exams. These graduates formed the backbone of the private sector. Hence, a premium was placed on them as vocational education was prioritized in the then West Cameroon (see Table 8.1).

Table 8.1. Educational system in the Cameroons, Pre- and Post-Reunification (modified from Gwanfogbe, 1996)

Age	Anglophone			Francophone
	Before 1964	After 1964	Technical Education	
4	Nursery 1	Nursery 1	Nursery 1	Maternel 1
5	Nursery 2	Nursery 2	Nursery 2	Maternel 2
6	Infants 1	Class 1	Class 1	cours d' initiation
7	Infant 2	Class 2	Class 2	Cours préparatoire
8	Standard 1	Class 3	Class 3	Cours élémentaire 1
9	Standard 2	Class 4	Class 4	Cours élémentaire 2
10	Standard 3	Class 5	Class 5	Cours moyen 1
11	Standard 4	Class 6	Class 6	Cours moyen 2: CEPE
12	Standard 5	Class 7 FSLC	Class 7 FSLC	Sixième
13	Standard 6 Certificate	Form 1	Form 1	Cinquième
14	Form 1	Form 2	Form 2	Quartrième
15	Form 2	Form 3	Form 3	Troisième: BEPC / CAP
16	Form 3	Form	Form 4	Seconde
17	Form 4	Form	Form 5 City and Guilds and CAP	Professional School
18	Form 5	Professional School	Professional School	Première: Probatoire
19	Lower Sixth	Lower Sixth	Lower Sixth	Terminale: BACC
20	Upper Sixth	Upper Sixth	Upper Sixth	
21	University	University	Univ. (Technical)	University and or Professional School
22	University/ Professional Schools	University Professional schools	University Professional School	

The Creation of the Bilingual Grammar School Buea

After the independence of both East and West Cameroon in 1960 and 1961, respectively, both entities opted for a bilingual Federal Republic of Cameroon with English and French as the two official languages. This remained a source of pride in the early years. President Ahidjo used it in his diplomatic overtures, placing bilingual Cameroonian diplomats in strategic positions. For example, he convinced African heads of state to appoint Nzo Ekangaki, a bilingual Anglophone diplomat, to the position of Secretary General of the continental body, the Organization of African Unity (OAU), which was founded in 1963 and was relaunched as the African Union in 2002. To continue along these lines and using bilingualism as a unifying factor, the government pursued educational policies to enhance bilingualism, such as the creation of a unique Bilingual Grammar School in Man O'War Bay in 1962, and later moved to Molyko Buea. The Ahidjo regime created other bilingual high schools such as the Bilingual High School Yaoundé (established in 1977). Other bilingual high schools were created in almost all the divisions of the country. Attempts were made during the Ahidjo regime to introduce bilingualism in primary schools. This policy of bilingualism, which made English and French compulsory for students at the primary and secondary levels of education and a requirement for admission into the university, continues to this day. *Français par la radio* (French by Radio) became an important part of primary school curricula in the main schools in Buea and Bamenda (see Chapter 7).

The Bilingual Grammar School Buea was a unique showcase of bilingual education in the Federal Republic of Cameroon, taking into consideration its success from inception to when interest in national integration waned after an unsuccessful coup d'état against President Paul Biya in 1984. Since then, the educational system has reverted to what has become the norm nationally – two separate Anglophone and Francophone sub-systems. In certain locations like Yaoundé, Anglophone and Francophone schools operate on the same premises, but the Anglophones have separate but inferior facilities. This represented abandoning the bilingual class format or the mélange (mixture) experiment.

Admission of students into the prestigious Bilingual Grammar school was through the end-of-course competitive exams for the Anglophones, the Common Entrance exams. This exam was conducted nationwide. The top candidates, those who scored above a certain threshold, were placed on List A, and second-tier candidates were placed on List B. Only those who selected the Bilingual Grammar School and who passed List A were invited for an admissions interview into "Lycée Bilingue" as it was widely known by its French acronym. Because of the strict criteria, only the *crème de la crème* from all over the nation were admitted. However, the system was not without flaws. Children of the West Cameroon elite and those who knew influential members of the selection committee (principals) got first preference. List A children from "poor" families were often passed over.

On the Francophone side, a special competitive exam was organized, and the best students were also selected. Upon admission into the BGS, the students were kept in separate streams – Form 1 Anglophone and *Sixième* Francophones were taught following the respective curriculum for their end-of-course exams at that level. However, in addition to the course load, the Anglophones were drilled with 10 hours of French weekly for two years, while the Francophones were drilled with 10 hours of intensive English for the next two years. Being a boarding school, the boys were mixed up in the dormitories named after political leaders of the unification era to facilitate language socialization. The school soon became coeducational, with the girls' dormitories off campus. A large day-student population also attended the school, so Molyko Village became a melting pot for bilingual students. These students were the *crème de la crème* and most were highly driven and competitive. The fact that French and English were weighted as highly as Mathematics made all the difference in the students' end-of-year scores. Students returned ready to succeed. They developed strategies that included forming language pairs, whereby Anglophones would speak to Francophones only in French, and Francophones would speak to Anglophones only in English. Another incentive was the annual scholarship given to those with an average of at least 60% in the end-of-year exams.

By the end of the first year, both Anglophones and Francophones were getting comfortable conversing in French and English even if the grammar remained a challenge to many of them, but they could get around. Interestingly, in the second year, the French teachers were French expatriates who drilled students in French language and culture. Their stories of Paris and other French cities made learning the French language enjoyable. This two-year intensive language immersion laid the foundation for the "Bilingual Classes" A and B, where half of the Anglophone form 2 (sophomores) went to Bilingual Form 3A and the other half to Bilingual Form 3B. The students studied all the subjects in the French curriculum and all the subjects in the English curriculum for the next two years. The goal was to prepare them to sit for the *Brevet d'Études du Première Cycle* (BEPC), the French equivalent of the Anglophone General Certificate of Education (GCE) Ordinary levels exams. In hindsight, the selection process and the academic grilling eliminated those students who could not stand the rigors of the system. Those who weathered the academic storm continued. This experience shaped their characters and outlook on life. Students could take over 18 courses, sometimes in a mixture of languages – e.g., Biology in English and Human Biology in English; Geography in English and Human Geography in French; European History in English and African History in French; Geology or Technology in French, etc. Intensive French as well as English were added to the mix. Students were further required to choose a second language – intensive English (a bonus for Anglophones) or Spanish and German for Francophones. The timetable was very heavy, and students were also expected to participate in extracurricular activities. The results were usually good. The Anglophone success rate was high even though they were competing with students whose first language was French. The Anglophone students proceeded to form five, the last year of secondary school, and had to work harder to catch up with high school students who attended non-bilingual high schools. This was especially true of science-oriented students who did not have enough training in subjects like Chemistry, Physics and Biology. However, the GCE results were also good as the students competed successfully with students from other top schools like Sacred Heart College, Cameroon Protestant College (CPC) Bali, Saint Joseph's College, Sasse and Government High School, Mamfe. The irony is that while all Anglophones were required to be part of the bilingual classes and eventually sit for the French-language BEPC, no official policy required or encouraged the Francophones to take the General Certificate of Education (GCE). This was clearly a system designed to assimilate Anglophones into the Francophone system. The system demonstrated subtly that assimilation was directed at Anglophones.

Educational infrastructures, Libraries, Sports and Recreational Facilities

Schultz (2019) postulates that language "acquisition requires meaningful interaction in the target language - natural communication - in which speakers are concerned not with the form of their utterances but with the messages they are conveying and understanding" (p. 3). Within the framework of Krashen's theory of second language acquisition, this can apply to the environment both on and off campus that favors language acquisition. Bilingual

Grammar School was a big sports school, and it took part in many sporting competitions against other high schools in the Buea area. Sports, or physical education, was not only a subject in class. It had practical aspects, such as physical performance and conditioning being part of physical education exams. As part of the school's recreation program, students had many opportunities to participate in any sport of their choice. Thursdays were "half days," with afternoons earmarked for physical education and club activities. The bulk of physical education courses were taught in French, as most of the instructors were French-speaking. The few English-speaking teachers were trained in the French language, had their notes in French and probably were more comfortable teaching in French than English. Most social clubs, such as the Cinema Club (Cine Club), The Drama Club, and the Photography Club (Club Photo), were supported by the French Cultural Center in Buea. Unlike church or "mission" institutions in the area, such as Saint Joseph's College, Sasse, Baptist Teachers' Training College (BTTC), and Bishop Rogan College, which had school libraries, the Bilingual Grammar School did not have its own library. So, students were encouraged to visit the well-stocked library of the French Cultural Center, which was five miles away. Bilingual Grammar School students could check out books, hold meetings, watch French movies, and present dramas in the center's auditorium. There was no such facility on the relatively big campus. All the books of the French Cultural Center Library were in French. The library, which had a reading room, was open to the public. Students and young people from the Buea area could go to that library to study for their examinations and participate in its summer activities. One of the highlights of the summer holiday season was the weekly *matinée* French films projected in the afternoons, followed by the distribution of French graphic magazines for youth, Kouakou, and *Kalao*, that the French Foreign Ministry produced. The stories of the magazines were set in Africa, and the characters were African primary school children. These magazines were intended to teach French grammar and vocabulary. The French Cultural Center was the first "public library" in Buea. It expanded its activities while the British Council, the American Cultural Center, and their libraries closed their doors (See Chapter 7). It is little wonder that French gradually became the go-to language in physical and sports education, as well as culture at the Bilingual Grammar School and among the young people in the Buea area.

The Bilingual Grammar school administration was Francophone-dominated. The pioneer French principals eventually handed over to Cameroonian (Francophone) principals, and in the 1970s, Anglophone administrators were appointed vice principals and disciplinary masters. The groundwork had been laid for the complete assimilation of Anglophones despite the rhetoric of national unity and integration by sycophantic politicians. It is interesting to note that many French expatriate teachers were at the Bilingual Grammar School. Not only were they teaching secondary school students, but they were also teaching Anglophone Advanced Level students French grammar, composition, literature, culture, and philosophy. Lectures were always paired with weekly film screenings at the French Cultural Center. Students watched film classics of the works of French playwrights and poets, including Molière, Racine, Corneille, and Beaumarché, at the French Cultural Center in Buea. French translation classes (mostly from English to French) were taught by Cameroon Francophone teachers. As a result, students from BGS did exceptionally well in

French both at the Ordinary Level and Advanced levels General Certificate of Education (GCE) examinations. This was part of the positive outcome of the subtle assimilation process to transform Anglophone youth into members of *la Francophonie*. This is critical in understanding French hegemony because after independence, France, unlike Britain, continued to offer robust assistance to Cameroon through cultural exchanges (French Cultural Centers, French language teachers, and other educational activities). French experts also collaborated with the various ministries of the Federal Republic of Cameroon: Education, Health, Defense, Agriculture, and Foreign Affairs) to sustain French interests. Therefore, all reforms generally reflected French policies and interests. In fact, in a declassified confidential memo No 6099 of 26th April 1967 sent from the Consul General of France in Buea, Michel Moreux, to the *Chargée d'Affaires* of France at the Embassy in Yaoundé, the diplomat in Buea stated that West Cameroon is still an Anglophone state speaking exclusively English, and therefore it was imperative to start training future generations to be able to speak and use French fluently. He buttresses his point by explaining that the French Cultural Center in Buea would serve as a cultural hub that brings the youths together for French cultural programming. He also said France would also use radio and French graphic magazines to introduce Anglophone youth to the French culture (see appendix). Additionally, France would sponsor a Linguistic Center that would teach Anglophone civil servants French.

University Education

After reunification, the University of Yaoundé was created, followed by the various specialized professional institutions or French-style Grandes Écoles. Generally, the language of instruction at the University of Yaoundé was French, and aside from the English Department and the Common Law section in the Faculty of Law, where lectures were taught in English, the rest were in French. Notices were posted in French with hardly any English translation. Anglophone student enrollment in the Faculty of Sciences was abysmally low and despite that, some Anglophone students succeeded in completing their degrees in the Faculty of Science and the medical school. Those who went through the Bilingual Grammar School and grew up in the French-speaking part of Cameroon formed the bulk of Anglophones who successfully graduated from the University of Yaoundé before the creation or expansion of state universities in 1993. Many Anglophone students of the sciences who could afford it went to Nigeria and pursued their educational dreams there. Anglophone consciousness never really died because many young people growing up have either experienced outright marginalization as second-class citizens or indignation in the face of dominant French radio or TV programming, police harassment, and brutality. The French-dominated educational system has been under attack for a long time, and generations of Anglophone students fought and held protest marches in Yaoundé to obtain the creation of the independent General Certificate of Education (GCE) Board to organize English-language examinations (alongside an *Office du Bac*, which the Francophone educational sub-system had not requested). This was a means of stopping the harmonization of the national educational curriculum, a process intended to eliminate the specificity of the English-language educational sub-system. The horrid tales of parents, especially from Anglophone Northwest and Southwest regions, dying in the Finance Ministry or the

Treasury in Yaoundé in the process of obtaining approval or payment of their retirement benefits, of the discriminatory treatment they received if they did not speak French led many young people to leave Cameroon in search of better opportunities abroad. These collective experiences of second-class citizenship contributed to building an Anglophone consciousness that will never die. The result has been internal dissent led by Barrister Gorji Dinka, Albert Mukong, and others, the launching of the Social Democratic Front (SDF) in Bamenda by John Fru Ndi, amid bloodshed, organization of the All Anglophone Conferences in Buea (1993) and Bamenda (1994) to call for constitutional reforms that recognize the specificity of the Anglophone regions, to the crisis that paralyzed Anglophone Cameroon beginning in 2016. The situation of Cameroon after reunification is summed up by Cynthia Petrigh, Founder and Director of Beyond Peace:

> La création de la République Fédérale en 1961 a entérine ces approches différentes et chacun des Gouvernement des deux États fédérés était doté d'un Secrétariat d'État a l'Enseignement Primaire. Le français et l'anglais sont depuis lors les deux langues officielles, or les ferments d'une politique assimilationniste qui ne dit pas son nom étaient déjà en place. En pratique, les Écoles publiques bilingues sont rares et le bilinguisme n'est ni enseigne ni encourager, ni pratique par l'administration, laquelle fonctionne exclusivement en français. Cette politique pénalise les anglophones non seulement pour l'accès à des postes d'emplois publics mais aussi pour l'accès à l'administration dans la vie courante" (Petrigh, 2020).

The formation of the Federal Republic in 1961 led to these different approaches and each government of the two federated states had a Secretariat of State for Primary Education. English and French have since been the two official languages, but the basis of a policy of hidden assimilation was already in place. Practically, public bilingual schools are rare, and bilingualism is neither taught nor encouraged, nor practiced by the administration, which functions exclusively in French. This policy penalizes the Anglophones not only in terms of access to government jobs but also to the government in their daily lives.

Education is power. The value system of any educational system is measured by the critical thinking ability of the recipients. A curriculum that encourages creativity, accountability, responsibility, questioning authority, and respecting the rule of law mirrors the evolution of the educational system in Anglophone Cameroon. Therefore, the evolution of the educational system in Anglophone Cameroon reflects the story of a resilient people—yesterday, today, and tomorrow. Anglophone consciousness and the Anglophone Revolt of 2016 were launched by teachers and lawyers. The assimilationist program of the Bilingual Grammar Schools had not succeeded in assimilating Anglophones into la Francophonie.

References

Ako D. (1967). Pressures and Constraints on the Development of Education in the West Cameroon. *Africa Today, 14*(2), 18-20.

Amaazee, V. (1994). The Role of The French Cameroonians in the Unification of Cameroon, 1916-1961. *Transafrican Journal of History, 23*, pp. 195-234.

Awasom, N. (2002). Negotiating Federalism: How Ready Were Cameroonian Leaders before the February 1961 United Nations Plebiscites? *Canadian Journal of African Studies / Revue Canadienne Des Études Africaines, 36*(3), 425-459.

Clignet, R., & Foster, P. (1964). French and British Colonial Education in Africa. *Comparative Education Review, 8(2), 191-198.*

Devernois, G. (1959). Cameroons 1958-1959: From Trusteeship to Independence. *Civilisations, 9*(2), 229-234.

Devernois, G. (1960). The New Institutions of the Cameroons. *Civilisations, 10*(2), 256-258

Eko, L. (2003). The English-Language Press and the "Anglophone Problem" in Cameroon: Group Identity, Culture, and the Politics of Nostalgia. *Journal of Third World Studies, 20*(1), 79-102

Fofung, A. (2019). Cameroon: From Biya, A Mea Culpa on the Anglophone Crisis at the Second Paris Peace Summit hosted by the Mo Ibrahim Foundation November 12th, 2019. Retrieved on 10/27/20 from https://panafricanvisions.com/2019/11/cameroon-from-biya-a-mea-culpa-on-the-anglophone-crisis-in-paris/

Gonondo, J. & Djiraro, L. (2016). The Challenge of Saving Two Languages in Cameroonian Higher Education: The Case of the Public Universities. *Asian Journal of Social Sciences, Arts and Humanities 4(3), 38-46.*

Gramsci, A., & Buttigieg, J. A. (1996). *Prison Notebooks, Volume 2* (Vol. 2). New York: Columbia University Press.

Jua, N., & Konings, P. (2004). Occupation of Public Space: Anglophone Nationalism in Cameroon. *Cahiers D'Études Africaines. 44, 609 - 33*

Konings, P. (2006). Assessing the Role of Autonomous Teachers' Trade Unions in Anglophone Cameroon, 1959-1972. *The Journal of African History, 47*(3), 415-436

Ndille, R. (2020). Schools with invisible fences in the British Southern Cameroons, 1916 – 1961: Colonial Curriculum and the other side of Modernist thinking. *Third World Quarterly* DO: 10.1080/01436597.2020.1744431

Ndille, R. (2015). From Adaptation to Ruralisation in Cameroon Education Policy, 1922 – 2002: Replacing six with half a dozen. *African Educational Research Journal 3(3): 153 - 160*

Ngoh, V. (1999). The Origin of the Marginalization of Former Southern Cameroonians (Anglophones), 1961-1966: An Historical Analysis. *Journal of Third World Studies, 16*(1), 165-185.

Okereke, C. (2018). Analysing Cameroon's Anglophone Crisis. *Counter Terrorist Trends and Analyses, 10*(3), 8-12.

Pessoa, C. (2003). On Hegemony, Post-Ideology and Subalternity. *Bulletin of Latin American Research, 22*(4), 484-490.

Petrigh, C. (2020). Éducation et pouvoir dans le conflit anglophone au Cameroun. Notes de L'Ifri, Retrieved October 30, from https://www.ifri.org/fr/publications/notes-de-lifri/education-pouvoir-conflit-anglophone-cameroun

Schutz, R. (2019). Stephen Krashen's theory of second language acquisition. Accessed June 10, 2022 from https://www.sk.com.br/sk-krash-english.html

Terretta, M. (2012). "We Had Been Fooled into Thinking that the UN Watches over the Entire World": Human Rights, UN Trust Territories, and Africa's Decolonization. *Human Rights Quarterly, 34*(2), 329-360

Tiewa, K., & Vubo, E. (2015). Celebrating Unity and Debating Unity in Cameroon's 2010: Independence Jubilees, the "Cinquantenaire." *Cahiers D'Études Africaines,55*(218), 331-357.

PART THREE

The Anglophone Question and the Anglophone Revolt Of 2016:
Human Rights and Humanitarian Issues

TEN

#BringBackOurInternet

Cameroon Government Internet Shutdown and Digital Activist Resistance during the
Anglophone Revolt

DIBUSSI TANDE

In the last two decades, Internet access in Africa has grown exponentially from 2.7% in 2005 to 28.2% in 2019 (International Telecommunication Union, 2019). This increase in Internet access is due to the ubiquity of affordable smartphones, and falling prices of mobile data and services, along with investment in telecommunications infrastructure across the continent (Attwell, 2019).

The Global System for Mobile Communications (GSMA) estimates that 477 million people, or 45% of inhabitants in Sub-Saharan Africa, were subscribed to mobile services at the end of 2019 (of whom 272 million were mobile Internet users) and predicts that there will be one billion mobile connections or a 50% subscriber penetration in the region by 2025 (GSMA Intelligence, 2020, p. 3).

The rapid growth of the Internet and mobile technologies has spurred economic growth across the continent. According to GSMA, mobile technologies contributed nine percent of GDP in sub-Saharan Africa in 2019, amounting to more than $155 billion, supported about 3.8 million jobs, and funded the public sector with about $17 billion (GSMA Intelligent, 2020, p. 4).

The growth of the Internet has also led to a burgeoning virtual public sphere where citizens express and organize dissent, mobilize, and hold their governments accountable (Tande, 2010). Increasingly, however, social media's role as a tool for social change and an igniter of revolutions (Al-Sharif, 2018) is increasingly being questioned. Deibert (2019), for example, argues that social media is not only contributing to society's ills but has also become one of "the most effective enablers" (p. 26) of authoritarian regimes who use it to "control people and to sow confusion, ignorance, prejudice, and chaos in order to undermine public accountability." (p. 31)

That said, the development of the Internet as a disruptor of traditional ways of generating and sharing information has created conflictual relations between governments and citizens. Thus, despite its economic and other benefits, African governments view the Internet as a threat to their hegemony because it empowers citizens in ways not possible in the offline space, where governments have largely succeeded in undermining the political opposition and civil society (Tkacheva et al., 2013). As Shirky (2011) points out, "authoritarian governments stifle communication among their citizens because they fear, correctly, that a better-coordinated populace would constrain their ability to act without oversight." African governments, therefore, view the Internet as a space that must be controlled, co-opted, contained, or simply coerced into submission (Tande, 2012).

Techniques to rein in online activism and the Internet range from draconian laws to regulate the Internet, bandwidth throttling, and blocking specific social media platforms such as Twitter, WhatsApp, and Facebook, to complete Internet shutdowns. Most recently, some African governments have instituted an Internet or social media tax supposedly because telephone companies and governments are losing revenue as more citizens use Internet data for communication ("Uganda: One year of social media tax," 2019). Critics argue that the tax is another attempt to "silence speech, to reduce the spaces where people can exchange information, and to really be able to control, with the recognition that online platforms have become the more commonly used way for sharing information" (Dreyfuss, 2018). This was indeed the case in Uganda, where the social media tax slashed Ugandan Internet users by five million and reduced Internet penetration from 47% to 35% in the first three months of its implementation (Nanfuka, 2019).

The most common technique of Internet control is the Internet shutdown, which Access Now defines as "an intentional disruption of Internet-based communications, rendering them inaccessible or effectively unavailable, for a specific population, location, or mode of access, often to exert control over the flow of information" (Internet Society, 2019, p. 1).

Internet shutdowns have become increasingly popular in Africa. In 2016, 11 of the 56 Internet shutdowns worldwide were on the continent, representing a 50% increase over 2015 (Mukeredzi, 2017). In 2017, there were 13 full or partial shutdowns in Africa (Muperi & Brown, 2019), 17 in 2018, at least 25 in 2019 (Access Now, 2020), and 18 in 2020 (Access Now, 2021).

States cite several reasons for shutting down the internet, namely to prevent the spread of fake news (Goel et al., 2018), to suppress anti-government protests (Dahir, 2018), restore law and order and prevent misinformation and violence (The Sunday Mail, 2019), "prevent speech that could further inflame ethnic tensions" (Ethiopia enters third week, 2020), prevent election-related violence (Protests, clashes, Internet, 2021) or outside interference in elections (Uganda bans social media, 2021), and even to curtail fraud in national exams (Gbere, 2019). Whatever the reasons for Internet shutdowns, they are disruptive to the economy, violate the right to free speech and access to information, and raise significant human rights concerns.

According to a report on the global cost of Internet shutdowns (Woodhams & Migliano, 2020), Internet disruptions cost the world economy about $8 billion in 2019 and the economy of sub-Saharan Africa about $1 billion.

The United Nations recognizes the Internet's pivotal role in promoting socioeconomic and political development around the world and has insisted that Internet rights are human rights and that Internet shutdowns violate international law (UNHRC, 2016; 2018). According to the UN Special Rapporteur on Freedom of Expression, "A general network shutdown is in clear violation of international law and cannot be justified by any means. Shutdowns are damaging not only for people's access to information, but also for their access to basic services" (OHCHR, 2019).

Despite the negative impact of Internet shutdowns on economic growth, innovation, free speech, and political participation, African countries now frequently restrict access to the Internet, but not without a fight by ordinary citizens, civil society, political parties, and digital activists who are mobilizing to #KeepItOn whenever there is an Internet disruption.

In this chapter, we will study the 2017 Internet shutdown in the English-speaking regions of Cameroon, which remains the longest total Internet blackout in Africa. We will examine events leading up to the shutdown, show how digital activists built a transnational multi-stakeholder coalition to pressure the Cameroon government to end the shutdown through the #BringBackOurInternet campaign, and how they leveraged online and offline tools and strategies to advocate for universal digital rights while reframing mainstream media perceptions about the Anglophone problem in Cameroon.

The Internet Shutdown

On January 17, 2017, the Ministry of Post and Telecommunications ordered CAMTEL, the state-owned incumbent telecoms operator which controls Cameroon's fiber optic backbone, to cut off all Internet communication in the Northwest and Southwest regions (Tobor, 2017). Although this was the most restrictive measure the government had taken thus far against Cameroon's burgeoning digital space, it was merely another chapter in its decade-long hostility towards the Internet and Internet activists (Tande, 2011b).

The Internet was officially introduced in Cameroon in 1998, and the telecom market liberalized the following year by selling CAMTEL's mobile phone unit to South Africa's MTN. The adoption of both technologies was slow largely due to the inadequate infrastructure. By 2006, Internet penetration was a mere 1.4%, while mobile phone penetration was only slightly better at 14.5% (Lange, 2008). The situation improved dramatically in the next decade as government made major investments in the ICT and telecom sectors such as establishing a 12,000 km national optical fiber network that connected all 10 regions of the country and covered about 60% of national territory and linking the country to undersea cable systems such as the South Atlantic 3/West Africa Submarine Cable (SAT-3/WASC), the South Atlantic Inter Link (SAIL) and the Nigerian-Cameroon Submarine Cable System (NCSCS). By 2018, Internet and mobile phone penetration rates increased significantly to 35% and 83% respectively (Agence De Regulation Des Telecommunications, 2018).

As the Internet gained a foothold in Cameroon, an increasingly contentious relationship developed between the government, determined to control the Internet and Internet activists (particularly in the Diaspora) bent on using it to highlight the failures of the former. In its bid to regulate the Internet, the government created institutions such as the National Agency for Information and Communication Technologies (ANTIC) and the Telecommunications Regulatory Board (ART) and adopted a cybercrimes law which critics viewed as an attempt to muzzle anti-regime activities online and rein in free speech (Tande, 2011b).

One of the first major clashes around the use of the Internet occurred in 2004 when the government accused a Diaspora-based online newspaper of spreading rumors of President Biya's death ("Cameroun: Un "fantôme," 2004). Thereafter, there were numerous attempts to rein in the Cameroonian cyberspace such as blocking Twitter via SMS service in 2011 to stave off Egypt-style protests in the country (Tande, 2011a).

In October 2016, Anglophone lawyers and teachers began a strike action against the "Francophonization" of the common law and educational systems in the English-speaking regions of Cameroon. The strike soon snowballed into widespread street protests over the socio-political marginalization of Anglophones, culminating in calls for a return to a federal system of government in which Anglophones would have an autonomous state.

These protests led to an Anglophone reawakening reminiscent of the revival of "Anglophone Nationalism" in the early 1990s (Jua & Konings, 2004). As the crisis intensified, activists who were for the most part out of Cameroon used social media to "build a massive show of solidarity around the struggle" (Jong, 2017), rally the Anglophone community in Cameroon and abroad around the idea that federalism was the answer to Anglophone marginalization, and to expose human rights abuses by government forces such as the attacks on lawyers in Bamenda and Buea, and the torture of students at the University of Buea. Activists also used social media to initiate and coordinate street protests, organize the school boycott and Ghost Town campaigns (Iaccino, 2017a) and even crowdfunding initiatives ("Cameroon: 'Hoodlums,'" 2017).

As the Internet's role in fueling the street protests became increasingly apparent, the government complained stridently about its "misuse." During the November 2016 parliamentary session, the Speaker of the National Assembly characterized the Internet as "a new form of terrorism" and urged authorities "to track down and neutralize the culprits of cybercrimes" (Tande, 2016). The Minister of Communication also warned that the government would impose an Internet blackout if social media was used to spread "anti-government propaganda" (Kindzeka, 2017).

A week prior to the shutdown, the Minister of Telecommunications, Minette Libom li Likeng, initiated a "civic education campaign" via bulk SMS messages to mobile phone subscribers: "Dear subscriber, publishing as well as spreading false news, including on the social media, are punishable by the Penal Code and the law" (Nanfuka, 2017). Subsequent variations of the SMS warned users that they could "incur 6 months to 2 years imprisonment, and 5-10 million [Frs CFA] fine if you publish or spread on the social media, information you can't prove," or "may be sentenced to 20 years in prison if found guilty of slander or propagating false declarations on the social media" (Tande, 2019). According to the minister, the campaign was initiated because social media was being used to spread false messages that created fear, threatened public order, and could potentially destabilize the country (Minpostel, 2017).

According to Ogola (2019), "the desire to control the Internet is rooted in governments' determination to control the political narrative. Many see the Internet as an existential threat that must be contained, no matter what consequences it will have on other sectors" because it disrupts governments' "stranglehold on the production and dissemination of information." Thus, "what [authoritarian] regimes fear above all is the power of public opinion, especially informed and mobilized public opinion" (Odugbemi, 2014).

In Cameroon, Anglophone activists successfully transformed social media into a public sphere beyond the control of government and used it to hold the government to account and mobilize the Anglophones around demands for autonomy. Unable to control, co-opt, contain, or coerce the Anglophone virtual public sphere into submission, the government decided to cut it off. On January 17, the government banned two leading Anglophone organizations, the Southern Cameroons National Council (SCNC) and the Cameroon Anglophone Civil Society Consortium, and arrested two consortium leaders, Felix Nkongho and Fontem Neba, then shut down the Internet.

Initially, the government refused to acknowledge that it had shut down the Internet, however, it eventually conceded that it had done so because Anglophone activists were "using social media to spread rumors, fuel anti-government protests, and threaten national unity" (Ngassa, 2017). The Minister of Communication claimed that "the shutdown was triggered by the propagation of false information on social media capable of inciting hate and violence in the crisis-hit regions" (AFEX, 2018, p. 39).

Clay Shirky's observation (2011) that "Authoritarian governments stifle communication among their citizens because they fear, correctly, that a better-coordinated populace would constrain their ability to act without oversight" held true in Cameroon. The shutdown was less about maintaining public order and more about giving the government free rein to (re)frame and control the narrative about the Anglophone crisis, make it impossible for activists to circulate videos and pictures of police brutality, cut off communication channels between Anglophone activists abroad and those on "Ground Zero," and contain the spread of federalist and secessionist ideas in the Anglophone regions in what amounted to "a crude attempt to quell dissent" (Africa Highlights, 2017). The clampdown extended to the print and audiovisual media when, on January 20, National Communication Council President, Peter Essoka, issued a statement warning "all national state and privately-owned media from publishing or broadcasting any statement tending to condone secession or federalism on pain of... temporary suspension [or] a permanent operations ban" (Reporters Without Borders, 2017).

Hashtag Activism

As soon as the shutdown went into effect, a group of Cameroonian activists launched a campaign on Twitter to pressure the government to restore the Internet. Twitter was the ideal platform for the campaign because, even though it is the least popular social media platform in Cameroon, coming a distant fourth after Facebook, WhatsApp and Instagram (Kemp, 2020), it is the leading source of news among social media sites in Europe and America (Barnard, 2018, p. 23) which were a major focus of the campaign. In addition, Twitter's open structure makes it a perfect "forum for spreading awareness and information on social justice (or activist) movements, as well as for dialogue between users on a given social justice subject" (Konnelly, 2015, p. 1). According to Moscato (2016), Twitter's innate ability "to diffuse and amplify information and ideas across social media" (p. 6) makes it a preferred tool for activists because it allows users "to cluster, rebroadcast, modify, or reply to ongoing messages and conversations" (p. 5) and to deliver "key information to a broader public, garnering newfound publicity by reaching other media, or attracting attention from local governmental authorities" (p. 5).

The campaign to restore the Internet adopted the #BringBackOurInternet hashtag reminiscent of #BringBackOurGirls used during the kidnap of the Chibok girls in Nigeria. The hashtag is a metadata tag that allows Twitter users to "cluster their tweets around a single issue or focus" (Moscato, 2016). Adding the hash symbol (#) before a word or phrase makes it easier to search for, follow, discuss, interact with, and build narratives around the hashtagged word (Yang, 2016), thereby creating "ad hoc publics" around specific issues or causes (Ofori-Parku & Moscato, 2018). Hashtags can be classified into two main categories. Routine hashtags that deal with everyday issues (#travel, #Soccer, etc.) and "do not usually evolve into contentious collective events online" (Yang, 2016, p. 14) and Cause hashtags that "increas[e] awareness of advocacy efforts and allow for 'bypassing the gatekeepers by giving a range of advocates, from everyday citizens to multi-million-dollar companies, an opportunity to get their messages out to others.'" (Konnelly, 2015, p. 14)

Cause hashtags generally have a narrative structure through which "individuals contribute to the co-production of narratives" (Yang, 2016). They generally consist of complete sentences, for example, #BlackLivesMatter, #FreeAllArrested, #FreeSouthernCameroons.

Figure 10.1. Bring Back Our Internet

#BringBackOurInternet

On January 22, Cameroonian IT entrepreneur and digital activist, Rebecca Enonchong (2017), tweeted: "#Cameroon govt blocked all internet access in English-Speaking regions. Join us in telling them to #BringBackOurInternet #KeepItOn Pls RT." This tweet, which officially kicked off the #BringBackOurInternet campaign, was not random. It was the outcome of a campaign by a core group of activists who had been holding group conversations (private conversations that occur via Direct Messages) on Twitter since November 2016 amidst reports of a possible Internet shutdown in Cameroon. The group was set up to brainstorm on ways to prevent an Internet shutdown, and strategies to adopt in the event of a shutdown (K. Ndongmo, personal communication, January 21, 2019).

This group, which ultimately became the nucleus of the campaign to restore the Internet in Cameroon, adopted #BringBackOurInternet as the campaign hashtag because it focused solely on the shutdown and was not overtly political or partisan. As group member Olivia Mukam Wandji explained,

> Everyone can relate to the frustration and unfairness of being cut off from a tool like the internet. So, this issue has brought people who didn't want to take a stand on political and linguistic debates to denounce the injustice of what we call 'digital apartheid' ("Footballer Turns Spotlight," 2017).

Thanks to this inclusive approach, the activists quickly established a movement that cut across Cameroon's linguistic and political divide to mobilize Anglophone and Francophone Twitter influencers, journalists, civil society activists, bloggers (Kouagheu, 2017), the tech community, which, prior to the shutdown, had generally steered clear of the political crisis (Bright, 2017), and regular Cameroonian Twitter users who all adopted the #BringBackOurInternet hashtag, and joined in "the co-production of alternative news discourses" (Wasserman, 2017).

Exploiting Twitter Affordances

One of Twitter's key strengths is "its open, fast-paced communicative structure" (Barnard, 2018, p. 5), which allows activists to mobilize community clusters and create broadcast networks around specific causes. Community clusters are small groups or hubs with their own "audience, influencers, and sources of information" that form around an issue and create a broader conversation around the issue, while Broadcast Networks leverage influencers, agenda setters and thought leaders to disseminate information about the issue to their followers. (Olson, 2016). Twitter's affordances, that is, "features of a technology that make certain actions possible" (Graves, 2007, p. 332), promote interaction, networking and collaboration, and amplify marginalized voices (Chachra, 2017), making it ideal for digital activism. The two features that promote activism are Mentions and Retweets, which "enable anyone with compelling content to generate a whirlwind of attention" (Barnard, 2018, p. 55).

Mentions

A twitter mention is when you tag another user to your tweet by including the @ sign followed by the user's username, for example @JohnDoe. Mentions allow users to bring their causes to the attention of the media, celebrities, influencers, politicians, and government officials, who can then amplify them to a broader community (Barnard, 2017, p. 55). For example, when a user mentioned American whistleblower Edward Snowden in a tweet criticizing the SMS messages from the Cameroonian government, the original tweet had only 140 retweets and 111 likes; however, when Snowden retweeted it, it generated 1,700 retweets and 1,400 likes (Snowden, 2017b).

Mentions also allow users to publicly call out other users and initiate public conversations about an issue (Newsom & Hayne, 2014, p. 152). #BringBackOurInternet activists used the mention as a call to action and to get the attention of different stakeholders in the shutdown. For example, activists "made sure the social media campaigns included the handles of Cameroon's president, key political officials, and institutions" (Bright, 2017).

Activists used the mention to rally celebrities to the campaign and leverage their broadcast networks. They also used it to draw the attention of the international media to the shutdown, the most notable case being that of Aljazeera's interactive news bulletin "News Grid" which "got caught up in the middle of the conflict" and ended playing an "outsized role" in the Crisis ("Cameroon's Hashtag War," n.d.)

Retweet

A retweet occurs when a user reposts or shares a tweet. Retweeting amplifies the original tweet as it "can carry the words of a user to an audience far beyond their own followers" (Chachra, 2017). According to Boyd et al. (2010), retweeting goes beyond mere rebroadcasting as it "contributes to a conversational ecology in which conversations are composed of a public interplay of voices that give rise to an emotional sense of shared conversational context."

It was primarily through retweets that #BringBackOurInternet became a "Twitter cause célèbre" (Bright, 2017). Within the first week, Enonchong's kickoff tweet was retweeted 2,765 times, liked 1,302 times, generated 900 hashtag clicks and was viewed by over half a million people (641,753). Barely three days after the campaign kicked off, it received a major boost when Snowden (2017b) used the hashtag in a tweet about the shutdown: "This is the future of repression. If we do not fight it there, it will happen here. #KeepItOn #BringBackOurInternet." It was retweeted 4,756 times and got 4,490 Likes.

(Re)framing the media narrative

Traditionally, mainstream media sets the agenda on how the public understands or perceives events (Weimann & Brosius, 2017). However, social media platforms have now "emerge[d] as additional role-players in the media discourse around protests and to a large extent shaping public perceptions of events away from mainstream media" (Jacobs & Wasserman, 2018). In her study of the #BringBackOurGirls campaign, Olson (2016, p. 12) explains how it generated media coverage by "guiding the mainstream media's attention and mobilizing public conversation" about the kidnappings. In the same manner, #BringBackOurInternet activists sought to control and reframe international media coverage of the Internet shutdown and the Anglophone crisis, and in the process, discredit the government's narratives about these events.

According to Gamson and Wolfsfeld (cited in Ofori-Parku and Moscato, 2018), social movements generally have three media-related goals: that the media takes them seriously (Standing), that the media provides accurate coverage of the movement and its views (preferred framing), and that they and their cause receive positive coverage in the media (sympathy). Let us look at how the #BringBackOurInternet campaign sought to achieve each of these goals.

Standing

The #BringBackOurInternet campaign sought to gain media standing by having activists actively occupy mainstream media spaces. From the beginning of the shutdown, activists appeared in audio-visual and print media to make their case. For example, Julie Owono and Albert Nchinda, two members of the core group, appeared on Al Jazeera to challenge Elvis Ngolle Ngolle, a former Minister of Special Duties in the Office of the President of Cameroon, dispatched to defend the government's position ("Is Cameroon," 2017).

A measure of how well the campaign had achieved standing was how quickly the international media adopted the hashtag. Examples include Deutsche Welle ("Follow the Hashtag," 2017) Jeune Afrique ("#BringBackOurInternet: Quand les Camerounais," 2017) Le Monde ("#BringBackOurInternet ou la Révolte," 2017), Radio France Internationale ("#Bringbackourinternet: Les Internautes," 2017), France24 ("#BringBackOurInternet: La Bataille," 2017), RT France ("Cameroun: #BringBackOurInternet," 2017) which began incorporating the hashtag into their reports barely days into the campaign.

Preferred Framing

Despite attempts by the government to frame the Internet shutdown as a legitimate reaction against individuals whom President Biya (2016) described as "a group of manipulated and exploited extremist rioters," digital activists successfully challenged this narrative, convincing the media and the international community that the shutdown was part of a broader narrative about the discrimination, marginalization, persecution and collective punishment of Cameroon's Anglophone community; the state's continued hostility towards legitimate Anglophone demands for constitutional and structural redress; and about the escalation of state repression in the Anglophone regions.

Although the #BringBackOurInternet hashtag had been adopted because of its apparent non-political tone, it became a vehicle for discussions about the Biya regime and the Anglophone crisis. Anglophone activists appropriated the hashtag and used it alongside other hashtags that specifically addressed the Anglophone revolt such as #FreeAllArrested, to draw attention to Anglophone activists in jail; #FreeSouthernCameroons, to call for a return to federalism and even independence; and #GhostTownMonday, to promote weekly Ghost Towns which continued even after the consortium was banned and its leaders arrested.

By appropriating #BringBackOurInternet to generate awareness about the Anglophone question, Anglophone activists ensured that the media covered the shutdown not as a standalone story but as an integral part of the Anglophone crisis. Thus, media reports about the shutdown also focused extensively on the plight of English-speaking Cameroonians who were described as "historically marginalized and discriminated against" (Sow, 2017), "massively underrepresented in key positions of power… treated as second-class… not to mention economic disenfranchisement" (Atabong, 2017a), and on whom the "imposition of French legal and education systems" had resulted in "longstanding grievances against the largely-francophone central government" (Monks, 2018). It was pointed out that Anglophone marginalization began when the promises of the 1961 reunification were, according to the French weekly news magazine, L'Obs, "quickly trampled by an authoritarian centralism encouraged and facilitated by the former French colonial power" (Haski,

2017). According to the magazine, the digital marginalization of Anglophone Cameroon bore the hallmarks of the social and economic marginalization that Anglophones had been complaining about for decades:

> What is playing out in Cameroon... is both local and universal. It concerns the ability of a modern state to live with its cultural differences within boundaries inherited from colonization. It also concerns the use of the Internet both as a tool of resistance and a tool for repression (Haski, 2017).

By successfully (re)framing the discussion about the shutdown on their own terms, activists were able to present it as a tool for Anglophone persecution and a desperate government strategy that raised troubling questions about online censorship and Internet freedoms. It was in this context that David Kaye, the UN's Special Rapporteur on freedom of expression, described the shutdown as "an appalling violation" of Anglophones' "right to freedom of expression" that violated international law, suppressed public debate and deprived Cameroonians of access to essential services and basic resources (OHCHR, 2017).

Sympathy

During a panel discussion at the University of Yaounde in February 2017, Cameroon's Minister of Communication insisted that the shutdown would be maintained as long as Anglophone activists continued to use the Internet "to exercise violence, to initiate and instigate political upheaval... destabilize and to destroy peace" (Tande, 2017). This narrative, however, never took hold in the media thanks to the #BringBackOurInternet campaign. Instead, the media was replete with tales of Anglophone victimhood, resilience, resistance, and ingenuity in the face of the state's willingness to destroy the socioeconomic fabric of the Anglophone regions to quell dissent. Most notable was the recurring story of the "Digital Refugees" of Silicon Mountain (Atabong, 2017a; Mutter, 2017), Cameroon's tech hub in the town of Buea, whose startups and tech entrepreneurs were severely affected by the shutdown, and who set up a makeshift Internet "refugee camp" on the border between the French-speaking Littoral region and the English-speaking Southwest region to get Internet access (Koigi, 2017). These human-interest stories generated immense sympathy for Anglophone Cameroonians and helped bring the #BringBackOurInternet campaign to communities (such as the global tech community) that would otherwise not pay attention to a political crisis in an African country. This significantly expanded the campaign's broadcast networks.

Offline Engagement

Critics of online activism describe it as Clicktivism or Slacktivism, a "feel-good" activism with "zero political or social impact" (Morovoz, 2009), which is limited to liking, sharing, or retweeting messages, or signing online petitions without any further action (Housley et al., 2018, p. 2). Critics argue that online activism merely creates "the impression of activism" (Tostevin, 2014) and that what movements for social change need are "deeper commitments and stronger ties than those found on Facebook or Twitter" (Gladwell, 2010).

Mazak and Stetka (2015, p. 4) point out the "profound gap between peoples' actions in the online and the offline world," and argue that engaging in online activism "might even lead to increasing passivity in relation to offline politics."

According to Valenzuela (2013, p.17), social movements succeed when their online activism is combined with offline forms of citizen participation. This was the case, for example, of the Arab Spring, where "the merging of online activism and offline engagement" was "at the core of the success of the Egyptian and Tunisian revolutions" (Tande, 2011b).

Like Arab Spring activists before them, #BringBackOurInternet activists realized that their campaign needed an offline component for building multi-stakeholder coalitions consisting of Cameroonians in the Diaspora, influential personalities and celebrities, international organizations, and sympathetic governments that could leverage their networks to pressure the government to end the shutdown. Thus, in addition to engaging the media, activists organized numerous offline events to draw attention to the shutdown. For example, demonstrations were held at the MTN headquarters in Johannesburg to ask the company to "bring back our internet" (Ayong, 2017), in Paris to show solidarity with the people of the northwest and southwest regions (Mintoogue, 2017), and in Abuja to support a free Southern Cameroons (Ndeh-Che, 2017).

Mobilizing Rights Groups and Governments

A key component of the offline campaign was building coalitions with Internet rights and civil society organizations to give visibility and legitimacy to the #BringBackOurInternet campaign. Central to this coalition-building effort was Internet Without Borders (IWB), a member of the #KeepItOn coalition, a global campaign bringing together over 170 organizations from over 60 countries to fight Internet shutdowns. IWB worked closely with Access Now and an array of local and international organizations to pressure the Cameroonian government to reinstate the Internet ("Victory in Cameroon," 2017).

Other prominent Internet rights groups joined the campaign, among them Africtivistes (Mayault, 2018), the Global Network Initiative ("GNI Concerned," n.d.), and the Association for Progressive Communications (APC) ("Cameroon Maintains," 2017).

The #BringBackOurInternet's offline advocacy included reaching out discretely to potential sympathizers within the Cameroonian government, the Cameroonian business community, and foreign governments and their representatives in Cameroon with enough clout to pressure the government to end the shutdown. Even the Vatican got involved (Ritzen, 2018), with the Pope urging President Biya to end the shutdown (Bright, 2017; International Crisis Group, 2017a).

In March 2017, Prime Minister Philemon Yang traveled to Bamenda to negotiate the resumption of schools. According to Deutsche Welle, "hundreds of youths shouted 'Bring back our internet! Bring back our internet!' on the streets… as the convoy… passed" ("Anglophone Cameroon Marks," 2017). This incident demonstrated how much the #BringBackOurInternet hashtag and campaign had spread beyond the narrow confines of Twitter to become a global rallying cry, including in the region that was cut off from the Internet.

#BringBackOurInternet activists successfully bridged the gap between online activism and offline engagement and established viable cluster communities and broadcast networks in both spaces, thereby increasing pressure on the Cameroonian government to end the shutdown and address Anglophone demands.

Internet is Restored

By March 2017, cracks began to appear in the government's resolve to maintain the shutdown. On March 13, the Minister of Post and Telecommunications assured the public that the Internet would be restored in a matter of time (Cameroonians stage 'silent protest', 2017) and on March 30, the Minister of Justice promised that the Internet would soon be restored to hospitals, universities and banks in Bamenda (UN News, 2017).

The pressure increased when, on April 13, the UN Special Representative of the Secretary-General for Central Africa, François Louncény Fall, described the shutdown as a "deplorable situation" and urged Cameroonian authorities "to examine with diligence the difficulties of the populations and entrepreneurs of the English-speaking regions… deprived of Internet since mid-January 2017" (UN News, 2017).

On April 20, the Minister of Communication announced that President Biya had instructed him to re-establish Internet connections in the Northwest and Southwest regions because conditions that led to the shutdown had improved (Cameroon orders internet, 2017). He, however, warned that "the Government… reserves the right to take… appropriate measures to prevent the Internet from being used again to incite hatred and discord between Cameroonians or to threaten public order" (Cameroon Restores, 2017).

According to Jeffrey Smith (Iaccino, 2017b),

> The #BringBackOurInternet campaign generated international interest and condemnation [and] definitely helped lead to the restoration of the Internet. Oftentimes, these repressive governments, those like Cameroon which have operated outside the international gaze, need to be spotlighted and shamed. I think that's what happened here. The Internet block became too costly for the regime.

The "rigorous widespread international campaign by pro-Anglophone activists and advocacy groups" (Jong, 2017) was, therefore, "largely credited for ratcheting up the pressure that forced the Cameroonian government to restore the Internet" (Mukeredzi, 2017) and the #BringBackOurInternet campaign viewed by activists as one "that could serve as a global model for countering government internet meddling" (Africa Roundup, 2017).

To activists, the end of the shutdown was a victory for digital activism. According to Deji Olukotun, who was responsible for Access Now's "Keep It On" campaign,

> This victory is a testament to the persistence, resilience, and strength of the people and organizations fighting to stop internet shutdowns in Cameroon and around the world. We stand together with a unified message to world governments: shutdowns violate human rights, and they will not be tolerated. They cannot, and will not, become the new normal, for the people of Cameroon or anywhere else ("Victory in Cameroon," 2017).

Conclusion

During the campaign to restore the Internet, activists used the #BringBackOurInternet hashtag to inform, mobilize, and reframe discussions about the Internet shutdown, the Biya regime, and the Anglophone crisis. Like #BringBackOurGirls in Nigeria, the #Bring-BackOurInternet campaign "served a journalistic role for a broad audience, a publicity role for activists, and a way to gain the attention of power elites" (Ofori-Parku & Moscato, 2018). It confirmed Olson's view (2016) that "online and offline activism are symbiotic, each strengthening and growing the other" (p. 773), with both converging to "move an issue from the margins and to the mainstream agenda" (p. 776).

The 93-day total shutdown confirmed that shutdowns rarely achieve their goals. The government had assumed that by shutting down the Internet, it would control the narrative about the Anglophone Crisis, shift international and media focus from the crisis, and prevent Anglophone activists from using social media to organize their supporters. It achieved none of these goals because a paradox of Internet shutdowns is that they draw international scrutiny, particularly "widespread media attention, which can increase attention to issues the shutdown may have aimed to obscure" (Global Network Initiative, n.d.). In Cameroon, the shutdown "ended up bringing more unwanted global attention to Biya's recalcitrant government" (Atabong, 2017b), particularly its treatment of the country's English-speaking minority (Searcey & Essomba, 2017).

Another paradox of Internet shutdowns is that they "seem to animate dissent and encourage precisely the kind of responses considered subversive by many governments" (Ogola, 2019). Cameroon's shutdown radicalized the English-speaking community and "greatly reinforced the sense of exclusion" in the community (Caxton, 2017, p. 23). When the shutdown began, the protest movement was dominated by nonviolent pro-federalist groups that coalesced around the Consortium. However, by the time the Internet was reinstated, a seismic shift had occurred with erstwhile marginal separatist groups operating under the banner of the Southern Cameroons Ambazonia United Front (SCACUF), dictating the political agenda ("State Crackdown," 2017).

The lessons of the Internet shutdown were not lost on government officials who realized that a complete Internet shutdown was more trouble than was worth. Thus, when Anglophone separatists declared the independence of Ambazonia on October 1, 2017, the government opted instead for a partial Internet shutdown, specifically targeting social media platforms, notably WhatsApp, Twitter, and Facebook. (Atabong, 2017c). This second shutdown, which lasted until February 28, 2018, drew far less international scrutiny and outrage largely due to its limited nature (and also because it was largely ineffective as users easily circumvented it with free VPN software).

The #BringBackOurInternet campaign laid bare the ineffectualness of the state's repressive machinery and traditional censorship tools in the face of an effective transnational online campaign spearheaded by multi-stakeholder coalitions, and its inability to control political messaging in the online space using traditional communication tools. The government tried to remedy the situation by establishing a more visible Internet presence to influence the prevailing narrative about the Anglophone crisis and the Biya regime. One measure was to ensure that key government ministries such as Defense and Communications establish a more active online presence to counter Anglophone – and opposition – activists. The increasing importance of the online space to the government was highlighted in July 2018 when President Biya shunned traditional and official media to formally announce his intention to seek a seventh term of office, first on his official Twitter account, then on his official Facebook page (Teke, 2018b).

The government's attempt to expand its online footprint was not limited to encouraging state institutions and personalities to go online. It also began to discreetly sponsor and support pro-government activists such as Honneur et Fidélité - Armée Camerounaise (https://www.facebook.com/hfarmee), Ma Kontri Pipo Dem (https://kontripipo.com) and Éloges et bravoures aux militaires (https://twitter.com/ElogeEt) that aggressively promoted the government's "one and indivisible" Cameroon agenda, extolled the professionalism of the heavily-criticized Cameroonian military, and showcased their military victories over Ambazonian fighters (usually spiced up with claims of high body counts and gruesome pictures of dead "Amba Boys"), while trying to discredit the separatist enterprise by routinely sharing videos and pictures of alleged human rights abuses and other "terrorist" activities by Ambazonian fighters, and trumpeting internal divisions within the separatist camp.

To further influence the online narrative about Cameroon, the government established what amounted to an unofficial digital task force of pro-government commentators and trolls charged with flooding social platforms with pro-government and anti-Ambazonian (and anti-opposition) content, challenging negative comments about government, and undermining trust in Ambazonian and opposition activists with misinformation and disinformation (Foute, 2020). Nicknamed the "Tchiroma Trolls," these commentators were particularly active during the controversial 2018 presidential election that the opposition Cameroon Renaissance Movement (MRC) claimed to have won. During these elections, the Ministry of Communication recruited members of the Cameroon Bloggers Association and other" web influencers" to promote the government's "peace and stability" message after the MDR supposedly threatened national unity with its election victory claim. The Minister of Communication also announced plans to establish a Virtual Information Agency, in collaboration with these influencers, to provide real-time and "authentic" information on Cameroon (Massang, 2018).

Pro-government activists also sought to muzzle Ambazonian activists and drastically reduce their online footprint by systematically flagging and having their social media accounts suspended or disabled and their posts deleted (particularly on Facebook) for content deemed objectionable. For example, the original personal Facebook accounts of Ivo Tapang and Mark Bareta, two activists who were at the forefront of the online mobilization of the Anglophone community at the beginning of the crisis, have since been disabled, and the vast trove of archival material that they contained deleted. In February 2020, Facebook deleted two other popular pages belonging to Bareta – Mark Bareta, with over 150,000 followers, and Bareta News, with over 60,000 followers. Bareta subsequently filed a data subject access request with the Ireland Data Protection Commission (Facebook's European headquarters is in Ireland), arguing that the contents of these pages are his personal data and requesting that Facebook give him unfettered access to the data under the EU's General Data Protection Regulation (GDPR) (M. Bareta, personal communication,

October 10, 2020).

This campaign to delete objectionable content online is part of an emerging global trend where, in a bid to control extremist and violent content from groups such as ISIS and to be on the good side of governments, social media platforms are inadvertently deleting evidence of war crimes and silencing activists who are documenting these crimes (Human Rights Watch, 2020; Perrigo, 2020).

In October 2021, The Intercept revealed Facebook's secret list of dangerous individuals and organizations ("Facebook dangerous individuals," 2021), in which the Ambazonia Defense Forces were designated as a Tier Two: Violent Non-State Actor (i.e., an entity that engages in violence against state or military actors but do not generally target civilians"). According to Facebook, Tier Two entities:

> are not allowed to have a presence on Facebook, or have a presence main-tained by others on their behalf. As these groups are actively engaged in violence, substantive support of these entities is similarly not allowed. We will also remove praise of violence carried out by these entities ("Dangerous individuals and organizations," 2021).

The designation of the ADF on Facebook's DIO list, alongside the near complete and systematic elimination of the personal accounts and pages of prominent Ambazonian activists, indicates that Cameroon's repeated attempts to lobby Facebook officials—which publicly began with great Fanfare in 2018 when Facebook officials visited Yaounde to discuss "threats to Internet security in Cameroon," specifically "public security threats" with Cameroonian officials (Atabong, 2018; Ngochi, 2021) - seemed to be paying off.

Like many other governments, the Cameroon government also uses the "fake news" argument to silence and discredit Ambazonian activists and even journalists (Kindzeka, 2018), accusing them of false information, particularly regarding reports about abuses by Cameroonian soldiers. This was the case when soldiers executed women and children in Zelevet in the Far North region in 2018 (Teke, 2018a) and Ngarbuh in the Northwest region in 2020 (Teke, 2020). In both cases, the government eventually acknowledged that the incidents did, in fact, happen after being confronted with evidence mostly from online sleuths ("Cameroon: The Truth Behind a Viral Video," 2018; "Cameroon Government Makes U-turn," 2020). This was a cautionary tale, if ever there was one, that the government's foray into the online space was a tenuous one, bogged down by a continuous reliance on outdated tactics used to get the traditional and national media in line—obfuscation, vehement denials, and threats—that were ineffective and even counterproductive in an era of transnational networks, online information crowdsourcing and open-source forensic investigation techniques.

Acknowledgments

The author thanks Julius Nganji of the University of Toronto, Canada, and Teke Ngomba of Aarhus University, Denmark, for reviewing the manuscript and giving very useful feedback.

References

#BringBackOurInternet: Quand les Camerounais se rebiffent contre la coupure du web en zone anglophone (2017, January 27). https://www.jeuneafrique.com/397978/politique/bringbackourinternet-camerounais-se-rebiffent-contre-coupure-web-zone-anglophone/

#BringBackOurInternet ou la révolte des Camerounais privés de réseau. (2017, January 27). https://www.lemonde.fr/afrique/reactions/2017/01/27/bringbackourinternet-ou-la-revolte-des-camerounais-prives-de-reseau_5070260_3212.html

Access Now. (2021). Shattered dreams and lost opportunities. A year in the fight to #KeepItOn. https://www.accessnow.org/cms/assets/uploads/2021/03/KeepItOn-report-on-the-2020-data_Mar-2021_3.pdf

Access Now. (2020). Targeted, cut off, and left in the dark. The #KeepItOn report on internet shutdowns in 2019. https://www.accessnow.org/cms/assets/uploads/2020/02/KeepItOn-2019-report-1.pdf

AFEX. (2018). Constricting Freedom of Expression Online: Annual Report on the State of Internet Freedom in Africa 2017. Legon, Ghana: AFEX.

Africa highlights: Friday 10 February 2017, as it happened. (2017, February 10). https://www.bbc.com/news/live/world-africa-38862473

Africa Roundup: Cameroon's #BringBackOurInternet succeeds, Nigeria's Cars45.com raises $5M. (2017, May 15). https://techcrunch.com/2017/05/15/africa-roundup-cameroons-bringbackourinternet-succeeds-nigerias-cars45-com-raises-5m/

Agence De Regulation Des Telecommunications (2018, July). Observatoire annuel 2017 du marché des communications électroniques. http://www.art.cm/sites/default/files/documents/Observatoire%20finale.pdf

Anglophone Cameroon marks 50 days without the internet. (2017, March 7). https://www.dw.com/en/anglophone-cameroon-marks-50-days-without-the-internet/a-37841760

Atabong A.B. (2018, September 14). Cameroon has been asking Facebook for help with fake news ahead of a contentious election. https://qz.com/africa/1390219/cameroon-asks-facebook-to-help-beat-fake-news-as-election-looms/

Atabong, A. B. (2017a, February 21). 'Digital refugees', repression and the death penalty – Cameroon's escalating language conflict. https://www.equaltimes.org/digital-refugees-repression-and?lang=en#.XHsNGYhKg2x

Atabong, A. B. (2017b, March 20). Political tensions are growing in Cameroon's troubled English-speaking regions. https://qz.com/africa/936788/cameroons-anglophone-protestors-are-facing-a-government-crackdown/

Atabong, A. B. (2017c, October 01). Cameroon is disrupting the internet in its English-speaking regions to stifle protests again. https://qz.com/africa/1091516/cameroon-internet-shut-down-as-southern-cameroons-ambazonia-protests-grow-in-bamenda-buea/

Attwell, W. (2019, January). Curbing of internet freedoms could affect Africa's digital revolution. https://www.businesslive.co.za/bd/opinion/2019-01-24-curbing-of-internet-freedoms-could-affect-africas-digital-revolution/

Ayong, G. [@ameck98]. (2017, January 28). @GraffiGirl @cfreymeyer Cameroonian's in South Africa storm MTN against internet blackout #BringBackOurInternet #cameroon [Tweet]. Twitter. https://twitter.com/ameck98/status/825428639122595840

Barnard, S. R. (2018). *Citizens at the gates: Twitter, networked publics, and the transformation of*

American journalism. Cham, Switzerland: Palgrave Macmillan.

Biya, P. (2016, December 31). Head of State's New Year Message to the Nation. https://www.prc.cm/en/multimedia/documents/5138-head-of-state-s-message-to-the-nation

Boyd, D., Golder, S., & Lotan, G. (2010, January 01). Tweet, Tweet, Retweet: Conversational Aspects of Retweeting on Twitter. *Hawaii International Conference on System Sciences*, 2, 1657-1666.

Bright, J. (2017, April 30). Tech and politics clash in Cameroon as government restores internet. https://techcrunch.com/2017/04/30/1483467/

Cameroon: 'Hoodlums' Attack and Burn Car of SG of Consortium Dr Fontem Neba. (2017, January 16). https://actucameroun.com/2017/01/16/cameroon-hoodlums-attack-and-burn-of-sg-of-consortium-dr-fontem-neba/

Cameroon: The truth behind a viral video murder (2018, September 28). BBC. https://www.bbc.com/news/world-africa-45681690

Cameroon government makes U-turn on Anglophone massacre in Ngarbuh (2020, April 22). RFI. https://www.rfi.fr/en/africa/20200422-cameroon-government-makes-u-turn-on-anglophone-massacre-in-ngarbuh.

Cameroon maintains internet shutdown despite international outcry. (2017, January 31). https://www.apc.org/en/news/cameroon-maintains-internet-shutdown-despite-inter.

Cameroon orders internet restored to restive Anglophone region. (2017, April 20). https://www.reuters.com/article/us-cameroon-protests/cameroon-orders-internet-restored-to-restive-anglophone-region-idUSKBN17M2EW.

Cameroon restores Internet to English-speaking areas after shutdown. (2017, April 21). https://www.jurist.org/news/2017/04/cameroon-restores-internet-to-english-speaking-areas-after-shutdown.

Cameroonians stage 'silent protest' to demand internet. (2017, April 17). https://www.dw.com/en/cameroonians-stage-silent-protest-to-demand-internet/a-38453649.

Cameroon's hashtag war. (n.d.). https://art19.com/shows/the-take/episodes/392600c2-cc26-429f-ae4a-d0e07f09cca0

Cameroun: #BringBackOurInternet fustige les autorités pour les coupures intempestives du réseau. (2017, January 28). https://francais.rt.com/international/33129-cameroun-internautes-protestent-contre-coupures-internet

Cameroun: Un «fantôme» nommé Paul Biya. (2004, June 10). http://www1.rfi.fr/actufr/articles/054/article_28598.asp.

Caxton, A. S. (2017, September 01). The Anglophone dilemma in Cameroon: The need for comprehensive dialogue and reform. *Conflict Trends*, 2017, 2, 18-26.

Chachra, D. (2017, October 18). Twitter's Harassment Problem is Baked into its Design. https://www.theatlantic.com/technology/archive/2017/10/twitters-harassment-problem-is-baked-into-its-design/542952/

Dahir, A. L. (2018, December 28). Sudan has blocked Facebook, Twitter and Instagram to counter anti-govt protests. https://qz.com/africa/1510229/sudan-shuts-down-facebook-twitter-instagram-amid-bread-protests/

Deibert, R. (2019). The Road to Digital Unfreedom: Three Painful Truths About Social Media. Journal of Democracy 30(1), 25-39. https://doi.org/10.1353/jod.2019.0002

Dreyfuss, E. (2018, July 19). Uganda's Regressive Social Media Tax Stays, at Least For Now. https://www.wired.com/story/uganda-social-media-tax-stays-for-now/

Enonchong, R. [@africatechie]. (2017a, January 22). *#Cameroon govt blocked all internet access in English-Speaking regions Join us in telling them to #BringBackOurInternet #KeepItOn Pls RT* [Tweet]. Twitter. https://twitter.com/africatechie/status/823106771573207040

Enonchong, R. [@africatechie]. (2017b, January 26). @BonaRichard please please join the #BringBackOurInternet campaign [Tweet]. Twitter. https://twitter.com/africatechie/status/824695115524542464

Ethiopia enters third week of internet shutdown after unrest. (2020, July 14). https://english.alarabiya.net/media/digital/2020/07/14/Ethiopia-enters-third-week-of-internet-shutdown-after-deadly-unrest

Facebook Dangerous Individuals and Organizations list (Reproduced Snapshot). (2021, October 12). https://theintercept.com/document/2021/10/12/facebook-dangerous-individuals-and-organizations-list-reproduced-snapshot/

Follow the Hashtag: Cameroon's English speakers demand #BringBackOurInternet. (2017, March 18). https://www.dw.com/en/follow-the-hashtag-cameroons-english-speakers-demand-bringbackourinternet/av-38008779

Footballer turns spotlight on Cameroon's anglophone crisis. (2017, February 14). https://www.ft.com/content/bf8f85d2-f1c9-11e6-8758-6876151821a6

Foute, F. (2020, June 16). Au Cameroun, la «brigade cybernétique» secrète des pro-Biya. https://www.jeuneafrique.com/1001123/politique/au-cameroun-la-brigade-cybernetique-secrete-des-pro-biya/.

France 24. (2017, February 22). #BringBackOurInternet: La bataille numérique au Cameroun anglophone [Video]. YouTube. https://www.youtube.com/watch?v=FTFt1tNahA4

Gbere, S. Cybersecurity. (2019, June 13). Exam Cheats Cited in Three-Day Internet Shutdown in Ethiopia. https://www.bloomberg.com/news/articles/2019-06-13/exam-cheats-cited-in-three-day-internet-shutdown-in-ethiopia.

Gladwell, M. (2010, September 27). Small Change: Why the revolution will not be tweeted. http://www.newyorker.com/reporting/2010/10/04/101004fa_fact_gladwell

Global Network Initiative. (n.d.). The Consequences of Network Shutdowns and Service Disruptions: A One-page Guide for Policymakers. https://globalnetworkinitiative.org/the-consequences-of-network-shutdowns-and-service-disruptions-a-one-page-guide-for-policymakers/

GNI Concerned About Restrictions on Internet Access in Cameroon. (n.d.). https://globalnetworkinitiative.org/gni-concerned-about-restrictions-on-internet-access-in-cameroon/

Goel, V., Kumar, H., & Frenkel, S. (2018, March 8). In Sri Lanka, Facebook Contends with Shutdown After Mob Violence. *New York Times.* https://www.nytimes.com

Graves, L. (January 01, 2007). The Affordances of Blogging: A Case Study in Culture and Technological Effects. *Journal of Communication Inquiry*, 31, 4, 331-346.

GSMA Intelligence. (2020). The Mobile Economy: Sub-Saharan Africa 2020. https://www.gsma.com/mobileeconomy/wp-content/uploads/2020/09/GSMA_MobileEconomy2020_SSA_Eng.pdf

Haski, P. (2017, March 07). Couper internet, nouvelle méthode de répression «soft». https://www.nouvelobs.com/monde/20170306.OBS6146/couper-internet-nouvelle-methode-de-repression-soft.html

Housley, W., Webb, H., Williams, M., Procter, R., Edwards, A., Jirotka, M., Williams, M. (2018). Interaction and Transformation on Social Media: The Case of Twitter Campaigns. *Social Media Society*, 4(1). https://doi.org/10.1177/2056305117750721

Human Rights Watch (2020, September). "Video Unavailable." Social Media Platforms Remove Evidence of War Crimes. https://www.hrw.org/report/2020/09/10/video-unavailable/social-media-platforms-remove-evidence-war-crimes#

Iaccino, L. (2017a, January 09). English speaking Cameroon on 'lockdown' as Operation Ghost Town begins. https://www.ibtimes.co.uk/english-speaking-cameroon-lockdown-operation-ghost-town-begins-1600075

Iaccino, L. (2017b, April 30). Residents in English-speaking Cameroon have access to the internet again as government lifts ban. https://www.newsweek.com/cameroon-anglophone-internet-587734

International Crisis Group. (2017a, August 2). Cameroon's Anglophone Crisis at the Crossroads. https://www.crisisgroup.org/africa/central-africa/cameroon/250-cameroons-anglophone-crisis-crossroads

International Telecommunication Union (2019). Key ICT indicators for developed and developing countries and the world (totals and penetration rates). https://www.itu.int/en/ITU-D/Statistics/Pages/stat/default.aspx

Internet Society. (2019, December). Internet Shutdowns. An Internet Society Public Policy Briefing. https://www.internetsociety.org/policybriefs/internet-shutdowns

Is Cameroon persecuting its English speakers? (2017, January 27). https://www.aljazeera.com/programmes/insidestory/2017/01/cameroon-english-speakers-170127041221360.html

Jacobs, S., & Wasserman, H. (2018). Social media and political violence in Cape Town. https://africasacountry.com/2018/05/beyond-the-smoke-and-flames-of-protest

Jong, Y. T. (2017, May 12). English-speakers mobilize to end their marginalization in Cameroon. https://wagingnonviolence.org/feature/anglophone-movement-cameroon/

Jua, N., & Konings, P. (2004, January 01). Occupation of public space: Anglophone nationalism in Cameroon. *Cahiers D'études Africaines*, 44, 609-633.

Kemp, S. (2020, February 17). Digital 2020 Cameroon. https://datareportal.com/reports/digital-2020-cameroon

Kindzeka, M.E. (2018, November 5). Cameroon Detains Journalists Reporting on Unrest for 'Propagating False Information'. https://www.voanews.com/africa/cameroon-detains-journalists-reporting-unrest-propagating-false-information

Kindzeka, M. E. (2017, January 19). Cameroon Cuts Internet in English-speaking Regions. https://www.voanews.com/a/cameroon-cuts-internet-in-english-speaking-regions/3682688.html

Koigi, B. (2017, August 01). A refugee camp inspires the freedom of speech in Africa. https://www.fairplanet.org/story/a-refugee-camp-inspires-the-freedom-of-speech-in-africa/

Konnelly, A. (2015, January 01). #Activism: Identity, Affiliation, and Political Discourse-Making Twitter. The Arbutus Review 6 (1) 1-16. https://doi.org/10.18357/ar.konnellya.612015

Kouagheu, J. (2017, January 27). #BringBackOurInternet ou la révolte des Camerounais privés de réseau. https://www.lemonde.fr/afrique/article/2017/01/27/bringbackourinternet-ou-la-revolte-des-camerounais-prives-de-reseau_5070260_3212.html

Lange, P. (2008, May). The Case for "Open Access" Communications Infrastructure in Africa: The SAT-3/WASC cable Cameroon case study. https://www.apc.org/sites/default/files/APC_SAT-3Cameroon_20080515.pdf

Massang, G. (2018, October 13). Cameroun: Issa Tchiroma prépare la création de l'Agence virtuelle d'informations avec des influenceurs web. https://www.digitalbusiness.africa/

cameroun-issa-tchiroma-prepare-la-creation-de-lagence-virtuelle-dinformations-avec-des-in-fluenceurs-web/

Mayault, I. (2018, June 02). How a pan-African network of cyber activists has been strengthening democracy online. https://qz.com/africa/1216713/pan-african-activists-network-africtivists-fight-online-to-strengthen-democracy-in-africa/

Mazak, J. and Stetka, V. (2015). Who's afraid of clicktivism? Exploring citizens' use of social media and political participation in the Czech Republic. In Frame, A. and Brachotte, G. (2018). *Citizen participation and political communication in a digital world*. London: Routledge, Taylor & Francis Group.

Meta. (2021, October 24). Dangerous Individuals and Organizations. https://transparency.fb.com/policies/community-standards/dangerous-individuals-organizations/

MINPOSTEL. (2017, January 16). "Declaration by the Minister of Posts and Telecommunications within the framework of the awareness campaign for a responsible use of social media in Cameroon [Press Release].

Mintoogue, Y. [@mintoogue]. (2017, February 22). Samedi 25 février 2017, Place de la Porte d'Auteuil (près de l'ambassade du Cameroun). 14h-18h.#FreeAllArrested [Tweet]. Twitter. https://twitter.com/mintoogue/status/834432269221765124

Monks, K. (2018, January 02). Cameroon goes offline after Anglophone revolt. https://www.cnn.com/2017/02/03/africa/internet-shutdown-cameroon/index.html

Moscato, Derek. (2016). Media Portrayals of Hashtag Activism: A Framing Analysis of Canada's #Idlenomore Movement. *Journalism*. 9. https://doi.org/10.17645/mac.v4i2.416

Morozov, E. (2009, May 19). The brave new world of slacktivism. https://foreignpolicy.com/2009/05/19/the-brave-new-world-of-slacktivism/

Mukeredzi, T. (2017). Uproar over Internet shutdowns. https://www.un.org/africarenewal/magazine/august-november-2017/uproar-over-internet-shutdowns

Muperi, W & Brown, L (2019, January 19). As more Africans reach for web, more leaders reach for 'off' switch. https://www.csmonitor.com/World/Africa/2019/0123/As-more-Africans-reach-for-web-more-leaders-reach-for-off-switch

Nanfuka, J. (2019, January 31). Social Media Tax Cuts Ugandan Internet Users by Five Million, Penetration Down From 47% to 35%. https://cipesa.org/2019/01/%EF%BB%BFsocial-media-tax-cuts-ugandan-internet-users-by-five-million-penetration-down-from-47-to-35/

Nanfuka, J. (2017, January 30). 13 Days Later, Cameroon Maintains Internet Shutdown Despite Global Outcry. https://www.opennetafrica.org/13-days-later-cameroon-maintains-internet-shutdown-despite-global-outcry/

Ndeh-Che, F. [@fnche]. (2017, January 27). Going on now! Abuja protests to #FreeSouthernCameroons at foreign affairs #BringBackOurInternet @prc_cellcom @pr_paul_biya @WirbaJoseph [Tweet]. Twitter. https://twitter.com/fnche/status/824912617538015232

Newsom, D., & Haynes, J. (2014). *Public relations writing: Form and style*. Boston, MA: Wadsworth Cengage Learning.

Ngassa, S. (2017, August 17). The Damage Caused by the 93-Day Internet Blackout in Cameroon. https://slate.com/technology/2017/08/the-damage-caused-by-cameroon-s-93-day-internet-blackout.html

Ngochi, E. A. (2018. August 8). Government officials and Facebook team discuss ways to check cyber crimes. https://www.crtv.cm/2018/08/government-officials-and-facebook-team-discuss-ways-to-check-cyber-crimes/

Odugbemi, S. (2014, February 20). The Dictator's Dilemma. https://blogs.worldbank.org/publicsphere/dictator-s-dilemma

Ofori-Parku, S., & Moscato, D. (2018). Hashtag Activism as a Form of Political Action: A Qualitative Analysis of the #BringBackOurGirls Campaign in Nigerian, UK, and U.S. Press. *International Journal of Communication*, 12, 23. https://ijoc.org/index.php/ijoc/article/view/8068

Ogola, G. (2019, March 08). Shutting down the internet doesn't work -- but governments keep doing it. https://theconversation.com/shutting-down-the-internet-doesnt-work-but-governments-keep-doing-it-111642

OHCHR. (2017, February 10). UN expert urges Cameroon to restore internet services cut off in rights violation. https://www.ohchr.org/EN/NewsEvents/Pages/DisplayNews.aspx?NewsID=21165&LangID=E

OHCHR (2019, January 17). UN expert urges DRC to restore internet services. https://www.ohchr.org/EN/NewsEvents/Pages/DisplayNews.aspx?NewsID=24057&LangID=E

Olson, C. C. (2016, September 02). #BringBackOurGirls: digital communities supporting real-world change and influencing mainstream media agendas. *Feminist Media Studies*, 16, 5, 772-787.

Perrigo, B. (2020, April 11). These Tech Companies Managed to Eradicate ISIS Content. But They're Also Erasing Crucial Evidence of War Crimes. https://time.com/5798001/facebook-youtube-algorithms-extremism/

Reporters Without Borders. (2017, January 25). Government censors coverage of anglophone minority unrest. https://rsf.org/en/news/government-censors-coverage-anglophone-minority-unrest

Ritzen, Y. (2018, January 29). Rising internet shutdowns aimed at 'silencing dissent'. https://www.aljazeera.com/news/2018/01/rising-internet-shutdowns-aimed-silencing-dissent-180128202743672.html

Saka, S. (2017, January 27). #Bringbackourinternet: Les internautes du Cameroun anglophone privés d'Internet [Video]. http://www.rfi.fr/video/20170127-bringbackourinternet-internautes-cameroun-anglophone-prives-internet

Searcey, D., & Essomba, F. (2017, February 10). African Nations Increasingly Silence Internet to Stem Protests. *New York Times*. https://www.nytimes.com

Shirky, C. (2011, Jan/Feb). The Political Power of Social Media. Technology, the Public Sphere and Political Change. https://www.foreignaffairs.com/articles/2010-12-20/political-power-social-media

Snowden, E. [@Snowden]. (2017a, January 25). This is the future of repression. If we do not fight it there, it will happen here. #KeepItOn #BringBackOurInternet [Tweet]. Twitter. https://twitter.com/Snowden/status/824312606596988933

Snowden, E. [@Snowden]. (2017b, January 27). Reports: Cameroon threatens citizens with prison via mass SMS after #BringBackOurInternet campaign. Anglophone internet blackout continues [Tweet]. Twitter. https://twitter.com/Snowden/status/825045034097602560

Sow, M. (2017, February 07). Africa in the news: Protests continue in English-speaking parts of Cameroon, AU summit concludes, and Liberian businesses strike. https://www.brookings.edu/blog/africa-in-focus/2017/02/03/africa-in-the-news-protests-continue-in-english-speaking-parts-of-cameroon-au-summit-concludes-and-liberian-businesses-strike/

State crackdown fuels independence push in Anglophone Cameroon. (2017, October 03). https://

www.reuters.com/article/cameroon-politics-separatists/rpt-state-crackdown-fuels-inde-pendence-push-in-anglophone-cameroon-idUSL8N1MD631

Tande, D. [@dibussi] (2019, January 12). #OnThisDay Jan 12, 2017. #Cameroon govt starts sending phone messages warning citizens of risks of spreading false news online. 5 days later, govt turns off Internet in Anglophone regions. It would become longest Internet shutdown in Africa. #BriingBackOurInternet #KeepItOn [Tweet]. Twitter. https://twitter.com/dibussi/status/1084093208660004864

Tande, D. [@dibussi]. (2017, April 21). Issa Tchiroma-Feb 10, 2017: Internet shutdown will continue for as long as they implement their hidden agenda #BringBackOurInternet #Cameroon [Tweet]. https://twitter.com/dibussi/status/855430845393457153

Tande, D. (2016, November 16). Cameroonian Government Launches Campaign Against Social Media, Calls It "A New Form of Terrorism." *Global Voices*. https://globalvoices.org/2016/11/16/cameroonian-government-launches-campaign-against-social-media-calls-it-a-new-form-of-terrorism/

Tande, D. (2012, September). Time to Rein in the Internet? An Overview of the Battle for the Control of Cyberspace. Paper presented at the joint 16th Highway Africa Conference and Global Forum for Media Development 3rd World Conference, Rhodes University, Grahamstown.

Tande, D. (2011a, March 14). The Digital Disconnect and Misconceptions about "Revolution 2.0". *Scribbles from the Den*. https://www.dibussi.com/2011/03/the-digital-disconnect-and-mis-conceptions-about-revolution-20.html

Tande, D. (2011b, September). Cracking down on the diaspora and dissent. *Rhodes Journalism Review*. 31, 68.

Tande, D (2010, September). Is the Blogosphere the New Public Sphere? What should the Role of the State Be, if Any? Paper presented at Africa Media Leadership Conference, Dar es Salaam, Tanzania.

Teke, E. (2020, February 19). NW/SW: Minister of Communication Refutes allegations against military. http://www.crtv.cm/2020/02/nw-sw-minister-of-communication-refutes-allegations-against-military/

Teke, E. (2018a, July 12). Communication Minister dismiss video attributed to military as fake. http://www.crtv.cm/2018/07/communication-minister-dismiss-video-attributed-to-military-as-fake/

Teke, E. (2018b, July 13). Presidential elections 2018: President Paul Biya's candidacy announced on Twitter. http://www.crtv.cm/2018/07/presidential-elections-2018-president-paul-biyas-candidature-announced-on-twitter/

The Sunday Mail. (2019, January 27). Internet shutdown was tactical: President. https://www.sundaymail.co.zw/internet-shutdown-was-tactical-president

Tkacheva, O., Schwartz, L. H., Libicki, M. C., Taylor, J. E., Martini, J., & Baxter, C. (2013). *Internet Freedom and Political Space*. Santa, CA; RAND Corporation.

Tobor, N. (2017, January 24). Cameroon's government has shut down the Internet in the English speaking regions of the country. https://www.iafrikan.com/2017/01/22/cameroons-govern-ment-has-shut-down-the-internet-in-the-english-speaking-regions-of-the-country/

Tostevin, R. (2014, March 14). Online activism: It's easy to click, but just as easy to disengage. https://www.theguardian.com/media-network/media-network-blog/2014/mar/14/online-activism-social-media-engage

Uganda: One year of social media tax (2019, July 20). https://www.dw.com/en/uganda-one-year-of-social-media-tax/a-49672632

Uganda bans social media ahead of presidential election. (2021, January 12). https://www.reuters.com/article/us-uganda-election/uganda-bans-social-media-ahead-of-presidential-election-idUSKBN29H0KH

UNHRC (2016, July 1). Resolution adopted by the Human Rights Council on the promotion, protection and enjoyment of human rights on the Internet.

UNHRC. (2018, June 29). The resolution on "the promotion and protection of human rights in the context of peaceful protests."

UN News. (2017, April 13). Cameroon: UN envoy encourages authorities to restore the Internet in country's English-speaking regions. https://news.un.org/en/story/2017/04/555382-cameroon-un-envoy-encourages-authorities-restore-internet-countrys-english

Valenzuela, S. (2013). Unpacking the Use of Social Media for Protest Behavior. *American Behavioral Scientist*, 57(7), 920-942. https://doi.org/10.1177/0002764213479375

Victory in Cameroon: After 94 days, the internet is back on. (2017, April 20). https://www.accessnow.org/victory-cameroon-94-days-internet-back/

Wasserman, H. (2017, May 31). The Social is Political: Media, Protest and Change in Africa. https://hermanwasserman.wordpress.com/2017/05/31/the-social-is-political-media-protest-and-change-in-africa/

Weimann, G., & Brosius, H.-B. (2017, January 01). Redirecting the agenda: Agenda-setting in the online Era. *The Agenda Setting Journal*, 1, 63-101.

Woodhams, S. & Migliano, S. (2020, January 7). The global cost of Internet shutdowns. https://www.top10vpn.com/cost-of-internet-shutdowns/

Yang, G. (2016). Narrative Agency in Hashtag Activism: The Case of #BlackLivesMatter. *Media and Communication*, 4 (4), 13-17. https://doi.org/10.17645/mac.v4i4.692

ELEVEN

Killing the Messenger

The English-language Press and the Anglophone Crisis in Cameroon

HANSEL W. NGALA

The media system in Cameroon is unique. In the name of harmonization – some critics would say assimilation –despite its official bilingualism, there really is no separation between the French-language and the English-language services of the government-controlled media, as is the case in Canada, Switzerland and other multicultural countries. The government newspaper, *Cameroon Tribune* is a mishmash of English and French government propaganda pieces written by civil-servant journalists and published side by side with no apparent journalistic, linguistic, or cultural logic. In broadcasting, Cameroon Radio and Television (CRTV) has a radio service that broadcasts in French and English at specific times of the day. The national news in French is followed by an English summary, while English news is broadcast during the period reserved for English programs. The sports department has reporters in French and English. These reporters take turns commenting on each game in each sport. Those who understand only one of the two languages essentially get only half the report in the language they understand. In certain programs, Francophone interviewers ask their guests questions in French, and the guests respond in English or vice versa.

In contemporary times, people need access to information to make the right decisions about the issues that affect their lives. However, governments worldwide have often tried to keep information deemed "harmful," from their citizens. They censor what can and cannot be said on TV, radio, newspapers, or the Internet. Cameroon is one such country with a verifiable history of media censorship. However, given that media freedom is one of the pillars of true democracy (Wasserman, 2013), it is important that citizens in any given country have access to information.

Bourdieu (1992) advanced the idea that journalism is an epistemological field that has, over time, and through acts of resistance against external threats to its independence, as well as internal threats to its values, succeeded in achieving certain "positive entitlements" that it guards jealously, and defends fiercely. From time to time, external and internal forces

306

emerge that seek, for one reason or another, to restrict the scope of freedom of expression of journalists, undermine their credibility or the public trust upon which their profession is grounded, or limit their room to maneuver, as they seek to write the right draft of history. This chapter seeks to examine media censorship in Cameroon. The chapter refers to media censorship instead of press censorship because the word "press" suggests that we are referring solely to the print media. In contrast, the word "media" is a much broader term encompassing all forms of media in physical and virtual spaces (the Internet). The chapter begins with a definition of censorship, then touches briefly on the country's history to better understand how censorship came about in Cameroon. It also gives a brief overview of censorship in Africa before looking at the various ways censorship plays out in Cameroon's media today, emphasizing the role of the National Communications Council (NCC). This national media watchdog is acting as a censor, instead of a regulator. The article concludes by looking at how this has affected the practice of independent journalism in the country.

What is censorship?

Censorship, according to the Oxford Advanced Learner's Dictionary, is a noun derived from the verb *censor,* which is defined as "removing the parts of a book, film/movie, etc. that are considered to be offensive, immoral or a political threat" (p. 230); while Jansen (1988) defines it as:

> … all socially structured proscriptions or prescriptions which inhibit or prohibit the dissemination of ideas, information, images and other messages through a society's channels of communication whether these obstructions are secured by political, economic, religious, or other systems of authority. It includes both overt and covert proscriptions and prescriptions (p. 221).

Censorship is an age-old practice by governments who often claim that the content being censored is for "the maintenance of an orderly state, whereas the underlying motive is to keep the public ignorant of information that can potentially threaten authorities" (Abbasi & Al-Sharqi, 2015, p. 2). Socrates is one of the earliest known victims of censorship. In 399 BC, he was sentenced to drink poison because of his acknowledgment of unorthodox divinities (Abbasi & Al-Sharqi, 2015, p. 3). The origin of official censorship may be traced back to Rome, where, in 443 BC, the office of censor was first established. In 300 AD, China introduced its first censorship law (Newth, 2010).

Censorship in Africa

According to Yang (2016), the Windhoek Declaration, released in 1991 by newspaper journalists from the African continent, is one of the most important documents in the struggle for the freedom of the press in Africa - a situation which remains very dire according to Reporters Without Borders, better known by its French abbreviation RSF, one of the world's foremost authorities in media freedom, who in a prelude to their 2019 press freedom index, stated:

Sub-Saharan Africa has not avoided the latest international decline in press freedom. Hatred towards journalists, attacks on investigative reporters, censorship (especially online and on social networks), and economic and judicial harassment all undermined independent reporting and quality journalism in a continent where press freedom saw significant changes in 2018" (RSF, 2019).

Some significant incidents included the shooting to death of Ghanaian investigative reporter, Ahmed Hussein Suale who was part of a team led by Annas Aremayaw Anas, the award-winning investigative journalist who exposed corruption in the Ghanaian Football Federation. In 2020, RSF, in the prelude to their 2020 Press Freedom Index, stated:

> This 2020 edition of the Index, which evaluates the situation for journalists each year in 180 countries and territories, suggests that the next ten years will be pivotal for press freedom because of converging crises affecting the future of journalism: a geopolitical crisis (due to the aggressiveness of authoritarian regimes); a technological crisis (due to a lack of democratic guarantees); a democratic crisis (due to polarisation and repressive policies); a crisis of trust (due to suspicion and even hatred of the media); and an economic crisis (impoverishing quality journalism) (RSF, 2020).

RSF Secretary General, Christophe Deloire noted that "We are entering a decisive decade for journalism linked to crises that affect its future. The coronavirus pandemic illustrates the negative factors threatening the right to reliable information and is itself an exacerbating factor. What will freedom of information, pluralism and reliability look like in 2030? The answer to that question is being determined today" (RSF, 2020).

Freedom House (2010) also points out that "repressive laws that hinder journalists' ability to do their job, illegal detentions, and other press freedom restrictions" continue to be major issues across Africa. Many countries which scored low on the 2010 RSF ranking on press freedom were African. Eritrea, for example, came at the 178th position out of 180 due to its highly restrictive media laws, with Djibouti at 176, Sudan at 159, and Equatorial Guinea at 165.

RSF explains that "there is a clear correlation between suppression of media freedom in response to the coronavirus pandemic, and a country's ranking in the Index" but clarifies that the Index "is a snapshot of the media freedom situation based on an evaluation of pluralism, independence of the media, quality of legislative framework and safety of journalists in each country and region. It does not rank public policies even if governments have a major impact on their country's ranking. Nor is it an indicator of the quality of journalism in each country or region" (RSF, 2020). The poor performance of the media in Africa is a general phenomenon across the continent – one that is reflected in the media landscape in Cameroon.

Censorship in Cameroon

Cameroon, a country of about 23 million people, is wedged between West and Central Africa. To understand censorship in Cameroon, it is important to know how present-day Cameroon came to be. Modern Cameroon was birthed from the unification of a larger French colony with a smaller former British colony. The country was first a German colony and was later split between Britain and France following Germany's defeat in the First World War. Hence, its colonial heritage can be traced to German, British, and French influences. In fact, Nyamnjoh (2005) states that many outsiders know of Cameroon solely as a former colony of France but that the country also has a lesser-known British colonial past. This dual heritage has influenced legislation in the country and how the media operate in Cameroon. Censorship has been a major issue in Cameroon with the country scoring very low points on Reporters Without Borders' (RSF) press freedom indexes over the years. Cameroon ranked 133 out of 180 countries in 2015; 126 in 2016 out of 180 countries and again fell to 130th out of 180 in 2017 according to the annual Press Freedom Index for those years published by Reporters Without Borders. Earlier in 2020, the country ranked 134th out of 180 countries and territories in RSF's 2020 World Press Freedom Index, three places lower than in 2019. This is because Cameroon has a system of law and disorder where draconian anti-terrorism laws ensure that national security, as defined by the government, takes precedence over the rights of freedom of expression (Eko, 2003).

The issue of censoring the media in Cameroon goes as far back as the country's first president, Ahmadou Ahidjo. Ahidjo was president since the independence of French Cameroun in 1960, i.e., for 22 years, and handed power to his prime minister, Paul Biya, in 1982 (Langmia & Nwokeafor, 2014, p. 129). Biya has been president for more than 42 years as of 2024. Under Ahidjo, the press was muzzled and censored, and only five newspapers and a network of provincial government radio stations that "relayed" (rebroadcast) national news and programming from Yaoundé existed (Gallagher, 1991). Local news consisted of accounts of the actions and pronouncements of district and divisional officers appointed by President Biya or reports of the meetings of the ruling CPDM party. There was no television network under Ahidjo (Bourdon-Higbee, 1975). Private radio broadcasting was also forbidden under Ahidjo, and censorship was the order of the day (Ali, 2017). Ali notes that in June 1962, Ahidjo's government began tightening its hold on all opposition, including the press. Several journalists were arrested, and what became known as the "law of silence" dampened the nation's previous enthusiasm for newspapers. He adds that:

> Before 1960, most reading material in the English-speaking part of Cameroon came from Europe and neighbouring Nigeria. The first two papers to spring up in this part of Cameroon were *Cameroon Times* and *Cameroon's Champion,* both founded on the eve of reunification in 1960. The first press laws in a reunited Cameroon were enacted in 1966, just six years after independence. They led to the closure of many papers" (p. 19).

Tanjong and Diffang (2007) describe the 1966 law as a piece of powerful censorship machinery that authorized pre- and post-publication censorship whereby government officials became "editors-in-chief" as they were supposed to read the papers two hours before publication, and anything deemed anti-government was blotted out or the paper simply suspended."

While under Ahidjo's successor Paul Biya, there has been a plurality of newspapers, radio stations and TV stations, the Committee to Protect Journalists (CPJ) says this multiplicity of media outlets does not necessarily translate to media freedom. CPJ, citing statistics from Cameroon's National Communications Council (NCC), says Cameroon today has a diverse media environment, with at least 600 newspapers, 30 radio stations, 20 television stations, and 15 news websites in operation, but that does not mean information flows freely (CPJ, 2017). Patrice Nganang, a US-based Cameroonian writer and academic, said in a 2013 interview that Biya can claim that newspapers and TV stations are flourishing in Cameroon, "but the consequence of "administrative tolerance" – a practice whereby government allows media outlets to be set up without licenses, is that the police can come down on anybody at any time, and the police do so particularly when those outlets criticize Paul Biya" (Olukotun, 2013). While there is much talk about how the media is free under Biya's regime, (Nyamnjoh, 2005) argues that not much has changed since most of the laws enacted under Ahidjo remain in force today.

National Communications Council (NCC)

The authoritarian government of President Paul Biya has used all repressive means in the book to control, coerce, censor, and silence the private and independent media. The *Commission Nationale de Communication* (CNC), an extra-judicial governmental organization that enforces press laws in Cameroon, routinely suspends journalists and newspapers from publication for signifcant periods of time. The NCC, using the sledgehammer of the Law to crush freedom of expression, imposed a one-month ban on Vision 4 TV in Yaounde for publishing fake news. Ernest Obama was banned from practicing journalism in Cameroon for one month for utterances that the CNC said could be construed as "incitement to tribal hatred and violence."

The National Communications Council (NCC), the country's national media regulatory body, claims to be independent. However, its members are appointed by the Prime Minister of Cameroon, leading some to question how independent it really is (Nyamnjoh, 2005). The NCC is often seen to level sanctions only towards media outlets that publish or broadcast content deemed critical of the regime (Ricchiardi, 2019). It is important to note how much the media has been targeted since the latest phase of the Anglophone Crisis in the country which erupted in late 2016. Lawyers and teachers were protesting the imposition of French-speaking judges in Anglophone courts and the assignment of French-speaking teachers in Anglophone classrooms (Adichie, 2018). Protests, which had been peaceful, turned violent in 2017 when the government outlawed a consortium of teachers and lawyers (Atabong, 2017) and shut down the internet in English-speaking regions for three months – a move which Internet Without Borders described as a violation of human rights and one of the most extended Internet shutdowns anywhere in Africa (Internet Without Borders, 2017).

The Anglophone Crisis and Journalism

The crisis has since evolved into calls for the secession of the English-speaking regions (Essa, 2017). This has been followed by a crackdown by authorities on both the secessionists and the media (Moki, 2018; O'Grady, 2017). Journalists covering the activities of the terrorist group Boko Haram, active in the north of the country, have also been targeted by authorities, and an anti-terror bill enacted in 2014 to fight Boko Haram has been used to silence journalists and censor the media (CPJ, 2017). CPJ has since decried the enactment of the law, arguing that:

> Cameroon is using anti-state legislation to silence criticism in the press. When you equate journalism with terrorism, you create an environment where fewer journalists are willing to report on hard news for fear of reprisal (CPJ, 2017).

Instances of Censorship and Hatred Towards Anglophone Journalists in Cameroon

The major problem for journalists in Cameroon is that the government uses draconian antiterrorism laws to subject journalists to arrest, detention, and physical violence (Cameron, 2020). Indeed, the government uses these laws to prosecute English-speaking journalists, teachers, lawyers and others in Napoleonic military courts where the official language is French, where there is no due process, no independence of the judiciary, and definitely no presumption of innocence. All persons charged with an offense before these military courts are presumed guilty until proven innocent and the burden of proof is upon them. Before pointing out a few instances of censorship in Cameroon, it is important to note that while the NCC's excuse for banning or shutting media outlets is usually that they were "unethical" or "threatened national security" (Ali, 2017), there are a few instances where some were outright unethical (completely disregarding journalistic norms and ethics) and indeed put national security in jeopardy. However, the NCC did not sanction them because they were expressing pro-government sentiments. For example, Banda Kani, a TV personality and a fellow tribesman of Paul Biya made death threats on the life of the US Ambassador to Cameroon, Peter Barlerin, in May 2018 after Barlerin called on Biya who at that point had been president for 36 years, to be "thinking about his legacy and how he wants to be remembered" (Agbaw-Ebai, 2018). The ambassador added that former US President George Washington and former South African President, Nelson Mandela were "excellent role models" Biya could learn from (Agbaw-Ebai, 2018). Kani did not take the diplomat's suggestions kindly and said Barlerin "will go home in a coffin" (Agbaw-Ebai, 2018). The NCC did not call Kani to order, nor was Afrique Media, the TV station that broadcast Kani's hate speech, sanctioned.

State-run broadcaster CRTV was equally so unethical that it brought impostors in October 2018 to pose as election observers for Transparency International after Cameroon's presidential election (Finnan, 2018). CRTV repeatedly aired footage of the trio saying that the elections were transparent despite a nationwide outcry of massive rigging. Again, the

NCC did not sanction CRTV, nor did CRTV apologize for such unethical behavior even after Transparency International's head office in Berlin and the Cameroon office both issued statements saying they had no election observers in Cameroon and that an attempt by CRTV to "knowingly portray non-affiliated individuals as employees of the anti-corruption watchdog is completely unacceptable" (Transparency International, 2018).

Also, no sanction was meted out against *Vision 4* TV journalists Ernest Obama and Jacques Ze who called demonstrating Anglophones "rats" that should be eliminated. Ernest Obama was also not punished for saying in 2017 that the government should plant bombs in schools that "will kill the Anglophones themselves" (Cameroon News Agency, 2017) and stem the growing secessionist movement in that part of the country. Forty-three English-speaking journalists signed a petition to the NCC, which was not promptly addressed. Obama again shocked viewers in March 2019 when, during a live broadcast, he told viewers how to beat up their wives by grabbing their necks (Cole, 2019).

However, there are instances where journalists were simply doing their job but were arbitrarily arrested or targeted by authorities. Below are a few such instances: Ahmed Abba, a correspondent for Radio France International (RFI), was arrested in July 2015 for what authorities described as "complicity" with the terrorist group Boko Haram and charged with "non-denunciation of terrorism" (CPJ, 2015). Abba's "crime" was that he had come in contact with Boko Haram in the course of his journalism and did not inform the authorities about that.

Figure 11.1. Mimi Mefo

Radio Hot Cocoa in the town of Bamenda was banned by the NCC from broadcasting because it ran a show about Anglophone grievances (CPJ, 2017). Filmmaker Achomba Hans was arrested in Bamenda while filming a documentary on the Anglophone Crisis (CPJ, 2017). BBC correspondent for Cameroon Randy Joe Sa'ah was arrested for interviewing a lawyer at the forefront of the Anglophone protests (CPJ, 2017).

According to Muluh (2012), radio stations such as *Magic FM* had their equipment seized for being overly critical of the government or for "instigating" the population to protest against the government. Muluh adds that *Radio Freedom* never went on air as it was banned from commencing broadcasts in 2003, and by the time the ban was lifted in July 2005, the equipment was out of use. In 2018, TV news anchor Mimi Mefo was arrested in October of that year for reporting that an American Baptist missionary who died in crossfire between soldiers and separatist fighters may have been killed by a bullet from a soldier's gun (Kindzeka, 2018; CPJ, 2018). Cameroonian authorities at the time said that such reporting "infringes on the territorial integrity of the Republic of Cameroon" (CPJ, 2018), but CPJ's deputy executive director, Robert Mahoney, countered, arguing that, "The charge of publishing information that infringes on territorial integrity is a laughable smokescreen for censorship, plain and simple (CPJ, 2018).

On November 8, 2018, the *Syndicat National des Journalistes du Cameroun* (Cameroon Journalists' trade Union, SNJ) and the Cameroon Association of English-speaking Journalists (CAMASEJ) issued a public declaration stating that all journalists and media in Cameroon would boycott all government activities for 10 days with effect from November 8, 2018, over the so-called "*affaire Mimi Mefo*." The journalists' union said that the decision to stop covering or reporting any news or event involving the government was taken in protest over the arrest and incarceration at the New Bell Prison in Douala, of one of their members, Mimi Mefo Takambou of Equinoxe TV. Mefo had been charged at the Douala Military Tribunal with "Endangering State security, publishing false news and cyber criminality." She was charged under the "Terrorism Act," which allows the government to court-martial civilians charged with national security and terrorism offenses before military tribunals. These charges carry penalties up to the death penalty (Eko, 2019). In effect, Mimi Mefo got into trouble with the Cameroon government and military because she republished on her Facebook page, reports from the Cameroon News Agency to the effect that an American Missionary, Charles Truman Wesco, had been shot to death by Cameroonian soldiers in Bambui, Bamenda, a town in the English-speaking region of Cameroon, where separatists were fighting for independence for a country they call Ambazonia. After intense pressure from international human rights groups, social media activists, and Equinoxe TV, the government of Cameroon released Mefo after she had spent three nights in jail. During those three days, her colleagues showed a huge portrait of Mefo, and reported that she was not in the studio reading the news because she was in jail for doing her job. The official government television, CRTV, did not mention the fate of Mimi Mefo or the dozen or so other reporters arrested or jailed in connection with the Anglophone crisis in Cameroon (O'Grady, 2018). Also, another Anglophone journalist, Kingsley F. Njoka, was arrested at his Douala home on May 15, 2020, according to *The Guardian Post* newspaper of June 16, 2020. According to the paper, Njoka was whisked off by two men identified as having come from the National Security Headquarters in Yaoundé. As of June 2023, Njoka was still in detention at the infamous Kondengui prison. He had been accused of being a supporter of Anglophone separatists and also of "carrying out acts of terrorism and complicity in the smuggling of arms" (Mughe, 2020, p. 1). On World Press Freedom Day, May 3, 2023, the Cameroon Association of English-speaking Journalists, or CAMASEJ organized a series of conferences in which they highlighted the fact that their colleagues, Thomas Awah Junior, Tsi Conrad, Mancho Bibixy and Kingsley Njoka, were being held at the Yaoundé-Kondengui prison for "threatening" Cameroon's sovereignty.

The reporters were accused of collaborating with Anglophone separatists, but they say they were doing their job as reporters. CAMASEJ said journalists are being charged under the infamous 2014 law on terrorism, which allows the military to arrest and charge reporters with supporting terrorism if they publish articles about the crisis–especially articles about military atrocities that the government does not like. They also get in trouble if they have information that any government or military official considers "sensitive" (Kindzeka, 2023).

Figure 11.2. Arrested Anglophone Journalist charged with terrorism. *The Guardian Post*, June 16, 2020.

The Arrest, Torture and Death of Samuel Wazizi in Military Custody

Samuel Ajiekah Abuwe, also known as Samuel Wazizi, 36, presenter for Chillen Muzik and Television (CMTV), met an even worse fate when he died while in military detention in 2019. Wazizi, who was investigating a Cameroon military massacre of civilians in the town of Ekona, in the Southwest region, was summoned to the police station in Buea and arrested for collaborating with "Amba Boys", Ambazonia separatist militias. He was transferred to a military barracks, and his lawyers and family were denied access to him. He was later transferred to a military installation in Yaoundé. Wazizi was never formally charged in a court of law. All attempts by his lawyer, Edward Ewule, to have Wazizi produced in court failed. According to RSF, after his death, Wazizi "was accused of speaking critically on air about the authorities and their handling of the crisis in Cameroon's English-speaking regions" (RSF, 2020). It turned out that he had died shortly after his arrest in August 2019 from torture-induced injuries, but authorities only admitted to this nearly ten months later, in June 2020, after local and international media reports of his death (Aljazeera, 2020). When reports of Wazizi's death caused a scandal, Cameroon army spokesman Cyrille Atonfack Ngumo claimed that Wazizi was coordinating "logistics for separatist fighters" and denied that Wazizi was tortured but had rather died from "severe sepsis" (Aljazeera, 2020). Human Rights Watch expressed skepticism about this claim in a statement, observing that "No autopsy was performed, and it is not clear on what basis Atonfack made the statement" (Human Rights Watch, 2020).

Figure 11.3. Samuel Wazizi

News of Wazizi's death led to journalists staging a protest at the office of the South West Governor in Buea. However, Governor Okalia Bilai "said only the central government in the capital Yaoundé could tell them what happened to Wazizi" (Kindzeka, 2020). Journalists (wearing face masks because of the coronavirus) in Yaoundé, Douala and Bamenda also staged protests in front of government offices (Kindzeka, 2020; Bambi, 2020; Journal du Cameroun, 2020). After the outcry over Wazizi's death, his lawyers received death threats from unnamed persons. The threats were so severe that the United States Ambassador to Cameroon, Peter Barlerin, wrote a letter to the two lawyers to let them know they had the support of the ambassador as they dealt with the fallout of the death of their client in military custody. This support amounted to "moral protection" for the lawyers. In a separate statement dated 16 June 2020, the director-general for UNESCO, Audrey Azoulay, called for an independent investigation into Wazizi's death, stating:

I am deeply concerned about the circumstances surrounding the death of Samuel Wazizi. I call on the authorities to shed light on the events that led to Wazizi's demise and ensure that any contravention to his rights as a journalist and as a detainee are brought to justice (UNESCO, 2020).

The Human Rights Watch statement quoted earlier further read in part: "The circumstances of Wazizi's death underscore the dangers faced by Cameroonian journalists, particularly those who report on and investigate the crisis in the Anglophone regions of the country," adding that "Under national and international human rights law, Cameroon's authorities have an obligation to account for every death in custody and should conduct an effective, thorough, and independent investigation into Wazizi's enforced disappearance and death. The investigation should be capable of establishing the facts surrounding Wazizi's disappearance and death, including whether he died following torture or other ill-treatment in custody, and identifying all those responsible with a view to bringing them to justice" (Human Rights Watch, 2020). A statement jointly signed by ten human rights organizations and media organizations, among them Amnesty International, the Committee to Protect Journalists (CPJ), Cameroon Journalists' Trade Union and Human Rights Watch on June 9, 2020 called for U.N. Security Council members to take advantage of a June 12, 2020 meeting with the U.N. Office of Central Africa and urge Cameroonian authorities to allow an independent, effective, thorough, and impartial investigation into the circumstances around Wazizi's death. Worthy of mention is the fact that the French ambassador to Cameroon, Christophe Guilhou, told the media after meeting with the country's president (June 5) that he brought up Wazizi's case and President Biya "promised to order immediate investigations to determine the true causes of his death" (Kindzeka, 2020).

Figure 11.4. When Practicing Journalism in Cameroon is a Crime, *The Guardian Post*, June 4, 2020

No action was ever taken to investigate Wazizi's death. No one was held accountable for Wazizi's death, and his body was never released to his family for burial. When his family sued the government requesting that it produce Wazizi dead or alive, the Fako High Court in Buea threw out the case claiming that it did not have jurisdiction over the matter.

Figure 11.5. Court throws out request to produce Wazizi dead or alive! *The Guardian Post*, June 19, 2020.

Anglophone Cameroonian journalist, Moki Edwin Kindzeka who was an anchor for state broadcaster, CRTV and a correspondent for VOA and DW, had been brutalized by security forces who also confiscated his equipment in Yaoundé on June 27, 2020. Kindzeka was accused of being "an 'Ambazonian' pretending to be a journalist" (DW, 2020).

This culture of intimidation of journalists by Cameroonian authorities has made Cameroonian journalists avoid critical reporting and tend to go with versions of events as narrated by officials even when there is clear evidence to the contrary. For example, in 2017, when Monique Koumateke died at the doorsteps of the public Laquintinie Hospital in Douala because upfront payment was being demanded before she could be attended to, the then minister of public health, Andre Mama Fouda told the media that Koumateke "had died 'at least two hours' before arriving at Laquintinie" (Africa News, 2016). Local media ran this version of the story, perhaps fearing reprisals from authorities should they do otherwise. Similarly, when the Organized Crime and Corruption Reporting Project (OCCRP) and the Global Investigative Journalism Network (GIJN) published reports in 2016 that accused Paul Biya of spending over four-and-a-half years at the Hotel Intercontinental in Switzerland since 1982 (his luxurious hotel of choice where each trip, according to the investigative journalists, costs 40.000 USD per day) no media outlet in Cameroon ran the story for fear of being targeted by authorities though it did go viral on social media. The government-owned *Cameroon Tribune*, published a rebuttal, claiming the reports were false and meant to destabilize Cameroon (Freudenthal et al., 2018).

President Paul Biya, who has been described by the BBC as "Cameroon's absentee president" because of his long absences from the country, was also not in the country when a train derailed in the country's center region, killing hundreds. Cameroonians took to social media to lambast the government. The government, shortly after, referred to social media as a "new form of terrorism" (Dahir, 2016). The Internet was later cut off for three months in the country's Anglophone regions, where residents complained of marginalization – a move which became recorded as the longest internet shutdown in Africa (Internet Without Borders, 2017).

Cameroon also does not have an access to information law (Ali, 2017), and coverage of the president's numerous trips out of the country is the exclusive preserve of the state-owned *Cameroon Radio Television* (CRTV) and *Cameroon Tribune* (Amabo, 2015). This means corruption goes unchecked as no one knows precisely what the president travels abroad for; or how much his trips cost. It is also unclear how much the president earns; no one knows how much ministers and governors earn. Public officials do not have to declare their assets before assuming or leaving office. Journalists are forced to speculate on these matters and, therefore, risk having their licenses revoked by the National Communications Council, or they can be jailed or fined heavily if authorities deem their reporting unsavory.

Conclusion

Censorship has made many Cameroonian journalists steer away from investigative journalism because of harsh penalties from the authorities. This has resulted in mediocre journalism, as Freedom House (2010) says that the government uses financial, legal, political, and repressive tools to silence journalists who write or talk unfavorably about it. The result is a timid journalism that refrains from good investigative journalism, practices self-censorship, or is unnecessarily neutral or unnecessarily pro-government. Cameroon has no access to information laws (Ali, 2017) like in the US or South Africa for example and this makes journalists tend to use anonymous sources (Lucas, 2019) and also rely heavily on event coverage as they can have sources at these events easily and also because they can ask for remuneration after covering a story – an unethical practice that has come to be termed *gombo journalism* in Cameroon (Ndangam, 2006). This, in part, owes to the low salaries which journalists earn. According to Muluh (2012), on average, a Cameroonian journalist earns about 50.000 CFA Francs per month (about 86 US Dollars).

Coverage of the president's numerous trips out of the country is the exclusive preserve of the state-owned CRTV and *Cameroon Tribune* (Amabo, 2015). This has allowed corruption to go unchecked, as no one really knows what the president travels for or exactly how much his numerous trips cost Cameroonian taxpayers. CRTV reporters are also not independent, as they are often grafted into the president's official entourage, raising ethical journalistic concerns.

Unless civil society in Cameroon takes a stand to push for legislation that can allow the media to do its job without harassment or interference by the government, corruption will remain unchecked in Cameroon, and most of its citizens will continue to be deprived of the information and services they are entitled to. Cameroon needs to enact legislation that protects its journalists and other media practitioners. A country-wide code of ethics should also be adopted by an independent media body (not the NCC). It would also be good to set up an independent, non-partisan broadcasting complaints commission that penalizes defaulters of journalistic codes of conduct.

Since 2017, the following Anglophone journalists have been arrested and jailed in Cameroon: Tsi Conrad, Mancho Bibixy Tse, Awah Dzenyagha Thomas, and Kingsley Njoka (Kondengui Central Prison). Ojong Joseph was arrested in Mamfe and "disappeared."

References

Abbasi, I. S., & Al-Sharqi, L. (2015). Media censorship: Freedom versus responsibility. *Journal of Law and Conflict Resolution*, 7(4), 21-24.

Adichie, C.N. (2018). The Carnage of the Cameroons. *The New York Times* (September 15). Retrieved from: https://www.nytimes.com/2018/09/15/opinion/sunday/chimamanda-ngozi-adichie-cameroon.html

Agbaw-Ebai, V.E. (2018). French and Southern Cameroons Crisis: In Defence of Ambassador Peter Henry Barlerin, Cameroon Intelligence Report (June 13th). Retrieved from http://www.cameroonintelligencereport.com/french-and-southern-cameroons-crisis-in-defence-of-ambassador-peter-henry-barlerin/

Ali, P. N. (2017). *The Impact of the Government Concealing Information on the Practice of Journalism: A Study of Anglophone Cameroonian Journalists*. Unpublished dissertation, Michigan State University.

Aljazeera (2020). Cameroonian journalist Samuel Wazizi dies in gov't detention. Retrieved on June 30, 2020: Retrieved from: https://www.aljazeera.com/news/2020/06/cameroonian-journalist-samuel-wazizi-dies-gov-detention-rsf-200604194930958.html#:~:text=Army%20confirmation,RSF%20said%20he%20was%20arrested.

Amabo, S. (2015). In Cameroon, press struggles with financial and official constraints. Committee to Protect Journalists (May 4th), Retrieved from: https://cpj.org/blog/2015/05/in-cameroon-press-struggle-with-financial-and-offi.php

Atabong, A. B. (2017). Political tensions are growing in Cameroon's troubled English-speaking regions. *Quartz* (March 20th). Retrieved from: https://qz.com/africa/936788/cameroons-anglophone-protestors-are-facing-a-government-crackdown/

Bambi, J. (2020). Outrage over reported death of Cameroonian journalist Wazizi. *Africanews,* (June 5th). Retrieved from: https://www.africanews.com/2020/06/05/outrage-over-death-of-cameroonian-journalist-wazizi//

BBC News (2018). Paul Biya, Cameroon's absentee president. (October 5) Retrieved from: https://www.bbc.com/news/world-africa-43469758

Berkowitz, D. & Eko L. (2007). Blasphemy as Sacred Rite/Right. *Journalism Studies. 10/2007;* 8:779-797. Retrieved from: https://www.tandfonline.com/doi/abs/10.1080/14616700701504757?journalCode=rjos20

Berlinger, J., (2016). Hospital investigated after pregnant woman dies *CNN* (March 17th) Retrieved from: https://edition.cnn.com/2016/03/17/africa/pregnant-woman-death-cameroon/index.html

Bourdieu Pierre (1994). *L'emprise du journalisme.* (Pressures on Journalism) *Actes de la recherche en sciences sociales.* Vol. 101 (102), (pp. 3-9); doi: 10.3406/arss.1994.3078.

Bourdon-Higbee, H. C. (1975). Cameroonian news media. Cameroon: Preliminary Report on Proceedings Against Detained Journalist Samuel Ajeka Abuwe (2020). American Bar Association (June 5th). Retrieved from: https://www.americanbar.org/groups/human_rights/reports/cameroon--a-preliminary-report-on-proceedings-against-detained-j/

Cameroon News Agency (2017). Over 40 Bitter Anglophone Journalists Petition NCC Over Hate Speech of Vision 4 Journalist on Anglophones. (October, 3rd) Retrieved from: https://cameroonnewsagency.com/40-bitter-anglophone-journalists-petition-ncc-hate-speech-vision-4-journalist-anglophones/

Cole, W. (2019, March). 'Grab her by the neck - the more she talks, the more you press': Outrage after TV show features demonstrations on how to physically abuse your wife in Cameroon. *Daily Mail* (March 7th). Retrieved from: https://www.dailymail.co.uk/news/article-6783197/Outrage-Cameroon-TV-features-demonstrations-physically-abuse-wife.html

Committee to Protect Journalists CPJ (2017, September). Journalists, not terrorists. From https://cpj.org/reports/2017/09/journalists-not-terrorists-cameroon-ahmed-abba-anti-terror-imprisoned.php

Dahir, L.A. (2016, November). Cameroon's government is calling social media "a new form of terrorism" Quartz (November 18). Retrieved from https://qz.com/africa/840118/cameroons-government-is-reacting-to-online-criticism-by-calling-social-media-a-new-form-of-terrorism/

Deutsche Welle (2020). DW correspondent Moki Edwin Kindzeka was on Saturday night part of hundreds of Cameroonians arrested and harassed by security forces. Retrieved on June 30, 2020, from https://www.facebook.com/dw.africa/posts/3112541858827017

Eko (2010). The Art of Criticism: How African Cartoons Discursively Constructed African Media Realities in the Post-Cold War Era. *Critical African Studies,2(4), 65-911*

Eko, L. (2003). Press Freedom in Africa. In Johnston, D. (Ed.), *Encyclopedia of International Media and Communications* (pp. 95-116). San Diego, California: Academic Press.

Essa, A. (2017). Cameroon's English-speakers call for independence. *Al-Jazeera* (October 1). Retrieved from https://www.aljazeera.com/news/2017/10/171001123925310.html

Finnan, D. (2018, October). Cameroon 'fake' election observers mask the truth about reality of presidential polls. *Radio France Internationale* (October 10) Retrieved from http://en.rfi.fr/africa/20181011-cameroon-fake-election-observers-mask-truth-about-reality-presidential-polls

Freudenthal, E., Batchou, F.W. and Tjat, G. (2018). Paul Biya, Cameroon's roaming president. Retrieved from https://www.occrp.org/en/investigations/7653-paul-biya-cameroon-s-roaming-president

Gallagher, D. (1991). Public and Private Press in Cameroon. Retrieved from Retrieved from: http://www.lightningfield.com/cameroon/isp2.html

Jansen, S. C. (1988). *Censorship: The knot that binds power and knowledge.* New York: Oxford University Press.

Kindzeka, M.E., (2023). Cameroonian Journalists Decry Violence as World Observes Press Freedom Day, *The Voice of America.* (May 3). Retrieved from: https://www.voanews.com/a/cameroonian-journalists-decry-violence-as-world-observes-press-freedom-day/7076814.html

Kindzeka, M.E., (2020). Cameroon Journalists Blast Government Silence on Case of Missing Colleague., *VOA News* (June 4th). Retrieved from: https://www.voanews.com/africa/cameroon-journalists-blast-government-silence-case-missing-colleague

Kindzeka, M.E., (2020). Cameroon Military Says Missing Journalist Died in Military Hospital. *VOA News*. (June 6th). Retrieved from https://www.voanews.com/press-freedom/cameroon-military-says-missing-journalist-died-military-hospital

Kindzeka, M.E., (2018). Cameroon Journalist Jailed in Anglophone Unrest. *VOA News* (November 8). Retrieved from: https://www.voanews.com/a/cameroon-journalist-jailed-in-anglophone-unrest/4650515.html#:~:text=A%20popular%20journalist%20from%20Cameroon's,the%20crisis%20in%20that%20region.

Kindzeka, M. E., (2018). Cameroon Detains Journalists Reporting on Unrest for 'Propagating False Information' *VOA News* (November 5th). Retrieved from: https://www.voanews.com/a/cameroon-detains-journalists-reporting-on-unrest-for-propagating-false-information-/4645362.html

Lucas, C. (2019). Press censorship in Cameroon: a cycle of fear. English Pen. Retrieved from: https://www.englishpen.org/campaigns/press-censorship-in-cameroon-a-cycle-of-fear/

Major, A. (1992) "Problematic" situations in press coverage of the 1988 US and French Elections. *Journalism Quarterly*, 69, 600-611.

Mughe, M.P., (2020,). Arrested Anglophone journalist charged with terrorism! *The Guardian Post* June 16, p. 1, p. 7

Muluh, H., Z. (2012). Trends in Private Radio Journalism Practice in Cameroon. *African Journal of Social Sciences* Vol 7 (8), pp 1-18.

Ndangam, L. N. (2006). 'Gombo': Bribery and the corruption of journalism ethics in Cameroon. *Ecquid Novi*, 27(2), 179-199.

Internet Without Borders (2017). New internet shutdown ordered in Cameroon (October 2). Retrieved from: https://internetwithoutborders.org/new-internet-shutdown-ordered-in-cameroon/

Nwokeafor, C. U., & Langmia, K. (2013). *Media Role in African Changing Electoral Process: A Political Communication Perspective*. University Press of America.

Nyamnjoh, F. B. (2005). *Africa's media: Democracy and the politics of belonging*. London, UK: Zed Books.

O'Grady, S. (2019). Divided by Language Cameroon's crackdown on its English-speaking minority is fueling support for a secessionist movement. *The Washington Post* (February 5). Retrieved from https://www.washingtonpost.com/graphics/2019/world/cameroon-anglophone-crisis/

O'Grady, S. (2018). In Cameroon, Journalists are being Jailed on Charges of "fake news." *The Washington Post*, December 16. Retrieved from: https://www.washingtonpost.com/world/africa/in-cameroon-journalists-are-being-jailed-on-charges-of-fake-news/2018/12/15/80bcb5c6-f9ad-11e8-8642-c9718a256cbd_story.html?utm_term=.f465a533fa1d

Olukotun, D. (2013). Five questions with Patrice Nganang, Cameroonian human rights advocate and author. Pen America (March 29). Retrieved from: https://pen.org/five-questions-with-patrice-nganang-cameroonian-human-rights-advocate-author/

RSF (2020). 2020 World Press Freedom Index: "Entering a decisive decade for journalism, exacerbated by coronavirus." Retrieved June 30, 2020, Retrieved from: https://rsf.org/en/2020-world-press-freedom-index-entering-decisive-decade-journalism-exacerbated-coronavirus

RSF (2020). Covid-19 in Africa: RSF joins a coalition of civil society organizations to demand the release of imprisoned journalists on the continent. Retrieved on June 30, 2020, Retrieved from https://rsf.org/en/news/covid-19-africa-rsf-joins-coalition-civil-society-organiza-tions-demand-release-imprisoned#:~:text=April%207%2C%202020-,Covid%2D19%20 in%20Africa%3A%20RSF%20joins%20a%20coalition%20of%20civil,imprisoned%20jour-nalists%20on%20the%20continent&text=Last%20week%2C%20the%20Committee%20 to,journalists%20imprisoned%20for%20their%20work.

Reporters Without Borders. Retrieved from: https://rsf.org/en/ranking/2016

Reporters Without Borders Retrieved from https://rsf.org/en/ranking/2019

Ricchiardi, Sherry (2019, March). Cameroonian journalists face ban on political report-ing. International Journalists' Network, Retrieved from https://ijnet.org/en/story/ cameroonian-journalists-face-ban-political-reporting

Sa'ah, R.J., (2016). Cameroon outcry over razorblade operation to save unborn twins. BBC News (March 30). Retrieved from: https://www.bbc.com/news/world-africa-35877272

Tanjong, E., & Diffang, F. (2007). Journalists' self-assessment in Cameroon: a survey. *Journal of the Cameroon Academy of Sciences*, 7(2), 195-206.

Transparency International (2018, October). International election observers in Cameroon are not affiliated with Transparency International. Retrieved from: https://www.transparency.org/news/ pressrelease/election_observers_in_cameroon_are_not_affiliated_with_TI"https://www.trans-parency.org/news/pressrelease/election_observers_in_cameroon_are_not_affiliated_with_TI

Turnbull, J., Lea, D., Parkinson, D., Phillips, P., Francis, B., Webb, S., ... & Ashby, M. (2010). *Oxford Advanced Learner's Dictionary. International Student's Edition.*

UNESCO (2020). UNESCO Director-General urges investigation into the death of jour-nalist Samuel Wazizi in Cameroon. Retrieved from: https://en.unesco.org/news/ unesco-director-general-urges-investigation-death-journalist-samuel-wazizi-cameroon

Wasserman, H. (2013). Journalism in a new democracy: The ethics of listening. *Communicatio*, 39(1), 67-84.

Yang, A. (2016). Censorship of Media in Africa. (March 2). Retrieved from: https://scholarblogs. emory.edu/violenceinafrica/2016/05/02/censorship-of-media-in-africa/

TWELVE

Chieftaincy Politics and the Explosion of the Anglophone (Ambazonian) Crisis in Cameroon

JUDE FOKWANG

This chapter is a continuation of my efforts to investigate and elaborate on the intercalary position of traditional rulers in Africa, specifically those in the Anglophone regions of Cameroon (Fokwang, 2005, 2009, 2011). Many scholars and activists continue to see traditional rulers as 'decentralized despots' (Mamdani, 1996) with little to offer other than acting as brokers for political capital between an unpopular centralized state machinery and a largely dispossessed rural peasantry (Fisiy, 1995; Jua, 1995). This seems to be the view of a growing number of young activists in Anglophone Cameroon who see no role for traditional authorities in a future democratic autonomous/semi-autonomous Southern Cameroons/Ambazonia, similar to aspirations expressed by activists against chiefly rule in rural South Africa during the final days of the apartheid era (Maloka, 1995, 1996). This chapter revisits Piet Konings' (1999) seminal article, which, two decades ago, examined the thorny relationship between the Francophone-dominated regime of Paul Biya and traditional leaders in the Anglophone regions. In the wake of a separatist conflict raging in the Anglophone territories (now self-declared Ambazonia), it is worthwhile interrogating what positions chiefs have taken, prior to and during the explosion of the conflict. Are there insights in Konings' article relevant to understanding today's crisis? What has changed, and is there a role for traditional authorities in resolving the conflict?

What is the Anglophone Problem?

Contrary to claims in certain academic and political circles, national and international media that the Anglophone problem is essentially a language issue, it is simply stated, a political crisis occasioned by the postcolonial state's failure to manage the relationship between its constituent parts —two former UN-Trust territories, the dominant section previously administered by France until 1960[1] and a smaller portion administered by Britain until

---

1 French Cameroon obtained its independence from France on 1st January 1960.

1961. On 1st October 1961, British Southern Cameroons obtained its independence, and both Cameroons jointly established a federation with limited constitutional guarantees to safeguard the sociocultural and political character of the territory previously administered by Britain and upon independence known as West Cameroon.[2] What has become known as the Anglophone problem initially emerged as far back as 1963 when Bernard Fonlon, a highly influential member of the Kamerun National Democratic Party (KNDP) raised concerns with Ahmadou Ahidjo about the growing marginalization of West Cameroonian leaders in decision-making processes within the Federal Republic.[3] By 1966, Ahidjo's desire for a highly centralized political system was achieved when multiparty politics was abolished in favor of a one-party state. By 1972, the federation was crushed through a highly staged process supposedly to foster national unity between the Francophone and Anglophone portions of the country (Anyangwe, 2009; Chem-Langhëe, 1995; Konings & Nyamnjoh, 1997, 2003; Ndi, 2016). Renamed the United Republic of Cameroon after Ahidjo's so-called peaceful revolution, Paul Biya, Ahidjo's successor in 1982, later renamed the country by presidential decree in 1984 – as the Republic of Cameroon, an act many saw as the final straw against West Cameroon's political identity (also see Ndangam, 2020). It was upon the heels of this executive fiat that Fon Gorji Dinka, a traditional ruler and lawyer, called for the independence of the Republic of Ambazonia (the territory previously known as Southern Cameroons and later West Cameroon) in 1985 (Konings, 1999, p. 185). Thus, the Anglophone problem can be briefly summarized as follows: it is the real and perceived marginalization or state-sanctioned attempts by the Francophone-dominated ruling class to undermine three principal domains of West Cameroonian sociocultural and political heritage: the educational and legal systems as well as the ethos or what Anthony Ndi (2016, p. xxxv) has referred to as the Anglophone moral fiber. A brief examination of one of these domains may further clarify the proper context and understanding of what is meant by the "Anglophone Problem."

Anglophone activists and intellectuals have protested against Francophone efforts to modify or undermine the Anglophone educational system dating as far back as 1983 when Paul Biya issued an executive order introducing French as a compulsory subject in the General Certificate of Education (GCE) without a corresponding requirement for English in Francophone exams (Konings, 1999, p. 184). Anglophone students, parents, and teachers later staged a prolonged struggle for the establishment of a GCE Board headed by a registrar, which was celebrated as a milestone in the preservation of Anglophone educational heritage (Nyamnjoh, 1996). Through another executive order in October 2018, Paul Biya eliminated the position of Registrar and converted the revered institution into a government parastatal[4] – a move that has attracted widespread condemnation, especially in the wake of the military campaign by Biya's forces in the Anglophone regions of the country. A consortium of teachers' trade unions has protested the reorganization of the

---

2 Although Title X, Article 47 (1) of the Federal Constitution states that "Any proposal for the revision of the present Constitution which impairs the unity and integrity of the federation shall be inadmissible," Ahmadou Ahidjo introduced a bill in 1972 seeking the dissolution of the federation (see (Ndi, 2016, p. xxxi).

3 Bernard Fonlon, (1964) *The Time is Now*, a secret memo addressed to Ahidjo.

4 See Presidential Decree No 2018/514 of 22 October 2018.

GCE Board as well as the fact that the decree clearly omits any references to "Anglophone" or the "Anglo-Saxon" character of the erstwhile board:[5]

> The fact that the Board no longer organises only GCE examinations, that it now organises an Advanced Professional Certificate with the possibility that it might henceforth organise more, means that the name "GCE Board" no longer captures the essence of that body. A name like, the "Cameroon Anglophone Examination Board" or "the Cameroon Examination Board" will make more sense. We should make bold to point out, Your Excellency, that we see no reason why attempts are being made to obliterate the word "Anglophone" or the expression "Anglo-Saxon" from our context – these words do not appear even once in the new text, giving the impression that this text, presented as having been born of a well-meaning disposition, might after all have been driven by ulterior motives.[6]

Activists have continued to decry the fact that most institutions of higher education in the Anglophone regions are not only poorly equipped compared to similar institutions in Francophone Cameroon but also that a steady increase in the number of Francophone-enrolled students has contributed to the erosion of the so-called "Anglo-Saxon" standards at these institutions. Most importantly, the appointment of French-speaking lecturers to Anglophone universities with minimal mastery of the English language has exacerbated the situation, pitting Anglophone activists against the Francophone-dominated regime. These concerns prompted members of the Higher Teachers' Trade Union (SYNES) at the University of Buea to join forces with the Anglophone Lawyers' Association to lead a civic protest against the regime between 2015 and 2016.[7] Their efforts culminated in forming the Cameroon Anglophone Civil Society Consortium (CACSC) in 2016. The consortium operated for a couple of weeks, during which its leaders entered into negotiations with members of Biya's government. Unexpectedly, the consortium was banned in January 2017, and its leaders were arrested and charged with treason, amongst other crimes.

What has become widely known within Cameroon and beyond as the Anglophone problem remains a major political challenge for the Francophone-dominated state. These issues have received significant intellectual scrutiny, and lately, more and more activists, politicians, and religious leaders have drawn attention to the plight of the Anglophone

---

5 Anglophone teachers slam Biya over GCE Board reorganization; https://www.journalducameroun.com/en/cameroonanglophone-teachers-slam-biya-over-gce-board-reorganistion/; accessed 12 Nov, 2018.

6 A Memo Addressed to His Excellency the President and Head of State of the Republic of Cameroon, CATTU, PEATTU, CEWOTU, BATTUC, and TAC; undated Memo, published by *Journal du Cameroun*.

7 Anglophone lawyers issued several resolutions to Paul Biya amongst which they demanded that civil law magistrates (Francophones) be redeployed from Anglophone courts and common law practitioners transferred to common law courts (Anglophone Cameroon). These resolutions were widely supported by traditional rulers in both the South West and North West regions as well as journalists and the cross-section of civil society actors in both regions. See "After Gov't Snubs Ultimatum, Anglophone Lawyers Begin Strike Oct 11" *Cameroon Postline*, October 11, 2016, https://cameroonpostline.com/after-govt-snubs-ultimatum-anglophone-lawyers-begin-strike-oct-11/ accessed November 8, 2018.

minority in Cameroon (Konings and Nyamnjoh, 1997, 2003; Konings, 2005; Nyamnjoh, 1996; Ndi, 2016; Atanga, 1994; Eyoh, 1998). In the wake of widespread unrest in the Anglophone regions in November 2016, the Bishops of the Catholic Church in Anglophone Cameroon addressed a 12-page memo to Paul Biya in which they cataloged the plight of Anglophones dating to the ill-conceived Plebiscite that denied Southern Cameroonians the choice of complete independence.[8] Whilst there is significant literature on Anglophone marginalization in socioeconomic, political, legal, and educational issues, there is relatively puny literature on the role of traditional authorities in the articulation/resolution of these concerns. This chapter is an attempt to fill that gap.

Chieftaincy and the Origins of the Anglophone Problem

Konings (1999, p. 189) contends that a full account of Anglophone struggles for autonomy would be incomplete without due credit to the role of chiefs, first, during campaigns for reunification and later federation in 1961. He credits, in particular, the role of Grasslands chiefs (known as Fons) in tilting the balance of the 1959 general elections in favor of the KNDP against the Kamerun National Convention (KNC) led by Dr. Emmanuel Mbella Lifafa Endeley. Whilst Dr. Endeley, an heir to the paramount chiefdom of Buea, who had passed up the opportunity of becoming paramount chief in favor of studying medicine abroad, was generally portrayed by his political rival, John Ngu Foncha, as disrespectful of chieftaincy institutions. Hence, during the campaigns, Foncha and his associates' "main strategy was to portray the KNDP as a party that upheld traditional norms and symbols and the KNC as inimical to tradition and traditional rulers" (Konings, 1999, p. 191). The KNDP leaders "succeeded in winning over the powerful chief of Bali, the most educated among the North Western chiefs who used to be a strong KNC supporter" (Konings, 1999, p. 191). This chief was Galega II, paramount Fon of Bali Nyonga, who mobilized his peers in the Grasslands and the Coastal regions to support the KNDP platform. In fact, the campaign against Endeley's position to join the Nigerian federation was portrayed as so unfavorable to traditional rulers that many Bakweri chiefs, including the paramount ruler of Buea, Chief G.M. Endeley, joined the KNDP. Dr. Endeley unsuccessfully tried to replace these chiefs with those sympathetic to his political platform.

The KNDP eventually won the general elections of 1959 and proceeded to fulfill one of their election pledges, namely, the creation of the Southern Cameroons House of Chiefs in 1960 (Chem-Langhëe, 1983, p. 672). Composed of 22 members, the House was divided into two categories: 4 ex-officio members and 18 elected members. The four ex-officio members were the paramount Fons of Kom, Bafut, Nso, and Bali (now classified as First Class Fons). The House's principal role was to advise the government, and should resolutions emerge from this body, the House of Assembly would debate them.

Following reunification and federation, the Southern Cameroons House of Chiefs became known as the West Cameroon House of Chiefs.[9] It was a casualty of Ahidjo's

---

8 Memorandum Presented to the Head of State, His Excellency President Paul Biya, By the Bishops of the Ecclesiastical Province of Bamenda on the Current Situation of Unrest in the Northwest and Southwest Regions of Cameroon, 22 December 2016, BAPEC/PRES/2016/30.

9 The Federal Constitution recognized and preserved the House of Chiefs although it did not elaborate on

so-called peaceful revolution when the federation was dismantled in 1972[10] and a unitary state established, this, against the wishes of West Cameroonians.[11] With decree 77/245 of 15 July 1977, traditional chieftaincy institutions were reorganized and assigned the role of auxiliaries of the administration. Thus, commenced what Konings refers to as the "bureaucratization of chieftaincy" – that is, the state's quest to align chieftaincy with state administration. One of the consequences of this bureaucratization is that the line between the modern state elite and chiefs has become blurred as both camps compete for pre-eminence as brokers between the central government and the local populations in their various regions or chiefdoms (also see Geschiere, 1993).

With the reintroduction of multiparty politics in 1990, Paul Biya and his surrogates began courting traditional rulers in Anglophone Cameroon.[12] This was initially marked by the high-profile appointment of Fon Angwafor III of Mankon as the First Vice-President of the ruling Cameroon People's Democratic Movement (CPDM) in 1990, following the resignation of John Ngu Foncha, who, ironically, had stepped down from this position on account of the marginalization of Anglophone Cameroonians.[13] Following the launch of the Social Democratic Front (SDF) led by John Fru Ndi, traditional rulers, especially in the North West became divided into pro-CPDM, pro-opposition and supposedly neutral camps. Traditional rulers who were believed to be pro-CPDM in opposition strongholds were often targeted by their subjects or the general population as evidenced by the burning of Angwafor's rest house in Bamenda and the temporary dethronement of Fon Galabe Doh Gah Gwanyin of Bali-Kumbat (Fokwang, 2009). These divisions were further ossified following the All Anglophone Conference (AAC) of 1993, in which a large delegation of chiefs participated. Later, the South West Chiefs' Conference (SWECC) dissociated itself from the resolutions of the AAC. A similar attempt by several Northwestern chiefs led by Fon Angwafor III failed as he met strong opposition from traditional rulers sympathetic to the SDF.

Since the mid-1990s, traditional rulers in both the South West and North West regions have remained torn between further attempts at bureaucratization by the Francophone-dominated state[14] and their efforts, real or perceived, in serving the interests of their subjects either as members of the ruling CPDM or by posing as neutral political actors (Fokwang,

---

their legislative role. See Title IX, Article 38 and Article 40 which stipulates that certain powers may be exercised in matters of legislation by the House of Chiefs.

10 In May 1972, "a presidential decree gave the House of Chiefs a maximum of six months to dissolve itself" (Chem-Langhëe, 1983, p. 673).

11 Ndi expresses surprise "how the entire Federal Republic of Cameroon could have been made to vote in the 1972 referendum over an issue which ten years previously, in February 1961 had involved only a fifth or 20% of the entire Federal Republic of Cameroon" (Ndi, 2016, p. xxxi).

12 Bolstered by his title as Fon of Fons – a title acquired upon his coronation by the Fons of the North West region in 1985, Paul Biya began to expect more from the Fons. They would be relied upon as vote-brokers for the CPDM's dwindling status in the villages and towns in the North West and South West regions.

13 See Foncha's resignation letter. Amongst other complaints, Foncha decried the fact that the people he had brought into the union had been frequently referred to as "the enemies in the house." See Cameroon: Fragile State? *Africa Report* N°160 – 25 May 2010.

14 Since September 2013, traditional rulers in Cameroon are paid a salary from the public treasury, perceived and lauded by traditional leaders as the personal decision of the President, Paul Biya.

2009). Many of the traditional rulers have defended their membership in the CPDM as the most persuasive strategy to channel development funds and infrastructure to their chiefdoms and that, given the patrimonial character of the state (cf. Gabriel, 1999), highly coveted pieces of the "national cake" would only come to regions that demonstrate loyalty and support for the national government and the head of state. This partly accounts for the splits and in-fighting within and between members of SWECC and their North West counterparts, the North West Fons' Union (NOWEFU).[15] These divisions notwithstanding, both SWECC and NOWEFU have remained vocal in their call for the need to address the root causes of the Anglophone problem and for long-lasting solutions.

Chieftaincy and the Explosion of the Anglophone Problem

A few months leading up to the events that contributed to the explosion of the Anglophone problem, 248 chiefs in the South West region met under the banner of SWECC in Kumba and denounced the continued marginalization of Anglophones in Cameroon.[16] Amongst their resolutions, they requested the head of state to respond to the lawyers' ultimatum[17] in order to save the unity of the country and to protect Anglophone institutions. The chiefs singled out the need to preserve the character of the Anglophone educational system: "SWECC humbly urges His Excellency Paul Biya, President of the Republic of Cameroon to urgently enact a law to preserve the distinct characteristics of the educational systems of Cameroon with particular attention to the Anglo-Saxon educational system of the English-speaking regions."[18] They also decried the predicament of Anglophone chieftaincy institutions which are "gradually being turned into a village civil service headed by the Divisional Officers" (SWECC Statement, 2015). The chiefs further called for criminalizing the neglect or non-treatment of English as an equal language in official government business.[19]

A few months after their proclamation on the Anglophone problem, SWECC members met again in February 2016 and, this time, paid homage to Paul Biya and his vision for the country even though the Biya government had addressed none of the items in their June 2015 resolution. SWECC, headed by Nfon V.E. Mukete, paramount ruler of the Bafaw

---

15 Francis Tim Mbom & Isidore Abah, SWECC Presidential Race Turns Hostile after NOWEFU Deadlock, *Cameroon Postline*, August 5, 2016; https://cameroonpostline.com/swecc-presidential-race-turns-hostile-after-nowefu-deadlock/ ; accessed Nov. 7, 2018. I should add that the NOWEFU is largely in disarray following a prolonged struggle for leadership within the association.

16 Ezieh Sylvanus, "SW Chiefs Back Anglophone Lawyers, Want Biya to Address Anglophone Banishment," *Cameroon Daily Journal*, June 8, 2015.

17 See Bouddih Adams & Chris Mbunwe "After Gov't Snubs Ultimatum, Anglophone Lawyers Begin Strike Oct 11" *Cameroon Postline*, October 11, 2016, https://cameroonpostline.com/after-govt-snubs-ultimatum-anglophone-lawyers-begin-strike-oct-11/ accessed November 8, 2018.

18 A Statement by the South West Chiefs Conference on the Implementation of the 1996 Constitution Bearing on the Nature of the State and the Decentralization Process, June 6, 2015. Also note how the 2018 presidential decree on the reorganization of the GCE board has further undermined the "Anglophone" character of the board, something the chiefs would have denounced in light of their memo to the president in June 2015.

19 A bilingual commission has since been created and headed by former Prime Minister, Mafany Musonge. However, this has made little impact in terms of advocating for parity in the official use of English and French. Most official documents are released exclusively in French.

and appointed CPDM-senator, reiterated chiefs' roles as auxiliaries of the government and declared their partnership as one of mutual benefit for both the government and the peoples:

> As custodians of traditions handed to us by our ancestors, and auxiliaries of the administration within our chiefdoms, even before these authorities were instituted, we do remind the State authorities not to forget so soon that we are, and, have always been, inseparable partners in nation building. They cannot do without the royal fathers who we are. Neither can we, in the present context of coexistence, also do without the administrative authorities. We are interdependent in a win-win partnership.[20]

Given the tide of events in October 2016, which rapidly culminated in the explosion of the Anglophone problem, a preliminary assessment of the developments in Anglophone Cameroon since October 2016 reveals that the aspired "win-win partnership" between chiefs and government authorities echoed by Mukete has not materialized. Three broad developments are worth highlighting in this chapter: a) that the ongoing crises has left many traditional rulers vulnerable to violence at the hands of both government and separatist forces, b) the explosion of the crisis has exacerbated some of the divisions and contestations for power within chieftaincy associations and finally c) the escalation of the Anglophone crisis has provided further opportunity for some chiefs and their associations to assert their claims for legitimacy as "genuine" representatives of their peoples in their advocacy to state authorities to address the root causes of the conflict.

Violence Against Traditional Rulers

In the summer of 2018, the Fon of Bali, Ganyonga III, an appointed senator in the Cameroon parliament, feared for his safety and his family and arranged for their evacuation to a safe location outside the kingdom. Ganyonga's unexpected departure from Bali sent shockwaves among subjects in the kingdom and the Bali diaspora, including North America. As heir to the highly celebrated Galega II, and one of the few leaders classified as a "first-class Fon," his departure was widely condemned by both his subjects and Anglophones in general.[21]

Soon after Ganyonga vacated his palace and sought refuge in Yaoundé, the Fon of Nso, another high-profile traditional ruler, was evacuated by a military helicopter on the pretext that he needed medical attention. Before his departure, he had refused to make any public statements as both government elite and separatist forces canvassed his support for their respective positions. Defenders of the Fon of Nso allege that one of his cousins, who

---

20 Maxcel Fokwen, "Nfon Mukete Rallies Southwest Chiefs to Support Biya", *Cameroon Postline*, February 15, 2016; https://cameroonpostline.com/nfon-mukete-rallies-southwest-chiefs-to-support-biya accessed Nov. 7, 2018.

21 Many see this as an abomination of sorts, given that the palace has never been vacated since the founding of the kingdom in the mid 19th century. On May 22, 2020 a video was issued by Ganyonga in which he stated that he had returned to the palace and that his doors were open to every subject interested in discussing the welfare of Bali.

had joined an Ambazonian separatist group, was determined to use the conflict to settle scores with the Fon. A rumor circulated on social media that the Fon had carried out a major sacrifice at which an unnamed virgin was killed, allegedly to neutralize the growing power of the Ambazonian fighters. Ambazonian fighters proceeded to avenge the death of the unnamed virgin by killing two of the Fon's sons and threatening his life as well. These events, his defenders contend, precipitated the Fon's evacuation from his kingdom.[22]

Of the classified first-class kingdoms in the North West region, only the Fon of Kom and Bafut have maintained residency in their kingdoms. The Fon of Kom, for example, reportedly refused to meet with a visiting general of the Cameroon army and sought to know through an intermediary why soldiers had been deployed to his kingdom. As tensions increased in the lead-up to the October 7, 2018, presidential election, the Fon of Bafut was allegedly abducted by unidentified gunmen and later returned to his palace.[23] Government forces later stormed his palace, following a tip-off that he was allegedly, providing a haven for separatist forces. Eventually, photos of the palace gates ridden with bullets were widely circulated on social media, and eyewitness accounts blamed the Cameroon military for the atrocities. The palace and a nearby museum were again looted by Cameroon soldiers in September 2019, this time attracting worldwide condemnation.[24] Earlier in the conflict, a widely circulated video on social media had shown the Fon of Bafut stating that as king, he would always side with his people against all outside forces:

> This palace belongs to the Bafut people. If anyone has any worry of any sort, the palace is where he or she will run to. I am pleased that you people have assembled here this morning to state your grievances against the government of Cameroon. I am equally pleased that you have done this peacefully, without any destruction and without holding any weapons. The announcement I am making is that I have heard you people. I want to make it very clear that I am the Fon of Bafut and I will never betray the Bafut people.[25]

Fons or chiefs in both Anglophone regions with less prestigious ranks have not been so lucky in the ongoing conflict. The Fon of Oku,[26] Sentieh II, for example, was kidnapped by separatist forces for his alleged close relationship with Philemon Yang, Cameroon's Prime Minister at the time.[27] His kidnappers submitted a long list of demands to the Prime

22 Joe Dinga Pefok, "Why Did Fons of Mankon, Bafut, Kom, Others Not Attend National Dialogue?" Oct 3, 2019, *Cameroon Postline*, http://www.cameroonpostline.com/why-did-fons-of-mankon-bafut-kom-others-not-attend-national-dialogue/ accessed Nov 18, 2019.

23 "Fon of Bafut released after hours in captivity", September 5, 2018, *Journal du Cameroun*, https://www.journalducameroun.com/en/fon-bafut-released-hours-captivity/ accessed, Nov. 7, 2018.

24 See "Statement Concerning Destruction of Cultural Patrimony in Bafut" by the Arts Council of the African Studies Association (ACASA), 20 November 2019.

25 Translated from the Bafut by Neba N.

26 A small kingdom in Bui division of the North west region, hometown of the former Prime Minister, Philemon Yang.

27 "Cameroon: Separatists kidnap Fon of Oku", August 31, 2018, *Journal du Cameroun*,

Minister, amongst which they called for the withdrawal of Cameroon's forces from their land and for the Fon to apologize to his subjects for taking sides with powerful elites and the Cameroon state against his people.[28] The Fon was eventually released after ten days in captivity.[29]

When the conflict took a turn for the worse in January 2018, many communities and traditional rulers became internally displaced persons. Since then, many citizens and traditional rulers have sought refuge in forests or remote areas.[30] Many traditional rulers report threats to their lives[31] and many like Ganyonga of Bali have left their palaces for safer abodes. Dozens of chiefs in the Meme Division of the South West region, for instance, who themselves were living in hideouts, were requested by the local Francophone administrator to convince their subjects to leave their hideouts in the forests. Their sense of insecurity seemed justified, given the murder of a local chief in Ngongo Bakundu village in January 2018.[32] At a meeting with local government administrators, the chiefs condemned the killings and burning but told the administrator that the task of trying to convince their subjects to come out of the forest was akin to a suicide mission.[33] The chiefs, conscious of the inability to exercise their powers as "auxiliaries of the administration," pressed instead for implementing the 1996 constitution, which requires the existing ten regions to be decentralized into semi-autonomous regions.

In July 2018, more news about kidnapped traditional rulers was reported in both print and social media. Eight chiefs were kidnapped in Buea, including Chief Njombe Njoke, 34, a second-class chief who was also vying for the presidency of SWECC.[34] He was recorded

https://www.journalducameroun.com/en/cameroon-fon-oku-kidnapped/ accessed Nov. 7, 2018.

28 "Kidnappers present conditions to PM Yang to release Oku Fon", *Journal du Cameroun*, September 5, 2018, https://www.journalducameroun.com/en/kidnappers-present-conditions-pm-yang-release-oku-fon/ accessed Nov. 7, 2018.

29 "Cameroon: Fon of Oku released", September 9, 2018, *Journal du Cameroun* https://www.journalducameroun.com/en/cameroon-fon-oku-released/ accessed Nov. 7, 2018.

30 Over 600,000 people have become internally displaced. The UNCHR has recorded over 50,000 refugees in Nigeria and others have fled to Europe, the United States and Canada. Anglophone Cameroonian refugees make up a substantial number of persons who have been stuck in Mexico following President's Trump's policy to return all refugees to await the processing of their applications in Mexico.

31 Maxcel Fokwen, "Meme Chiefs to Petition Gov't Over Insecurity, Death Threats", *Cameroon Postline*, 19 January 2018, https://cameroonpostline.com/meme-chiefs-to-petition-govt-over-insecurity-death-threats/ accessed Nov. 7, 2018. This followed the murder of Chief Johannes Ekebe Niongo of Ngongo Village on 12 January 2018 by unidentified gunmen. Also see "SW Chiefs, Minister Want Fleeing Anglophones Brought Back Home" *Cameroon Postline*, 6 April 2018, https://cameroonpostline.com/sw-chiefs-minister-want-fleeing-anglophones-brought-back home/ accessed Nov. 7, 2018.

32 Maxcel Fokwen, "Anglophone Crisis – Chiefs Remain in Hideouts Despite Asking Villagers to Come Out," Cameroon Postline, April 23, 2018, https://cameroonpostline.com/anglophone-crisis-chiefs-remain-in-hideouts-despite-asking-villagers-to-come-out/ , accessed Nov. 7, 2018. Also see, Maxcel Fokwen, "Village Chief Shot Dead, Colleagues on-the-run," *Cameroon Postline*, 15 January 2018, https://cameroonpostline.com/village-chief-shot-dead-colleagues-on-the-run/ accessed Nov. 7, 2018.

33 Maxcel Fokwen, "Gov't Orders Meme Chiefs to Bring Population Out of Forest," 9 April 2018, *Cameroon Postline* https://cameroonpostline.com/govt-orders-meme-chiefs-to-bring-population-out-of-forest/ accessed Nov. 7, 2018.

34 Andrew Nsoseka, "Buea Chiefs Vamoose Following Abduction of Chief Njombe, Others," *Cameroon Postline*, July 17, 2018, https://cameroonpostline.com/Buea-Chiefs-Vamoose-Following-Abduction-of-Chief-Njombe-Others/, accessed Nov. 7, 2018.

in a widely circulated video in which he called for the cancellation of the presidential elections on account of the Anglophone problem:

> The election now is not necessary. To me, it is premature because you cannot come to your house, the tap is bad, there is water all over your house and you start cleaning the carpet without first stopping the flow of water from the tap. So that election is uncalled for. The Ambazonia problem should first be resolved before they can think of any election.[35]

Further reports of a kidnap included the chief of Bukari, a village in the kingdom of Bafut[36] and early in 2019, news was reported about the murder of the chief of Fuh village in Ndu subdivision by Cameroon soldiers. He was accused of leading a separatist group that operated in his chiefdom. Even the highly respected first-class chief of the Bafaw, Nfon Mukete, has not been spared by the conflict. One of his palaces in Konye was attacked and looted by the Ambazonia Defence Forces (ADF), one of the separatist groups seeking to defend the territorial borders of its self-declared state, Ambazonia.[37]

Faced with threats to their lives, some chiefs in Meme Division, South West region, have resorted to altering their dress code in order to blend with those of the general population. Chiefs in this region of the country can be easily spotted with their uniquely decorated hats (often with cowrie shells), ivory necklaces, and "traditional" brooms. Because of their acute sense of insecurity, many chiefs have opted to move about hatless or to minimize, as much as possible, the sartorial and symbolic paraphernalia that tend to distinguish them from their subjects. Questioned about this trend, one of the chiefs responded thus:

> Things have gone out of hand. We didn't expect this…. When people, for no reason, begin to target custodians of tradition, then, it means something has gone out of place in the society. Even enemies of some traditional rulers may want to use this current crisis to settle personal scores.[38]

Evidently, these attacks are not "for no reason" and must be placed within the broader context of the evolution and politicization of chieftaincy in Anglophone Cameroon. It therefore begs the question, why are traditional rulers the subject of death threats, kidnap, and attacks?

A House Divided Against Itself: Chieftaincy and Elite Politics

A major consequence of the bureaucratization of chieftaincy is the proliferation of

35 "Gunmen kidnap eight Fako chiefs", *Journal du Cameroun*, 7 July 2018 https://www.journalducameroun.com/en/gunmen-kidnap-eight-fako-chiefs/ accessed Nov. 8, 2018.

36 "Gunmen kidnap traditional ruler in Bafut," *Journal du Cameroun*, 20 July 2018, https://www.journalducameroun.com/en/gunmen-kidnap-traditional-ruler-bafut/ accessed, Nov. 7, 2018.

37 Maxcel Fokwen, "Fon Mukete's Palace Attacked, Royal Artefacts Looted," *Cameroon Postline*, 9 August 2018, https://cameroonpostline.com/fon-muketes-palace-attacked-royal-artefacts-looted/ accessed Nov. 7, 2018.

38 Maxcel Fokwen, "Anglophone Crisis Makes Chiefs to Stop Wearing Caps," *Cameroon Postline*, 26 January 2018, https://cameroonpostline.com/anglophone-crisis-makes-chiefs-to-stop-wearing-caps/

chiefs' associations. In both Anglophone regions, chiefs are organized into divisional associations and then at regional levels. In the South West region, divisional chiefs' unions constitute the membership of SWECC, and in the North West region, NOWEFU remains the dominant chiefs' association, although it has recently been plagued by factional disputes between rival leaders.[39] I argue that these internal rivalries have undermined their quest for legitimacy both in the eyes of their subjects, the elites with whom they seek alliances, and ultimately with the state. It is precisely on account of their diminished legitimacy that their voices and efforts concerning the ongoing Anglophone revolts have gone largely unheeded.

The bureaucratization of chieftaincy in Cameroon has led to the crystallization of hierarchies amongst chiefs in Anglophone Cameroon. The 1977 chieftaincy decree ranks chiefs in terms of prestige from first-class to third-class chiefs. In the North West Region, for example, only four Fons are classified as first-class chiefs, and in the South West, four chiefs are ranked thus. This bureaucratization has led to contestations for power and primacy between the first-class Fons and hundreds of lesser-ranked chiefs. For instance, following the end of Nfon Victor Mukete's tenure as president of SWECC in 2016, Chief Njombe of Wokaka, Buea, was selected by a faction of chiefs in Fako as a potential candidate to succeed Mukete. Njombe's nomination triggered dissent within the ranks of some chiefs in Fako, many of whom objected to the fact that Njombe was a "third-class" chief and they would not entertain a chief of such low rank to run SWECC affairs, whereas there were more qualified first-class and second-class chiefs to replace Mukete.[40] Due to the Fako chiefs' inability to agree on a single candidate, SWECC floated the idea of giving the Manyu division the option of presenting a candidate to replace Mukete, but security challenges prevented them from convening. These disputes resulted in Mukete holding on to the office of SWECC president for two years, beyond the end of his tenure. Similar disputes led to him holding on to the position of president of the Meme Chiefs' Conference due to security challenges posed by the ongoing conflict.[41]

These associations have often aligned themselves very closely with regional elites, especially in the South West region, where the South West Elites' Association (SWELA) remains a powerful force in negotiating access to state resources (see Paul Nchoji Nkwi, 1997; W. G. Nkwi, 2006; Orock, 2013, 2015). Many of these associations are perceived as bodies whose primary functions, far from catering to the needs of their subjects, generally aim at coveting political and economic benefits for their members. By aligning themselves with elite politics, chiefs have also extended the politics of divide and rule initiated by successive colonial governments and, since independence, by Cameroon's Francophone-dominated regimes (Fokwang, 2019). The basic mechanism of divide and rule in Anglophone Cameroon

---

39 Isidore Abah, "North West Region: Atanga Nji tells Fons to down royal guns, sue for peace" *Journal du Cameroun*, 15 March 2018, https://www.journalducameroun.com/en/north-west-region-atanga-nji-tells-fons-royal-guns-sue-peace/ accessed Nov. 7, 2018.

40 Francis Tim Mbom & Isidore Abah, "SWECC Presidential Race Turns Hostile After NOWEFU Deadlock," *Cameroon Postline*, 5 August, 2016, https://cameroonpostline.com/swecc-presidential-race-turns-hostile-after-nowefu-deadlock/ accessed Nov. 7, 2018.

41 Maxcel Fokwen, "Infighting, Anglophone Crisis Maintain Nfon Mukete as SWECC President," *Cameroon Postline*, 26 January 2018, https://cameroonpostline.com/infighting-anglophone-crisis-maintain-nfon-mukete-as-swecc-president/ accessed Nov. 7, 2018.

consists of playing the North West region against its fellow English-speaking province, the South West, in matters of politics and infrastructural developments. Government appointments of personnel from one region often create the impression that this comes at the expense of potential technocrats from the other region, a mechanism that has been particularly salient with the appointment of Anglophone Prime Ministers.[42] The case of the installation of a new Vice-Chancellor (a presidential appointment) may illustrate this point. Disheartened that the new Vice Chancellor, a member of the Iroko ethnic group in the Ndian Division, was replacing Nalova Lyonga, a member of the Bakweri ethnic group in the Fako Division, Fako chiefs boycotted the installation, despite an overwhelming attendance by other members of SWECC. Stunned by this boycott, one of the attendees sought to know what the Fako chiefs would have done if the incoming Vice Chancellor had been from the North West or a Francophone.[43] Chiefs are often fast to galvanize symbolic capital in favor of an appointed son or daughter to high office and to emphasize such kinship in ways that underscore the instrumentalist character of ethnic politics in Cameroon. Thus, amidst the escalation of the Anglophone crisis, members of the North West Fons' Union undertook a trip to Yaoundé in 2018 to celebrate the appointment of Paul Atanga Nji as the first Anglophone Minister of Territorial Administration – the same minister who has been tasked with crushing the Anglophone revolt.

Following the kidnap of the Divisional Officer (DO) for Momo Division in the North West region in February 2018, SWECC and SWELA dispatched a delegation to Batibo tasked with enlisting the support of Momo chiefs in the search for their kidnapped "son." The abducted DO was reported to be from a remote area of the Ndian Division and was the first in his community to hold such an administrative post. Predictably, the chiefs' efforts made no difference, and a new DO was appointed to replace the abducted one. Thus, chiefs and administrative officers have become victims in the ongoing crisis, raising major concerns about the ability of the former to serve as legitimate brokers between their subjects and the state. As auxiliaries of the administration, they are generally seen to be in cahoots with the Francophone-dominated state and, therefore, ill-placed to speak on behalf of their people. Despite this widely held opinion, traditional leaders, through their associations, have continued to voice concerns about the plight of their people, albeit with limited results. Hence, it is worth reviewing the mechanisms through which they have channeled their discontent and what results they have produced, if any.

Chiefs in the Corridors of Power

Following the dismantling of the West Cameroon House of Chiefs in 1972, traditional rulers in Anglophone Cameroon have had no constitutional role in the country other than the much-recited *auxiliaries of the administration*. The return to multiparty democracy in

---

42 See for instance the alternations between prime ministers from the South West and North West regions. In 2018, Philemon Yang from the North West region was replaced as prime minister by Joseph Dion Ngute from the South West region. This alternation also follows a long-standing principle initiated by Ahmadou Ahidjo known as regional balance (cf. P. N. Nkwi & Nyamnjoh, 1997).

43 Andrew Nsoseka, "Cracks Between SWECC, Fako Chiefs Widen," *Cameroon Postline*, July 25, 2017, https://cameroonpostline.com/cracks-between-swecc-fako-chiefs-widen/ accessed Nov. 7, 2018.

1990 also provided chiefs with a new platform to seek relevance as old political actors – despite widespread campaigns for chiefs to exercise neutrality (cf. Fokwang, 2009). Many of these chiefs opted to retain their membership in the CPDM, often at loggerheads with subjects who clamored for regime change by throwing their weight behind opposition parties like the SDF. The creation of the Cameroon Senate in 2013, as provided for in the 1996 constitution, saw the appointment of several traditional rulers from both the South West and North West regions of the country.[44] These appointments are widely believed to have benefitted the chiefs individually rather than their communities or subjects given their reluctance or inability to hold the government to account for the war it declared on the Anglophone populations. In this section, I review evidence of chiefs' articulation of the Anglophone problem, prior to and following the escalation of the Anglophone revolts. Some of the areas in which chiefs have spoken out include the need to revisit the form of the state (that is, the root causes of the ongoing civil war), the need to address gross inequalities in the educational and legal systems as well as issues concerning infrastructural developments in the Anglophone regions.

As previously seen, South West chiefs delivered a very strongly worded statement in June 2015, backing the Anglophone Lawyers who had issued an ultimatum to Paul Biya to resolve the root causes of the Anglophone problem.[45] The nonchalance of the Biya government to the lawyers' ultimatum provoked the escalation of the Ambazonian revolts.

Inspired by the Anglophone Bishops' letter to President Biya in December 2016, the North West Fons' Union (NOWEFU) submitted a similar memo to the President in which they documented what, in their view, traced the origins of the Anglophone problem and why – to use their metaphor - the festering wound had become cancerous. According to Fons, the origins of the Anglophone problem are traced to Ahidjo's abolition of West Cameroon's multiparty political system in 1966. According to them, this was quickly followed by the dismantling of the federal structure in 1972. The "illegal" abrogation of the 1961 Federal Constitutional provisions that safeguarded the status of the Anglophone minority in Francophone-dominated Cameroon remains a watershed moment in Cameroon's political history. The Fons further argued that the government's failure to "respect and implement some of the articles of the various Constitutions that uphold and safeguard what Anglophone Cameroonians came with into the union since February 1961"[46] has led to the "slow but sure destruction of the cultural identity as can be seen in [the] education

---

44 An exhaustive list of all traditional leaders in the Senate is currently unavailable. However, in an address to SWECC by the secretary general of the National Council of Traditional Rulers, Fon Chafah Isaac, stated that 19 members of the senate were traditional leaders, some of them elected and others appointed. 70 senate members are directly elected by their regions and 30 are nominated by the president, Paul Biya. Some of the prominent traditional leaders who were appointed in 2013 are: Nfon Mukete and Chief Anja Simon Onjwo from the South West region and Fon Doh Ganyonga III and Fon Teche Njei II from the North West region. See presidential decree No. 2013/149 of 8 May 2013 which details all 30 appointed senators.

45 Prior to this, South West chiefs in 2009 had threatened to lead a peaceful strike action due to the continued discrimination of Anglophones in Limbe. See Francis Tim Mbom, "Chiefs to Confront Biya on Anglophone Marginalisation" *Cameroon Post*, Monday, May 11, 2009.

46 The Plebiscite itself was held in February 1961 but the official date of Southern Cameroons' independence was 1st October 1961. It remains unclear why the Fons identify the date of February 1961 as their point of origin.

and legal systems"[47] in the Northwest and Southwest regions of the country. Echoing their counterparts in SWECC, the Fons called for general amnesty to all arrested Anglophone protesters, the withdrawal of Francophones from Anglophone courts, and equity in the representation of Anglophones and Francophones in competitive examinations.[48]

One of the traditional leaders who was consistent in his statements about the need to revisit the form of the state was Nfon Victor Mukete. In his submission during a senate debate on a bill concerning decentralization, Mukete advocated the view that only a return to federation and specifically a ten-state federation[49] would bring an end to the civil war that had engulfed the Anglophone regions:

> The system has failed, federation is the only way. Ten states federation so each region can manage its affairs. Why are people afraid of federation? I am not talking like this because the country should be divided. No! I fought very hard for the reunification of Former Southern Cameroons and Former *La Republique du Cameroun*. And I can never destroy it. But the country should be federated. Look at America, South Africa, Switzerland, Nigeria, Canada, Belgium, Germany, Mexico, Russia and Rwanda…. What is all these (sic) nonsense? My people are dying; they are suffering and we are playing games here in Yaoundé. We should be careful. I don't care. Go and tell anybody. Go and tell Paul [Biya]. Quote me anywhere.[50]

In July 2017, members of SWECC also complained to the administration of the University of Buea concerning its admission policy. As the pioneer English-speaking university in the country, the University of Buea also admits French-speaking students who attend a short summer preparatory course in English after admission has already been granted. According to the chiefs and many other activists, the university's admission policy is partial to Francophone students at the expense of Anglophone students, who are often refused admission on the grounds that they failed the English Language subject in the General Certificate of Education (GCE) - Ordinary Level (OL). The chiefs recommended

47 North West Fons' Union Memo to President Biya

48 Yerima Kini Nsom, February 13, 2017, Issues at Stake: The Fons' Voice of Reason, *Cameroon Postline*; https://comeroonpostline.com/issues-at-stake-the-fons-voice-of-reason/ accessed Nov. 7, 2018.

49 Whilst some, like Mukete and SWECC have advocated a ten-state federation as a solution to the crisis, others have advocated a return to the two-state federation as it were in 1961. There is no consensus amongst chiefs as to what sort of federation would be ideal for Anglophones. None of the chiefs have publicly supported the separatists' efforts to seek complete autonomy from the Cameroon Republic.

50 Mukete also granted an interview to the legendary French-language magazine *Jeune Afrique* in which in reiterated his call for a ten-state federation. In a rare admission, he also suggested that the creation of the National Commission for the Promotion of Bilingualism and Multiculturalism, set up in January 2017 had come a little too late. He further stated that "None of the different English-speaking prime ministers in this country has ever been sufficiently honest or courageous to sound the warning bells and try to limit frustrations." "Ten-State Federation is solution to Anglophone crisis - Chief Mukete" *Journal du Cameroun*, February 19, 2018; https://www.journalducameroun.com/en/ten-state-federation-solution-anglophone-crisis-chief-mukete/, accessed May 28, 2020. Also see "Cameroon: Will parliament finally discuss Anglophone problem?" *Journal du Cameroun*, 10 June 2019 https://www.journalducameroun.com/en/cameroon-will-parliament-finally-discuss-anglophone-problem/ accessed May 28, 2020.

that Anglophones seeking admission with an English Language pass at the GCE should be granted the same opportunity as Francophones in the summer preparatory course.[51] A few months after the chiefs' request, the University of Buea revised its admission policy with respect to the status of the English Language in the GCE. In preparation for the 2017-2018 academic year, the university put out a statement encouraging Anglophone applicants, including those who had not obtained a pass in the English Language at the GCE Ordinary Level, to submit their applications for admission to the University of Buea.[52]

One of the central issues of the Anglophone problem concerns the gross neglect in developing the regions' infrastructure, especially in the South West region from where a substantial amount of the country's GDP is extracted.[53] One of these infrastructural projects is the promised Limbe Deep Seaport, whose status has been pending for over two decades. In the wake of the Anglophone revolts, chiefs from the city of Limbe headed by Otto Molungu submitted a memo to the government in which they requested the immediate construction of the promised seaport – as a show of good faith if indeed the government were interested in resolving the Anglophone problem.[54] The chiefs further requested that English be the exclusive language of instruction in government-run professional schools in the English-speaking regions.[55] Currently, French is the exclusive language of instruction in all four government professional schools in the South West region. Besides the chiefs of Limbe, many other chieftaincy associations, especially in the South West, have continued to put out statements calling for a general amnesty to separatist forces and, subsequently, for an all-inclusive dialogue.[56] Along with elites from their respective divisions or regions,

51 Andrew Nsoseka, "SW Chiefs Decry Anglophone Marginalisation in UB," *Cameroon Postline*, 21 July 2017; https://cameroonpostline.com/sw-chiefs-decry-anglophone-marginalisation-in-ub/ accessed Nov. 7, 2018.

52 However, applicants would be "expected to sit and pass an English Proficiency Test which will be organised by the Department of English, Faculty of Arts, at a cost." Andrew Nsoseka, "Following SWECC's Criticism, UB Adjusts Discriminatory Admission Rules," *Cameroon Postline*, 28 October 2017, https://cameroonpost-line.com/following-sweccs-criticism-ub-adjusts-discriminatory-admission-rules/ accessed Nov. 7, 2018.

53 The region is host to SONARA and the Cameroon Development Corporation (CDC) that traces its origins to German agro-industrial development in the 19th century (Konings, 2003). Whatever remained of the CDC prior to the civil war has been largely decimated.

54 On May 5th, Paul Biya signed decree No. 2020/249 reorganizing the Limbe sea port. It remains uncertain what this development will mean for Anglophones or citizens of Limbe specifically.

55 Francis Tim Mbom & Erna Mouyeme, "Anglophone Crisis Solution: Limbe Chiefs Want Immediate Construction of Seaport" *Cameroon Postline*, 20 October 2017, https://cameroonpostline.com/anglo-phone-crisis-solution-limbe-chiefs-want-immediate-construction-of-seaport/ accessed Nov. 7, 2018. The creation of the Bilingual Commission in January 2017 has hardly achieved anything in the promotion of the equality of both English and French in the conduct of government business – itself a demonstration that the Anglophone problem is far from being just a linguistic problem.

56 Andrew Nsoseka, "Manyu Chiefs, Elite Appeal for General Amnesty, Urgent Dialogue" *Cameroon Postline*, 18 June 2018, https://cameroonpostline.com/manyu-chiefs-elite-appeal-for-general-amnesty-urgent-dialogue/ accessed Nov. 7, 2018. Following repeated calls by the international community for an inclusive dialogue, the Cameroon government staged a national dialogue without first declaring a cease-fire. Although it supposedly brought citizens from all over the country to Yaoundé between September 30 and Oct 4, 2019, the event was largely attended by what some have referred to as IDP-Fons – that is, traditional rulers who were already living in exile, far from their chiefdoms. Also see Joe Dinga Pefok, "Why Did Fons of Mankon, Bafut, Kom, Others Not Attend National Dialogue?" Oct 3, 2019, *Cameroon Postline*, http://www.cameroonpostline.com/why-did-fons-of-mankon-bafut-kom-others-not-attend-national-dialogue/ accessed Nov 18, 2019.

such demands have largely gone unheeded, including a carefully stage-managed National Dialogue that took place without key members representing Ambazonian/Anglophone interests. Regrettably, the Cameroon government seems determined to resolve a political crisis by military means.

Conclusion

This chapter has built on and extended Konings' (1999) findings on the role of chieftaincy in the struggles for Anglophone autonomy in Cameroon. It has examined, in particular, the situation of chiefs and their associations prior to and during the insurgency that continues to wreak havoc in most of the countryside in the Anglophone territories. The chapter reveals that traditional rulers have been the target of violence perpetrated by both the Cameroon military and separatist forces. That local chiefs have been killed, kidnapped, and their properties looted is far from new. What we see today is an increase in the scale and gravity with which such violence is meted out to chiefs, especially those associated with the Francophone-dominated regime. Chiefs have been kidnapped in Buea, Oku, and Bafut while others have fled their palaces, as in Bali and Nso, or killed, as seen in the case of a chief in Kumba and the fon of Fuh village in the Ndu subdivision. Why these attacks, especially in the North West region where chiefs commanded considerable reverence?

One may read these attacks in two ways: first, as a continued diagnostic of the intercalary position of chiefs since they became compromised by the colonizing project (cf. Fallers, 1960). Since the dismantling of the House of Chiefs in 1972, traditional rulers have seen their powers continuously eroded, thanks to their cooptation as "auxiliaries" of an overwhelmingly unpopular Francophone-dominated regime. The ongoing conflict and the fact that they are targeted indexes their marginal position within the hierarchy of postcolonial power, but they also represent a state that has lost relevance in the eyes of the masses. More and more young people are acutely disconnected from chieftaincy institutions whose role they see as mainly self-serving. The politicization of culture or custom has further dealt a heavy blow to the image of those who claim to be the guardians of tradition, given that chiefs are seen to be in cahoots with the elites (see, for example, the Fon of Oku's supposed alliance with the then prime minister, Philemon Yang), or are perceived to be seeking elite status themselves through senate appointments, board membership in government institutions and parastatals. The fact that many of the senatorial appointees from the Anglophone regions are traditional rulers further underscores the view that these traditional rulers have been fully captured by and are serving the interests of the Francophone-dominated elite rather than their subjects.

The above argument may be buttressed by a cursory examination of the relationship between Fon Ganyonga III of Bali Nyonga and his subjects – a relationship that has been strained since the reintroduction of multiparty politics in 1990 (Fokwang, 2009). However, things took a turn for the worse following Ganyonga's appointment to the Cameroon Senate as a member of the CPDM. Prior to the eruption of the conflict, the kingdom's most celebrated festival – Lela – had not been held for several years. Richard Fardon (2006) contends that Lela could be understood as a "barometer of the state of play in Bali politics: a ceremony that has adjusted to reflect the changing composition and external relations of the community" (2006, p. 2). This argument could be extended as follows: Lela's absence over several consecutive years could also index the state of politics – one that shows the growing dissonance between the ruled and the rulers (Fokwang, 2020). This growing dissonance became even more apparent in the council and senatorial election of 2013 when the Fon and the Bali traditional council allegedly enlisted the powers of a revered Bali cult known as the Voma – aimed at coercing his subjects to vote in favor of the ruling CPDM. Remarkably, the Fon also became one of the first traditional rulers to flee his palace once separatist forces established themselves in the kingdom. That chiefs and their allies are attacked by their subjects speaks to the fact that they are perceived to have aligned themselves with elites whose self-serving pursuits have brought nothing but turmoil and further dispossession to the masses.

A second reading of these attacks against traditional rulers falls within the scope of what I refer to as *symbolic dethronement*. Symbolic dethronement operates in two ways – by demystifying the sacred powers of the chiefs through their abduction and by exercising the threat of violence that results in chiefs "downgrading" their dress forms in order to blend in with those of ordinary people. Big men could easily be replaced once their fortunes declined in the precolonial horticultural communities of the forest and coastal lands (Chem-Langhëe, 1983). These decentralized communities had no patience with individuals who failed to meet society's expectations – either in their generosity or ability to mediate in conflict situations. Village members would simply switch allegiance to a new big man. In the Grasslands, chiefs could be dethroned by members of the regulatory society, variously known as Kwifo or Ngumba. These mechanisms for checking the excesses of traditional rulers have all but disappeared, leaving many of them convinced about their invincibility, especially when backed by the brutal power of the postcolonial state. In this sense, Mahmood Mamdani refers to chiefs as *decentralized despots* (Mamdani, 1996) – partly in the sense that they drew their authority initially from the colonial state and now from the postcolonial state. Thus, when young people scorn or refuse these chiefs' directives, they actively resist an institution that has increasingly lost its legitimacy. Here, it is important to emphasize that in contemporary times, few people distinguish between the institution and its office-bearer. In the eyes of many, a despotic ruler undermines the legitimacy of the institution as young people grapple with finding solutions that meet their present needs. It is also against this backdrop that chieftaincy has come to be associated with the things of the "old" rather than as a forward-looking institution. Here, we see parallels with the violent backlash that confronted chiefs in rural South Africa during the final years of apartheid (Fokwang, 2009; Oomen, 2000, 2002, 2005; van Kessel & Oomen, 1997) - when most chiefs were accused of having been lackeys of successive apartheid regimes and that they had no relevance in a post-apartheid democratic dispensation.

If we consider that many traditional rulers are alienated from their subjects, are themselves the target of both symbolic and physical violence, and their associations in disarray, it becomes comprehensible why their memos, open letters, and ultimatums to government authorities often fall on deaf ears. I argue that the internal squabbles that plague chiefs' unions or associations have prevented them from acting decisively as the Anglophone problem erupted into civil war. It is the rare case that their recommendations are considered (such as in the admission policy at the University of Buea).[57] The record is replete with chieftaincy rivalries: first, to occupy offices within their respective associations; to seek relevance in a patrimonial state where allegiance to the state and its functionaries supposedly ensures access to resources and finally; to build alliances with their elites or upstage them in their jostling for power and influence. Hence, chieftaincy politics have not only failed to be decisive in seeking solutions to the Anglophone problem but rather, are widely believed to have exacerbated the problem prior to and during the conflict.

This chapter argues that traditional rulers have not only failed in playing a mediatory role during the conflict but that their track record of aligning themselves with the Francophone-dominated state has largely alienated them from their subjects and the masses in general – a fact that leaves them too tarnished to serve as neutral or trustworthy brokers. Evidently, a semi-autonomous or autonomous Anglophone state would have a constitutional role for chiefs akin to the House of Chiefs prior to its dissolution in 1972. Thus, chiefs, irrespective of their political affiliations, must recognize that they stand to gain as much as their subjects should a negotiated settlement on this conflict be achieved. Chiefs are not only stakeholders in the political process but must galvanize forces within their ranks to act decisively on behalf of their people. This, I contend, would enable them to regain legitimacy and make a case for the relevance of chieftaincy in the 21st century.

References

Anyangwe, C. (2009). *Betrayal of too Trusting a People: The UN, the UK and the Trust Territory of the Southern Cameroons*. Bamenda: Langa Research & Publishing CIG.

Chem-Langhëe, B. (1983). The Origin of the Southern Cameroons House of Chiefs. *International Journal of African Historical Studies, 16*(4), 653-673.

Chem-Langhëe, B. (1995). The Road to the Unitary State of Cameroon 1959-1972. *Paideuma, 41,* 17-25. Retrieved from http://www.jstor.org/stable/40341689

Fallers, L. (1960). The Predicament of the Modern African Chief: An Instance From Uganda. In S. Ottenberg & P. Ottenberg (Eds.), *Cultures and Societies of Africa* (pp. 504-521). New York: Random House.

Fardon, R. (2006). *Lela in Bali: History through Ceremony in Cameroon*. Oxford: Berghahn Books.

Fisiy, C. F. (1995). Chieftaincy in the Modern State: An Institution at the Crossroads of Democratic Change. *Paideuma, 41*

Fokwang, J. (2005). Tribal Innovators? Traditional Leadership and Development in Africa. *Codesria Bulletin, Nos. 3 & 4,* 41-43.

Fokwang, J. (2009). *Mediating Legitimacy: Chieftaincy and Democratisation in Two African Chiefdoms*. Bamenda: Langaa Research and Publishing.

Fokwang, J. (2011). Chieftaincy at the Crossroads: Society and Customary Reform in Bali Nyonga. In J. Fokwang & K. Langmia (Eds.), *Society and Change in Bali Nyonga: Critical Perspectives* (pp. 148-165). Bamenda: Langaa Research and Publishing.

Fokwang, J. (2019). *Alterity as Political Capital: Chieftaincy and the Politicization of Ethnicity in Anglophone Cameroon*. Paper presented at the 62nd African Studies Association Annual

---

57 But even when such is achieved, this cannot be credited to their advocacy only.

Conference, Nov. 20-24, 2019, Boston, MA.

Fokwang, J. (2020). The Cultural Diffusion and Analysis of a Symbol Complex: Lela and its Antecedents among the Bali Chamba of the Cameroon Grassfields. Retrieved from https://judefokwang.com/the-cultural-diffusion-and-analysis-of-a-symbol-complex/

Gabriel, J. M. (1999). Cameroon's Neopatrimonial Dilemma. *Journal of Contemporary African Studies, 17*(2), 173-196.

Geschiere, P. (1993). Chiefs and Colonial Rule in Cameroon: Inventing Chieftaincy, French and British Style. *Africa, 63*(2), 151-175.

Jua, N. (1995). Indirect Rule in Colonial and Postcolonial Cameroon. *Paideuma, 41*, 39-47.

Konings, P. (1999). The 'Anglophone Problem' and Chieftaincy in Anglophone Cameroon. In E. A. B. van Rouveroy van Nieuwaal & R. van Dijk (Eds.), *African Chieftaincy in a New Socio-Political Landscape* (pp. 181-206). Hamburg: LIT Verlag.

Konings, P. (2003). Organised labour and neo-liberal economic and political reforms in west and central Africa. *Journal of Contemporary African Studies, 21*(3), 447-471.

Konings, P., & Nyamnjoh, F. B. (1997). The Anglophone problem in Cameroon. *Journal of Modern African Studies, 35*(2), 207-229.

Konings, P., & Nyamnjoh, F. B. (2003). *Negotiating an Anglophone Identity: A Study of the Politics of Recognition and Representation in Cameroon.* Leiden & Boston: Brill.

Maloka, E. (1995). Traditional Leaders and the Current Transition. *The African Communist, Second Quarter*, 35-43.

Maloka, T. (1996). Populism and the Politics of Chieftaincy and Nation-building in the New South Africa. *Journal of Contemporary African Studies, 14*(2), 173-196.

Mamdani, M. (1996). *Citizen and Subject: Contemporary Africa and the Legacy of Late Colonialism.* Princeton, NJ: Princeton University Press.

Ndangam, A. (2020). *Ceded at Dawn: The Aborted Decolonization of the UN Trust Territory of British Southern Cameroons.* Denver, Colorado: Spears Media Press.

Ndi, A. (2016). *The Golden Age of Southern Cameroons: Vital Lessons for Cameroon.* Denver, CO: Spears Media Press.

Nkwi, P. N. (1997). Rethinking the role of elites in rural development: A case study from Cameroon. *Journal of Contemporary African Studies, 15*(1), 67-86.

Nkwi, P. N., & Nyamnjoh, F. B. (Eds.). (1997). *Regional Balance and National Integration in Cameroon.* Yaounde: African Studies Centre/ICASSRT.

Nkwi, W. G. (2006). Elites, Ethno-regional Competition in Cameroon and the Southwest Elites Association (SWELA), 1991-1997. *African Study Monographs, 27*(3), 123-143.

Oomen, B. (2000). 'We must now go back to our history': Retraditionalisation in a Northern province Chieftaincy. *African Studies, 59*(1).

Oomen, B. (2002). *Chiefs! Law, Power and Culture in Contemporary South Africa.* (PhD Thesis). University of Leiden, PhD Thesis.

Oomen, B. (2005). *Chiefs in South Africa: Law, Power and Culture in the Post-Apartheid Era.* Oxford: James Currey.

Orock, R. T. E. (2013). Manyu youths, belonging and the antinomies of patrimonial elite politics in contemporary Cameroon. *Cultural Dynamics, 25*(3), 269-290.

Orock, R. T. E. (2015). Elites, Culture, and Power: The Moral Politics of "Development" in Cameroon.

Anthropological Quarterly, 88(2), 533-568.

van Kessel, I., & Oomen, B. (1997). 'One chief, one vote': the revival of traditional authorities in post-apartheid South Africa. *African Affairs, 96*(385), 561-585.

THIRTEEN

Caught in the Sickening Crossfire

The Healthcare Sector and the Anglophone Crisis in Cameroon

LYOMBE EKO

"When two bull elephants in musth fight for dominance, the grass and the ants get
trampled."
African Proverb

War is one of the most devastating phenomena against human, animal, and environmental health and safety. War is a destroyer of human beings, healthcare workers, and health institutions. War prevents physicians, who are bound by the Hippocratic Oath, to practice medicine according to professional ethical standards and treat patients humanely and confidentially, from fully exercising their healing crafts. The grim realities of war led the European powers to create the principle of medical neutrality in times of war and civil unrest. The first international convention protecting the wounded and the sick in military conflicts was signed in 1864. The fundamental humanitarian value that underpins the principle of medical neutrality is that medical facilities, medical transports, and healthcare personnel are neutral caregivers who must not be interfered with. Physicians and allied medical workers must be allowed to care for sick and wounded combatants irrespective of the affiliations of these combatants. Furthermore, article 19 of the Geneva Convention (I) provides that medical establishments should be considered sacrosanct and inviolable institutions whose neutrality has to be respected by all in times of war and civil conflict: "Fixed establishments and mobile medical units of the Medical Service may in no circumstances be attacked, but shall at all times be respected and protected by the Parties to the conflict." (ICRC, 2016). The principle of medical neutrality and noninterference with medical institutions personnel and patients in their care applies to international conflicts as well as conflicts that are non-international (Geneva Convention (1), 1949). These principles have been crystallized into international human rights law, international humanitarian law (the laws of war), and medical ethics.

The Anglophone Problem in Cameroon and the subsequent civil war that it degenerated into is a result of the political intransigence of the Biya regime, which opted to use military means to solve a political problem. By failing to discuss and resolve the political grievances of the Anglophone minority, the Biya regime allowed the problem to fester and develop into an armed conflict that engulfed the healthcare sector. That conflict has become the paradigmatic case of manifest, and reckless authoritarian disrespect of medical neutrality, international human rights law, and the laws of war as they apply to an internationalizing conflict. In effect, as a result of the intransigent decision of the Biya regime to opt for top-down cosmetic measures, coupled with a military solution to the essentially political Anglophone Problem in Cameroon, medical institutions in the Anglophone regions became caught in the crossfire of the conflict. As the war progressed, it became clear that the Cameroon military, led by the Israeli-trained and armed *Bataillon d'Intervention Rapide* (BIR), did not have the most rudimentary notion of the Hippocratic Oath, medical ethics, medical neutrality, and international humanitarian law (Edelstein, 1996). The Cameroon military invaded the sacrosanct precincts of impartial hospitals, health centers, and clinics and removed wounded and sick combatants whom they subsequently executed. The Cameroon military also entered hospitals and health care centers from time to time and demanded the full list of all patients treated or admitted into those facilities and forced physicians to violate the Hippocratic Oath by revealing confidential medical information about the nature of their diseases. The Hippocratic Oath requires physicians to make the following oath:

> I will respect the privacy of my patients, for their problems are not disclosed to me that the world may know. Most especially must I tread with care in matters of life and death..." (Lasagna, 1964).

Soldiers also attacked, detained, killed, and wounded healthcare workers accused of treating sick and wounded Anglophone non-state combatants in accordance with their medical ethics. The Cameroon military's practice of invading healthcare facilities and forcefully removing wounded non-state combatants from hospital beds and executing them caused the separatists to accuse the healthcare centers of colluding with the military through identifying wounded separatists and revealing their presence in healthcare facilities. This led the Anglophone combatants, many of whom are not schooled in international law or the laws of war, to threaten, target, and even attack certain healthcare facilities in retaliation. As a result of these egregious violations of international law, governmental public hospitals, religious denominational or mission hospitals, clinics, and health centers, private humanitarian clinics, and impartial international humanitarian organizations all became caught in the crossfire of the battles between the government and Anglophone non-state armed groups, the so-called Amba Boys. Tragically, the medical institutions that sought to bind the wounds of war in the Anglophone Northwest and Southwest regions became part of the theater of the conflict. While Cameroon soldiers imposed a reign of terror and exactions on the people in the Anglophone regions, burnt hundreds of villages as part of their scorched-earth policy, tortured and killed journalists, invaded, and ransacked hospitals and health centers looking for wounded non-state combatants, the independentists blockaded roads throughout the region to enforce anti-government "ghost-town" strikes, and school boycotts. These roadblocks made it impossible for people to travel to healthcare centers. The inhuman actions of the Cameroon military and the Amba Boys transformed the region into a healthcare disaster area (Kongeh, 2019).

Aim of the Chapter

This chapter aims to survey, describe, analyze, and explain the events and occurrences affecting the healthcare sector in Southern Cameroons (the Anglophone Northwest and Southwest regions) in the context of the Anglophone Revolt that began in 2016, degenerated into a vicious conflict between the Cameroon security forces, led by the Israeli-trained and armed *Bataillon d'Intervention Rapide* (BIR), on the one hand, and an assemblage of non-state armed Anglophone groups, ranging from federalists to independentists. The analysis was carried out within the framework of international humanitarian law (Protocol 1, article 3 of the Geneva Convention of 1949 for the Amelioration of the Conditions of the Wounded and Sick in Armed Forces in the Field). This provision of international human rights law sets forth the laws of war protecting civilians in "internal" non-international armed conflicts, "[p]ersons taking no active part in the hostilities, including members of armed forces who have laid down their arms and those placed *hors de combat* by sickness, wounds, detention, or any other cause." The laws of war also set forth the role and place of impartial medical institutions and medical personnel, and their obligation to treat ex-combatants no longer participating in hostilities humanely in all circumstances. This chapter presents several case studies that illustrate the dilemma of a healthcare sector that strives to serve the population amid a terrible humanitarian crisis triggered by the Anglophone Revolt of 2016, the government's repressive reaction to it, as well as the total disregard for the Geneva Convention and the laws of war on the part of the Cameroon military and the non-state armed groups locked in combat in the Anglophone Northwest and Southwest regions of Cameroon. The case studies show examples of brave medical professionals who resisted attempts by the belligerents to transform them into a partial group.

Background: Hospitals and Health Centers in the Crossfire of the Civil War

The healthcare system in Southern Cameroons is part of the highly centralized national healthcare system of Cameroon that is controlled and administered (mismanaged is a more appropriate term) by the Ministry of Health. Cameroon has a historical legacy of missionary medical work on which a highly centralized, French-style bureaucratic medicine has been superimposed. The system is thus an amalgamation of: 1) Poorly funded, poorly equipped, corrupt, and poorly-run government hospitals mismanaged from the center (Yaoundé). These are hospitals and health centers that would probably not be accredited or licensed to operate in most parts of the world, 2) the legacy, pre-independence and pre-unification "mission" healthcare institutions. These are church-affiliated hospitals, clinics, and health centers operated mostly by the Roman Catholic Church, the Cameroon Baptist Convention, and the Presbyterian Church in Cameroon and licensed by the government, and 3) private clinics and health centers of diverse levels of quality and professionalism authorized by the Ministry of Health. In terms of quality, professionalism, and health outcomes, the church-affiliated "mission" hospitals, so-called because they were started by missionaries and religious orders have the best reputation for providing professional and compassionate healthcare to the people at affordable rates.

When the Anglophone Revolt began in 2016, and the Cameroon government responded to demands for political change on the part of lawyers, teachers, university students and members of Anglophone civil society with repression and excessive violence, many of the victims who survived beatings, shootings, arrests and torture ended up in hospitals and health centers. Generally speaking, under international law, healthcare facilities are regarded as safe havens, oases of humanitarian care where wounded combatants seek medical treatment. In some cases, hospitals and health centers are sanctuaries where refugees seek refuge during armed conflicts. Unfortunately, this has not been the case with the ongoing armed conflict in Cameroon. When the Anglophone crisis degenerated into a full-blown insurgency due to the bad faith and political intransigence of the government, the Cameroon military began a policy of raiding hospitals and health centers to capture sick or wounded Amba Boys (armed Anglophone separatists fighting to create a separate state of Ambazonia in the English-speaking Northwest and Southwest regions). Cameroon security forces and Anglophone separatist groups also launched attacks against medical institutions and medical personnel treating wounded and sick soldiers and non-state fighters. German international media organization Deutsche Welle (Kindzeka, 2018) summarized the precarious situation of medical institutions and personnel in the Northwest and Southwest regions as follows:

> …they are being threatened by both sides of the conflict: government security forces accuse them of treating armed fighters and hiding some in hospitals while the armed separatists accuse medical staff of disclosing their [wounded separatist patients'] identities to the military….

An official of the international humanitarian organization, Human Rights Watch, told the German broadcaster *Deutsche Welle,* that medical personnel in the Northwest and Southwest region are:

> caught on the one hand between an insurgency that has been using problematic tactics to advance its goals, and on the other hand, a government that is using scorched earth tactics against anyone they suspect is supportive of the pro-independence agenda… (Kindzeka, 2018).

Eyewitnesses in healthcare clinics and hospitals in the Northwest and Southwest regions confirm that the Cameroon military routinely raids hospitals suspected of treating wounded Anglophone separatists, beat doctors and nurses for treating these hospitalized fighters, and drag the wounded fighters out of their hospital beds and summarily execute them. The United Nations Office for the Coordination of Humanitarian Affairs (OCHA) reported that one such incident occurred at the Baptist Hospital in Mutengene, Southwest Region, on 1st October 2018 (Northwest and Southwest Crisis Report, 2019). After a gunfight between the Cameroon military and Ambazonian separatist fighters, the military raided the hospital in search of patients being treated for gunshot wounds. The military burst into the surgical ward and asked the nurse in charge to identify all patients being treated of gunshot wounds. When she hesitated, the military seized the medical records, read every patient's information, and identified a male patient who was allegedly being treated for gunshot wounds. The patient was dragged from his hospital bed and taken away by the military. The following day, he was found shot to death in Tiko, a nearby town. The Cameroon Baptist Convention Medical authorities declined to comment on the incident for fear of retaliation by the Cameroon military and the non-state armed groups.

In Mbengwi, Momo Division, a husband-and-wife team, Nancy Azah and Njong Paddisco, who were nurses in two different clinics, were shot to death by the Cameroon military in 2019 while they were on their way to attend to people wounded in a clash between Cameroon security forces and Anglophone independentists (Kindzeka, 2018). This was a lesson to all medical personnel who treated non-state actors in the Cameroon civil war. The people of Mbengwi came out in large numbers to denounce the targeted killing of healthcare workers by the military. In another instance, Dr. Roland Fonkwa, a medical doctor at Aduck Health Center in Fundong, Boyo Division, was arrested and detained by the Gendarmerie on suspicion that he had provided medical care to wounded, non-state combatants. The evidence against him was a bag of medications in his car and pictures of known separatist fighters on his cell phone at the time the gendarmes stopped his car. The doctor explained that he had traveled to Bamenda for a meeting, bought the much-needed medications there, and was traveling back to his health center. He said the pictures of the Amba Boys on his phone were essentially a type of *laissez-passer* he needed to pass through their multiple roadblocks. He said that as a medical doctor, he had to be on good terms with all parties in the Anglophone conflict to ensure his health center's and its patients' safety and security. The Gendarmes concluded that by "associating" with separatists and possibly giving them medical care, the doctor had committed a serious crime. He was arrested and taken into Gendarmerie custody. He was locked up at the Fundong Gendarmerie post and denied access to a lawyer or members of his family. His patients were also denied medical care during the period of his detention (Health worker detained for "associating" with separatist fighters, 2020). He was never formally charged with a crime in a court of law, but he was detained for weeks by the Gendarmerie in Fundong. His family members paid bribes equivalent to $250 just to see the doctor and provide him with food. The Gendarmerie in Fundong also ordered his family to pay bribes of more than $4000 for his release "or 6 months of prison." The Gendarmerie seized the medication the doctor had purchased from Bamenda for use in his clinic. Clearly, the Gendarmerie in Cameroon had not heard of the Geneva Convention and international humanitarian law. The arrest and arbitrary detention of the only medical doctor in the area amid the Coronavirus (COVID-19) pandemic worsened the medical situation. The detention also damaged the physician's reputation among the military and non-state armed groups. All attempts to get the Minister of Health, the boss of all public sector doctors in Cameroon to intervene and secure the release of the physician proved fruitless (Mimi Mefo Info, 2020). Dr. Roland Fonkwa is lucky to be alive. Cameroon security forces have been known to kill nurses and other medical personnel in Muyuka, Kumbo, Batibo, Kembong (Manyu), and Njinikom. Ambulances have also been shot at in Bamenda, wounding doctors and nurses. There have also been incidents of military atrocities on healthcare facilities and healthcare workers in Kumba, Mutengene, and Menji in Lebialem.

Figure 13.1. Dr. Roland Fonkwa, medical doctor of the Aduck Health Center in Fundong, Boyo Division, under arrest and handcuffed at the Gendarmerie brigade in Fundong for "associating" with armed non-state actors and providing them medical care.

Denying the People Access to Medical Care: Government and Separatist Bans on the Circulation of Motorbikes and Vehicles

From the beginning of the Anglophone Revolt in 2016, the Biya government, led by Paul Atanga Nji, Permanent Secretary of the *Conseil National de Sécurité* (National Security Council), and Minister of Territorial Administration, banned the movement of commercial motorbikes, the most common means of public transportation in Cameroon, in most parts of Anglophone Southwest and Northwest regions. These bans lasted for specific periods, depending on the "security situation." Taking a cue from their boss, the government's appointed administrators – prefects and sub-prefects – used their extensive powers to impose bans on specific localities for different periods of time. These bans seriously affected the freedom of movement of people, goods, and services in the name of public security. The Cameroon government banned motorbikes from time to time because it believed these bikes facilitated the mobility of Anglophone non-state armed groups (SDO bans movement of bikes in Manyu, 2018; Mbonwoh, 2018; Cameroon: Fako SDO bans circulation of bikes throughout the division, 2021; Territorial Administration, 2018). In addition to the bans, government officials and security forces seized and burned motorbikes whose owners or riders failed to obey orders or bribe police or gendarmerie officers at checkpoints. Taken together with the widely observed Monday "kontri Sunday or ghost towns" strikes imposed by the separatists, these administrative decrees severely restricted the movement of people in both regions. To make matters worse, armed Ambazonian independentist groups operating in several parts of the Northwest and Southwest regions, erected roadblocks on all roads outside and between the main towns: Buea, Bamenda,

Kumba, Mamfe, Mbengwi, Bali, Kumbo, Nkambe, Ndu, Wum, and other localities, to hamper the movement of Cameroon military forces to their villages and strongholds. These roadblocks enforced Monday "ghost town strikes," and frequent "lockdowns" decreed by the leadership of separatist groups in the United States and other parts of the Diaspora. These separatist roadblocks also enforced a ban on the beer and other products of *Brasseries du Cameroun*, the major, French-owned brewery that has operated in French Cameroon since independence. Separatists also blocked the movement of people, goods, and services from the busy Nigerian border post at Ekok to Anglophone Cameroon, thereby depriving the government of customs revenue for periods of time.

The most notable motorbike ban of the Anglophone Revolt was a three-month, renewable ban imposed on 20 July 2021 in Bali by the Prefect of Mezam, Mr. Simon Emile Mooh. This was in response to an Improvised Explosive Device (IED) attack on Cameroon security forces on July 18, 2018 in Bali Nyonga. Ambazonian separatist fighters posted a video on social media showing the detonation of their IED under a Chinese-made armored police pickup truck that was driving through the town. The video showed that the IED blew up the police truck and rendered it immobile. A gun battle ensued between the security forces and armed, non-state attackers. When the dust settled, the five Cameroon security officers in the vehicle were dead (Azonwhi, 2021). The video next showed jubilating Bali Buffaloes, the Ambazonian the non-state armed group that operated in Bali, and controlled sections of the strategic Bamenda-Ekok road, emerging from their hideouts and seizing the weapons of the dead Cameroon security forces. This viral video led to the Prefect's ban on the circulation of motorbikes in Bali.

In response to the Prefect's motorbike ban, Grandpa, leader of the Bali Buffaloes, imposed a ban on the circulation of motor vehicles on the Bamenda-Bali-Mbengwi road for three months, renewable to match the Prefect's decree against motorbikes (Fungwe, 2021). This and other tugs-of-war between the Cameroon military and Ambazonian separatist groups severely restricted the movement of people, goods, and services, and especially access to healthcare and medical facilities. People walked long distances to reach hospitals and health centers. Some very sick people were ferried on wheelbarrows and handcarts (Njinikom: Separatists Impose Ban on the Circulation of Motorbikes, 2021). Under these difficult circumstances, many healthcare workers fled for their lives, resulting in the closure of public and church-affiliated health centers in many parts of the Northwest and Southwest region. This left the people who had not fled their villages without access to medical care. The Prefect lifted his ban on the circulation of motorbikes three months later. The Bali Buffaloes followed suit and lifted their ban on motor vehicles.

It did not take long for other non-state armed groups to mimic the bans of the Cameroon government. One notable example was a ban that took place in May 2021. A separatist group operating in Njinikom, Boyo division, imposed a ban on the circulation of motorbikes after a military ambush resulted in the death of two of their fighters, one of whom was a Nigerian mercenary who was instructing the separatists on how to use automatic weapons, and how to manufacture improvised explosive devices that targeted the Cameroon military. The separatists indicated that the ban was to "punish the people for cooperating with the military, leaking their [separatist] movement details thereby causing several casualties on them" (Njinikom: Separatists impose ban on the circulation of motorbikes, 2021). The motorbike ban ultimately became a month-long lockdown. The separatists imposed a resistance tax ranging from $10 to $20 on all businesses in the Njinikom area (Timfuchi, 2021). The lockdown was lifted only after all the small businesses had paid the tax. The people were once again caught between the Cameroon government, which opted for a military solution to the Anglophone Revolt, and Ambazonia separatist groups that attacked anyone who collaborated with the security forces. These acts of collective punishment essentially stopped most people in the division from leaving their homes and traveling to health centers, including the nearby Mbingo Baptist Hospital, which served people from all parts of Cameroon, and has a medical training center that served as the site of tropical medicine practicums for African, European and American medical centers, including Georgetown University School of Medicine in Washington DC.

Billeting Cameroon Soldiers in Health Centers

One of the outcomes of the Cameroon government's decision to resolve the Anglophone conflict through military means rather than through concerted and inclusive dialogue was the massive militarization of all parts of the Northwest and Southwest regions. Moving thousands of soldiers into these regions, which are known for lengthy rainy seasons, severe dry seasons, dense forests, mountainous terrain, and deplorable roads, required accommodations for thousands of soldiers. The result is that the Cameroon military decided to billet troops anywhere generals could find shelter from the elements. These impromptu military barracks included churches, church halls, community halls, requisitioned hotels, primary schools and boarding schools, airports, and, in many cases, health centers. These billeting practices disrupted the activities of many institutions. In one case, soldiers of the Cameroon military lived in the dormitories of Sacred Heart College, Mankon, Bamenda, a well-known, all-boys Catholic high school. The reason for this billeting was ostensibly to provide security for the students. Videos soon surfaced on social media of armed soldiers making the boys in one dormitory perform sexually indecent and lascivious dance routines while the soldiers watched in amusement. This grotesque performance in a Roman Catholic high school raised a hue and cry among parents and alumni of the institution. In another instance, soldiers billeted at the Cameroon Protestant College (CPC) Bali transformed the stagnant pools of water in the road in front of the college into a place of torture for girls suspected of separatist tendencies or of associating with separatists (see Chapter 14 Mama Amba Drama).

The Bali Kumbat hospital was a theater of clashes between the Cameroon military, including members of the elite *Bataillon d'Intervention Rapide (BIR)*, and separatist groups like the Bali Buffaloes of Bali Nyonga. This was because the Cameroon military transformed the hospital into a military barracks. In a 2020 report, the independent international human rights organization, Human Rights Watch, noted that both the Cameroon army and separatist groups had attacked hospitals and medical staff on multiple occasions. In 2020, Cameron soldiers including members of the Rapid Intervention Battalion (BIR), fired a grenade into the courtyard of the district hospital in Bali Kumbat, leading to the death of a cardiac patient, injuring at least four others, and destroying four vehicles (Human

Rights Watch, 2020). The protestations of the institution's medical director did not make any difference. In Cameroon, the military has the power to forcibly enter hospitals and health centers looking for wounded non-state actors, whom they drag out of hospital beds, never to be seen alive again. In response to these military violations of international humanitarian law, separatist groups attacked some hospitals and healthcare facilities after accusing them of collaborating with the military and identifying wounded separatists receiving treatment in healthcare institutions. They have also been known to loot hospital supplies to treat their wounded comrades in their camps in the bush. This reality put the healthcare facilities in a difficult ethical quandary; they were repeatedly presented with "damned if you do and damned if you don't" life and death situations.

On March 11, 2019, Senator Henry Kemende Gamsey of the Northwest constituency wrote a letter to the Minister of Health in Yaoundé through the President of the Senate, Marcel Niat Njifenji, posing a number of questions about the healthcare situation in the region. The letter said inter alia:

> Concerning the Balikumbat Hospital in Ngoketunjia Division of the Northwest region, which premises have been transformed into a Barrack, what is your ministry doing to either reestablish that medical facility or transfer same somewhere else for the health personnel to return in order that the local population can have access to health facilities? (Kemende, 2019). (See Appendix I)

Senator Henry Kemende Gamsey's letter was an attempt to get the Cameroon Minister of Health and the President of the do-nothing, rubber-stamp Senate to comment on the status of the healthcare sector in the crisis-stricken Northwest and Southwest regions. There is no official record of a response by either the minister of health or the president of the Senate to Senator Henry Kemende Gamsey's probing questions. This deafening silence was not strange given that since the Anglophone Revolt began in 2016, the National Assembly and the Senate steadfastly refused to officially discuss the crisis in parliament. Indeed, the Anglophone Problem was the hot potato that neither of the legislative bodies of Cameroon dared to touch. Neither house held even a single debate on the crisis despite desperate attempts by members of the opposition Social Democratic Front, which is majority Anglophone, to put the crisis on the agenda of the rubber-stamp Cameroon National Assembly and the Senate (When Parliament speaks truth to Biya but avoids armed conflict in NW, SW, 2022). The fear of the Speaker of the National Assembly, Honorable Cavaye Yegue Djibril, and the President of the Senate, Marcel Niat Njifenji, to even discuss the Anglophone Problem reflected the Biya regime's policy of treating the crisis as a movement of political insubordination, a secessionist revolt that could only be dealt with through the top-down, Napoleonic-style, rule-by-decree, as well as the use of military and security forces to impose the diktats of the authoritarian *chefferie républicaine*. While the legislative bodies of the United States, Canada, the United Kingdom, Switzerland, and Germany discussed the Anglophone Problem and passed resolutions calling for a negotiated settlement and decentralization, the Biya regime turned a deaf ear to all these calls and clung steadfastly to the military option. The only action both houses of parliament are known to have taken was to rubberstamp a government proposal to grant the Anglophone regions a French-style "special status" without discussion and without the consent of these regions. The special status was essentially meaningless and did not address the demands of the English-speaking minority. Senator Henry Kemende Gamsey was murdered by unknown gunmen in Bamenda on the night of January 11, 2022. The government made no official statement about the senator's assassination. No formal investigation was opened into the killing.

Transformation of Esu Hospital into a Military Barracks

The practice of billeting Cameroonian soldiers in schools, colleges, and health centers that Senator Henry Kemende Gamsey questioned in his letter essentially transformed these institutions into military torture centers and sometimes theaters of war. This was the case with the Esu Health Center in Menchum Division, which the military transformed into a barracks. From the premises of this health center, the military and its civilian Mbororo/ Fulani allies carried out joint operations against the separatist "Amba Boys." On the night of May 26, 2019, the Amba Boys counter-attacked the Cameroon Army billeted at the Esu Health Center. According to media reports, one person was killed, while windows and medical equipment in the hospital were damaged (One killed, medical equipment damaged in Esu shootout, 2019).

Figure 13.2. Cameroonian soldier in front of Esu Health Center that had been transformed into a fortified military barracks (May 2019).

Case Study #1: Cameroon Army "Invasions" of Saint Elizabeth's Catholic General Hospital Cardiac Center, Shisong

On November 15, 2021, Dr. Sr. Anshoma Helen Mbuoh, Director and cardiologist of Saint Elizabeth's Catholic General Hospital Cardiac Center, Shisong, Bui Division, a hospital complex run by the Roman Catholic Order, the Tertiary Sisters of Saint Francis, wrote a letter to "The Provincial Leadership Team, Tertiary Sisters of St. Francis, Shisong," the leaders of her Roman Catholic religious order. The letter's subject was "REPORT ON THE MILITARY INVASION OF THE ST. ELIZABETH CATHOLIC GENERAL HOSPITAL, SHISONG" (Capitals in the original). The letter began, "Once again, the Cameroon military orchestrated a surprise invasion of Shisong Hospital" (Mbuoh, 2021). It went on to state that this was the second time in four months that the Cameroon military had launched a surprise raid on the hospital since she became its director. The first time was in July 2021. On this occasion, she reported that on Sunday, the 14th of November, at about 1:30 pm:

> …the Cameroon Military again entered the St. Elizabeth Catholic General Hospital and Cardiac Center, Shisong. The number of military men could not be easily determined but they came in three (03) armoured cars. They were armed with sophisticated weapons and dressed in combat attire. A frightful scene for all, especially for patients in a Hospital setting…The Military requested the Emergency Unit of the Hospital, as they claimed to be searching for Amba boys [Ambazonia separatists] that were brought for treatment to the hospital that same morning. The director took them to the Out Patient Department, which serves as the emergency unit, and where all consultations in the Hospital begin…they insisted to be taken to the Emergency Unit with the inscription on the door but were calmly told that all cases are brought to the Out Patients' Unit for consultation….They took the Register and went through it, thoroughly. Then they resorted to a thorough search of the entire hospital. They moved from Ward to Ward and from Unit to Unit. The Dispensary, Admission Room, Men's Medical Unit, the Pediatric Unit, the Females' Medical Unit, the Surgical Units I & II, the Maternity and the Theatre were all bumped into, with patients and little children and babies and pregnant women in them. All the Private Wards were opened and searched…Nothing suspicious was found…Not finding the Amba Boys they were looking for, they started insulting and threating the Reverend Sisters. They even threatened to shoot the Sisters in the leg if they did not indicate where they had hidden and are treating the Amba Boys in the Hospital...the two Security Officers on Duty were arrested and systematically interrogated. They were asked, at gun point, to show where the Amba Boys were hidden…the military exercised brute force on the Security Officers. They were severely beaten with the butts of the guns and kicked with their military boots. They all sustained injuries and swollen faces…. Thereafter, the military insisted they wanted to see the Consultation Area of the Cardiologist…They requested to go down to the Basement of the Cardiac Center and there they searched everywhere. At the end of the search, some of the Military men expressed remorse… However, some of them promised that the next time they would be back, they will set the entire hospital on fire…They left the hospital at 3:45 pm (Mbuoh, 2021).

This frightening narrative, which was copied to the government officer, the hand-picked representative of the President of Cameroon in the area, the Senior Divisional Officer for Bui, and the Bishop of the Diocese of Kumbo, was widely reported by the independent, English-language media because Shisong Hospital is noted for the excellence of its holistic healthcare and humanitarian services.

The letter from Dr. Sr. Anshoma Helen Mbuoh, Director and cardiologist of Saint Elizabeth's Catholic General Hospital Cardiac Center, Shisong, went viral. Its detailed contents and reporting by the English-language press provided a close look at the now common modus operandi of the Cameroon army, as well as its violations of the Geneva Convention of 1949, and the international laws of war in the troubled Anglophone North-west and Southwest regions since the Anglophone crisis began in 2016. Dr. Sr. Anshoma Helen Mbuoh, Director of Shisong Hospital, one of the largest healthcare facilities in Cameroon, and the only cardiac hospital of its kind in West and Central Africa, told the world that this was the second time the military had ransacked the hospital in four months, and the third time the armed soldiers had invaded the hospital since the beginning of the Anglophone crisis. The official Cameroon government media and its branches in the Northwest and South regions ignored the event and did not mention it in their broadcast, print, or online versions. However, the independent, English-language media did not fail to note the egregious violation of international humanitarian law. The headline of the Anglophone *Guardian Post* newspaper screamed in indignation: "Soldiers in search of Amba fighters ransack Shisong hospital" (Kongeh, 2021). The expression 'Amba Boys" is the generic name for Anglophone separatist fighters. Due to the reckless atrocities of some non-state actors against civilians, this term is an epithet to some Anglophones and a term of endearment to others.

Letter from Dr. Sr. Anshoma Helen Mbuoh, Director of Shisong Hospital (2021)

The Shisong Hospital Invasion of 2019

According to Radio Evangelium, the radio station of the Roman Catholic Diocese of Kumbo, the first time the Cameroonian military, led by a squadron of the dreaded, Israeli-trained and equipped BIR, "invaded" Saint Elizabeth's Catholic General Hospital Cardiac Center, Shisong, was Sunday, February 17th, 2019, at the height of the Anglophone civil war in Bui. Radio Evangelium reported that five heavily armed members of the Cameroon military descended unannounced on the premises of the hospital when the Revered Sisters who run the institution were observing a day of "recollection" and prayer. The radio stated that the Cameroon soldiers came to the hospital:

> …in search of wounded separatists who might have been admitted into the hospital…. They moved into the Cardiac Centre section of the hospital. They proceeded to the inner sections of the hospital, went to the Surgical II Unit, and moved into one of the wards. The soldiers are said to have fired some gunshots inside the hospital premises… Some of the Sisters

immediately came to the hospital where they met the soldiers. According to the Director of the Hospital, Sr. Mary Aldrine Kinyuy, T.S.S.F, the Sisters requested that the soldiers discontinue any activity and leave the hospital premises. The Sisters then accompanied the soldiers to the hospital gate… At press time, it was unclear whether there was any causal link between the activity of the soldiers in the hospital and the death of one patient in the Female Medical Unit within those moments (Uproar as Cameroon's Defense Forces Get into Shisong Hospital, 2019).

Radio Evangelium noted that though gun battles between the Cameroon military and Anglophone separatist Amba Boys had taken place near Shisong Hospital premises on several occasions, this was the first time uniformed and armed members of the Cameroon military had actually entered the protected precincts of the hospital and gone through its units in search of wounded Anglophone separatists. The irony is that Bui has been one of the theatres of military clashes between Cameroon soldiers and armed non-state actors. In addition to gun battles, on multiple occasions, Anglophone independentists had used improvised explosive devices to attack members of the Cameroon armed forces. Some of the wounded Cameroon soldiers had been treated at the Shisong Hospital and the nearby Banso Baptist Hospital. It should be noted that the Shisong Hospital also serves as a place of refuge. In 2020, more than 200 people whom the conflict had displaced sought refuge on the premises of the hospital. The Tertiary Sisters of Saint Francis, who operate the hospital, proceeded to feed the internally displaced persons who had taken refuge there.

Case Study #2: St Mary Soledad Catholic Health Centre in the Crossfire of the Anglophone War

Roman Catholic healthcare institution, St Mary Soledad Catholic Health Centre in Bamenda, experienced something common in health centers in the Anglophone Northwest and Southwest regions. It found itself in the crossfire of the conflict between Cameroon security forces and armed, non-state actors in late 2021. On December 9th, Capo Daniel, the Europe-based Deputy Defense Chief of the Ambazonia Defense Force (ADF), one of the armed separatist groups fighting the Cameroon military for an independent Ambazonia in the former Southern Cameroons, posted a video on social media (Facebook, YouTube, WhatsApp, Telegram) that put St Mary Soledad Catholic Health Centre in Bamenda in an unenviable situation. Capo Daniel demanded an explanation from the Roman Catholic Church for the deaths of two of its "commanders," whose *noms de guerre* were: "Commander Talk and Do" and "Commander Brandy" (ADF DDC Issues Warning to Saint Mary Soledad Health Centre, 2021). The Ambazonia Defense Force spokesman revealed that the two non-state fighters had masterminded an improvised explosive device (IED) attack against a Cameroon military armored car. The attack had resulted in the death of a Cameroon military officer. The two ADF commanders had also been wounded by shrapnel from a grenade launched by the Cameroon military. They managed to escape, but because their wounds were severe, they were taken to the St Mary Soledad Catholic Health Centre in Bamenda for treatment. The hospital provided the two separatist commanders with urgent care, stabilized them, and admitted them. Before leaving the hospital, their comrades took videos of them lying on their beds in the health center, speaking jovially. Capo claimed that at night, the Cameroonian military raided the health center, dragged the wounded ADF fighters from their beds, and took them to Ntarikon, a neighborhood in Bamenda, executed them summarily, and left their bodies on the street. The ADF demanded that St Mary Soledad Catholic Health Centre make a public statement denouncing the Cameroon military's violation of the Geneva Convention or risk being considered a party to the human rights violations of the Cameroon military. The ADF threatened to shut down the health center (ADF DDC Issues Warning to St Mary Soledad Catholic Health Centre, 2021). The Roman Catholic Church and the St Mary Soledad Catholic Health Centre declined to comment on the incident for fear of retaliation. The Cameroon army also refused to comment on the incident. This incident essentially put the Roman Catholic Church and its healthcare services in the crossfire of the military conflict.

Figure 13.3. Soldiers in search of Amba fighters ransack Shisong Hospital, *The Guardian Post*, Nov. 17, 2021

Case Study #3: Arbitrary Withdrawal of Consent to Médecins Sans Frontières
Under international humanitarian law, impartial humanitarian bodies have a right to offer humanitarian services to the Parties in a non-international armed conflict. Article 3(2) of the Geneva Convention (I) of 1949, which governs conflicts "not of an international character," provides that the arbitrary withdrawal of consent for impartial international organizations to provide humanitarian aid constitutes a violation of international humanitarian law. Such a violation of international humanitarian law through denial of consent occurred in Bamenda, in the Northwest region, on December 8, 2020. In one of the most blatantly authoritarian, inhuman, governmental interference with humanitarian aid in the Anglophone conflict, President Biya's hand-picked, proconsul, the unelected governor

of the Northwest region, Mr. Adolphe Lele L'Afrique Tchoffo Deben, issued a decree: "Regional Decision 966 RD/E/GNWR.22/IGRS suspending the partnership between the independent and neutral international humanitarian organization, *Médecins Sans Frontières* (Doctors Without Borders) and St Mary Soledad Catholic Health Centre, Bamenda, as well as related partnerships with other health facilities in the Northwest Region pending definition of a framework of activities for Doctors Without Borders (DWB/MSF) by the Minister of Public Health (MINSANTE)." This decree was more than a bureaucratic act. It was tantamount to an expulsion of the independent, impartial international humanitarian organization, which had been taking care of the sick and wounded victims of the civil war in the Northwest and Southwest regions since the crisis began in 2016. Subsequent events would explain the real reason why the Cameroon government expelled MSF from the Northwest. In effect, it turns out that military necessity precipitated the Cameroon government's arbitrary withdrawal of consent from *Médecins Sans Frontières*. MSF had partnered with local clinics and doctors, who had virtually no resources, to treat internally displaced persons, civilians who had been caught in the crossfire between government forces and Anglophone separatists. Many of these displaced people had run into the bush to escape the fighting and were suffering from snake bites, bullet, and machete wounds, falls, broken bones, malnutrition, malarial and other infections. *Médecins Sans Frontières* also provided first aid and other medical assistance to government security forces, soldiers, and civilian officials who had been targeted by Ambazonia separatist fighters. In short, *Médecins Sans Frontières* partnered with all kinds of local health care centers to provide much-needed humanitarian medical services to the public, non-combatants caught in the crossfire of the armed conflict, internally displaced persons, as well as state and non-state combatants in the conflict. The decree of Governor Lele L'Afrique terminating the services of *Médecins Sans Frontières* in the war zones of the Northwest region amounted to an arbitrary withdrawal of consent from an impartial humanitarian organization to render humanitarian services in a war zone in collaboration with a local Cameroonian healthcare delivery partner. This violated international humanitarian law. Under the Geneva Convention I, Article 3 (1949): Conflicts not of an international character. The military situation on the ground precipitated this withdrawal of consent. In effect, the Cameroon military did not want MSF to provide any medical care to wounded Ambazonian separatists who were killing Cameroon security forces. According to the International Committee of the Red Cross:

> Since 1949, international law has developed to the point where the consent may not be arbitrarily withheld by any of the Parties to a non-international armed conflict…Military necessity is no valid ground under humanitarian law to turn down a valid offer of services or to deny in their entirety the humanitarian activities proposed by impartial humanitarian organizations" (ICRC Commentary on Geneva Convention 1, 2016).

In effect, *Médecins Sans Frontières*, a well-known, impartial international humanitarian organization, was attending, for the most part, to the medical needs of the civilian population affected by the non-international armed conflict in Anglophone Southern

Cameroons. The role of *Médecins Sans Frontières* in the conflict had been crucial because the regular hospitals and clinics in Southern Cameroons, are anemic, poorly equipped, and notoriously short of medical supplies even in the best of times. Steeped in ignorance of international human rights law, the Cameroon army and their non-state opponents carried out all kinds of atrocities. Separatists, alleged separatists, their mothers, sisters, girlfriends, and children were all targeted, as was anyone suspected of collaborating with the military. Six months after the arbitrary withdrawal of consent from MSF to provide humanitarian assistance in the Northwest region, the international organization indicated that discussions with the government of Cameroon to resume their humanitarian services in the Northwest region had not been fruitful because "Cameroonian authorities accused us of being too close to non-state armed groups in the area" (People in Northwest seek healthcare as MSF Denied Providing medical services, 2021). The withdrawal of consent to provide humanitarian aid was arbitrary because under Article 3 of the Geneva Convention (I) of 1949: "Military necessity is no valid ground under humanitarian law to turn down a valid offer of services or to deny in their entirety the humanitarian activities proposed by impartial humanitarian organizations." Months of negotiations between MSF and the Ministries of External Affairs and Health did not change the hostility of the Cameroon government towards the impartial international humanitarian organization. If anything, the situation got worse. The Cameroon government did not countenance any hospital or international humanitarian organization that was suspected of having treated wounded Ambazonian independentist fighters. The irony is that the Cameroon Ministry of Health did not provide any humanitarian services to replace those that had been offered by MSF.

Figure 13.4. Doctors Without Borders quits Northwest, *The Sun*, August 4, 2021.

Doctors Without Borders Forced to Cease Operations in the Southwest Region

We saw earlier that MSF was forced to stop providing humanitarian services to the war-ravaged Northwest region in 2021. What had happened to MSF in the Northwest region, also happened to the impartial international humanitarian organization in the Southwest region. On March 29, 2022, MSF wrote an open letter to the "community leaders" in the region announcing that it was suspending its humanitarian health services in the war-torn region due to governmental harassment and false accusations of collusion with Anglophone separatists. The MSF letter announced: "the immediate and indefinite suspension of activities …to support health facilities and communities…The ability of Doctors Without Borders to conduct its activities in the region has been hampered by a difficult relationship with the government authorities amidst false accusations of complicity to (sic) secessionists in the Southwest region" (Habaasa, 2022). This was a blow to the healthcare sector because Doctors Without Borders provided humanitarian services, including one of the few emergency ambulance services to the people of the region. Its clients included internally displaced persons and persons living in war-torn areas under Letters of Agreement (LoA) signed with local public, religious, and private healthcare facilities. All those letters of agreement became null and void with immediate effect. The explanation for the Cameroon government's hostility towards Doctors Without Borders is that despite the much-needed humanitarian services DWB provided, the Cameroon government considered it an obstacle to its policy of military subjugation of Southern Cameroons by all means. MSF is, after all, an independent, impartial international humanitarian organization whose work in local communities puts it in a position to monitor and denounce atrocities, war crimes, and crimes against humanity committed by the Cameroon military and Anglophone separatists. MSF also provided humanitarian aid to those who needed medical services, including sick and wounded soldiers and non-state armed groups.. That policy of impartiality, which is consistent with the Geneva Convention of 1949 and international humanitarian law, was clearly unacceptable to the Cameroonian military and government, which did not want MSF to provide medical aid to armed, non-state actors. This was made very clear in December 2021 when the leaders of two non-state armed groups called an MSF ambulance requesting humanitarian assistance for two wounded separatists after a clash with the Cameroon military. The MSF ambulance went and picked up the wounded non-state actors, but the Cameroon military was tipped off about the mission of the MSF ambulance and intercepted it. The MSF healthcare workers treating the wounded Anglophone separatists were arrested, along with their patients, one of whom later died. Cameroon Army spokesman Captain Cyrille Atonfack Guemo and the governor of the Southwest region, Okalia Bilai, denounced MSF for responding to a call for medical assistance from Anglophone non-state combatants wounded in battle. The Cameroon government expressed dismay that MSF would extend humanitarian aid to notorious separatists whom they said were responsible for many atrocities (Kindzeka, 2021). This was the latest incident in which the Cameroon government and the military wanted MSF to abandon its neutrality and impartiality under the Geneva Convention and treat only those patients approved by the government. Clearly, the Cameroon government officials were not well acquainted with the Geneva Convention, international humanitarian law, and the role of impartial, independent humanitarian organizations in international and non-international conflicts. Nevertheless, the MSF workers were released from custody a few days later. Nothing further was heard of the wounded separatist taken into custody by the government. Ironically, a Doctors Without Borders community health worker in the same Southwest region had been killed by armed non-state actors after they accused him of collaborating with the military and divulging the identities of separatists he was treating to the military (Human Rights Watch, 2020). MSF was clearly caught in the crossfire and decided that for the safety and security of its personnel, the best cause of action was to quit the Southwest region. Clearly, the actions of the Cameroon military and government in arbitrarily withdrawing consent from MSF in the Northwest region and putting pressure on the medics to offer humanitarian services only to patients approved by the government in the Southwest region made the situation of the international humanitarian organization untenable. This was clearly a violation of the Geneva Convention.

Trial by Fire: Healthcare Services as Targets of Arson in the Anglophone Crisis

As we saw above, in her protest letter of November 15, 2021, Dr. Sr. Anshoma Helen Mbuoh, Director and cardiologist of Saint Elizabeth's Catholic General Hospital Cardiac Center, Shisong, wrote that when members of the Cameroon military invaded her hospital and found no wounded Amba Boys (non-state combatants) being treated therein, they became frustrated. Some of the soldiers "promised that the next time they would be back, they will set the entire hospital on fire." The military's threat to incinerate the hospital was not an idle one, so it was taken seriously. The use of fire as an instrument of terror and as a reprisal against opponents had been a common, well-documented military strategy in the Anglophone conflict. Hundreds of villages in the Northwest and Southwest regions were burnt to ashes by the Cameroon military and security forces as a reprisal for allegedly playing host to, sheltering, or assisting Anglophone separatists (Willis et al., 2019). Indeed, according to the Cameroon-based Center for Human Rights and Development in Africa (CHRDA) and the Raoul Wallenberg Center for Human Rights (2019): "Burning and razing homes and villages are established military tactics and the signature human rights violation perpetrated in the conflict" (p. 27). Burning of whole villages was the most common reprisal visited on civilians when separatists killed government security personnel.

Figure 13.5. Little girl in the burnt remains of her home in Bali Nyonga. Credit: anonymous

From the beginning of the Anglophone crisis, Radio Evangelium, the Roman Catholic Radio station based in Kumbo, Bui, reported extensively on the pyromaniacal tendencies and scorched-earth tactics of the elite, Israeli-trained and armed BIR, and other branches of the Cameroon security forces. The army, marines, gendarmerie, and police left burnt and smoldering villages in their wake across Bui and other parts of the Anglophone Northwest and Southwest regions. (Onslaught in Kumbo Continues, 2018).

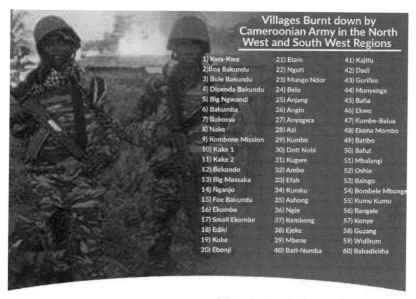

Villages Burnt down by Cameroonian Army in the North West and South West Regions		
1) Kwa-Kwa	21) Etam	41) Kajifu
2) Boa Bakundu	22) Nguti	42) Dadi
3) Bole Bakundu	23) Mungo Ndor	43) Gurifen
4) Dipenda Bakundu	24) Belo	44) Munyenge
5) Big Ngwandi	25) Anjang	45) Bafia
6) Bakumba	26) Angin	46) Ekwe
7) Bokosso	27) Anyagwa	47) Kumbe-Balua
8) Nake	28) Azi	48) Ekona Mombo
9) Kombone Mission	29) Kumbo	49) Batibo
10) Kake 1	30) Doti Nobi	50) Bafut
11) Kake 2	31) Kugwe	51) Mbalangi
12) Bekondo	32) Ambo	52) Oshie
13) Big Massaka	33) Efah	53) Balngo
14) Nganjo	34) Kumku	54) Bombele Mbonge
15) Foe Bakundu	35) Ashong	55) Kumu Kumu
16) Ekombe	36) Ngie	56) Bangele
17) Small Ekombe	37) Kembong	57) Konye
18) Ediki	38) Ejeke	58) Guzang
19) Kuke	39) Mbene	59) Widikum
20) Ebonji	40) Bati-Numba	60) Babadiekha

Centre for Human Rights and Democracy in Africa

CHRDA
promoting human rights and democracy

"*Extrajudicial killings, burning down entire villages, shooting unarmed civilians and forced disappearances in the South West and North West Regions must be investigated. We urge for a commission of inquiry to fully investigate these crimes.*"

Barrister Agbor Nkongho

Figure 13.6. CHRDA poster of villages burnt with Cameroon soldiers burning a village. (2018)

As noted above, hospitals, health centers and clinics suspected of treating wounded Amba Boys (non-state actors) are known to have been set ablaze by the Cameroon military on multiple occasions, in total disregard of the laws of war. Sometimes, separatists whose comrades were snatched from health centers by the military attacked the health center in retaliation for colluding with the military. The most egregious act of arson as a military tactic took place at the Kumba District Hospital in Meme Division in 2019. That public hospital had been touted as one of the earliest success stories of the World Bank's Performance Based Financing (PBF) health initiative in Cameroon. PBF is an innovative World Bank-funded project to improve the availability, accessibility, and quality of health services in Cameroon and other low and medium-income countries. The system subsidizes healthcare structures according to the quantity and quality of the care they provide (Fritsche et al., 2014). On the night of February 10/11, 2019, unidentified armed men attacked and set fire to a section of the Kumba District Hospital in the center of town, killing four persons, including two patients. The perpetrators of the criminal act were never found. However, the Cameroon government immediately blamed Anglophone separatists for setting fire to the hospital, while the separatists blamed the Cameroon military for setting fire to the hospital because it was known to have treated wounded Anglophone separatists. One thing is clear – on the night of the attack, Cameroon security forces were guarding the hospital. A video soon surfaced on social media showing the silhouettes of French-speaking Cameroon soldiers standing and chatting calmly inside the section of the hospital that was not on fire. Three soldiers are seen calmly pushing a motorbike out of harm's way as the fire rages in the background (see below for a screenshot from the video). No formal investigation was ever carried out on the event. On the night of March 30, 2019, the Muyuka District Hospital suffered the same fate as the Kumba District Hospital. It was set ablaze by unknown persons who had grudges against the hospital, persons who were apparently not acquainted with the Geneva Convention and international humanitarian law. A few months later, one of the buildings of the Banso Baptist Hospital in Bui Division was also burnt. At any rate, the pyromaniacal attacks against these hospitals continued to demonstrate that the Anglophone problem was a festering political wound that the Cameroon government had refused to take good-faith measures to bind.

Figure 13.8. Screenshot of Cameroon security forces moving a motorbike inside the burning Kumba District Hospital on the night of February 12, 2019.

The Anglophone Problem, the Healthcare Sector, and International Humanitarian Law

One of the realities of the Anglophone Revolt of 2016 is that the Cameroon government uses repressive military means to try and crush a social and political movement. The security forces, led by the Israeli-trained and equipped BIR, shot, arrested, and jailed unarmed civilian demonstrators in a bid to subjugate the English-speaking regions of Cameroon once and for all and accomplish the dream of assimilating it into the Francophone *la République du Cameroun*. Arrested Anglophone lawyers, teachers, students, and civil society groups that had led the revolt or participated in it were deported to French Cameroon where French-only military tribunals held kangaroo trials that did not meet the most elementary standards of presumption of innocence, due process, fairness and justice. These Anglophone activists and demonstrators were subsequently handed lengthy sentences in overcrowded, insalubrious dungeons in French Cameroon. As a result of the Biya regime's decision to opt for a military solution to the purely political Anglophone problem – the demand by Anglophones for federalism and decentralization – the crisis degenerated into a bloody military conflict. The government's response to the emerging Anglophone resistance was a scorched-earth policy that razed hundreds of villages. This high-handed repression resulted in the deaths of thousands of civilians and triggered an exodus of hundreds of thousands of refugees to Nigeria. Hundreds of thousands of others became internally displaced persons (IDPs). The conflict quickly morphed into a horrendous Anglophone war of independence from French Cameroon. Both sides engaged in horrendous human rights violations. Hospitals, health centers, and healthcare givers in Southern Cameroons (Northwest and Southwest regions) became caught in the crossfire of fierce battles between the Cameroon security forces and the Anglophone separatists.

The evidence shows that some of the actions of the belligerents, and particularly the Cameron military, led by the elite, Israeli-trained and equipped BIR, have been at variance with international humanitarian law. Nay, invasions of hospitals by the military, transformation of medical institutions into military barracks, burning of hospitals and healthcare facilities, and attacks against healthcare workers violated the letter and spirit of the Geneva Convention of 1949, and specifically, its humanitarian law provisions applicable to international and non-international armed conflicts. The Geneva Convention protects the sanctity of medical personnel and medical institutions, as well as sick and wounded prisoners who are treated in medical facilities. As the discussion above demonstrates, the Geneva Convention is definitely not applicable in Cameroon. The Cameroon government and the Cameroon military showed a reckless disregard for that convention. The Anglophone war has been executed with utmost savagery. The scorched-earth policy aimed at denying sanctuary and humanitarian aid to the separatists, led to invasions and attacks on hospitals for purposes of denying non-state actors humanitarian aid and succor. Military atrocities led to separatist counterattacks on healthcare institutions that were viewed as colluding with the military in its search for separatists hospitalized in these facilities. These separatist counterattacks compounded the gross disregard for human rights and humanitarian law in the Anglophone conflict.

The Geneva Conventions, which govern international human rights and humanitarian law, stipulate that medical and religious personnel should be protected in international and non-international conflicts, like the Anglophone crisis in Cameroon.

1. Medical and religious personnel shall be respected and protected and shall be granted all available help for the performance of their duties. They shall not be compelled to carry out tasks which are not compatible with their humanitarian

mission.

2. All the wounded, sick and shipwrecked, to whichever Party they belong, shall be respected and protected.

3. In all circumstances, they shall be treated humanely and shall receive, to the fullest extent practicable and with the least possible delay, the medical care and attention required by their condition. There shall be no distinction among them founded on any grounds other than medical ones (Protocol Additional to the Geneva Conventions of 12 August 1949 Protocol II (1977).

The Cameroon government is a signatory to the Protocol Additional to the Geneva Conventions, having signed it on 16 March 1984. According to the International Committee of the Red Cross (2016), humanitarian law that is applicable to non-international armed conflict was developed precisely to regulate situations of violence against unarmed and defenseless persons, in particular, and to protect all persons not or no longer actively participating in hostilities:

> The protection of persons not or no longer participating in hostilities is at the heart of humanitarian law... 'persons taking *no* active part in the hostilities, including members of armed forces who have *laid down* their arms and those placed *hors de combat* by sickness, wounds, detention, or any other cause' (emphasis added). Parties to a non-international armed conflict are under the categorical obligation to treat these persons humanely, in all circumstances and without any adverse distinction.
>
> ...
>
> To this end, the following acts are and shall remain prohibited at any time and in any place whatsoever with respect to the above-mentioned persons: (a) violence to life and person, in particular murder of all kinds, mutilation, cruel treatment and torture (Convention (I) for the Amelioration of the Condition of the Wounded and Sick in Armed Forces in the Field. Geneva, 12 August 1949).

As noted above, the Geneva Conventions apply to "Conflicts not of an international character." This refers to conflicts within states like the Anglophone conflict in Cameroon. The most recent non-international conflicts to which the Geneva Conventions were applied were the genocidal ethnic conflicts that convulsed and precipitated the disintegration of the multi-ethnic former Federal Republic of Yugoslavia. The International Criminal Tribunal for the Former Yugoslavia (1993-2017) relied on provisions of the Geneva Conventions in its rulings on the alleged and real human rights violations and war crimes that were committed by different state, non-state, and international parties involved in the Yugoslav civil wars. NATO became a Party and belligerent in the conflict when it launched an aerial bombing campaign against Serbia, the rump of the Federal Socialist Republic of Yugoslavia. The military activities of NATO in the NATO-Yugoslav War of 1999 were held up to the searchlight of international humanitarian law (*Bankovic v. Belgium* & 16 Other States, 2002; Eko, 2003).

Torture as an Instrument of War in the Anglophone Revolt

The English-language media in Cameron – the much-censored and prosecuted independent private press, surreptitiously used English-language programs on government radio to criticize the excesses of the Ahidjo-Biya Napoleonic *chefferie républicain*, while emerging independent TV stations and Internet-based media platforms have been at the forefront of promoting Anglophone identity and cultural specificity in Cameroon (Eko, 2019b; Eko, 2003). As a result, the Biya regime undertook coercive and censorious measures to control this segment of the Cameroonian media. These authoritarian measures have included censorship, the arrest of journalists, the cooptation of token Anglophone journalists into leadership positions in the architecture of censorship and media control, especially the *Conseil National de Communication* (CNC), the arrest, torture, and imprisonment of Anglophone and Francophone journalists who criticize the injustices visited on Anglophones (Eko, 2019). One of the most draconian censorious measures was the lengthy, 91-day Internet shutdown in the Anglophone regions in 2017 (See Dibussi Tande, Chapter 10). Torture is a widely used instrument of war in the Anglophone crisis. The Cameroon security forces systematically arrested, beat, and tortured students, lawyers, teachers, and members of the civil society suspected or accused of championing federalism or a separate Southern Camerons or Ambazonian state. They also arrest and torture lawyers suspected of defending separatists, as well as journalists suspected of associating with separatists, writing pro-separatist articles, or having federalist ideas or tendencies. Torture is in the DNA of the security forces in Cameroon. The International Criminal Tribunal for the former Yugoslavia (ICTY) defined torture under international humanitarian law as "the intentional infliction, by act or omission, of severe pain or suffering, whether physical or mental, for such purposes as to obtain information or a confession, to punish, intimidate or coerce the victim or a third person, or to discriminate, on any ground, against the victim or a third person" (International Committee of the Red Cross, 2016).

The Death of Samuel Wazizi in Military Custody

Two persons stand out as iconic victims in the sea of torture of the Anglophone crisis. The journalist, Samuel Ebuwe Ajiekia, also known as Samuel Wazizi, of the independent broadcaster, Chillen Muzik and Television (CMTV), was arrested in Buea in 2019 by the Cameroon military on charges of associating with terrorists and complicity in acts of terrorism. He was deported to Yaoundé, where he was tortured to death by Cameroon security forces. His death was revealed one year after it had occurred in military custody. His body was never released to his family for burial (See Hansel Ngala, Chapter 11). The death of Wazizi made international news because it demonstrated how Cameroon security forces torture and kill dissidents and journalists with impunity. The Secretary General of the United Nations Educational, Scientific, and Cultural Organization (UNESCO), Audrey Azoulay, and human rights organizations around the world denounced the murder of Wazizi and called for an investigation into his arrest and death in military custody (UNESCO

Director-General urges investigation into the death of journalist Samuel Wazizi in Cameroon, 2020; ABA President Judy Perry Martinez statement, 2020). Despite the international hue and cry, the Cameroon government did absolutely nothing, knowing that the international community would soon forget and move on to other things. That is precisely what happened. The arrest, torture, and death of Wazizi in Cameroon military custody have been forgotten, as have the arrest, torture, trial, and imprisonment of Anglophone journalists: Mancho Bibixy, Tsi Conrad, Penn Terrence, Kingsley F. Njoka, and others.

Mass Transfer of Medical Facilities from Anglophone Cameroon to French Cameroon

To survive the crisis that decimated the healthcare sector in the Anglophone Northwest and Southwest regions, many doctors employed in the government healthcare system fled the regions, and their health centers closed, leaving the people without any healthcare facilities. Virtually all the major church-related healthcare institutions run by the Baptist, Presbyterian, and Roman Catholic churches relocated, transferred, or opened branches in French Cameroon, mostly in Bafoussam, Yaoundé, and Douala. They also opened branches of their health institutions in Anglophone towns like Mutengene, Buea, and Limbe, which were relatively safe from the exactions of the Cameroon military and the separatist Amba Boys. Incidentally, hundreds of thousands of internally displaced persons had moved to these towns and swelled their populations.

Discussion and Conclusion

In Cameroon, the first casualty of war is the innocent person. The second casualty of war is healthcare: healthcare givers and healthcare institutions. This chapter explored the precarious existence of hospitals, health centers, and clinics in the context of the Anglophone crisis in Cameroon, where, despite the fact that Cameroon is a signatory to the Geneva Conventions and their regime of international human rights, international humanitarian law, and the laws of war, the repressive activities of the Cameroon military – and to a lesser extent, the Anglophone non-stake actors–reflected a reckless disregard for international humanitarian law and international public opinion. When the Anglophone Revolt began in 2016, the first casualties of the war were healthcare institutions –hospitals, health centers, and clinics, as well as healthcare providers. Displaced persons who sought refuge in the compounds and buildings of health centers soon found out that the Cameroon military did not respect the sanctity and specificity of healthcare facilities as stipulated in the humanitarian law provisions of the Geneva Conventions and the laws of war. The Cameroon military invaded the precincts of healthcare centers and hospitals to look for wounded separatists who were allegedly being treated in these facilities. Once non-state parties to the conflict realized that the Cameroon military was using healthcare institutions of all sorts as locations to easily capture wounded non-state combatants who had been placed *hors de combat* by sickness or their wounds, these institutions became soft targets. Their personnel and facilities were soon caught in the crossfire between the Cameroonian army and the Southern Cameroons independentist groups. Neither side cared for the niceties of the Geneva Convention of 1949 or the protections they granted civilians, sick and wounded combatants, doctors, nurses, hospitals, health centers, and clinics in war zones. Just as the Biya regime gave a deaf ear to international diplomatic calls to resolve the Anglophone crisis peacefully through frank and inclusive dialogue, the Cameroon military and government officials in the Northwest and Southwest displayed a total, willful disregard for international humanitarian law.

Afterword

The fundamental problem of Cameroon is the autocratic denialism of the ruling Francophone elite in Yaoundé and their Anglophone partners. Even as the situation has deteriorated since the Anglophone Revolt began in 2016, and thousands of people have been killed while more than one million people have become internally displaced or refugees in Nigeria, Ghana, and other countries, the out-of-touch leaders in their Yaoundé cocoon insist that: "There is no Anglophone Problem." While the autocrats of the republican chiefery in Yaoundé sip the choicest French wines, the most prized champagne, wear the most expensive French suits, and pad their Swiss bank accounts, the Anglophone crisis drags on. The normally anemic medical infrastructures of the Northwest and Southwest Anglophone regions continue to be caught in the crossfire between Cameroon security forces and Anglophone/non-state combatants. The first major casualty of 2022 was the government-owned and operated Mamfe General Hospital, which was razed to the ground on the night of June 7, 2022. The next day, stunned patients gathered and watched helplessly at the remains of what had been their only functioning healthcare facility in the midst of the crisis. Reports say it was probably burnt down by Ambazonian fighters in retaliation against Cameroon military officers who had entered the hospital, dragged their wounded comrades from their beds and took them away for execution, their modus operandi in multiple healthcare institutions since the start of the Anglophone crisis. There is no end in sight… Due to a complete lack of visionary leadership, the Anglophone crisis is becoming yet another "frozen conflict" that will hinder development for decades.

Figure 13.8. The remains of Mamfe General Hospital after a June 7, 2022 attack.

References

ADF DDC Issues Warning to Saint Mary Soledad Health Center (2021). YouTube, December 9. Retrieved from: https://www.youtube.com/watch?v=t-ovBvLr6p4

Ajumane, F. (2018). SDO bans movement of bikes in Manyu, *Journal du Cameroun.com*, April 5. Retrieved from: https://www.journalducameroun.com/en/sdo-bans-circulation-bikes-manyu/

American Bar Association (2020). ABA President Judy Perry Martinez statement Re: Reported Death of Cameroon Journalist Samuel Ajekah Abuwe, also known as "Samuel Wazizi" June 5. Retrieved from: https://www.americanbar.org/news/abanews/aba-news-archives/2020/06/statement-of-aba-president-re--death-of-cameroon-journalist--sam/

Anglophone regions: Covid-19 Scare rises as doctors abandon rural hospitals for fear of their lives (2020). *Mimi Mefo Info* (April 13). Retrieved from: https://mimimefoinfos.com/anglophone-regions-covid-19-scare-rises-as-doctors-abandon-rural-hospitals-for-fear-of-their-lives/

Onslaught in Kumbo Continues (2018). *Atlantic Chronicles* (December 6th). Retrieved from: https://www.atlanticchronicles.com/everyday-people/grim-story-of-kumbo-war-woes-as-narrated-by-radio-evangelium/

Azohnwi, A. (2021). Cameroon–Anglophone Crisis: Motorbikes banned in Bali after separatists ambushed, killed five police officers. Cameroon-Info-Net, July 20. Retrieved from: http://www.cameroon-info.net/article/cameroon-anglophone-crisis-motorbikes-banned-in-bali-after-separatists-ambushed-killed-five-police-officers-403059.html

Mimi Mefo Info (2021). Bali locals resort to trekking as bike/car circulation banned (July 30). Retrieved from: https://mimimefoinfos.com/bali-locals-resort-to-trekking-as-bike-car-circulation-banned/?fbclid=IwAR12I8gKdqMruNbeFd0Vaewiex4EdPmCkDoK_l-hPq7I9m-m35ZTfptguyQ4

Bankovic v. Belgium and 16 Other States, European Court of Human Rights (Grand Chamber) App. No. 52207/99, Dec. 12, 2001, 41 ILM 517 (2002).

Brilman, M. (2017). *Trial Observation Report – Cameroon: Case of Nkongho Felix Agbor Bala, Fontem Neba and Others. Hearing 27 April 2017, Military Tribunal Yaoundé*. The Law Society of England and Wales.

Territorial Administration: New Measures restrict circulation of commercial Motorbikes (2018), *Cameroon Radio Television (CRTV)*. (March 10). Retrieved from: https://www.crtv.cm/2018/03/territorial-administration-new-measures-restrict-circulation-of-commercial-motorbikes/

Convention (I) for the Amelioration of the Condition of the Wounded and Sick in Armed Forces in the Field. Geneva, 12 August 1949). Commentary of 2016, Article 3: Conflicts not of an international character. Retrieved from: https://ihl databases.icrc.org/applic/ihl/ihl.nsf/Comment.xsp?action=openDocument&documentId=59F6CDFA490736C1C1257F7D-004BA0EC#_Toc465169884

Edelstein, L. (1996). *The Hippocratic oath: text, translation and interpretation*. Baltimore, MD: Johns Hopkins University Press.

Eko, L. (2019). African Television in the Age of Globalization, Digitization, and Media Convergence. In *The Routledge Companion to Global Television*, Shawn Shimpach (ed., pp. 421-435). London: Routledge

Eko, L. (2019b). Couching Political Criticism in Humor: The Case of Musical Parodies of the Military in Cameroon and Congo-Brazzaville. In Uche Onyebadi (ed). *Music and Messaging in the African Political Arena* (pp, 87-107). Hershey, PA: IGL Global.

Eko, L. (2002). Bombs and Bombast in the NATO Yugoslav War of 1999: The Attack on Radio Television Serbia and the Laws of War. *Communications and the Law* 24 (3) 1-35.

Eko, L. (2003). The English-language Press and the "Anglophone Problem" in Cameron: Group Identity, Culture and the Politics of Nostalgia, *Journal of Third World Studies* XX (1) 79-102.

Foguem A. (2020). Cameroon: Anglophone inmates protest after Thomas Tangem dies, chained to hospital bed. *Journal du Cameroun.com* June 8th. Retrieved from: https://www.journalducameroun.com/en/news-in-brief/ cameroon-anglophone-inmates-protest-after-thomas-tangem-dies-chained-to-hospital-bed/

Freudenthal, E. (2019). Inside Cameroon's Bunker: Different guys had different torture techniques. *African Arguments*, May 7. Retrieved from: https://africanarguments.org/2019/05/ inside-cameroon-torture-bunker/

Fritsche, G., Soeters, R., Meessen, B. (2014). *Performance-Based Financing Toolkit. World Bank Training*. Washington, DC: World Bank. Retrieved from: https://openknowledge.worldbank. org/handle/10986/17194.

Fungwe, N. (2021). Separatist fighters prohibit movements of vehicles in Bali, Mimi Mefi Info, July 21. Retrieved from: https://mimimefoinfos.com/ separatist-fighters-prohibit-movement-of-vehicles-in-bali/

Habaasa, D. (2022). Suspension DWB Activities in Southwest region. Doctors Without Borders (Letter of March 29). Retrieved from: <iframe src="https://www.facebook.com/ plugins/post.php?href=https%3A%2F%2Fwww.facebook.com%2Fagbor.balla%2F-posts%2F10158215972252063&show_text=true&width=500" width="500" height="698" style="border:none;overflow:hidden" scrolling="no" frameborder="0" allowfullscreen="true" allow="autoplay; clipboard-write; encrypted-media; picture-in-picture; web-share"></iframe>

Cameroon: Civilians killed in Anglophone Regions (2020). *Human Rights Watch* (July 27th). Retrieved from: https://www.hrw.org/news/2020/07/27/cameroon-civilians-killed-anglophone-regions#

International Committee of the Red Cross (1949). Geneva Convention (I) for the Amelioration of the Condition of the Wounded and Sick in Armed Forces in the Field. Geneva, 12 August 1949. Retrieved from: https://ihl-databases.icrc.org/applic/ihl/ihl.nsf/Article. xsp?action=openDocument&documentId=D8F87DF50E554BC2C12563CD0051A030

International Committee of the Red Cross (1977). Protocol Additional to the Geneva Conventions of 12 August 1949 and relating to the Protection of Victims of Non-International Armed Conflicts (Protocol II), 8 June 1977.

Article 9, Protection of medical and religious personnel. Retrieved from: https://ihldatabases.icrc. org/applic/ihl/ihl.nsf/Treaty.xsp?action=openDocument&documentId=AA0C5BCBAB-5C4A85C12563CD002D6D09

International Committee of the Red Cross (2016). Convention (I) for the Amelioration of the Condition of the Wounded and Sick in Armed Forces in the Field. Geneva, 12 August 1949.

Article 3: Conflicts not of an international character Commentary of 2016. Retrieved from: https:// ihldatabases.icrc.org/applic/ihl/ihl.nsf/Comment.xsp?action=openDocument&documen-tId=59F6CDFA490736C1C1257F7D004BA0EC#_Toc465169884

Cameroon: Fako SDO bans circulation of bikes throughout the division (2021). *Journal du Cameroun.com* (January 1). Retrieved from: https://www.journalducameroun.com/en/

cameroon-fako-sdo-bans-circulation-of-bikes-throughout-division/

One killed, medical equipment damaged in Esu shootout (2019). *Journal du Cameroun. com* Cameroon *(*May 27). Retrieved from: https://www.journalducameroun.com/en/ cameroon-one-killed-medical-equipment-damaged-in-shootout-in-esu/

Kindzeka, M, (2018). Medical staff targeted in Cameroon's English-speaking regions, *Deutsche Welle*, August 17. Retrieved from: https://www.dw.com/en/ medical-staff-targeted-in-cameroons-english-speaking-regions/a-45119170

Kindzeka, M. (2021). Cameroon Releases MSF Workers Held After Helping Rebel Leader. The Voice of America. December 28. Retrieved from: https://www.voanews.com/a/cameroon-releases-msf-health-workers-held-after-helping-rebel-leader/6372803.html

Kongeh, S. (2019). Soldiers in search of Amba fighters ransack Shisong Hospital! *The Guardian Post*, Nov. 16, 2021, p. 1.

Lasagna, L. (1964). The Hippocratic Oath: Modern version. *Public Broadcasting Corporation, Nova Doctors' Diaries*. Retrieved from: https://www.pbs.org/wgbh/nova/doctors/oath_modern.html

Mbonwoh, N. (2018). Cameroon: Ban on Moto-Bikes-Worrying Causes Effects. Cameroon Tribune, March 13. Retrieved from: https://allafrica.com/stories/201803130563.html

Mbuoh, A (2021). Report of the Military Invasion of the St. Elizabeth Catholic General Hospital, Shisong. Open Letter, November 25.

People in Northwest seek healthcare as MSF Denied Providing medical services (2021), *Médecins Sans Frontières (June 22). Retrieved from: https://www.msf.org/ msf-denied-providing-badly-needed-healthcare-northwest-cameroon.*

Health worker detained for "associating" with separatist fighters (2020). *Mimi Mefo Info* (March 16). Retrieved from: https://mimimefoinfos.com/ health-worker-detained-for-associating-with-separatist-fighters/

Njinikom: Separatists impose ban on the circulation of motorbikes (2021). *Mimi Mefo Info* Retrieved from: https://mimimefoinfos.com/njinikom-separatists-impose-ban-on-circulation-of-motorbikes/

Ndi, E. (2020). Outrage After Detainee Dies Chained to Hospital Bed. The Daily Nation (Nairobi). August 7. Retrieved from: https://allafrica.com/stories/202008100372.html

Northwest and Southwest Crisis Report No. 8-As of 3 June (2019). OCHA. Retrieved from: https:// reliefweb.int/report/cameroon/cameroon-north-west-and-south-west-crisis-situation-report-no-8-30-june-2019

UNESCO Director-General urges investigation into the death of journalist Samuel Wazizi in Cameroon (2020). *UNESCO* (June 16). Retrieved from: https://en.unesco.org/news/ unesco-director-general-urges-investigation-death-journalist-samuel-wazizi-cameroon

When Parliament speaks truth to Biya but avoids armed conflict in NW, SW. (2022). *The Guardian Post* April 13, p. 4.

Timfuchi, A. (2021). Njinikom: Separatist Fighters lift over one-month lockdown after compulsory payments by shopkeepers. *Mimi Mefo Info*, July 17th. Retrieved from: https://mimimefoinfos. com/njinikom-separatist-fighters-life-over-one-month-lockdown-after-compulsory-payment-by-shopkeepers/

Willis, R., McAulay, J., Ndeunyema, N., & Angove, J. (2019). *Human Rights Abuses in the Cameroon Anglophone Crisis: A Submission of Evidence to UK Parliament*. Faculty of Law, Oxford University.

FOURTEEN

Na Mama Amba Drama

A Soyinkan Reading of Language, Torture and Resistance in the Anglophone Revolt

LYOMBE EKO

Memorandum to: My former French Teachers, Madame Le Sage, Madame Chabret, Monsieur Van Dorpe, Lycée Bilingue/ Bilingual Grammar School, Molyko, Buea
Cc: Monsieur Meva Ondo Henri, Principal, Monsieur Ava Ava Ndzié,
Monsieur Nguimbus Nkou (Francophone Cameroun French teachers), Monsieur Yves X, teacher, *Français Par la Radio*, Radio Buea

From: Lyombe Eko, former student at Bilingual Grammar School, Molyko, Buea

Subject: The Intellectual Dissonance of a Former Anglophone French Student

Date: May 20, 2021
My Dear French Teachers,

This unusual letter may come as a bolt from the blue, a total surprise to you. I was a student at the Bilingual Grammar School, Molyko, about 40 years ago. I had the good fortune of having all of you from France and French Cameroon as my French teachers. Your classes were, for me, a gateway to the French language, culture, and civilization. You taught me about *Liberté, égalité, fraternité,* secular humanism (*laïcité*), moral philosophy (ethics), universal human rights, and human dignity. You taught me that France is the civilizational lighthouse that guides the ship of humanity in the stormy ocean of universal barbarianism and irrationality. You introduced me to the problem of evil, of human existence (existentialism), and its philosophical rejection of a world system founded on the hideous and harrowing suffering (torture) of children (Dostoevsky). You taught me memorable lessons like: "*If there is no God, everything is permitted,*" and "*The degree of civilization in a society can be judged by entering its prisons*" (Dostoevsky); "*Freedom is what you do with what's been done to you*" (Sartre), and "*I rebel; therefore, I exist*" (Camus). These words stayed with me and colored my worldview as I went to university in the United States and became an international professional communicator, translator, and, ultimately, a university professor. I am eternally grateful to you all because you taught me how to think and what to think about. I have traveled around the world looking at the problem of human existence from the prism of the ideas of Pascal, Descartes, Kant, Voltaire, Montesquieu, Diderot, Moliere, Sartre, Dostoyevsky, Senghor, and so on. I became a Francophile, a professional French-English translator, a researcher, and an author in comparative and international communication law and policy, France being my starting point. I admired French universal humanitarianism and your country's human rights posture…until I had a head-on collision with reality, the sad reality of the role of France and the French language in the atrocities and massive human rights violations of the so-called "Anglophone crisis" in Cameroon.

This is the reality for me and millions of Anglophones from the former Southern Cameroons: French has become the language of violence for us. It is the language of death. We are legislated in French, dictated to, and decreed in French, arrested in French, tortured in French, tried arbitrarily in French, sentenced to death in French, and executed with French bullets. The last harsh expressions of dehumanization, of man's inhumanity to man, are enunciated in the French language, African-accented French language. This Francophile has developed acute cognitive dissonance, a burning ambivalence bordering on revulsion toward the French language.

Through my exploration of the political and cultural history of the Anglophone Question in Cameroon, I stumbled upon confidential correspondence from the first French Ambassador to the Federal Republic of Cameroon, His Excellency Jean-Pierre Bernard, to the first French Consul in Buea, West Cameroon, Monsieur Yves Robin. These letters, the first of which was dated 8 January 1962, indicated that the posting of French teachers to Bilingual Grammar School Molyko was part and parcel of a French postcolonial *mission assimilisatrice* (assimilating mission) to English-speaking Cameroon. This was the extension of the "famous" colonial *"mission civilisatrice* (civilizing mission) to the English and Pidgin-speaking State of West Cameroon. This assimilating mission consisted of muting the cultural and identitarian specificity of the State of West Cameroon, and assimilating it into *la Francophonie*, the French linguistic and cultural sphere. The French language you taught Anglophones was essentially the passport and entry visa into this imagined superior French civilizational community where English-speaking West Cameroonians would be transformed into speakers of the French language. That diplomatic correspondence was indeed an eye-opener. It explained many historical events in Cameroon, including the illegal dissolution of the Federal Republic of Cameroon and its replacement with a highly centralized, Napoleonic, United Republic of Cameroon, renaming the country the "Republic of Cameroon," the original name of Francophone East Cameroon, and division of the former State of West Cameroon into the Northwest and Southwest provinces for easier dispersal into the Francophone national, and faster assimilation into *la Francophonie*.

The aim of this missive from Middle America, where I live and ply my trade as an educator, is to acquaint you with the unfortunate outcome of French extension of the colonial "civilizing and assimilationist mission" to English and Pidgin-speaking State of Southern Cameroons after the reunification of British Southern Cameroons and la République du Cameroun in 1961. Since the situation has taken a dramatic turn for the worse since France and la République du Cameroun set their assimilationist program in motion in 1962, I present this sad postcolonial African hegemonic domination and dehumanization in the form of a collection of dramatic vignettes.

Act I

Scene 1

Na Mama Amba Drama: Women's Spoken-word Poetry of Resistance Against the Cameroon Army's Human Rights Violations

Video: https://www.facebook.com/isaac.zama.9828/videos/171645178188354

Setting: Market place in Wum, Menchum County (Northwest region). Late evening. Group of women in their "meeting best" attire, beautiful, multi-colored head ties, nice blouses, modest but elegant "wrappers" and long dresses or "kabas". Two burnt-out buildings, evidence of military atrocities, form the background of this colorful assembly of mothers, aunts, sisters, wives, mothers-in-law, newly-weds, and mothers-to-be.

This beautiful and colorful scene of singing and chanting women could have been in any African country, any African town where women gather to celebrate the birth of children, rejoice at the successes of their grown children, welcome newly married ladies to their midst, commiserate and condole with bereaved friends, "celebrate" the death of relatives, engage in charitable work or just hold a "meeting" to relax, sing, dance, and forget their ever-present heavy travails to keep the bodies and souls of their family members together. However, attentive listening to the song and dance these women were performing reveals that this was no ordinary women's meeting. It was a spontaneous and creative speech, chant and dance performance. It was an African call-and-response performativity of resistance at its best. In Pidgin English, it was described alliteratively as: "Na mama Amba drama" (It is the drama of the Amba mamas/mothers).

"Se le Mama Amba, Se le Mama Amba, passay ici là ! passay ici là !" (It is the Amba Mama, it is the Amba Mama, Get over here! Get over here!). The women were imitating orders Cameroon soldiers shout at them in a mixture of garbled "Franci" (French) and Aghem or Bafu'wum, the language of the area. This was the women's exaggerated mimicry, their mocking imitation of the insulting and accusatory epithet, "C'est une maman Amba, passez ici-là!" (That is an Amba mother/mother of an Ambazonian fighter, get over here!) that Cameroon soldiers hurl at women and mothers in Southern Cameroons at every turn. These French, Israeli, and American-trained soldiers march unannounced into localities and transform schools, health centers, private homes, church-owned buildings and even churches themselves into temporary barracks. They subsequently proceeded to burn down entire villages suspected of harboring Ambazonian independentist fighters. The old, infirm, and very young who cannot escape into the bush perish in the village infernos. Accusing a woman of being a Maman Amba, the mother, wife, girlfriend, or sister of an Ambazonian resistance fighter, is grounds for arrest, rape, torture, detention and even murder.

The "Na Mama Amba drama" of Wum is one of the most dramatic acts of defiance and resistance to come out of Anglophone Cameroon since the Cameroon government decided to crush unarmed Anglophone civilian demonstrators in 2016 and triggered the so-called Anglophone crisis. These women from Wum were bravely defying and resisting brutal and notorious Israeli, French, and American-trained Cameroon soldiers who descend in the middle of the night without warning on villages suspected of harboring or being friendly to Anglophone independentist fighters, break into their houses, kill their husbands and sons with impunity, torture and rape them along with their daughters, and burn down their villages. These women are the victims of collective punishment meted out by the *Bataillon d'Intervention Rapide* (BIR), the notorious, armed military unit known for its crimes against humanity. The BIR does its dastardly scorched-earth job along with other branches of the Cameroon army, and gendarmerie.

Figure 14.1. Screenshot of "Mama Amba": performative resistance of women in Wum. They use Aghem, the local language) and "Franci" (broken French) spoken-word mimicry in front of a destroyed building in Wum.

What crimes are these women accused of?
"Se le Mama Amba, se le Mama Amba, passez ici-la."
They are accused of being: "Maman Amba! Maman Amba! Get over here!" The women made this highly humiliating and accusatory epithet the source of poetic inspiration. They recite and sing it with defiant facial gestures, ironic smiles, and symbolic hand movements. They sing, chant, and perform their resistance in the marketplace, thereby reclaiming their human dignity. They proclaim loud and clear, repeat again and again, their ironic, poetic mimicry of the Francophone soldiers' degrading accusation that is leveled at them on a daily basis, the penal sentence that is pronounced on them before they are harassed, jailed, tortured, raped and murdered with impunity by soldiers trained by Western custodians of

human rights and human dignity.

14.2. Screenshot of Women of Wum chanting their parodic rhyme of resistance against harassment by the Cameroon security forces.

"Se le Mama Amba, Se le Mama Amba, passay ici là ! passay ici là !"

This is their parody of the humiliating accusation and imputation of guilt that gives the Cameroon soldier a license to abuse and impose collective punishment. The "sins" of the children are now being visited on their mothers on a daily basis, to paraphrase and invert the Biblical saying. These women had had enough. These women defiantly used a staple of African musicology and oral literature, the rhythmic call-and-response, spoken-word chant, recitation, pronouncement and incantation. These poetic recitations are punctuated and accompanied by choral refrains, musical interludes, and choruses that add emphasis, fervency and immediacy to the music and poetry of defiance of the "Mama Amba." These women use the African spoken-word poetry, chants and ululations as instruments of resistance and defiance against these French-speaking perpetrators of crimes against humanity who deploy the French language as a weapon of war designed to mute them. These women demonstrate once again that in Cameroon, in Africa, French is the language of violence and human rights violations, the language of oppression, death and destruction:

« *Se le Mama Amba, Se le Mama Amba, passay ici là ! passay ici là !* »

The defiant mothers then engage in an imaginary dialogue with their harassers,

"When you were infants suckling in your mothers' breasts, did they advise you to become soldiers, killers of innocent men, women and children? Are your mothers responsible for your atrocities? If your mothers are not responsible for your acts of violence, why are you holding us responsible and punishing us for the acts of our sons who decided to become Ambazonia fighters? Violence is not passed on to children through their mother's breast milk. Who said so? The peaceful women you insult: *"Se le Mama Amba, Se le Mama Amba, passay ici la! passay ici la!"* and harass as they struggle daily to feed their families"

14.3. Screenshot of Women performing their protests against the military (Wum).

Ultimately, these defiant mothers of Wum turned this French epithet that the Cameroon army and BIR hurl at them into a tool of empowerment. They turn the slur, the insult, that is meant to be an instrument of dehumanization, on its head. They bravely and proudly embrace it, drain it of its oppressive poison by mimicking it. They engulf it in their African language, parody it, drain it of its oppressive venom, and turn it against their tormentors, the occupying force from *la République du Cameroun.*

"Se le Mama Amba, Se le Mama Amba, passay ici là ! passay ici là !"

Misuse of grammar, whether deliberate or not, is one of the most powerful instruments of resistance against the French, whose language is their religion. These Anglophone mothers of Wum were deliberately blaspheming the French language, satirizing the Cameroon military and, by extension, Francophone Cameroon. Who said so?

"Se le Mama Amba, Se le Mama Amba, passay ici là ! passay ici là !"

As the defiant women of Wum performed their resistance against being muted and erased, they chanted the Pidgin proverb: "You born pikin, you no born ye heart," (You give birth to a child, you don't give birth to that child's mind). Meaning, all individuals have free will. Mothers should not be punished for the actions of their children.

Figure 14.4. Object of the satire of the "Mama Amba": Late Israeli Defense Forces Col. Avi Sivan, Technical/Security Adviser at the Presidency of Cameroon in charge of the *Bataillon d'Intervention Rapide* (BIR) and the *Guarde Présidentiel* (Presidential Guard) handing soldiers awards and diplomas after their training at Man O'War Bay, Limbe (2010).

Scene II

Enter Wole Soyinka

My Dear French Teachers from France,

The lessons you taught me about French universal humanitarianism, human rights, and democracy suddenly rang hollow and hypocritical as I watched the army of the authoritarian, neo-patrimonial regime of President Paul Biya attempt to subjugate the English and Pidgin-speaking Northwest and Southwest region, and forcefully assimilate it into *la Francophonie* in order to seize its rich natural resources–oil, natural gas, agricultural products, timber, iron ore, and so on – once and for all. Pascal, Descartes, Kant, Voltaire, Montesquieu, Diderot, Moliere, Sartre, Dostoyevsky, and even Senghor, had not provided me with tools to analyze and understand the monstrous human rights violations funded by Switzerland, France, China, and the United Kingdom, and carried out by the Israeli-trained and equipped killing automatons of the BIR in Anglophone Cameroon (Melman, 2010). These partnerships in crimes against humanity did not make sense.

I soon lost faith in the "Western" universal humanitarianism and the human dignity that is touted by France at every turn. I became skeptical about the rationality, the positive, structured and structuring power of the French language and culture as a civilizing force. In international affairs, human rights violators have strange bedfellows. In Cameroon, it is always French, Israeli, Chinese, British, American, Russian and Swiss interests über alles. Human rights be damned. Rather than look to European philosophers to explain the conundrum of French, British, and Israeli high ideals and their base, inhuman conduct in the postcolonial context of Cameroon, I turned to Wole Soyinka, winner of the Nobel Prize for Literature, for inspiration. Soyinka provides intellectual insights on fear, power, and human rights violations that help me make sense of the contradictions of "the French Problem" in Cameroon. The elements of this contradiction are the role of France – and its exalted humanitarian ideals, the so-called French civilizing mission, and the French language as instruments for the furtherance of the subjugation of Anglophones in Cameroon.

Wole Soyinka is a philosopher of the arbitrary power, oppression, and the political deployment of fear as an instrument of human control and subjugation. From his lived experience in the treacherous shoals of alternating civilian chieftaincy and autocratic military regimes in Nigeria, Soyinka has developed theories that explain how authoritarian regimes and individuals control and subjugate others. In his collection of essays, "*Climate of Fear: Quest for Dignity in a Dehumanized World*," Soyinka suggests that dictators and powerful autocrats who are "lodged in the hermetic enclosure of absolutism," use fear as a weapon and deploy rhetoric [language] as the "readiest killing device." According to Soyinka, Nigerian military regimes did not care for the niceties of the rule of law. The legally questionable public executions that they carried out were "defiant acts of murder" that flouted the most elementary principles of justice, for purposes of creating a climate of fear in the populace. However, fear is not instilled in the populace for the sake of it. Soyinka adds that fear is a weapon, fear is deployed as an instrument of control, "a prelude to the domination of the mind and the triumph of power." The dictatorial state, he suggests, "represents power at its crudest," and dictatorial African states are intimately acquainted with the "exegesis of [interpretations and manifestations] of power…the thrill of power… the pure ambiance of power." Dictatorial power humiliates, humbles, and dehumanizes others. One of the enduring traits of literature is its timelessness, its clairvoyant relevance across time, space, and cultures. Soyinka may have been speaking of Southern Cameroons when he wrote in 2004 about the deterritorialized reality of alien forces in science fiction: "in order to ensure absolute submission, that alien force must first lay a track of fear on which it rolls its juggernaut of domination." In Cameroon, that "alien" force is the notorious, Israeli-trained and equipped BIR, which is a "dispenser of life and death…a purveyor of terror," which has no moral restraints as it leaves violence and atrocities in its wake in the English-speaking West Cameroon.

As one who lived under the climate of fear imposed by military dictatorships in Nigeria, Soyinka advanced the idea that the response to the climate of fear, power and domination is resistance, the resolve not to yield to dehumanization, the determination to assert human dignity and freedom, the refusal to "forego our fundamental right of existence." In his prison memoirs, *The Man Died*, Wole Soyinka sends out a clarion call: those who keep silent in the face of injustice, brutality, and violence, die! Our humanity dies, we lose our human dignity when we succumb to the pathology of fear, embrace and become molded by the Climate of Fear, with a capital F.

These ideas of Soyinka serve as the framework within which I explore videos of happenings in the Anglophone Revolt that illustrate the themes of fear, torture, dehumanization, violence, and of language as an instrument of power, violence, and subjugation. They say that power corrupts, and absolute power corrupts absolutely. That is true of run-of-the-mill dictatorships and military juntas. In the kleptocratic, tribalistic, republican chiefdom of Cameroon, things have been notched up by an order of magnitude: raw power intoxicates and corrupts, absolute power corrupts absolutely. It kills, and tortures with absolute impunity.

The Mama Amba Drama that took place in Wum in April 2021 was dramatized resistance through parody and linguistic mimicry. Though enveloped by a climate of fear, humiliation and dehumanization that came with the "civilized" language, "Franci," the women of Wum refused to lie down, be muted and erased, take the "forced diet of indignity," to use the expression of Soyinka, suffer in silence, and die! Viva Mama Amba!

Scene III

Resistance to French Assimilation in English and Pidgin-Speaking Southern Cameroons

My Dear French Teachers from France,

The French language, which I studied with such eagerness under your tutelage at Bilingual Grammar School, Molyko, has become problematic in English and Pidgin-speaking Southern Cameroons. This is a result of the authoritarian policy of assimilating English speakers into *la Francophonie*. The Anglophone Question in Cameroon – and I summarize it as arrogant lack of respect for the identitarian and cultural specificity of the English and Pidgin-speaking minority in Cameroon – is one of the last unresolved problems of 19th-century European imperialism in Africa. It is also an unresolved problem of World War I, the Treaty of Versailles of 1919, the United Nations Trusteeship system, and decolonization. It is the outcome of European power dynamics and postcolonial hegemonic relationships between Anglophone and Francophone Cameroon. The French language and culture have become problematic in English-and Pidgin-speaking Northwest and Southwest regions due to high-handed assimilationist measures on the part of the over-centralized, authoritarian, republican chieftaincy of Cameroon, with the backing of France, the UK, Israel and Russia. The Anglophone "problem" is a problem of resistance, resistance against the imposition of the asphyxating, postcolonial Francophone African hegemonic system on the English-medium educational system and the common law courts of the former West Cameroon. The Mama Amba of Wum were only the latest English and Pidgin-speaking group in West Cameroon to take issue with and resist the French language and what it has come to represent for us, the objects of forced assimilation and relentless repression.

Let us rewind to 2016. In effect, the heirs and custodians of the two bulwarks of Anglophone culture and identity, lawyers and teachers, went on strike to resist forced "harmonization," assimilation and dispersal of the English-medium common law and educational systems of the minority Southern Cameroons into the majority Francophone East Cameroon system. Common law lawyers donned their robes and wigs and took to the streets in desperation, and peacefully demanded a halt to measures taken to assimilate and marginalize the common law legal system that obtained in the Northwest and Southwest regions. These measures had included flooding English-medium, common law courts with French-speaking judges and magistrates, who did not have mastery of the English language, having been trained in the French Napoleonic civil law system. For their part, English-medium teachers in the Northwest and Southwest regions went on strike to protest government flooding of primary schools in these English-speaking regions with Francophone teachers who did not have mastery of the English language and were not competent enough to teach English-speaking students in the English-medium sub-system. That was the beginning of the so-called, Anglophone crisis. Since the start of the Anglophone crisis in 2016, the Cameroon military has carried out a scorched earth policy that has created climates of fear, forcing hundreds of thousands to flee to Nigeria as refugees. Hundreds of thousands more have become internally displaced persons. While these human rights violations were going on, France, the African Union, the United Nations, and the international community have offered only the most tepid and insipid "condemnations," to use the formulation of Wole Soyinka.

Act II

Scene I

The Predecessors of Les Mamans Amba
My Dear French Teachers from France,
The French Language has always been a variable in the Anglophone "crisis." We have examined the problematic situation of the French language in Anglophone Cameroon through the lenses of the resistance of the Mamans Amba, the common law lawyers and English-medium teachers. The Anglophone crisis in Cameroon is, at its core, a problem of absolute power, lack of democracy, tolerance and an authoritarian rejection of political compromise. We now turn to the narrative of two brave Cameroonians, one from the English-speaking zone and the other from the French-speaking zone, who presented the "French problem" in Cameroon to a national and international audience. In December 2016, human rights lawyer, Felix Nkongho Agbor Balla, President of the Fako Lawyers' Association, and of the Anglophone Civil Society Consortium, a collective of common law lawyers and teachers in Anglophone Cameroon, told Equinoxe Television in Douala, that for the English and Pidgin-speaking minority linguistic community of Cameroon: "French is the language of oppression." That declaration, on a television station in French Cameroon, was stunning as it was perceptive. However, it was not farfetched. It aptly and pithily described and explained the predominant role of the French language in the political repression and ferocious military subjugation by force of arms and draconian military tribunals, of the Anglophone minority that had dared to revolt against Francophone assimilation and marginalization. The repressive instruments of the State – the *Guarde présidentielle*, the army, the Israeli-trained and equipped BIR, all branches of military, the paramilitary Gendarmerie, the police, and even prison warders all do government business in French. All proceedings before Military Tribunals are in French. The rule of thumb is: "*l'armée n'est pas bilingue*" (the army is not bilingual).

As a result of this reality, for the Anglophone minority, oppression speaks French. Suspects are arrested in French, they are imprisoned in French, jailed in French, tortured

380

in French, tried in French, sentenced in French, incarcerated in French. Villages are burned in French, and civilians are summarily executed in French. Military Tribunal proceedings against civilians are in French, convictions and sentences are handed down in French. In Cameroon, life, and especially death, come in French. As the Amba Mamas' resistance against "Franci" demonstrates, to Anglophones in Cameroon, French is the language of cultural subjugation, oppression, intimidation, injustice, exploitation, rape, and violence. Even the climate of fear and the infrastructure of repression that reigns over Anglophones has a red, white and blue French tinge to it. The armored cars that strike terror are French – in addition to those of Russian, Chinese, Israeli, and British vintage–but they were, first and foremost, French. The guns are French (and Israeli and Russian –the hand grenades are French, the rocket-propelled grenades are French. To English and Pidgin-speaking Cameroonians in Southern Cameroons, death speaks French.

The Cameroonian authorities were not amused by Agbor Balla's Anglophone federalist, common law activism. He was arrested at his home in Buea, blindfolded, and transferred to the dungeons of the *Secretariat d'État à la Defense* in Yaoundé, and later tried at the Yaoundé Military Tribunal, along with other members of the Anglophone Civil Society Consortium. That essentially meant transferring them from the common law jurisdiction of Southern Cameroons to the civil law jurisdiction of Francophone Cameroon. On 20 January 2017, they were charged with "terrorism, hostility against the motherland, secession, insurrection, contempt of public authorities, and collective rebellion"; "incitement to civil war by bringing the inhabitants of the South- and Northwest regions to arm themselves against other citizens"; and "attempt[ing] to modify the constitutional laws, notably the federalist system, through violence." Though Agbor Balla and his co-accused are civilians, they were charged in the Military Tribunal because their alleged offenses fell under Law No. 2014/028 of 23 December 2014 on the Suppression Acts of Terrorism. Though Agbor Balla and his co-accused are part of the Anglophone minority, the proceedings were carried out in French, and they did not have the benefit of English interpreters. This is also the case in military tribunals throughout the country. Proceedings against civilians are in French, convictions and sentences are handed down in French; and they are imprisoned in hellish French-speaking prisons. In Cameroon, life, and especially death, comes in French. To Anglophones in Cameroon, French is the language of military subjugation, cultural assimilation, intimidation, exploitation, rape, and violence. Military torturers issue orders in perfect French as they mete out harsh, inhuman, and dehumanizing treatment on their Anglophone victims in public places and prison dungeons. French is the language of postcolonialism, of brutality and death. Even the climate of fear and the infrastructure of repression that reigns over Anglophones has a red, white, and blue, as well as an Israeli Star of David (Melman, 2010). The armored cars are French; the guns are French and Israeli; the hand grenades are French and Israeli; the rocket-propelled grenades are French, and their sonorous explosions sound like French and Hebrew…. In Limbe, Buea, Ekona, Muyuka, Kumba, Mamfe, Bamenda, Bambalang, Kom, Wum, Bui, and Donga Mantung, Death, with a capital D., speaks French. Cameroon prisons are hell on earth, their official language is French.

Scene II

Patrice Nganang and the Criminalization of the French Language in NOSO

Another person who had issues with – it is perhaps more accurate to say, "took exception to" – the French language as an instrument of oppression was Prof. Patrice Nganang. A Francophone Cameroonian-American scholar, notable writer and professor of Comparative Literature at Stony Brook University (SUNY), Nganang has written extensively about the atrocities the French colonial army visited on anti-colonial freedom fighters in French Cameroon from the 1950s to the 1970s. Nganang has also written about the Anglophone Revolt. In 2021, he declared that Ambazonian separatists had succeeded in making French a "criminal language." The professor, who has written about the Cameroonian street slang, *Camfranglais*, a hodge-podge of French, Pidgin English, and African dialects, had traveled to Buea in the English and Pidgin-speaking region of Cameroon, and written critically about the government's massive human rights violations in response to the political occurrence that is the Anglophone Revolt. The Cameroon government was not amused by the trenchant criticism of Professor Nganang. As he was about to board a flight at the Douala International Airport, he was arrested and "disappeared" for a few days. His wife and friends raised the alarm. Days later, it turned out that he was being held in the dungeons of the Gendarmerie headquarters, the *Sécretariat d'État à la Defense* (SED). He was later transferred to the notorious Kondengui prison in Yaoundé. After intense pressure from the United States government (Nganang has American citizenship), he was released 14 days later, stripped of his Cameroonian citizenship, and deported to the United States (Maher, 2018).

The cases of Barrister Agbor Balla and Professor Patrice Nganang describe and explain perceptions of France and the French in the context of the Anglophone Revolt. As the Anglophone uprising took a turn for the worse, English-speaking Cameroonian demonstrators in the Diaspora – Brussels, London, Berlin, Paris, New York, Washington D.C, and South Africa –demonstrated in front of French embassies, blaming France and its subalterns in Yaoundé for the oppression of Anglophones, and calling for a world-wide boycott of French goods. Furthermore, Ambazonian separatists attacked and burned Brasseries du Cameron beer trucks, as well as trucks carrying timber out of Southern Cameroons. In response, France issued a travel advisory warning to its citizens from traveling to Limbe, Buea, and other locations in the English-speaking regions of Cameroon. Alarmed, the French ambassador, His Excellency Gilles Thibault, made known the position of France with regard to the Anglophone problem in a speech delivered at the French Embassy in Yaoundé on July 14, 2017, the French national day. In the middle of his speech, suddenly and without warning, the ambassador switched to English, an unprecedented departure from the traditional French government requirement that all official speeches be made in French.

The Ambassador Thibault told his invitees (who included Anglophone politicians and academics) in English:

"I am proud that my country has never made a difference between English and French-speaking areas" [of Cameroon].

That is precisely the problem. France has consistently refused to respect the identitarian and cultural specificity of English and Pidgin-speaking Southern Cameroons in its assimilationist drive. Apparently, Ambassador Thibault had not read the correspondence of his predecessors, who implemented the French government policy of working with the French Cameroon authorities to extend the French civilizing mission, and the frontiers of la Francophonie to the State of West Cameroon. Nevertheless, the Ambassador implied that France does not discriminate against Anglophones. At least he invited Anglophones and spoke in English, something President Biya had never done in his 40 plus years in power. Perhaps there is a difference between the French and Francophones after all!

My Dear French Teachers from France,

As the cases above demonstrate, the French language and culture that you taught me and hundreds of other English-speaking or Anglophone students in Bilingual Grammar School Molyko, have become problematic in the context of the Anglophone Revolt. France and the French language, I am sorry to say, have become part of the architecture of repression in Cameroon. This is particularly true in situations where the government and its unelected administrators issue oppressive decrees – in perfect French administrative form – that displace and dehumanize helpless people, as the *Préfet* Oum II Joseph did in Manyu in 2017. It is also problematic in military circles. In short, the French language has become associated with arbitrariness, oppression, subjugation, and crimes against humanity. The thought that the French language that you schooled us to appreciate has become an instrument that facilitates the commission of crimes against humanity by the government and the military in Cameroon causes emotional distress and intellectual dissonance.

Act III

The Anglophone Human-Swine Mud Bath of Molyko

My Dear French Teachers from France,

I have shown, through the episode of the Mama Amba in Wum, and the legal troubles of Barrister Felix Nkongho Agbor Balla and Professor Patrice Nganang that French and Francophone Cameroon imposed assimilationist measures had left a bitter taste in the mouths of English-and Pidgin-speaking Cameroonians in the Northwest and Southwest regions. These authoritarian measures had also shaken to the core, my heretofore favorable views of French universalist humanism and French commitment to human rights. The resistance that was marshaled by the victims of oppression and human rights abuses was a desperate response to atrocities that had been going on with impunity since the Anglophone Revolt began in 2016. The next two acts in this horrible drama actually preceded the performativity of resistance of the Mama Amba of Wum. They are video recordings of public torture. One of these horrific episodes took place not too far from Molyko, Buea, where our paths crossed many years ago as students and teachers.

In traditional, run-of-the-mill dictatorships and regimes obsessed with power, "national security," torture is an instrument of governance, a weapon of power, that is often meted out on political opponents, dissidents, naysayers, refusniks and other "enemies of the state," "enemies of the people" or "enemies of development" in dark, poorly lit underground dungeons and torture chambers. Torture chambers exist at the SED in Yaoundé and prisons across Cameroon to be sure, but the most blatant form of torture carried out in the English and Pidgin-speaking Southern Cameroons is a particularly dehumanizing form of torture as public spectacle – "baptism by mud" – at gunpoint. This consists of making the torture victim immerse himself or herself in mud, wallow like a human pig in the mirey, clayey muck, and marinate slowly in the slimy filth and dirt until the yuck penetrates every pore. This torture is generally carried out under the supervision of Israeli, French, and American-trained Cameroon soldiers at gunpoint. Power, dehumanizing power does indeed emanate from the barrel of the gun as Chinese Communist Party leader, Mao Zedong wrote in 1938. Bizarrely, these torture videos were recorded by the soldier-torturers, and posted on Facebook and other social media outlets.

Scene I

Son of Mama Amba: The Human-Swine Mud Bath at Gunpoint

Location: Unpaved, muddy, water-logged side road in a banana/plantain plantation in the Molyko/Muea area of Buea. The rainy season has turned the road into a muddy pool.
https://www.facebook.com/100003132982390/videos/pcb.1460277920753293/1460277810753304

Figure 14.5 Cameroonian soldier administering a human-swine mud bath torture at gun point to an Anglophone demonstrator (Molyko, 2018).

The one-minute forty-eight-second video is shot over the shoulder of a woman, a background female voice expressing consternation at what was happening, an indication that it was recorded surreptitiously. The sound of birds, the banana plantation in the background, wetness, the mud, and the pool of water in the middle ground tell us we are off the beaten path, somewhere in the Molyko or Muea or Ekona areas in the Buea sub-division. The eye of the viewer is immediately drawn to the center of the screen. The first perceptible image is the black silhouette of a man in greenish Cameroon army combat fatigues and a green beret. The soldier is standing on jet-black volcanic rock, the coarse-grained, sometimes sharp basaltic rock common in parts of the Fako division due to the eruptions of Mount Fako over time. The soldier is holding what looks like an AK-47 assault rifle and looking at a muddy pool filled with water in front of him. The weapon provides the directional cue the viewer needs to make sense of the scene. The legendary Russian weapon is pointed towards the ground and invites the eye to see what it is aimed at. Just then, what had seemed like an inanimate object in the muddy pool, starts rolling like a log towards the soldier. This log was clearly rolling uphill against the laws of gravity. A closer look reveals that it is a human being, a naked human log, hands outstretched over his head, rolling in a muddy pool of rainwater. He was heading towards the soldier who had the human-log's life in his hands. This is what Wole Soyinka (2005) called "power at its crudest, ...[an] exercise of raw power" (p. 30, 42). When the human log reached the feet of the soldier, he stopped and immediately started rolling in the opposite direction as if his life depended upon it. It was a parody of a swimmer training for the Olympic Games, only this was a one-man race to survive, to comply with the orders of a gun-wielding torturer! The man seemed to be acutely conscious of the menace that hung over him. Disobedience or hesitation of any sort meant death.

The first indication that this episode of dehumanization, this séance of torture, was a linguistic, cultural, and civilizational affair came in the form of an order barked by the demi-god of a soldier to the man whose life he had in his hands:

Figure 14.6. The Cameroon soldier making a torture victim to take his human-swine mud bath (Molyko, 2018).

"Porte! Ça! ...Tu mets sur la tête...Porte la boue la!" the soldier ordered, pointing to a pile of mud he wanted the victim to put on his head.

The victim quickly rolled over to the pile of mud, grabbed it with both hands, and rubbed it into his head with the gesture of someone rubbing and savoring the finest soap or shampoo into every pore of his head, every hair on his head. He did it slowly, deliberately, as if he were really enjoying it, desperately seeking to prolong his life, even by a few more minutes.

The next sound that was heard is the voice of a girl who was perhaps standing near the person recording the video:

"Hmmmm...Jesus, Oh God, Oh!

The mud on the young man's head must have seemed like the crown of thorns shoved down the scalp of Jesus Christ, as the good European missionaries, from Our Lady of Lourdes, and other Roman Catholic parishes had taught her. Her voice clearly had the surprise, mingled with revulsion of one who was scandalized that God would allow such cruelty on one of his children!

Figure 14.7. Anglophone mud shampoo at gun point (Molyko, 2018).

The soldier did not allow the man much time to "soap" his hair with the mud.

"*Roule maintenant comme ça!*" he ordered, indicating with his free hand, the direction in which he wanted the victim to roll!.

"*Monte sur les cailloux...quand tu roule tu tends les bras,*" the soldier ordered his victim to roll on the sharp basaltic volcanic rock while stretching his arms.

"Voila!" he exclaimed with satisfaction as the victim did what he was told.

As the victim came close to him, the soldier warned him that if one spot of mud appeared on his uniform, the victim will pay the penalty for it.

As the soldier followed his victim on the volcanic rocks, the camera revealed a road construction crew that was laying the volcanic rock from a wheelbarrow. Apparently, these workers had not been part of the anti-government Anglophone demonstrations. The workers focused on their work, ignoring the man who was being forced at gunpoint to roll on the volcanic rocks they were laying on the muddy road. The tension and urgency of the moment were palpable. The video was heading towards the climax of the episode. Mercifully for the viewer, the human swine rolled out of the frame, followed slowly by his

386

torturer. Fade to black.

No one knows who the anonymous victim was, who the soldier was, and who had shot the video. The camera was very steady and the action well framed. Perhaps it was recorded by another soldier or someone hiding in the nearby shed. Wole Soyinka suggests the army is the "laboratory of power," power that force feeds [its victims and opponents] with a diet of humiliation." One thing is certain: the video soon appeared on Facebook. Some Anglophones were scandalized by it…but nothing came of their indignation. The Cameroon army is notorious for torturing, even executing women and children with impunity. Videos like the Molyko torture video abound on social media. That is the legacy of one of the most ignored conflicts on the face of the earth.

Figure 14.8. Rock torture: rolling on sharp volcanic rocks at gun point (Molyko, 2018)

Scene II
Daughters of "Mama Amba": The Human-Swine Mud Bath of Bali
Location: Muddy, waterlogged road in front of Cameroon Protestant College, Bali, Mezam, Northwest region.
Characters: Two teenage girls and a group of French-speaking Cameroonian soldiers
Video: https://www.facebook.com/victor.samkoh/videos/1885517288153298/

The African human swine mud bath torture is the "exercise of raw power," "power at its crudest," a "lacerating memory [display] of antihumanism," to use the expressions of Wole Soyinka. The dehumanizing public, human swine mud bath is designed to create a climate of fear. It sends a public message, a warning to all who might be tempted to rebel or balk at conforming or obeying degrading orders. The Cameroon soldier has been conditioned by his Israeli, French, and Russian instructors to be judge, jury and executioner of unarmed civilians. Members of the Israeli-trained BIR are strangers to human rights and human dignity. They demonstrated this amply on the campus of the Cameroon Protestant College, Bali, Northwest region in 2018.

The video is just under five minutes long. Watching it feels like an eternity. This is because it is yet another demonstration of the raw display of inhumanity and power – in its military sense of force, domination, and control, as well as its ballistic sense (dynamite).

The video shows "power at its crudest," it portrays the "obsession to dominate," as Africa's Nobel Laureate, Wole Soyinka put it in his collection of essays entitled, *Climate of Fear.* For his part, Stendhal stated that: "power is the greatest of all pleasures." He was not far from the truth. The video is an excellent piece of visual narrative, a masterpiece of tragic visual storytelling. As a parent, the father of two daughters, it is one of the most grotesque displays of inhumanity I have watched.

The scene opens on a muddy road that looks like a flooded, mirey cesspool. We hear a low cough that sounded as if it emanated from a quaking female and then a loud masculine voice barking out four words:

"Go, go, go...Go!"

Figure 14.9. "Human-swine" girl; the mud bath with shadow of a gun-toting soldier supervising her torture (Bali, 2018).

We see the form of a woman lying face down in the cesspool, her head lifted, struggling to drag herself forward in terrified obedience of the male voice, a gun-toting shadow that hovered over her, ordering her to move forward. Only a touch of blue at the back of her dress tells us that she wore a blue dress before she was forced into the muddy cesspool.

Figure 14.10. Screenshot of Cameroon soldier administering mud bath torture of young girl in Bali (2018).

388

We are about to witness another episode in the tortured life of women caught up in the life and death-struggles of the Anglophone Revolt in Cameroon. It is the African swine mud bath, a form of public torture to which the French, Israeli, and American-trained Cameroon Army routinely subjects men and women suspected of participating in anti-government demonstrations or of belonging to Anglophone independentist or Ambazonian resistance groups.

The woman in the muddy cesspool groaned as she dragged herself painfully in the muck. The military videographer pans to reveal a second woman going through the swine mud bath torture, a uniformed Cameroonian soldier cradling an AK-47 assault rifle standing over her and supervising the torture. Suddenly, a French-accented torturer's voice orders the groaning girls:

"Ho ho... Shut up...shut up!" The voice drowns out the tortured girls' muffled groans!

In the background, we hear a soldier telling another in French:

"*Arme d'abord! arme d'abord.*" (Arm the weapon first, arm the weapon first).

The girl at the top of the cesspool lifts her head, turns it in fear at the direction of the voices. She did not understand what was being said. She thought she was being ordered to do something. Another soldier screams:

"*Fais vite!*" (Hurry up!).

Figure 14.11. Screenshot of soldier "inspecting" tortured girl's breasts in the mud, while the other girl is ordered to continue wallowing in the mud (Video shot by Cameroon soldiers in Bali, 2018).

The torture soon took on a sexual turn. The soldier who seemed to be in charge tells the others:

"*Il faut tremper les seins*" (You must soak their breasts).

Whereupon a second soldier orders the girls in French-accented "Francophone" Pidgin English:

"Moa di bobbi for wata!" (Immerse your breasts deeper in the muddy water!).

The victim lowers her chest in the cesspool to comply.

"Put ya bobbi inside wata, put ya bobbi inside wata, put ya bobbi inside wata" the soldiers repeated again and again. One soldier stooped and reached into the girl's chest to ensure that her breasts were well-soaked in the cesspool.

"*Tu ne vas pas mourir!*" (You are not going to die!), a soldier said, seeing the terror in the victim's uplifted, tearful, pleading face. She was divided between moving forward and soaking her breasts in the cesspool.

The soldiers uttered a number of untranslatable dehumanizing obscenities in French about the impact of the swine mud bath on the genitalia of the girls... In the midst of the sexual insults, the voice of the commanding officer barked at the girls:

"Avance!"

The groaning girls dragged themselves painfully in the muck towards the soldiers standing beside a fence.

"*Avancez*" the soldier who seemed to be in charge barked at the girls.

"Shut up! *Allez! Avancez! Arrête de pleurer ! Ho, ne pleures plus la bas*, No Cry!"

A soldier walked down the grassy median between the two sides of the road that were now pools of torture, stooped down, and groped one of the girl's breasts to satisfy himself that they were really soaked in the mud.

Figure 14.12. Screenshot of soldier administering mud torture on two girls suspected of harbouring separatist sentiments. (Video shot by Cameroon soldiers in Bali, 2018)

Mercifully, that sexualized orgy of power soon moved to a drier location. The girls were told to get out of the mirey cesspool. Amid a string of sexual innuendos hurled at them in French by the soldiers, they were frog-marched towards the military barracks, which, on closer examination, turned out to be the Cameroon Protestant College (CPC).

As they walked towards the military camp, the mud from their bodies and feet left footprints on the road. One of the girls stumbled, walking unsteadily on her feet.

"Si tu tombes ici, je vais te taper" (if you fall down here, I am going to hit you!) shouted a soldier.

"My woman welcome, you are welcome," said a soldier mockingly as the muddied girls were matched towards the CPC Bali campus.

"If you cry again...*Moi je vous dis en Francais, si vous pleurez encore...la Vitesse qui va passer...en tout cas je declare le centre d'instruction ouvert.*" (I declare the investigation center open).

Figure 14.13. Screenshot: Soldier supervising mud bath of Bali girl accused of supporting separatists (2018).

The girls were made to sit in their muddy dresses on a grassy area at the CPC Bali entrance for interrogation. In effect, this grotesque episode of torture and humiliation took place in front of the Cameroon Protestant College (CPC), Bali, one of the premier Christian secondary schools in English and Pidgin-speaking Southern Cameroons. CPC Bali was started by Presbyterian and Baptist missionaries and is part of the religious and cultural collective memory of English and Pidgin-speaking Southern Cameroons.

What crimes did these teenage girls commit? The Cameroon army had taken over the campus of CPC Bali and was using it as their barracks. The two girls were walking near the high school when they were arrested and accused of being spies for Ambazonian fighters in Bali.

The video ended as it had started, in *media res*, in the middle of things. No one knows what became of those girls. No one knows whether they are dead or alive.

One thing is sure: a human being cannot become a pig no matter how long he/she is forced to wallow in the mud at gunpoint.

The French, Israeli, and American-trained and equipped military of Cameroon have achieved the incredible feat of adding to the global vocabulary of human torture. Its human-swine public mud bath is definitely a novel form of water torture.

Figure 14.14. Screenshot of the girls being interrogated in front of CPC Bali after the human-swine bath torture. One soldier is videotaping the incident for the record (2018).

Scene III

President Emmanuel Macron and Human Rights Violations in Anglophone Cameroon
My Dear French Teachers

A happening that contributed to my intellectual and cognitive dissonance vis-à-vis France, the French language and French culture was one of the most surreal and dramatic public moments of the presidency of French President, Emmanuel Macron. It was the kind of unscripted, uncontrollable occurrence that political relations practitioners, image managers, and spinmeisters dread. It happened on February 22, 2020, at the *Salon de l'Agriculture de Paris*. As reported by *Radio France Internationale*, President Emmanuel Macron was touring the agricultural fair when a loud male voice from the crowd of spectators loudly interpellated him with fierce and desperate urgency, ignoring decorum and protocol:

"Monsieur Macron...Monsieur Macron," the voice shouted in desperation.

President Macron paused and instinctively looked in the direction from which his name was being shouted. He hesitated momentarily and scanned the crowd to find out who was shouting his name. The President's aides and the omnipresent pack of journalists took a cue from the president and paused, waiting to see what Macron would do. That brief pause gave the desperate male voice in the crowd a little opening, which the shouter deftly exploited:

Il y a Paul Biya qui tue les Camerounais Monsieur Macron…Il y a un genocide au Cameroun Monsieur Macron…Paul Biya tue les Camerounais M. Macron…

Nous sommes des Camerounais et nous sommes des morts Monsieur Macron…
Monsieur Macron, Monsieur Macron s'il vous plait !
S'il vous plait, Monsieur Macron !

Mr. Macron, Mr. Macron. Paul Biya is killing Cameroonians, Mr. Macron. There is a genocide in Cameroon, Mr. Macron. Biya is killing Cameroonians, Mr. Macron. We are Cameroonians and we are dead Mr. Macron, Mr. Macron, Mr. Macron. Please, please, Mr. Macron.

The Anglophone Question in Cameroon had gate-crashed a political exercise that President Emmanuel Macron was going through in the heart of Paris. The voice was that of Abdoulaye Thiam, a.k.a. 'Calibri Calibro,' a Cameroonian immigrant who was one of the leaders of a Europe-based group known as *le Brigade Anti-Sardinard* (BAS). The group consisted of Cameroonians whose residency status in Europe ranged from dissidents and exiles, to immigrants of all states of legality or lack thereof. Calibri Calibro was referring to the horrendous crimes against humanity visited on innocent people and whole villages in the Anglophone regions of Cameroon. Specifically, he was referring to the gruesome massacre of 38 innocent women and children at Ngarbuh, in the Donga Mantung Division of the Northwest region on February 14, 2020. The atrocities were carried out by members of the Cameroon army and their Fulani herdsmen militias and partners. France's direct and indirect role in the human rights violations of the Anglophone crisis was thus the cause of the dramatic interpellation of President Macron in Paris on February 20, 2020. To everyone's surprise, President Macron turned and walked towards the voice, his eyes scanning the crowd. As Macron approached, Calibri Calibro waved his hands excitedly and continued his denunciation of the Biya regime:
Monsieur Macron, il y a un genocide au Cameroun M. Macron…
(Mr. Macron, there is a genocide in Cameroon, Mr. Macron).
"Oui," *(yes),* answered President Macron, standing near the security perimeter surrounded by a phalanx of reporters and cameras, audio and video recording devices of all kinds. Calibri Calibro continued from the other side of the security barrier.
"*Il y a un genocide au Cameroun M. Macron…C'est un enorme plaisir de vous voir Monsieur Macron…*"
(There is a genocide in Cameroon, Mr. Macron…It is a pleasure to see you, Mr. Macron).
"*Moi aussi*" (Me too), responded President Macron.
The activist lowered his voice and stopped his frantic waving. Once he was certain he had attracted President Macron's attention. The man

struggled to milk the fleeting moment fate had granted him.

"Il y a plus de 22 morts… qui sont morts calcines, Monsieur Macron"

(There are more than 22 dead… who were burned to death, Mr. Macron"), Calibri Calibro said, referring to the Ngarbuh massacre in Donga Mantung, Cameroon.

"Je sais…Je sais ça…"

(I know… I know that), responded President Macron.

That impromptu exchange between President Macron and Calibri Calibro lasted a good 10 minutes. That lengthy, public conversation/debate ended with President Macron promising to call President Paul Biya and putting pressure on him to solve the Anglophone problem.

Figure 14.15. American Embassy, Yaoundé: American diplomats providing Covid-19 and military aid to the Cameroon army (May 8, 2021).

Figure 14.16. French Embassy Yaoundé: French diplomats present equipment to aid operational capacity of the *Gendarmerie Nationale* (May 27, 2021).

Nothing came of President Macron's promised call to President Biya. The massacres and killings in Anglophone Northwest and Southwest Cameroon continued.

On May 27, 2021, the French Embassy in Yaoundé announced that France was donating military equipment—including drones—to the paramilitary *Gendarmerie Nationale* in support of its operational capabilities against terrorism (see Appendix II). Military equipment from France, Israel, Russia and China is used extensively in the war to crush the Anglophone Revolt and subjugate the former State of West Cameroon.

Conclusion

My Dear French Teachers, Promoters of the French Civilizing Mission in English- and Pidgin-Speaking Southern Cameroons

The Anglophone Revolt and the failure of President Biya's *"chefferie républicaine"* (republican chiefdom) to militarily subjugate the English and Pidgin-speaking regions that used to be called Southern Cameroons demonstrates the failure of French and Francophone Cameroon's assimilating mission. Using military means as a final solution, the ultimate means to impose a linguistic and cultural hegemony, is a demonstration of failure. The most successful hegemonies are those to which the subaltern State voluntarily acquiesces. Taken together, the torture and resistance videos that have been the subject of this study demonstrate that for English and Pidgin-speaking Cameroonians, the French language is an instrument of dehumanization and human rights violations. The Anglophone Revolt is marked by unspeakable atrocities and human rights violations. The videos present different dimensions of the harsh, inhuman reality of the conflict. The world has come to know of these acts of human cruelty to other human beings through the now ubiquitous cellphone camera and social media platforms. Thanks to this new technology, the world had been able to see episodes of the Anglophone Revolt, and specifically its brutality and depravity, as recorded either by perpetrators and participants or surreptitiously by third parties whose intent was to expose these human rights violations on the part of the Cameroon military and the diabolical Ambazonian armed groups. The thread that runs through the Francophone torture videos is the problematic role of France and the French language in the atrocities of the Anglophone crisis in Cameroon. To my mind, French universal humanism and human rights hit rock-bottom, nay dissolved under the blistering, sarcastic mimicry of the Mama Amba, the "human swine" wallowing and suffering silently in the muck at gunpoint in Molyko, and under the silent groans of the tortured village maidens of Bali.

Dear French Teachers from France,

One of the things I learned in your classes was that intellectuals have a role in denouncing human predatory activities against other humans. You taught me to denounce injustice and human rights violations. You taught me about Émile Édouard Charles Antoine Zola and his famous open letter, *J'accuse* (I accuse), that fearlessly denounced the wrongful conviction of a Jewish officer, Alfred Dreyfus. In the spirit of Zola, I end this lengthy epistle with accusations:

J'accuse Paul Biya (of crimes against humanity), *J'accuse* Emmanuel Macron, *J'accuse*

Benjamin Netanyahu, *J'accuse la Swiss* of complicity in human rights violations, *J'accuse* Xi Jinping, J'accuse Vladimir Putin, *J'accuse*, Theresa May, Boris Johnson and Rishi Sunak (of of being partners in crimes against humanity in Cameroon), J'accuse Muhammadu Buhari, *J'accuse* the UN Security Council of making a mockery of the international human rights regime and offering nothing but the "most tepid statements of condemnation," to borrow the expression of Wole Soyinka (2005, p. 18), of the massive human rights violations in Southern Cameroons. Ah talk ah die, ah no talk, ah die!

Respectfully Submitted

References

Maher, J. (2018). Cameroonian Author, Patrice Nganang Freed from Prison. Publishers Weekly, (January 23) Retrieved from: https://www.publishersweekly.com/pw/by-topic/industry-news/people/article/75883-cameroonian-author-patrice-nganang-freed-from-prison.html

Melman, Y. (2010). Ex-IDF Top Officer Dies in Cameroon Helicopter Crash. *Haaretz* (November 22). Retrieved from: https://www.voanews.com/a/cameroonian-journalists-decry-violence-as-world-observes-press-freedom-day/7076814.html"https://www.voanews.com/a/cameroonian-journalists-decry-violence-as-world-observes-press-freedom-day/7076814.html

Soyinka, W. (2005). *Climate of Fear*. New York: Random House

REPUBLIC OF CAMEROON
Peace-Work-Fatherland

SOUTH WEST REGION

MANYU DIVISION

DIVISIONAL OFFICE, MAMFE

REPUBLIQUE DU CAMEROUN
Paix-Travail-Patrie

REGION DU SUD-OUEST

DEPARTEMENT DE LA MANYU

PREFECTURE DE MAMFE

No G.38/C.... L9/K III/523

MAMFE, THE ... 1 DEC 2017

COMMUNIQUE

The Senior Divisional Officer for Manyu communicates for the attention of the populations resident in the under mentioned villages viz:

- Akwaya Sub Division: Bodam, Dadi, Kesham, Badjie, Abonado, Beteme, Ebinsi and Bakem villages.
- Eyumojock Sub Division: Otu, Nsanaragati, Nsanakang, Agborkem German, Nduap and Esaghem,
- Mamfe Sub Division: Egbekaw village

To relocate to safer neighbourhoods of their choices in the hours that follow; failure of which they will be treated as accomplices or perpetrators of ongoing criminal occurrences registered on security and defense forces.

Business men and persons ploughing the Manyu River are equally advised to immediately suspend their activities till further notice

On a related note, the Senior Divisional Officer officially cautions motor bike riders to strictly observe without provocation the suspension of their circulation from 07pm to 06am daily.

CC
-One Family Radio
-MRC/Mamfe
-VOM Radio/Mamfe } for continuous broadcast
The Traditional Rulers of the villages concerned

Oum II Joseph
Administrateur Civil Principal

Appendix II
Historic Stamps of German Kamerun, French Cameroun, British Southern Cameroons, la République du Cameroun, and the Federal Republic of Cameroon

Cameroun Francais 1940

Stamp to commemorate the Centenary of Victoria (1958)

Independence of La Republique du Cameroun, January 1, 1960

Flag of the Federal Republic of Cameroon (1961-1972)

Appendix III
CHRI Submission to the Ministerial Action Group on Cameroon

CHRI

working for the *practical* realisation of human rights in the countries of the Commonwealth

SUBMISSION TO THE COMMONWEALTH MINISTERIAL ACTION GROUP ON CAMEROON

19 September 2017

The Commonwealth Human Rights Initiative (CHRI) writes to draw the attention of the Commonwealth Ministerial Action Group (CMAG) to the human rights and civil liberties situation in Cameroon. We urge the CMAG to take effective steps towards release all political prisoners, investigate allegations of illegal detention, ensure an enabling environment for dialogue and honour its international human rights obligations. CHRI also welcomes the release of Felix Balla, Fontem Neba, Mancho Bibixy and Justice Paul Ayah detained for over six months, and hopes that this will continue in the process of building a stable, peaceful and democratic Cameroon.

Beginning with the lawyers' strike on 11 October 2016 in Bamenda, the provinces of Northwest and Southwest Cameroon have witnessed continued protests and demonstrations against the government's linguistic and cultural policies and practices; "francophinisation" of courts, the education system and the marginalisation of the Anglophone population are some of the long-standing grievances against the central Francophone administration. Anglophones comprise approximately 19 percent of Cameroon's 23 million population. To counter the protests, the government in Yaoundé has repeatedly responded with excessive use of force by security forces. The Anglophone crisis has further curtailed civil and political rights in an already restrictive space. Cameroon's military operations against the armed regional group Boko Haram in the country's Far North has led to severe restrictions on the exercise of fundamental freedoms and widespread violations of human rights.

Use of Excessive Force
During the 21 November 2016 teachers' strike and rally, several people were severely beaten, dozens were arrested and at least two persons were shot dead, according to a report by the National Commission of Human Rights and Freedoms (*Commission nationale des droits de l'homme et des libertes*). A peaceful march organised by the students of Buea University was met with brutal repression by the police, including female students being beaten, stripped, rolled in mud and one was allegedly raped.[i] The violence elicited response from the UN Special Rapporteur on the rights to freedom of peaceful assembly and association regarding the use of excessive force by security forces during the demonstrations.[ii] Between October 2016 and February 2017, at least nine people were killed and many sustained gunshot wounds

CHRI

Arbitrary Arrests and Illegal Detentions

In the same period, the Cameroonian communications minister reported 82 arrests, including journalists and lawyers; the opposition party Social Democratic Front (SDF) says 150 have been arrested. According to the Centre for Human Rights and Peace Advocacy (CHRAPA) in Cameroon, approximately 200 youths were arrested after the November teachers' strike. Those who could not furnish the bail amount were moved to Yaoundé and detained in unknown places. Others such as Fomsoh Ivo Feh and his two friends have been imprisoned for 10 years for sharing a private joke about Boko Haram by text message.[iii]

Freedom of Speech and Expression

In January 2017, the government of Cameroon shutdown Internet services in the two Anglophone provinces. Albeit restored after 92 days, the UN Special Rapporteur on the Right to Freedom of Opinion and Expression described the move as "an appalling violation of their right to freedom of expression."[iv] Freedom of opinion and expression are guaranteed under Article 19 of the International Covenant on Civil and Political Rights (ICCPR) to which Cameroon is a signatory. Further, the Human Rights Council (HRC) passed a resolution in 2016 which condemned measures to intentionally prevent or disrupt access to or dissemination of information online in violation of international human rights law."[v]

Since the protests have started, the government has taken action against 20 journalists for allegedly flouting professional ethics.[vi] Bamenda-based Radio Hot Cocoa was shut down ostensibly on the grounds of illegal exploitation and broadcasting which incited violence.[vii] The government also banned three newspapers, including the French language weekly newspapers, *Aurore* and *Aurore Plus*, and prohibited its publisher from practising journalism in the country.[viii]

Media Freedoms

The Anglophone crisis and the government's response to it has further deepened Cameroon's democratic and human rights deficit. The country's war against Boko Haram in its Far North has allowed the discourse of securitization to overshadow freedoms of speech, expression and basic civil liberties.

On 24 April 2017, Ahmed Abba, a correspondent for Radio France International covering Boko Haram, was sentenced to ten years in prison for "non-denunciation of terrorism" and "laundering of the proceeds of terrorist acts".[ix] Others journalists and media personnel—Atia Azohnwi, Amos Fofung, Thomas Awah Junior, Mfor Ndong, Medjo Lewis, Jean Claude Agbortem, Tim Finnian and Hans Achomba—too have been arrested for exercising their freedom of expression.[x]

Counter-Terrorism and Civil Liberties

Since Cameroon began security operations in its Far North in 2014, instances of arbitrary arrest, enforced disappearance, torture, custodial deaths and unlawful killings have increased manifold.[xi] In December 2014, more than 200 people were arrested during cordon-and-search operations in the villages of Magdeme and Doublé in the Far North region. Of those arrested, at least 25 died in custody on the night of the arrests; 130 continue to remain unaccounted for without any information from the government on their whereabouts.[xii]

CHRI

Torture and Custodial Deaths

Amnesty International's latest report on Cameroon focusses on illegal detention, torture and custodial deaths.[xiii] Based on testimonies which are corroborated with satellite imagery, photographic and video evidence, the report documents 101 cases of incommunicado detention, custodial torture and deaths between 2013 and 2017 at over 20 different sites across the country, which are in violation of Cameroon's international human rights obligations, including the Convention Against Torture and Other Cruel, Inhuman or Degrading Treatment or Punishment.[xiv]

According to the report, a school in the northern town of Fotokol continues to be partially used by Cameroon's elite security force where they held detainees. Using the school as a military base while children are present violates Cameroon's obligations under international humanitarian law to protect civilians in armed conflict and puts children at risk.[xv]

Recommendations

The situation in Cameroon is characterized by flagrant violations of human rights, lack of space for opposition and systematic constraints on civil society and the media. As part of its mandate which includes "serious or persistent violation of Commonwealth values" and the "systematic denial of political space, such as through detention of political leaders or restriction of freedom of association, assembly or expression", CHRI urges CMAG to press upon the country to[xvi]:

- Release from detention all political prisoners, including civil society leaders and human rights advocates; drop terrorism charges against journalists and media personnel and cease military court proceedings against them.
- Investigate allegations of illegal detention, enforced disappearance and torture of civilians by state security and intelligence officials, and hold perpetrators to account.
- Honour its international human rights and Treaty Body obligations.
- Ensure an enabling environment for dialogue between the central government and Anglophone representatives to address concerns regarding minority linguistic and cultural rights issues.

CHRI

References:

[I] International Crises Group, *Cameroon's Anglophone Crisis at the Crossroads*, Africa Report N°250, August 2017, p. 10, available at: https://www.crisisgroup.org/africa/central-africa/cameroon/250-cameroons-anglophone-crisis-crossroads

[II] United Nations, Department of Public Information, *Cameroon: UN Experts Urge Government to Halt Violence Against English-speaking Minority Protests*, 21 December 2016, available at: http://www.ohchr.org/EN/NewsEvents/Pages/DisplayNews.aspx?NewsID=21054&LangID=E

[III] Amnesty International, *Cameroon: Release of Anglophone Leaders A Relief But Others Still Languish in Prison*, 30 August 2017, available at: https://www.amnesty.org/en/press-releases/2017/08/cameroon-release-of-anglophone-leaders-a-relief-but-others-still-languish-in-prison/

[IV] United Nations, Department of Public Information, *UN Expert Urges Cameroon to Restore Internet Services Cut Off in Rights Violation*, 10 February 2017, available at: http://www.ohchr.org/EN/NewsEvents/Pages/DisplayNews.aspx?NewsID=21165&amp%3BLangID=E

[V] UN Human Rights Council, *The Promotion, Protection and Enjoyment of Human Rights on the Internet*, 27 June 2016, A/HRC/32/L.20, available at: https://www.article19.org/data/files/Internet_Statement_Adopted.pdf

[VI] Ndi Eugene Ndi, "Cameroon Bans Three Newspapers for Flouting Rules", *Daily Nation*, December 2016, available at: http://www.nation.co.ke/news/africa/Cameroon-bans-three-newspapers/1066-3478484-1052mpxz/

[VII] African Centre for Democracy and Human Rights Studies, *Resolution on the Anglophone Crisis in Cameroon*, CRES/002/05/17, May 2017, available at: http://www.acdhrs.org/2017/06/4305/

[VIII] Ndi Eugene Ndi, "Cameroon Bans Three Newspapers for Flouting Rules", *Daily Nation*, December 2016, available at: http://www.nation.co.ke/news/africa/Cameroon-bans-three-newspapers/1066-3478484-1052mpxz/

[IX] Al Jazeera, "Military Court Convicts Cameroon Journalist Ahmed Abba", April 2017, available at: http://www.aljazeera.com/news/2017/04/military-court-convicts-journalist-ahmed-abba-170421034120487.html

[X] Committee to Protect Journalists, *Cameroonian Police Detain Freelance Documentary Maker on Terrorism Charges*, August 2017, available at: https://cpj.org/amp/028174.html

[XI] Amnesty International, *Right Cause, Wrong Means: Human Rights Violated and Justice Denied in Cameroon's Fight Against Boko Haram*, 2016, available at: https://www.amnesty.org/en/documents/afr17/4260/2016/en/

[XII] https://www.amnesty.org/en/latest/news/2016/08/cameroon-130-people-still-missing-20-months-after-their-arrest/

[XIII] Amnesty International, *Cameroon : 130 People Still Missing 20 Months After their Arrest*, August 2016, available at: https://www.amnesty.org/en/latest/news/2016/08/cameroon-130-people-still-missing-20-months-after-their-arrest/

[XIV] Forensic Architecture, *Torture and Detention in Cameroon*, available at: http://www.forensic-architecture.org/case/cameroon/

[XV] Amnesty International, *Cameroon: Amnesty Report Reveals War Crimes in Fight Against Boko Haram, Including Horrific Use of Torture*, July 2017, available at: https://www.amnesty.org/en/latest/news/2017/07/cameroon-amnesty-report-reveals-war-crimes-in-fight-against-boko-haram-including-horrific-use-of-torture/

[XVI] Commonwealth Secretariat, *Strengthening the Role of the Commonwealth Ministerial Action Group (CMAG)*, 2012, p. 9, available at: http://thecommonwealth.org/sites/default/files/news-items/documents/120131.pdf

Appendix IV
European Parliament Resolution on the Situation in Cameroon

European Parliament
2019-2024

Plenary sitting

B9-0573/2021

23.11.2021

MOTION FOR A RESOLUTION

with request for inclusion in the agenda for a debate on cases of breaches of human rights, democracy and the rule of law

pursuant to Rule 144 of the Rules of Procedure

on the human rights situation in Cameroon
(2021/2983(RSP))

Barry Andrews, Petras Auštrevičius, Dita Charanzová, Olivier Chastel, Bernard Guetta, Irena Joveva, Ilhan Kyuchyuk, Karen Melchior, Frédérique Ries, Michal Šimečka, Nicolae Ştefănuţă, Ramona Strugariu, Dragoş Tudorache, Hilde Vautmans
on behalf of the Renew Group

RE\P9-B(2021)0573_EN.docx

PE699.915v01-00

EN

United in diversity

EN

B9-0573/2021

European Parliament resolution on the human rights situation in Cameroon (2021/2983(RSP))

The European Parliament,

–   having regard to the Universal Declaration of Human Rights of 10 December 1948,

–   having regard to the 1966 International Covenant on Civil and Political Rights,

–   having regard to the African Charter on Human and Peoples' Rights of June 1981, which Cameroon has ratified,

–   having regard to the Constitution of the Republic of Cameroon,

–   having regard to the Convention on the Rights of the Child, ratified in 1993 by Cameroon,

–   having regard to the resolution of 11 March 2021 of the Joint Parliamentary Assembly of the African, Caribbean and Pacific Group of States (ACP) and the EU on democracy and the respect for constitutions in EU and ACP countries,

–   having regard to the United Nations Sustainable Development Goals,

A.   Whereas, since 2017, Cameroon's Anglophone Regions have been engulfed by a dramatic and growing civil war that has killed thousands of people and led to a full-blown humanitarian crisis;

B.   Whereas the initial peaceful protests promoted by the Cameroon Anglophone Civil Society Consortium against the Federal Government's marginalisation of Cameroon's Anglophone regions in 2016 were suppressed with extreme violence by the state authorities, fuelling support for separatism and the emergence of several separatist militias calling for a new state, Ambazonia, and prompting a bloody military conflict;

C.   Whereas dialogue is a precondition for peace, and President Paul Biya's government has consistently rejected direct talks with any separatist leaders from the Anglophone Regions;

D.   Whereas the ongoing conflict in Cameroon has internally displaced over 1 million people; whereas according to the European Civil Protection and Humanitarian Aid Operations (ECHO) report on Cameroon of 5 October 2021 there are over 2.2 million people requiring humanitarian assistance and over 66,000 have sought refuge in neighbouring Nigeria;

E.   Whereas Cameroon hosts more than 447,000 refugees and asylum seekers; whereas the spill over of this crisis affects the Cameroon West and Littoral regions;

F.   Whereas this conflict has had a disproportionate impact on children, with 700,000 students having been deprived of their right to education due to a forced school boycott across the Anglophone Regions and, according to OCHA, teachers and students have been attacked, kidnapped, threatened, and killed in the Anglophone Regions;

G. whereas civilians carry the brunt of the violence and conflict between government and separatist forces and make up the vast majority of casualties; whereas government forces and separatist forces alike continuously perpetrate reprisal attacks against one another, purposefully targeting civilians and vulnerable parts of the population;

H. Whereas, as of August 2021, children make up 28% of all survivors of Gender Based Violence and face a heightened risk of child recruitment, child labour and child abuse, with over 50% of children in Cameroon having reportedly been abused; whereas, according to the UN Population Fund, 38% of women aged 20-24 were married before age 18 and 13% were married before age 15;

I. Whereas the rule of law is not upheld by the state of Cameroon, with independent monitors including Human Rights Watch and Amnesty International, having previously documented military trial proceedings marred by serious substantive and procedural defects, in which the presumption of innocence, the right to an adequate defence, and the independence of proceedings and of the judiciary overall are all seriously undermined;

J. Whereas the Courts in Cameroon continue to impose the death penalty; whereas the African Commission on Human and People's Rights has long called on governments to abolish the death penalty;

K. Whereas the situation in the northern part of the country is still dominated by the struggle against Boko Haram; whereas the members of BIR (Bataillon d'Intervention rapide) executed civilian women and children and they have not yet been criminally prosecuted, the security of the civilian population in the areas where Boko Haram operates is precarious and requires that the Cameroonian authorities take full responsibility and needed action;

1. Urges President Paul Biya's government and the Anglophone separatists to initiate, without further ado, peace talks to avoid a further dramatic escalation of the humanitarian situation in Cameroon and to put an end to the human rights violations this conflict has prompted; calls on both sides of the conflict to cease staging reprisal attacks against one another, which purposefully target civilians suspected of affiliation with either government or separatist forces;

2. Condemns the arbitrary arrests of political opponents and peaceful protesters, independent press and other civilians, and deplores the use of a military tribunal to try civilians, which is in violation of international law; is concerned by serious procedural irregularities, including depriving the accused of their right to challenge the evidence against them and to present evidence in their own defence; deplores the use of torture against any person by any party to the conflict;

3. Calls on the Cameroonian authorities to stop railroading people into a sham trials before a military tribunal, with a predetermined outcome, capped with the imposition of the death penalty, which is unlawful under international human rights law;

4. Insists that the Cameroonian authorities ensure that victims of the ongoing conflict have the right to an independent, fair and effective investigation into their case, and that those responsible for human rights violations and abuses be brought to justice in a fair trial; stresses that facilitating corrupt trials amounts to impunity;

EN

5. Calls on the Cameroon government to, without further delay, ratify the Second Optional Protocol to the International Covenant on Civil and Political Rights on the abolition of the death penalty and to ratify the Rome Statute of the International Criminal Court; calls upon the Government to, in the meantime, put an end to impunity and ensure absolute judicial independence, which are core components of the rule of law and the foundation of a functioning democratic state;

6. Deplores the attacks against teachers and students across the Anglophone Regions in Cameroon; urges separatists to cease immediately all attacks against schools and to end the forced education boycotting, allowing the safe return to school of all students and teachers; implores the Cameroon authorities to prioritize the rights and safety of children above any other political motive; condemns the instrumentalisation of children and communities during attacks which lead to killings, rape, looting and abduction by terrorist organizations such as Boko Haram;

7. Condemns the excessive use and abuse of force against political opponents, and peaceful protestors; deplores the abuse of lockdown measures, such as curfews or banning public meetings, under the veil of the COVID-19 pandemic in order to constrain freedom of expression, the press and the right to peaceful assembly;

8. Expresses concern at the status of freedom of speech and freedom of the press in Cameroon; deplores the arbitrary arrest and harassment of journalists and opposition politicians and the silencing of political dissent; calls on the government of Cameroon to promote and ensure the protection of the right to freedom of speech, freedom of expression, freedom of assembly and the right to protest; calls for the strengthening of an inclusive democratic dialogue between all stakeholders and political players throughout all regions of Cameroon;

9. Insists that all parties to the conflict immediately provide unfettered humanitarian access, given that 2.2 million people are now in humanitarian need and stresses that humanitarian assistance currently provides life-saving support and protection to large portions of the population, including refugees from Nigeria and Central African Republic; deplores, therefore, the fact that over 40,000 people were denied food assistance due to insecurity and roadblocks in the North-West and the South-West regions, as well the recent attacks on health facilities and the fact that humanitarian activities were banned under lockdown;

10. Condemns the attacks against humanitarian workers, including their abduction, harassment and murder in the North West and South West regions of Cameroon and, equally, condemns the escalating intimidation towards independent monitors and human rights defenders, especially women rights defenders, whose work is more important than ever in the context of serious human rights violations by all parties to this conflict;

11. Urges the international community, notably the African Union, Central African States, United Nations and the European Union to exert pressure on the Cameroon authorities to put an end to the violence, enable humanitarian access, and develop and apply a sustainable, peaceful and democratic solution to the ongoing crisis; considers that a UN Human Rights Council Fact-Finding Mission to Cameroon would be appropriate to determine the degree to which international human rights law and international humanitarian law have been violated and by whom; recommends that the UN Security

Council formally add the situation in Cameroon's Anglophone regions to its agenda and that the UN Secretary General provide a briefing on the situation without further delay;

12. Calls upon the High Representative of the Union for Foreign Affairs and Security Policy to consider adopting targeted sanctions towards those individuals responsible for human rights violations, by means of the Global Human Rights Sanctions Regime;

13. Instructs its President to forward this resolution to the Council, the Commission, the Vice-President of the European Commission /High Representative of the Union for Foreign Affairs and Security Policy, the EU Special Representative for Human Rights, the ACP-EU Council, the institutions of the African Union, and the Government and Parliament of Cameroon.

Appendix V
Letter from Nkoto Emane David, Director General of Camtel Confirming
"Suspension of Internet Service to Certain Sensitive Regions" (January 18, 2017)

Yaoundé, le 1 8 JAN 2017

N° 006 /DG

A la haute attention de
Madame Le Ministre des Postes et
Télécommunications.
YAOUNDE

Objet : Suspension du service internet
dans certaines Régions sensibles.

Madame Le Ministre,

J'ai l'honneur de porter à votre haute connaissance que comme suite à vos hautes instructions, la CAMTEL a pris toutes les dispositions nécessaires pour la suspension mentionnée en objet. Toutefois, il se trouve que certains opérateurs n'ont pas exactement suivi à lettre vos recommandations.

Aussitôt informé, j'ai personnellement mobilisé une équipe sur les sites CAMTEL des villes de Yaoundé, Douala, Kribi et Limbé entre le mardi 17 janvier 2017 à 20 H 30 et le mercredi 18 janvier 2017 à 01 H 30 aux fins de procéder de manière coercitive au respect de vos hautes instructions susdites.

Cette opération a abouti à la suspension du service internet de tous les opérateurs et fournisseurs d'accès internet (FAI) sur toute l'étendue du territoire national. Après un engagement ferme, pris par ces différents partenaires sur le respect des actions arrêtées en étroite collaboration avec le Gouvernement, le service a été rétabli.

Elle nous a permis de constater que certains opérateurs à l'instar de MTN offrent le service internet à d'autres fournisseurs tels que CREOLINK, VODAFONE et AFRIMAX, ceci en marge de la réglementation en vigueur. Des investigations sont en cours pour le cas VIETTEL.

Par ailleurs, elle pose clairement la problématique non seulement du contrôle du service internet au niveau des différents aéroports numériques que sont les câbles optiques sous-marins et les accès satellitaires, mais aussi d'acquisition d'outils modernes pouvant garantir notre souveraineté.

Veuillez agréer, **Madame Le Ministre,** l'expression de ma haute considération.

CAMEROON TELECOMMUNICATIONS
B.P. : 1571 Yaoundé - Cameroun TELEPHONE (237) 222 234 065
Fax : (237) 222 230 303 Site Web : www.camtel.cm
N° Contribuable M 0998 0000 9853 S

409

Appendix VI
Letter from Senator Henry Kemende Gamsey

REPUBLIQUE DU CAMEROUN
Paix - Travail - Patrie

REPUBLIC OF CAMEROON
Peace - Work - Fatherland

Le SENAT

The SENATE

From the DESK of: Senator/Barrister **KEMENDE** Henry **GAMSEY** *of the*
North West Constituency, Member of the Resolutions and Petitions Committee
(P. O. Box 851 - BAMENDA. Tel.: 677760752 / 694034171. Email: kemendelaw@yahoo.com)

<u>DATE:</u> **11/03/2019**

<u>*Through:*</u> *The* PRESIDENT,
CAMEROON SENATE,

<u>*To:*</u> *H. E. The* MINISTER,
MINISTRY OF PUBLIC HEALTH,
YAOUNDE.

<u>*Subject Matter:*</u> <u>ORAL QUESTIONS DIRECTED TO THE MINISTER
OF PUBLIC HEALTH PURSUANT TO SECTION 35
OF THE CONSTITUTION AND SECTION 90(New)
OF THE STANDING ORDERS OF THE SENATE</u>

1- *Your Excellency, Mr.* MINISTER, out of the number of **Public Health
Services** known to have been affected by the ongoing crisis in the **North
West** and **South West** Regions of our country, how many have your Ministry rehabilitated and are functional? To those yet to be rehabilitated or shut
down, what is your Ministry doing to make sure that the local populations are
medically attended to?

2- Concerning the **BALIKUMBAT HOSPITAL** in the NGOKETUNJIA
Division of the North West Region which premises have been transformed
into a **Barrack**, what is your Ministry doing to either re-establish that Medical facility or transfer same elsewhere for the **health personnel** to return
in order that the local population can have access to health facilities?

3- Under what circumstances are **HEALTH DISTRICTS** created? What
is the **Ministry of Public Health** doing to ensure that the number of these
Health Districts within each **Region** reflect the population to be cartered
for?

Sign.: Senator Henry G. **KEMENDE**

Appendix VII
Letter from Dr. Sr. Anshoma Helen Mbuoh, Director of Shisong Hospital-

ST. ELIZABETH'S CATHOLIC GENERAL HOSPITAL CARDIAC CENTER SHISONG
P.O. Box 8, Kumbo, Bui Division, North West Region, Cameroon
Tel (237) 650-268-462. 650-268-656, 653-807-563, 69948-8412
Email: info@shisonghospital.org / cardiacadm@gmail.com

November 15, 2021.

The Provincial Leadership Team
Tertiary Sisters of St. Francis,
Shisong.

SUBJECT: **REPORT ON THE MIITARY INVASION OF**
THE ST ELIZABETH CATHOLIC GENERAL HOSPITAL, SHISONG.

Once again, the Cameroon Military orchestrated a surprised invasion of the Shisong Hospital. The last time they did was on Monday the 19th of July, 2021, at about 2:15am.

This time, today Sunday the 14th of November, 2021, at about 1:30pm, the Cameroon Military again entered the St. Elizabeth Catholic General Hospital and Cardiac Centre, Shisong. The number of the military men could not be easily determined but they came in three (03) armoured cars. They were armed with sophisticated weapons and dressed in combat attire. A frightful scene for all, especially for patients in a Hospital setting.

The Director of the Hospital (Dr. Sr. Anshoma Helen Mbuoh, Cardiologist) was immediately alerted. She came and met the military. The Military requested for the Emergency Unit of the Hospital, as they claimed to be searching for Amba boys that were brought for treatment in the Hospital that same morning. The Director took them to the Out Patient Department, which serves as the emergency unit and where all consultations in the Hospital begin.

Not satisfied with this, they insisted to be taken to the Emergency Unit with the inscription on the door but were calmly told that all cases are brought to the Out

1

Patients' Unit for consultation. Here too, they were told that emergency treatment is administered and those with indication of admission are normally sent to the appropriate units. They took the Registers and went through it, thoroughly. Then they resorted to a thorough search of the entire Hospital. They moved from Ward to Ward and from Unit to Unit. The Dispensary, Admission Room, Men's Medical Unit, the Pediatric Unit, the Females' Medical Unit, the Surgical Units I & II, the Maternity and the Theatre were all bumped into, with patients and little children and babies and pregnant women in them. All the Private Wards were opened and searched. All the toilets and rooms the Hospital were searched. Nothing suspicious was found.

Not finding the Amba Boys they were looking for, they started insulting and threatening the Reverend Sisters. They even threated to shoot the Sisters in the leg if they did not indicate where they had hidden and are treating the Amba Boys in the Hospital.

In the meantime, the two (02) Security Officers on Duty were arrested and systematically interrogated. They were asked, at gun point, to show where the Amba Boys were hidden. The response from the Guards was clear and concise. Their responsibility starts with receiving all the patients and then forward to the Out patients' Department, where the cases are taken over by the Nurses and Doctors. From there, they go back to their duty posts.

Not satisfied with this explanation, the Military exercised brute force on the Security Officers. They were severely beaten with the butts of the guns and kicked with their military boots. They all sustained injuries and swollen faces. The Administration later asked the Security Officers to go for consultation and to have a medical checkup.

Coming out to the Hospital parking lot, the Military insisted that all the bikes should be identified, else they will be burnt. All those who parked their bikes were called and each one of them identified his bike by starting the engine and was asked to park where the military indicated to them. (It should be noted that the Administration had issued a Public Order whereby only bikes of the Staff, patients, guardians, hospital should be parked in the hospital premises and records are kept).

2

Thereafter, the military insisted they wanted to see the Consultation Area of the Cardiologist. The Director, being the Cardiologist, identified herself. She was asked to escort them to consultation room and the exploratory laboratories (the echocardiogram and electrocardiogram Room). They entered the Out Patients' Department of the Cardiac Centre and all the consultation rooms. They requested to go down to the Basement of the Cardiac Centre and there they searched everywhere.

At the end of the search, at about 3:30pm, some of the Military men expressed remorse and indicated that their action was exaggerated. However, some of them continued with their threats to the Sisters and the Hospital. They promised that the next time they would be back; they will set the entire hospital on fire.

They left the hospital at about 3:45pm

Submitted by,

Dr. Sr. Anshoma Helen Mbuoh
Director

CC:

The Senior Divisional Officer, Bui
The Bishop, Diocese of Kumbo

3

CONTRIBUTORS

LYOMBE EKO is the William S. Morris endowed professor in Innovation, Information and Journalism at the College of Media and Communication, Texas Tech University. He was born in the colonial Buea Native Authority, Southern Cameroons as a "native subject" of Her Majesty the Queen of England. He attended the Baptist Bible College in Ndu, Donga Mantung, and the Bilingual Grammar School in Molyko, Buea. He earned his B.A. in Foreign Language Studies & Media Communication at the University of Sioux Falls, South Dakota, his M.A. in Media Communication from Wheaton College Illinois, and his doctorate in Journalism and Mass Communication from Southern Illinois University at Carbondale.

Before he joined Texas Tech in 2015, he was an associate professor and Director of Graduate Studies at the University of Iowa School of Journalism and Mass Communication. He was also Director of the African Studies Program at the University of Iowa. He has also taught at the University of Maine in Orono, Maine. Before his academic career, he was a journalist at Cameroon Radio and Television (CRTV) Yaoundé, and an editor/translator at the African Broadcasting Union (URTNA) in Nairobi, Kenya. His documentary, *Kip Keeps Kids*, which focuses on Kenyan Olympic multi-gold medal winner Kipchoge Keino, won an international prize at the Prix Futura TV Festival in Germany. He has published multiple refereed journal articles, and five books on comparative and international communication law and policy. He is the winner of a Texas Tech University President's Book Award, an Independent Publisher Book Award, and an International Book Award.

HANSEL WENDA NGALA was born in January 1992 at the Banso Baptist Hospital (BBH) and later attended CBC Primary School, PS Kumbo and Saint Augustine's College (SAC), Nso and Government Bilingual High School (GBHS), Kumbo.

He later earned qualifications in journalism from CityVarsity School of Media and Creative Arts in Cape Town, South Africa. He also has a B.A. and an M.A. in journalism from the University of the Witwatersrand (Wits), South Africa. His thesis at Wits analyzed the contents of a community radio station that broadcasts from the embattled Northwest Region of Cameroon.

Hansel currently serves as political affairs editor for the Cameroon News Agency, commentator on West Africa for South Africa's *eNCA* TV network and as a staff writer for The Gospel Coalition Africa where his works examine the intersection of contemporary developments in Africa with Christianity. His journalism focuses on democratic issues in Africa, health and the role of religion more broadly in Africa.

He has previously served as a communications officer for the Cameroon Baptist Convention (CBC) Health Services, communications consultant for Mission Aviation Fellowship (MAF) in Chad and is currently rounding off a stint as a writer for Mercy Ships in Madagascar, where he focuses on telling health stories about the impact of life-saving surgeries in poor communities in Madagascar.

WOMAI SONG is Assistant Professor of History, Assistant Professor and Chair of the African and African American Studies Program at Earlham College in Indiana, USA. Born and raised in Cameroon, Dr. Song earned his B.A. and M.A. degrees in History from the University of Buea and holds a PhD from Howard University in Washington DC. Before he joined Earlham College in 2017, he was a lecturer at Morgan State University. He is a scholar of African History and the modern African Diaspora Experience. Womai's primary research interests include transitions in colonial and postcolonial erstwhile African German colonies, memory and heritage of enslavement, coloniality, anti-Black racism, decoloniality, political assassinations, Pan-Africanism, and Neo-colonialism in Africa and the global African world. Besides having presented his research at a plethora of conferences, he has co-authored and published articles in the *Journal of Humanities and Social Sciences* and the *International Journal of Humanities, Social Sciences, and Education*. He is a recent recipient of the Emerging Scholar Award for the Twenty-third International Conference on Diversity in Organizations, Communities, and Nations. Dr. Song is the co-editor of *Heritage and History in Africa: Social and Ethno-Historical Perspectives on Heritage Elements in Cameroon* (2024) and is completing his first solo book entitled *In the Eye of the Storm: Augustine Ngom Jua and Anglophone Cameroon Nationalism*. He is currently serving as a member of the Academic Council of the Pan-African Heritage World Project, the Secretary General of the North American Association of Scholars on Cameroon (NAASC), and co-editor of Spears Media's African & African Diaspora History Book Series.

DIBUSSI TANDE is a political scientist, writer and poet who lives in Chicago. His articles have appeared in a variety of print and online publications such as the *Rhodes Journalism Review, Focus on Africa Magazine, African Writing Online* and *African Muckraking, 75 Years of Investigative Journalism from Africa*. He is the author of *No Turning Back: Poems of Freedom 1990-1993 (2007)* and co-editor of *Their Champagne Party Will End! Poems in Honor of Bate Besong (2008)*. His poems have been published in several anthologies, including *Treasured Poems of America* (1994) and *Hiraeth-Erzolirzoli: A Wales – Cameroon Anthology (2018)*. Dibussi is also the author of *Scribbles from the Den. Essays on Politics and Collective Memory in Cameroon* (2009), and he produces the award-winning blog, *Scribbles from the Den* [https://www.dibussi.com].

His Twitter handle, @dibussi, is a leading source of news and analysis on Cameroon. Dibussi obtained a "Licence" in Public law and a "Maitrise" in Political Science from the University of Yaoundé. He also holds Master's degrees in Political Science and Instructional Technology from Northeastern Illinois University, Chicago, and Northern Illinois University, DeKalb, respectively. He previously served as an Associate Editor for *Cameroon Life Magazine* and *Cameroon Today*.

JUDE FOKWANG is Professor of Anthropology at Regis University, Denver. He attended Sacred Heart College, Bamenda and earned his Bachelor's degree in Sociology and Anthropology from the University of Buea, his MA from the University of Pretoria and PhD in

Sociocultural Anthropology from the University of Toronto. He has held previous teaching positions at the University of Cape Town and Rhodes University in South Africa, Trent University and the University of Toronto in Canada. His ethnographic film, *Something New in Old Town* (2016), won the best documentary film category at the Lekki International Film Festival, Lagos, Nigeria (2019). He is the author of *Cultivating Moral Citizenship: An Ethnography of Young People's Associations, Gender and Social Adulthood in the Cameroon Grasslands* (2023). He serves on the advisory board of *Africa: The Journal of the International Africa Institute* and the *Nordic Journal of African Studies*.

INNOCENT AWASOM is Associate Librarian and STEM Team Lead at Texas Tech University Libraries in Lubbock, with Liaison responsibilities to the College of Agricultural Sciences and Natural Resources (CASNR), the Departments of Biological Sciences, Chemistry and Biochemistry and the International Center for Arid and Semi-Arid land Studies (ICASALS). He was born in Mankon, Bamenda in the Federal Republic of Cameroon. He attended P.S. Azire, Mankon and the prestigious Bilingual Grammar School Buea, graduating from the bilingual classes thus obtaining the BEPC (French) and GCE O Levels (English), and returning to Sacred Heart College Mankon for his GCE A' Levels. He holds graduate degrees in Information Sciences (M.Inf.Sc.) from the African Regional Center for Information Science (ARCIS) and in Zoology (M.Sc.) - Hydrobiology & Fisheries, from the University of Ibadan. He was the University Librarian and lecturer of Library and Information Sciences at the University of Ngaoundere, Cameroon, before relocating to the USA. His over two decades of professional librarianship experience has taken him across the USA, Europe, and Africa, most recently to the Bindura University of Science Education (BUSE), Bindura – Zimbabwe, where he was a Fulbright Scholar in residence. His research interests are in the areas of International Librarianship, Information/Media/ Digital literacy, scholarly communications, Research Metrics, and Knowledge Management.

TANJONG ASHUNTANTANG, PhD, is an award-winning Barrister-at-law and a legal scholar based in Cameroon. He attended St Joseph's College Sasse, Buea. He was called to the Nigerian bar in 1991 and the Cameroon bar a year later; he earned his LL.B. degree from the University of Benin in Nigeria and proceeded to the Nigerian law school, Lagos, where he earned the certificate of proficiency for the call to bar. A Chevening scholar, he earned a Master's in Conflict, Security, and Development at the University of Exeter, England, and a Doctor of Philosophy in Conflict Resolution from the University of Buea, Cameroon. Barrister Ashuntantang is a founding partner of Amity Law Offices, which has been operating in the Southwest region of Cameroon since 1997. Co-founder of the Cameroon Common Law Report and pioneer member of its editorial board, he is a legal historian who has written and presented papers extensively on the common law in English-speaking Cameroon and legal harmonization with the civil law system of Francophone Cameroon.

INDEX

Made in the USA
Middletown, DE
25 January 2025